BRITISH LOCO1
CATALOGU L
1825-1923

compiled by the late Bertram Baxter
edited by the late David Baxter and Peter Mitchell

Volume 6
Great Eastern Railway
North British Railway
Great North of Scotland Railway
Midland & Great Northern Joint Railway
Remaining Companies in the LNER Group

Printed and bound by CPI Group (UK) Ltd, Croydon, CR0 4YY.

ISBN 978-1-905505-26-5

Kestrel Railway Books
PO Box 269
SOUTHAMPTON
SO30 4XR

www.kestrelrailwaybooks.co.uk

Cover picture:
Eastern Counties Railway 0-4-2 No 164 *Tiger*, built in 1848 (see page 28).

Contents

Editorial Note and Acknowledgements

The late Bertram Baxter's *British Locomotive Catalogue 1825-1923* was originally produced between 1977 and 1988, starting with a general summary, and ending (prematurely) with Volume 5B, which covered the Great Northern and Great Central Railways. Published originally by the Moorland Publishing Company, Derbyshire, there were planned to be three further volumes to complete the LNER group of companies and to add the GWR and Southern Railway constituents; these volumes were never published. However, much of the work for Volume 6 had been done, and is presented here, albeit nearly 25 years after the last volume was published. In the intervening years, Bertram Baxter's son David, who had painstakingly marshalled his father's data into the original volumes, has himself died, but he had been assisted by Peter Mitchell, and it is he who we must thank for completing this final volume.

And it will be the final volume. Things have moved on somewhat since the 1980s, and the locomotives of the Great Western and Southern companies have both been covered by other publications in the intervening years. The same can also be said about the LNER, with the publication of Willie Yeadon's comprehensive locomotive registers, but it was felt that this volume would represent a more fitting conclusion to the Baxters' work than for it to be left petering out where it did.

In addition to the work that has been done by Peter Mitchell to complete this volume, we must also thank Keith Dexter, who made it his mission to see the final one printed. Keith has also helped with a bibliography that had ossified in the mid-1990s, and needed a considerable amount of work to bring it up to date. Given the plethora of published material that has appeared in the intervening years, a decision has been made to limit the new entries to only major articles and books.

The publishers also wish to acknowledge the help provided by the relevant societies in their contribution to the updated bibliography. Web addresses for each society are given on page 262, but here we must thank David Chappell (Mid-Suffolk Light Railway Museum), Keith Fenwick (Great North of Scotland Railway Association), James Hay and Allan Rodgers (North British Railway Study Group), John Hobden (Midland & Great Northern Circle), Bill King (Great Eastern Railway Society) and Paul Lemon (Colne Valley Railway).

Howard Sprenger
Kestrel Railway Books
February 2012

Abbreviations

BHS	Boiler heating surface (feet/inches)
Blr	Boiler (diameter x length of barrel in feet/inches)
Cyls	Cylinders (diameter x stroke in inches)
diam	diameter
DW	Driving (coupled) wheels (diameter in feet/inches)
HP	High pressure
LP	Low pressure
LW	Leading wheels (diameter in feet/inches)
no(s)	number(s)
O/S	outside
S'heat	superheated
THS	Total heating surface (square feet)
TW	Trailing wheels (diameter in feet/inches)
TWB	Total wheelbase (feet/inches)
WB	Wheelbase (feet/inches)
WP	Working pressure (pounds per square inch)
WT	Weight in working order (tons/hundredweights)

Other abbreviations in text.

GREAT EASTERN RAILWAY

Introduction

The Eastern Counties Railway was incorporated on 4th July 1836 with the object of opening a line to Norwich and Yarmouth from London via Ipswich with a gauge of 5ft 0in. The scheme met with many difficulties under its engineer, John Braithwaite, both physically and financially. Beyond the London area the territory was completely rural with little potential for goods traffic other than agricultural produce, and investors were not attracted in great numbers. Furthermore, difficulties in constructing the line over the Essex boulder clay, particularly in the river Lea area at Stratford, escalated costs as it had originally been thought to be favourable for building.
In addition, landowners proved to be particularly greedy and the company was faced with sluggish capital investment and mounting expenditure rendering it in an almost continual financial crisis.
The first section from a temporary station near the Mile End Road to Romford was opened in 1839, and by March 1843, the construction of the line had struggled to reach Colchester, at which point the company was forced to call a halt and delay plans for further construction.
Meanwhile, the Northern and Eastern Railway which was incorporated on the same date as the ECR, was authorised to build a 5ft 0in gauge line to the north via Cambridge, and had met with even greater financial difficulties. Unable to build a London terminal of its own, it made connection with the ECR at Stratford, and ran its trains into the ECR terminus at Bishopsgate (originally named Shoreditch and opened in 1840). The ECR demanded a totally uneconomic charge for this, and the N&E line reached no further than Bishops Stortford, opened in 1842 with a branch to Hertford opened in 1834, by which time it was almost bankrupt.
The ECR were thus able to lease the N&E at advantageous rates in 1844. Later in the same year, the decision was taken to alter the gauge of the EC and N&E lines to standard gauge 4ft 8½in, which was carried out during September and October 1844.
The ECR also carried on construction of the N&E line from Bishops Stortford to Brandon, opened in 1845.
In October of that year, George Hudson succeeded in becoming Chairman of the ECR, his principal interest being in using the N&E line as a means of providing a northern link with the Midland Railway to defeat plans for the future Great Northern Railway.
At Brandon, connection was made with the Norfolk Railway which was an amalgamation of the Yarmouth and Norwich Railway (incorporated 1842) and the Norwich and Brandon Railway (incorporated 1844), and opened from Yarmouth to Brandon via Norwich (Thorpe) in 1844/5. This provided a route via Cambridge and Ely. In 1846 the Norwich Railway leased the Lowestoft Railway and Harbour and in 1848 concluded a working agreement with the ECR. A further working agreement was reached in 1850 with the Newmarket Railway (incorporated 1846, opened 1848).
At Ely the Norfolk Railway connected with the East Anglian Railway, incorporated in 1847 by the amalgamation of the Lynn and Ely, Dereham and Ely, and Ely and Huntingdon Railways, and was opened between these places in 1846/7. By 1850 however it was officially bankrupt, and was initially leased by the Great Northern Railway in 1851, but the ECR successfully blocked the lease by court action and leased the EAR itself on 1st January 1852. By virtue of these independent schemes the ECR was first able to extend its system without capital outlay despite its continuing financial problems.
Standards of safety and service were abysmally low and accidents were frequent, culminating in an official enquiry by Norwich City Council in November 1855, which reported to the Board of Trade, who compelled the ECR to carry out remedial works in 1856/7.
Meanwhile the powers of the EC to construct a line beyond Colchester to Ipswich had been taken over by the Eastern Union Railway. By amalgamating with the Ipswich, Bury and Norwich Railway, a more direct route to Norwich (Victoria), the one originally intended by the ECR, was opened between 1846 and 1849. Intense competition between the ECR and the EUR followed, with the ECR doing everything possible to deter passengers from using this route, which lasted until 1854 when the EUR admitted defeat and accepted the ECR's terms for a lease, whereupon the ECR began to promote the shorter route, which it had formerly discouraged.

The complicated system of leases and working arrangements was formalised in 1862 when the ECR, East Anglian, East Suffolk (which the ECR had worked since its opening in 1854, and which provided a line to the south from Lowestoft), Newmarket and Norfolk Railways were amalgamated as the Great Eastern Railway.

Standards of operation however did not really improve until 1867 when Lord Cranborne became Chairman. He later became Marquis of Salisbury and Prime Minister. During his four years as Chairman he did much to improve the company's image and its finances.

In 1866, the GE leased the London and Blackwall Railway, which had been in operation since 1840 but, which was not connected to the ECR until 1854. The L&B was unusual in that until 1848, it was cable-operated with two winding engines at Minories and Blackwall. It had double track, but each was operated independently in either direction giving a journey time for the 3½ miles of eight minutes. Carriages left the Fenchurch Street terminus by gravity to Minories where they were attached individually to the cable. The Blackwall engine then hauled the carriages and any carriages attached at intermediate stations without stopping, carriages for intermediate stations being detached from the cable and brought to a stand in the rear by their brakesmen. At Blackwall, carriages continued into the station by their momentum as at Fenchurch Street and left again by gravity for the return with the Minories engine hauling. The process was repeated on the other line fifteen minutes later, which gave a fifteen minute frequency of service on alternate lines, or every half an hour when one of the cables was broken. Unfortunately this happened rather often - sometimes as often as two or three times a week. The other objection was that it was not possible to travel between intermediate stations between Minories and Blackwall except via the termini.

The L&B also owned three river steamers operating from Blackwall Pier to Woolwich, Gravesend and other river destinations.

After conversion to locomotive operation, it also had connections with the North London and London Tilbury and Southend Railways. The latter was worked by the GE until 1880, and also operated into Fenchurch Street station. The connection to the GE was between Stepney and Bow.

When Lord Cranborne left the Board, his place was taken by Lord Claud Hamilton, who became Chairman in 1893, and remained in that capacity until the LNER was formed.

Four further small locomotive owning companies were taken over by the GE, the Waveney Valley by amalgamation in 1863, the Thetford and Watton by purchase in 1880, the Felixstowe in 1887, and the Wivenhoe and Brightlingsea in 1893.

From 1874 to 1893, the Chairman was CH Parkes, after whom the Parkeston Quay is named which was opened in 1883. The name is a composite of his name and Stone, the engineer for the project.

The ECR took over four river steamers operating on the rivers Orwell and Stour in 1854, and under the GE, three more river steamers were registered. Freight shipping services from Harwich to Rotterdam started in October 1863 using three chartered vessels. In 1864, a passenger ship and two cattle carriers were acquired, and a second passenger paddle steamer was added in 1865. When Parkeston Quay was opened, the GE had ten North Sea ferries operating to Rotterdam and Hamburg. The passenger service was transferred from Rotterdam to the new Hook of Holland terminal in 1893.

One of the most important developments improving the company's prosperity was the opening of the joint line with the Great Northern from March via Spalding, Sleaford, Lincoln and Gainsborough to Doncaster on 1st August 1882 utilising some former GN lines (see Vol 5B). Until this was in operation, the GE had little freight traffic, which had been one of the main disadvantages since the EC was opened. The GE, like the GN, was granted running powers over the North Eastern Railway to York from 1st November 1892. The aspirations of the original Northern and Eastern Railway had at last been achieved.

The other development was the phenomenal growth of London suburban passenger traffic into Liverpool Street station (opened in 1874 alongside the North London Broad Street terminus but on street rather than viaduct level) and Fenchurch Street.

As the price of getting Parliamentary permission for the short extension from Bethnal Green on a 1 in 70 grade and other suburban extensions, the GE introduced a two penny workmen's fare in 1872 for journeys from Walthamstow and later from the Enfield line. With this inducement many suburbs grew rapidly at Ilford, Leytonstone, Walthamstow and Tottenham. No other railway had such cheap fares, completely reversing the ECR fares policy, although the trains provided only the most spartan accommodation with wooden seats in the third class. Congestion, however, quickly became acute. By 1903 220,000 passengers a day were using Liverpool Street, 75,000 of them arriving before 10.30am. This was the most intensive suburban passenger train service in the country worked by steam locomotives, and with the advent of the tube and electric railways at the turn of the century rival commercial schemes were promoted.

A scheme in 1894 for a surface electric railway, the London, Walthamstow and Epping Forest Railway had lapsed, but two companies were formed to build tube lines into the area, the North East London Railway to Tottenham and the City and North Eastern Suburban Railway to Waltham Abbey. Although an obvious case for electrification, the GE maintained that the low fares could not possibly recoup the capital cost. Instead it embarked on an elaborate bluff to counter the pro-electrification critics by instructing James Holden to design a locomotive capable of accelerating a train of fifteen four-wheel carriages faster than electricity. This he did, but it was never used as the improvements to track and bridges that would have been necessary would themselves have imposed a heavy capital expenditure.

This locomotive was the famous 'Decapod' – an enormous 0-10-0WT. At any rate it succeeded in defeating the tube schemes or, at least, assisted to that end, and despite a 1905 Royal Commission report recommending electrification and extension of the tube lines two years later, the company made no further move, claiming that the advent of the electric tram had removed some of the short-distance traffic. The bluff had worked. In its turn the LNER continued to resist electrification on the same grounds, and only in 1935 when the Treasury was prepared to guarantee interest on loans for capital schemes to relieve unemployment, did the electrification and tube extensions receive sanction. The programme was interrupted by the war and was not completed until 1960.

On the GE, suburban traffic grew from 8 million a year in 1897 to 10½ million in 1919, and the General manager Sir Henry Thornton (who had been recruited from the USA) and the Operating Superintendent FV Russell, introduced a new service increasing capacity by 75% in the morning up service and 50% in the evening down service at a modest cost of £80,000. Engine spurs were provided at the departure end of each platform so that the platform could be quickly cleared for the next arrival, and the engine from the spur would then head this train out. Fifty-one suburban trains left between 5.0pm and 6.0pm, twenty seven to Hackney Downs for Broxbourne and beyond, Chingford and Enfield, eight for the Loughton line, and sixteen for Ilford and beyond. To enable passengers to find their carriages quickly, first class carriages had a yellow line painted on them and third class were blue. This gave rise to the terms 'Jazz Trains' and 'Jazz Service', which persisted into the LNER and BR periods.

In terms of route mileage, the GE ranked sixth in the UK, but in terms of passengers carried, largely because of the volume of London suburban traffic, it was second. In the LNER group, it was larger than the GN and came second only to the NE. Like the NE, it enjoyed a virtual monopoly in its area no other major railway encroaching in Suffolk and only the M&GNR Joint line to Norwich and Cromer offering any opposition in Norfolk.

The company's coat of arms contained the cross and dagger of the City of London and the shields of Maldon, Ipswich, Norwich, Cambridge, Hertford, Northampton, Huntingdon and Middlesex, although the GE only just reached Northamptonshire at Peterborough. The GE worked the Lynn and Hunstanton Railway, which opened in 1862, just after the then Prince of Wales purchased Sandringham House served by Wolferton station on this line. The L&H was absorbed by the GE in 1890. A branch to Cromer (High) from Norwich was opened in 1877, and a second line to Southend was opened from Shenfield to Southend (Victoria) in 1888/9. The expected merger with the London, Tilbury and Southend Railway had failed to materialise, and the working arrangement with the GE had ceased in 1880 when the LT&S began working its own trains.

From 1st July 1870 until 15th January 1917, and for the summers of 1922 and 1923, the GE operated certain trains to Norwich and Hertford from St Pancras over the Tottenham and Hampstead line to which the GE and the Midland Railways subscribed. The GE granted access for Midland goods trains from this line to reach the docks via Temple

Mills and Stratford, and in return, the GE gained access to St Pancras for passenger trains, which was considered more accessible for the West End and relieved pressure on Liverpool Street. Royal trains to Wolferton and Newmarket race specials also used St Pancras. In the case of royalty, the use of St Pancras avoided the formalities that would have been necessary when the monarch entered the City.

The GE also built the Wisbech and Upwell tramway to Outwell alongside the Wisbech and Outwell canal in 1883, and extended to Upwell in 1884. This ran along public roads on which a speed limit of 8mph was imposed. Traffic was passengers, for whom special coaches were provided, and agricultural goods. Special locomotives were built with noiseless blast and enclosed motion, known as 'tram engines'.

Another agricultural branch was the Kelvedon, Tiptree and Tollesbury Pier Light Railway, opened to Tollesbury in 1904 and Tollesbury Pier in 1907. It served local fruit growers and Wilkins jam factory, and was worked by the GE.

Three other small railways, the Colne Valley and Halstead, the Mid-Suffolk Light and the Southwold Railways remained independent from the GE. The CV&H is dealt with on page 247 of this volume, and the Mid-Suffolk Light on page 250, as being included in the LNER group.

Despite its uncertain origins, the GE eventually became a reasonably profitable railway, and from 1880-1914, paid a dividend of nearly 3% on its shares. Much of the credit for its success must be attributed to Lord Hamilton. The company was a good employer, and was the first railway to introduce a pension scheme.

During the First World War, the GE was very much in prominence with the Home Fleet operating from Harwich and the forty-four additional military camps set up in East Anglia.

The GE always had a distinctive character of its own with its Westinghouse braked passenger stock, and this distinctiveness survived even after Nationalisation and to the end of the steam era.

There was a high standard of loyalty amongst the staff to the company and to the public. Probably only on the former GE London suburban lines could one see station staff polishing outdoor platform seats with furniture polish as late as the 1950s.

Locomotive Superintendents Eastern Counties Railway
    William Fernihough 1839-1846
    John Hunter 1846-1850
    John Viret Gooch 1850-1856, Retired
    Robert Sinclair 1856-1866, Resigned (GE from 1862)

Locomotive Superintendents Great Eastern Railway
    Samuel Waite Johnson 1866-1873, Resigned
    William Adams 1873-1878, Resigned
    Massey Bromley MA 1878-1881, Resigned
    James Holden 1885-1907, Retired
    Stephen Dewar Holden 1908-1912, Resigned
    Alfred John Hill 1912-1923, Formation of LNER
        (Chief Mechanical Engineer from 1915)

William Fernihough the first locomotive superintendent of the Eastern Counties Railway established a locomotive works at Gidea Park near Romford. He had been a pupil of Edward Bury, and agreed with the decision of John Braithwaite to build the line with a gauge of five feet to allow for engines with larger boilers with additional water space between the tubes. The site at Gidea Park was too restricted however, and his successor John Hunter opened a new works in 1847 at Stratford, then a rural site on the edge of the River Lea. The first locomotives to be built there however were designed by JV Gooch. His elder brother Thomas Longridge Gooch was a civil engineer for several railways and chief engineer of the Manchester and Leeds Railway from 1841-44 and his younger brother, Daniel, was the celebrated locomotive superintendent and later, as Sir Daniel, Chairman of the GWR. John Viret, who had been a pupil under Joseph Locke, had designed locomotives for his previous company, the London and South Western Railway. All his locomotives were without domes.

Robert Sinclair came from the Caledonian Railway (see Volume 4) to the Eastern Counties Railway, and immediately decided to modernise and standardise the motley collection of locos acquired from absorbed railways. A system of letter classification of locomotives was introduced at this time, but it is not entirely clear whether this was introduced by Sinclair or Gooch.

In addition to the post of Locomotive Superintendent, Sinclair succeeded the civil engineer Peter Shuyler Bruff, holding the dual positions until his resignation in 1866, by which time of course, the GE had been formed. He also acted as consultant to foreign railways, and owing to his training under Buddicom on the Liverpool and Manchester Railway, tended to favour outside cylinders. He introduced the first standard classes to be built in any great number, a mixed traffic 2-4-0 class Y and a 2-2-2 class W.

As well as being a good manager, he was also innovative introducing the Bissel leading truck on twenty 2-4-2Ts (class V). The Bissel, or 'pony truck', was patented in America on 4th August 1857. Sinclair also pioneered the development of cabs on locomotives, the use of steel for axles and tyres, and the installation of injectors invented by Henri Giffard in 1859. He even experimented with roller bearings, but was defeated by the inferiority of the materials available at the time.

SW Johnson served his pupilage under James Fenton at EB Wilson & Co in Leeds, and worked under Sturrock on the GNR before becoming acting locomotive superintendent on the Manchester, Sheffield and Lincolnshire Railway, and in 1864, Locomotive Superintendent of the Edinburgh and Glasgow Railway. His designs for the GE exhibited many characteristics of his later work for the Midland Railway for which he is most renowned - rimmed chimneys, combined domes and safety valves and short cabs. The system of classifying locomotives built at Stratford by the order number of the first batch was also introduced at this time. The system was similar to that used at Doncaster on the Great Northern Railway, but whereas the GN did not use it for locomotive classification purposes, the GE did. Locomotives built solely by outside firms continued to be referred to by the number of the first one of the class.

William Adams spent his early years as a marine engineer including four years as an engineer in the Sardinian navy. In 1853, at the age of 30, he was appointed Locomotive Superintendent to the North London Railway, helping with the erection of its works at Bow. Whilst on the NLR, he designed an inside cylinder 4-4-0T with outside-framed bogie, which became widely used. His designs for the GE were not so successful however, and his 2-6-0 goods engines, introduced after his resignation and the first 'moguls' in the UK, were a failure. He is, of course, better known for his work on the LSWR after leaving the GE. On the GE he introduced a 'stovepipe' chimney tapering inwards, and changed the locomotive livery from green (Johnson had used a darker shade) to black with red lining.

Massey Bromley graduated as an MA at Brasenose College, Oxford and served his pupilage under Johnson at Stratford, becoming Works Manager under Adams in 1874 at the age of 28. His 4-2-2 locomotives were similar to the GN singles, but with driving wheels of only 7ft 6in. For the increasing London suburban service he built 0-4-4Ts (class E10) similar to those of Johnson and Adams, and introduced an 0-6-0T (class M12) for shunting. He also greatly increased the number of locomotives built at Stratford. He resigned in 1881 to join John C Wilson in business. While returning from Manchester on 16th July 1884, he was one of 24 passengers killed in the Penistone accident on the MS&LR (see Volume 5B p.155)

After training at Crewe and his uncle's engineering works at Birmingham, TW Worsdell worked at Altoona on the Pennsylvania Railroad before returning to Crewe as Works Manager. Whilst with the GE he patented, with A von Borries, a two-cylinder compound system which he applied on the GE and more extensively on the North Eastern Railway later (see Volume 5A). His eleven compound 4-4-0s (class G16) were soon converted to simple expansion by Holden, but his saturated 2-4-2Ts (class M15) for suburban traffic were more successful, despite being initially so heavy on coal that they were known as 'gobblers'. Holden improved the design and greatly added to their number. Worsdell also introduced a very workmanlike 0-6-0 goods engine (class Y14) which was also continued by Holden and became LNER class J15, nearly 300 being built.

In 1882, Worsdell changed the engine livery to the famous Royal Blue to coincide with the commencement of Royal trains to Wolferton for Sandringham.

James Holden was apprenticed to Edward Fletcher at the Gateshead works of the York, Newcastle and Berwick Railway, Fletcher being married to his aunt. After a period as works manager of an engineering works in Sunderland, he joined the carriage and wagon department of the GWR in 1865, later to become manager of the GW carriage and wagon works at Swindon and assistant to William Dean. He succeeded Worsdell on the GER in 1885 as Locomotive and Carriage and Wagon Superintendent, and quickly brought to bear his technical and organising abilities, improving the efficiency of Stratford works and introducing much more standardisation.

The GE had been unfortunate in having lost a succession of locomotive engineers to other companies, but Holden brought a period of stability to the management which, with the valuable help of his chief draughtsman, Frederick V Russell (later to become Operating Superintendent), who did most of the design work, he completely revolutionised the GE locomotive department. It was to be these designs which came to epitomise the classic GE lines, and were continued by his successors.

He continued construction of the Y14 0-6-0s and M15 2-4-2Ts, having improved the design of the latter. In addition to these, nearly 900 locomotives of Holden's own design were built at Stratford during his 22 years in office. Two new classes of 2-4-0 were introduced for the main line traffic, and with the vogue in the 1890s for the reintroduction of singles following the invention of steam sanding, a limited number of 2-2-2 and 4-2-2 singles. With the increasing weight of trains however, it was found necessary to rebuild the T19 2-4-0s as 4-4-0s, and the singles were soon withdrawn.

Holden's most celebrated class were the *Claud Hamilton* 4-4-0s, the first of which was exhibited at the Paris Exhibition in 1900.

2-4-2Ts (Worsdell's M15 and Holden's C32) were used on suburban trains in addition to 0-4-4Ts and, in response to increasing traffic, Holden switched to concentrating on the construction of class R24 0-6-0Ts to provide more powerful haulage power. These became known as 'Buckjumpers' due to the GE practice of keeping steam on as long as possible to keep the tight schedules and frequent stops, relying on the Westinghouse brake to stop the train sharply. On starting with full regulator for rapid acceleration, the locomotive gave a visible jump. Even so, these small tank engines were severely tested on suburban trains.

It is not known whether Holden seriously contemplated building more 'Decapods'. This 0-10-0WT, totally without precedent in British locomotive design being the first ten-coupled locomotive produced in Britain (and the most powerful), proved itself capable in tests of doing everything expected of it but, as already mentioned, the scheme was never proceeded with. Holden introduced his own design of 0-6-0 goods engine, N31 class, in 1893, and this was his only design that was not so successful. Two further designs, F48 and G58, were introduced in 1900 and 1905.

Holden was responsible for the introduction of oil burning locomotives. Experiments started in 1887 to use up oil waste from the company's oil-gas plant, which had hitherto been polluting the River Lea. The oil was a mixture of coal tar and creosote, and was heated by the exhaust steam to 200° F, 30 degrees below its flashpoint. The oil was sprayed into the firebox twelve inches above the fire bars by an annular steam jet in the centre of each burner and then atomised and distributed by small steam jets with a mixture of air. Petroleum residues were also tried, but whilst being more efficient, supplies were not sufficiently plentiful. From 1891, about eighty locomotives and tenders were adopted for oil fuel or coal burning but Stratford did not produce enough oil and some was imported. In the early 1900s, the price of oil rose and the practice was discontinued as being no longer economic. Holden also adopted the Belpaire firebox boiler in 1901 for all subsequent main line locomotives, and rebuilt earlier ones with these also when boiler renewals became necessary. He also fitted his locomotives with the Macallen variable blast pipe.

The GE was a pioneer of connecting omnibus services in country districts, and twelve double deck open top buses were built at Stratford in 1904.

Under Holden, a wagon works was built at Temple Mills and a chemical laboratory at Stratford. A dormitory for enginemen was also opened at Stratford, which had good standards of comfort and convenience. Slippers were provided to avoid disturbing those asleep.

A JP and a Quaker, Holden was highly respected by all above and below him, and on his retirement in 1907 at the age of 70, he left the railway with a well-equipped fleet of locomotives, and a reputation which placed the GE amongst the leading companies in the country.

He was succeeded by his son SD Holden, who had been with the GE since he was 16 doing a four-year pupilage at Stratford. He subsequently became Inspector, District Locomotive Superintendent, Chief of Running Department and then Assistant Locomotive Superintendent to his father.

Lacking his father's exceptional qualities as an engineer and administrator, he was fortunate in having a very able chief draughtsman, ES Tiddeman, on whom he relied for much of the design work, just as his father had relied on FV Russell.

Three classes emerged from this combination, the class Y65 2-4-2Ts nicknamed 'Crystal Palace Tanks' because of their very large cabs, the G69 2-4-2Ts with side window cabs and, most significantly, the first 4-6-0 passenger engines on the GE, the S69 '1500' class.

The GE had always had a small engine policy due to the lightly engineered lines bequeathed to it by the impecunious ECR, but by 1911, sufficient improvements had been made on the main lines to permit 4-6-0s badly needed for express work. These locomotives turned out to be highly useful on the LNER, with their dual braking systems and small loading gauge, being able to go anywhere and do a wide variety of duties.

Their design followed that of the *Claud Hamilton* 4-4-0s in their general style, with Belpaire fireboxes and superheaters. Construction of J Holden's designs also continued, including further *Claud Hamiltons*, which were also now being superheated. Although still only in his early forties SD Holden suddenly resigned in October 1912, just short of completing his fifth year in office. We can only speculate on his reasons, but presumably he did not feel happy with his position.

His place was taken by AJ Hill, who had also apprenticed at Stratford some nine years before SD Holden. He had obtained a Whitworth scholarship at the GER Mechanics Institute, and had been Stratford Works Manager since 1899. He also continued the traditions in design set during J Holden's period, but greatly increased the size and power of his locomotives.

In 1915 he brought out his class L77 0-6-2T with inside Walschaerts valve gear for suburban passenger work, which as LNER class N7, was continued by Gresley as a standard LNER class. More powerful six-coupled tanks were also built, and the superheated goods 0-6-0 class E72 had the same boiler as the *Claud Hamilton* 4-4-0s. In 1920, he brought out an even more powerful 0-6-0 goods engine, class D81, with the same cylinders as class E72, but with the 4-6-0 boiler and superheating. These were the most powerful 0-6-0s in the country, and remained so until the Bulleid Q1 class on the Southern Railway in 1942.

The ultimate in GE locomotive development, not completed until 1923, were Hill's development of the Holden *Claud Hamilton* 4-4-0, with a larger superheated boiler, which became known as 'Super Clauds'. Regrettably the First World War caused the magnificent Royal Blue livery to be discontinued in 1915 for grey.

Hill was active in work for the Government concerning railways during the war for which he was awarded the CBE. A JP, he was keenly interested in ambulance work, and for many years was Honorary Secretary of the GE ambulance corps.

His title with the company was altered to Chief Mechanical Engineer in 1915. In 1923, when the GE went into the LNER, he was 61 and he retired.

Locomotive building was discontinued by the LNER at Stratford in 1924, a total of 1702 locomotives having been built there since 1851. However, a large repair shop, built in 1914, continued in use, subsequently being converted to diesel repairs in 1957. Driving position on GE locomotives was on the right.

Duplicate List

The original method of designating locomotives placed on the duplicate list was by adding a 0 after the number, but during 1879 the method was changed and the 0 was placed in front of the number.

LNER renumbering

Under the temporary scheme introduced in 9/1923, GE numbers were suffixed by the letter E. From 2/1924 until the 1946 renumbering, GE numbers had 7000 added.

BR renumbering

In common with other LNE locomotives, BR added 60000 to the 1946 LNER numbers.

Eastern Counties Railway(5ft gauge)

Incorporated 4/7/1836.
Opened: Dog Row, Mile End Road - Romford 18/6/1839 (ceremony, ordinary traffic from
20/6/1839); Webb's Square, Shoreditch - Mile End Road 1/7/1840 (Shoreditch station
named Bishopsgate from 1846); Romford - Brentwood 1/7/1840; Brentwood - Colchester
7/3/1843 (goods) 29/3/1843 (passenger). Leased Northern and Eastern Railway (*qv*)
1/1/1844. Gauge changed to standard 9-10/1844. Bishops Stortford (Northern and
Eastern Railway) to Brandon 30/7/1845 linking N&E line to Norfolk Railway (*qv*);
Woolwich branch (Eastern Counties and Thames Junction Railway, incorporated 1844, and
North Woolwich Railway and Pier, incorporated 1845, but both worked by ECR) Stratford
- Canning Town 29/4/1846; to North Woolwich 14/6/1847; Ely North Junction -
Peterborough Junction 10/12/1846 (goods) 14/1/1847 (passenger); March - Wisbech
3/5/1847 (goods, passenger later); Chesterton Junction (Cambridge) - St Ives 17/8/1847
- March South Junction 1/2/1848 (goods, passenger later). Took over working of
Norfolk Railway (*qv*) 8/5/1848; Witham - Maldon, Witham - Braintree 5/8/1848 (goods)
2/10/1848 (passenger); Water Lane (Angel Road) - Enfield 1/3/1849; Great Shelford -
Shepreth (GN) 1/8/1851; East Anglian Railway (*qv*) leased 1/1/1852; Eastern Union
Railway (*qv*) 1/1/1854; Newmarket Railway (*qv*) purchased 30/3/1854; Newmarket - Bury St
Edmunds 1/4/1854; Manningtree - Harwich 15/8/1854; Stratford Market, Sheet Factory
Junction - Victoria Park (North London Railway) 16/10/1854 (goods, passenger later)
worked by NLR until 1866 then by GE and NL in alternative years until 1874, then by GE
alone; Loughton branch 22/8/1856; Ipswich, East Suffolk Junction - Woodbridge 1/6/1859
and East Suffolk Railway taken over (incorporated 1851 as Halesworth, Beccles and
Haddiscoe Railway opened 20/11/1854, goods, 4/12/1854, passenger worked by ECR;
throughout Great Yarmouth, South Town to Woodbridge as East Suffolk Railway and
Lowestoft to Beccles 1/6/1859); Saxmundham to Leiston, Framlingham and Snape Maltings
goods branch, 1/6/1859; Leiston to Aldeburgh 12/4/1860. Amalgamated with Norfolk,
Eastern Union, East Suffolk, East Anglian and Newmarket Railways as Great Eastern
Railway 1/8/1862.

31 Locomotives built to 5ft gauge, altered to standard gauge 1844 as follows:

0-4-0 Built by Braithwaite Milner & Co.
DW 5ft 0in, Cyls 14 x 18. Ballast engines not at first numbered.

Name	Date	No	Date	no	date	
				Renumbered		
Essex	1838	151	c1839			Scrapped by 1846
Middlesex	1838	152	c1839			Scrapped by 1846
Norfolk	1838	153	c1839			Scrapped by 1846
Suffolk	1838	154	c1839	188	6/1848	Rebuilt 0-4-2ST by Kitson,
						Cyls 14 x 24 6/1848
						Sold in the period 1856-65
No name	6/1839	7	6/1839	92	12/1845	
				141	6/1846	Sold 1849
No name	6/1839	8	6/1839	93	12/1845	
				142	6/1846	Sold 1849

2-2-0 Built by Braithwaite Milner & Co.
DW 6ft 0in, LW 4ft 6in, Cyls 12 x 18. Four sold, two scrapped but dates not recorded.
Dome on raised firebox with safety valves 2nd safety valve on boiler.

No	Date	
1	6/1839	Nos 1-4 replaced 1852, disposal not known
2	6/1839	
3	6/1839	
4	6/1839	
5	6/1839	Replaced 1846, disposal not known
6	6/1839	Replaced 1852, disposal not known

Steam Carriage built by Walter Hancock, Stratford 1840.
Vertical cylinders, variable chain drive.
Not numbered in EC stock and further history not known.

2-2-0 Built by E Bury & Co.
DW 5ft 6in, Cyls 13 x 18

No	Date	Renumbered no	date	
9	5/1840	121	4/1852	Withdrawn by 1862, some records give DW 5ft 0in, Cyls 12 x 18
10	5/1840	122	4/1852	Lent to Midland Railway for a period from 10/1846 Withdrawn by 1862
11	5/1840			Sold or scrapped 11/1849

2-2-0 Built by Jones, Turner and Evans,
DW 6ft 0in, 13in diam cyls (stroke not recorded). Bury type safety valves on dome and on boiler.

No	Date	Renumbered no	date	
12	4/1841			Lent to Midland Railway for a period from 10/1846 Scrapped 1850
13	5/1841			Scrapped 1850
14	6/1841	123	1852	Withdrawn by 1862
15	6/1841			Lent to Midland Railway for a period from 10/1846 Replaced 1854

2-2-0 Built by Bury, Curtis & Kennedy.
DW 5ft 6in, Cyls 14 x 18. Rebuilt with splashers and shorter chimney.

No	Date	Renumbered no	date	
18	5/1842	126	1852	Withdrawn by 1862
19	1842	127	1852	Withdrawn by 1862
20	1842			Scrapped c1851
21	1842	128	4/1852	Withdrawn by 1862
22	1842	129	4/1852	Replaced 1856
23	6/1842	5	6/1846	
		118	4/1852	Withdrawn by 1862
24	1842	6	6/1846	
		119	4/1852	Withdrawn by 1862
25	6/1842	16	6/1846	Rebuilt 2-2-2 at unknown date. O/s cyls.
		124	4/1852	Replaced 1856

2-2-0 Built by Bury, Curtis and Kennedy.
Dimensions not known, but said to have been of smaller dimensions than 18 class above (Locomotive Magazine Vol 7 page 8).

No	Date		
26	6/1842		
	6/1846	Renumbered 17	
	4/1852	Renumbered 125	Withdrawn by 1862

2-4-0 Built by Stothert & Slaughter.
Dimensions not known.

No	Date	Renumbered no	date	
16	12/1841	94	1845	
		143	1846	Replaced 1850.
17	12/1841	95	1845	
		144	1846	Lent to Midland Railway for a period from
		218 or		10/1846 which may account for duplication
		219	1854	of number between 1850 and 1854
		169	1855	Withdrawn by 1862

254 Locomotives built to standard gauge as under:

1845-56 period.
Locomotive Superintendents:
     William Fernihough 1845-6
     John Hunter   1846-9
     John Viret Gooch   1850-6

2-2-2 Built by Jones & Potts.
DW 6ft 0in, Cyls 15 x 22 o/s. Haystack firebox.

No	Date	
41	7/1845	Replaced 1847, probably scrapped 1850
42	8/1845	Probably scrapped 1850
43	10/1845	Withdrawn by 1862
44	11/1845	Withdrawn by 1862
45	12/1845	Renumbered 201 by 1850. Withdrawn by 1862.
46	12/1845	Probably scrapped 1850.
47	2/1846	Renumbered 202 by 1850. Withdrawn by 1862.
49	4/1846	Withdrawn by 1862
(50)	3/1846	Transferred to Norfolk Railway on delivery (no 12), EC 204 from 1850. Renumbered 124 in 1856. Withdrawn by 1862.

2-2-2 Built by Stothert & Slaughter.
DW 6ft 0in, Cyls 15 x 22 o/s. Dome on firebox. All withdrawn by 1862.

No	Date	No	Date
51	6/1845	56	1845
52	6/1845	57	1845
53	6/1845	58	1845
54	7/1845	59	1845
55	7/1845	60	11/1845

2-2-2 Built by Stothert & Slaughter.
DW 6ft 0in, Cyls 15 x 22, inside cylinders and shorter wheelbase than 51-60 above.
Dome on firebox. Rebuilt with extended wheelbase and canopy type cab later.

No	Date	GE no 1862	Rebuilt	Duplicate no	year	Scrapped
61	1/1846	**61**	10/1864	610	1875	5/1878
62	1846	**62**	7/1868	620	1875	5/1879
63	1846	**63**	1/1863			1/1875
64	1846	**64**	5/1863			11/1873
65	1846	**65**	7/1868	650	1875	5/1878
66	1846	**66**	11/1864			5/1873
67	9/1846	**67**	6/1860	670	1875	8/1878

2-2-2 Built by EB Wilson & Co.
DW 5ft 6in, Cyls 15½ x 20 o/s. Long boiler.

No	Date	Renumbered no	year	Rebuilt 2-4-0ST	GE no 1862	Scrapped
116	5/1847	215	1854			
		18	1855	1855	**18**	6/1870
117	5/1847	216	1854			
		19	1855	1855	**19**	8/1871

2-2-2 Built by EB Wilson & Co.
Dimensions uncertain. Larger than 105-7 below. Centre dome. Safety valve on
firebox. Weatherboard.

No	Date	GE no 1862	Scrapped
103	6/1847	**103**	6/1874
104	9/1847	**104**	7/1868

2-2-2 Built by EB Wilson & Co.
DW 6ft 0in, Cyls 15 x 20. Similar to 103/4.

No	Date	GE no 1862	Scrapped
105	10/1848	**105**	11/1867
106	11/1848	**106**	10/1869
107	12/1848	**107**	4/1869

(2-2)-2-0 Built by R & W Hawthorn & Co Works no 385 (probable)
DW 5ft 6in, Cyls 13 x 18 o/s, 'smoke consuming'.

No	Date	
8	11/1845	Renumbered 120 about 1853. Withdrawn by 1862.

(2-2)-2-0 Built by Jones & Potts.
DW 6ft 0in; Cyls 15 x 24 o/s; Blr 13ft 7in long, no dome.

No	Date	
88	10/1846	All withdrawn by 1862.
89	12/1846	
90	4/1847	

(2-2)-2-0 Built by Jones & Potts.
DW 6ft 0in; Cyls 15 x 24; Domes. Safety valves on boiler and firebox.

No	Date	
91	7/1847	All withdrawn by 1862.
92	10/1847	
93	10/1847	

(2-2)-2-0 Built by Jones & Potts.
DW 6ft 0in; Cyls 15 x 22; Domes. All withdrawn by 1862. Similar to 91 class.

No	Date	
94	1847	Rebuilt (2-2)-2-2 at unknown date. Replaced 1857.
95	1847	Replaced by 1856
96	1847	Withdrawn by 1862
97	1847	Rebuilt (2-2)-2-2 at unknown date. Withdrawn by 1862.

(2-2)-2-0 Built by EB Wilson & Co.
DW 7ft 0in; LW 4ft 6in and 3ft 9in; Cyls 16 x 20 o/s. Boilers from these Cramptons were used for building 0-6-0 234 class (see page 21) and were officially regarded as rebuilds. A sixth Crampton built by Wilson went to the North British Railway (see page 157).

No	Date	Renumbered 1852	Boilers to 0-6-0 234 class
108	10/1848	233	8/1855
109	11/1848	234	10/1854
110	11/1848	235	11/1855
111	12/1848	236	9/1855
112	12/1848	237	10/1854

(2-2)-2-2 Built by R Stephenson & Co. Works nos 560-4.
DW 6ft 6in; Cyls 15 x 24 o/s; All rebuilt 2-2-2.

No	Date	Rebuilt 2-2-2	
98	10/1846	no date	Withdrawn by 1862
99	11/1846	no date	To GE **99** 1862. Scrapped 12/1866.
100	12/1846	no date	Withdrawn by 1862
101	12/1846	1859	To GE **101** 1862. Scrapped 12/1866.
102	1/1847	no date	Withdrawn by 1862

2-4-0 Built by Jones & Potts.
DW 6ft 0in; Cyls 15 x 22 o/s; ordered as 2-2-2.

No	Date		
50	9/1845	Rebuilt by Wilson & Co date unknown	
	8/1862	To GE **50**. Scrapped 2/1868.	

2-4-0 Built by Jones & Potts.
Dimensions uncertain.

No	Date		
48	2/1846	Rebuilt by Wilson & Co date unknown	
	by 1850	Renumbered 203	
	8/1862	To GE **203**. Scrapped 4/1876.	

2-4-0 Built by Jones & Potts.
DW 5ft 0in; Cyls 15 x 24 o/s. Long boiler.

No	Date	
102	6/1846	Renumbered 170 c1847
	8/1862	To GE **170**
	5/1866	Rebuilt
	7/1872	To duplicate list 1700. Scrapped 3/1879.
103	7/1846	Renumbered 171 c1847
	8/1862	To GE **171**
	11/1864	Rebuilt. Scrapped 8/1877 (Stratford Works Register gives 11/1876 – 9/1877).

2-4-0 Built by R Stephenson & Co. Works No 534 (no 68, others not certain).
DW 6ft 0in; Cyls 15 x 22 o/s. Long boiler. Centre dome when rebuilt.

No	Date	Rebuilt	GE no 1862	Duplicate no	year	Scrapped	
68	7/1846	9/1860	**68**	680	1876	6/1878	
69	7/1846	6/1861	**69**	690	1876	3/1876	
70	8/1846		**70**			7/1868	Accident Halesworth 26/9/1865

2-4-0 Built by R Stephenson & Co. Works no 358 9/1842.
Transferred from Midland Railway (ex-North Midland Railway), see Vol 3A page 21.
DW 4ft 6in; Cyls 14 x 20; Outside frames.

No	Date	
140	3/1847	Renumbered 217 1854 and 95 1856. Sold to Colne Valley & Halstead Railway 1861 (see page 247).

2-4-0 Built by Jones & Potts.
DW 5ft 6in; Cyls 15 x 24 o/s. No dome. Long boiler. Rebuilt with centre dome and weatherboard.

No	Date	Rebuilt	GE no 1862	Duplicate no	year	Scrapped	
78	10/1846	12/1863	**78**	780	1877	8/1880	
79	2/1847	12/1861	**79**	790	1877	8/1880	
80	2/1847	5/1863	**80**	800	1877	10/1881	Possibly withdrawn 7/1881
81	4/1847					10/1869	
82	11/1847						Probably numbered 82 in error see page 17

Renumbered

| 182 | 12/1847 | 7/1862 | **182** | 1820 | 1878 | 12/1878 |

2-4-0 Built by EB Wilson & Co.
DW 6ft 0in; Cyls 15 x 22 o/s. Long boiler. Rebuilt with centre dome and small upright cab.

No	Date	GE no 1862	Rebuilt	Scrapped
37	12/1846	**37**	12/1863	10/1878
38	1/1847	**38**	4/1864	8/1879
39	2/1847	**39**	11/1863	8/1880
40	2/1847	**40**	8/1865	8/1879
41	3/1847	**41**	1/1868	2/1882

2-4-0 Built by R Stephenson & Co.
DW 6ft 0in; Cyls 15 x 22 o/s. Centre dome. Small upright cab later.

No	Date	Rebuilt	GE no 1862	Duplicate no	year	Scrapped	
71	3/1847	5/1860	**71**	710	1876	5/1878	
72	4/1847	6/1867	**72**	720	1876	8/1878	Possibly withdrawn 9/1877
73	5/1847		**73**			11/1869	
74	5/1847					4/1859	After explosion at Ilford 17/4/1859
75	8/1847	6/1867	**75**	750	1876	4/1881	
76	9/1847		**76**			7/1868	
77	9/1847		**77**			8/1871	

2-4-0 Built by Vulcan Foundry Co. Works nos 289-298.
DW 5ft 0in; Cyls 15 x 24 o/s. Centre dome, weatherboard added.

No	Date	Rebuilt	GE no 1862	Scrapped
172	8/1847	3/1862	**172**	3/1874
173	9/1847		**173**	1856-65 period
174	9/1847	3/1860	**174**	6/1878
175	9/1847	4/1860	**175**	5/1879
176	10/1847		**176**	5/1870
177	11/1847	6/1861	**177**	1/1875
178	11/1847	4/1860	**178**	9/1875.
179	11/1847		**179**	1856-65 period
180	11/1847		**180**	3/1871
181	12/1847	12/1859	**181**	1/1878

2-4-0 Built by R Stephenson & Co. Works nos 713-5.
DW 5ft 0in; Cyls 15 x 24 o/s. Centre dome. Safety valve on raised firebox.

No	Date	GE no 1862	Scrapped
190	5/1849	**190**	7/1870
191	5/1849	**191**	7/1870
192	6/1849	**192**	2/1869

2-4-0 Built by R Stephenson & Co. Works no 669.
DW 5ft 6in; Cyls 15 x 24 o/s. Similar to 190.

No   Date
189 11/1847   To GE **189** 1862. Scrapped 11/1868

2-4-0 Built by B Hick & Son under sub-contract from R Stephenson & Co.
DW 5ft 6in; Cyls 15 x 22 o/s; Dome behind chimney, safety valve on firebox. Intended to be nos 182-7 and probably delivered with these numbers.

No	Date	GE no 1862	
82	10/1847	**82**	Scrapped 2/1869
83	10/1847	**83**	Scrapped 10/1869
84	5/1848	**84**	Scrapped 7/1870

```
85   6/1848   85   Replaced 1873
86   7/1848   86   Scrapped 2/1868
87   8/1848   87   To duplicate list 870 1868.  Scrap date not recorded.
```

2-4-0 Built by Jones & Potts.
DW 5ft 0in; Cyls 15 x 24 o/s; Centre dome. Intended to be nos 83-7 and 83-5 delivered
with these numbers.

No	Date	Rebuilt	GE no 1862	Duplicate no	date	Scrapped
183	1/1848		**183**			2/1869
184	2/1848	6/1859	**184**			12/1875
185	3/1848	5/1863	**185**	1850	10/1872	7/1875
186	12/1848	6/1862	**186**	1860	7/1872	4/1876
187	12/1848	5/1859	**187**	1870	7/1872	7/1875

2-4-0 Built by EB Wilson & Co.
DW 5ft 0in; Cyls 15 x 22.

No	Date	GE no 1862	Scrapped
193	12/1848	**193**	4/1869
194	12/1848	**194**	11/1868
195	12/1848	**195**	11/1868
196	12/1848	**196**	2/1871
197	1/1849	**197**	1/1870
198	1/1849	**198**	4/1869
199	2/1849	**199**	1/1870
200	2/1849	**200**	2/1871

0-4-2 Built by Longridge & Co.
DW 4ft 9in; Cyls 15 x 24 o/s; Long boiler; Rebuilt 2-4-0 DW 5ft 0in by Kitson & Co.

No	Date	Renumbered 1847/8	Rebuilt 2-4-0	
104	4/1846	145	1848	Both withdrawn
105	6/1846	146	1849	by 1862

0-6-0 Built by Stothert & Slaughter.
DW 4ft 0in; Cyls 16 x 24. Dome on firebox.

No	Date	Renumbered 1846/7	GE no 1862	Rebuilt	Duplicate no	date	Scrapped
97	3/1846	155	**155**		1550	2/1865	1865
98	3/1846	156	**156**		1560	2/1865	1865
99	4/1846	157	**157**	5/1866	1570	2/1865	5/1866
100	4/1846	158	**158**	6/1866	1580	2/1865	8/1880
101	4/1846	159	**159**		1590	2/1865	4/1873

0-6-0 Built by Kitson & Co. Works no 68.
DW 4ft 9in; Cyls 15 x 24. Long boiler.

No	Date
90	7/1846 Renumbered 149 about 1847. Withdrawn by 1862.

0-6-0 Built by Tayleur & Co. Works no 244.
DW 4ft 7½in; Cyls 15 x 24; Transferred on delivery from Norfolk Railway.

No	Date
91	3/1846 Renumbered 50 in 1847. Withdrawn by 1862.

0-6-0 Built by Jones & Potts.
DW 4ft 9in; Cyls 15 x 24; Coupled wheels later 5ft 0in. Long boiler.

No	Date	
151	11/1846	Withdrawn by 1862
152	1/1847	Rebuilt 1858 to GE **152** 1862. To duplicate list 1520 in 1864
	9/1973	Scrapped

0-6-0 Built by R Stephenson & Co. Works no 667.
DW 4ft 9in; Cyls 15 x 24.

No	Date	
188	10/1847	Renumbered 154 in 1848. Scrapped 1862.

0-6-0 Built by Stothert & Slaughter.
DW 4ft 9in; Cyls 16 x 24; Three locomotives returned to S&S in dispute as below.

No	Date	GE no 1862	
160	10/1847	**160**	Scrapped in period 1856-65
161	11/1847	**161**	Scrapped 12/1866
162	11/1847		Returned to makers in dispute
163	12/1847	**163**	Scrapped 12/1866
164	2/1848		Returned to makers in dispute
165	2/1848	**165**	Scrapped in period 1856-65
166	2/1848	**166**	Scrapped 6/1867
167	4/1848	**167**	Scrapped 6/1867
168	4/1848	**168**	Scrapped in period 1856-65
169	4/1848		Returned to makers in dispute

0-6-0 Built by P Rothwell & Co, Bolton.
DW 4ft 9in; Cyls 15 x 24; Inside frames, long boiler type with 'haystack' firebox.
Transferred on delivery from Midland Railway (86 class), see Vol 3A page 77.

No	Date	
106	11/1846	Renumbered 153 in 1846. Sold 1857.

0-6-0 Built by Kitson & Co. Works nos 96/7.
DW 4ft 9in; Cyls 15 x 24; Similar to no 90 above with larger firebox. Wt 23 tons.

No	Date	Renumbered no	year	
170	3/1847	147	c1847	No record of scrapping date
171	4/1847	148	c1847	Both replaced 1865, but probably withdrawn by 1862

0-2-2T Built by WB Adams, Bow 4/1847.
DW 3ft 4in; Cyls 3½ x 6; Vertical boiler 1ft 7in diam x 4ft 3in high; THS 43.5 sq ft; Wt 1¼ tons.

Name	
Express	Steam powered carriage seating 7. Originally named *Little Wonder* and also known as *Lilliputian*, possibly a nickname. Not numbered in EC locomotive stock and no record of disposal.

2-2-0T Built by WB Adams, Bow 1/1849.
DW 5ft 0in; Cyls 8 x 12 o/s; Horizontal boiler 2ft 6in o/s diam; THS 255 sq ft; Wt 15 tons 7 cwt.

Name	
Enfield	Combined locomotive and carriage on four wheels seating 42 passengers. Rebuilt as 2-2-2T at unknown date. Not numbered in EC stock and no record of disposal.

2-2-0WT Built by WB Adams, Bow 8/1849.
DW 4ft 9in; Cyls 8 x 12 o/s; Separate locomotive and four wheel carriage.
Name
Cambridge   Engine to stationary use 1872. Not numbered in EC stock.

See also page 26 Norfolk Railway for 2-2-0T *Eagle*.

Gooch locomotives 1851-9

2-2-2 Built by Brassey, Jackson & Betts. Works nos below (B).
                EC Railway at Stratford. Works nos 28-33 (S).
DW 6ft 11/8in; LW & TW 3ft 8in; WB 6ft 9in + 7ft 3in; Cyls 15 x 22 o/s;
Boiler 3ft 7^1/8in diam. 274-9 had no domes. Stratford locomotives had boilers built by
Beyer Peacock & Co with dome behind chimney and tenders by Kitson & Co, and are
thought to have been renewals of earlier locos. Classified 'C' by Sinclair. Rebuilt
with cab, dome and 'stovepipe' chimney.

No	Date	Works no	GE nos 1862	Duplicate no	year	Scrapped
274	12/1855	B 42	274			1/1875
275	7/1856	B 43	275			1/1875
276	7/1856	B 44	276			10/1875
277	8/1856	B 45	277			7/1878
278	9/1856	B 46	278			7/1875
279	9/1856	B 47	279			9/1874
27	10/1856	S 28	27			1/1878
94	2/2857	S 29	94			8/1876
280	1/1859	S 30	280	2800	1879	5/1879
281	1/1859	S 31	281	2810	1879	2/1879
282	1/1859	S 32	282	2820	1879	5/1879
283	1/1859	S 33	283	2830	1879	12/1879

2-4-0 Built by Sharp Stewart & Co. Works nos below (SS).
                Kitson & Co. Works nos below (K).
                Brassey, Jackson & Betts (B).
DW 5ft 6in; Cyls 15 x 24 o/s; Sharp Stewart locomotives had a dome on firebox. The
others had no domes. Known as *Butterflies*.

No	Date	Works no	GE no 1862	Duplicate no	year	Scrapped
238	5/1855	SS 853	238			1/1873
239	5/1855	SS 854	239			12/1875
240	5/1855	SS 855	240			12/1875
241	7/1855	SS 865	241			7/1875
242	7/1855	SS 866	242			1/1873
243	7/1855	SS 867	243			12/1875
244	5/1855	K 434	244			1/1876
245	6/1855	K 435	245			1/1875
246	6/1855	K 436	246			1/1873
247	7/1855	K 437	247			8/1875
248	7/1855	K 438	248			10/1873
249	8/1855	K 439	249	0249	1879	12/1879
214	1/1856	B	214	2140	1875	8/1879
215	1/1856	B	215	2150	1875	8/1879
216	2/1856	B	216			6/1874
217	2/1856	B	217	2170	1875	2/1879
218	4/1856	B	218			9/1874
219	6/1856	B	219	2190	1875	1/1876

0-6-0 Built by EC Railway at Stratford. Works nos 13-17.
DW 5ft 6in; Cyls 15 x 24; No domes. O/s frames. Regarded officially as rebuilds
using the boilers from former Cramptons (see page 15). Known as *Floating Batteries*.

		GE no		Duplicate		
No	Date	1862	Rebuilt	no	year	Scrapped
234	10/1854	**234**	10/1867	0234	1880	4/1882
237	10/1854	**237**	4/1870	0237	1880	10/1883
233	8/1855	**233**	6/1869	0233	1880	1/1883
236	9/1855	**236**	10/1867	0236	1880	11/1884
235	11/1855	**235**	12/1869	0235	1880	1/1883

0-2-2WT Built by EB Wilson & Co 1851.
DW 5ft 6in; Cyls 10 x 17; O/s bearings on LW and TW. Ordered by Norfolk Railway.

No	Date	
1	3/1852	All withdrawn
2	3/1852	by 1862
3	3/1852	

2-2-2WT Built by EC Railway at Stratford. Works nos below (S).
                   RB Longridge & Co (L).
DW 6ft 6in; Cyls 11 x 22 o/s (later 12 x 22); No dome;
WP of Stratford locomotives 110 lbs/sq in; Wt 23¾ tons. Classified 'A' by Sinclair.

		Works	GE no	Duplicate		
No	Date	no	1862	no	year	Scrapped
20	9/1851	S 1	**20**			3/1871
21	11/1851	S 2	**21**			3/1871
22	1/1852	S 3	**22**	022	1/1878	12/1879
23	1/1852	S 4	**23**			3/1871
24	1/1852	S 5	**24**			6/1873
25	8/1852	S 6	**25**			11/1871
4	4/1852	L	**4**			1/1874
5	10/1852	L	**5**			11/1871
6	10/1852	L	**6**			11/1871

2-2-2WT Built by EC Railway at Stratford. Works Nos 7-12, 18-27.
DW 6ft 6in; LW & TW 3ft 8in; WB 6ft 9in + 7ft 11in; Cyls 12 x 22 o/s (7-12),
14 x 22 o/s (250-9); Wt 27 tons 1½ cwt. Sinclair class B. Weatherboards added later.

		GE no		Duplicate		
No	Date	1862	Rebuilt	no	year	Scrapped
7	6/1853	**7**				6/1874
8	8/1853	**8**	12/1874 2-2-4T			
			Inspection saloon			
			7/1876 4-2-4ST	08	12/1877	3/1883
9	4/1854	**9**				8/1874
10	4/1854	**10**				11/1871
11	4/1854	**11**				3/1871
12	4/1854	**12**				1/1874
250	12/1854	**250**		0250	1879	12/1879
251	12/1854	**251**				8/1878
252	12/1854	**252**		0252	1879	12/1879
253	12/1854	**253**		0253	1879	12/1879
254	1/1855	**254**				5/1873
255	1/1855	**255**		2550	1877	12/1879
256	2/1855	**256**				10/1875
257	4/1855	**257**				1/1876
258	5/1855	**258**		2580	1877	12/1878
259	5/1855	**259**		2590	1877	12/1878

Sinclair locomotives 1858-61

2-4-0 Built by P Rothwell & Co. Works nos 183-8.
DW 5ft 1in; Cyls 18 x 22 o/s; Inclined cyls. Dome behind chimney with safety valve.
Second safety valve on firebox. Weatherboard. **Class Z**

		GE no	
No	Date	1862	Scrapped
301	2/1858	**301**	4/1873
302	3/1858	**302**	10/1873
303	10/1858	**303**	4/1873
304	10/1858	**304**	1/1873
305	11/1858	**305**	11/1875
306	12/1858	**306**	1/1873

2-4-0 Built by Neilson & Co. Works nos below.
R Stephenson & Co. Works nos below.
R&W Hawthorn & Co. Works nos below.
DW 6ft 1in; Cyls 18 x 24 o/s; Coupled WB 9ft 0in; WP 120 lbs/sq.in.
Class Y. Dome over firebox. Cylinders altered to 17in diam.

The following were built by Neilson & Co. Works nos 496-515, and had no cabs when
built. Class U13 rebuilds had DW 6ft 3in. All rebuilds had centre domes and cabs.

		GE no			Duplicate		
No	Date	1862	Rebuilt		no	year	Scrapped
307	7/1859	**307**	1882	U13	0307	1888	11/1893
308	8/1859	**308**	11/1878	4-4-0			
			11/1883		0308	1888	8/1894
309	9/1859	**309**	6/1875		0309	1888	6/1888
310	9/1859	**310**					1886
311	10/1859	**311**	10/1877	4-4-0	0311	1888	3/1889
312	10/1859	**312**	12/1876	4-4-0	0312	1888	10/1890
313	10/1859	**313**	4/1872				2/1885
314	10/1859	**314**	3/1878	4-4-0	0314	1888	5/1891
315	11/1859	**315**	12/1881		0315	1888	6/1890
316	11/1859	**316**	3/1881		0316	1888	1892
317	12/1859	**317**	12/1878	4-4-0	0317	1888	10/1888
318	12/1859	**318**					3/1884
319	1/1860	**319**	6/1882		0319	1888	10/1892
320	1/1860	**320**	10/1878	4-4-0	0320	1888	12/1890
321	2/1860	**321**	10/1882	U13	0321	1888	6/1893
322	3/1860	**322**					10/1883
323	3/1860	**323**					5/1883
324	3/1860	**324**	10/1878	4-4-0	0324	1888	5/1891
325	3/1860	**325**	10/1878	4-4-0	0325	1888	10/1889
326	3/1860	**326**					5/1883

The following were built by R Stephenson & CO. Works nos 1361-75, with cabs.
No 327 was exhibited at the International Exhibition 1862.
Class U13 rebuilds DW 6ft 3in.

		GE no			Duplicate		
No	Date	1862	Rebuilt		no	year	Scrapped
327	2/1861	**327**	4/1872				
			10/1876	4-4-0	0327	1888	11/1888
328	2/1861	**328**	12/1882	U13	0328	1890	1892
329	3/1861	**329**	10/1877	4-4-0	0329	1888	1/1890
330	3/1861	**330**	12/1880		0330	1888	11/1892
331	4/1861	**331**	4/1882		0331	1888	5/1891
332	4/1861	**332**	9/1883		0332	1888	6/1892
333	5/1861	**333**					5/1885
334	6/1861	**334**					11/1886
335	7/1861	**335**	12/1879		0335	1888	1892

```
336    7/1861    336    9/1875           0336    1888    11/1888
337    8/1861    337                                      6/1886
338    8/1861    338    6/1880                            8/1889
339    9/1861    339                      0339    1890    2/1892
340    9/1861    340    8/1883            0340    1890    12/1891
341   10/1861    341   10/1882    U13     0341    1890    4/1894
```

The following were built by R&W Hawthorn & Co. Works nos 1105-19.
Class U13 rebuilds DW 6ft 3in.

		GE no			Duplicate		
No	Date	1862	Rebuilt		no	year	Scrapped
342	2/861	342	12/1876	4-4-0			3/1889
343	3/1861	343	12/1888				3/1889
344	3/1861	344	9/1882	U13	0344	1890	10/1893
345	4/1861	345	6/1880		0345	1890	7/1892
346	4/1861	346	6/1875				2/1885
347	5/1861	347	6/1875				11/1886
348	5/1861	348					4/1886
349	6/1861	349	3/1878	4-4-0	0349	1890	7/1890
350	7/1861	350					12/1887
351	8/1861	351	5/1879		0351	1890	1892
352	8/1861	352	6/1879		0352	1890	6/1892
353	9/1861	353	7/1880				10/1889
354	10/1861	354					10/1883
355	10/1861	355	12/1880		0355	1890	1892
356	11/1861	356	1882	U13	0356	1890	6/1893

Class continued by Great Eastern Railway. See page 36.
For other Sinclair locomotives built by Great Eastern Railway see page 35.

Northern and Eastern Railway (5ft gauge)

Incorporated 4/7/1836.
Opened: Stratford (ECRailway) to Broxbourne 15/9/1840; extended to Harlow 9/8/1841; to
Spelbrook 19/11/1841; to Bishop's Stortford 16/5/1842; Broxbourne to Hertford
31/10/1843. Lines to Cambridge, Peterborough, Lincoln and Norwich north of Bishop's
Stortford were not proceeded with and the company was leased to the Eastern Counties
Railway on 1/1/1844. The ECR altered the gauge to standard together with its own
system in 9-10/1844, and opened the line from Bishop's Stortford to Brandon (Norfolk
Railway) on 30/7/1845 creating a through route via Cambridge and Ely to Norwich.

14 locomotives as under: Although taken over in 1844, ECR numbers were not applied
until 4/1846, by which time the original intention of numbering them 27-40 had been
superseded and they were given the numbers 23-36. There is no record of a numbering
system on the N&E Railway, and there are discrepancies in various accounts of the
original ECR numbers of certain locos.

2-2-2 Built by Longridge & Co. Works Nos 142 (possibly), 156-60 (No 25 not known).
DW 6ft 0in; Cyls 14 x 18. Other dimensions varied. No 29 had a WB of 8ft 6½in + 6ft
4in and No 30 6ft 8in + 7ft 2in. Nos 35/6 and 23/5 had a WB of 7ft 6in + 6ft 11in.
Haystack firebox. O/s frames.

	ECR no	Renumbered		
Date	6/1846	no	year	
9/1840	33	28	1852	Withdrawn by 1862
11/1841	29			Withdrawn by 1862
12/1841	30			Withdrawn by 1862
1/1842	35	27	1852	Replaced 1856
2/1842	36			Scrapped about 1850
4/1842	23	26	1852	Withdrawn by 1862
4/1842	25			Scrapped 1850-2

2-2-2 Built by Tayleur & Co. Works nos 120 & 121 (or 124/5), 154.
DW 6ft 0in; Cyls 14 x 18. Dome behind chimney and on firebox.

	ECR no	
Date	6/1846	
10/1840	27	All scrapped
10/1840	28	in period
10/1841	34	1850-2

2-2-2 Built by R Stephenson & Co. Works nos 321/2.
DW 6ft 0in; Cyls 14 x 18; WB 6ft0in + 5ft 9in. Similar to Longridge batch.

	ECR no	
Date	6/1846	
5/1841	31	Scrapped 1850-2
6/1841	32	(one in 1850)

2-2-2 Built by R Stephenson & Co. Works no 323.
DW 5ft 6in; Cyls 14 x 20; Long boiler type.

Date	
12/1841	To ECR no 24 6/1846. Scrapped about 1850.

2-2-2 Built by Bury, Curtis & Kennedy.
Dimensions not known. O/s frames. Haystack firebox.

Date	
5/1843	to ECR no 26 6/1846
1852	Renumbered 143
1854	Renumbered 218 or 219
1856	Renumbered 129
	Rebuilt 2-4-0ST DW 4ft 3in at unknown date
	Withdrawn by 1862

Norfolk Railway

Incorporated 30/6/1845 by amalgamation of Yarmouth & Norwich Railway (incorporated
18/6/1842) and Norwich & Brandon Railway (incorporated 1844). Y&N Railway opened
Yarmouth (Vauxhall) to Norwich (Thorpe) 1/5/1844; Norwich (Trowse) to Brandon (opened
30/7/1845), Norwich (Thorpe Jct) to Trowse 15/12/1845; leased Lowestoft Railway &
Harbour 1846 (opened from Reedham 3/5/1847 (goods), 1/7/1847 (passenger)). Wymondham
to Dereham (East Anglian Railway) 15/2/1847 (passenger), 7/12/1847 (goods); Dereham to
Fakenham 20/3/1849. Connection with Eastern Counties Railway (formerly Northern &
Eastern) at Brandon. Worked by ECR from 1848, and amalgamated Eastern Counties,
Eastern Union, East Suffolk, East Anglian and Newmarket Railways as Great Eastern
Railway 1/8/1862.

40 locomotives as under. ECR numbers applied in 1850.

Type and dimensions unknown. Probably ex-contractor's locomotive.

	Approximate	
No	date	
1	1844	Both sold prior
2	1844	to ECR working

2-2-2 Built by R Stephenson & Co. Works nos 396-8.
DW 5ft 6in; Cyls 14 x 22 o/s. The sale of nos 3 & 5 to the Liverpool, Crosby &
Southport Railway was not completed until 9/1849 due to dispute about the price of
£1500 which was eventually reduced by £100. See Vol 3B pp 17/18.

No	Date	
3	5/1844	Sold 8/1848 to Liverpool, Crosby and Southport Railway
4	5/1844	To ECR no 45 1850 and GE **45** 1862. Scrapped 7/1868.
5	5/1844	Sold 8/1848 to Liverpool, Crosby and Southport Railway

2-2-2 Built by R Stephenson & Co. Works nos 427-32.
DW 6ft 0in; Cyls 15 x 24 o/s. Haystack firebox. Ordered by Yarmouth & Norwich
Railway.

No	Date	ECR no 1850			
6	6/1845	46 7	7/1845	47	All withdrawn
8	8/1845	48	by 1862		
9	10/1845	140			
10	12/1845	141			
11	11/1845	142			

(No 12 was 2-2-2 ex-Eastern Counties no 50, see page 14.)

0-6-0 Built by Tayleur & Co. Works nos uncertain.
DW 4ft 9in; Cyls 15 x 24. Long boiler. Rebuilt with conventional boiler with centre
dome.

No	Date	ECR no 1850	Rebuilt	GE no 1862	
21	6/1845	225		**225**	Scrapped 7/1867
22	8/1845	226	4/1856		
			9/1866	**226**	Scrapped 2/1883
23	9/1845	227	12/1863	**227**	Scrapped 4/1881
24	9/1845	24			Sold to Royal Danish Railways 6/1853

(2-2)-2-0 Built by Tayleur & Co. Works nos 234-6.
DW 6ft 0in; Cyls 15 x 24 o/s. Long boiler.

No	Date	ECR no 1850	GE no 1862	
13	7/1846	42	**42**	Scrapped 7/1868
14	7/1846	143		Replaced 1852. Scrapped 1856-65.
15	7/1846	144		Scrapped 1856-65

0-6-0 Built by Tayleur & Co. Works no uncertain.
DW 4ft 9in; Cyls 15 x 22. Centre dome. No cab or weatherboard.

No	Date	
20	1/1846	To ECR no 224, 1850 and GE **224**, 1862
	8/1861	Rebuilt
	1877	To duplicate list 2240. Scrapped 1/1882.

0-6-0 Built by Tayleur & Co. Works nos 244-53.
DW 4ft 7½in; Cyls 15 x 24; Long boiler. Rebuilt with conventional boiler, centre
dome. First locomotive (Tayleur 244) transferred on delivery to Eastern Counties
Railway (see page 15).

No	Date	ECR no 1850	Rebuilt	GE no 1862	Duplicate no	year	Scrapped
16	8/1846	220	9/1960	**220**			9/1872
17	10/1846	221	2/1861	**221**	2210	1877	10/1881
18	10/1846	222	5/1863	**222**	2220	1877	10/1881
19	10/1846	223	5/1864	**223**	2230	1877	11/1881
25	10/1846	228	1/1863	**228**			9/1873
26	10/1846	229		**229**			1856-65
27	11/1846	230		**230**			1856-65
28	11/1846	231	6/1867	**231**	2310	1878	10/1881
29	12/1846	232		**232**			12/1867

2-4-0 Built by R Stephenson & Co. Works nos 571-80.
DW 5ft 7in; Cyls 15 x 22 o/s. Long boiler. Rebuilt with conventional boiler, centre
dome.

No	Date	ECR no 1850	Rebuilt	GE no 1862	Duplicate no	year	Scrapped
30	11/1846	130		**130**			11/1868
31	11/1846	131	2/1861	**131**			1/1882
32	1/1847	132	6/1861	**132**			9/1880
33	2/1847	133	12/1861	**133**			8/1877
34	4/1847	134		**134**			11/1870
35	4/1847	135	1/1861	**135**	1350	1872	8/1878
36	8/1847	136		**136**			11/1868
37	9/1847	137		**137**			12/1866
38	10/1847	138	4/1860	**138**	1380	1872	8/1879
39	11/1847	139		**139**			12/1866

2-2-0WT Built by J&E Headly Bros, Cambridge 1849.
DW 4ft 6in; Cyls 7 x 14; LW 2ft 6½in; WT approximately 2 tons empty; Overall length
12ft. Named *Eagle*. Domeless boiler, raised firebox with well tank beneath footplate.
Intended as Engineer's locomotive and not numbered into Norfolk or EC Railway stock.
Later altered as 2-2-2WT with built in saloon. Scrapped 1868.

Eastern Union Railway

Incorporated 19/7/1844 to take up lapsed ECR powers.
Opened: Colchester to Ipswich 1/6/1846 (goods), 11/6/1846 (official ceremony),
15/6/1846 (passenger). Amalgamated with Ipswich, Bury & Norwich Railway (incorporated
21/7/1845 as Ipswich & Bury St Edmunds Railway) 1/1/1847; opened Ipswich to Bury St
Edmunds 30/11/1846 (goods), 7/12/1846 (official ceremony), 24/12/1846 (passenger).
Purchased Eastern Union and Hadleigh Junction Railway (incorporated 1846) in 1847;
opened Bentley to Hadleigh 21/8/1847 (goods), 2/9/1847 (passenger). Haughley Junction
(on Bury St Edmunds line) to Finningham opened 7/6/1848, extended to Burston 2/7/1849
and to Norwich (Victoria) 3/12 1849 providing alternative route to Norwich in
competition with ECR. Leased by ECR 1854, and amalgamated with Eastern Counties,
Norfolk, East Anglian and Newmarket Railways as Great Eastern 1/8/1862.

31 Locomotives as under:

2-2-2 Built by Sharp Brothers. Works nos as below.
DW 5ft 0in (1-3), 5ft 6in (4-6); LW & TW 3ft 6in; Cyls 15 x 20; Blr 3ft 6in x 10ft
0in; Wt 18 tons 12 cwt. O/s frames. Dome behind chimney with safety valve. No cab.
Hugh Moffat, *East Anglia's First Railway* (Terence Dutton, 1987) states that numbers 1-
3 were intended for the Blackburn and Preston Railway and gives a list of names which
is quite different to that given in the Locomotive Magazine articles. In the
following list the Locomotive Magazine names are shown first. Naming was discontinued
after No 6.

No	Name	Date	Works no	ECR nos 1854	1855	GE no 1862	Rebuilt	Duplicate no	year	Scrapped
1	*Ipswich* or									
	Colchester	5/1846	346	260		**260**	5/1869	2600	1877	12/1879
2	*Bury* or									
	Ipswich	5/1846	347	261		**261**	4/1864			10/1874
3	*Colchester* or									
	City of Norwich									
		5/1846	348	262		**262**	5/1863	2620	1877	12/1879
4	*Diss* or									
	Bury St Edmunds									
		10/1846	368	263		**263**	7/1862			1/1873
5	*Stowmarket* or									
	Orwell	10/1846	372	264		**264**	6/1868	2640	1877	8/1877

```
 6  Haughley or
    Stour      10/1846  388  265        265  12/1865             3/1874
14             12/1846  389  266        266  12/1862             7/1875
15             12/1846  390  267        267   3/1869  2670  1876  8/1880
16              3/1847  406  268        268   4/1866             3/1874
17              3/1847  407  269        269   9/1865             3/1874
18               1848*       270        270  11/1863             2/1875
19               1848*       271  116    116                     6/1867
26               1849*       272  117    117  10/1865            2/1875
```

* Nos 18, 19 & 26 were delivered in early 1849 and 18/19 were probably built in 1848, but have not been positively identified in Sharp's list. Works no of no 26 was either 565 or 566. They had central dome.

2-2-2 Built by Stothert & Slaughter.
DW 5ft 0in; LW & TW 3ft 6in; Cyls 15 x 22; Blr 10ft 6in long. Haystack firebox. All were rebuilt as 2-4-0 in 1852. Wt 34 tons 9 cwt.

		ECR no	GE no	
No	Date	1854	1862	Scrapped
7	1846	205	205	c1860
8	1846	206	206	6/1867
20	1848	209	209	c1860
21	1848	210	210	2/1868

0-4-2 Built by Stothert & Slaughter.
DW 5ft 0in; TW 3ft 6in; Cyls 15 x 22; Blr 10ft 6in long.
Moffat (above) gives *Essex* or *Suffolk* as the name for no 9.

			ECR nos		GE no	
No	Name	Date	1854	1856	1862	Scrapped
9	*Suffolk*	1846	207		207	by 6/1867
10	(naming	1846	208		208	by 6/1867
22	discontinued)	1848	211		211	6/1867
23		1848	212		212	by 6/1867
24		1848	213		213	by 6/1867
25		1848	214	204	204	6/1867

2-2-2 Built by R & W Hawthorn & Co. Works nos 471-3.
DW 6ft 0in; LW & TW 3ft 6in; Cyls 15 x 21; Blr 3ft 7in x 11ft 6in; Wt 20tons 6cwt. O/s frames. Centre dome. No cab. Ordered by Ipswich & Bury Railway.

		ECR no		
No	Date	1854		
11	1846	273		All
12	1846	274	Renumbered 271 1855	withdrawn
13	1846	275	Renumbered 272 1855	by 1862

2-2-2WT Built by Sharp Brothers. Works no 595.
DW 5ft 6in; Cyls 14 x 18 or 15 x 20. O/s frames. Dome behind chimney. Weatherboard. Possibly converted from undelivered Ipswich and Bury tender engine.

No	Date	
27	11/1849	To ECR no 16 1854 and GE **16** 1862. Scrapped 2/1871

2-2-0WT Built by Kitson, Thompson & Hewitson. Works no 270.
DW 5ft 0in; LW 3ft 0in; Cyls 9 x 15; Blr 2ft 6in x 10ft 6in.

No	Name	Date	
28	*Ariels Girdle*	1851	To ECR 17 1854 and GE **17** 1862
		1868	Rebuilt 2-4-0T Wt 10¾ tons; DW 4ft 0in. Later worked on Millwall Extension Railway. No 17 was re-used in 5/1875 for a class T7 0-4-2T, and until scrapped in 5/1879, this locomotive was recorded at Stratford as 17A.

2-2-2WT Built by Sharp Brothers. Works nos 765/6/8.
DW 5ft 0in; LW & TW 3ft 6in; Cyls 14 x 18; Blr 3ft 6in x 9ft 6in; Wt 19 tons approx.

		ECR no	GE no	
No	Date	1854	1862	Scrapped
29	2/1854	13	13	11/1871
30	2/1854	14	14	11/1871
31	2/1854	15	15	11/1871

Newmarket Railway

Incorporated 16/7/1846 as the Newmarket and Chesterford Railway (name changed 1847).
Opened: Great Chesterford (ECR) to Newmarket 3/1/1848 (goods) 4/4/1848 (passenger);
Six Mile Bottom to Cambridge 9/10/1851 (Six Mile Bottom to Chesterford closed).
Company worked by ECR from 1850, purchased 30/3/1854.
6 Locomotives as under:

2-4-0 Built by Gilkes Wilson & Co, Middlesbrough. Works nos 2-7.
DW 5ft 6in; Cyls 15 x 22 o/s. Dome and safety valve behind chimney. Weatherboard.
ECR 1850 numbers possibly not applied until 1852.

Name	ECR no 1850	GE no 1862	Scrapped	
Beeswing	31	31	2/1869	
Queen of Trumps	32	32	12/1866	
Van Tromp	33	33	7/1868	
Flying Dutchman	34	34	7/1868	
Eleanor	35	35	12/1866	
Alice Hawthorn	36	36	4/1870	Possibly to duplicate list 1869

East Anglian Railway

Incorporated 27/7/1847 by amalgamation of Lynn and Ely, Lynn and Dereham and Ely and
Huntingdon Railways (all incorporated 1846).
Lynn and Ely opened King's Lynn to Downham Market and to Kings Lynn Harbour
27/10/1846. Lynn and Dereham opened King's Lynn to Narborough 27/10/1846. Narborough
to Swaffham opened 10/8/1847 extended to Sporle 26/10/1847 and to Dereham 11/9/1849.
St Ives to Huntingdon opened 17/8/1847, Downham Market to Ely North Junction (ECR)
26/10/1847. Company initially leased to Great Northern Railway 1851 but lease taken
over by ECR 1/1/1852. Amalgamated with Eastern Counties, Norfolk, Eastern Union, East
Suffolk and Newmarket Railways as Great Eastern Railway 1/8/1862.
10 Locomotives as under (plus 1 ballast engine of which no details are recorded):

2-2-2 Built by Sharp Brothers. Works nos 369-70, 383, 428/9, 503, 507.
DW 5ft 6in; Cyls 15 x 20. Dome and safety valve behind chimney. No cab.

Name	Date	ECR no 1852	GE no 1862	Rebuilt	Scrapped	
Eagle	1846	108	108	8/1862		Stationary use Peterton 7/1875
Vulture	1846	109	109		6/1867	
Ostrich	1846	110	110		1/1870	
Falcon	1846	111	111		9/1868	
Hawk	1847	112	112		10/1869	
Kite	1847	113	113		10/1869	
Raven	1848	114	114		3/1870	
Heron	1848	115	115		1/1870	

0-4-2 Built by Sharp Brothers. Works nos 533, 536.
DW 5ft 0in; Cyls 16 x 22. Dome behind chimney. No cab. Safety valve on firebox.

Name	Date	ECR no 1852	GER no 1862	
Lion	1848	162	162	To duplicate list 1620 7/1872. Scrapped 12/1872.
Tiger	1848	164	164	Scrapped 11/1871. See cover picture.

EASTERN COUNTIES RAILWAY NUMBER INDEX

1	1839	2-2-0		28	1846	ex-N&E
-3	1852	0-2-2WT			1852	ex-N&E 2-2-2 33
4	1839	2-2-0		29	1846	ex-N&E
	1852	2-2-2WT		-30		
5	1839	2-2-0		31	1846	ex-N&E
-6	1846	2-2-0 ex-23/4		-36	1850-2	ex-Newmarket
	1852	2-2-2WT		37	1846	2-4-0
7	1839	0-4-0		38	1847	2-4-0
	1845	Blank		-40		
	1853	2-2-2WT		41	1845	2-2-2
8	1839	0-4-0			1847	2-4-0
	1845	(2-2)-2-0		42	1845	2-2-2
	1853	2-2-2WT			1850	ex-Norfolk
9	1840	2-2-0		43	1845	2-2-2
-10	1853	Blank		-44		
	1854	2-2-2WT		45	1845	2-2-2
11	1840	2-2-0		-46	1850	ex-Norfolk
	1850	Blank		47	1846	2-2-2
	1854	2-2-2WT			1850	ex-Norfolk
12	1841	2-2-0		48	1846	2-4-0
	1851	Blank			1850	ex-Norfolk
	1854	2-2-2WT		49	1846	2-2-2
13	1841	2-2-0		50	1845	2-4-0
	1851	Blank		51	1845	2-2-2
	1854	ex-E Union		-60		
14	1841	2-2-0		61	1846	2-2-2
	1853	Blank		-67		
	1854	ex-E Union		68	1846	2-4-0
15	1841	2-2-0		-70		
	1854	ex-E Union		71	1847	2-4-0
16	1841	2-4-0		-73		
	1846	2-2-0/2-2-2 ex-25		74	1847	2-4-0
	1853	Blank			1860	Blank
	1854	ex-E Union		75	1847	2-4-0
17	1841	2-4-0		-77		
	1846	2-2-0 ex-26		78	1846	2-4-0
	1853	Blank		79	1847	2-4-0
	1854	ex-E Union		-81		
18	1842	2-2-0		82	1847	2-4-0
-19	1853	Blank			1847	2-4-0
	1855	2-4-0ST ex-215/6		83	1847	2-4-0
20	1842	2-2-0		84	1848	2-4-0
-21	1851	2-2-2WT		-87		
22	1842	2-2-0		88	1846	(2-2)-2-0
	1852	2-2-2WT		-89		
23	1842	2-2-0		90	1846	0-6-0
	1846	ex-N&E			1847	(2-2)-2-0
	1852	2-2-2WT		91	1846	0-6-0 (from Norfolk)
24	1842	2-2-0			1847	(2-2)-2-0
	1846	ex-N&E		92	1845	0-4-0 ex-7/8
	1850	ex-Norfolk		-93	1847	(2-2)-2-0
	1852	2-2-2WT		94	1845	2-4-0 ex-16
25	1842	2-2-0			1847	(2-2)-2-2
	1846	ex-N&E			1857	2-2-2 C class
	1852	2-2-2WT		95	1845	2-4-0 ex-17
26	1842	2-2-0			1847	(2-2)-2-0
	1846	ex-N&E			1856	2-4-0 ex-217
	1852	N&E 2-2-2 ex-23		96	1847	(2-2)-2-0
27	1846	ex-N&E		97	1846	0-6-0
	1852	N&E 2-2-2 ex-35			1847	(2-2)-2-0/(2-2)-2-2
	1856	2-2-2 C class				

98	1846	0-6-0	160	1847	0-6-0
-101	1846	(2-2)-2-2/2-2-2	-161		
102	1846	2-4-0	162	1847	0-6-0 (returned)
	1847	(2-2)-2-2/2-2-2		1848	Blank
103	1846	2-4-0		1852	ex-E Anglian
	1847	2-2-2	163	1847	0-6-0
104	1846	0-4-2/2-4-0	164	1848	0-6-0 (returned)
	1847	2-2-2		1849	Blank
105	1846	0-4-2/2-4-0		1852	ex-E Anglian
	1848	2-2-2	165	1848	0-6-0
106	1846	0-6-0 ex-Midland	-168		
	1847	Blank	169	1848	0-6-0 (returned)
	1848	2-2-2		1849	Blank
107	1848	2-2-2		1855	2-4-0 ex-218 or 219
108	1848	(2-2)-2-0	170	1847	0-6-0
-112	1852	ex-E Anglian	-171	c1847	2-4-0 ex-102/3
113	1848	Blank	172	1847	2-4-0
-115	1852	ex-E Anglian	-181		
116	1847	2-2-2	182	1847	2-4-0 ex-82
-117	1855	E Union 2-2-2 ex-271/2	183	1848	2-4-0
118	1852	2-2-0 ex-5/6	-187		
-119			188	1847	0-6-0
120	c1853	(2-2)-2-0 ex-8		1848	0-4-0/0-4-2ST ex-154
121	1852	2-2-0 ex-9/10	189	1847	2-4-0
-122			190	1849	2-4-0
123	1852	2-2-0 ex-14	-192		
124	1852	2-2-0/2-2-2 ex-16	193	1848	2-4-0
	1856	2-2-2 ex-204	-196		
125	1852	2-2-0 ex-17-19	197	1849	2-4-0
-127			-200		
128	1852	2-2-0 ex-21	201	by 1850	2-2-2 ex-45
129	1852	2-2-0 ex-22	202	by 1850	2-2-2 ex-47
	1856	N&E 2-2-2 ex-218 or 219	203	by 1850	2-4-0 ex-48
130	1850	ex-Norfolk	204	ex-Norfolk (EC 50)	
-139				1856	EU 0-4-2 ex-214
140	1847	2-4-0 ex-Midland	205	1854	ex-E Union
	1850	ex-Norfolk	-213		
141	1846	0-4-0 ex-92/3 1850	214	1854	ex-E Union
-142	1850	ex-Norfolk		1856	2-4-0
143	1846	2-4-0 ex-94	215	1854	2-2-2 ex-116/7
	1850	ex-Norfolk	-216	1856	2-4-0
	1852	ex-N&E 2-2-2 26	217	1854	2-4-0 ex-140
	1855	Blank		1856	2-4-0
144	1846	2-4-0 ex-95	218	1854	ex-143 or 144
	1850	ex-Norfolk		1856	2-4-0
145	1847/8	0-4-2/2-4-0 ex-104/5	219	1854	ex-143 or 144
-146				1856	2-4-0
147	c1847	0-6-0 ex-170/1	220	1850	ex-Norfolk
-148			-232		
149	c1847	0-6-0 ex-90	233	1852	(2-2)-2-0 ex-108
150	1847	0-6-0 ex-91		1855	0-6-0
151	c1839	0-4-0 ex-*Essex*	234	1852	(2-2)-2-0 ex-109
	1846	0-6-0		1854	0-6-0
152	c1839	0-4-0 ex-*Middlesex*	235	1852	(2-2)-2-0 ex-110/111
	1847	0-6-0	-236	1855	0-6-0
153	c1839	0-4-0 ex-*Norfolk*	237	1852	(2-2)-2-0 ex-112
	1846	0-6-0 ex-106		1854	0-6-0
	1858	Blank	238	1855	2-4-0
154	c1839	0-4-0 ex-*Suffolk*	-249		
	1848	0-6-0 ex-188	250	1854	2-2-2WT Class B
155	1846/7	0-6-0 ex-97-101	-253		
-159			254	1855	2-2-2WT Class B
			-259		

260	1854	ex-E Union		280	1859	2-2-2 Class C
-270				-283		
271	1854	ex-E Union		284	1859	Blank
-272	1855	2-2-2 ex-274/5		-300		
273	1854	ex-E Union		301	1858	2-4-0 Class Z
274	1854	ex-E Union		-306		
	1855	2-2-2 Class C		307	1859	2-4-0 Class Y
275	1854	ex-E Union		-318		
	1856	2-2-2 Class C		319	1860	2-4-0 Class Y
276	1856	2-2-2 Class C		-326		
-279				327	1861	2-4-0 Class Y
				-356		

London and Blackwall Railway (5ft 0½in gauge)

Incorporated 1839 as the Commercial Railway.
Opened: Blackwall to The Minories 6/7/1840 with cable haulage. Extended to Fenchurch
Street 2/8/1841. Converted to standard gauge locomotive haulage 1848. Stepney to Bow
Junction (ECR) opened 2/4/1849 (but not physically connected until 1854). Leased by
GE 1/1/1866, but not taken over until absorbed by LNER in 1923.

11 Locomotives as under:

2-2-2WT Built by Jones & Potts. Works nos 281-6.
DW 5ft 6in, Cyls 13½ x 18 o/s. Inclined cylinders. Dome on firebox. Safety valves
(2) on boiler. Weatherboard. Names removed by GE.

No	Name	Date	Rebuilt	GE no 1866	Duplicate no	year	Scrapped
1	*Stepney*	1848	1865	91	910	1878	10/1880
2	*Shadwell*	1848	1864	92	920	1878	4/1882
3	*Blackwall*	1848	1864	93	930	1878	4/1883
4	*London*	1848	1864	95			4/1873
5	*Bow*	1848	1865	96	960	1878	10/1880
6	*Thames*	1848	1864	97			11/1875

2-2-2WT Built by Jones & Potts. Works no 292.
DW 5ft 6in; Cyls 15 x 18 o/s. Dome on firebox. Safety valves on dome and boiler.
Name removed by GE.

No	Name	Date	
7	*Victoria*	1850	To GE **98** 1866
		3/1871	Rebuilt
		1878	To duplicate list 980. Scrapped 8/1880.

Two locomotives built speculatively by George England & Co, both 2-2-2T in 9/1849 and
1/1850 named *Dwarf* and *Pigmy Giant* were obtained, but were returned in exchange for
Samson and *Hercules* below. It is possible, although not certain, that these were
resold as LNW PW Dept *Dwarf* and Sandy and Potton Railway no 2 *Little England*. When
the S&P became part of the LNW the latter locomotive replaced *Dwarf* as a PW engine and
assumed its name. See Vol 2A page 49, Vol 2B page 303.

2-2-2WT Built by George England & Co.
DW 5ft 6in; Cyls 15 x 18 o/s. Similar to 1 class. Names removed by GE.

No	Name	Date	GE no 1866	Rebuilt	Duplicate no	year	Scrapped
8	*Samson*	1852	**99**	1/1872	990	1878	10/1881
9	*Hercules*	1852	**100**				4/1870

2-4-0T Built by George England & Co.
DW 4ft 0in; Cyls 15 x 22 o/s.

No	Date	GE no 1866	Duplicate no	year	Scrapped
10	1860	**101**	1010	1879	1/1882
11	1860	**102**	1020	1879	2/1882

Waveney Valley Railway

Incorporated 3/7/1851
Opened: Tivetshall (EUR) to Harleston 1/12/1855, to Bungay 2/11 1860 and to Beccles (E Suffolk Railway) 2/3/1863. Worked by ECR until 1861, then took over own working. On completion of railway the company was amalgamated with the GE in 3/1863.

One locomotive as under:

2-2-2T Built by Sharp Stewart & Co. Works no 1228.
DW 5ft 6in; Cyls 15 x 22 o/s

Date
1861   To GE **30**   3/1863
5/1864 Rebuilt 2-4-0T. Scrapped 11/1881.

Wivenhoe and Brightlingsea Railway

Incorporated 1861
Opened: (with Tendring Hundred incorporated 1859 and Clacton-on-Sea Railways incorporated 1877) Hythe (EUR) to Wivenhoe 8/5/1863, to Weeley 8/1/1866; Wivenhoe to Brightlingsea 18/4/1866; Weeley to Kirby Cross 28/7/1866, to Walton-on-the-Naze 17/5/1867; Thorpe-le-Soken to Clacton-on-Sea 4/7/1882. Worked by GER except between 8/1876 and 1879 when a dispute resulted in independent operation from Brightlingsea to a point short of Wivenhoe station. Company purchased by GE 6/1893.

One locomotive as under:

0-6-0ST Built by Hudswell Clarke & Rodgers. Works no 184.
DW 3ft 3in; Cyls 13 x 20 o/s.

Name   Date
Resolute   1876 to GE 203
           1879 Name removed
           3/1888 to stationary work

Thetford and Watton Railway

Incorporated 1866
Opened: Roudham Junction (GE) to Watton 26/1/1869 (goods by contractor until 22/7/1869), 18/10/1869 (passenger). Also worked Watton and Swaffham (incorporated 1869, opened 20/9/1875 (goods), 15/11/1875 (passenger)) and Bury St Edmunds and Thetford (incorporated 1865, opened 1/3/1876). Acquired by GE 1/1/1880.

7 locomotives as under:

2-4-0T Built by Manning Wardle & Co. Works nos 298/9.
DW 4ft 6in; Cyls 13 x 20 o/s.

No	Date	GE No 1/1880	Duplicate no	year	Scrapped
1	1870	**802**	0802	1886	10/1887
2	1870	**803**	0803	1886	5/1888

0-6-0ST Built by Stothert & Slaughter for Monmouthshire Railway & Canal in 1850 (Vol 7).
DW 4ft 0in; Cyls 13 x 20; WB 5ft 0in + 6ft 0in; Wt 23 tons 1½ cwt.
Purchased from Budd & Holt 3/1874.

No	Date		
3	3/1874	To GE **801**	Scrapped 6/1884

2-4-0T Built by Sharp Stewart & Co. Works nos 2474/5.
DW 4ft 6½in; Cyls 15 x 20.

		GE No	Duplicate		
No	Date	1/1880	no	year	Scrapped
4	1875	**804**	0804	1886	8/1887
5	1875	**805**	0805	1886	8/1887

0-4-2 Built by Sharp Stewart & Co. Works nos 2595/6.
DW 5ft 0in; Cyls 15 x 22.

		GE No	Duplicate		
No	Date	1/1880	no	year	Scrapped
6	1876	**806**	0806	1886	12/1891
7	1876	**807**	0807	1886	12/1890

Felixstowe Railway and Pier

Incorporated 1875 by sole proprietor and landowner Colonel George Tomline.
Opened: 1/5/1877 (passenger), 1/6/1877 (goods) from connection with GE at Westerfield.
Name changed 1879 to **Felixstowe Railway and Dock** on abandonment of plan to build a
tidal basin. Worked by GE from 1/9/1979 and locomotives transferred to GE stock.
Railway only purchased by GE 1887 and changed to **Felixstowe Dock and Railway**.

3 locomotives as under:

2-4-0T Built by Yorkshire Engine Co. Works nos 328-30.
DW 4ft 7½in; Cyls 14 x 20 o/s.

		GE No	Duplicate		
No	Date	9/1879	no	year	Scrapped
1	1877	**808**	0808	1886	5/1888
2	1877	**809**	0809	1886	5/1888
3	1877	**810**	0810	1886	5/1888

GREAT EASTERN RAILWAY

Sinclair Locomotives 1862-7

See pages 22-3 for Sinclair locomotives built for the Eastern Counties Railway.

2-2-2 Built by Wm Fairbairn & Sons (F)
              Slaughter Gruning & Co. Works nos below. (SG)
              Kitson & Co. Works nos below. (K)
              Schneider & Cie. Works nos below. (Sc)
DW 7ft 1¼in; LW & TW 3ft 7in; TWB 15ft 0in; Cyls 16 x 24 o/s; Blr 4ft 0in x 12ft 1¼in; THS 1051 sq ft; WP 120 lbs/sq in; WT 29¼ tons (Sc 30½ tons).
Class W Side window cab; o/s sandwich frames; Allan type cylinders; Gooch valve gear. Rebuilt by Johnson. WP 140 lbs/sq in; DW 7ft 3in; Wt 33-4 tons. 4-2-2 rebuilds had 17in diameter cylinders and were painted canary yellow similar to LBSC livery (as also no 60, some Sharp singles and tank locomotives). Rebuilds had conventional cab and Westinghouse brake.

No	Date	Works no	Tender Works no	Rebuilt	Renumbered No	year	Duplicate No	year	Scrapped
284*	10/1862	F		9/1879			0284	1886	1889
285	11/1862	F		12/1879			0285	1886	1888
286	11/1862	F		12/1880			0286	1886	1889
287	12/1862	F		1/1880					1885
288	12/1862	F					0288	1886	1892
51	4/1864	SG 541		7/1873 (4-2-2)					
					275	1880			
				6/1882			0275	1886	1890
52	5/1864	SG 542			**276**	1880	0276	1886	1891
53	5/1864	SG 543		5/1879	**277**	1880	0277	1886	1889
54**	5/1864	SG 544							9/1874**
55	5/1864	SG 545			**278**	1880	0278	1886	1889
56	6/1864	SG 546			**279**	1880			1874
57**	6/1864	SG 547		6/1880	**280**	1880	0280	1886	1892
58	6/1864	SG 548		9/1881	**281**	1880	0281	1886	1890
59	6/1864	SG 549		6/1882	**282**	1880	0282	1886	1893
60	6/1864	SG 550		5/1873	**283**	1880	0283	1886	1888
291	5/1865	K 1191	1196	11/1873 (4-2-2)					
				9/1880			0291	1886	1893
292**	5/1865	K 1192	1197	3/1882			0292	1886	1890
293* **	5/1865	K 1193	1198	8/1872					1883
294**	8/1865	K 1194	1199	11/1872					1883
295**	8/1865	K 1195	1200	11/1881			0295	1886	1894
296	8/1865	K 1201	1206				0296	1886	1887
297	9/1865	K 1202	1207				0297	1886	1887
298	9/1865	K 1203	1208						1885
289	9/1865	K 1204	1209	12/1880			0289	1886	1889
290	9/1865	K 1205	1210	10/1881			0290	1886	1894
88	9/1866	Sc 949			302	1878			1885
89	9/1866	Sc 950		5/1881	303	1878	0303	1886	1891
90	9/1866	Sc 951			304	1878			1883
299	9/1866	Sc 952					0299	1886	1888
300	9/1866	Sc 953		4/1882			0300	1886	1893
87*	5/1867	Sc 1079		7/1881	301	1878	0301	1886	1890

*   No 284 was painted cream for wedding of the Prince of Wales in 1863.
      No 87 was exhibited at the Paris Exhibition in 1867.
** The following were involved in accidents:
      No 54 at Cringleford 1/7/1865 and at Thorpe (Norwich) 10/9/1874 after
         which it was scrapped.
      No 57 at Bradfield 15/7/1864.   No 292 at Kelvedon 17/10/1872.

No 294 at Manningtree 8/12/1879.   No 295 at Helpringham 25/10/1882.
No 302 at March 9/11/1882.
*** No 293 was lent to the Great Northern Railway in 1868.

2-4-0 Built by Kitson & Co. Works nos below. (K)
                Vulcan Foundry Co. Works nos below. (V)
                Schneider & Cie. Works nos below. (Sc)
DW 6ft 1in; Cyls 17 x 24; THS 1179 sq ft; Wt 30tons 16cwt. **Class Y** mixed traffic
class continued from Eastern Counties (see page 22). Open splashers, canopy type cab.
Rebuilds, some as 4-4-0, were modernised with conventional cabs with large cut-outs
and solid splashers. DW 6ft 3in; WP 140 lbs/sq in.
Original cabs of Vulcan and Schneider locomotives were more substantial. Westinghouse
brake fitted 1878-83 (except 381). U13 rebuilds also had DW 6ft 3in.

No	Date	Works no	Tender works no	Rebuilt	Duplicate no	year	Scrapped
357	12/1863	K 1131	1136	5/1880	0357	1890	1890
358	1/1864	K 1132	1137	4/1880	0358	1890	1892
359	1/1864	K 1133	1138	6/1882	0359	1890	1893
360	1/1864	K 1134	1139	11/1878 4-4-0	0360	1890	1892
361	2/1864	K 1135	1140	3/1882	0361	1890	1892
362	2/1864	K 1141	1146	4/1880	0362	1890	1890
363	2/1864	K 1142	1147	7/1879			1888
364	3/1864	K 1143	1148	10/1875			1889
365	3/1864	K 1144	1149	4/1879	0365	1890	1890
366	3/1864	K 1145	1150	2/1878 4-4-0	0366	1890	1890
367	4/1864	K 1151	1156	12/1879			1888
368	4/1864	K 1152	1157				1883
369	4/1864	K 1153	1158	11/1871, 4/1879			1888
370	5/1864	K 1154	1159	9/1877 4-4-0	0370	1890	1893
371	5/1864	K 1155	1160				1886
372	5/1864	K 1161	1166	6/1882	0372	1890	1892
373	6/1864	K 1162	1167	6/1882	0373	1890	1892
374	6/1864	K 1163	1168				1886
375	6/1864	K 1164	1169	12/1881	0375	1890	1893
376	7/1864	K 1165	1170	1882 U13	0376	1890	1892
377	9/1864	K 1171	1173	10/1883	0377	1890	1894
378	10/1864	K 1172	1174	1882 U13	0378	1890	1890
379	2/1865	K 1183		11/1879	0379	1890	1892
380	2/1865	K 1184		8/1881	0380	1890	1893
381	7/1865	K 1272		3/1877 4-4-0			1886
387	6/1864	V 511					1883
388	6/1864	V 512					1884
389	6/1864	V 513		6/1882	0389	1890	1892
390	6/1864	V 514					1883
391	7/1864	V 515					1886
392	8/1864	V 516		9/1881			1889
393	8/1864	V 517		7/1881	0393	1890	1891
394	9/1864	V 518					1884
395	9/1864	V 519					1885
396	9/1864	V 520		6/1880	0396	1890	1894
397	9/1864	V 521		9/1879	0397	1890	1893
398	12/1864	V 526					1884
399	12/1864	V 527					1885
400	12/1864	V 528					1887
401	2/1865	V 530					1885
382	6/1865	V 540		1882 U13	0382	1890	1894
383	7/1865	V 541					1885
384	7/1865	V 542		1882 U13	0384	1890	1893
385	7/1865	V 543		12/1876 4-4-0	0385	1890	1893
386	8/1865	V 544		3/1881	0386	1890	1891
402	8/1865	V 545					1886

403	8/1865	V 546				1884
404	9/1865	V 547				1884
405	9/1865	V 548	6/1882		0405	1890	1891
406	9/1865	V 549	12/1877 4-4-0	0406	1890	1890
407	7/1866	Sc 928	2/1881	0407	1890	1891
408	7/1866	Sc 929	9/1883	0408	1890	1893
409	7/1866	Sc 930	6/1879	0409	1890	1890
410	7/1866	Sc 931				1885
411	7/1866	Sc 932	6/1881	0411	1890	1890
412	7/1866	Sc 933	12/1876 4-4-0	0412	1890	1891
413	8/1866	Sc 934	5/1879	0413	1890	1892
414	8/1866	Sc 935	12/1880	0414	1890	1890
415	8/1866	Sc 936	10/1883	0415	1890	1894
416	8/1866	Sc 937	12/1877 4-4-0	0416	1890	1891

2-4-0WT Built by GER at Stratford. Works nos 34-8.
DW 4ft 1in; Cyls 12 x 18 o/s.
Class X Boilers built by Slaughter Gruning & Co.

No	Date	
120	12/1862	Scrapped 10/1880
121	12/1862	Possibly to 121A. Scrapped 7/1882.
122	12/1862	To duplicate 1220 1884. To stationary work 7/1885 until 1907.
123	12/1862	Scrapped 4/1882
124	12/1862	Scrapped 7/1883

2-4-2WT Built by Neilson & Co. Works nos 1083-1102.
DW 5ft 7in; LW & TW 3ft 7¼in; Cyls 15 x 22; Blr 3ft 11in x 13ft 6in;
THS 1035 sq ft; WP 120 lbs/sq in; Wt 36¼ tons. **Class V** Leading Bissel truck. Known
as 'The Scotchmen'.

No	Date	Duplicate no	year	Scrapped
140	11/1864	1400	1880	1883
141	11/1864	1410	1880	1886
142	12/1864	1420	1880	1884
143	12/1864	1430	1880	1886
144	2/1865	1440	1880	1886
145	2/1865	1450	1880	1884
146	3/1865	1460	1880	1886
147	3/1865	1470	1880	1886
148	3/1865	1480	1880	1883
149	4/1865	1490	1880	1884
150	4/1865			1888
151	5/1865			1886
152	5/1865			1886
153	5/1865			1883
154	5/1865			1886
155	6/1865			1883
156	6/1865			1886
157	6/1865			1886
158	7/1865			1886
159	7/1865			1887

Johnson Locomotives 1867-74

2-2-2 Built by GER at Stratford. Works nos 47/8.
DW 5ft 6in; Cyls 15 x 20; Possibly used parts from scrapped locomotives.

No	Date	Duplicate no	year	Scrapped
73	10/1870	730	1876	8/1877
74	10/1870	740	1876	12/1879

2-4-0 Built by Neilson & Co. Works nos 1294-6, 1300/1.
DW 6ft 0½in; Cyls 16 x 20; Originally intended for North British Railway.
Four-wheel tenders.

No	Date	Duplicate no	year	Scrapped
125	2/1867			2/1885
126	2/1867			2/1886
127	4/1867			2/1885
128	5/1867			3/1884
129	5/1867	1290	1885	2/1886

2-4-0 Built by Sharp Stewart & Co. Works nos below (SS).
         GER at Stratford. Works nos below (GE) (**Class L7**)
DW 5ft 7in; Cyls 16 x 22; THS 979.9 sq ft; TWB 31ft 4in; WP 140 lbs/sq in;
Wt 29 tons 3 cwt; Mixed traffic. Some were lent to the London, Tilbury & Southend
Railway. Known as 'Little Sharpies'. Rebuilt DW 5ft 8in; WP 160 lbs/sq in;
Wt 30¾ tons.

No	Date	Works no	Rebuilt	Renumbered no	year	Duplicate no	year	Scrapped
1	10/1867	SS 1803	1890, 1906			01	1911	3/1914 (Replaced 1911)
2	10/1867	SS 1804	1890					1902
3	10/1867	SS 1805	1889					1904
26	10/1867	SS 1806	1889, 1904	30	1898			by 1913
28	5/1868	SS 1807	1889, 1904					by 1913
29	5/1868	SS 1808	1889					1902
32	5/1868	SS 1809	1892					1901
35	6/1868	SS 1810	1890					1903
43	7/1868	SS 1811	1890, 1908					1910
44	8/1868	SS 1812	1893					1904
46	12/1868	SS 1813	1893					1903
47	12/1868	SS 1814	1892					1903
48	1/1869	SS 1815	1892, 1902					1911
49	1/1869	SS 1816	1892					1903
33	3/1869	SS 1817	1891, 1901					1914
34	4/1869	SS 1818	1893					1903
36	5/1869	SS 1819	1891					1901
42	5/1869	SS 1820	1892, 1904					1908
45	5/1869	SS 1821	1891					1901
50	5/1869	SS 1822	1891, 1901					by 1913
31	11/1870	SS 2044	1893					1902
100	11/1870	SS 2045	1889, 1901	103	1878	0103	11/1905	1912
104	11/1870	SS 2068	1889, 1902			0104	11/1905	1911
105	11/1870	SS 2069	1890, 1906			0105	11/1905	by 1913
106	11/1870	SS 2070	1889					1903
107	3/1871	SS 2113	1890, 1907			0107	2/1906	1912
160	3/1871	SS 2114	1892			0160	6/1901	1902
161	3/1871	SS 2115	1889			0161	6/1901	1901
173	3/1871	SS 2116	1890	108	1878			1903
176	4/1871	SS 2117	1889	117	1878		possibly	by 1909
112	10/1869	GE 42	1892					1905
113	10/1869	GE 43	1891					1902

110	12/1869	GE 44	1893					1904
114	7/1870	GE	1891, 1902					2/1911
115	7/1870	GE	1892					1901
119	10/1871	GE 52	1890, 1905	**27**	1884			by 1913
118	11/1871	GE 53	1892					1903
5	7/1872	GE 54	1889					1901
6	7/1872	GE 55	1890					1904
10	8/1872	GE 56	1891	**4**	1878			1905

2-4-0 Built by GER at Stratford. Works nos 39-41.
DW 5ft 6in; Cyls 15 x 20. Possibly renewals of ex-E Union & E Anglian locos with same nos.

No	Date	Scrapped
116	8/1868	10/1881
109	9/1868	3/1884
111	1/1869	1/1882

0-4-0ST Built by Manning Wardle & Co. Works no 414.
DW 3ft 0in; Cyls 12 x 18; THS 374.5 sq ft; WP 140 lbs/sq in; WB 5ft 4in;
Wt 17½ tons. For shunting in Stratford works yard/

No	Date	Name
200	12/1872	*The Chairman* (name removed 1895)
	1894	To 'Works A'
	1895	Rebuilt. Withdrawn 2/1922. Scrapped 1923.

0-4-2T Built by GER at Stratford. Works nos 49-51, 57-68.
DW 5ft 3in; Cyls 15 x 22 **Class T7**

No	Date	Scrapped	No	Date	Scrapped
81	3/1871	1892	**11**	12/1874	1893
82	3/1871	1891	**12**	12/1874	1892
83	4/1871	1892	**15**	4/1875	1894
84	6/1873	1892	**16**	4/1875	1893
85	6/1873	1893	**17**	5/1875	1893
86	9/1873	1892	**18**	5/1875	1891
13	11/1873	1891	**19**	6/1875	1894
14	12/1873	1894			

0-4-4T Built by Neilson & Co. Works nos below. (N)
                 Avonside. Works nos below. (A)
DW 5ft 3in; TW 2ft 10in; Cyls 17 x 24; THS 1084 sq ft; WP 140 lbs/sq in;
Wt 45 tons 9 cwt (other weights 42¾ and 44¾ tons also quoted). Weather boards only when built. Rebuilt with cabs and rear weather board. DW 5ft 4in; WP 160 lbs/sq in. First side tank locomotives in England.

No	Date	Works no	Rebuilt	Renumbered no	year	Duplicate no	year	Withdrawn or scrapped
134	11/1872	N 1707	1890, 1899	**201**	1897	0201	1897	12/1910 (wdn)
135	11/1872	N 1708	1892			0135	1903	1903
136	11/1872	N 1709	1893			0136	1903	1906
137	12/1872	N 1710	1889, 1901			0137	1908	12/1912 (wdn)
138	12/1872	N 1711	1893					1902
139	12/1872	N 1712	1885, 1902			0139	1908	5/1912 (wdn)
162*	12/1872	N 1713	1894			0162	1901	1902
163	12/1872	N 1714	1889			0163	1901	1904
164	12/1872	N 1715	1891			0164	1901	1903
165	12/1872	N 1716	1885, 1897			0165	1901	1905
166	2/1873	N 1736	1889			0166	1901	1902
167	3/1873	N 1737	1885, 1896			0167	1901	1906
168	3/1873	N 1738	1887, 1896			0168	1901	1905
169	3/1873	N 1739	1890, 1900			0169	1901	1907

170	4/1873	N 1740	1892	**133**	1878			
				200	1897	0200	1899	1904
186	10/1872	A 917	1885, 1900					1907
187	10/1872	A 918	1893					1903
188	11/1872	A 919	1886, 1898			0188	1909	4/1911 (wdn)
189**	11/1872	A 920	1886, 1899			0189	1900	1902
185	3/1873	A 921	1885, 1899					1905
190	3/1873	A 922	1894			0190	1900	1902
191	3/1873	A 923	1886			0191	1900	1902
192	4/1873	A 924	1885			0192	1900	1902
193	5/1873	A 925	1887***			0193	1900	1901
194	5/1873	A 926	1886, 1900			0194	1900	1906
195	7/1873	A 978	1893			0195	1900	1904
196	7/1873	A 979	1887, 1899			0196	1900	1904
197	7/1873	A 980	1887, 1897			0197	1900	1904
198	8/1873	A 981	1887, 1901			0198	1900	1906
199	9/1873	A 982	1885, 1897			0199	1899	1904

*   No 162 was in an accident at Witham 1/1/1899.
** No 189 was the first locomotive to receive the royal blue livery under
     TW Worsdell.
*** No 193 fitted with Holden's patent oil burning system.

0-6-0ST Built by Hudswell Clarke & Co. Works no 80.
DW 3ft 0in; Cyls 13 x 18.

No	Date		
201	4/1867	Rebuilt 3/1883.	Scrapped 3/1888.

0-6-0ST Built by Hudswell Clarke & Co. Works no 87.
DW 3ft 8in; Cyls 15½ x 22 o/s.

No	Date	
202	11/1867	Scrapped 6/1886

0-6-0T Built by Ruston, Proctor & Co, Lincoln.
DW 4ft 0in; WB 6ft 9in + 6ft 9in; Cyls 16 x 22; Blr 3ft 10in x 9ft 1in;
THS 684.5 sq ft; WP 140 lbs/sq in; Wt 34 tons 9 cwt. Rebuilt with half cabs. Crane
tanks had WB 6ft 9in + 7ft 9in; Blr 4ft 2in diameter;
THS 966.05 sq ft (1891), 974.05 sq ft (1894), 983.21 sq ft (1907),
990.21 sq ft (1909). LNE class Z4, J92 from 4/1927

No	Date	Half cabs	Rebuilt crane tank (3 tons capacity)	LNE no 6/1946	BR no	applied	Withdrawn or scrapped
204	5/1868	8/1881	12/1893				
			To Works 'B' 1894	8667	68667	2/1949	5/1952
205	7/1868	12/1881	5/1891				
			To Works 'C' 1894				
			Departmental 35 9/1952	8668	68668	2/1950	11/1952
206	9/1868	not	12/1893				
		fitted	To Works 'D' 1894	8669	68669	3/1950	10/1950
207	1868	9/1881					1889
208	1868	10/1882					1892

0-6-0 Built by Neilson & Co.   Works nos below. (N)
             Worcester Engine Co.   Works nos below. (W)
DW 5ft 6in; Cyls 16½ x 24; THS 1072.66 sq ft; WP 140 lbs/sq ft;
Wt 31¾ tons; Rebuilt with closed domes, Ramsbottom safety valves, lengthened cab roofs
and DW 5ft 4in.

No	Date	Works no	Rebuilt	Duplicate no	year	Scrapped
417	1867	N 1330				1889
418	1867	N 1331				1889
419	1867	N 1332	1888	0419	1891	1895

420	1867	N 1333					1889
421	1867	N 1334					1888
422	1867	N 1335	1888		0422	1891	1898
423	1867	N 1336	1887		0423	1891	1892
424	1867	N 1337					1888
425	1867	N 1338					1889
426	1867	N 1339	1888		0426	1891	1895
427	1867	N 1340					1888
428	1867	N 1341					1890
429	1867	N 1342					1890
430	1867	N 1343	1888		0430	1891	1898
431	1867	N 1344					1890
432	1868	N 1345	1887		0432	1891	1896
433	1868	N 1346					1888
434	1868	N 1347					1888
435	1868	N 1348	1879				1889
436	1868	N 1349					1889
437	1867	W 17	1887		0437	1891	1894
438	1867	W 18					1888
439	1867	W 19	1887		0439	1891	1895
440	1868	W 20	1885		0440	1891	1895
441	1868	W 21					1890
442	1868	W 22	1885		0442	1891	1891
443	1868	W 23					1889
444	1868	W 24					1888
445	1868	W 25					1888
446	1868	W 26					1889
447	1868	W 40	1885		0447	1891	1892
448	1868	W 41	1886		0448	1891	1894
449	1868	W 42	1886		0449	1891	1894
450	1868	W 43	1887		0450	1891	1895
451	1868	W 44					1890
452	1868	W 45					1888
453	1868	W 46					1889
454	1868	W 47					1889
455	1869	W 48					1891
456	1869	W 49					1889
457	1869	W 50					1890
458	1869	W 51					1889
459	1869	W 52			0459	1891	1892
460	1869	W 53	1879		0460	1891	1893
461	1869	W 54					1888
462	1869	W 55					1889
463	1869	W 56					1889
464	1869	W 57	1886		0464	1891	1896
465	1869	W 58	1888		0465	1891	1899
466	1869	W 59					1890
467	1869	W 60					1891
468	1869	W 61			0468	1891	1892
469	1869	W 62	1880		0469	1891	1891
470	1869	W 63	1887		0470	1891	1895
471	1869	W 64	1887		0471	1891	1894
472	1869	W 65					1888
473	1869	W 66	1887		0473	1891	1894
474	1869	W 67					1889
475	1869	W 68	1879				1888
476	1869	W 69					1890

0-6-0 Built by Beyer Peacock & Co. Works nos below. (BP)
              R Stephenson & Co. Works nos below. (S)
              Dubs & Co. Works nos below. (D)
              Nasmyth Wilson & Co. Works nos below. (NW)
              Yorkshire Engine Co. Works nos below. (Y)
DW 5ft 1in; WB 7ft 7in + 7ft 11in; Cyls 17 x 24; Blr 3ft 11in x 10ft 0in;
THS 1081.4 sq ft; WP 140 lbs/sq ft; Wt 32 tons 13 cwt. Some had hinged chimneys for
working on the Woolwich branch. Rebuilt with closed domes, Ramsbottom safety valves,
lengthened cab roofs and DW 5ft 2in.

		Works		Duplicate		
No	Date	no	Rebuilt	no	year	Scrapped
477	1871	BP 1014	1889	0477	1894	1901
478	1871	BP 1015	1893	0478	1894	1902
479	1871	BP 1016	1888	0479	1894	1898
480	1871	BP 1017	1879, 1888	0480	1894	1898
481	1871	BP 1018	1893	0481	1894	1902
482	1871	BP 1019	1888	0482	1894	1898
483	1871	BP 1020	1891	0483	1894	1899
484	1871	BP 1021	1892	0484	1894	1900
485	1871	BP 1022	1888	0485	1894	1900
486	1871	BP 1023	1892	0486	1894	1902
487	1872	BP 1024	1893	0487	1894	1900
488	1872	BP 1025	1893	0488	1894	1902
489	1872	BP 1026	1893	0489	1894	1901
490	1872	BP 1027	1892	0490	1894	1899
491	1872	BP 1028	1895	0491	1894	1899
492	1872	BP 1029	1892*	0492	1894	1901
493	1872	BP 1030	1893	0493	1894	1899
494	1872	BP 1031	1891	0494	1894	1901
495	1872	BP 1032	1894	0495	1894	1901
496	1872	BP 1033	1895	0496	1894	1902
497	1872	S 1998	1891	0497	1896	1899
498	1872	S 1999	1894	0498	1896	1901
499	1872	S 2000	1893	0499	1895	1901
500	1872	S 2003	1892	0500	1896	1904
501	1872	S 2004	1894	0501	1896	1901
502	1872	D 503	1894	0502	1896	1901
503	1872	D 504	1893	0503	1896	1901
504	1872	D 505	1894	0504	1896	1899
505	1872	D 506	1893	0505	1896	1901
506	1872	D 507	1892	0506	1896	1900
507	1872	NW 120	1894	0507	1899	1902
508	1872	NW 121	1894	0508	1899	1902
509	1872	NW 122	1888	0509	1899	1900
510	1872	NW 123	1893	0510	1899	1902
511	1872	NW 124	1894	0511	1899	1902
512	1873	Y 195	1893	0512	1899	1902
513	1873	Y 196	1894	0513	1899	1901
514	1873	Y 197	1892			1898
515	1873	Y 198	1892			1899
516	1873	Y 199	1893	0516	1899	1901
517	1873	Y 200	1891			1898
518	1873	Y 201	1893	0518	1899	1899
519	1873	Y 202	1892			1897
520	1873	Y 203	1892	0520	1899	1901
521	1873	Y 204	1889	0521	1899	1901
522	1873	Y 205	1893			1898
523	1873	Y 206	1892			1898
524	1873	Y 207	1895			1898
525	1873	Y 208	1892			1898

526   1873   Y 209   1893   1898
* No 492 was fitted with an American made *Weston* boiler in 1879 until 1881.

4-4-0 Built by GER at Stratford. Works nos 69/70.
DW 6ft 6in; LW 3ft 8in; Cyls 17 x 24; THS 1181 sq ft; WP 140 lbs/sq in;
Wt 39 tons 13 cwt. Designed and ordered by Johnson but completed by Adams.
Rebuilt DW 6ft 7in. **Class C8** No engine brakes.

		Renumbered			
No	Date	no	year	Rebuilt	Scrapped
301	7/1874	305	1878	7/1888	11/1898

Adams Locomotives 1874-9

4-4-0 Built by Dubs & Co. Works nos below. (D)
        R&W Hawthorne. Works nos below. (H)
DW 6ft 1in; Cyls 18 x 26 o/s; Blr 4ft 3in x 11ft 5in; THS 1109 sq ft;
WP 140 lbs/sq ft; Wt 45 tons 1 cwt. Side window cabs, raised frames. Known as
'Ironclads'. Relegated to fast goods work.

		Works	Duplicate		
No	Date	no	no	year	Scrapped
265	1876	D 893	0265	1896	1896
266	1876	D 894			1895
267	1876	D 895			1895
268	1876	D 896	0268	1896	1896
269	1876	D 897	0269	1896	1896
270	1876	D 898			1894
271	1876	D 899			1895
272	1876	D 900			1895
273	1876	D 901			1894
274	1876	D 902	0274	1896	1897
255	1877	H 1705			1895
256	1877	H 1706			1895
257	1877	H 1707			1895
258	1877	H 1708	0258	1896	1897
259	1877	H 1709			1894
260	1877	H 1710			1894
261	1877	H 1711	0261	1896	1896
262	1877	H 1712	0262	1896	1897
263	1877	H 1713			1894
264	1877	H 1714			1895

0-4-0ST Built by Neilson & Co. Works nos below.
DW 3ft 6in; WB 5ft 9in; Cyls 12 x 20 o/s; Blr 3ft 4¼in x 8ft 7^{15}/$_{16}$in;
THS 530 sq ft; WP 120 lbs/sq in; Wt 17 tons 14 cwt. Rebuilt with cabs.
DW 3ft 7in; THS 514.55 sq ft; WP 140 lbs/sq in; Wt 21 tons 4 cwt.
LNE Class Y5

		Works		Duplicate		LNE	LNE	Withdrawn
No	Date	no	Rebuilt	no	date	1923 no	1924 no	Applied
209	5/1874	1940	10/1894			209E	7209	11/1926
210	3/1875	1942	7/1894					9/1914
228	4/1876	2118	12/1894	0228*	7/1914	0228E	07228	1926 6/1927
								(service stock)
229	4/1876	2119	2/1895					2/1917*

* No 229 had Westinghouse pump, vacuum & heating apparatus fitted for brake testing.
  It was sold to the Admiralty then to Fairfield Shipbuilding Co., Chepstow.
  Preserved at North Woolwich. 0228 was fitted for brake testing as 229 in 11/1919.
  Class continued by Holden, see page 85. LNE Class Y5.

0-4-0T 'Tram' Built by Kitson & Co.
DW 2ft 0in; Cyls 6 x 10; Replacement for *Ariels Girdle* on Millwall Extension Railway.

No	Date	
230	1878	To stationary use 1889 (replaced 1884)

0-4-2T Built by GER at Stratford. Works nos 71-80.
DW 4ft 10in; TW 3ft 8in; Cyls 15 x 22; THS 967.24 sq ft; WP 140 lbs/sq in;
Wt 38 tons 11 cwt. **Class K9**. Half cabs.

No	Date	Rebuilt	Renumbered no	year	Scrapped	
20	5/1877		020*	1902	1906	*Duplicate list
21	6/1877	1893			1904	
23	6/1877	1892			1905	
24	6/1877	1892			1905	
25	6/1877	1894			1905	
7	12/1877	1890, 1899			1907	
9	12/1877	1892			1903	
8	2/1878	1893			1903	
10	4/1878	1894	26	1898	1904	
22	5/1878	1893			1903	

0-4-4T Built by Neilson & Co. Works nos below. (N)
                R Stephenson & Co. Works nos uncertain possibly 2311-20. (S)
                Kitson & Co. Works nos below. (K)
DW 4ft 10in; TW 2ft 10in; Cyls 17 x 24 (N), 17½ x 24 (S&K); THS 1084 sq ft; WP 140
lbs/sq ft; Wt 48¾ tons (N), 49 tons 4 cwt (K); Relegated to goods work due to
excessive weight. Rebuilt DW 4ft 11in; WP 160 lbs/sq in. **61 Class**

No	Date	Works no	Rebuilt	Fitted for oil fuel	Duplicate no	date	Withdrawn or scrapped
211	1875	N 2013	1889, 1905	1893	0211	1907	10/1910 (wdn)
212	1875	N 2014	1894				1906
213	1875	N 2015	1891	1893	0213	1907	1907
214	1875	N 2016	1889				1906
215	1875	N 2017	1894	1893	0215	1907	1907
216	1875	N 2018	1889, 1906	1893	0216	1907	5/1912 (wdn)
217	1875	N 2019	1892	1893			1906
218	1875	N 2020	1894				1907
219	1875	N 2021	1894				1906
220	1875	N 2022	1894		0220	1907	1907
61	1875	N 2023	1889	1893			1906
62	1875	N 2024	1891				1906
63	1875	N 2025	1889	1893			1907
64	1875	N 2026	1893				1907
65	1875	N 2027	1889, 1905	1893			12/1913 (wdn)
66	1875	N 2028	1891, 1906	1893			12/1913 (wdn)
67	1875	N 2029	1893	1893			1906
68	1875	N 2030	1894				1907
69	1875	N 2031	1895	1893			1907
70	1875	N 2032	1889, 1901				1909
71	1875	N 2033	1895		071	1909	6/1911 (wdn)
72	1875	N 2034	1892	1893			1907
73	1875	N 2035	1892	1893			1908
74	1875	N 2036	1894				1908
75	1875	N 2037	1892, 1900	1893			1908
76	1876	RS*	1894				1907
77	1876	RS*	1892, 1898				1907
78	1876	RS*	1889				1907
79	1877	RS*	1890				1907
80	1877	RS*	1894				1906
221	1877	RS*	1889				1907
222	1877	RS*	1893		0222	1907	190

No	Date	Works no		Renumber	Date	Scrapped
223	1877	RS*	1893			1906
224	1877	RS*	1890	0224	1907	1908
225	1877	RS*	1892	0225	1907	1908
170	1878	K 2201	1893			1906
171	1878	K 2202	1890, 1905	0171	1908	12/1913 (wdn)
172	1878	K 2203	1891			1906
173	1878	K 2204	1891, 1904	0173	1908	7/1913 (wdn)
174	1878	K 2205	1891, 1903	0174	1908	12/1913 (wdn)
175	1878	K 2206	1891			1907
176	1878	K 2207	1890	0176	1908	1908
177	1878	K 2208	1893			1907
178	1878	K 2209	1889, 1905	0178	1908	8/1911 (wdn)
179	1878	K 2210	1894			1907
180	1878	K 2211	1890, 1906	0180	1908	12/1913 (wdn)
181	1878	K 2212	1891, 1897	0181	1908	1910
182	1878	K 2213	1893			1908
183	1878	K 2214	1893			1906
184	1878	K 2215	1893, 1906	0184	1908	2/1911 (wdn)

* Works nos uncertain, see above.

2-6-0 Built by Neilson & Co. Works nos 2393-2407.
DW 4ft 10in; LW 2ft 10in; WB 7ft 5in + 7ft 3in + 8ft 6in; Cyls 19 x 26 o/s;
Blr 4ft 6^1/8in x 11ft 5in; THS 1393 sq ft; WP 140 lbs/sq in; Wt 46 tons 12 cwt.
Adams design, modified by Bromley, and the first 2-6-0 in the UK, although this
arrangement was already established in America where it as known as the 'mogul' after
the Moguls of India. No 527 (and one other according to some accounts) carried the
name *Mogul* until 1885. Radial pony truck, side window cab, cab to running plate
doors, o/s valves. Designed to haul 400 ton coal trains they suffered from boiler
incapacity and did not last long.

No	Date	Scrapped	
527	1878	1887	Named *Mogul* until 1885
528	1878	1887	
529	1878	1885	
530	1878	1887	
531	1878	1886	
532	1879	1885	
533	1879	1886	
534	1879	1887	
535	1879	1886	
536	1879	1887	
537	1879	1887	
538	1879	1887	
539	1879	1887	
540	1879	1886	
541	1879	1887	

Bromley Locomotives 1878-83

4-2-2 Built by Dubs & Co. Works nos below. (D)
        Kitson & Co. Works nos below. (K)
DW 7ft 6in; LW & TW 4ft 0in; Cyls 18 x 24 o/s; Blr 4ft 1in x 11ft 5¼in;
THS 1205 sq ft; WP 140 lbs/sq in; Wt 41 tons 14 cwt. Cab to running plate doors.
Open splashers, later solid. Cylinders reduced to 17½in diameter from 1885 as below
on Kitson locomotives. Steam sanding, o/s valves with rocking bar.

No	Date	Works no	17½in cyls	Scrapped
245	1879	D 1223		1891
246	1879	D 1224		1892
247	1879	D 1225		1892

248	1879	D 1226		1890	
249	1879	D 1227		1890	
250	1879	D 1228		1890	
251	1879	D 1229		1891	Equipped by Holden to burn oil fuel
252	1879	D 1230		1891	
253	1879	D 1231		1890	
254	1879	D 1232		1890	
600	1881	K 2420	1886	1892	
601	1882	K 2421	1885	1893	
602	1882	K 2422	1885	1893	
603	1882	K 2423	1886	1890	Accident Streatham Fen 28/7/1882
604	1882	K 2424	1885	1890	
605	1882	K 2425	1885	1893	
606	1882	K 2426	1885	1893	
607	1882	K 2427	1886	1893	
608	1882	K 2428	1888	1892	
609	1882	K 2429	1886	1890	Accident Streatham Fen 28/7/1882

0-4-4T Built by GER at Stratford. Works nos 81-120, 131-143, 154-160.
DW 4ft 10in; TW 2ft 10in; Cyls 16½ x 22; THS 983.21 sq ft; WP 140 lbs/sq in;
Wt 44 tons 16 cwt. Rebuilt DW 4ft 11in; WP 160 lbs/sq in.
Class E10 Half cabs.

No	Date	Rebuilt etc	Duplicate no	year	Withdrawn or scrapped
87	1878	1892	087	1904	1905
88	1878	1895	088	1904	1905
89	1878	1892	089	1904	1904
90	1878	1892			1903
91	1878	1892			1904
92	1878	1892	092	1905	1905
93	1878	1895	093	1905	1907
94	1878	1888			1903
95	1879	1890, 1900	095	1905	1907
96	1879	1893 and fitted for oil fuel	096	1905	12/1911 (withdrawn)
97	1879	1890, 1901	097	1905	11/1912 (withdrawn)
98	1879	1892			11/1904 (withdrawn)
99	1879	1893	099	1905	1906
100	1879	1894	0100	1905	1906
101	1879	1892	0101	1905	1906
102	1879	1895	0102	1905	2/1911 (withdrawn)
51	1879	1892	051	1904	1905
52	1879	1896	052	1904	1907
53	1879	1894	053	1904	1906
54	1879	1888, 1902	054	1904	1910
55	1879	1891	055	1904	1907
56	1879	1888	056	1904	1907
57	1879	1888, 1907	057	1904	1907
58	1880	1890, 1900	058	1904	1904
59	1880	1893	059	1904	1907
60	1880	1891	060	1904	7/1910 (withdrawn)
231	1880	1890	0231	1903	1904
232	1880	1892			1907
233	1880	1891			1906
234	1880	1888, 1898			1908
235	1880	1890			1906
236	1880	1892			1903
237	1880	1893			1905
238	1880	1894			1904
239	1880	1888			1904
240	1880	1890, Oil fuel 1893	0240	1906	1906

No	Date	Rebuilt	Duplicate no	year	Scrapped
241	1880	1892, Oil fuel 1893			1905
242	1880	1887			1903
243	1880	1893, 1903	0243	1906	1909
244	1880	1891	0244	1906	1908
572	1881	1890			1906
573	1881	1890			1905
574	1881	1891			1904
575	1882	1890			1905
576	1882	1892	0576	1907	1907
577*	1882	1891, 1902			1905
578	1882	1895	0578	1907	1907
579*	1882	1895	0579	1907	1907
580	1882	1893			1906
581	1882	1894	0581	1907	12/1911 (withdrawn)
582	1882	1893	0582	1907	1908
583	1882	1894			1906
584	1882	1894			1906
585	1883	1892	0585	1907	1907
586	1883	1892	0586	1907	1907
587	1883	1892, 1899	0587	1907	7/1910 (withdrawn)
588	1883	1892			1906
589	1883	1893	0589	1907	1907
590	1883	1891	0590	1907	1908
591	1883	1892	0591	1907	1909

* No 579 was in collision with Midland Railway no 1722 at Crouch End 19/3/1887.
　No 577 was in an accident in collision with T18 0-6-0T 344 at Stratford
　　　Market 7/4/1905.

0-4-4T Built by R&W Hawthorn & Co. Works nos 1822-31.
DW 5ft 4in; Cyls 16 x 22; THS 974.5 sq ft; WP 140 lbs/sq in; Wt 40 tons 18 cwt.

No	Date	Rebuilt 0-4-2T	Duplicate no	year	Scrapped
140	1880	1892	0140	1903	1903
141	1880	1891	0141	1903	1903
142	1880	1891	0142	1903	1903
143	1880	1892	0143	1903	1905
144	1880	1890	0144	1903	1903
145	1880	1892	0145	1903	1904
146	1880	1894	0146	1903	1903
147	1880	1895	0147	1903	1905
148	1880	1895	0148	1903	1904
149	1880	1895	0149	1903	1903

0-6-0T Built by GER at Stratford. Works nos 121-30.
DW 4ft 10in; Cyls 16 x 22; THS 974.05 sq ft; WP 140 lbs/sq in; Wt 40 tons 6 cwt.
Shunting tanks. **Class M12** Half cabs.

No	Date	Rebuilt	Duplicate no	year	Scrapped
542	1881	1887			1896
543	1881	1887			1896
544	1881	1888			1896
545	1881	1895	0545	1898	1902
546	1881	1895	0546	1898	1902
547	1881				1895
548	1881				1898
549	1881		0549	1898	1899
550	1881		0550	1898	1899
551	1881				1897

0-6-0 Built by Kitson & Co. Works nos 2430-6, 2438-40.
DW 5ft 2in; Cyls 17 x 24; THS 1081.4 sq ft; WP 140 lbs/sq in; Wt 36 tons 3 cwt. Side
window cab, o/s frame, raised running plate. Cylinders increased to 17½in diameter.

No	Date	Rebuilt	Scrapped
552	1882	1895	1904
553	1882	1895	1906
554	1882	1895	1906
555	1882	1896	1905
556	1882	1896	1905
557	1882	1893	1905
558	1882	1893	1905
559	1882	1894	1905
560	1882	1894	1905
561	1882	1896	1906

Worsdell Locomotives 1882-97

2-4-0 Built by GER at Stratford. Works nos 161-70, 181-90.
DW 7ft 0in; LW 4ft 0in; WB 8ft 9in + 8ft 9in; Cyls 18 x 24; Blr 4ft 2in x 11ft 9¼in;
THS 1228 sq ft; WP 140 lbs/sq in; Wt 41 tons 3 cwt. **Class G14** Joy valve gear
replaced by link motion, continuous splasher, LW radial axlebox.

No	Date	Rebuilt	Duplicate no	year	Scrapped
562*	1882		0562	1898	1899
563	1882				1897
564	1882				1896
565	1883				1897
566	1883	1891			1897
567	1883				1897
568	1883		0568	1898	1899
569	1883				1895
570	1883				1896
571	1883				1895
640	1883	1891	0640	1899	1899
641	1883	1891			1898
642	1883	1891	0642	1899	1901
643	1883	1892	0643	1899	1900
644	1883	1892			1897 Fitted with Morton's valve gear.
645	1883				1899
646	1883				1899
647	1883	1891			1899
648	1883				1898
649	1883	1891			1899

* No 562 cylinders reduced to 17½in diameter in 1886

4-4-0 Compound built by GER at Stratford. Works nos 244, 267-76.
DW 7ft 0in; LW 3ft 1in; WB 6ft 3in + 7ft 7½in + 8ft 9in; Cyls 18 x 24 hp, 26 x 24 lp;
Blr 4ft 2in x 11ft 5¼in; THS 1200 sq ft; WP 160 lbs/sq in; Wt 44½ tons. **Class G16**.
Von Borries compound. Joy valve gear. Similar to G14 2-4-0 except for leading bogie.
All rebuilt simple expansion 18 x 24 cyls in 1892.

No	Date	Rebuilt simple	Duplicate no	year	Scrapped
230	1884	1892	0230	1903	1904
700	1885	1892	0700	1892	1904
701	1885	1892	0701	1892	1903
702	1885	1892	0702	1892	1902
703	1885	1892	0703	1892	1902
704	1885	1892	0704	1892	1903
705	1885	1892	0705	1892	1903
706	1885	1892	0706	1892	1902 Fitted with extended smokebox 1901

707	1885	1892	0707	1892	1903
708	1885	1892	0708	1892	1904
709	1885	1892	0709	1892	1904

2-4-2T Built by GER at Stratford. Works nos 214-23 (order no M15)
224-43 (order no E16)

DW 5ft 4in; LW + TW 3ft 9in; Cyls 18 x 24; Blr 4ft 2in x 10ft 2½in; THS 1054.1 sq ft; WP 140 lbs/sq in; WB 7ft 6in + 8ft 0in + 7ft 6in; Wt 51 tons 18 cwt. **Class M15** Joy radial valve gear.

As built, these locomotives were exceptionally heavy on coal consumption earning them the nickname 'gobblers' and Holden (who succeeded Worsdell in 1885) had no 674 fitted with Stephenson instead of Joy valve gear and with cylinder diameter reduced to 17½in diameter. All were reboilered with 2-ring instead of 3-ring boilers, with the dome further forward on the first ring instead of in the centre ring of the original three ring boiler. The new boiler had WP increased to 160 lbs/sq in from 1896. 17½in cylinders and Stephenson link motion replaced the original Joy valve gear at the dates below.

Replacement boilers between 1886 and 1896 had THS 1107, 1133.2 and 1110.8 sq ft, and from 1907, 2-ring telescopic boilers with 1116.4 sq ft THS were fitted instead of the original butt-jointed type (except on 652/61/72). Nos 650-9 were fitted with condensers in 1895/6 for working over the East London line. LNE class F4.

Svg = Stephenson valve gear.

No	Date	Rebuilt Svg & 17½in cyls	160 lbs blr	LNE no 1923	LNE no 1924	Withdrawn
650	7/1884	10/1895	9/1909	650E	7650*	6/1927
651	7/1884	12/1895	9/1909			12/1914
652	8/1884	12/1896	12/1896			10/1913
653	9/1884	10/1895	1/1911	(653E)		8/1923
654	9/1884	11/1896	11/1896	654E	7654*	11/1927
655	9/1884	12/1895	7/1909	655E	(7655)	10/1926
656	11/1884	12/1895	12/1908			12/1922
657	11/1884	7/1896	5/1909	657E	(7657)	5/1926
658	11/1884	4/1896	7/1909			6/1914
659	11/1884	5/1896	2/1909	659E	(7659)	9/1925
660	12/1884	9/1925	11/1910	660E	(7660)	1/1926
661	1/1885	11/1897	11/1897			9/1913
662	3/1885	8/1896	10/1909	662E	7662	11/1926
663	3/1885	8/1895	10/1907	663E	(7663)	9/1925
664	4/1885	11/1895	4/1910			9/1915
665	5/1885	12/1895	6/1911	665E	(7665)	8/1926
666	6/1885	1/1897	1/1897	666E	(7666)	3/1926
667	7/1885	7/1896	11/1908			12/1922
668	7/1885	7/1896	4/1911	668E	(7668)	3/1926
669	7/1885	5/1896	3/1911	669E	(7669)	9/1926
670	8/1885	10/1897	10/1897	670E	7670	9/1927
671	9/1885	10/1896	10/1896			12/1922
672	10/1885	1/1898	1/1898			9/1913
673	12/1885	3/1896	7/1909			12/1914
674	10/1885	as built	2/1897	674E	(7674)	2/1926
675	12/1885	1/1897	1/1897	675E	7675*	8/1927
676	1/1886	10/1896	10/1896	676E	(7676)	2/1926
677	2/1886	5/1896	9/1910	677E	(7677)	4/1925
678	3/1886	10/1895	3/1910	678E	7678	11/1928
679	2/1886	8/1896	6/1909	679E	(7679)	7/1925

* LNE number possibly not applied.

James Holden continued construction of this class as rebuilt (see page 77).

0-4-0T 'tram' built by GER at Stratford. Works nos below. Order nos G15, N17, C29, F40.
DW 3ft 1in; WB 6ft 6in; Cyls 11 x 15; Blr 2ft 9⁵/₈in x 6ft 10in; THS 308.9 sq ft; WP 120 lbs/sq in; Wt 20 tons 19 cwt (1883-92); 1897 locomotives had THS 349.46 sq ft; WP 140 lbs/sq in; Wt 21¼ tons. This higher pressure boiler was fitted to the earlier locomotives as below. All except 7132 had boilers with 348.08 sq ft THS from 1929 for various periods.

Class G15 Designed to work on the Wisbech and Upwell Tramway, much of which ran on public roads. The wheels and motion were cased in with steel plates and with 'cowcatchers' at each end to conform with Board of Trade regulations. They could be driven from either end, and the upper parts were enclosed in a wooden body rather like a brake van. They were also used on the Yarmouth Union Tramway from Vauxhall to the fish wharf. LNE class Y6.

No	Date	Works no	140 lbs blr	Duplicate no	year	LNE no 1923	LNE no 1924	LNE no 1946	Applied	Withdrawn
130	6/1883	191	10/1898							12/1909
131	6/1883	192	not fitted							9/1907
132	8/1883	193	6/1899			132E	7132			10/1931
128	3/1885*	255	3/1906							3/1913
129	4/1885*	256	2/1898	0129	1921	0129E	07129			4/1933
125	12/1891	649	4/1904	0125	1921	0125E	07125			2/1940
126	1/1892	650	9/1901	0126	1921	0126E	07126			2/1940
127	1/1892	651	9/1902							12/1913
133	8/1897	923	as built			133E	7133	8082	5/1946	5/1951
134	8/1897	924	as built			134E	7134	8083	4/1946	11/1952

* No 128 to stock 12/1885, No 129 to stock 10/1885.

0-6-0 Built by GER at Stratford. Works nos below.
               Sharp Stewart & Co. Works nos below.
DW 4ft 10in; WB 7ft 7in + 8ft 6in; Cyls 17½ x 24; Blr 4ft 4in x 10ft 0in; THS 1160.6 sq ft; WP 140 lbs/sq in; Wt 36½ tons.

Class Y14 Introduced to cope with increasing traffic from the Joint Line to Doncaster opened in 1882. Replacements to the original 3-ring butt jointed boilers from 1900 were 2-ring telescopic. THS 1199.5 sq ft and from 1908 1164.7 sq ft; WP 160 lbs/sq in. These, and later locomotives built to the same pattern by J Holden, had level grates ('square bottom' in Stratford works parlance) until Holden introduced sloping grates in 1890. DW increased to 4ft 11in and Wt to 37 tons 2 cwt after reboilering and with thicker tyres. LNE class J15.
The following were built at Stratford: Works nos 171-80 (order no Y14), 194-213 (order no K15), 245-54 (order no N16), 257-266 (order no P17) and originally had only tender hand brakes until fitted with steam brakes between 1896-1901.

No	Date	160 lbs boiler*	LNE no 1923	LNE no 1924	Withdrawn	
610	7/1883	1908	610E	7610	10/1929	Fitted for oil fuel 7/1894
611	7/1883	10/1897	611E	7611	8/1926	Fitted with Serve tubes THS 985.4 sq ft 12/1891 until 10/1897. Also fitted for oil fuel 7/1894.
612	7/1883	1908	612E	7612	1/1932	
613	8/1883	1898	613E	7613	6/1931	Accident Roudham Crossing, Thetford 27/10/1926
614	8/1883	1906	614E	7614	9/1926	
615	9/1883	1908	615E	7615	10/1926	
616	9/1883	1907	616E	7616	7/1929	To ROD 1917-19
617	9/1883	11/1906	617E	7617	10/1926	Fitted with Serve tubes THS 998.48 sq ft 1/1896 until 11/1906
618	10/1883	1897	618E	7618	7/1929	
619	10/1883	11/1906			5/1922	Serve tubes 1896-1906 as 617
620	3/1884	1908	620E	7620	10/1926	
621	3/1884	1906	621E	7621	7/1932	

622	3/1884	1906	622E	7622	10/1926	
623	3/1884	1897	623E	7623	7/1933	
624	3/1884	1909			5/1922	
625	3/1884	1896	625E	7625	6/1932	
626	3/1884	1896			5/1922	
627	3/1884	1899	627E	7627	11/1933	
628	3/1884	1897	628E	7628	12/1931	
629	3/1884	1898	629E	7629	9/1926	
630	5/1884	1896	630E	7630	6/1929	
631	5/1884	1897	631E	7631	12/1933	
632	5/1884	1896			5/1922	
633	6/1884	1903	633E	7633	8/1926	
634	6/1884	1898	634E	7634	1/1929	
635	6/1884	1896	635E	7635	4/1936	
636	7/1884	1903	636E	7636	5/1929	
637	7/1884	1897			5/1922	
638	7/1884	1903	638E	7638	6/1936	
639	8/1884	1905	639E	7639	6/1928	
680	2/1885	1896	680E	7680	6/1932	
681	2/1885	1896	681E	7681	10/1932	
682	2/1885	1907	682E	7682	1/1932	
683	2/1885	11/1903	683E	7683	11/1931	Serve tubes as 611 until 11/1903
684	2/1885	1900	684E	7684	6/1932	
685	2/1885	1897	685E	7685	10/1929	
686	2/1885	1896	686E	7686	6/1928	
687	2/1885	1896			5/1922	
688	2/1885	1899			5/1923	
689	2/1885	1898	689E	7689	6/1936	
690	11/1885	1896	690E	7690	6/1938	Sold to Bairds & Scottish Steel Ltd. To ROD 1917-19. Scrapped 1960.
691	11/1885	1898	691E	7691	3/1929	
692	12/1885	1897	692E	7692	4/1929	
693	12/1885	1898	693E	7693	7/1928	
694	1/1886	1897	694E	7694	10/1931	
695	1/1886	1899			3/1922	To ROD 1917-19
696**	12/1885	1897	696E	7696	3/1938	
697	1/1886	1897	697E	7697	10/1929	
698	2/1886	1899	698E	7698	10/1936	Sloping grate blr fitted 8/1933
699	3/1886	1899	699E	7699	7/1934	Accident Bethnal Green, 29/8/1899

* Locos fitted with 160 lbs/sq in boilers before 1900 initially had a 2-ring butt-jointed type with a THS of 1221.68 sq ft.

** No 696 exchanged cylinders with no 674 M15 2-4-2T together with Joy valve gear during construction to enable experiments to be carried out with Stephenson valve gear on the M15 class. It was thus fitted with 18in diameter cylinders and Joy valve gear until 1/1897.

The following were built by Sharp Stewart & Co, works nos 3146-64 and were fitted with steam brakes when built.

No	Date	160 lbs boilers*	LNE no 1923	LNE no 1924	Withdrawn	
37	4/1884	1897			8/1923	
38	4/1884	1906	38E	07038	8/1932	To duplicate list 9/1923
39	4/1884	1897	39E	07039	3/1933	To duplicate list 9/1923
40	4/1884	1909			10/1922	
41	5/1884					
	Renumbered					
600	7/1912	1896	600E	7600	6/1934	
119	5/1884	1896	119E	7119	9/1929	

120	5/1884	1898	120E	7120	2/1928
121	5/1884	1909	121E	7121	3/1933
122	5/1884	1910	122E	7122	1/1930
123	5/1884	1897			7/1922
124	5/1884	1896	124E	7124	7/1933
592	5/1884	1905	592E	7592	8/1928
593	6/1884	1906	593E	7593	12/1926
594	6/1884	1896	594E	7594	7/1926
595	6/1884	1897	595E	7595	6/1929
596	7/1884	1905	596E	7596	11/1932
597	7/1884	1899	597E	7597	4/1928
598	7/1884	1907	598E	7598	9/1926
599	7/1884	1906	599E	7599	5/1931

* See note above (Stratford batch) for locomotives fitted with 160 lbs boilers before 1900.

Class continued by J Holden (see page 67).

J Holden Locomotives 1886 - 1911

2-2-2 Built by GER at Stratford. Works nos 388 (1888), 589-98 (1891), 753-62 (1893).
DW 7ft 0in; LW & TW 4ft 0in; WB 7ft 9in + 8ft 9in; Cyls 18 x 24; Blr 4ft 4in x 10ft
0in; THS 1230.46 sq ft; WP 140 lbs/sq in (1888-91). 160 lbs/sq in (1893); Wt 40 tons
3½ cwt.
Class D27 1888-91 locomotives reboilered at 160 lbs pressure.
Steam sanding, o/s bearings on LW. Designed for express work but soon rendered
redundant by increasing train weights. Nos 1004-9 fitted for oil fuel with water
scoop tenders for working non stop expresses to Cromer.
1893 locomotives had 18 x 25 cyls.

			Renumbered		Duplicate		
No	Date		no	year	no	date	Scrapped
740	1888	Cylinder design	789	1888			
		improved 1891	780	1892			1905
770	1891	Improved cylinder			0770	7/1904	1906
771	1891	design on all 1891/3			0771	7/1904	1904
772	1891	locomotives with angle of			0772	7/1904	1905
773	1891	inclination reduced					1902
774	1891	to 1 in 8			0774	7/1904	1905
775	1891						3/1904
776	1891				0776	7/1904	1907
777	1891				0777	7/1904	1905
778	1891				0778	7/1904	1907
779	1891				0779	7/1904	1907
1000	1893						1901
1001	1893						1902
1002	1893						1901
1003	1893						1902
1004	1893						1904
1005	1893						1901
1006	1893						1904
1007	1893						1901
1008	1893						1903
1009	1893						1903

4-2-2 Built by GER at Stratford. Works nos 967-76.
DW 7ft 0in; LW 3ft 9in; TW 4ft 0in; WB 6ft 6in + 7ft 3in + 9ft0in; Cyls 18 x 26; Blr
4ft 4in x 11ft 0in; THS 1292.73 sq ft; WP 160 lbs/sq in; Wt 52 tons 4¾ cwt.

Class P43 Steam sanding, Westinghouse brake, Double frames with single-framed bogie and o/s bearings on DW & TW. Oil fired but easily convertible for coal firing. Brass rimmed built up chimney in place of usual 'stovepipe' pattern. Swindon influence on Holden was very evident as they had a distinctly GW appearance, and were undoubtedly very elegant machines. Regrettably, however, they too proved inadequate with heavier trains despite the advantages of freer running and were soon withdrawn. Tenders were rounded inwards at the top. 2790 gallons of water and 720 gallons of oil.

No	Date	Scrapped	
10	1898	1908	
11	1898	1908	
12	1898	1910	Extended smokebox fitted 1902.
13	1898	1910	
14	1898	1907	
15	1898	1908	
16	1898	1908	
17	1898	1908	
18	1898	1907	
19	1898	1909	

2-4-0 Built by GER at Stratford. Works nos below.
DW 7ft 0in; LW 4ft 0in; WB 7ft 9in + 8ft 9in; Cyls 18 x 24; Blr 4ft 4in x 10ft 0in; THS 1230.46 sq ft (1886), 1208.3 sq ft (1890), 1217.08 sq ft (1892); WP 140 lbs/sq in (1886-95), 160 lbs/sq in (1897); Wt 42 tons.

Class T19 Similar in size to Worsdell class G14 but with shorter wheelbase. Boiler as class Y14 0-6-0, and parts were interchangeable with the D27 2-2-2, T26 2-4-0 and C32 2-4-2T. Increasing traffic demands resulted in 21 being rebuilt with 4ft 9in diameter boilers THS 1476.2 sq ft. These had Belpaire firebox, the barrels being 2-ring telescopic type instead of the original 3-ring butt-jointed type used from 1886 to 1890 and the 2-ring butt-jointed ones from 1892. With the introduction of the latter type, the dome (which had been positioned on the centre ring) was moved forward to the front ring. This was again the position with the rebuilt locomotives but the larger diameter boiler increased the pitch by a foot resulting in a rather top heavy appearance and getting them the nickname 'Humpty-Dumpty'. Working pressure on these rebuilds increased to 180 lbs/sq in. Other locomotives had 2-ring telescopic boilers of the original diameter with 160 lbs/sq in pressure from 1899.
The rebuilds had new cabs similar to the class S46 4-4-0s, but with only one side window due to the shorter length, and their weight was 45 tons 9 cwt. Commencing in January 1905, sixty were rebuilt as 4-4-0s with 4ft 9in diameter boilers, but with the dome on the rear ring. THS and WP as on the 2-4-0 rebuilds, but from 1907, THS was 1452.7 sq ft. The bogies for these 4-4-0s were taken from withdrawn Bromley class E10 0-4-4Ts and Worsdell G16 4-4-0s, the latter with their original 3ft 1in wheels and the former with new 3ft 1in wheels. WB 6ft 3in + 6ft 4½in + 8ft 9in.
Schmidt superheaters (190.5 sq ft) were fitted from 1913 (THS 1297.3 sq ft including superheater) and Robinson superheaters (136.8 sq ft) from 1921 (THS 1243.6 sq ft including superheater). From 1940, boilers with THS 1234 sq ft including superheater were fitted. Superheated locomotives had a larger smokebox with chimney further forward. Wt of 4-4-0s 47 tons 16 cwt (saturated), 48 tons 6 cwt (superheated). Steam heating apparatus fitted from 1906. All built with Westinghouse brake. The following had vacuum ejectors in addition: 713/46 (from 1890), 760-4 when new, 1030-9 when new and 704/72 (from 1906). Some twenty five, both rebuilt and unrebuilt, are believed to have had 25in stroke pistons at some time. The 4-4-0 rebuilds survived to become LNE class D13. As such, all those still remaining were fitted with vacuum ejectors in addition to their Westinghouse brakes from 4/1927 to 1929 (7719 in 4/1927) although 7704 had this removed before 1923.
The following were built with level grates and had hand-screw reverse and Worsdell 2755 gallon tenders. Works nos 337-46 (order no T19), 358-67 (order no 520), 378-87 (order no F21), 429-38 (order no 022) and 439-48 (order no R22).

No	Date	160 lb blr	Rebuilt Belpaire	4-4-0	Super-heated	Vacuum ejector	LNE no 1923	LNE no 1924	Wdn
710	11/1886	12/1898	1/1908	1/1908	10/1916	1/1929	710E	7710	12/1929
711	5/1887								1908
712*	5/1887	5/1900	5/1906	5/1906*	11/1925	4/1929	712E	7712	11/1931
713	5/1887	7/1898	1/1907	1/1907	3/1922	5/1890	713E	7713	5/1933
714	1887								1909
715	6/1887	9/1897	12/1906	12/1906*					12/1922
716	6/1887								1909
717	6/1887	11/1896	1/1907	1/1907					3/1930
718	6/1887	6/1897	3/1905	3/1905*	3/1914	7/1929	718E	7718	5/1933
719	6/1887	9/1895	5/1906	5/1906*	3/1914	4/1927	719E	7719	3/1932
720	1888								1909
721	1888**								1909
722	1888								1909
723	1888								1908
724	1888		1904						1914
725	1888		1904						1919
726	1888								1910
727	1888		1903						1915
728	1888	7/1900	5/1906	5/1906*	4/1914	3/1929	728E	7728	4/1931
729	4/1888	6/1898	2/1905	2/1905	2/1915	5/1929	729E	7729	4/1936
730	5/1888	11/1896	2/1907	2/1907					8/1923
731	5/1888	9/1897	2/1907	2/1907*					8/1931
732	5/1888	8/1898	4/1908	4/1904*	5/1921	1929	732E	7732	5/1933
733	5/1888	4/1898	7/1908	7/1908*	12/1920	11/1928	733E	7733	9/1931
734	5/1888	10/1900	6/1907	6/1907	9/1919	3/1929	734E	7734	10/1931
735	6/1888	8/1900	10/1907	10/1907*	12/1913	12/1928	735E	7735	4/1932
736	6/1888								1910
737	6/1888	6/1899	6/1907	6/1907	3/1916	6/1929	737E	7737	4/1933
738	6/1888	5/1900	2/1908	2/1908	2/1921	2/1929	738E	7738	7/1931
739	6/1888	5/1902	10/1907	10/1907	6/1916	5/1929	739E	7739	9/1931
740	1889								1911
741	4/1889	3/1900	6/1907	6/1907	2/1920	10/1928	741E	7741	12/1935
742	4/1889	9/1896	9/1896	2/1907*	11/1914	10/1928	742E	7742	11/1935
743	1889		1904						1913
744	5/1889	8/1902	10/1907	10/1907	8/1915	1/1929	744E	7744	4/1935
745	5/1889	6/1902	6/1906	6/1906	3/1918	8/1929	745E	7745	1/1933
746	5/1889				1890				1908
747	5/1889	11/1900	1/1908	1/1908*					12/1922
748	5/1889	3/1896	2/1905	2/1905*	5/1914	8/1929			9/1931
749	1889								1908
750	1889		1903						1915
751	6/1889	7/1899	6/1907	6/1907*	5/1914	7/1928	751E	7751	1/1933
752	1889								1910
753	1889								1909
754	1889								1908
755	1889								1910
756	9/1889	2/1901	6/1908	6/1908	6/1915	10/1929	756E	7756	12/1938
757	1889								1910
758	1889								1908
759	1889								1911

* 25in stroke at this time on nos 712/8/28/31/2/3/42/8 which were retained.
  Nos 718/9/28/35/48/51 had stepped instead of sloping framing in front of
  the smokebox. No 712 was built for oil burning as well as coal.

** No 721 had the coupling rods removed for period in 6/1888 for experiments
  with singles.

The following were built with sloping (bevel-bottom) grates and crescent shaped
balance weights in place of square ended ones. Holden 2640 gallon tenders, screw

reverse. Works nos 509-18 (order no T24). Nos 760, 762-7 were built for oil fuel. No 760 was named *Petrolea* for a time. 762-7 had water scoops fitted in 1896 and others later.

No	Date	160 lb blr	Rebuilt Belpaire	4-4-0	Super heated	Vacuum ejector	LNE no 1923	LNE no 1924	Wdn
760	1890		1903			as new			1914
761	1890					as new			9/1908
762	1890		1903			as new			1913
763	1890		1903			as new			1913
764	1890					as new			1911
765	6/1890	3/1905	3/1905*	3/1905	3/1917	1/1929	765E	7765	1/1930
766	6/1890	4/1902	2/1908	2/1908	8/1919	8/1928	766E	7766	1/1935
767	6/1890	4/1902	1/1908	1/1908	2/1923	4/1929	767E	7767	12/1934
768	1890								1913
769	1890		1902						1913

* 25in stroke at this time which was retained.

The following were built with 2-ring boilers with the dome on the front one and sloping grates. 2640 gallon tenders. The air brake cylinder was moved from underneath the cab to a position within the rear frame spacer casting, and a single brake cylinder replaced the former pair of smaller cylinders. Macallan variable blast pipes were fitted. Nos 1020-9 exchanged tenders with those from class P43 4-2-2s in 1901, but without the oil tanks they had originally carried with a capacity of 2790 gallons. Works nos 672-81 (order no S29), 682-91 (order no V29), 743-52 (order no V32), 853-62 (order no H35).

No	Date	7/1904 no	Reblt Belpaire	160 lbs blr* 4-4-0	Super heated	Vacuum ejector	LNE no 1923	LNE no 1924	Wdn
700	5/1892		3/1905	3/1905	3/1920	1929	700E	7700	10/1935
701	5/1892								1909
702	5/1892		1903						1919
703	5/1892								1909
704	5/1892		2/1906	2/1906**	6/1914	9/1906**	704E	7704	12/1932
705	6/1892		10/1907	10/1907**			705E	7705	12/1926
706	6/1892		3/1905	3/1905**	6/1925	3/1929	706E	7706	6/1938
707	6/1892		1/1905	1/1905**	11/1913	1929	707E	7707	5/1937
708	6/1892		4/1906	4/1906**	11/1917	8/1929	708E	7708	11/1935
709	6/1892								1910
781	6/1892	770	1903						1914
782	6/1892	771	1903						1919
783	6/1892	772	2/1906	2/1906**	10/1914	10/1906	772E	7772	9/1938
784	6/1892	773							1909
785	6/1892	774	1903						1914
786	6/1892	775	2/1905	2/1905**	11/1913	6/1929	775E	7775	5/1936
787	6/1892	776	1904						1920
788	6/1892	777	3/1906	3/1906**	5/1914	5/1928	777E	7777	6/1934
789	1892	778	1904						1920
790	7/1892	779	5/1906	5/1906**	5/1918	10/1928	779E	7779	4/1935
1010	1893		1904						1915
1011	1893		1904						1914
1012	6/1893		5/1906	5/1906**	4/1915	8/1929	1012E	8012	12/1935
1013	6/1893		4/1906	4/1906	6/1922	5/1929	1013E	8013	10/1935
1014	6/1893		1904						1915
1015	6/1893		5/1906	5/1906	11/1916	6/1928	1015E	8015	10/1934
1016	7/1893		2/1906	2/1906**	4/1914	3/1929	1016E	8016	5/1938
1017	7/1893		1904						1915
1018	7/1893		7/1907	7/1907			1018E	(8018)	6/1925

No	Date	Belpaire	4-4-0	Super heated		LNE no 1923	LNE no 1924	Wdn
1019	1893							1910
1020	6/1895	3/1907	3/1907	12/1914	2/1929	1020E	8020	4/1936
1021	6/1895	3/1906	3/1906	10/1919	12/1928	1021E	8021	8/1936
1022	1895	1904						1913
1023	7/1895	5/1906	5/1906**	4/1914	12/1928	1023E	8023***	1/1944
1024	7/1895							1908
1025	7/1895	3/1906	3/1906	10/1914	6/1928	1025E	8025	10/1937
1026	8/1895	4/1906	4/1906	5/1926	6/1928	1026E	8026	2/1937
1027	8/1895	5/1906	5/1906	3/1915	8/1928	1027E	8027	1/1936
1028	8/1895	3/1907	3/1907	5/1918	3/1929	1028E	8028	1/1938
1029	9/1895	3/1907	3/1907	10/1919	1/1929	1029E	8029	3/1938

* Nos 705 and 1018 received 160 lbs boilers in 2/1900 and 3/1901 respectively.
** Nos 704/5/6/8/72/7/9, 1012 had 25in stroke at this time which were retained.
Nos 704/7/75/7, 1016/23 had stepped framing in front of the smokebox instead of sloping frames.
No 704 had the vacuum ejector removed before 1923 which was reinstated in 2/1929.
*** No 8023 was allotted the number 2057 in the 1943 renumbering scheme.

The following were built with two ring boilers of 160 lbs pressure and vacuum ejectors. Works nos 913-22 (order no M39).

No	Date	Rebuilt Belpaire	4-4-0	Super heated	LNE no 1923	LNE no 1924	Wdn
1030	3/1897	4/1906	4/1906	9/1916	1030E	8030	11/1938
1031	3/1897	3/1908	3/1908		1031E	8031	12/1926
1032	3/1897	5/1906	5/1906*	3/1921	1032E	8032	9/1936
1033	3/1897	3/1905	3/1905		1033E	8033	6/1927
1034	1897	1904					1913
1035	4/1897	1/1905	1/1905	3/1918	1035E	8035	5/1943
1036	4/1897	2/1907	2/1907*	4/1918	1036E	8036	2/1937
1037	4/1897	5/1908	5/1908	12/1920	1037E	8037	12/1934
1038	1897						1909
1039	5/1897	10/1907	10/1907	12/1921	1039E	8039	3/1944**

* Nos 1032 and 1036 had 25in stroke at this time which was retained.
** No 8039 was allotted the number 2058 in the 1943 renumbering scheme.

2-4-0 Built by GER at Stratford. Works nos below.
DW 5ft 8in; LW 4ft 0in; WB 7ft 9in + 8ft 9in; Cyls 17½ x 24 (some 17in and 18in diam, see below); Blr 4ft 4in x 10ft 0in; THS 1208.3 sq ft (1891), 1217.08 sq ft (1892), 1199.5 sq ft (1899); WP 140 lbs/sq in (1891), 160 lbs/sq in (1896); Wt 40 tons 6 cwt.
Class T26 Design derived from T19 class but with smaller DW for secondary passenger and perishable or livestock traffic. The improved cylinder design already adopted on class D27 2-2-2s decreasing the inclination from 1 in 30 to 1 in 8 with shorter exhaust passages improved performance. As they were intended for 'intermediate' traffic they became known throughout their existence as 'Intermediates'. 2-ring telescopic boilers were introduced in 1899 and were fitted on the 1902 locomotives when built. A modified version was introduced in 1907 (THS 1164.7 sq ft) and the LNER fitted boilers of 1147.1 sq ft and 1137.69 sq ft THS in 1940. Macallan variable blast pipes were originally fitted but were removed by the LNER. (422/47/81 had the Stones type fitted in 1914). Gravity sanding, 2640 gallon tenders. In addition to the Westinghouse brake, sixty were built with vacuum ejectors as well in view of the amount of exchange traffic they dealt with from other railways and others were so equipped later. No 490 built in 1895 was the last 2-4-0 in traffic when withdrawn in 1959 and after restoration to GER condition at Stratford is now at the National Railway Museum at York. LNE class E4.
The following were built with 3-ring butt-jointed boilers with the dome on the centre ring. Nos 417-26 had 17½ in diameter cylinders. The others had 17in diameter cylinders originally, but these were increased to 17½ in between 1/1896 and 3/1902. Working pressure increased to 160 lbs/sq in from 1897 when reboiling commenced with nos 417/8. Later reboilerings had the 1899 2-ring telescopic type and the modified

1907 version of this. Works nos 559-68 (order no T26), 569-78 (order no Y26), 579-88 (order no A27), 692-701 (order no Z30).

No	Date	Vacuum ejector	LNE no 1923	LNE no 1924	Renumbered no	Renumbered date	BR no applied	Wdn
417	2/1891		417E	7417				1/1930
418	3/1891	6/1930		7418				9/1934
419	3/1891		419E	7419				5/1926
420	4/1891		420E	7420				3/1927
421	4/1891	9/1931	421E	7421				11/1938
422	4/1891	4/1929	422E	7422				9/1939
423	3/1891		423E	7423				1/1926
424	3/1891		424E	7424				1/1929
425	3/1891		425E	7425				2/1927
426	3/1891		426E	7426				10/1926
427	4/1891	as new	427E	7427	7797	1/1943		
					2780	1/1947	62780	
							6/1950	9/1955
428	4/1891	as new	428E	7428				5/1929
429	4/1891	as new	429E	7429				10/1929
430	4/1891	as new	430E	7430				4/1926
431	4/1891	as new	431E	7431				6/1926
432	4/1891	as new	432E	7432				7/1929
433	5/1891	as new	433E	7433				4/1927
434	4/1891	as new	434E	7434				12/1935
435	4/1891	as new	435E	7435				3/1928
436	5/1891	as new	436E	7436				6/1929
437	5/1891		437E	7437				1/1927
438	5/1891		438E	7438				5/1926
439	5/1891		439E	7439				8/1927
440	5/1891		440E	7440				6/1929
441	5/1891	4/1930	441E	7441				6/1937
442	6/1891		442E	7442				12/1927
443	6/1891	6/1929	443E	7443				10/1931
444	6/1891	8/1931	444E	7444				6/1934
445	6/1891		445E	7445				1/1927
446	6/1891		446E	7446				4/1926
447	9/1892	as new	447E	7447				9/1926
448	9/1982	as new	448E	7448				1/1930
449	9/1892	as new	449E	7449				2/1930
450	9/1892	as new	450E	7450				5/1927
451	9/1892	as new	451E	7451				2/1929
452	10/1892	as new	452E	7452				9/1929
453	10/1892	as new	453E	7453				3/1935
454	10/1892	as new	454E	7454				6/1928
455	10/1892	as new	455E	7455				3/1934
456	11/1892	as new	456E	7456				12/1928

The following were built with 2-ring butt-jointed boilers, with the dome on the front ring. Nos 457-76 had 17in diameter cylinders originally but these were increased to 17½in in 1896-1902 period. The others were built with 17½in cylinders which became standard except 487 which was built with 18in cylinders as an experiment, but this was not perpetuated. Working pressure increased to 160 lbs/sq in as on 1891/2 locomotives above. Works nos 702-11 (order no A31), 712-21 (order no C31), 823-32 (order no I34), 833-42 (order no X34).

No	Date	Vacuum ejector	LNE no 1923	LNE no 1924	Renumbered no	Renumbered date	BR no applied	Wdn
457	11/1892	as new	457E	7457				6/1931*
458	11/1892	as new	458E	7458				8/1937
459	11/1892	as new	459E	7459				3/1935

460	11/1892	as new	460E	7460					4/1929
461	11/1892	as new	461E	7461					9/1931
462	11/1892	as new	462E	7462					5/1937
463	11/1892	as new	463E	7463**	2781	10/1946	62781		
								1/1949	1/1956
464	11/1892	as new	464E	7464					12/1933
465	12/1892	as new	465E	7465					7/1928
466	12/1892	as new	466E	7466	2782	6/1946	62782		
								8/1948	12/1954
467	12/1892	7/1930	467E	7467					4/1937
468	12/1892		468E	7468					8/1929
469*	12/1892		469E	7469					6/1929
470*	12/1892	2/1931	470E	7470					5/1934
471*	12/1892		471E	7471					9/1924
472	12/1892	5/1928	472E	7472					5/1938
473	1/1893	12/1932	473E	7473					12/1935
474	1/1893	8/1901	474E	7474					4/1929
475	1/1893	8/1929	475E	7475					5/1931
476	1/1893	8/1929	476E	7476					3/1937
477	10/1894	as new	477E	7477	2783	11/1946	62783		
								1/1952	12/1954
478	10/1894	as new	478E	7478**	2784	11/1946	62784		
								8/1950	5/1955
479	10/1894	as new	479E	7479					3/1938
480	10/1894	as new	480E	7480					1/1935
481	10/1894	as new	481E	7481					6/1935
482	11/1894	as new	482E	7482					9/1929
483	11/1894	as new	483E	7483					6/1929
484	11/1894	as new	484E	7484					3/1936
485	11/1894	as new	485E	7485					1/1940
486	11/1894	as new	486E	7486					6/1931*
487	12/1894	12/1928	487E	7487					12/1929
488	12/1894		488E	7488					12/1928.
489	12/1894	8/1929	489E	7489					3/1936
490	1/1895	4/1931	490E	7490	7802	11/1942			
					2785	12/1946	62785		
								2/1951	12/1959***
491	1/1895	8/1931	491E	7491					1/1935
492	1/1895	3/1930	492E	7492	2786	10/1946	62786		
								6/1948	7/1956
493	1/1895		493E	7493					7/1929
494	1/1895	8/1929	494E	7494	2787	3/1946	62787		
								6/1948	11/1956
495	1/1895		495E	7495					5/1928
496	1/1895	10/1929	496E	7496**	7805	10/1942			
					2788	1/1947	62788		
								10/1948	3/1958

*   Nos 7457 and 7486 were in head on collision with each other at Fakenham on
      27/5/1931 and were both withdrawn the following month.
      Nos 7469 and 7470 were involved in an accident at Saxilby 26/12/1927.
      No 471 was in collision with S69 4-6-0 no 1506 at Colchester on 2/7/1913.
**   Fitted on the following dates with more substantial side window cab when
      transferred to the NE area, adding 2 cwt to the weight.
          7463 8/1936; 7478 7/1936; 7496 12/1936.
*** Preserved in National Railway Museum collection at York.

The following were built to the higher working pressure of 160 lbs/sq in. The 1902
batch originally had the 2790 gallon tenders with the inward turning curve at the top,
which had been designed to carry oil fuel or coal and were known as 'water cart'

tenders. These had been intended for class S46 *Claude Hamilton* 4-4-0s nos 1880-9, but it was decided to provide these with larger ones (*qv*). They were at times attached to other T26s. Works nos 893-902 (order no L37), 1118-27 (order no S50).

No	Date	1/1920 no	Vacuum ejector	LNE no 1923	LNE no 1924	Renumbered no	date	BR no applied	With-drawn
497	7/1896		as new	497E	7497*	2789	3/1946	62789	
								12/1949	12/1957
498	8/1896		as new	498E	7498				1/1935
499	8/1896		as new	499E	7499				3/1935
500	8/1896		as new	500E	7500				6/1936
501	9/1896		as new	501E	7501				10/1938
502	9/1896		as new	502E	7502				1/1939
503	9/1896		as new	503E	7503	2790	9/1946	62790	
								7/1949	1/1956
504	10/1896		as new	504E	7504				11/1938
505	10/1896		as new	505E	7505				2/1931
506	10/1896		as new	506E	7506	2791	10/1946	62791	
								6/1949	4/1955
1250	6/1902	407	as new	407E	7407	7791	11/1942		
						2792	9/1946	62792	
								1/1950	6/1956
1251	6/1902	408	as new	408E	7408**	2793	9/1946	62793	
								10/1949	2/1955
1252	6/1902	409	as new	409E	7409	2794	10/1946	62794	
								4/1950	8/1955
1253	6/1902	410	as new	410E	7410				1/1935
1254	6/1902	411	as new	411E	7411**	7794	10/1942		
						2795	10/1946	62795	
								12/1951	3/1955
1255	7/1902	412	as new	412E	7412				8/1935
1256	7/1902	413	as new	413E	7413				10/1931
1257	7/1902	414	as new	414E	7414	2796	9/1946	62796	
								5/1950	5/1957
1258	8/1902	415	as new	415E	7415				6/1937
1259	8/1902	416	as new	416E	7416**	2797	9/1946	62797	
								5/1949	3/1958

* Back cab fitted later with circular spectacles.
** Fitted with more substantial cab with side window when transferred to NE area.
     7408 9/1936; 7411 5/1936; 7416 10/1936.

4-4-0 Built by GER at Stratford. Works nos below.
DW 7ft 0in; LW 3ft 9in; WB 6ft 6in + 8ft 0in + 9ft 0in; Cyls 19 x 26;
Blr 4ft 9in x 11ft 9in; THS 1630.5 sq ft; WP 180 lbs/sq ft; Wt 50 tons 6 cwt.
Class S46 *Claud Hamilton*. This class, and the improved D56 that succeeded it, are Holden's most celebrated class of locomotive although *Locomotives of the LNER Part 3C* (RCTS) records that the original design was mostly the work of Frederick V Russell, the Stratford works Chief Draughtsman, in Holden's absence abroad for health reasons. No 1900 won a gold medal at the 1900 Paris Exhibition for which it was named *Claud Hamilton*, and numbered 1900, although GER capital account numbers had not reached 1200 at this period. Subsequent 4-4-0s were numbered backwards in blocks of, ten but the gap in the numbering was never completely closed. They were at that time the largest express passenger engines on the GER. THS from 1908 was 1624.38 sq ft with some new boilers fitted in 1913 being 1626 sq ft. These were all round-topped as originally designed (LNE class D14). All were rebuilt with Belpaire fireboxes as class D56 (LNE D15) over an extended period from 1915 to 1931 (*qv* for details). Some were given extended smokeboxes and the LNE recorded these (from 12/27) as D15/2 whether superheated or not.

By 1935 all had the extended smokeboxes and superheating had been completed by 1933, so the sub-division was discontinued and all became D15 again. Details of the superheaters are given under class D56 following. From 1933, most of the original class S46 locos were rebuilt again as class D16/3 with a 5ft 1$\frac{1}{8}$in diameter round-topped boiler pitched 4in higher at 8ft 9in; THS 1429.4 sq ft + 204.4 sq ft superheater (1933), 302.5 sq ft superheater (1936), some with 8in and 9½in piston valves and some with slide valves. Weight with piston valves: 55 tons 18 cwt, with slide valves: 54 tons 18 cwt. GN chimneys fitted 11/35-7/36 except 8860/1/3/5/6/9/70/6/8/900. As built, a double side window cab (subsequently widened as below) was provided which was retained in the rebuilds. Compressed air from the Westinghouse brake pump could be used to operate the reversing gear and the water scoop on the tender together with the usual hand operation. These were powered by a subsidiary reservoir fed from the main reservoir by a non-return valve which ensured that there was always a supply of air for the braking. Sanding could also be applied by compressed air. All of this class was equipped for burning either coal or oil and all had reverted to coal by 1911. Three (1860/2/4) were reconverted to oil between 6/1916 and 2/1917, 1865/72/93 in 1/1921, and 1860/1/6/8/70/1/3/5/6/8/80/3/4/5/7/7/8/9/92/5/7 in May and June 1921 until the end of the 1921 coal miner's strike. In the 1926 strike 8868/73/5/6 (D14) and 8860-4/6/9-72/86/9/91 (D15) were reconverted 6-8/1926 until 1-7/1927. E suffixes to GE nos 9/1923-2/1924.

The following were built with 6ft 3in wide cabs and had 2790 gallon ('water cart') tenders holding 720 gallons of oil and 30 cwt of coal (used during lighting up). Works no 1027 (order no S46), 1048-57 (order no L47).

Below, R = Royal Train engine - white plus red lining; p/v = piston valves; s/v = slide valves; Sat = saturated; S'heat = superheated.

No	Date	Rebuilt	Vacuum ejector	LNE no 1924	Renumbered no	date	BR no	App-lied	With-drawn
1900	3/1901	3/1925 D15 S'heat							
Named *Claud*		1/1929 D15/2	6/27		7770	12/42			
Hamilton		2/1933 D16/3 8in p/v		8900	2500	4/46			5/1947*
1890	4/1900	2/1916 D56 S'heat							
		4/1929 D15/2	1906	8890	2501	12/46	62501	8/49	6/1951
1891	4/1900	3/1916 D56 S'heat							
		6/1932 D15/2	1906	8891	2502	10/46	62502	3/50	2/1952
1892	4/1900	10/1927 D15 S'heat							
		5/1932 D15/2	1906	8892	2503	11/46	62503	12/48	2/1951
1893	5/1900	12/1926 D15 S'heat							
		5/1931 D15/2	1906	8893	2504	9/46	(62504)		6/1948
1894	5/1900	1/1918 D56 S'heat			7764	1/43			
		4/1932 D15/2	1906	8894**	2505	3/46	62505	10/49	11/1951
1895	6/1900	11/1926 D15 S'heat							
		2/1930 D15/2	1906	8895	2506	9/46	62506	2/50	4/1952
1896	6/1900	8/1915 D56 S'heat							
		6/1933 D15/2	1906***	8896	2507	11/46	62507	10/49	4/1952
1897	6/1900	9/1919 D56 S'heat							
		5/1929 D15/2	1906	8897	2508	11/46	62508	11/48	10/1950
1898	7/1900	6/1915 D56 S'heat							
		4/1933 D15/2	1906***	8898	2509	11/46	62509	4/48	9/1952
1899	7/1900	2/1922 D56 Sat							
		6/1925 D15 S'heat							
		7/1929 D15/2 Sat							
		4/1933 D15 S'heat							
		3/1935 D15/2	1906						
		9/1943 D16/3 s/v		8899	2510	11/46	62510	2/49	10/1957

*   The nameplate *Claud Hamilton* was transferred to D16/3 no 2546 (ex-GE class D56 no 1855) in 8/1947.

**   No 8894 was involved in the accident at Saxham on 26/12/1927.

*** Nos 1896 and 1898 had the vacuum ejector removed by 1923. It was reinstated in 12/1924 and 4/1933 respectively. No 8896 was in an accident at Wormley on 27/11/1934.

The following had the cabs widened to 7ft 2in with a higher arched roof and the front sandbox below the running plate to beneath the front footsteps being brought further back to conceal it. The pistons were provided with tail rods and of the first batch, 1890/3/8 and 1900 were so fitted, but these were all removed by the LNER. Within three months of no 1880 being completed, it was decided to provide them with larger 3300 gallon tenders and the original 2790 gallon tenders were passed to class T26 2-4-0s as already noted. 1880-3/5 were given larger tenders in 7/1901, 1889 in 1/1902, 1886/8 in 2/1902, 1884/7 in 3/1902. Five of the first batch also acquired larger tenders, no 1900 in 5/1912, 8890 in 9/1925, 8894 in 4/1932, 1897 in 1919 and 8898 in 7/1926. Oil burning facilities continued to be supplied until 1904 after which it was discontinued. Works nos 1128-37 (order M51).
Abbreviations as for previous batch.

No	Date	Rebuilt	Vacuum ejector	LNE no 1924	Renumbered no	date	BR no	Applied	Withdrawn
1880	4/1901	2/1918 D56 S'heat							
		3/1928 D15/2	8/28						
		9/1942 D16/3 s/v		8880	2511	11/46	62511	5/48	12/1959
1881	5/1901	5/1930 D15/2	1/29	8881	2512	10/46	62512	5/48	8/1950
1882	5/1901	12/1919 D56 S'heat							
		5/1933 D15/2	11/28						
		9/1942 D16/3 s/v		8882	2513	6/46	62513	10/49	11/1958
1883	5/1901	1/1916 D56 S'heat							
		8/1928 D15/2	8/28						
		5/1943 D16/3 s/v		8883	2514	6/46	62514	1/49	3/1957
1884	5/1901	3/1922 D56 Sat							
		12/1928 D15/2	12/28						
		1/1943 D16/3 s/v		8884	2515	8/46	62515	9/48	4/1958
R1885	5/1901	5/1919 D56 S'heat							
		12/1928 D15/2	12/28						
		7/1937 D16/3 s/v		8885	2516	6/46	62516	2/49	8/1957
1886	6/1901	10/1925 D15 Sat							
		3/1929 D15/2	7/27						
		4/1940 D16/3 s/v		8886	2517	8/46	62517	1/49	9/1959
1887	6/1901	2/1918 D56 S'heat							
		4/1933 D15/2	5/29						
		8/1943 D16/3 s/v		8887	2518	6/46	62518	12/48	10/1958
1888	6/1901	11/1918 D56 S'heat							
		2/1929 D15/2	6/24						
		6/1939 D16/3 s/v		8888	2519	6/46	62519	3/49	1/1957
1889	6/1901	3/1917 D56 S'heat							
		2/1930 D15/2	5/27	8889	2520	9/46	62520	12/48	8/1951

The following differed in having circular spectacles in the cab replaced by larger shaped ones that followed the shape of the cab roof and the firebox, and an improved design of reversing gear was fitted. Earlier batches were also later fitted with this. Works nos 1170-9 (order no F33), 1201-10 (order no L55).
Abbreviations as above.

No	Date	Rebuilt	Vacuum ejector	LNE no 1924	Renumbered no	date	BR no	Applied	Withdrawn
R1870	3/1902	4/1924 D15 S'heat							
		6/1928 D15/2	4/24		7740	12/42			
		5/1935 D16/3 s/v		8870	2521	3/46	62521	8/49	2/1958
R1871	3/1902	4/1924 D15 S'heat							
		7/1929 D15/2	4/24						
		5/1938 D16/3 s/ v		8871	2522	6/46	62522	4/49	8/1958

```
1872  3/1902   3/1924 D15 S'heat
               4/1928 D15/2          3/24
               5/1940 D16/3 s/v             8872   2523   6/46  62523   5/48   8/1956
1873  3/1902    /1930 D15 Sat
               3/1933 D15/2          3/29
               6/1939 D16/3 s/v        .    8873   2524   6/46  62524  12/50   3/1960
1874  3/1902   5/1919 D56 S'heat
              12/1932 D15/2          7/28
               6/1938 D16/3 s/v             8874   2525   3/46  62525   5/49   9/1955
1875  4/1902   3/1931 D15/2          6/24
               8/1937 D16/2 s/v             8875   2526   8/46  62526   7/48   5/1957
1876  4/1902   6/1929 D15/2          8/27
               3/1935 D16/2 s/v             8876   2527   6/46  62527   8/48   7/1952
1877  4/1902   2/1928 D15/2         10/29   8877   2528   6/46  62528  10/48   6/1951
1878  5/1902   3/1929 D15 Sat
               7/1931 D15/2          6/15
               5/1935 D16/3 s/v             8878   2529   6/46  62529   4/50  11/1959
1879  5/1902  12/1927 D15/2          6/15
               4/1938 D16/3 s/v             8879   2530   6/46  62530  10/48   9/1958
1860  5/1903   5/1919 D56 S'heat
               6/1928 D15/2          6/24
               6/1934 D16/3 s/v             8860   2531   6/46  62531   8/48   3/1955
1861  5/1903  11/1921 D56 Sat
              11/1929 D15/2          6/27
               4/1936 D16/3 9½in p/v
                                            8861   2532   9/46  62532   7/48  11/1956
1862  5/1903  12/1923 D15 S'heat
               5/1930 D15/2          5/27
               6/1940 D16/3 s/v             8862   2533  11/46  62533   6/49   9/1957
1863  6/1903  11/1921 D56 Sat
               6/1926 D15 S'heat
               4/1933 D15/2          4/29
               4/1935 D16/3 s/v             8863   2534  12/46  62534  12/48  11/1958
1864  6/1903   5/1923 D15 S'heat
               3/1932 D15/2          5/27
              10/1936 D16/3 9½in p/v
                                            8864   2535  10/46  62535   8/48  11/1957
1865  9/1903   4/1930 D15/2         10/28
               7/1936 D16/3 9½in p/v
                                            8865   2536  11/46  62536   3/48   7/1955
1866  9/1903   6/1923 D15 S'heat
               6/1928 D15/2          6/28        allotted
               3/1933 D16/3 8in p/v   8866   2537                              9/1945
1867 10/1903   5/1923 D15 S'heat
              12/1933 D15/2          2/27   8867   2538   6/46  62538   8/48   4/1952
1868 10/1903   9/1929 D15/2          5/27
               7/1940 D16/3 s/v             8868   2539   6/46  62539   4/49  10/1957
1869 11/1903   1/1922 D56 Sat
               2/1924 D15 S'heat
               7/1928 D15/2          7/28
               6/1934 D16/3 s/v             8869   2540   6/46  62540  11/48   8/1959
```

4-4-0 Built by GER at Stratford. Works nos below.
DW 7ft 0in; LW 3ft 9in; WB 6ft 6in + 8ft 0in + 9ft 0in; Cyls 19 x 26;
Blr 4ft 9in + 11ft 9in; Belpaire THS 1706.58 sq ft (1903), 1678.84 sq ft (1907);
WP 180 lbs/sq in; Wt 52 tons 4 cwt.

Class D56 In 1903, Holden, having built the foregoing S46 class with round-top boilers, changed the design and introduced boilers with Belpaire fireboxes. Apart from the boiler and of course, the weight, all the other dimensions remained the same and the boiler still had the same overall dimensions. The same 7ft 2in cabs were retained and the S46 were gradually rebuilt as above with Belpaire firebox boilers so both classes have been described as *Clauds* after no 1900 *Claud Hamilton*. Superheaters were fitted to four locomotives of the final batch in 1911 (see below) two with Schmidt superheaters THS 1275.1 sq ft + 226 sq ft superheater and two with Swindon pattern THS 1362.8 sq ft + 188 sq ft superheater. From 1914, a Robinson superheater with the same heating as the Schmidt was fitted to existing locos. From 1921, short return loops in the superheater elements instead of long ones reduced the heating surface of this to 154.8 sq ft. From 1940, THS was 1263.9 sq ft + 154.8 sq ft superheater. The class became LNE D15 and when the LNER began fitting them with extended smokeboxes in 1926 these were classed as D15/2, the unrebuilt ones being D15/1. When this programme was complete in 1933 the subdivision was discontinued. In the closing months of the GE's separate existence, Hill designed a further improvement using a Belpaire firebox boiler 5ft $1\frac{1}{8}$in diameter and a larger superheater which became known as *Super Clauds* (class H88, LNE class D16) (*qv*). These were not actually completed until 1923. At the same time, existing class D15s were fitted with this boiler (with some variations in the framing) as class D16. The same subdivision was used, ie D16/1 and D16/2, to distinguish between those with short and long smokeboxes, as with the D15s from 1926 until 1934 when all had the extended smokebox. Finally, all but four were rebuilt by Gresley with 5ft $1\frac{1}{8}$in diameter round-top boiler with higher pitch and Robinson superheater (see under class S46 for details) some with slide valves and some 8in and 9½in piston valves. The following summary of the LNER classifications may be found helpful in making reference.

    D15/1 4ft 9in boilers Belpaire firebox short smokebox saturated and superheated (12/1927 to 1933)

    D15/2 As D15/1 but with extended smokeboxes (12/1927 to 1933)

    D16/1 5ft $1\frac{1}{8}$in boilers Belpaire firebox short smokebox superheated (12/1927)

    D16/2 As D16/1 but with extended smokeboxes (12/1927)

    D16/3 5ft $1\frac{1}{8}$in round top boilers, superheated with slide and piston valves (1933)

GN chimneys fitted to 8791/3/7-9/803/6-8/11/5/20/3-5/30/5/6/44/50/5/7/8 2/1930-7/1936. E suffix added to GE nos 9/1923-2/1924.

The following were built with oil burning facilities and 3300 gallon tenders. Works nos 1223-32 (order no D56).

Below S'heat = superheated; s/v = slide valves; p/v = piston valves'; R = Royal train engine - white plus red lining.

No	Date	Rebuilt	Vacuum ejector	LNE no 1924	Renumbered no	date	BR no	Applied	Withdrawn
1850	12/1903	12/1921 S'heat							
		2/1932 D15/2	11/28						
		7/1939 D16/3 s/v		8850	2541	6/46	62541	4/49	10/1955
1851	12/1903	11/1918 S'heat							
		6/1927 D16/2	6/27						
		6/1938 D16/3 s/v*		8851	2542	5/46	62542	10/48	10/1056
1852	12/1903	7/1922 S'heat							
		2/1928 D16/2	6/27						
		2/1949 D16/3 s/v*		8852	2543	9/46	62543	5/48	10/1958
1853	12/1903	5/1926 D16/1							
		11/1929 D16/2	10/28						
		3/1947 D16/3 s/v*		8853	2544	11/46	62544	7/48	11/1959
1854	1/1904	6/1916 S'heat	5/29						
		3/1933 D16/3 s/v		8854	2545	8/46	62545	2/49	9/1958
1855	2/1904	11/1914 S'heat**							
		9/1928 D15/2	9/28						
		1/1934 D16/3 s/v		8855	2546	9/46	62546	10/48	6/1957
1856	3/1904	9/1923 S'heat							
		5/1927 D16/2	8/28	8856	2547	6/46	62547	6/48	2/1951

```
1857   3/1904  11/1916 S'heat
               10/1933 D15/2        6/27              7727 12/42
               7/1939 D16/3 s/v           8857   2548  5/46  62548  6/48 10/1957
R1858  3/1904  5/1927 S'heat
               5/1930 D15/2         6/04              7728  1/43
               3/1938 D16/3 s/v           8858   2549  3/46  62549  2/49 12/1955
R1859  4/1904  5/1931 D15/2         6/04
               5/1934 D16/3 s/v           8859   2550  9/46         11/1946
```

* Decorative valances over driving wheels retained.
** Also top feed until 3/1920.

The following were built without oil burning facilities, which were now discontinued,
as a result of which tender water capacity was increased to 3450 gallons.
Works nos 1323-32 (order no G61), 1373-82 (order no A64), 1418-27 (order no B66),
1438-47 (order no D67), 1449-58 (order no P67), 1469-78 (order no E69).
Abbreviations as above batch.

```
                                     Vacuum   LNE no  Renumbered         App-  With-
No    Date     Rebuilt               ejector  1924    no    date  BR no  lied  drawn
1840  11/1906  8/1923 S'heat
               2/1929 D15/2          2/29
               3/1935 D16/3 s/v               8840    2551  6/46  62551  4/49  7/1956
1841  11/1906  1/1929 D16/2          4/29
               2/1949 D16/3 s/v*             8841    2552  8/46  62552  2/49 10/1955
1842  11/1906  9/1930 D16/2          12/28                 7712 12/42
               9/1949 D16/3 s/v*             8842    2553  3/46  62553  5/48  1/1957

1843  11/1906  7/1927 D16/2          10/28
               11/1938 D16/3 s/v*            8843    2554 10/46  62554  6/49 11/1955
1844  11/1906  10/1914 S'heat
               11/1928 D15/2         10/26
               3/1939 D16/3 s/v              8844    2555 10/46  62555  5/48  3/1958
1845  11/1906  10/1914 S'heat**
               5/1929 D16/2          5/29
               4/1946 D16/3 s/v*             8845    2556  9/46  62556  5/48  1/1957
1846  12/1906  12/1924 D16/1
               3/1934 D16/2          2/29
               4/1944 D16/3 s/v*             8846    2557 12/46  62557  6/49 10/1955
1847  12/1906  5/1921 S'heat
               7/1926 D16/1
               10/1933 D16/2         6/07
               9/1948 D16/3 s/v*             8847    2558 11/46  62558  9/48  5/1957
R1848 1/1907   9/1918 S'heat
               4/1929 D15/2  as new
               1/1933 D16/3 s/v              8848    2559  6/46  62559  3/49 12/1955
R1849 1/1907   5/1919 S'heat
               5/1928 D15/2  as new
               4/1933 D16/3  8in p/v         8849    2560 12/46 (62560)       9/1948
1830  3/1908   1/1925 S'heat
               5/1929 D15/2          1/25
               3/1940 D16/3 s/v              8830    2561 10/46  62561  2/49  2/1958
1831  3/1908   4/1916 S'heat
               4/1928 D16/2          8/28
               2/1946 D16/3 s/v*             8831    2562  8/46  62562  5/48 10/1957
1832  3/1908   7/1919 S'heat
               11/1930 D15/2         1/29
               7/1936 D16/3 9½in p/v         8832    2563 10/46 (62563)       8/1948
1833  4/1908   1/1930 D16/2          3/26
               1/1948 D16/3 s/v*             8833    2564 10/46  62564  2/50  3/1958
1834  4/1908   3/1929 D16/2          6/27
               6/1945 D16/3 s/v*             8834    2565  9/46  62565  8/49  1/1957
```

```
1835   5/1908   3/1925 S'heat
                5/1929 D15/2          7/14
                1/1939 D16/3 s/v            8835    2566 10/46   62566   10/48 12/1958
1836   5/1908   6/1928 S'heat
                2/1930 D15/2          5/27
               10/1937 D16/3 s/v
               (GN chimney 2/30 -
               10/35 & from 6/36)           8836    2567 10/46   62567    4/49 12/1956
1837   6/1908   7/1931 D15/2         10/29           7707 11/42
                5/1933 D16/3 8in p/v        8837    2568  4/46   62568    4/48  4/1958
1838   7/1908  11/1929 D16/2  as new                7708 11/42
                5/1948 D16/3 s/v*           8838    2569  3/46   62569    5/48 11/1956
1839   7/1908   2/1922 S'heat
                4/1928 D16/2  as new
                9/1949 D16/3 s/v*           8839    2570 11/46   62570    9/49 11/1959
1820   6/1909   5/1932 D15/2          3/30
                5/1939 D16/3 s/v            8820    2571 10/46   62571    9/48  1/1959
1821   6/1909   5/1920 S'heat         2/24
                5/1933 D16/3 s/v            8821    2572 11/46   62572    8/49  7/1958
1822   9/1909   6/1930 D16/2          5/29           7692 12/42
                3/1947 D16/3 s/v*           8822    2573  4/46   62573    4/49 10/1955
1823  11/1909  12/1921 S/heat**
               12/1929 D15/2          1/25
                4/1938 D16/3 s/v            8823    2574 11/46   62574    4/48 12/1955
1824  11/1909   4/1918 S'heat
                1/1930 D15/2          6/24
                2/1940 D16/3 s/v            8824    2575 11/46   62575   12/48  5/1957
1825  11/1909   5/1922 S'heat
                6/1928 D15/2          5/27           7695 12/42
                3/1937 D16/3 9½in p/v       8825    2576  4/46   62576    6/48  9/1957
1826  12/1909   7/1922 S'heat**
                4/1929 D16/2**        1/27
                5/1949 D16/3 s/v*           8826    2577 11/46   62577    5/49 10/1956
1827  12/1909   7/1927 D16/2          7/27
                9/1944 D16/3 s/v*           8827    2578 11/46   62578    4/48 10/1957
R1828 12/1909   6/1928 D15/2  as new
                3/1934 D16/3 s/v            8828    2579 11/46   62579    6/48  3/1955
R1829 12/1909   2/1930 D16/2  as new
                4/1948 D16/3 s/v*           8829    2580 12/46   62580    4/48  6/1958
1810   3/1910   4/1922 S'heat**
                3/1931 D15/2         11/26
                7/1936 D16/3 9½in p/v       8810    2581  9/46   62581    8/48  3/1953
1811   3/1910   4/1922 S'heat
                3/1932 D15/2          3/29
               12/1939 D16/3 s/v            8811    2582 10/46   62582    1/50  1/1959
1812   3/1910   3/1922 S'heat
                4/1934 D15/2          1/25
                6/1936 D16/3 9½in p/v       8812    2583  9/46  (62583)        11/1948
1813   4/1910   7/1914 S'heat
                4/1926 D16/2          8/28
                9/1947 D16/3 s/v*           8813    2584  9/46   62584    4/50 12/1957
1814   4/1910  11/1921 S'heat
               12/1931 D15/2          6/27
                2/1935 D16/3 s/v            8814    2585  9/46   62585    5/49  4/1955
1815   5/1910  11/1922 S'heat
                5/1931 D15/2          4/29
                8/1939 D16/3 s/v            8815    2586  9/46   62586    8/50  3/1958
```

```
1816   6/1910   5/1920 S'heat
                12/1929 D15/2              5/27
                 3/1934 D16/3 8in p/v        8816    2587  9/46   62587  5/48  12/1956
1817   6/1910   5/1924 S'heat
                 5/1930 D15/2              6/27
                 7/1934 D16/3 8in p/v        8817    2588  9/46   62588  8/48  10/1958
1818   6/1910   6/1923 D16/1
                11/1933 D16/2  as new
                 3/1947 D16/3 s/v*           8818    2589  9/46   62589  2/49   5/1959
1819   6/1910   6/1919 S'heat
                 1/1926 D15/2  as new
                 1/1928 D16/2                8819    2590  9/46   62590  9/49   1/1952
1800   7/1910   7/1927 D16/2              7/28  8800  2591  9/46   62591  4/49   4/1950
1801   7/1910   6/1919 S'heat
                 4/1929 D16/2              4/29
                 6/1945 D16/3 s/v*           8801    2592  9/46   62592 11/49   4/1958
1802   8/1910   5/1928 D15/2              3/26
                 4/1933 D16/3 s/v           8802    2593  9/46   62593  1/50  10/1957
1803   8/1910   9/1927 D15/2              6/29
                 4/1937 D16/3 9½in p/v      8803    2594  4/46  (62594)        3/1949
1804   8/1910  12/1928 D15/2              6/27
                 3/1934 D16/3 8in p/v        8804    2595 11/46               11/1946
1805   9/1910   3/1923 D16/1
                11/1931 D16/2              6/27
                 3/1947 D16/3 s/v*           8805    2596 11/46   62596  4/49  10/1957
1806   9/1910   8/1929 D15/2              8/29
                 1/1940 D16/3 s/v           8806    2597 10/46   62597  1/50   1/1960
1807  10/1910   6/1914 S'heat
                12/1929 D15/2              1/29
                 1/1942 D16/3 s/v           8807    2598  6/46   62598  6/49   5/1952
1808  10/1910   7/1929 D15/2             11/24
                 6/1937 D16/3 9½in p/v      8808    2599  8/46   62599 11/49   9/1958
1809  11/1910   7/1929 S'heat             7/29
                 6/1933 D16/3 8in p/v        8809    2600  9/46  (62600)        6/1948
1790   2/1911   8/1927 D15/2
                 4/1929 D16/2              3/24
                 9/1944 D16/3 s/v*           8790    2601 10/46   62601  4/50   1/1957
1791   3/1911   4/1923 S'heat
                 5/1928 D15/2              6/27
                 2/1937 D16/3 9½in p/v      8791    2602 10/46  (62602)        9/1948
1792   3/1911   7/1914 S'heat             9/28
                 3/1928 D16/2                8792    2603 11/46   62603  5/48   9/1951
R1793  4/1911***
                 5/1929 D15/2**            3/27
                 7/1937 D16/3 s/v           8793    2604 11/46   62604  6/48   2/1960
R1794  5/1911***
                 2/1929 D16/2**            2/25
                 3/1940 D16/3 s/v*           8794    2605 10/46   62605 10/48   6/1957
1795   7/1911   4/1931 D16/2              5/29   7665 12/42
                 3/1946 D16/3 s/v*           8795    8795  7/44
                                                     2606 11/46   62606  6/50   9/1959
1796   7/1911   4/1925 S'heat
                12/1928 D16/2              6/27
                12/1946 D16/3 s/v*           8796    2607 12/46   62607  1/49  11/1955
1797   7/1911   7/1914 S'heat
                 4/1928 D15/2              9/28
                 7/1937 D16/3 s/v           8797    2608 10/46   62608  8/49   1/1957
1798   8/1911***
                 4/1932 D15/2              6/27
                 4/1934 D16/3 8in p/v        8798    2609  9/46   62609  4/48   2/2957
```

1799 8/1911***

2/1934 D15/2		2/29					
2/1940 D16/3 s/v			8799	2610 11/46	62610 12/49	1/1959	

*   Decorative valance retained.
** The following also had top feed:
     1845 10/1914 until 1/1922
     1823 1/1914 until 6/1916
     1826 9/1913 (Churchward system) until 3/1922 (boiler ex-1823 from 8/1917)
           and 12/1926 until 4/1929 (boiler ex-8810)
     1810 4/1922 until 9/1926
     8793 5/1929 until 4/1931
     1794 10/1921 until 4/1927
*** Nos 1793/4 were built with Schmidt superheaters
       1798/9 were built with Swindon pattern superheaters

0-6-0 Built by GER at Stratford. Works nos below.
DW 4ft 10in (1886), 4ft 11in (1891); WB 7ft 7in + 8ft 6in; Cyls 17½ x 24;
Blr 4ft 4in x 10ft 0in; THS as below; WP 140 lbs/sq in (1886), 160 lbs/sq in (1896);
Wt 37 tons 2 cwt.
Class Y14 Continuation of Worsdell class introduced in 1883. LNE class J15.
The following were built with 3-ring butt-jointed boilers THS 1230.46 sq ft, with
square bottom (level) grates. Replacement boilers were - 1893: 2-ring butt-jointed
THS 1221.68 sq ft; 1899: 2-ring telescopic THS 1204.1 sq ft; 1907: 1169.3 sq ft.
Locomotives fitted with bevel bottom firebox (bvl btm firebox in list below) with a
sloping grate had THS 1147.1 sq ft (1137.69 from 1940); DW later 4ft 11in; 2755 gallon
tenders. As built, only tender brakes were provided until 1896-1901 when steam brakes
were added.
Works nos 277-86 (order no M18), 287-96 (order no X18), 348-57 (order no D20)

No	Date	bvl btm firebox	LNE no 1923	LNE no 1924	Renumbered no	date	Allotted BR no	Withdrawn
800	4/1886							
Renumbered								
609	1/1892	8/32	609E	7609				10/1935
801	4/1886		801E	7801				1/1935
802	5/1886		802E	7802				1/1929
803	5/1886		803E	7803				12/1935
804	5/1886							5/1922
805	7/1886		805E	7805				4/1928
806	7/1886	8/32	806E	7806				10/1939
807	7/1886		807E	7807				3/1929
808	8/1886							5/1922
809	8/1886	8/33	809E	7809				8/1936
810	11/1886*		810E	7810				1/1929
811	12/1886							3/1922
812	12/1886		812E	7812				2/1929
813	12/1886	9/45	813E	7813	5850	8/46	(65350)	2/1951
814	12/1886	8/32	814E	7814				8/1938
815	1/1887		815E	7815				6/1936
816	1/1887		816E	7816				1/1930
817	2/1887*		817E	7817				3/1936
818	2/1887*	8/32	818E	7818				11/1936
819	2/1887	8/32	819E	7819				4/1938
820	9/1887		820E	7820				7/1928
821	9/1887		821E	7821	5851	5/46	(65351)	5/1949
822	9/1887							10/1922
823	9/1887		823E	7823				5/1937
824	9/1887		824E	7824				1/1936

825	9/1887		825E	7825	5352	11/46	(65352)		5/1948
826	9/1887*		826E	7826					9/1929
827	9/1887		827E	7827					2/1929
828	9/1887	10/42	828E	7828	5353	10/46	(65353)		12/1949
829	9/1887		829E	7829					8/1936

* To ROD 1917-19

The following originally had 2612 gallon tenders. Works nos 368-77 (order no U20).

No	Date	bvl btm firebox	LNE no 1923	LNE no 1924	Renumbered no	date	BR no	Applied	Withdrawn
527	10/1887		527E	7527	5354	6/46	(65354)		2/1951
528*	10/1887		528E	7528					2/1930
529	11/1887		529E	7529					12/1931
530	11/1887	6/32	530E	7530	5355	12/46	(65355)		4/1951
531	11/1887**		531E	7531					8/1928
532	1/1888**	10/39	532E	7532	5356	6/46	65356	9/50	4/1957
533*	1/1888**		533E	7533					5/1928
534	1/1888**		534E	7534					5/1929
535	1/1888		535E	7535					3/1936
536	1/1888								5/1923

* Nos 528 and 533 were fitted for working on oil fuel during 1921 coal strike
** To ROD 1917-19. No 532 had vacuum ejector fitted in 1933.

The following originally had 2755 gallon tenders.
Works nos 399-408 (order no R21, 449-58 (order no T22).

No	Date	bvl btm firebox	LNE no 1923	LNE no 1924	Renumbered no	date	BR no	Applied	Withdrawn
537	10/1888								8/1923
538	10/1888		538E	7538					12/1938
539	10/1888*		539E	7539					6/1936
540	10/1888		540E	7540	5357	9/46	(65357)		9/1949
541	10/1888		541E	7541					9/1936
830	10/1888		830E	7830	5358	11/46			8/1947
831	10/1888		831E	7831					11/1936
832	10/1888								8/1923
833	10/1888	6/37	833E	7833	5359	10/46	65359	1/50	12/1955
834	10/1888	5/32	834E	7834	5360	10/46			11/1947
835	7/1889		835E	7835					9/1936
836	7/1889	10/44	836E	7836	5361	1/47	65361	1/50	9/1962
837	7/1889	9/42	837E	7837	5362	10/46	(65362)		7/1951
838	7/1889		838E	7838					7/1934
839	7/1889	8/32	839E	7839					7/1936
840	7/1889	5/44	840E	7840	5363	9/46	(65363)		8/1949
841	7/1889*		841E	7841					6/1936
842	7/1889		842E	7842					11/1934
843	7/1889	8/32**	843E	7843	5364	11/46	(65364)		6/1949
844	7/1889		844E	7844					8/1936

* To ROD 1917-19
** No 7843 reverted to square bottom (level) firebox in 1/1944

The following had 2640 gallon tenders. Works nos 459-68 (order no R23), 469-78 (order
no T23), 479-88 (order no X23), 519-28 (order no U25), 529-38 (order no Y25).

No	Date	bvl btm firebox	LNE no 1923	LNE no 1924	Renumbered no	date	BR no	Applied	Withdrawn
845	10/1889		845E	7845					12/1938
846	10/1889	3/47	846E	7846	5365	10/46	(65365)		7/1950
847	10/1889*		847E	7847	5366	9/46	(65366)		6/1952
848	10/1889*		848E	7848	5367	10/46	(65367)		1/1950

849**	10/1889*		849E	7849	5368	10/46	(65368)		5/1948
850	10/1889		850E	7850	5369	10/46	(65369)		2/1951
851	10/1889		851E	7851					10/1936
852	10/1889	9/45	852E	7852	5370	1/47	65370	9/48	4/1956
853	10/1889	6/35	853E	7853	5371	11/46	(65371)		12/1949
854	10/1889	11/46	854E	7854	5372	11/46	65372	5/49	9/1949
855**	10/1889	4/41	855E	7855	5373	11/46	(65373)		10/1950
856	10/1889*		856E	7856					10/1936
857	11/1889*	3/43	857E	7857	5374	1/47	(65374)		11/1950
858**	11/1889								3/1923
859	11/1889		859E	7859					6/1939
860	11/1889	8/38	860E	7860	5375	6/46	(65375)		11/1949
861	11/1889		861E	7861					9/1936
862**	11/1889		862E	7862					11/1938
863	11/1889		863E	7863					10/1936
864	11/1889		864E	7864					4/1939
865	11/1889	11/41	865E	7865	5376	6/46	(65376)		6/1949
866	12/1889		866E	7866	5377	11/46	(65377)		2/1951
867	12/1889		867E	7867					5/1937
868	12/1889		868E	7868					10/1934
869	12/1889*	9/45	869E	7869	5378	1/47	65378	8/48	4/1951
870	12/1889		870E	7870					10/1934
871	12/1889	2/46	871E	7871	5379	11/46	(65379)		9/1949
872	12/1889*	6/32	872E	7872	5380	1/47			1/1948
873	12/1889		873E	7873					12/1934
874	12/1889	1/40	874E	7874	5381	12/46	(65381)		11/1948
875	8/1890	5/32	875E	7875	5382	6/46	(65382)		3/1952
876	8/1890*	7/45	876E	7876	5383	8/46			2/1948
877***	8/1890	5/36	877E	7877	5384	1/47	65384	9/48	4/1955
878	8/1890		878E	7878	5385	11/46	(65385)		1/1949
879	8/1890		879E	7879					4/1929
880	9/1890	5/37	880E	7880	5386	12/46	(65386)		1/1950
881**	9/1890	4/35	881E	7881	5387	11/46	(65387)		8/1949
882	9/1890								7/1922
883	9/1890	12/39	883E	7883	5388	6/46	65388	2/50	5/1959
884	9/1890								7/1922
885**	9/1890								5/1922
886**	10/1890	5/35	886E	7886	5389	11/46	65389	2/49	4/1960
887	10/1890*	11/46	887E	7887**	5390	11/46	65390	2/49	12/1958
888**	10/1890	4/43	888E	7888**	5391	10/46	65391	3/50	12/1958
889	10/1890		889E	7889					10/1935
890	10/1890		890E	7890					2/1935
891	11/1890		891E	7891					1/1935
892	11/1890*		892E	7892	5392	4/46	(65392)		5/1949
893	11/1890*		893E	7893	5393	6/46	(65393)		8/1949
894	11/1890*		894E	7894	5394	1/47	(65394)		5/1948

*   To ROD 1917-19
**   Nos 849/55/8/62/81/5/6/8 were fitted for oil fuel during the 1921 coal strike.
      No 7887 was fitted with vacuum brake ejector in 5/1933.
      No 7888 was fitted with vacuum brake ejector in 6/1932 and steam heating
      apparatus in 5/1933 for working passenger trains on the Colne Valley line.
      In 8/1934 a side window cab (single window) was fitted.
*** No 877 was in an accident at Temple Mills on 19/8/1901 with 934.

The following had a modified frame and valve gear and were built with bevel bottom
(sloping) grates. The 3-ring butt-jointed boiler had a THS of 1208.3 sq ft. DW was
increased to 4ft 11in. Replacement boilers were of the 2-ring telescopic type and
with the dome on the front ring. THS 1199.5 sq ft (1900), 1164.7 sq ft (1908), 1147.1
sq ft (some only 1914), 1137.69 sq ft (1940).

Works nos 599-608 (order no L28), 609-18 (order no N28), 619-28 (order no P28).

No	Date	LNE no 1923	LNE no 1924	Renumbered no	date	BR no	Applied	Withdrawn
895	9/1891	895E	7895	5395	1/47	(65395)		5/1949
896	9/1891	896E	7896					3/1939
897	9/1891	897E	7897	5396	12/46	(65396)		3/1951
898	9/1891	898E	7898	5397	11/46	(65397)		9/1949
899	9/1891	899E	7899					1/1938
900	9/1891	900E	7900					12/1934
901	10/1891	901E	7901	5398	12/46	65398	4/48	2/1952
902	10/1891	902E	7902	5399	1/47			3/1948
903	10/1891	903E	7903					2/1938
904	10/1891*	904E	7904	5400	11/46			2/1948
905	10/1891	905E	7905					3/1939
906	10/1891	906E	7906	5401	8/46	(65401)		9/1951
907	10/1891	907E	7907	5402	7/46	(65402)		10/1950
908	10/1891	908E	7908	5403	11/46			8/1947
909	11/1891	909E	7909					1/1935
910	11/1891	910E	7910	5404	11/46	65404	10/48	10/1956
911	11/1891*	911E	7911**	5405	12/46	65405	2/49	8/1958
912	11/1891	912E	7912					10/1938
913	11/1891	913E	7913	5406	12/46	(65406)		4/1951
914	11/1891	914E	7914	5407	12/46	65407	5/48	4/1951
915	11/1891	915E	7915	5408	1/47	65408	12/48	12/1951
916	11/1891*	916E	7916					4/1937
917	11/1891	917E	7917					3/1939
918	11/1891*	918E	7918	5409	8/46	(65409)		11/1949
919	12/1891	919E	7919					6/1936
920	12/1891*	920E	7920	5410	5/46			2/1948
921	12/1891*	921E	7921	5411	12/46	(65411)		4/1949
922	12/1891	922E	7922	5412	12/46	65412	8/48	10/1949
923	12/1981	923E						10/1934
924	12/1891	924E	7924	5413	8/46	(65413)		11/1950

*   To ROD 1917-19

** No 7911 was equipped with vacuum ejector in 4/1932 and steam heating
     apparatus in 5/1933 for working passenger trains on the Colne Valley line.
     In 1934 a side window cab (single window) was fitted.

The following were built with a 2-ring butt-jointed boiler THS 1217.08 sq ft.
Replacement boilers were of the 2-ring telescopic type THS as 895-924 above.   No 930
was built and in steam in 9 hours 47 minutes as a publicity exercise.
Works nos 629-38 (order no S28), 639-48 (order no X28).

No	Date	LNE no 1923	LNE no 1924	Renumbered no	date	BR no	Applied	Withdrawn
925	12/1891*	925E	7925	5414	12/46	(65414)		11/1949
926	12/1891*	926E	7926	5415	8/46	(65415)		5/1949
927	12/1891*	927E	7927	5416	11/46	(65416)		12/1949
928	12/1891*	928E	7928	5417	11/46	65417	7/48	8/1956
929	12/1891	929E	7929	5418	7/46			3/1948
930	12/1891	930E	7930					1/1935
931	1/1892	931E	7931	5419	12/46	(65419)		2/1950
932	1/1892	932E	7932	5420	8/46	65420	9/48	8/1962
933	1/1892	933E	7933					3/1936
934**	1/1892	934E	7934	5421	8/46			3/1948
936	8/1892	936E	7936					4/1937
937	8/1892	937E	7937	5422	12/46	65422	8/48	7/1955
938	8/1892	938E	7938					10/1934
939	8/1892	939E	7939					2/1936
940	8/1892*	940E	7940	5423	12/46	(65423)		11/1950

941	8/1892	941E	7941***	5424	6/46	65424	3/49	12/1959
942	9/1892	942E	7942	5425	1/47	65425	3/49	10/1956
943	9/1892	943E	7943	5426	8/46	65426	7/48	5/1951
944	9/1892	944E	7944					2/1935
945	11/1892	945E	7945	5427	1/47	(65427)		10/1950

* To ROD 1917-19.
** No 934 was in an accident at Temple Mills in 19/8/1901 with 877.
*** No 7941 was fitted with vacuum ejector and train heating apparatus in 5/1933 for working passenger trains on the Colne Valley line. In 7/1934 a side window cab (single window) was fitted.

The following were built with a 2-ring telescopic boiler THS 1199.5 sq ft (1164.7 sq ft from 1908). Later replacements as 895-924 above.
Works nos 1007-16 (order no I45), 997-1006 (order no S45).

No	Date	LNE no 1923	LNE no 1924	Renumbered no	date	BR no	Applied	Withdrawn
507	5/1899*	507E	7507					1/1935
508	5/1899*	508E	7508	5428	11/46	(65428)		8/1949
509	5/1899	509E	7509	5429	12/46	(65429)		11/1950
510	5/1899*	510E	7510	5430	11/46	65430	9/48	1/1956
511	5/1899	511E	7511	5431	11/46	65431	4/48	3/1951
512	5/1899	512E	7512**	5432	9/46	65432	11/48	3/1958
513	5/1899*							8/1920
514	5/1899	514E	7514	5433	11/46	65433	2/50	1/1958
515	6/1899	515E	7515	5434	11/46	65434	1/50	11/1959
516	6/1899	516E	7516	5435	9/46	65435	8/48	10/1956
517	6/1899*	517E	7517	5436	11/46	(65436)		12/1949
518	6/1899*	518E	7518					4/1937
519	6/1899	519E	7519					12/1934
520	6/1899	520E	7520	5437	11/46	(65437)		9/1950
521	6/1899	521E	7521					6/1939
522	9/1899*	522E	7522					3/1936
523	9/1899	523E	7523**	5438	10/46	65438	7/49	6/1958
524	10/1899	524E	7524					3/1936
525	10/1899	525E	7525					10/1935
526	10/1899	526E	7526	5439	12/46	(65439)		11/1951

* To ROD 1917-19. No 513 was returned damaged and withdrawn 8/1920.
** Nos 7512 and 7523 were fitted with vacuum ejector, steam heating apparatus and side window cab (single window) for working passenger trains on the Colne Valley line in 1/1935 and 7/1934 respectively.

The following originally had 3066 gallon tenders. All were equipped with Westinghouse brake and 640-4 had vacuum ejectors as well. Works nos 1017-26 (order no X45).

No	Date	Vacuum ejector	LNE no 1923	LNE no 1924	Renumbered no	date	BR no	Applied	Withdrawn
640	7/1899	as new	640E	7640	5440	10/46	65440	8/49	10/1960
641	7/1899	as new	642E	7641	5441	12/46	65441	10/49	10/1958
642	7/1899	as new	642E	7642	5442	12/46	65442	4/49	5/1958
643	7/1899	as new	643E	7643*	5443	11/46	65443	8/49	12/1959
644	7/1899	as new	644E	7644	5444	9/46	65444	2/51	10/1958
645	8/1899	9/31	645E	7645	5445	12/46	65445	4/49	8/1962
646	8/1899	1/32	646E	7646	5446	11/46	65446	10/49	12/1960
647	8/1899	2/32	647E	7647	5447	8/46	65447	7/48	4/1959
648	9/1899	11/31	648E	7648	5448	10/46	65448	9/48	3/1960
649	9/1899	2/32	649E	7649	5449	9/46	65449	10/48	12/1959

* No 7643 was in an accident at Brentwood on 8/7/1926.

The following were originally provided with second-hand 2640 gallon tenders. All were
dual fitted with both Westinghouse brakes and vacuum ejectors.
Works nos 1303-12 (order no A60).

No	Date	LNE no 1923	LNE no 1924	Renumbered no	date	BR no	Applied	Withdrawn
552	5/1906	552E	7552	5450	1/47	65450	5/49	10/1961
553	5/1906	553E	7553	5451	10/46	65451	6/48	9/1959
554	6/1906	554E	7554	5452	1/47	65452	5/49	12/1959
555	6/1906	555E	7555	5453	6/46	65453	9/49	8/1962
556	6/1906	556E	7556	5454	6/46	65454	3/51	5/1959
557	6/1906	557E	7557	5455	6/46	65455	6/49	3/1960
558	6/1906	558E	7558	5456	10/46	65456	4/48	9/1958
559	6/1906	559E	7559	5457	10/46	65457	2/49	2/1962
560	7/1906	560E	7560	5458	9/46	65458	5/49	10/1961
561	7/1906	561E	7561	5459	9/46	65459	6/49	2/1960

The following, ordered by SD Holden, were built with 2-ring telescopic boilers THS
1164.7 sq ft (1137.69 sq ft from 1940), and were all dual-fitted with both
Westinghouse brakes and vacuum ejectors.
Works nos 1504-13 (order no B70), 1544-53 (order no G73).

No	Date	LNE no 1923	LNE no 1924	Renumbered no	date	BR no	Applied	Withdrawn
562	2/1912	562E	7562	5460	9/46	65460	8/49	9/1962
563	2/1912	563E	7563	5461	12/46	65461	10/48	4/1960
564	3/1912	564E	7564	5462	11/46	65462	2/49	9/1962*
565	3/1912	565E	7565	5463	12/46	65463	4/48	11/1959
566	3/1912	566E	7566	5464	1/47	65464**	6/50	9/1962
567	3/1912	567E	7567	5465	11/46	65465	8/49	9/1962
568	4/1912	568E	7568	5466	11/46	65466	10/48	7/1958
569	4/1912	569E	7569	5467	11/46	65467	4/48	2/1959
570	5/1912	570E	7570	5468	11/46	65468	3/49	9/1959
571	5/1912	571E	7571	5469	11/46	65469	12/50	8/1962
542	6/1913	542E	7542	5470	12/46	65470	8/50	12/1959
543	6/1913	543E	7543	5471	9/46	65471	11/49	6/1960
544	6/1913	544E	7544	5472	12/46	65472	11/48	12/1959
545	6/1913	545E	7545	5473	1/47	65473	6/48	3/1960
546	7/1913	546E	7546	5474	12/46	65474	5/49	2/1960
547	8/1913	547E	7547	5475	1/47	65475	9/50	9/1959
548	8/1913	548E	7548	5476	10/46	65476	12/48	9/1962
549	8/1913	549E	7549	5477	12/46	65477	5/48	2/1960
550	9/1913	550E	7550	5478	12/46	65478	9/49	10/1961
551	9/1913	551E	7551	5479	12/46	65479	12/48	8/1960

* No 564 is preserved on the North Norfolk Railway at Sheringham.
** No 65464 was used in 9/1953 for the film *O'Leary Night*, as a CIE (Irish
Railways) locomotive.

0-6-0 Compound built by GER at Stratford. Works no 347 (order no DP 203).
DW 4ft 10in; WB 7ft 7in + 8ft 6in; Cyls (2), HP 18 x 24, LP 26 x 24;
Blr 4ft 4in x 10ft 0in; THS 1217.08 sq ft; WP 140 lbs/sq in; WT 38½ tons.
Worsdell von Borris system of two cylinder compounding; 2-ring butt-jointed boiler
barrel with sloping firebox grate (bevel bottom); DW increased to 4ft 11in with
thicker tyres after 1891.

No	Date	
127	1887	
	7/1891	Renumbered **935**
	7/1895	Rebuilt simple expansion as class N31
	1901	Reboilered THS 1199.5 sq ft (telescopic barrel)
	9/1913	Withdrawn

0-6-0 Built by GER at Stratford. Works nos below.
DW 4ft 11in; WB 7ft 7in + 8ft 6in; Cyls 17½ x 24; Blr 4ft 4in x 10ft 0in; THS 1217.08
sq ft; WP 140 lbs/sq in; Wt 38 tons 19 cwt.
Class N31 Cyls as T19 2-4-0 with valve steam chests below the cylinders instead of
between. The boiler was interchangeable with T26 2-4-0, C32 2-4-2T, Y14 0-6-0 and the
later T19 2-4-0. It was originally of the 2-ring butt-jointed type of barrel, and the
firebox had a sloping grate (level bottom). Replacement boilers from 1900-08 were of
the telescopic type with THS 1199.5 sq ft (1164.7 from 1907). Working pressure was
increased to 160 lbs/sq in from 1896. Macallan variable blast pipes were provided.
2640 gallon tenders. Only tender hand brake was provided until 1897/8 when steam
brakes were fitted although some had Westinghouse brakes for working excursion
passenger trains and some were fitted as below. The amended arrangement of the steam
chests compared with the class Y14 which they resembled (although with higher-pitched
boiler) was not a success, as over extended steam passages resulted in sluggish
response to the regulator. By 1908 the demand for light-haul goods engines was
falling, and being catered for by the more successful class Y14, so the decision was
taken to withdraw them rather than rebuild. However the process was not completed
until after the LNER was formed. LNE class J14.

The following were built with WP 140 lbs/sq in increased to 160 lbs/sq in after 1896.
Works nos 722 (order no N31), 763-72 (order no H33), 773-82 (order no L33), 813-22
(order no E34). Locomotives to order no L33 were built with Westinghouse brakes.

No	Date	LNE no 1923	LNE no 1924	Withdrawn	
999	1892			1920	
979	1893			1913	
980	10/1893	980E		9/1923	
981	10/1893	981E	(7981)	4/1925	Built with steam brake
982	10/1983			1910	
983	10/1893	983E	(7983)	1/1925	
984	10/1893	984E	(7984)	2/1925	
985	10/1893	985E		12/1923	
986	10/1893			1922	Built with steam brake
987	10/1893	987E	(7987)	4/1925	
988	1893			1911	
989	1894			1910	Nos 989-98 to order no L33
990	1894			1910	built with Westinghouse brake
991	1894			1910	
992	1894			1922	
993	7/1894	993E		8/1923	
994	7/1894			1916	
995	7/1894			1922	
996	7/1894			1912	
997	7/1894			1911	
998	7/1894	998E	(07998)	3/1925	To duplicate list 0998E 9/1923
969	1894			1909	
970	9/1894	970E		12/1923	
971	9/1894			1908	
972	9/1894			1909	
973	9/1894	973E	(7973)	3/1925	
974	9/1894			1910	
975	9/1894			1909	
976	9/1894			8/1923	Built with steam brake Collision Marks Tey 29/9/1897
977	10/1894	977E	(7977)	1/1924	
978	10/1894	978E	(7978)	7/1924	

The following were built with Westinghouse brakes. Nos 959-63 were dual-fitted with
vacuum ejectors also. WP 160 lbs/sq in. Works nos 903-12 (order no N37).

		LNE no	LNE no	
No	Date	1923	1924	Withdrawn
959	11/1896	959E		12/1923
960	1896			1911
961	1896			1911
962	1896			1910
963	12/1896	963E	(7963)	7/1924
964	12/1896	964E	(7964)	2/1924
965	1896			1921
966	1896			1909
967	1896			1912
968	1896			1912

The following were built with steam brakes. Works nos 927-36 (order no H40), 937-46 (order no O41), 947-56 (order no G42).

		LNE no	LNE no		
No	Date	1923	1924	Withdrawn	
949	1897			1912	
950	1897			1909	
951	7/1897	951E	(7951)	2/1924	
952	1897			1912	
953	1897			1909	
954	1897			1909	
955	1897			1909	
956	1897			1910	
957	1897			1909	
958	1897			1911	
602	1897			1909	
603	1897			1910	
604	10/1897	604E	(7604)	3/1925	
605	1897			1909	
606	1897			1910	
607	1897			1913	
608	1897			1909	
946	1897			1915	
947	1897			1914	
948	1897			1922	
542	1898			1910	
543	1898			1920	To duplicate list 0543 1913
544	1898			1912	
545	1898			1914	To duplicate list 0545 1913
546	1898			1909	
547	1898			1911	
548	1898			1922	
549	1898			1909	
550	1898			1910	
551	1898			1911	

The following were built with 2-ring telescopic boiler THS 1199.5 sq ft (1164 sq ft from 1907) and steam brakes. Works nos 957-66 (order no K43).

No	Date	Withdrawn	
562	1898	1911	
563	1898	1910	
564	1898	1914	To duplicate list 0564 1912
565	1898	1909	
566	1898	1909	
567	1898	1911	
568	1898	1910	
569	1898	1910	

570	1898	1909
571	1898	1909

0-6-0 Built by GER at Stratford. Works nos below.
DW 4ft 11in; WB 8ft 10in + 8ft 10in; Cyls 19 x 26; Blr 4ft 9in x 11ft 9in; THS 1630.5
sq ft; WP 180 lbs/sq in; Wt 44 tons 11 cwt.
Class F48 More powerful goods engine for heavier loads with round-top firebox, double
side window cab, Macallan variable blast pipe (later Stones type fitted, removed by
LNER) and steam brakes. 3500 gallon tenders except as indicated below. Replacement
boilers 1908-13 were 1624.38 sq ft. LNE class J16. All rebuilt with Belpaire
fireboxes and superheating as class G58 (LNE class J17) below.

The following originally had second-hand Worsdell tenders 3066 gallon capacity.
Works nos 1058-67 (order no F48).

No	Date	Rebuilt G58/J17	LNE no 1923	LNE no 1924	Renumbered no	date	BR no	App-lied	Withdrawn
1150	9/1900	5/1929	1150E	8150	5500	6/46	65500	3/51	3/1958
1151	9/1900	4/1929	1151E	8151	5501	12/46	65501	5/49	1/1958
1152	9/1900	9/1929	1152E	8152	5502	9/46	65502	10/50	9/1959
1153	9/1900	12/1922	1153E	8153	5503	9/46	65503	3/49	8/1960
1154	10/1900	9/1924	1154E	8154	5504	10/46	65504	6/49	10/1958
1155	10/1900	12/1924	1155E	8155	5505	10/46	65505	1/49	11/1959
1156	10/1900	4/1922	1156E	8156	5506	12/46	65506	7/48	8/1960
1157	10/1900	2/1923	1157E	8157	5507	12/46	65507	7/49	9/1961
1158	11/1900	6/1929	1158E	8158	5508	12/46	65508	4/51	6/1958
1159	11/1900	5/1929	1159E	8159*	5509	11/46	65509	12/49	1/1958

* No 8159 was fitted with vacuum ejector in 10/1942

The following originally had 2640 gallon tenders. Works nos 1088-97 (order no H50).

No	Date	Rebuilt G58/J17	LNE no 1923	LNE no 1924	Renumbered no	date	BR no	App-lied	Withdrawn
1160	11/1900	5/1928	1160E	8160	5510	12/46	65510	12/48	3/1955
1161	11/1900	9/1923	1161E	8161	5511	12/46	65511	3/51	11/1960
1162	11/1900	4/1925	1162E	8162	5512	5/46	65512	1/51	12/1959
1163	11/1900	10/1931	1163E	8163	5513	11/46	65513	6/51	3/1961
1164	12/1900	4/1923	1164E	8164	5514	5/46	65514	12/49	1/1960
1165	1/1901	7/1929	1165E	8165	5515	9/46	65515	1/49	9/1958
1166	1/1901	1/1925	1166E	8166	5516*	6/46	65516	11/50	3/1955
1167	1/1901	12/1926**	1167E	8167	5517	5/46	65517	6/49	5/1955
1168	1/1901	12/1929	1168E	8168	5518	10/46	65518	8/49	9/1958
1169	2/1901	9/1922	1169E	8169	5519	9/46	65519	5/48	3/1960

* No 5516 was fitted with vacuum ejector in 1/1948
** No 8167 had a saturated Belpaire boiler in 12/1926, superheater boiler 11/1930.

The remainder had the standard 3500 gallon tender, which was the same as the 3250
gallon tender attached to passenger engines, but without the water pick up apparatus
that accounted for the extra 250 gallons capacity.
Works nos 1138-47 (order no L52), 1148-56 (order no P52).

No	Date	Rebuilt G58/J17	LNE no 1923	LNE no 1924	Renumbered no	date	BR no	App-lied	Withdrawn
1170	9/1901	12/1921	1170E	8170	5520	1/47	65520*	9/48	2/1961
1171	9/1901	8/1928	1171E	8171	5521	9/46	65521	12/48	2/1962
1172	9/1901	1/1926	1172E	8172	5522	9/46	65522	3/49	9/1958
1173	10/1901	6/1921	1173E	8173	5523	6/46	65523	10/48	5/1957
1174	10/1901	2/1922	1174E	8174	5524	10/46	65524	10/49	3/1955
1175	10/1901	1/1927**	1175E	8175	5525	9/46	65525	2/50	4/1959
1176	10/1901	6/1927	1176E	8176	5526	11/46	65526	1/50	8/1959
1177	10/1901	6/1924	1177E	8177	5527	10/46	65527	12/49	4/1959
1178	10/1901	3/1923	1178E	8178	5528	5/46	65528	12/50	11/1961

1179	10/1901	1/1931	1179E	8179	5529	11/46	65529	5/48	5/1958
1180	11/1901	8/1929	1180E	8180	5530	6/46	65530	11/50	1/1960
1181	11/1901	11/1929	1181E	8181	5531	6/46	65531	8/48	4/1959
1182	11/1901	1/1929	1182E	8182	5532	12/46	65532	9/48	2/1962
1183	11/1901	3/1928	1183E	8183***	5533	12/46	65533	7/48	1/1960
1184	11/1901	10/1929	1184E	8184	5534	10/46	65534*	9/49	5/1958
1185	12/1901	2/1929	1185E	8185	5535	9/46	65535	9/48	5/1958
1186	12/1901	8/1929**	1186E	8186	5536	11/46	65536	5/48	3/1960
1187	12/1901	2/1928	1187E	8187	5537	12/46	65537	4/48	1/1957
1188	12/1901	3/1923	1188E	8188	5538	6/46	65538	5/50	4/1959

*   Nos 65520 and 65534 were fitted with tender cabs in 2/1958 and 1/1952
    respectively
** Nos 8175 and 8186 had saturated Belpaire boilers on these dates, superheated
    boilers 10/1930 and 8/1931 respectively.
*** No 8183 was fitted with vacuum ejector in 6/1944.

The last locomotive built to order no P52, works no 1157, was the prototype for the
following class G58. Although built with saturated Belpaire firebox boiler, it was
still officially classed by the GE as F48 although, of course, when these had all been
rebuilt it became LNE J17 in common with them.

No	Date	
1189	2/1902	To LNE 1189E 1923, 8189 1924
	10/1929	Superheated
	6/1946	Renumbered 5539
	1/1949	Renumbered BR 65539. Withdrawn 8/1960.

The construction of further locomotives with round-top boilers continued as below.
Works nos 1180-9 (order no B54), 1190-9 (order no P54).

No	Date	Rebuilt G58/J17	LNE no 1923	LNE no 1924	Renumbered no	date	BR no	Applied	Withdrawn
1190	9/1902	5/1928	1190E	8190	5540	9/46	65540	9/48	4/1959
1191	9/1902	11/1930	1191E	8191	5541	10/46	65541	8/51	9/1962
1192	9/1902	8/1923	1192E	8192	5542	8/46	65542	2/49	5/1959
1193	9/1902	3/1921	1193F	8193	5543	9/46	65543	10/48	5/1955
1194	9/1902	2/1922	1194E	8194	5544	9/46	65544	5/49	11/1959
1195	10/1902	7/1926	1195E	8195*	5545	9/46	65545	6/48	10/1959
1196	10/1902	1/1924	1196E	8196	5546	10/46	65546	2/50	1/1960
1197	10/1902	4/1922	1197E	8197	5547	1/47	65547	8/49	9/1954
1198	10/1902	12/1921	1198E	8198	5548	9/46	65548	2/51	3/1960
1199	11/1902	7/1923	1199E	8199	5549	6/46	65549	7/51	12/1960
1200	11/1902	1/1932	1200E	8200	(5550)**				11/1944**
1201	12/1902	12/1921	1201E	8201	5551	1/46	65551*	9/49	2/1960
1202	12/1902	1/1922	1202E	8202	5552	3/46	65552*	5/48	1/1955
1203	12/1902	3/1925	1203E	8203	5553	5/46	65553	9/48	4/1959
1204	12/1902	1/1923	1204E	8204	5554	5/46	65554	3/52	9/1961
1205	1/1903	9/1926	1205E	8205	5555	8/46	65555	9/50	3/1960
1206	1/1903	2/1925	1206E	8206	5556	8/46	65556	11/48	3/1961
1207	2/1903	12/1921	1207E	8207	5557	2/46	65557*	2/49	4/1959
1208	2/1903	7/1928	1208E	8208	5558	6/46	65558*	6/48	1/1960
1209	2/1903	6/1928	1209E	8209*	5559	6/46	65559	6/46	11/1959

* These locos were fitted with vacuum ejector on the following dates
    8195 10/1942, 65551 9/1949, 65552 1/1951, 65557 2/1949, 65558 6/1948.
** No 8200 was allotted the number 5550 in the 1943 renumbering scheme but was
    destroyed by V2 rocket at Stratford.

0-6-0 Built by GER at Stratford. Works nos 1263-72 (order no G58, 1293-1302 (order no S59), 1459-68 (order no T67). DW 4ft 11in; Cyls 19 x 26; THS 1706.58 sq ft (1905), 1678.84 sq ft (1910); Wt 45 tons 8 Cwt. Other dimensions as class F48.
Class G58 Belpaire firebox version of class F48. Robinson superheaters fitted by Hill. THS 1275.1 sq ft + 226 sq ft superheater, later 1263.9 sq ft + 154.8 sq ft superheater. LNE class J17.

No	Date	Super-heated	LNE no 1923	LNE no 1924	Renumbered no	date	BR no	Applied	Withdrawn
1210	4/1905	10/1927	1210E	8210	5560	8/46	65560	6/48	6/1962
1211	4/1905	1/1917	1211E	8211	5561	8/46	65561	12/50	12/1959
1212	4/1905	3/1916	1212E	8212*	5562	6/46	65562	6/49	8/1958
1213	5/1905	7/1916	1213E	8213	5563	3/46	65563	9/49	1/1960
1214	5/1905	6/1916	1214E	8214	5564	5/46	65564	5/48	8/1960
1215	5/1905	10/1915	1215E	8215	5565	8/46	65565	9/51	4/1960
1216	5/1905	10/1923	1216E	8216	5566	4/46	65566*	12/48	7/1960
1217	5/1905	9/1923	1217E	8217*	5567	4/46	65567	9/50	8/1962**
1218	5/1905	7/1932	1218E	8218	5568	4/46	65568***	7/49	9/1958
1219	6/1905	5/1922	1219E	8219	5569	4/46	65569	10/48	2/1955
1220	1/1906	8/1921	1220E	8220	5570	8/46	65570	6/48	4/1960
1221	1/1906	8/1921	1221E	8221	5571	5/46	65571	11/48	2/1958
1222	1/1906	9/1923	1222E	8222	5572	8/46	65572	3/49	12/1957
1223	1/1906	9/1929	1223E	8223	5573	5/46	65573	1/49	10/1958
1224	1/1906	12/1930	1224E	8224	5574	5/46	65574*	8/51	4/1955
1225	2/1906	3/1920	1225E	8225	5575	4/46	65575***	7/48	2/1958
1226	2/1906	6/1919	1226E	8226	5576	4/46	65576	8/48	9/1962
1227	2/1906	4/1920	1227E	8227	5577	12/46	65577	6/51	2/1962
1228	3/1906	3/1921	1228E	8228	5578	7/46	65578	3/51	3/1962
1229	3/1906	6/1921	1229E	8229*	5579	7/46	65579	4/49	11/1954
1230	10/1910	8/1919	1230E	8230	5580	7/46	65580	10/50	11/1959
1231	11/1910	3/1919	1231E	8231*	5581	8/46	65581	1/49	4/1962
1232	11/1910	11/1919	1232E	8232	5582	9/46	65582	9/48	9/1962
1233	11/1910	6/1924	1233E	8233	5583	8/46	65583	9/48	2/1962
1234	11/1910	6/1925	1234E	8234	5584	5/46	65584	5/48	2/1960
1235	11/1910	7/1927	1235E	8235	5585	5/46	65585	7/48	11/1954
1236	12/1910	6/1930	1236E	8236*	5586	8/46	65586	5/50	4/1962
1237	12/1910	9/1919	1237E	8237	5587	8/46	65587	10/48	12/1958
1238	1/1911	3/1928	1238E	8238*	5588	8/46	65588	2/50	5/1961
1239	1/1911	2/1925	1239E	8239	5589	8/46	65589	5/48	1/1961

*   These locos were fitted with vacuum ejectors at the following dates.
     8212 5/1944, 65566 4/1951, 8217 1/1943, 65574 8/1951, 8229 6/1944, 8231 6/1945,
     8236 5/1944, 8238 8/1942.
     No 8231 was in an accident at Bishop's Stortford 10/5/1926.
** No 1217 is preserved at Bressingham.
*** Nos 65568 and 65575 had tender cabs fitted in 10/1952.

2-4-2T Built by GER at Stratford. Works nos below.
DW 5ft 4in; LW & TW 3ft 9in; WB 7ft 6in + 8ft 0in + 7ft 6in; Cyls 17½ x 24; Blr 4ft 2in x 10ft 2½in; THS 1107 sq ft (1886), 1133.2 sq ft (1903), 1116.4 sq ft (later series from about 1907); WP 140 lbs/sq in (1886), 160 lbs/sq in (1896); Wt 51 tons 11 cwt.
Class M15 As Worsdell design, but with Stephenson link motion instead of Joy radial valve gear and 17½in diameter cylinders instead of 18in. The last batch of the Worsdell order was still under construction when Holden took over, and it fell to him to modify the design following the successful application of these features on no 674 (see page 49). The boiler was also 2-ring butt-jointed instead of 3-ring as on the Worsdell engines, and the dome was now on the front ring. Replacement boilers had 1133.2 sq ft THS from 1903 and from 1907 2-ring telescopic boilers were provided (THS 1116.4 sq ft). Working pressure was increased to 160 lbs/sq in in 1896. Having completed the Worsdell order and successfully modified the design in 1886, Holden

built no more until 1903 when construction was restarted. From 1911, thirty two were rebuilt with 180 lbs/sq in, THS 1114.7 sq ft as fitted to class G69 (SD Holden *qv*) increasing the weight to 53 tons 19 cwt. These were referred to as M15 rebuilt on the GE, but the LNE classified them as F5 and the unrebuilt ones as F4.

The following were built to order no 018, Works nos 287-296. No 794 had a condenser fitted by the GE subsequent to being built which was retained.

No	Date	160 lbs boilers	LNE no 1923	LNE no 1924*	Withdrawn
790	9/1886				
Renumbered					
800	7/1892	4/1897	800E	7800	2/1927
791	9/1886	2/1898	791E	(7791)	11/1924
792	10/1886	6/1889	792E	7792	10/1926
793	10/1896	10/1896			8/1923
794	11/1886	7/1896	794E	(7794)	6/1925
795	11/1886	9/1898	795E	7795	6/1927
796	12/1886	10/1896	796E	(7796)	10/1924
797	1/1887	3/1897	797E	7797	5/1927
798	1/1887	4/1897	798E	7798	3/1927
799	1/1887	4/1897	799E	7799	3/1926

* Possibly other 1924 numbers were not applied.

When construction was resumed in 1903, single slide bars replaced the original four, and working pressure was now 160 lbs/sq in THS 1133.2 sq ft.
Works nos 1211-20 (order no P55), 1253-62 (order no F58, 1273-82 (order no R58).
Below C = condenser; V = vacuum ejector; P = push/pull equipment.

No	Date	Rebuilt (LNE F5)	LNE no 1923	LNE no 1924	Renumbered no	date	BR no	Applied	Withdrawn
140	6/1903		140E	7140					3/1932
141	6/1903	9/1915 V 12/36	141E	7141	7188	5/46	67188	5/49	12/1955
142	6/1903	11/1911 V 2/29	142E	7142	7189	5/46	67189	1/50	12/1956
143	6/1903	10/1911 V 7/35	143E	7143	7190	5/46	67190	12/48	11/1955
144	6/1903	6/1916 V 7/37	144E	7144	7191	4/46	67191	4/49	11/1955
145	7/1903	9/1913 C 9/23-c1954							
		V 7/31	145E	7145	7192	4/46	67192	7/48	4/1958
146	7/1903		146E	7146					1/1930
147	7/1903	4/1914 V 1/36							
		P 9/49	147E	7147	7193	5/46	67193	9/48	11/1957
148	8/1903		148E	7148					8/1931
149	8/1903		149E	7149					5/1931
781	10/1904	11/1911 V 6/35	781E	7781	7194	9/46	67194	9/49	10/1956
782	11/1904	12/1911 V 10/28	782E	7782	7195	9/46	67195*	12/50	5/1958
783	11/1904	12/1911 V 9/31	783E	7783	7196	9/46	67196	5/48	3/1955
784	11/1904	12/1911 C 9/23-11/36**							
			784E	7784**	7197	5/46	67197	5/51	3/1955
785	11/1904	1/1912 V 6/29	785E	7785	7198	12/46	67198	11/49	8/1955
786	11/1904	3/1912 C by GE - 9/36							
		V 12/28							
		P 11/49	786E	7786	7199	8/46	67199	11/48	2/1957
787	11/1904	12/1911 V 3/37							
		P 9/49	787E	7787	7200	12/46	67200	3/49	12/1957
788	11/1904	12/1911 V 2/29	788E	7788	7201	12/46	67201	9/49	12/1956
789	12/1904	7/1912***							
		C by GE - c1954							
		V 4/39							
		P 11/49	789E	7789	7218	9/46	67218	4/48	3/1958
790	12/1904	7/1912***							
		C by GE - 2/37							
		V 9/27	790E	7790	7219	12/46	67219	11/49	11/1956

```
 91  7/1905 10/1913 C by GE - 9/49
                     V  5/29
                     P  9/49  91E  7091  7202  8/46  67202  3/48 12/1957
 92  7/1905          V  4/33  92E  7092                           4/1933
 93  7/1905                   93E  7093                           5/1932
 94  7/1905  4/1913 C by GE - 9/49
                     V  3/29
                     P  9/49  94E  7094  7203 11/46  67203  4/48 12/1957
 95  8/1905  6/1913 C by GE - c1935
                     V 11/31  95E  7095  7204  5/46  67204  8/49  9/1955
 96  9/1905  9/1911 C by GE - 9/37
                     V  4/29  96E  7096  7205  8/46  67205  7/48 11/1955
 97  9/1905                   97E  7097                          12/1929
 98  9/1905                   98E  7098                          11/1929
 99 10/1905                   99E  7099                           5/1932
100 10/1905  1/1912 C by GE - 12/36
                     V  2/29 100E  7100  7206 10/46  67206  6/50  9/1955
```

*   67195 ran with BR 'E' suffix before 12/1950.

**   7784 was transferred to the War Department in 7/1940 to haul coastal defence
     Trains, and was fitted with armour plate and painted in army camouflage. It bore
     the letter M, and was based at Spalding. With armour plating, weight was 59 tons
     18 cwt. It was returned in 7/1943 and armour plating removed. Vacuum ejector was
     probably fitted at this time.

*** Nos 789/90 were given side window cabs when rebuilt as class G69 (LNE F6). In
     1923 the LNE wrongly classified them as F6 and this was not rectified until
     12/1948. This resulted in their being given the wrong numbers in 1946.

The following were built with condensers. Some were removed by the GE and some by the
LNE (CR below). Other abbreviations as above. Works nos 1283-92 (order no C59),
1313-22 (order no I60), 1333-42 (order no A62).

```
                 Rebuilt            LNE no LNE no  Renumbered            App-  With-
No   Date        (LNE F5)           1923   1924    no    date   BR no    lied  drawn
101  11/1905                 CR by GE 101E  7101                                11/1929
102  11/1905             V  9/16
                             CR by GE 102E  7102                                 2/1931
103  11/1905  9/1911 V 12/28
                             CR 5/36  103E  7103    7207 12/46  67207    5/48 12/1955
104  11/1905  9/1911 V  3/29          104E  7104    7208  5/46  67208    9/49  1/1957
105  11/1905         V  2/31          105E  7105                                 3/1935
106  11/1905                 CR by GE
                     V  1/31          106E  7106                                 2/1933
107   2/1906                 CR by GE 107E  7107                                12/1929
108   1/1906  9/1911 V  2/29          108E  7108    7209  8/46  67209   11/48  2/1957
109   2/1906  9/1911 V  5/31          109E  7109    7210  5/46  67210    1/50  7/1955
110   1/1906  7/1913 V  4/31
                             CR 6/36  110E  7110    7211  8/46  67211    6/48 10/1956
236   7/1906         V after 1931*
                             CR after 1931*
                     P  1941 236E  7236*   7151  3/46  67151    6/48  8/1951
237   7/1906                          237E  7237                                 9/1929
238   7/1906                          238E  7238**                               7/1929
239   8/1906                          239E  7239                                11/1929
240   8/1906                          240E  7240                                 6/1937
241   8/1906                          241E  7241                                10/1933
242   9/1906                          242E  7242                                10/1937
243   9/1906                          243E  7243                                12/1934
244   9/1906                 CR 3/37
                     V  9/47 244E  7244*** 7152  9/46  67152   11/48  2/1952
780   7/1906 10/1914 V  5/31          780E  7780    7212 10/46  67212   11/48  5/1958
572   2/1907                          572E  7572                                 3/1933
```

No	Date	Rebuilt (LNE F5)	LNE no 1923	LNE no 1924	Renumbered no	date	BR no	Applied	Withdrawn
573	3/1907	CR 1941/2***							
		V 11/47	573E	7573***	7153	1/47	(67153)		7/1951
574	3/1907	V 12/16							
		CR 12/36	574E	7574	7154	1/47	67154	12/48	9/1951
575	3/1907	CR 6/26	575E	7575					1/1931
576	3/1907		576E	7576					5/1937
577	4/1907		577E	7577					1/1931
578	4/1907	CR after 1931							
		V 8/33	578E	7578	7155	12/46	67155	4/50	8/1951
579	4/1907	V 5/33							
		CR 6/36	579E	7579	7156	1/47	(67156)		11/1950
580	4/1907		580E	7580					7/1937
581	5/1907	V 6/33							
		CR after 1935							
			581E	7581*	7157	11/46	67157	6/50	6/1956

*   Nos 7236/581 were transferred to the Scottish area, 7236 in 1931 and 7581 in 1948. Both were at various times fitted with 'cowcatchers' for working the Fraserburgh – St Combs branch. The condenser on 7236 was removed in Scotland at Inverurie.

** 7238 was in an accident at Fenchurch Street on 16/1/1927.

*** Nos 7244/573 were transferred to the War Department in 6 & 7/1940 respectively to work coastal defence trains, and were armoured and camouflaged as 7784 above. No 7244 was lettered 'E' and stationed at Ashford. It was returned in 7/1943 and armour plating was removed in 9/1943. No 7573 was lettered 'K' and stationed at Longniddry. It was returned in 1/1945 and armour plating removed in 2/1945.

The following were built without condensers although no 583 had one fitted subsequently. Works nos 1343-52 (order no D63). Abbreviations as above.

No	Date	Rebuilt (LNE F5)	LNE no 1923	LNE no 1924	Renumbered no	date	BR no	Applied	Withdrawn
582	5/1907		582E	7582					3/1936
583	5/1907	C by GE - 1/31							
		V 11/16	583E	7583					5/1937
584	5/1907	V 3/35	584E	7584	7158	1/47	67158	4/49	1/1953
585	5/1907		585E	7585					3/1933
586	6/1907	V 6/34*	586E	7586*	7159	1/47	(67159)		4/1948
587	6/1907		587E	7587					10/1933
588	6/1907	V 5/33	588E	7588	7160	1/47	(67160)		4/1950
589	6/1907 6/1915	V 2/29							
		P 9/49	589E	7589	7213	9/46	67213	2/49	2/1955
590	7/1907 7/1915	V 11/35	590E	7590	7214	12/46	67214	5/49	5/1958
591	7/1907		591E	7591					3/1933

* 7586 was transferred to the War Department in 1/1941 to work coastal defence trains and was armour plated as above and camouflaged. It was held as a spare engine until 6/1943 when it was returned and armour plating removed 7/1943. The vacuum ejector was removed when transferred to the War Department.

The following were all built with condensers although some were subsequently removed (CR below) when sent out of the London area. Works nos 1353-62 (order no G63), 1363-72 (order no H63), 1386-95 (order no S64), 1396-1405 (order no A65), 1406-15 (order no I65). Abbreviations as above.

No	Date	Rebuilt (LNE F5)	LNE no 1923	LNE no 1924	Renumbered no	date	BR no	Applied	Withdrawn
211	8/1907		211E	7211					8/1934
212	8/1907		212E	7212					12/1933
213	9/1907		213E	7213					12/1933
214	9/1907	CR 5/36							
		V 9/47	214E	7214*	7162	12/46	67162	5/50	8/1955
215	9/1907	V 1/31	215E	7215					5/1935
216	9/1907	V as new	216E	7216					3/1934

```
217   9/1907              V as new 217E   7217                                4/1935
218  10/1907              V as new
                          CR 10/25 218E   7218                                3/1933
219  10/1907              V as new
                          CR  3/34 219E   7219    7163 12/46  67163  10/48 12/1951
220  10/1907              V as new
                          CR 10/30 220E   7220                                5/1934
111  11/1907              CR  9/37 111E   7111*   7161  9/46 (67161)         4/1948
221  11/1907              V  10/18 221E   7221                                6/1934
222  11/1907              V after 1931
                          CR after 1931
                                   222E   7222*   7164  9/46  67164** 8/48  8/1951
223  11/1907                       223E   7223                                2/1935
224  11/1907              V   2/31 224E   7224                                2/1935
225  11/1907                       225E   7225                                5/1935
232  11/1907              CR by GE
                          V  10/30 232E   7232    7165 12/46  67165   8/48  1/1951
233  12/1907              V   8/33 233E   7233    7166 12/46  67166   3/49  4/1951
234  12/1907                       234E   7234                                4/1933
235  12/1907                       235E   7235                                6/1935
170   8/1908  1/1915 V    5/31 170E   7170    7215  4/46  67215  11/49  9/1955
171   9/1908              CR  7/36
                          V   5/41 171E   7171    7167  8/46  67167   2/49  9/1952
172   9/1908              CR by GE 172E   7172*   7168  9/46 (67168)         4/1948
173   9/1908              CR before 1933
                                   173E   7173*   7169 10/46 (67169)         4/1948
174   9/1908              V   2/32-9/40
                          CR  2/37 174E   7174*   7170  8/46 (67170)         4/1948
175  10/1908              V  12/16
                          CR  2/32 175E   7175    7171 11/46  67171   4/49  8/1951
176  10/1908              CR after 1931
                          P  1941 176E   7176**                              4/1943
177  10/1908              CR c1940/1 177E 7177*   7172 11/46 (67172)         4/1948
178  10/1908              CR c1940/1 178E 7178*   7173 12/46 (67173)         4/1948
179  11/1908 12/1914 V    2/29
                          CR  7/37 179E   7179    7216  4/46  67216   6/51 12/1956
180  11/1908              CR  4/37
                          V  11/47 180E   7180*   7174 12/46  67174  11/49 12/1954
181  11/1908              V   6/31 181E   7181                               11/1935
182  12/1908                       182E   7182***                           1/1931
183  12/1908                       183E   7183                              10/1934
184  12/1908              V   2/34 184E   7184    7175 12/46  67175   4/49  8/1951
185   1/1909              V   2/32
                          CR  7/36 185E   7185    7176  9/46  67176  11/48  7/1953
186   1/1909              V   5/34
                          CR  7/36 186E   7186    7177 12/46  67177   8/48  3/1951
187   2/1909              CR 10/34
                          V  10/34 187E   7187    7178 12/46  67178  10/48  8/1952
188   2/1909  6/1920 V   10/28
                          CR  5/37 188E   7188    7217  4/46  67217   8/48 11/1955
189   2/1909              CR c1940/1 189E  7189*   7179  5/46 (67179)         4/1948
 71   3/1909              CR c1940/1  71E  7071    7180 12/46 (67180)         4/1948
 72   3/1909              CR c1940/1  72E  7072    7181  9/46 (67181)         4/1948
 73   3/1909                        73E   7073                                3/1935
 74   3/1909              V  11/30  74E   7074    7182  9/46  67182  10/48  1/1953
 75   4/1909              V   7/34
                          CR 12/36  75E   7075    7183  9/46 (67183)         4/1950
 76   4/1909              V   6/33
                          CR after 1935
                                    76E   7076    7184  1/47  67184   5/49 12/1952
```

```
77  4/1909        CR c1940/1  77E  7077*   7185  9/46  (67185)      4/1948
78  4/1909        CR by GE
                  V  8/35     78E  7078    7186 12/46  67186   7/48  7/1953
79  5/1909        CR by GE
                  V  4/31     79E  7079    7187 12/46  67187   1/50  8/1955
80  5/1909                    80E  7080                              2/1936
```

*   Engines to War Department as below were armour plated and camouflaged as 7784,
    7244, 7573/86 above. Lettered and stationed as below:

	Letter	Stationed	Period	Armour removed
7214	C	Westerfield and Canterbury	6/1940-7/1943	10/1943
7111	-	Spare	2/1941-6/1943	7/1943
7172	A	Hitchin	6/1940-5/1943	7/1943
7173	L	Aberdeen	7/1940-1/1945	4/1945
7174	-	Spare	1/1941-1/1945	3/1945
7177	-	Spare	1/1941-6/1943	6/1943
7178	D	Mistley	6/1940-7/1943	9/1943
7180	J	Stirling	7/1940-1/1945	2/1945
7189	G	Heacham	6/1940-5/1943	6/1943
7071	H	Canterbury	7/1940-7/1943	7/1943
7172	B	Canterbury	6/1940-5/1943	6/1943
7077	F	Tilbury	6/1940-3/1943	5/1943

**   Nos 7222 & 7176 were sent to the Scottish area in 1931 where condensers were
     removed. Both at various times were fitted with 'cow catchers' for working the
     Fraserburgh-St Combs branch. No 67164 continued to carry LNE lettering and 7164
     number on tanks and buffer beams after 8/1948 although full BR number was carried
     on the smokebox plate.
*** No 7182 was in an accident at Ware 31/10/1927.

2-4-2T Built by GER at Stratford. Works nos below.
DW 5ft 8in; LW & TW 4ft 0in; WB 7ft 6in + 8ft 9in + 7ft 0in; Cyls 17½ x 24; Blr 4ft
4in x 10ft 0in; THS 1217.08 sq ft (1893), 1199.5 sq ft (1902); WP 140 lbs/sq in
(1893), 160 lbs/sq in (1902); Wt 58 tons 12 cwt.
Class C32 Tank engine version of the T26 2-4-0 but with 3in shorter wheelbase
intended for longer distance stopping trains rather than suburban or local traffic.
Boilers were standard with class T26 and N31 0-6-0s, also post-1891 Y14 0-6-0s. Most
replacement boilers had THS 1164.7 sq ft from 1907, some having 1147.1 sq ft later.
After 1940, THS was 1137.69 sq ft. Outside framing on LW and TW. In common with
other classes vacuum ejectors were fitted by the LNER in addition to the Westinghouse
brakes. LNE class F3.

The following order no C32 works nos 733-42 and order no O33 works nos 793-802.

No	Date	160 lbs boiler	Vacuum ejector	LNE no 1923	LNE no 1924	Renumbered No	date	BR no	Applied	Withdrawn
1090	4/1893	11/1905	no date	1090E	8090					10/1936
1091	4/1893	1/1906	12/1928	1091E	8091					7/1938
1092	5/1893	9/1906	8/1929	1092E	8092	7114	10/46	(67114)		3/1948
1093	5/1893	10/1904	12/1928	1093E	8093	7115	3/46	(67115)		5/1948
1094	5/1893	11/1907	9/1928	1094E	8094	7116	11/46			11/1947
1095	6/1893	5/1906	7/1929	1095E	8095	7117	11/46	(67117)		5/1948
1096	6/1893	12/1906	4/1929	1096E	8096	7118	11/46			8/1947
1097	6/1893	10/1905	9/1928	1097E	8097	7119	11/46			2/1948
1098	6/1893	9/1903	no date	1098E	8098					12/1937
1099	6/1893	9/1906	1/1930	1099E	8099	7120	11/46			12/1947
1070	11/1893	9/1906	6/1929	1070E	8070	7121	5/46			4/1947
1071	11/1893	10/1907	10/1928	1071E	8071	7122	5/46			11/1947
1072	12/1893	8/1906	11/1928	1072E	8072	7123	5/46			3/1947
1073	12/1893	12/1905	1/1929	1073E	8073					11/1938
1074	12/1893	4/1909	11/1929	1074E	8074					2/1937

```
1075 12/1893  5/1908 10/1929 1075E 8075   7124  5/46 (67124)       3/1950
1076  1/1894  9/1903  6/1929 1076E 8076                            3/1937
1077  1/1894  8/1905  8/1930 1077E 8077   7125 11/46               8/1947
1078  1/1894  4/1906  4/1929 1078E 8078   7126  5/46 (67126)       1/1950
1079  1/1894 12/1928  9/1928 1079E 8079   7127  5/46  67127   1/49 4/1953
```

The following were built with condensers to order no R33 works nos 803-12. Some condensers were removed by the GE but only 1087 recorded. 8080/2 removed by 1939 others by 1933.

No	Date	160 lbs boiler	Vacuum ejector	LNE no 1923	LNE no 1924	Renumbered No	date	BR no	Applied	Withdrawn
1080	2/1894	3/1905	6/1929	1080E	8080					12/1938
1081	2/1894	6/1909	12/1928	1081E	8081	7128	12/46	67128	6/48	12/1950
1082	2/1894	12/1905	3/1930	1082E	8082	7129	5/46			8/1947
1083	3/1894	5/1905	4/1930	1083E	8083					2/1938
1084	3/1894	5/1905	no date	1084E	8084					5/1938
1085	4/1894	6/1905	11/1928	1085E	8085	7130	12/46			11/1947
1086	4/1894	9/1905	4/1929	1086E	8086					4/1938
1087	4/1894	12/1905	11/1928	1087E	8087					10/1938
1088	4/1894	5/1906	8/1929	1088E	8088	7131	10/46			11/1947
1089	4/1894	3/1905	11/1929	1089E	8089	7132	10/46			11/1947

The following were built to order G35 works nos 843-52 without condensers.

No	Date	160 lbs boiler	Vacuum ejector	LNE no 1923	LNE no 1924	Renumbered No	date	BR no	Applied	Withdrawn
1060	5/1895	11/1907	2/1930	1060E	8060	7133	5/46			6/1947
1061	5/1895	10/1910	2/1929	1061E	8061	7134	5/46	(67134)		5/1948
1062	5/1895	11/1906	8/1928	1062E	8062	7135	5/46			11/1947
1063	5/1895	7/1908	7/1929	1063E	8063	7136	5/46			11/1947
1064	5/1895	3/1908	10/1928	1064E	8064	7137	5/46			11/1947
1065	5/1895	7/1909	4/1930	1065E	8065					3/1938
1066	5/1895	4/1905	8/1929	1066E	8066	7138	5/46			8/1947
1067	5/1895	10/1904	6/1929	1067E	8067	7139	5/46	(67139)		12/1950
1068	5/1895	6/1907	6/1929	1068E	8068	7140	5/46	(67140)		3/1949
1069	5/1895	7/1907	6/1929	1069E	8069					3/1937

The following, built to order no D53 works nos 1160-9, had condensers and 160 lbs/sq in boilers THS 1199.5 sq ft when built. Condensers are known to have been removed from 1040/1/3/5/9 by the GE and the others by the LNE by 1933.

No	Date	Vacuum ejector	LNE no 1923	LNE no 1924	Renumbered No	date	BR no	Applied	Withdrawn
1040	5/1902	6/1930	1040E	8040	7141	5/46	(67141)		5/1948
1041	5/1902	3/1929	1041E	8041	7142	5/46			4/1947
1042	5/1902	9/1928	1042E	8042	7143	5/46			7/1948
1043	5/1902	12/1929	1043E	8043	7144	5/46			11/1947
1044	5/1902	10/1929	1044E	8044	7145	5/46			4/1947
1045	6/1902	8/1928	1045E	8045	7146	5/46			8/1947
1046	6/1902	12/1929	1046E	8046	7147	5/46			11/1947.
1047	6/1902	9/1928	1047E	8047	7148	5/46			7/1947
1048	6/1902	10/1928	1048E	8048	7149	4/46	67149	11/48	7/1949
1049	6/1902	10/1928	1049E	8049	7150	4/46	(67150)		10/1949

0-4-4T Built by GER at Stratford.
DW 4ft 11in; TW 3ft 1in; WB 7ft 7in + 9ft 9in + 5ft 0in; Cyls 17 x 24; Blr 4ft 2in x 10ft 0in; THS 1081.4 sq ft; WP 160 lbs/sq in; Wt 52 tons 3 cwt.
Class S44 Designed for heavy suburban trains on the Chingford and Enfield lines, they are reputed to have had sluggish acceleration, but could run at speed on non-stop workings. After 1923, most were transferred to work branch line passenger and light goods traffic. Replacement boilers had THS 1084 sq ft. Water tanks were increased in

capacity from 1100 gallons to 1349 gallons reducing coal capacity from 3 tons to 2.5 tons and increasing weight to 53 tons 8 cwt. The final order (L50) is reputed to have been built with this larger tank capacity. LNE class G4.

The following had the front and rear steps integral with the valance. Order no S44, works nos 977-86.

No	Date	Vacuum ejector	LNE no 1923	LNE no 1924	Withdrawn
1100	12/1898	4/1924	1100E	8100	7/1931
1101	12/1898		1101E	8101	2/1933
1102	12/1898		1102E	8102	1/1930
1103	12/1898		1103E	8103	10/1929 Accident Liverpool Street 9/5/1925
1104	1/1899	4/1924	1104E	8104	1/1931
1105	1/1899	4/1930	1105E	8105	1/1938
1106	1/1899		1106E	8106	7/1931
1107	2/1899	8/1924	1107E	8107	10/1931
1108	2/1899		1108E	8108	8/1930
1109	2/1899		1109E	8109	6/1933

The remainder had the footsteps separate from the valance. Works nos 1028-37 (order no F47), 1068-77 (order no R28).

No	Date	Vacuum ejector	LNE no 1923	LNE no 1924	Withdrawn
1110	10/1899		1110E	8110	4/1932
1111*	10/1899		1111E	8111	5/1930
1112	10/1899		1112E	8112	12/1931
1113*	11/1899	6/1924 until 10/1925	1113E	8113	2/1931
1114	11/1889	3/1924	1114E	8114	9/1931
1115	11/1899	6/1924 until 10/1925	1115E	8115	7/1931
1116	11/1899		1116E	8116	12/1933
1117*	11/1899		1117E	8117	2/1933
1118	11/1899		1118E	8118	1/1930
1119*	11/1899		1119E	8119	4/1933
1120	5/1900		1120E	8120	11/1929
1121	5/1900	3/1924 until 10/1925	1121E	8121	2/1930
1122	5/1900	7/1924	1122E	8122	12/1932
1123	5/1900	3/1924	1123E	8123	8/1938
1124	5/1900	7/1924	1124E	8124	9/1934
1125	5/1900	4/1924 until 10/1925	1125E	8125	6/1931
1126	5/1900		1126E	8126	12/1933
1127	5/1900	8/1924	1127E	8127	1/1931
1128*	6/1900	5/1924	1128E	8128	2/1930
1129	6/1900	5/1924 until 10/1925	1129E	8129	12/1932

* These locos were transferred to the War Department during the First World War to Richborough, the main embarkation point for supplies to the Western Front.

The following, with separate footsteps as above, are reputed to have been built with the larger capacity water tanks. Works nos 1098-1107 (order no L50).

No	Date	Vacuum ejector	LNE no 1923	LNE no 1924	Withdrawn
1130	12/1900		1130E	8130	2/1932
1131	12/1900		1131E	8131	6/1934
1132*	12/1900		1132E	8132	2/1932
1133	12/1900	3/1924 until 10/1925	1133E	8133	4/1929.
1134	1/1901		1134E	8134	9/1936
1135	1/1901		1135E	8135	6/1931
1136	2/1901		1136E	8136	12/1931
1137	2/1901		1137E	8137	8/1934
1138	2/1901		1138E	8138	3/1931
1139	3/1901	9/1924	1139E	8139	12/1938

* Transferred to the War Department, Richborough during the First World War as above.

0-4-0ST Built by GER at Stratford.
Works nos 925/6 (order no G40), 1221/2 (order no R55).
DW 3ft 7in; WB 5ft 9in; Cyls 12 x 18; Blr 3ft 4¼in; x 8ft $7^{15}/16$ in; THS 514.55 sq ft;
WP 140 1lbs/sq in; Wt 21 tons 4 cwt.
Continuation of Adams 209 class as rebuilt by Holden (see page 43). LNE class Y5.

No	Date		LNE no 1923	LNE no 1924	Renumbered no	date	Withdrawn
226	6/1897	To duplicate list 0226 1907					8/1911
227	6/1897	To duplicate list 0227 1907					12/1911
230*	3/1903	To LNE Service stock S7230	230E	7230	8081	12/46	4/1948
231**	4/1903		231E	7231			7/1931

* No 230 had Westinghouse brakes & vacuum ejector fitted 5/1916 until 1944.
** No 231 had 'cowcatcher,' side aprons & warning bell fitted at Hythe (Colchester)
   later removed.

0-6-0T Built by GER at Stratford. Works nos below.
DW 4ft 0in; WB 6ft 4in + 7ft 0in: Cyls 16½ x 22; Blr 4ft 2in x 9ft 1in;
THS 967.24 Sq ft (1886), 959.24 Sq ft (1888); WP 14o lbs/sq in; Wt 40 tons 6 cwt.
Class T18 Primarily intended for shunting duties only, hand brakes were provided on
the first 40, steam brakes being fitted in 1893 and 1895-9. The final order provided
for Westinghouse brakes so that they could be used on suburban passenger services
following the experimental fitting of Westinghouse brake to no 294. These duties were
taken over by class R24, and 317-26 reverted to shunting duties in 1890 and the
Westinghouse brake equipment was transferred to class R24. Working pressure was
increased to 160 lbs/sq in with the fitting of 2-ring telescopic boilers in place of
the original 2-ring butt-jointed type from 1898, which had THS 979.4 sq ft (987.4 sq
ft from 1908). Macallan variable blast pipes were removed by the LNER in 1924-6.
LNE class J66. Sometimes called 'Jubilee Tanks'.

The following originally had 2-ring butt-jointed boilers THS 967.24 sq ft.
Works nos 297-306 (order no T18), 307-11 and 322-6 (order no K19).

No	Date	LNE no 1923	LNE no 1924	Renumbered no	date	BR no	Applied	Withdrawn
275	6/1886	275E	7275					6/1938*
276	5/1886	276E	7276					7/1937
277	6/1886	277E	7277					7/1938*
278	6/1886	278E	7278					10/1936*
279	6/1886	279E	7279					5/1937
280	6/1886	280E	7280					7/1936
281**	6/1886	281E	7281	8370	4/46	68370	12/48	9/1962**
282	6/1886	282E	7282					2/1940
283	7/1886	283E	7283					7/1939
284	7/1886	284E	7284					5/1937
285	2/1887	285E	7285					10/1939
286	2/1887	286E	7286					9/1939
287	3/1887	287E	7287					10/1936*
288	3/1887	288E	7288	8371	5/46	68371	8/49	4/1954
289	3/1887	289E	7289	8372	1/46	68372	4/48	2/1951
290	4/1887	290E	7290	8373	1/46	68373	2/49	1/1952
291	4/1887	291E	7291					2/1939.
292	4/1887	292E	7292					10/1936*
293	5/1887	293E	7293	8374	1/46	68374	12/48	6/1954
294***	4/1887	294E	7294					7/1937

* Locos sold:
   7275 11/1938 to Ashington Coal Co no 18. Scrapped 2/1953.

7277 7/1938 to Ashington Coal Co no 19. Scrapped 12/1944.

7278 10/1936 to Sir Robert McAlpine & Co no 78. Scrapped 1938-9.

7287 10/1936 to Sir Robert McAlpine & Co no 76. Scrapped 1938-9.

7292 10/1936 to Guest, Keen & Baldwins Iron & Steel Co, Cardiff no 16.
Renumbered 10 in 1952. Scrapped 1/1959.

** No 281 was converted to burn oil fuel in 9/1886 and again in 11/1893. It was in
Service Stock at Stratford by 1923. Renumbered 'Departmental 32' in 9/1952.

*** No 294 had Westinghouse brake as a passenger engine from 7/1887 until 10/1930.

The following originally had butt-jointed boilers with THS 959.24 sq ft. Works nos
327-36 (order no K19); 389-98 (order no H21).

No	Date	LNE no 1923	LNE no 1924	Renumbered no	date	BR no	App-lied	Withdrawn
295	5/1887	295E	7295					12/1938*
296	10/1887	296E	7296	8375	1/46	68375	4/50	11/1952
297	6/1887	297E	7297			ME 3	1948	6/1950*
298	6/1887	298E	7298	8376	3/46	(68376)		7/1951
299	9/1887	299E	7299					6/1937
300	9/1887	300E	7300					4/1939
301	9/1887	301E	7301					8/1939
302	9/1887	302E	7302					5/1939
303	9/1887	303E	7303					10/1936*
304	9/1887	304E	7304	8377	5/46	(68377)		5/1951
307	6/1888	307E	7307	8378	6/46	68378	7/49	1/1959**
308	6/1888	308E	7308					10/1936*
309	7/1888	309E	7309	8379	5/46	68379	9/48	11/1950
310	7/1888	310E	7310	8380	6/46	(68380)		3/1952
311	7/1888	311E	7311	8381	4/46	(68381)		10/1950
312	7/1888	312E	7312					1/1939
313	8/1888	313E	7313	8382	5/46	68382	5/49	11/1959**
314	8/1888	314E	7314					7/1937
315	11/1888	315E	7315					2/1937
316	8/1888	316E	7316					7/1937

* Locos sold

7295 12/1938 to Ocean Coal Co, Treorchy. Scrapped 1951.

7297 5/1939 to Mersey Railway no 3. BR ME 3 1948.

7303 10/1936 to Sir Robert McAlpine no 75. Scrapped 1938-9.

7308 10/1936 to Sir Robert McAlpine no 77. Scrapped 1938-9.

** No 68378 to service stock 9/1952. Renumbered 'Departmental 36' 11/1952.

No 68382 to service stock 6/1952. Renumbered 'Departmental 31' 8/1952.

The following were built with Westinghouse brakes and screw reverse for passenger
work, with longer bunkers increasing coal capacity to 2½ tons.
Wt 40 tons 11 cwt following the successful use of no 294 on passenger trains. In 1890
the brake gear was transferred to R24 class as below, and lever reverse was
substituted in 1896. Works nos 409-18 (order no T21).

No	Date	LNE no 1923	LNE no 1924	Renumbered no	date	BR no	App-lied	Withdrawn
317	11/1888	317E	7317					6/1937
318	11/1888	318E	7318					3/1937
319	11/1888	319E	7319	8383	4/46	68383	11/51	10/1955
320	11/1888	320E	7320	8384	6/46	(68384)		4/1950
321	11/1888	321E	7321	8385	5/46	68385	5/48	6/1951
322	12/1888	322E	7322	8386	7/46	(68386)		4/1950
323	12/1888	323E	7323	8387	6/46	(68387)		2/1951
324	12/1888	324E	7324	8388	4/46	68388	1/49	4/1952
325	12/1888	325E	7325					7/1937
326	12/1888	326E	7326					7/1937

0-6-0T Built by GER at Stratford. Works nos below.
DW 4ft 0in; WB 6ft 4in + 7ft 6in; Cyls 16½ x 22; Blr 4ft 2in x 9ft 1in;
THS 959.24 sq ft and 922.09 sq ft (1890), 979.4 sq ft (1899);
WP 140 lbs/sq in (1890); Wt 40 tons.
Class R24 Designed for either passenger or shunting work, a large number of the
former were ordered in preference to four-coupled locomotives. The passenger engines
had Westinghouse brake and screw reverse, screw couplings and wheels with balance
weights. The shunting engines had hand brakes (later steam brakes by 1898), lever
reverse, unbalanced wheels and three link couplings. The wheelbase was longer than
class T18, but the front and rear overhangs were less so that overall length was 6½ in
shorter. Replacement boilers from 1899 were of the telescopic type instead of butt-
jointed, both having two rings THS 979.4 sq ft (987.4 sq ft from 1908), WP 160 lbs/sq
ft. From 1902, most of the passenger engines were rebuilt with higher pressure
boilers 180 lbs/sq in and larger fireboxes, THS 988.17 sq ft (996.17 sq ft from 1908).
From 1903, 4 in wider tanks were fitted, increasing water capacity from 1000 gallons
to 1140 gallons, and from 1904, tanks were widened by 5 in (wider than the cab sides)
increasing capacity to 1180 gallons. The locomotives rebuilt in 1902 eventually were
given the 5 in wider tanks. The weight of the rebuilds, known on the GE as 'class R24
rebuilt', was 42 tons 9 cwt. The unrebuilt locomotives were classed as J67 and the
rebuilt ones as J69 by the LNER. In 12/1938 a distinction was made in the
classification system for certain locos which had (from 1912) reverted to 160 lbs
boilers but retaining the larger tanks. Unrebuilt locos with small tanks became
J67/1, and those with 160 lbs boilers and large tanks J67/2. From 12/1952, a similar
sub-division of J69 class took account of certain shunting locomotives with small
tanks which were given 180 lbs boilers, J69/1 covering 180 lbs boilers with large
tanks and J69/2 180 lbs boilers with small tanks. Condensers were fitted to the
passenger locomotives in 1893 and to all those built from 1894, but when the
locomotives were downgraded from passenger work the condensers were removed and steam
brakes substituted for Westinghouse, usually at the same date. Below V/E = vacuum
ejector fitted; CR = condenser removed; S = with steam brake substituted for
Westinghouse brake; W = Westinghouse brake retained or refitted. Suffix E added to GE
numbers 9/1923-2/1924. 1924 LNE numbers applied from 2/1924

The following were passenger engines with Westinghouse brakes etc. Nos 337-46 had the
brake equipment removed from T18 317-26 above. Condensers fitted in 1893. Works nos
489-98 (order no R24), 499-508 (order no S24).

No	Date	Rebuilt		V/E	CR	LNE nos no	date	BR no	App-lied	With-drawn
327	3/1890	7/1904	R24 rbt							
		6/1912	R24 blr*		6/12S	7327	1924			
		5/1950	J69/1			8490	9/46	68490	5/50	5/1958
328	3/1890	7/1908	R24 rbt							
		8/1912	160 lbs*		8/12S	7328	1924			
		2/1917	180 lbs	5/35		8491	9/46	68491	4/48	6/1958
329	3/1890	9/1902	R24 rbt**		11/12S	7329	1924			
		11/1912	160 lbs*			8492	3/46	68492	6/50	6/1956
330	3/1890				11/12S	7330	1924			
						8493	9/46	68493	10/48	10/1954
331	3/1890	9/1904	R24 rbt							
		11/1912	160 lbs*		11/12S	7331	1924			
		7/1945	J69/1			8494	9/46	68494	3/51	4/1958
332	4/1890	7/1902	R24 rbt**							
		9/1912	160 lbs*		9/12S	7332	1924			
		12/1940	J69/1			8495	9/46	68495	12/50	5/1958
333	4/1890	8/1908	R24 rbt							
		5/1912	160 lbs*		5/12S	7333	1924			9/1939
334	4/1890	2/1903	R24 rbt**			7334	1924			
		9/1912	160 lbs*		9/12S	8496	10/46	68496	2/49	5/1956

```
335  4/1890  12/1903 R24 rbt**          10/1912 160 lbs*                    7335  1924
                2/1917 180 lbs   11/35  10/12S 8497   3/46   68497  12/50   9/1960
336  4/1890   8/1951 J69/2              12/12S 7336   1924
                                               8498   3/46   68498   8/48   9/1962***
337  4/1890   7/1904 R24 rbt     12/27  12/27S 7337   1924
                                               8499   5/46   68499  10/48   9/1962
338  5/1890  12/1909 R24 rbt     10/28  10/28S 7338   1924
                                               8500  10/46   68500   3/51   1/1961.
339  5/1890  10/1904 R24 rbt
                8/1939 J67/2      8/24  10/26S 7339   1924
                6/1946 J69/1                   8501  12/46   68501  12/48   8/1960
340  5/1890  12/1903 R24 rbt**          10/29S 7340   1924
                                 10/29         8502  10/46   68502   5/50   2/1961
341  5/1890   9/1902 R24 rbt**          11/28S 7341   1924
                                  3/24         8503  11/46   68503  12/49   1/1957
342  5/1890   9/1902 R24 rbt**           8/27S 7342   1924
                                               8504  11/46   68504   5/52   1/1956
343  5/1890   8/1903 R24 rbt**           4/28S 7343   1924
                                               8505  11/46   68505   2/51  11/1953
344  5/1890  10/1913 R24 rbt      4/35   1932W 7334   1924                 10/1940***
345  5/1890   9/1903 R24 rbt**    2/30   2/30S 7345   1924
                                               8507  11/46   68507  12/48   6/1960
346  5/1890   1/1904 R24 rbt**    2/30   2/30S 7346   1924
                                               8508  11/46   68508   1/50   2/1961
```

*   Nos 327-36 were downgraded to shunting engines in 1912. No 327 was reboilered
      with an R24 boiler with small firebox but retaining large tanks. Nos 328/9/31-5
      retained the rebuilt boilers but with pressure reduced to 160 lbs/sq in. Nos
      328/35 had the pressure restored to 180 lbs/sq in in 2/1917, the latter with a new
      boiler and were classed as J69 by the LNER despite being shunting engines. The
      others except 7332 eventually had J67 boilers until rebuilt as above. Lever
      reverse substituted. Condenser tanks retained.
**   Nos 329/32/41/2 had the tanks widened by 5in subsequently (1180 gallons).
      Nos 334/5/40/3/5/6 had tanks widened by 4 in (1140 gallons).
***   No 68498 to service stock no 44 8/1959.
      No 7344 to War Department as no 88 (later 70088) 10/1940. Sold to Steel Breaking
      and Dismantling Co Ltd, Chesterfield 3/1947. Scrapped 1949. 1946, no 8506 was
      left blank in case the locomotive was returned. As 344, was in accident at
      Stratford Market 7/4/1905.

The following were built as shunting engines. Works nos 539-48 (order no A26).

No	Date	Rebuilt	LNE no 1924	no	date	BR no	Applied	Withdrawn
397	11/1890		7397	8509	9/46	68509	6/51	3/1954
398	11/1890	3/1950 J69/2	7398	8510	9/46	68510	3/50	9/1959
399	11/1890		7399	8511	9/46	68511	5/49	12/1956
400	11/1890	2/1951 J69/2	7400	8512	9/46	68512	2/51	4/1957
401	11/1890	6/1952 J69/2	7401	8513	10/46	68513	6/49	10/1960
402	11/1890		7402					5/1937
403	12/1890		7403	8514	10/46	68514	6/52	7/1955
404	12/1890		7404					5/1937
405	12/1890		7405	8515	11/46	68515	6/49	1/1957
406	12/1890		7406					7/1937

The following, also shunting engines had steel fireboxes THS 922.09 sq ft.
Works nos 549-58 (order no B26).

No	Date	Renumbered no date	Rebuilt	LNE no 1924	no	date	BR no	App- lied	With- drawn
407	12/1890	11 1/1920		7011	8516	1/47	68516	1/49	5/1957
408	12/1890	12 1/1920	2/1951 J69/2	7012	8517	1/47	68517	2/51	3/1956
			9/1953 J67/1						

409	12/1890	13 1/1920			7013	8518	9/46	68518	8/48	2/1958
410	1/1891	14 1/1920	4/1950	J69/2	7014	8519	11/46	68519	4/50	8/1958
411	1/1891	15 1/1920	2/1950	J69/2	7015	8520	8/46	68520	12/48	8/1959
412	1/1891	16 1/1920			7016	8521	11/46	68521	10/49	8/1956
413	1/1891	17 1/1920			7017					6/1937
414	1/1891	18 1/1920	3/1950	J69/2	7018	8522	12/46	68522	3/50	3/1961
415	1/1891	19 1/1920			7019	8523	9/46	68523	5/49	12/1955
416	1/1891	20 1/1920			7020					6/1937

The following were passenger engines THS 959.24 sq ft. Condensers fitted in 1893.
Works nos 652-61 (order no P29), 662-71 (order no R29).

No	Date	Rebuilt	V/E	CR	LNE nos no	date	BR no	App- lied	With- drawn
347	2/1892	1/1905 R24 rbt	7/24	8/28W	7347	1924			
					8524	10/46	68524	9/48	6/1959
348	2/1892	12/1903 R24 rbt*	12/27	12/27W	7348	1924			
					8525	1/47	(68525)		12/1953
349	3/1892	5/1904 R24 rbt	11/29	11/29S	7349	1924			
					8526	11/46	68526	10/48	10/1960
350	3/1892	12/1909 R24 rbt	3/29	3/29S	7350	1924			
					8527	12/46	68527	2/50	6/1958
351	3/1892	12/1903 R24 rbt*		12/28S	7351	1924			
					8528	8/46	68528	10/51	10/1959
352	3/1892	8/1906 R24 rbt							
		10/1938 J67/2			7352	1924			
		5/1954 J69/1		7/29S	8529	9/46	68529	3/48	8/1958
353	3/1892	1/1905 R24 rbt	8/35	11/28S	7353	1924			
					8530	12/46	68530	1/50	2/1961
354	3/1892	10/1903 R24 rbt*			7354	1924			
		10/1943 J67/2*	9/29	9/29S	8531	10/46	68531	6/49	10/1955
355	3/1892	5/1904 R24 rbt	7/24	1930W	7355	1924			
					8532	11/46	68532	11/50	8/1959**
356	3/1892	10/1911 R24 rbt	2/28	2/28W	7356	1924			
					8533	12/46	68533	5/49	7/1953
357	4/1892	11/1904 R24 rbt		4/28S	7357	1924			
					8534	9/46	68534	4/51	11/1954
358	4/1892	12/1904 R24 rbt		3/28S	7358	1924			
					8535	8/46	68535	10/48	8/1959
359	4/1892	6/1904 R24 rbt	12/29	12/29S	7359***	1924			
					8536	4/46	68536	6/49	2/1958
360	4/1892	10/1903 R24 rbt*							
		7/1940 J67/2			7360	1924			
		10/1945 J69/1		1/29S	8537	3/46	68537	4/48	6/1958
361	4/1892	9/1906 R24 rbt	7/24		7361	1924			
					8538	6/46	68538	10/49	9/1961
362	4/1892	3/1917 R24 rbt	4/35	5/30W	7362	1924			10/1940**
363	5/1892	11/1904 R24 rbt			7363	1924			
		1/1939 J67/2	9/29	9/29S	8540	5/46	68540	2/49	1/1956
364	5/1892	5/1919 R24 rbt			7364	1924			1/1931**
365	5/1892	11/1904 R24 rbt	2/24	10/24S	7365	1924			
					8541	9/46	68541	12/48	8/1958
366	5/1892	9/1905 R24 rbt							
		6/1939 J67/2			7366	1924			
		2/1945 J69/1		12/28S	8542	9/46	68542	11/48	9/1962

* Nos 348/51/4/60 had tanks widened by 4in (1140 gallons).
No 7354 was rebuilt J67/2 at Gorton. The date was officially recorded as 12/1944.
** No 68532 to service stock no 43 1/1959.

No 7362 to War Department no 89 (later 70089). Scrapped c1947. No 8539 kept blank
1943.
No 7364 was in an accident at Northumberland Park 7/1/1931.
*** No 7359 did not carry E suffix in 1923 being lettered 'L&NE 359'.

The following were passenger engines. THS 979.4 sq ft. From this date, condensers
were provided to all passenger engines as built. Works nos 783-92 (order no N33),
863-72 (order no F36), 873-82 (order no Y36).

No	Date	Rebuilt	V/E	CR	LNE nos no	date	BR no	App- lied	With- drawn
367	4/1894	7/1904 R24 rbt		8/29S	7367	1924			
					8543	5/46	68543	6/49	9/1962*
368	4/1894	10/1906 R24 rbt		6/28S	7368	1924			
					8544	10/46	68544	8/49	1/1955
369	4/1894	11/1904 R24 rbt	6/37	8/29S	7369	1924			
					8545	10/46	68545	11/48	2/1961
370	5/1894	12/1904 R24 rbt		10/28S	7370	1924			
					8546	9/46	68546	11/51	5/1958
371	5/1894	2/1907 R24 rbt			7371	1924			
		4/1944 J67/2**	6/24	12/26S	8547	9/46	68547	4/49	4/1956
372	5/1894	12/1904 R24 rbt	5/24		7372	1924			
					8548	4/46	68548	12/49	11/1953
373	5/1894	11/1906 R24 rbt	8/24		7373	1924			
					8549	5/46	68549	2/49	2/1962
374	6/1894	12/1904 R24 rbt		7/28S	7374	1924			
					8550	10/46	68550	5/50	7/1961
375	6/1894	11/1904 R24 rbt	1/28	1/28W	7375	1924			
					8551	9/46	68551	7/49	6/1957
376	6/1894	7/1906 R24 rbt	3/24	1939W	7376	1924			
					8552	10/46	68552	6/48	9/1961
377	10/1895	10/1906 R24 rbt							
		10/1938 J67/2			7377	1924			
		8/1946 J69/1	4/24	8/26S	8553	8/46	68553	10/49	12/1958
378	10/1895	7/1904 R24 rbt	10/36	3/29S	7378	1924			
					8554	11/46	68554	9/50	7/1961
379	10/1895	1/1904 R24 rbt		8/28S	7379	1924			
					8555	9/46	68555	11/50	5/1958
380	10/1895	7/1904 R24 rbt	1/30	1/30S	7380	1924			
					8556	3/46	68556	10/49	9/1962
381	10/1895	11/1907 R24 rbt	2/30	2/30S	7381	1924			
					8557	10/46	68557	12/48	10/1959
382	11/1895	2/1905 R24 rbt							
		7/1938 J67/2			7382	1924			
		8/1946 J69/1	4/24	9/26W	8558	8/46	68558	4/49	1/1961
383***		7/1904 R24 rbt	1/30	1/30S	7383	1924			
	11/1895				8559	8/46	68559	3/49	4/1956
384	11/1895	3/1908 R24 rbt**							
		7/1939 J67/2			7384	1924			
		11/1945 J69/1	12/29	12/29W	8560	9/46	68560	8/49	1/1961
385	11/1895	10/1907 R24 rbt	11/23	7/26S	7385	1924			
					8561	11/46	68561	4/50	7/1958
386	12/1895	2/1904 R24 rbt		11/27S	7386	1924			
					8562	5/46	68562	11/51	8/1956
387	12/1895	2/1906 R24 rbt	1/30	1/30S	7387	1924			
					8563	5/46	68563	2/49	10/1960
388	12/1895	12/1904 R24 rbt	4/24	4/32W	7388	1924			10/1940*
389	12/1895	9/1904 R24 rbt	3/30	3/30S	7389	1924			
					8565	7/46	68565	11/48	8/1962

```
390 12/1895   9/1905 R24 rbt   6/37     1/29S 7390 1924
                                               8566 10/46  68566 10/50   9/1962
391  1/1896   5/1913 R24 rbt   1/24    1932W  7391 1924
                                               8567 11/46  68567  6/48   8/1957
392  1/1896   9/1904 R24 rbt             9/27S 7392 1924
                                               8568  8/46  68568  4/56   5/1958
393  1/1896   8/1906 R24 rbt 12/29    12/29S  7393 1924
                                               8569 11/46  68569  1/49   6/1960
394  1/1896   8/1909 R24 rbt 10/26    10/26S  7394 1924
                                               8570  9/46  68570  2/50   9/1961
395  2/1896  11/1910 R24 rbt   2/30     2/30S 7395 1924
                                               8571  7/46  68571 12/49  12/1960
396  2/1896  10/1909 R24 rbt             7396 1924
                3/1938 J67/2    8/24   11/26S 8572  9/46  68572 12/48  11/1954
*    No 68543 to service stock no 45 11/1959.
     No 7388 to War Department no 84 (later 70084). Sold 5/1948 to John Lysaght Ltd,
     Scunthorpe No 27.  Scrapped 1/1958.  No 8564 kept blank.
**   No 7371 was rebuilt J67/2 at Gorton.  The date was officially recorded as 12/1944.
     No 384 had front section of coupling rod removed for working the Kelvedon branch.
*** No 383 was in an accident at Temple Mills 19/8/1901.
```

The following passenger engines had steel fireboxes THS 922.09 sq ft.
Works nos 883-92 (order no C37).

```
                                        LNE nos          App-   With-
No  Date    Rebuilt          V/E   CR    no   date    BR no lied   drawn
265  4/1896 12/1908 R24 rbt  11/29 11/29S 7265 1924
                                               8573  5/46  68573 10/48   8/1960
266  4/1896 12/1907 R24 rbt   8/24       7266 1924
                                               8574 10/46  68574  7/51   1/1959
267  4/1896  5/1912 R24 rbt   8/24       7267 1924
                                               8575  7/46  68575  6/51  10/1960
268  4/1896 12/1910 R24 rbt   1/29       7268 1924
                                               8576  3/46  68576  9/49   3/1958
269  5/1896  2/1912 R24 rbt   4/29       7269 1924
                                               8577  1/46  68577  3/49  11/1960
270  5/1896  4/1910 R24 rbt   7/29  by    7270 1924
                                  1947W         8578  5/46  68578  7/49   1/1961
271  5/1896 11/1908 R24 rbt   3/29*      7271 1924
                                  5/44W         8579 12/46  68579  1/52   1/1960
272  6/1896  2/1908 R24 rbt  10/39*      7272 1924                      10/1940**
273  6/1896  1/1908 R24 rbt  10/29  ***  7273 1924
                                               8581  3/46  68581 10/48   9/1959
274  6/1896  3/1908 R24 rbt  10/39* ***  7274 1924                      10/1940**
*    No 7271 had vacuum ejector removed 1/1940.  Refitted 6/1940.
     No 7272 had vacuum ejector removed 4/1940.
     No 7274 had vacuum ejector removed 5/1940.
**   Nos 7272/4 to War Department nos 79 and 78 respectively (later 70079 & 70078).
     Sold to Metal Industries Ltd, Faslane (70078 becoming their no 3).  70079 was
     later sold to G Wimpey & Co Ltd.  Both were scrapped in 1955.  Nos 8580/2 kept
     blank.
*** Condensers on nos 273 & 274 were removed by the GE.  273 had steam brake
     substituted for Westinghouse in 10/1929.  274 retained Westinghouse brake.
```

The following were shunting engines with telescopic type boiler barrels. THS 979.4 sq
ft, WP 160 lbs/sq in. Works nos 987-96 (order no H45), 1038-47 (order no G47).

```
                          LNE no  Renumbered
No  Date    Rebuilt       1924     no    date    BR no  Applied  Withdrawn
255  3/1899               7255                              5/1937
256  3/1899               7256   8583  12/46  68583   5/49   4/1958
```

No	Date	Rebuilt	Works no	LNE no	date	BR no	date	Withdrawn
257	3/1899		7257	8584	7/46	68584	3/49	8/1955
258	3/1899	9/1947 J69/2	7258	8585	1/46	68585	3/49	6/1958
259	3/1899		7259					5/1937
260	3/1899		7260	8586	3/46	68586	7/50	5/1956
261	4/1899	6/1946 J69/2	7261	8587	1/46	68587	8/49	10/1959
262	4/1899	6/1953 J69/2	7262	8588	3/46	68588	12/50	5/1958
263*	4/1899		7263	8589	3/46	68589	3/49	1/1956
264	4/1899		7264	8590	3/46	68590	10/48	9/1955
199	12/1899		7199					7/1937
200	12/1899		7200	8606**	9/46	68606	7/48	3/1955
201	12/1899		7201					7/1937
202	12/1899		7202					7/1937
203	12/1899	11/1948 J69/2	7203	8591	9/46	68591	11/48	1/1960
204	12/1899		7204	8592	4/46	68592	3/49	7/1955
205	12/1899		7205					5/1937
206	12/1899		7206	8593	9/46	68593	11/50	1/1958
207	1/1900		7207	8594	9/46	68594	11/48	11/1955
208	1/1900		7208	8595	5/46	68595	11/48	1/1957

* No 263 was in an accident at Bethnall Green 29/8/1899.
** 1946 no out of sequence in error.

The following were passenger engines with the same dimensions as above batch of shunting engines. Works nos 1078-87 (order no S48), 1108-17 (order no R50).

No	Date	Rebuilt	V/E	CR	LNE no	date	BR no	Applied	Withdrawn
189	6/1900								
Renumbered					7305	1924			
305	1/1909	9/1910 R24 rbt	1/30	1/30S	8596	9/46	68596	5/49	11/1959
190	7/1900	8/1913 R24 rbt			7190	1924			
		3/1939 J67/2	12/35	*	8597	4/46	68597	8/49	10/1955
191	7/1900	4/1913 R24 rbt	9/27	*	7191	1924			
					8598	4/46	68598	6/48	5/1957
192	7/1900	12/1911 R24 rbt			7192	1924			
		7/1939 J67/2							
		10/1944 J69/1		11/29W	8599	4/46	68599	9/49	11/1959
193	7/1900	7/1914 R24 rbt			7193	1924			
		9/1938 J67/2							
		1/1945 J69/1	2/42	7/36W	8600	4/46	68600	11/48	9/1962
194	7/1900	4/1915 R24 rbt	2/24	8/26S	7194	1924			
					8601	9/46	68601	12/50	10/1959
195	7/1900	10/1913 R24 rbt	3/30	3/30S	7195	1924			
					8602	5/46	68602	5/48	10/1959
196	8/1900	12/1916 R24 rbt	2/24	3/30W*	7196	1924			
					8603	9/46	68603	7/48	3/1958
197	8/1900	3/1912 R24 rbt	9/24**	3/31W	7197	1924			10/1940***
198	8/1900	10/1916 R24 rbt	4/37	10/28S	7198	1924			
					8605	9/46	68605	10/48	7/1958
160	6/1901	4/1913 R24 rbt	6/33	after 7/40W	7160	1924			
					8607	9/46	68607	12/48	5/1958
161	6/1901		12/39	*	7161	1924			
					8608	9/46	68608	10/49	10/1958
162	6/1901	8/1915 R24 rbt			7162	1924			
		9/1938 J67/2							
		6/1952 J69/1	5/35	*	8609	10/46	68609	11/48	9/1962
163	6/1901	12/1921 R24 rbt			7163	1924			
		4/1940 J67/2	11/26	11/26S	8610	9/46	68610	4/51	1/1957
164	6/1901		7/36	7/36W	7164	1924			
					8611	9/46	68611	8/48	7/1955
165	7/1901	5/1912 R24 rbt	5/24	4/31W*	7165	1924			
					8612	9/46	68612	7/49	6/1961

```
166  7/1901  5/1911 R24 rbt 10/39        7166 1924
                                         8613  9/46 68613  5/48  9/1961
167  7/1901  7/1910 R24 rbt  1/35**      7167 1924              10/1940***
168  8/1901  4/1912 R24 rbt  3/24** 4/40W 7168 1924             10/1940***
169  8/1901              10/39  7/36W    7169 1924
                                         8616  9/46 68616 11/49 11/1958
```

*   Nos 190/1 and 161/2 had condensers removed by GE. No 190 steam brake substituted in 12/1927. 191 and 161/2 retained Westinghouse brake. No 7196 had condenser refitted after 3/1942 and no 7165 after 7/1940.
** No 7197 had vacuum ejector removed in 4/1940, 7167 in 10/1939 and 7168 in 4/1940.
*** Nos 7197 and 7167/8 to War Department 81, 90 & 82 respectively (later 70081/90/82). 70081/2 sold to British Industrial Solvents Ltd, Margam nos 1 & 2 in 12/1947. No 1 (ex-7197) scrapped in 1953, no 2 (ex-7168) scrapped 9/1955. No 70090 sold to Metal Industries, Faslane, later no 3 in 1946, scrapped in 1962 (ex-7167). Nos 8604/14/15 kept blank.

0-6-0T Built by GER at Stratford. Works nos 1233-42 (order no S56), 1243-52 (order no P57).
DW 4ft 0in; Cyls 16½ x 22; THS 988.17 sq ft; WP 180 lbs/sq in; Wt 42 tons 9 cwt. Other dimensions as class R24 rebuilt.
Class S56 Built with 180 lbs boilers as fitted to rebuilds of R24 class, all were passenger engines with Westinghouse brakes and condensers. Tank capacity was increased to 1200 gallons and tank and cab sides were flush. THS 996.17 sq ft from 1908. LNE class J69 (J69/1 from 12/1952). Abbreviations as for R24 class above.

No	Date	Rebuilt	V/E	CR	LNE no	date	BR no	Applied	Withdrawn
51	5/1904		5/40	12/27S	7051	1924			
					8617	12/46	68617	12/49	7/1958
52	5/1904			12/27S	7052	1924			
					8618	9/46	68618	11/48	8/1958
53	5/1904		1/35	1/35W*	7053	1924			
					8619	1/47	68619*	6/53	10/1961
54	5/1904		5/24**	9/30W	7054	1924			10/1940**
55	5/1904		8/37	*	7055	1924			
					8621	1/47	68621	10/48	9/1962
56	6/1904			*	7056	1924			10/1940**
57	6/1904			10/28S	7057	1924			
					8623	7/46	68623	4/51	2/1961
58	6/1904		11/36**	11/36W	7058	1924			10/1940**
59	6/1904		8/32	1948W	7059	1924			
					8625	9/46	68625	2/50	1/1959
60	6/1904		6/40	12/27W	7060	1924			
					8626	10/46	68626	1/50	5/1962
81	8/1904		12/33**	12/36W	7081	1924			10/1940**
82	8/1904	8/1938 J67/2	9/32	9/35W	7082	1924			
					8628	9/46	68628	9/50	2/1958
83	8/1904		3/29		7083	1924			
					8629	6/46	68629	10/49	11/1959
84	8/1904		11/28		7084	1924			
					8630	1/47	68630	7/49	1/1959
85	8/1904		11/28	*	7085	1924			
					8631	1/47	68631	11/48	7/1958
86	9/1904	1/1940 J67/2							
		3/1944 J69/1		12/27S	7086	1924			
		at Gorton. Official			8632	9/46	68632	7/51	5/1958
		date 2/1945							
87	9/1904		10/39		7087	1924			
					8633	4/46	68633	1/49	11/1960***
88	9/1904		11/31**	4/34W	7088	1924			10/1940**

89	9/1904	12/25	4/28W	7089	1924
				8635	9/46 68635 7/48 9/1962
90	9/1904		9/24	3/30W	7090 1924***
				8636	9/46 68636 11/50 1/1959

* No 7053 had condensers refitted 8/1940. Carried BR 'E' prefix 1948.
    No 55 had condensers removed by GE. Steam brake was substituted in 4/1933.
    No 56 had condensers removed by GE.
    No 85 had condensers removed by GE and refitted in 11/1923.
** No 7054 had vacuum ejector removed in 10/1939. To War Department no 86 (later
    70086). Sold to Metal Industries Ltd, Faslane no 1. Scrapped 6/1954.
    No 7056 to War Department no 87 (later 70087). Sold 1946 to Metal Industries Ltd,
    Faslane no 2. Scrapped 6/1954.
    No 7058 had vacuum ejector removed in 4/1940. To War Department no 83 (later
    70083). Sold 1946 to Metal Industries Ltd, Faslane no 3. Scrapped 6/1954.
    No 7081 had vacuum ejector removed in 5/1940. To War Department no 80 (later no

    70080). Sold 2/1948 to John Lysaght Ltd, Scunthorpe no 25. Scrapped 1958/9.
    No 7088 had vacuum ejector removed in 10/1939. To War Department no 91 (later
    70091). Sold 5/1948 to John Lysaght Ltd, Scunthorpe no 26. Scrapped 10/1960.
*** No 87 is preserved at the National Railway Museum at York.
    No 7090 was in an accident at Liverpool Street 9/5/1925.

0-6-0T Built by GER at Stratford. Works nos 419-28 (order no E22), 723-32 (order no
B32).
DW 4ft 0in; WB 6ft 4in + 7ft 0in; Cyls 14 x 22; Blr 4ft 2in x 9ft 1in;
THS 922.09 sq ft (1889), 930.09 sq ft (no 159 and 1893 batch) except as below; WP 140
lbs/sq in; Wt 36 tons 16 cwt (1889), 36 tons 11 cwt (1893).
Class E22 Smaller version of class T18 for light duties with smaller cylinders and
shorter frames, all fitted with Westinghouse brake for passenger working and screw
reverse. Replacement boilers from 1899 were 979.4 sq ft, and from 1908, telescopic
type boilers replaced the original butt-jointed type with THS 987.4 sq ft and working
pressure was raised to 160 lbs/sq in.
he 1889 batch held 600 gallons of water and, despite being 5 cwt lighter, the 1893
locos had a capacity of 650 gallons. No 159 and the 1893 batch had steel fireboxes
with THS as above, no 158 also had a steel firebox with THS 978.4 sq ft, and nos
157/250/1/3 had boilers with steel fireboxes fitted later as below. Macallan variable
blast pipes removed by the LNER about 1924. NE pattern chimneys were fitted from
about 1930. LNE class J65. Some ran for a time with front connecting rod removed as
2-4-0s.

No	Date	Vacuum ejector	LNE no 1923	LNE no 1924	Renumbered no	date	BR no	Applied	Withdrawn
150	2/1889	10/25	150E	7150					6/1937
151	2/1889	10/31	151E	7151					7/1937
152	2/1889		152E	7152					10/1935
153	2/1889		153E	7153					9/1931
154	2/1889		154E	7154					4/1932
155	2/1889		155E	7155	8211	10/46	68211	3/51	11/1953
156	3/1889	10/31	156E	7156					8/1937
157*	3/1889		157E	7157	8212	9/46			11/1947
158	3/1899		158E	7158					3/1932
159	6/1889		159E	7159					5/1937
245	2/1893		245E	7245					1/1931
246	2/1893		246E	7246					12/1930
247	2/1893		247E	7247	8213	4/46			2/1948
248	3/1893	11/25	248E	7248					5/1936
249	3/1893		249E	7249					7/1937
250	3/1893	9/25	250E	7250	8214	6/46	68214	8/51	10/1956
251*	3/1893	9/25	251E	7251					12/1931
252	3/1893	10/25	252E	7252					8/1935

```
253*  4/1893           253E    7253    8215 11/46 (68215)        5/1949
254   4/1893   9/24    254E    7254                              6/1937
```
* Nos 157 and 250 had boilers with steel fireboxes THS 978.4 sq ft in 1918, no 251 in
  1920 and no 253 after 1920.

0-6-0T ('tram') Built by GER at Stratford. Works and order nos below.
DW 3ft 1in; WB 3ft 4in + 3ft 4in; Cyls 12 x 15 o/s; Blr 2ft 10½ in x 6ft 10in; THS
348.08 sq ft; WP 180 lbs/sq in; Wt 27 tons 1 cwt.
Class C53 Designed for Wisbech and Upwell tramway, and also used on Yarmouth fish
dock, they largely supplanted the earlier 0-4-0 'tram' engines (see page 50). With
outside Walschaerts valve gear and Westinghouse brake, these locos were remarkably
powerful for their size. All-over wooden cover and side sheeting over motion, with
'cow catchers' and safety chains at the ends to satisfy legal requirements as with
0-4-0 engines. Screw reverse.
LNE class J70.

No	Date	o/no	Works nos	LNE no 1923	LNE no 1924	Renumbered no	date	BR no	Applied	Withdrawn
135	10/1903	C53	1158	135E	7135	8216	5/46	68216	2/49	11/1953
136	11/1903	C53	1159	136E	7136	8217	5/46	68217	9/49	3/1953
137	9/1908	C64	1383	137E	7137	8218	5/46	(68218)		9/1949
138	9/1908	C64	1384	138E	7138					1/1942
139	10/1908	C64	1385	139E	7139	8219	4/46	68219	11/50	8/1953
130	4/1910	I67	1448	130E	7130	8220	9/46	68220	6/50	2/1953
127	6/1914	P75	1570	127E	7127	8221	5/46	68221	8/48	5/1951
128	6/1914	P75	1571	128E	7128	8222	9/46	68222	3/49	1/1955
131	6/1914	P75	1572	131E	7131	8223	9/46	68223	8/49	7/1955
125	3/1921	D85	1640	125E	7125	8224	10/46	68224	3/50	3/1952
126	3/1921	D85	1641	126E	7126	8225	5/46	68225	5/50	3/1955
129	3/1921	D85	1642	129E	7129	8226	5/46	68226	5/48	8/1955

0-10-0WT Built by GER at Stratford. Works no 1200 (order no A55).
DW 4ft 6in; WB 4ft 11in + 4ft 11in+ 4ft 11in + 4ft 11in; Cyls (3) 18½ x 24 (2 o/s);
Blr 5ft 10in x 15ft 6¼ in (5ft 3in x 15ft 10⁷/8 in mean inside diameter x distance
between tube plates); THS 3013 sq ft; WP 200 lbs/sq in; Wt 78¼ tons.
Holden's answer to the problem of increasing train capacity on the Enfield line where
existing engines were hauling trains of 200 tons at maximum speeds, between the
sixteen stations on the 10½ mile line, of 20 mph. It was also seen as an alternative
to electrification, which the GE claimed they could not afford in the face of two
proposed tube railways into GE territory (see introduction). The locomotive was
designed to haul 300-ton trains at maximum speeds of 30 mph which speed was to be
reached in 30 seconds from starting.
The result was one of the most remarkable locomotives built in the UK which quickly
became known as the 'Decapod'. The enormous boiler, in four sections with dome
between the second and third rings and 8in chimney, was pitched at 9ft from rail
level, and the total height was 12ft 11in. The boiler was thus about twice the size
of the average express engine, and with the three large cylinders and high pressure a
tractive effort of some 16 tons (by Pambour's formula) could be obtained. All three
cylinders were horizontal, the outside connecting rods driving the third pair of
wheels, and the inside cylinder was connected to the second axle with a massive
connecting rod machined out of solid steel. The leading axle was cranked and revolved
inside a fork in the inside connecting rod. The firebox was of the 'Wooten' type
spread over the frames and contained three grates and ashpans, two smaller ones at the
sides complimenting the main one, and giving a firebox area of 131.2 sq ft and a grate
area of 42 sq ft, which could itself hold a ton of coal in addition to 2 tons in the
bunker. Water capacity was 1300 gallons.
Two steam chests were provided, one supplying the left-hand cylinder and the other the
two other cylinders. The smokebox had two lower doors for ash removal. Compressed
air sanding could be applied when the regulator was opened with one movement of the
driver's hand. This system was the same as that already used by Holden and did not

affect the supply of air to the brakes. The cranks were set at 120° thus the coupling rods were not at 90° which caused difficulty in calculating stresses so that coupling rods were made over strong to be on the safe side, being machined out of solid steel forgings that did nothing to lessen the weight. The whole of the reciprocating weights were balanced instead of the customary two thirds. The third pair of wheels were flangeless and there was about an inch of side play (½in each way) in the trailing wheels. The coupling rods were fitted with ball and socket joints to assist in rounding curves. There were six 3½in Ramsbottom safety valves, four on the boiler and two over the firebox.

The locomotive cost £5000 and was much praised by the technical press who predicted that many more would be built. Before this could have happened a considerable amount of money would have had to be spent on bridge strengthening to permit such heavy locomotives to operate. Whilst Holden and Frederick Vernon Russell his locomotive designer responded to the technical challenge in a thoroughly competent manner, the motives of the Board are more suspect. Did they really evaluate the cost of line improvements against the cost of electrification or did they first see the exercise as a means of defeating the opposition? Certainly in the event, the latter would seem more likely as once the threat of competition had been removed, nothing further happened. The 'Decapod' did little work, despite having been proved capable in tests of everything required of it. In 1906 Holden carried out a very extensive rebuild retaining only the two outside cylinders and some of the wheels as a rather ungainly 0-8-0 tender locomotive with 4ft 9in diameter boiler, Belpaire firebox and standard double window side cab. As such it was sent to March to work freight traffic but did not prove to be very much more efficient than the existing 0-6-0s, and lasted only a further seven years.

No   Date
20 12/1902
        1906 Rebuilt 0-8-0 Cyls (2) 18½ x 24; Blr 4ft 9in x 12ft 11¾in (between tube
             plates); THS 1869 sq ft; WP 180 lbs/sq in; WB 7ft 6in + 8ft 9in +
             7ft 0in; Wt 54 tons 6¾ cwt; 3500 gallon tender.
     6/1913 Scrapped. Tender to no 8578 4-6-0 (built 1928) after accident 16/1/1931
             until 12/1952 then to 4-6-0s 61556 (5/1955) & 61535 (12/1957) until
             scrapped 12/1959.

SD Holden Locomotives 1909-20

2-4-2T Built by GER at Stratford. Works nos 1416/7 (order no Y65), 1428-37 (order no A67).
DW 4ft 10in; LW & TW 3ft 6in; WB 6ft 3in + 7ft 0in + 6ft 3in; Cyls 15 x 22;
Blr 3ft 11½in x 9ft 1in; THS 872.9 sq ft; WP 160 lbs/sq in; Wt 45 tons 14 cwt.
Class Y65 Intended to replace E22 class 0-6-0Ts on light branch work, but in fact, the six-coupled tanks were preferred. Their large cabs got them the nickname 'Crystal Palace tanks' or, when nos 8301/8/10 were transferred to Scotland, 'Tomato Houses'. All had Westinghouse brake. Steam brake and vacuum ejector substituted on the above three sent to Scotland. Six fitted for push/pull operation by compressed air system as below. LNE class F7.

No	Date	Steam brake	Push pull	LNE no 1923	LNE no 1924	Renumbered no	date	Allotted BR no	Withdrawn
1300	6/1909			1300E	8300				8/1938
1301	7/1909	4/33		1301E	8301	7593	10/42		4/1943
1302	11/1909			1302E	8302				5/1931
1303	11/1909		1/21	1303E	8303				4/1939
1304	11/1909		11/15	1304E	8304	7594	12/42		3/1944
1305	11/1909		2/21	1305E*	8305	7595	10/42		4/1943
1306	12/1909			1306E	8306				4/1931
1307	12/1909		12/24**	1307E	8307	7596	10/42		6/1943
1308	12/1909	5/32		1308E	8308	7597	10/42		
						7093	8/46	(67093)	11/1948
1309	12/1909		5/20	1309E	8309				1/1931
1310	1/1910	9/32		1310E	8310	7598	10/42		

                                      7094 11/46   (67094)   11/1948
1311 1/1910   10/14   1311E   8311   9/1931
* No 1305E was in an accident at Palace Gates on 22/11/1923.
** Vacuum ejector additionally fitted to 8307.

2-4-2T Built by GER at Stratford. Works nos 1479-88 (order no G69), 1489-98 (order no
A71).
DW 5ft 4in; LW & TW 3ft 9in; WB 7ft 6in + 8ft 0in + 7ft 6in; Cyls 17½ x 24; Blr 4ft
2in x 10ft 2½in; THS 1114.7 sq ft; WP 180 lbs/sq in; Wt 56 tons 9 cwt.
Class G69 Final development of radial tank used extensively on London suburban
services. Thus all had condensers in addition to Westinghouse brake. Condensers
removed at dates below (C/R) Vacuum ejectors (V/E below) fitted additionally by the
LNER. High arched roof was replaced by an elliptical one $7^5/8$in lower (both being of
wood as was Stratford practice) about 1924, and from 1930, steel roofs of similar
shape to the previous one were provided as with other tank engines. Steam heating
apparatus fitted 1921/2. NE type taper chimneys fitted from 1930. LNE class F6.

No	Date	V/E	C/R	LNE no 1923	LNE no 1924	Renumbered no	date	BR no	Applied	Withdrawn
61	4/1911	9/27	1/37	61E	7061	7220	12/46	67220	7/51	7/1955
62	4/1911	9/27	1/37	62E	7062	7221	10/46	67221	12/49	10/1957
63	4/1911	10/27	4/38	63E	7063	7222	12/46	67222	10/48	8/1955
64	5/1911	9/27	9/36	64E	7064	7223	9/46	67223	5/48	12/1955
65	5/1911	9/27	6/37	65E	7065	7224	7/46	67224	6/50	11/1956
66	5/1911	9/27	10/37	66E	7066	7225	12/46	67225	4/49	5/1956
67	5/1911	10/27	4/37	67E	7067	7226	12/46	67226	4/50	11/1955
68	5/1911	10/27	2/38	68E	7068	7227	10/46	67227	9/48	5/1958
69	6/1911	10/27	6/36	69E	7069	7228	12/46	67228	5/50	4/1958
70	6/1911	2/29	9/36	70E	7070	7229	9/46	67229	1/49	3/1958
1	10/1911	10/27	8/36	1E	7001	7230	12/46	67230	11/49	5/1958
2	10/1911	9/27	8/37	2E	7002	7231	10/46	67231	11/49	3/1958
3	11/1911	9/27	9/37	3E	7003	7232	12/46	67232	6/49	11/1955
4	11/1911	9/27	11/36	4E	7004	7233	12/46	67233	10/50	12/1955
5	11/1911	9/27	10/36	5E	7005	7234	9/46	67234	1/49	8/1956
6	12/1911	9/27	6/37	6E	7006	7235	10/46	67235	6/49	1/1956
7	12/1911	9/27	2/37	7E	7007	7236	5/46	67236	12/49	8/1955
8	1/1912	10/27	4/37	8E	7008	7237	5/46	67237	3/48	8/1955
9	1/1912	10/27	12/36	9E	7009	7238	5/46	67238	1/51	11/1955
10	1/1912	9/27	7/37	10E	7010	7239	5/46	67239	8/50	12/1955

4-6-0 Built by GER at Stratford. Works nos below.
              William Beardmore & Co Ltd. Works nos below.
DW 6ft 6in; LW 3ft 3in; WB 6ft 6in + 8ft 0in +7ft 0in + 7ft 0in;
Cyls 20 x 28; Blr 5ft $1^1/8$in x 12ft 6in; THS 1632 sq ft + 286 sq ft superheater (later
201.6 sq ft); WP 180 lbs/sq in; Wt 63 tons.
Class S69 Design of this compact and highly adaptable class was mainly, if not
purely, the work of Stratford Works drawing office under its Chief Draughtsman, ES
Tiddeman. As such it was essentially an enlarged 'Claud' with the same decorative
valance, extended of course to cover the six-coupled wheels. Axle weights were kept
within the limits necessary to ensure a wide route availability and overall length to
permit use of the many fifty-foot turntables still in use. DW size was 6in smaller
than the 4-4-0 'Clauds'. They were thus rather on the small size for 4-6-0s but this
did not detract from their usefulness. Nos 1500-12 and 1515-35 were built with
Schmidt superheaters. Nos 1513/14 were fitted experimentally with Robinson
superheaters, which were adopted as standard from 1536 on. Nos 1500-40 had Stone's
variable blast pipes (nos 1500-4 fitted subsequently to building dates) but these were
removed by the LNER between 1925 an 1929. Air operated reverse gear and water scoops
were fitted. 3700 gallon tenders. THS was later 1609.1 sq ft + 201.6 sq ft

superheater. The LNE fitted vacuum ejectors in addition to the Westinghouse brakes, making them dual fitted, and several carried ACFI feed water heaters for a period. Some were also fitted with Lentz valve gear for a while. The LNE classification was B12 and in the 1930s when weight restrictions on the GE section had been eased, 43 were rebuilt from 1932, with Gresley round-top boilers in place of the original Belpaire firebox type 5ft 6in x 12ft 7½in; THS 1559 sq ft + 315 sq ft superheater; Wt 69½ tons, with screw reverse and without decorative valance. These rebuilds were classed as B12/3. The classification B12/2 had already been given to ten more B12s built in 1928 not listed here. A number of the B12s had however been transferred to Scotland by this time, and this rebuild would not have been appropriate for them so from 1943, nine were rebuilt with round-top boilers of the same dimensions as before THS 1498.1 sq ft + 201.6 sq ft superheater, Wt 64 tons 19 cwt, as B12/4. By coincidence the 1946 LNE numbers were the same as the GE ones. E suffix added to GE nos 9/1923-2/1924.

The following were built at Stratford, works nos 1499-1503 (order no S69), 1504-6, 1537-43 (order no A73), 1555-9 (order no E75), 1573-82 (order no R75), 1787-92 (order no M77), 1603-7 (order no B78). From no 1504, 1½in side play was allowed in the trailing axle box in a manner similar to that adopted in the 'Decapod'. Working pressure of nos 1522/3 was initially only 170 lbs/sq in. No 1535 was a replacement for no 1506 lost in the Colchester accident as below. Later batches came out in the wartime grey livery from 1915. V/E = vacuum ejector fitted; Sc = transferred to Scotland;
ACFI = ACFI feed water heater fitted for period indicated; v/g = valve gear

No	Date	V/E	Sc	Rebuilt	LNE nos no	date	BR no	App-lied	With-drawn
1500	12/1911	7/28	1/32	ACFI 12/31-c/40	8500	1924			
				10/1947 **B12/4**	1500	6/46	(61500)		6/1948
1501	2/1912	7/28	7/31	ACFI 7/31 - c41	8501	1924			
					1501	9/46	61501	6/48	5/1953
1502	2/1912	1/29	4/31		8502	1924			
					1502	8/46	61502	6/48	4/1954
1503	3/1912	4/28	4/31	ACFI 4/31-11/37	8503	1924			
					1503	9/46	61503	4/48	5/1951
1504	5/1912	8/28	6/31	ACFI 4/31-after	8504	1924			
				5/42 3/1945 **B12/4**	1504	10/46	61504	5/48	6/1950
1505	2/1913	5/28	3/39	ACFI 12/27-c39	8505	1924			
				11/1944 **B12/4**	1505	9/46	61505	4/49	3/1952
1506	2/1913								1913*
1507	3/1913	5/24	5/40	ACFI 6/32-after	8507	1924			
				8/41 3/1944 **B12/4**	1507	11/46	61507	1/49	2/1953
1508	3/1913	7/24	7/40	ACFI 10/31-after	8508	1924			
				8/41 7/1943 **B12/4**	1508	6/46	61508	10/48	4/1953
1509	4/1913	6/28		ACFI 2/32-4/35**	8509	1924			
				4/1935 **B12/3**	1509	9/46	(61509)		10/1948
1510	4/1913	8/28		ACFI 6/31-12/37	8510	1924			
				12/1937 **B12/3**	1510	9/46	(61510)		6/1949
1511	5/1913	5/24	3/42	ACFI 11/31-6/41	8511	1924			
				8/1946 **B12/4**	1511	8/46	61511	5/48	5/1952
1512	6/1913	7/28		ACFI 12/32-10/37	8512	1924			
				10/37 **B12/3**	7426	1/43			
					1512	10/46	61512	11/48	1/1957
1513	6/1913	8/25	6/40	ACFI 10/31-9/41	8513	1924			
					1513	8/46	61513	3/48	2/1953
1514	6/1913	3/29		ACFI 11/32-2/38	8514	1924			
				2/1938 **B12/3**	1514	10/46	61514	7/48	10/1959
1515	11/1913	11/28		ACFI 5/32-7/38	8515	1924			
				7/1938 **B12/3**	1515	10/46	61515	3/49	11/1951

```
1516 11/1913  6/28       Lentz v/g 12/26-
                         11/32            8516  1924
                         11/1932 B12/3    1516  1/47   61516   4/49   7/1958
1517 11/1913  7/28       ACFI 12/27-2/34  8517  1924
                         2/1934 B12/3     1517  11/46  (61517)        10/1948
1518 12/1913  9/27       Lentz v/g 6/29-6/32
                         ACFI 6/32-5/35   8519  1924
                         5/1935 B12/3     1519  11/46  61519   5/49   12/1957
1520  4/1914  8/25       ACFI 4/32-1/40   8520  1924
                         1/1940 B12/3     1520  7/46   61520   9/48   6/1957
1521  4/1914 12/28  2/42 ACFI 12/31-c41   8521  1924
                                          1521  10/46  61521  10/48   7/1952
1522  4/1914  5/28       ACFI 3/33-2/37   8522  1924
                         2/1937 B12/3     1522  11/46                 8/1947
1523  5/1914  5/28       ACFI 12/27-9/35  8523  1924
                         9/1935 B12/3     7437  11/42
                                          1523  8/46   61523   4/48   3/1955
1524  5/1914  7/24  4/33 ACFI 6/31-6/41** 8524  1924
                         9/1946 B12/4     1524  9/46   61524   7/48   11/1953
1525  6/1914  3/27       Lentz v/g 9/28-
                         1/34             8525  1924
                         1/1934 B12/3     1525  1/47   61525   7/49   8/1951
1526  6/1914  6/28  3/37 ACFI 2/32-after
                         11/42            8526  1924
                         1/1948 B12/4     1526  11/46  61526   2/49   10/1951
1527  8/1914  4/27       ACFI 1/32-1/35   8527  1924
                         1/1935 B12/3     1527  12/46                 9/1947
1528  8/1914  3/28  5/33 ACFI 4/33-c39    8528  1924
                                          1528  8/46   61528  11/48   7/1953
1529  9/1914  2/29  7/39 ACFI 11/31-c40   8529  1924
                                          1529  8/46   61529   4/48   2/1950
1530 11/1914 11/28       ACFI 4/32-5/38   8530  1924
                         5/1938 B12/3     1531  9/46                  11/1947
1532 12/1914  7/24  8/40 Lentz v/g 4/30-
                         5/32 ACFI 5/32-
                         after 8/41       8532  1924
                         2/1948 B12/4     1532  8/46   61532   5/49   7/1953
1533 12/1914  5/24       Lentz v/g 9/29-
                         2/33             8533  1924
                         10/1937 B12/3    1533  12/46  61533   4/48   11/1959
1534  2/1915  7/28       ACFI 8/32-7/41   8534*** 1924               6/1945
1535  3/1915  7/24       ACFI 5/32-10/35  8535  1924
                                          1535  6/46   61535  12/48   12/1959
1536  5/1915  7/25  4/33 ACFI 6/31 until  1536  3/46   61536   7/48   12/1949
1537  7/1915  7/28       ACFI 9/32-4/39   8537  1924
                         4/1939 B12/3     1537  3/46   61537   6/48   4/1957
1538  7/1915  3/28       ACFI 12/32-6/37  8538  1924
                         6/1937 B12/3     1538  5/46   61538   8/49   1/1957
1539  6/1917  8/25  6/33 ACFI 3/32- after 8539  1924
                         11/40            1539  8/46   61539   9/48   11/1954
1540  7/1917  6/28       Lentz v/g 7/29-6/32
                         ACFI 6/32-10/34  8540  1924
                         10/1934 B12/3    1540  5/46   61540   8/48   10/1957
```

*   Scrapped after accident at Colchester 12/7/1913. Tender to 1530-5 batch
     (order M77)
** No 8509 also fitted with Worthington Simpson feedwater heater 2/1926-5/1929.
     No 1524 fitted for oil fuel briefly in 6/1921.
*** No 1530 carried BR 'E' prefix 1948
     No 8534 originally lettered LNE 1534.

The following were built by William Beardmore & Co Ltd (works nos below), order no
W82. Abbreviations as above.

No	Date	Works no	V/E	Rebuilt	LNE nos no	LNE nos date	BR no	Applied	Withdrawn
1541	6/1920	135	5/28	5/1936 **B12/3**	8541	1924			
					1541	6/46	61541	2/49	1/1957
1542	7/1920	136	4/29	ACFI 2/32-2/35	8542	1924			
				2/1935 **B12/3**	1542	9/46	61542	8/49	7/1958
1543	7/1920	137	5/28	ACFI 7/32 until	8543*	1924			
				after 12/41	1543	5/46	61543	11/48	6/1953
1544	7/1920	138	7/25	ACFI 7/32-2/35	8544	1924			
				2/1935 **B12/3**	1544	9/46			9/1947
1545	8/1920	139	2/28	11/1936 **B12/3**	8545	1924			
					1545	10/46	61545	9/50	1/1957
1546	9/1920	140	3/27	ACFI 2/32-2/38	8546	1924			
				2/1938 **B12/3**	1546	9/46	61546	3/49	5/1959
1547	9/1920	141	7/27	7/1937 **B12/3**	8547	1924			
					1547	9/46	61547	9/48	10/1958
1548	5/1921	143	7/27	ACFI 10/31 until	8548*	1924			
				unknown date.	1548	12/46			12/1946
1549	6/1921	144	4/28	ACFI 7/32-7/41	8549	1924			
				1/1944 **B12/3**	1549	5/46	61549	12/48	1/1959
1550	10/1920	142	5/28	5/1936 **B12/3**	8550	1924			
					1550	10/46	61550	7/48	1/1957
1551	10/1920	145	7/24	ACFI 3/34 until	8551*	1924			
				unknown date	1551	9/46			1/1947
1552	12/1920	146	1/24	ACFI 4/34 until	8552*	1924			
				unknown date	1552	10/46	61552	10/48	7/1952
1553	12/1920	147	8/27	ACFI 6/32-5/37	8553	1924			
				5/1937 **B12/3**	1553	9/46			
					7467	11/42	61553	11/49	8/1958
1554	1/1921	148	6/24	ACFI 8/32-11/35	8554	1924			
				11/1935 **B12/3**	1554	10/46	61554	1/49	9/1958
1555	1/1921	149	3/27	10/1935 **B12/3**	8555	1924			
					1555	9/46	61555	9/49	10/1957
1556	2/1921	150	3/29	ACFI 1/32-5/35	8556	1924			
				5/1935 **B12/3**	7470	11/42			
					1556	11/46	61556	11/48	12/1957
1557	2/1921	151	4/27	12/1934 **B12/3**	8557	1924			
					1557	10/46	61557	1/50	1/1957
1558	2/1921	152	6/24	11/1935 **B12/3**	8558	1924			
					7472	1/43			
					1558	10/46	61558	6/48	4/1959
1559	2/1921	153	5/28	5/1936 **B12/3**	8559	1924			
					1559	7/46	61559	8/48	9/1951
1560	4/1921	154	5/28	ACFI 11/32-c41	8560*	1924			
					1560	9/46	61560	10/48	5/1952

* Transferred to Scotland as under:
  8543 1/1939; 8548 6/1933; 8551 6/1939; 8552 7/1939; 8560 3/1939.

The following were built at Stratford. Works nos 1630-9 (order no H82).

No	Date	V/E	Rebuilt	LNE nos no	LNE nos date	BR no	Applied	Withdrawn
1561	3/1920	3/24	4/1937 **B12/3**	8561	1924			
				1561	10/46	61561	1/49	9/1958
1562	4/1920	2/29	4/1938 **B12/3**	8562	1924			
				7476	12/42			
				1562	7/46	61562	8/48	8/1955

1563	4/1920	6/24	ACFI 9/32-c40	8563*	1924			
				1563	5/46	61563	4/48	4/1953
1564	4/1920	9/27	ACFI 11/32-7/35	8564	1924			
			7/1935 **B12/3**	1564	10/46	61564	1/49	11/1958
1565	5/1920	5/28	2/1937 **B12/3**	8565**	1924			
				7479	12/42			
				1565	9/46	61565	3/49	1/1957
1566	5/1920	5/28	5/1936 **B12/3**	8566	1924			
				1566	10/46	61566	4/48	1/1959
1567	5/1920	4/24	ACFI 4/32-4/35	8567	1924			
			4/1935 **B12/3**	1567	10/46	61567	2/50	11/1958
1568	6/1920	4/24	ACFI 10/31-4/41	8568	1924			
				7482	10/42			
				1568	9/46	61568	10/48	8/1959
1569	6/1920	12/28	ACFI 5/32-12/33	8569	1924			
			12/1933 **B12/3**	1569	11/46	61569	5/49	1/1957
1570	6/1920	3/29	ACFI 4/32-6/41	8570	1924			
			11/1943 **B12/3**	1570	6/46	61570	4/48	3/1958

* No 8563 was transfered to Scotland in 6/1939.
** No 8565 was in an accident at Brentwood 18/7/1926.

Ten more of this class, with some modifications, were built by the LNER in 1928, nos 8571-80.

Hill Locomotives 1912-23

0-6-0 Built by GER at Stratford. Works nos 1524-33 (order no E72).
DW 4ft 11in; WB 8ft 10in + 8ft 10in; Cyls 20 x 28; Blr 4ft 9in x 11ft 9in;
THS 1275.1 sq ft + 226 sq ft superheater; WP 160 lbs/sq in; Wt 47 tons 8 cwt.
Class E72 Development of class G58 with Schmidt superheaters with long front overhang
caused by the use of tail rods for the pistons.
LNE class J18 as built, but three rebuilt as J19 (GE class T77 below) and all rebuilt
with 5ft 1^1/8in diameter round-top boilers in place of the original Belpaire pattern
as were class T77 (details below). Steam brakes were provided but vacuum ejectors
were added when rebuilt with the larger boilers as LNE class J19/2. Nos 8241/7 fitted
with Robinson superheater 5/1929 and 8249 in 4/1929.

		Rebuilt		LNE no	LNE no	Renumbered		App-	With-
No	Date	J19	J19/2	1923	1924	no	date	BR no	lied	drawn
1240	11/1912	7/1935	1/1938	1240E	8240	4640	12/46	64640	6/48	1/1959
1241	11/1912		10/1936	1241E	8241	4641	12/46	64641	6/48	1/1960
1242	11/1912		1/1936	1242E	8242	4642	10/46	64642	8/51	3/1960
1243	11/1912		4/1935	1243E	8243	4643	12/46	64643	8/48	11/1961
1244	11/1912		2/1935	1244E	8244	4644	6/46	64644	4/50	7/1959
1245	11/1912		5/1935	1245E	8245	4645	3/46	64645	12/49	12/1958
1246	11/1912	11/1935	1/1938	1246E	8246	4646	2/46	64646	10/48	10/1961
1247	12/1912		2/1936	1247E	8247	4647	4/46	64647	6/48	3/1960
1248	12/1912		1/1936*	1248E	8248	4648	4/46	64648	8/50	8/1959
1249	1/1913	5/1935	4/1937	1249E	8249	4649	11/46	64649	7/48	1/1959

* No 8248 had cylinder diameter reduced to 19½in from 11/1942.

0-6-0 built by GER at Stratford. Works nos 1593-1602 (order no T77); 1608-12 (order no
H80); 1613-7 (order no X80); 1618-22 (order no A81).
DW 4ft 11in; WB 8ft 10in + 8ft 10in; Cyls 20 x 28; Blr 4ft 9in x 11ft 9in; THS 1275.1
sq ft + 226 sq ft superheater (1916), 154.8 sq ft (5/1918); WP 160 lbs/sq in;
Wt 47 tons 8 cwt.

Class T77 As class E72, but with Robinson superheater instead of Schmidt and without tail rods reducing the front overhang by 1ft 6½in. Classified J19 by LNE until October 1934, when no 8146 was rebuilt with larger round-top boiler 5ft 1¹/₈in x 11ft 9in; THS 1429.4 sq ft + 204.4 sq ft (superheater with twin anti-vacuum valves as fitted by GE) and 302.5 sq ft (superheater fitted with Gresley single anti-vacuum valves). All were subsequently rebuilt with this boiler, together with class E72 above, and became J19/2 (Wt 50 tons 7 cwt) the others becoming J19/1 until rebuilt. The rebuilt Gresley boiler was the same as that used for the rebuilt 'Clauds' (LNE diagram 28A). A new cab with steel rather than wood was provided on class J19/2, and the working pressure increased to a nominal 170 lbs/sq in, although they were operated at 180 lbs on the 'Clauds', and reduced to 160 lbs in 1945/6. Five locomotives had cylinders altered to either 19 in or 19½ in diameter for a period as detailed below. From 1947 (all having been rebuilt by 1939) the classification reverted to J19 again. All had vacuum ejectors when built.

| | | Rebuilt | LNE no | LNE no | Renumbered | | | | |
No	Date	J19/2	1923	1924	no	date	BR no	Applied	Withdrawn
1140	8/1916	2/1937	1140E	8140	4650	3/46	64650	5/51	10/1960
1141	8/1916	4/1937	1141E	8141	4651	5/46	64651	5/49	1/1959
1142	8/1916	6/1937	1142E	8142	4652	3/46	64652	7/48	1/1961
1143	9/1916	2/1935	1143E	8143	4653	5/46	64653	1/49	1/1961
1144	10/1916	6/1937	1144E	8144	4654	8/46	64654	3/49	10/1960
1145	11/1916	1/1936*	1145E	8145	4655	12/46	64655	5/49	8/1961
1146	11/1916	10/1934	1146E	8146	4656	10/46	64656	3/49	5/1960
1147	11/1916	1/1938	1147E	8147	4657	12/46	64657	5/48	9/1962
1148	12/1916	4/1938	1148E	8148	4658	12/46	64658	8/48	11/1959
1149	1/1917	10/1935*	1149E	8149	4659	10/46	64659	1/50	4/1960
1260	12/1917	4/1937	1260E	8260	4660	12/46	64660	12/50	8/1960
1261	12/1917	7/1936	1261E	8261	4661	9/46	64661	2/49	8/1959
1262	1/1918	9/1935*	1262E	8262	4662	4/46	64662	5/48	1/1959
1263	3/1918	10/1935	1263E	8263	4663	11/46	64663	4/49	10/1960
1264	9/1918	2/1939	1264E	8264	4664	11/46	64664	12/50	9/1962
1265	11/1918	8/1938	1265E	8265	4665	11/46	64665	3/49	12/1959
1266	11/1918	8/1936	1266E	8266	4666	11/46	64666	11/48	1/1961
1267	12/1918	11/1938	1267E	8267	4667	11/46	64667	9/48	9/1961
1268	1/1919	10/1935	1268E	8268	4668	10/46	64668	1/49	12/1959
1269	3/1919	11/1936*	1269E**	8269	4669	10/46	64669	7/48	9/1961
1250	9/1920	3/1938	1250E	8250	4670	12/46	64670	3/49	11/1959
1251	10/1920	1/1939	1251E	8251	4671	6/46	64671	3/49	2/1962
1252	10/1920	11/1935*	1252E	8252	4672	4/46	64672	9/50	1/1959
1253	10/1920	10/1936	1253E	8253	4673	4/46	64673	1/49	8/1962
1254	11/1920	8/1936	1254E	8254	4674	6/46	64674	12/50	1/1961

* The following had cylinder diameter reduced as under:
   No 8145 19½in from 7/1935-8/1939.
       8149 19in from 10/1935-7/1944
       8252 19in from 11/1935-9/1950
       8262 19in from 1/1938-2/1944
       8269 19in from 11/1936-1/1942
** No 1269 did not carry 'E' suffix being lettered 'LNE 1269'.

0-6-0 Built by GER at Stratford. Works nos 1623-7 (order no D81); 1653-62 (order no M87); 1663-72 (order no Y87).
DW 4ft 11in; WB 8ft 10in + 10ft 0in; Cyls 20 x 28; Blr 5ft 1¹/₈in x 12ft 6in; THS 1632.6 sq ft (later 1609.1 sq ft) + 201.6 sq ft superheater; WP 180 lbs/sq in; Wt 54 tons 15 cwt.
Class D81 Boiler, cylinders, valve gear etc as S69 4-6-0. Rebuilt with Gresley round-top boiler in place of the original Belpaire firebox type. THS 1498.1 sq ft + 201.6 sq ft superheater; Wt 54 tons. Robinson superheaters, vacuum ejectors. LNE class J20, J20/1 as rebuilt.

No	Date	Rebuilt J20/1	LNE no 1923	LNE no 1924	Renumbered no	date	BR no	Applied	Withdrawn
1270	4/1920	10/1947	1270E	8270	4675	6/46	64675	11/50	12/1959
1271	12/1920	1/1956	1271E	8271	4676	12/46	64676	8/49	9/1961
1272	12/1920	9/1947	1272E	8272	4677	12/46	64677	5/51	9/1961
1273	12/1920	1/1944	1273E	8273	4678	12/46	64678	4/48	9/1960
1274	12/1920	1/1945	1274E	8274	4679	12/46	64679	6/48	1/1961
1275	9/1922	5/1947	1275E	8275	4680	10/46	64680	5/50	1/1961
1276	9/1922	2/1945	1276E	8276	4681	12/46	64681	12/50	11/1960
1277	9/1922	8/1947	1277E	8277	4682	11/46	64682	6/50	9/1960
1278	9/1922	5/1951	1278E	8278	4683	12/46	64683	4/50	11/1959
1279	9/1922	7/1944	1279E	8279	4684	12/46	64684	10/49	6/1960
1280	10/1922	5/1944	1280E	8280	4685	2/46	64685	11/49	10/1960
1281	10/1922	7/1944	1281E	8281	4685	1/46	64686	10/50	8/1960
1282	10/1922	3/1953	1282E	8282	4687	2/46	64687	2/51	9/1962
1283	11/1922	12/1943	1283E	8283	4688	2/46	64688	6/51	1/1959
1284	11/1922	7/1951	1284E	8284	4689	2/46	64689	5/49	1/1961
1285	12/1922	9/1949	1285E	8285	4690	2/46	64690	9/49	9/1962
1286	12/1922	12/1944	1286E	8286	4691	5/46	64691	8/48	9/1962
1287	12/1922	12/1949	1287E	8287	4692	5/46	64692	12/49	9/1961
1288	12/1922	9/1947	1288E	8288	4693	2/46	64693	4/51	8/1960
1289	12/1922	9/1947	1289E	8289	4694	2/46	64694	11/50	1/1960
1290	12/1922	11/1944	1290E	8290	4695	2/46	64695	11/50	1/1960
1291	12/1922	9/1953	1291E	8291	4696	2/46	64696	12/50	4/1962
1292	12/1922*	10/1943	1292E	8292	4697	1/46	64697	1/49	9/1961
1293	12/1922*	2/1955	1293E	8293	4698	5/46	64698	10/48	3/1961
1294	12/1922*	11/1943	1294E	8294	4699	5/46	64699	4/49	9/1962

* To traffic 1/1923.

0-4-0T Built by GER at Stratford. Works nos 1554 (order no B74); 1583/4 (order no
B77); 1628/9 (order no A82).
DW 3ft 10in; WB 6ft 0in; Cyls 17 x 20; Blr 4ft 2in x 9ft 1in; THS 980.5 sq ft;
WP 180 lbs/sq in; Wt 38 tons 1 cwt.
Class B74 Belpaire firebox. No bunker. LNE class Y4.

No	Date	LNE no 1923	LNE no 1924	Renumbered no	date	BR no	Applied	Withdrawn
227	7/1913*	227E	7227	8125	6/46	68125	11/49	9/1955
226	9/1914	226E	7226	8127	4/46	68127	5/49	4/1956
228	10/1914	228E	7228	8126	6/46	68126	6/49	10/1957
210	1/1921	210E	7210	8129	5/46	68129	10/48	12/1963**
229	1/1921	229E	7229	8128	6/46	68128	12/49	10/1956

* To stock 11/1913.
** No 68129 to service stock no 33 1952.

0-6-0T Built by GER at Stratford. Works nos below.
DW 4ft 0in; WB 6ft 4in + 7ft 6in; Cyls 16½ x 22; Blr 4ft 2in x 9ft 1in; THS 996.17 sq
ft; WP 180 lbs/sq in; Wt 42 tons 9 cwt.
Class C72 Based on S56 class of 1904 (J Holden) with 1200 gallon tanks.
A high arched roof cab with side windows was provided with square instead of round
front and rear spectacles. Parallel sided chimneys with rims instead of tapered
'stovepipe' type. As with the S56 class they were divided between passenger and
shunting engines as below. LNE class J68.

The following were passenger engines and were provided with screw reverse and
condensers. Nos 7042/3/5/8/9/50 had lever reverse substituted by the LNER.
Works nos 1514-23 (order no C72). V/E = vacuum ejector added.
CR = condenser removed. Macallan variable blast pipe removed by LNE.

No	Date	V/E	C/R	LNE no 1923	LNE no 1924	Renumbered no	date	BR no	Applied	Withdrawn
41	6/1912	2/24*			41E	7041				10/1940*
42	6/1912	3/24	3/37		42E	7042	8638	1/47	68638	9/50 2/1959
43	6/1912	5/23			43E	7043	8639	1/47	68639	9/49 4/1959
44	7/1912	4/24	8/37		44E	7044	8640	9/46	68640	2/49 4/1959
45	7/1912	1/24	11/37		45E	7045	8641	9/46	68641	9/48 11/1959
46	8/1912	4/23	8/37		46E	7046	8642	5/46	68642	2/50 9/1961
47	8/1912	3/29	1919		47E	7047**	8643	9/46	68643	10/48 11/1959
48	9/1912	9/24	3/37***		48E	7048	8644	11/46	68644	12/49 11/1960
49	9/1912	5/29	6/36		49E	7049	8645	12/46	68645	7/51 11/1959
50	9/1912	11/28	7/38		50E	7050	8646	1/47	68646	4/49 9/1961

* No 7041 had vacuum ejector removed in 10/1939 and was transferred to War Department on withdrawal no 85 (later 70085). Sold 1946 to Metal Industries Ltd, Faslane. Scrapped 1952.

** No 7047 was rebuilt with 160 lbs boiler and reclassified as J67/2 in 9/1939but, of course, retaining J68 cab. It was rebuilt back to J68 in 7/1945.

*** No 7048 had condensing equipment refitted in 6/1940.

The following were shunting engines with lever reverse and no condensers. Works nos 1560-9 (order no G75).

No	Date	Vacuum ejector	LNE no 1923	LNE no 1924	Renumbered no	date	BR no	Applied	Withdrawn
21	12/1913	9/37	21E	7021	8647	12/46	68647	4/50	12/1960
22	12/1913	1/37	22E	7022	8648	9/46	68648	6/48	8/1959
23	12/1913	2/24	23E	7023	8649	12/46	68649	6/50	9/1961
24	12/1913	5/40	24E	7024	8650	12/46	68650	8/51	10/1960
25	12/1913	7/23	25E	7025	8651	9/46	68651	3/50	5/1958
26	12/1913	3/35	26E	7026	8652	1/47	68652	6/49	9/1959
27	12/1913	7/36	27E	7027	8653	1/47	68653	12/49	7/1958
28	1/1914	3/35	28E	7028	8654	1/47	68654	10/51	3/1960
29	1/1914		29E	7029	8655	8/46	68655	1/49	11/1959
30	2/1914	4/35	30E	7030	8656	10/46	68656	4/49	4/1960

The following, also shunting engines, had elliptical roofs. Works nos 1683-92 (order no I89).

No	Date	Vacuum ejector	LNE no 1924	Renumbered no	date	BR no	Applied	Withdrawn
31E	10/1923	8/37	7031	8657	9/46	68657	2/50	8/1958
32E	10/1923		7032	8658	9/46	68658	4/51	4/1959
33E	10/1923		7033	8659	9/46	68659	10/50	8/1958
34E	10/1923	9/36	7034	8660	9/46	68660	3/49	12/1960
35E	10/1923	6/36	7035	8661	9/46	68661	12/49	12/1959
36E	11/1923	5/40	7036	8662	1/47	68662	4/48	8/1958
37E	11/1923	2/37	7037	8663	1/47	68663	1/49	10/1960
38E	11/1923	5/35	7038	8664	1/47	68664	4/52	9/1958
39E	11/1923	8/36	7039	8665	1/47	68665	3/51	12/1959
40E	11/1923	8/37	7040	8666	1/47	68666	4/48	8/1958

0-6-2T Built by GER at Stratford. Works nos 1585/6 (order no L77); 1643-52 (order no K85).

DW 4ft 10in; TW 3ft 9in; WB 7ft 6in + 8ft 9in + 6ft 9in; Cyls 18 x 24; Blr 4ft 9in x 9ft 7in; THS 1394.2 sq ft; WP 180 lbs/sq in; Wt 61 tons 12 cwt.

Class L77 The GE was late in adopting this wheel arrangement, surprisingly so in view of the heavy suburban traffic which it handled into Liverpool Street - a Holden design for an 0-6-2T in 1907 having been shelved. Consequently, full development of the design was carried out by the LNER after the grouping. The full advantages of superheating had not been realised at this time, so that although no 1001 was provided with a Robinson superheater with 12 elements (THS 1189.3 sq ft + 102.4 sq ft superheater) the others were saturated. They had inside Walschaerts valve gear with 9-inch piston valves and cut-outs at the cab entrance together with a single side window at the front of the cab.

Nos 1001/2 (1915) differed from the 1921 locomotives in that the cut-out extended some 8 or 9 inches into a high-arched roof, whereas the later ones had flatter roofs the cut-out stopping at the roof edge. All had the, by now, standard GE Belpaire firebox design of boiler. The 1921 locomotives also had the dome 9 inches further forward on the 2-ring telescopic boiler barrel. All were provided with Westinghouse brakes and condensers. Built up chimneys were provided with a brass rim. Although the later locomotives built by the LNER from 1923 all had vacuum ejectors, the GE locomotives below were never fitted with them. The LNE did however fit them with 18-element superheaters with a heating surface of 134.2 sq ft. Stones variable blast pipes, fitted when built, were removed by the LNE, and condensers were also removed as below.

LNE class N7. When Gresley adopted the design, with modifications as standard in 1925 (see summary below), the new locomotives became N7/1 and the GE design N7/GE. Two further variations extended the Gresley part numbers to N7/2 and N7/3. From 1940 the GE locos were rebuilt with round-top boilers (THS 938.1 sq ft + 134.2 sq ft superheater) and reclassified N7/4.

CR - condenser removed. E suffix 9/1923-2/1924.

No	Date	super-heated	CR	Rebuilt N7/4	LNE no 1924	Renumbered no	date	BR no	App-lied	With-drawn
1000*	1/1915	12/1929	11/36	7/1943	8000	7978	8/44			
						9600	12/46	69600	9/50	2/1959
1001	2/1915	as				7979	8/44			
		built	10/36	11/1944	8001	9601	10/46	69601	10/48	5/1958
1002	7/1921	5/1929	1/37	6/1949	8002	7980	8/44			
						9602	10/46	69602	6/49	7/1959
1003	7/1921	2/1929	3/37	7/1940	8003	7981	8/44			
						9603	11/46	69603	5/49	7/1959
1004	9/1921	3/1929	6/37	3/1941	8004	7982	8/44			
						9604	12/46	69604	3/48	8/1959
1005	9/1921	7/1929	9/36	4/1942	8005	7983	8/44			
						9605	6/46	69605	8/48	10/1958
1006	9/1921	9/1931	12/36	3/1942	8006	7984	8/44			
						9606	8/46	69606	6/49	8/1958
1007	10/1921	9/1930	9/37	9/1941	8007	7985	8/44			
						9607	5/46	69607	9/48	7/1958
1008	10/1921	5/1929	11/37	3/1942	8008	7986	8/44			
						9608	9/46	69608	7/48	8/1958
1009	10/1921	6/1928	5/37	8/1948	8009	7987	8/44			
						9609	12/46	69609	8/48	4/1958
1010	11/1921	10/1929	2/37	10/1943	8010	7988	8/44			
						9610	12/46	69610	8/50	1/1959
1011	11/1921	11/1929	12/36	4/1940	8011	7989	8/44			
						9611	1/47	69611	10/48	11/1960

* Only no 1000 had blue livery.

10 more were built by the LNE to the GE design in 1923/4 nos 7990-9 (N7/GE) and these were the last locomotives built at Stratford works.

When the design was adopted with modifications as an LNE standard class 50 more were built in 1925-7 (N7/1 Belpaire firebox, short travel valves), 30 in 1927-8 (N7/2 Belpaire firebox, long travel valves) and 32 in 1927-28 (N7/3 round top boiler, long travel valves).

4-4-0 Built by LNE at Stratford. Works nos 1673-82 (order no H88).

DW 7ft 0in; LW 3ft 9in; WB 6ft 6in + 8ft 0in + 9ft 0in; Cyls 19 x 26; Blr 5ft 1$\frac{1}{8}$in x 11ft 9in; THS 1507.9 sq ft + 180.5 sq ft superheater; WP 180 lbs/sq in; Wt 54 tons 18 cwt.

Hill's development of Holden's *Clauds* (class S46 and D56) with larger diameter superheated boiler which would have been class H88, but construction was completed by the LNE when they became D16. They have always popularly been referred to as 'Super Clauds'. They had the same decorative valances as the Holden locos, and 1785-9 had dual braking systems, Westinghouse and vacuum ejector. The LNE fitted nos 1780-4 with vacuum ejectors in addition to Westinghouse as below. Nos 1783/7 were Royal train engines. All were finished in LNE green livery with the E suffix after the number. From 12/27, the original design became D16/1 when extended smokeboxes were fitted which became D16/2. They were eventually rebuilt with Gresley round-top boiler in place of the original Belpaire firebox type, and then had THS 1429 sq ft + 302.5 sq ft superheater, and were designated D16/3. The decorative valances were retained except on no 8783*.

V/E = vacuum ejector fitted.

No	Date	V/E	Rebuilt D16/2	D16/3	LNE no 1924	Renumbered no	date	BR no	Applied	Withdrawn
1780E	6/1923	11/28	11/1928	9/1944	8780	2611	12/46	62611	12/48	1/1957
1781E	6/1923	8/28	8/1928	4/1949	8781	2612	11/46	62612	4/49	11/1959
1782E	6/1923	6/27	5/1931	12/1948	8782	2613	11/46	62613	12/48	10/1960
1783E	7/1923	3/27	6/1928	12/1939	8783	2614	11/46	62614	11/49	8/1958*
1784E	7/1923	6/27	6/1929	4/1947	8784	2615	11/46	62615	3/49	10/1958
1785E	7/1923	as new	6/1928	5/1944	8785	2616	11/46	62616	11/48	2/1953
1786E	8/1923	as new	6/1929	1/1945	8786	7656	11/42			
						8786	8/44			
						2617	11/46	62617	9/48	5/1957
1787E*	8/1923	as new	1/1929	8/1944	8787	2618	11/46	62618	10/49	11/1959
1788E	9/1923	as new	12/1928	12/1948	8788	2619	11/46	62619	10/50	10/1957
1789E	9/1923	as new	12/1928	3/1948	8789	2620	10/46	62620	11/49	10/1955

* No 8783 was in an accident at Hilgay on 1/6/1939. Nos 1783/7E had been Royal train engines fitted with brass capped chimneys which 8783 retained until the accident. When rebuilt as D16/3 the decorative valances were removed.

Simplex petrol tractor built by Motor Rail & Tram Co. Works no 1931.
3ft 1in wheels; WB 5ft 6in; 40 hp; Wt 8 tons approx.
Purchased in 1919, not included in GE stock. Used for shunting in Brentwood goods yard in place of a horse named *Peggy* and this name bestowed on the tractor. Transferred to engineer's yard at Lowestoft in 1925. LNE class Z6. Reclassified Y11 12/1943.

Date	Name	
12/1919	*Peggy*	To LNE running stock 9/1925. Cab added about 1925.
7/1930		Numbered 8430.
6/1946		Renumbered 8188 (BR no 68188 not applied).
5/1949		Renumbered 15098. Withdrawn 9/1956

Narrow gauge Simplex tractor built by Motor Rail & Tram Co.
2ft 11¾in gauge; 17¾in wheels; Wt 4 tons.
Date
5/1920 Still in use 1958.

GREAT EASTERN RAILWAY

NUMBER INDEX (for Eastern Counties number index, see page 29)

No	Date	
1	1862	Blank
	1867	2-4-0 1 class (L7)
	1911	2-4-2T class G69
2	1862	Blank
	1867	2-4-0 1 class (L7)
	1903	Blank
	1911	2-4-2T class G69
3	1862	Blank
	1867	2-4-0 1 class (L7)
	1905	Blank
	1911	2-4-2T class G69
4	1862	ex-E Counties
	1875	Blank
	1878	2-4-0 ex-10
	1906	Blank
	1911	2-4-2T class G69
5	1862	ex-E Counties
	1872	2-4-0 1 class (L7)
	1902	Blank
	1911	2-4-2T class G69
6	1862	ex-E Counties
	1872	2-4-0 1 class (L7)
	1905	Blank
	1911	2-4-2T class G69
7	1862	ex-E Counties
	1875	Blank
	1877	0-4-2T class K9
	1908	Blank
	1911	2-4-2T class G69
8	1862	ex-E Counties
	1878	0-4-2T class K9
	1904	Blank
	1912	2-4-2T class G69
9	1862	ex-E Counties
	1875	Blank
	1877	0-4-2T class K9
	1904	Blank
	1912	2-4-2T class G69
10	1862	ex-E Counties
	1872	2-4-0 1 class (L7)
	1878	0-4-2T class K9
	1898	4-2-2 class P43
	1909	Blank
	1912	2-4-2T class G69
11	1862	ex-E Counties
	1872	Blank
	1874	0-4-2T class T7
	1894	Blank
	1898	4-2-2 class P43
	1909	Blank
	1920	0-6-0T ex-407

No	Date	
12	1862	ex-E Counties
	1874	0-4-2T class T7
	1893	Blank
	1894	4-2-2 class P43
	1911	Blank
	1920	0-6-0T ex-408
13	1862	ex-E Counties
	1872	Blank
	1873	0-4-2T class T7
	1892	Blank
	1898	4-2-2 class P43
	1911	Blank
	1920	0-6-0T ex-409
14	1862	ex-E Counties
	1872	Blank
	1873	0-4-2T class T7
	1895	Blank
	1898	4-2-2 class P43
	1908	Blank
	1920	0-6-0T ex-410
15	1862	ex-E Counties
	1872	Blank
	1875	0-4-2T class T7
	1895	Blank
	1898	4-2-2 class P43
	1909	Blank
	1920	0-6-0T ex-411
16	1862	ex-E Counties
	1872	Blank
	1875	0-4-2T class T7
	1894	Blank
	1898	4-2-2 class P43
	1909	Blank
	1920	0-6-0T ex-412
17	1862	ex-E Counties
	1875	0-4-2T class T7
	1894	Blank
	1898	4-2-2 class P43
	1909	Blank
	1920	0-6-0T ex-413
18	1862	ex-E Counties
	1871	Blank
	1875	0-4-2T class T7
	1892	Blank
	1898	4-2-2 class P43
	1908	Blank
	1920	0-6-0T ex-414
19	1862	ex-E Counties
	1872	Blank
	1875	0-4-2T class T7
	1895	Blank
	1898	4-2-2 class P43
	1910	Blank
	1920	0-6-0T ex-415

20	1862	ex-E Counties
	1872	Blank
	1877	0-4-2T class K9
	1902	0-10-0WT
	1914	Blank
	1920	0-6-0T ex-416
21	1862	ex-E Counties
	1872	Blank
	1877	0-4-2T class K9
	1905	Blank
	1913	0-6-0T class C72
22	1862	ex-E Counties
	1878	0-4-2T class K9
	1904	Blank
	1913	0-6-0T class C72
23	1862	ex-E Counties
	1872	Blank
	1877	0-4-2T class K9
	1906	Blank
	1913	0-6-0T class C72
24	1862	ex-E Counties
	1874	Blank
	1877	0-4-2T class K9
	1906	Blank
	1913	0-6-0T class C72
25	1862	ex-E Counties
	1872	Blank
	1877	0-4-2T class K9
	1906	Blank
	1913	0-6-0T class C72
26	1862	Blank
	1867	2-4-0 1 class (L7)
	1898	0-4-2T ex-10
	1905	Blank
	1913	0-6-0 class C72
27	1862	ex-E Counties
	1879	Blank
	1884	2-4-0 ex-119
	1913	0-6-0T class C72
28	1862	Blank
	1868	2-4-0 1 class (L7)
	1914	0-6-0T class C72
29	1862	Blank
	1868	2-4-0 1 class (L7)
	1903	Blank
	1914	0-6-0T class C72
30	1862	Blank
	1863	ex-Waveney Valley
	1882	Blank
	1898	2-4-0 ex-26
	1914	0-6-0T class C72
31	1862	ex-E Counties
	1870	2-4-0 1 class (L7)
	1903	Blank
32	1862	ex-E Counties
	1867	Blank
	1868	2-4-0 1 class (L7)
	1902	Blank

33	1862	ex-E Counties
	1869	2-4-0 1 class (L7)
	1915	Blank
34	1862	ex-E Counties
	1869	2-4-0 1 class (L7)
	1904	Blank
35	1862	ex-E Counties
	1867	Blank
	1868	2-4-0 1 class (L7)
	1904	Blank
36	1862	ex-E Counties
	1869	2-4-0 1 class (L7)
	1902	Blank
37	1862	ex-E Counties
	1879	Blank
	1884	0-6-0 class Y14 (Worsdell)
38	1862	ex-E Counties
	1880	Blank
	1884	0-6-0 class Y14 (Worsdell)
39	1862	ex-E Counties
	1881	Blank
	1884	0-6-0 class Y14 (Worsdell)
40	1862	ex-E Counties
	1880	Blank
	1884	0-6-0 class Y14 (Worsdell)
41	1862	ex-E Counties
	1883	Blank
	1884	0-6-0 class Y14 (Worsdell)
	1912	0-6-0T class C72
42	1862	ex-E Counties
	1869	2-4-0 1 class (L7)
	1909	Blank
	1912	0-6-0T class C72
43	1862	Blank
	1868	2-4-0 1 class (L7)
	1911	Blank
	1912	0-6-0T class C72
44	1862	Blank
	1868	2-4-0 1 class (L7)
	1905	Blank
	1912	0-6-0T class C72
45	1862	ex-E Counties
	1869	2-4-0 1 class (L7)
	1902	Blank
	1912	0-6-0T class C72
46	1862	Blank
-47	1868	2-4-0 1 class (L7)
	1904	Blank
	1912	0-6-0T class C72
48	1862	Blank
	1869	2-4-0 1 class (L7)
	1912	0-6-0T class C72
49	1862	Blank
	1869	2-4-0 1 class (L7)
	1904	Blank
	1912	0-6-0T class C72

50	1862	ex-E Counties
	1869	2-4-0 1 class (L7)
	1912	0-6-0T class C72
51	1862	Blank
-57	1864	2-2-2 class W
	1879	0-4-4T class E10
	1879	0-4-4T class E10
	1904	0-6-0T class S56
58	1862	Blank
-60	1864	2-2-2 class W
	1880	0-4-4T class E10
	1904	0-6-0T class S56
61	1862	ex-E Counties
-62	1875	0-4-4T 61 class
	1907	Blank
	1911	2-4-2T class G69
63	1862	ex-E Counties
	1875	0-4-4T 61 class
	1908	Blank
	1911	2-4-2T class G69
64	1862	ex-E Counties
	1874	Blank
	1875	0-4-4T 61 class
	1908	Blank
	1911	2-4-2T class G69
65	1862	ex-E Counties
-66	1875	0-4-4T 61 class
	1911	2-4-2T class G69
67	1862	ex-E Counties
	1875	0-4-4T 61 class
	1907	Blank
	1911	2-4-2T class G69
	1875	0-4-4T 61 class
	1907	Blank
	1911	2-4-2T class G69
68	1862	ex-E Counties
-69	1875	0-4-4T 61 class
	1908	Blank
	1911	2-4-2T class G69
70	1862	ex-E Counties
	1869	Blank
	1875	0-4-4T 61 class
	1910	Blank
	1911	2-4-2T class G69
71	1862	ex-E Counties
	1875	0-4-4T 61 class
	1909	2-4-2T class M15 (Holden)
72	1862	ex-E Counties
	1875	0-4-4T 61 class
	1908	Blank
	1909	2-4-2T class M15 (Holden)
73	1862	ex-E Counties
	1870	2-2-2 no 73
	1875	0-4-4T 61 class
	1909	2-4-2T class M15 (Holden)
74	1862	Blank
	1870	2-2-2 no 74
	1875	0-4-4T 61 class
	1909	2-4-2T class M15 (Holden)

75	1862	ex-E Counties
	1875	0-4-4T 61 class
	1909	2-4-2T class M15 (Holden)
76	1862	ex-E Counties
	1869	Blank
	1876	0-4-4T 61 class
	1908	Blank
	1909	2-4-2T class M15 (Holden)
77	1862	ex-E Counties
	1872	Blank
	1876	0-4-4T 61 class
	1908	Blank
	1909	2-4-2T class M15 (Holden)
78	1862	ex-E Counties
	1876	0-4-4T 61 class
	1908	Blank
	1909	2-4-2T class M15 (Holden)
79	1862	ex-E Counties
	1877	0-4-4T 61 class
	1908	Blank
	1909	2-4-2T class M15 (Holden)
80	1862	ex-E Counties
	1877	0-4-4T 61 class
	1907	Blank
	1909	2-4-2T class M15 (Holden)
81	1862	ex-E Counties
	1870	Blank
	1871	0-4-2T class T7
	1893	Blank
	1904	0-6-0T class S56
82	1862	ex-E Counties
	1870	Blank
	1871	0-4-2T class T7
	1892	Blank
	1904	0-6-0T class S56
83	1862	ex-E Counties
	1870	Blank
	1871	0-4-2T class T7
	1893	Blank
	1904	0-6-0T class S56
84	1862	ex-E Counties
	1871	Blank
	1873	0-4-2T class T7
	1893	Blank
	1904	0-6-0T class S56
85	1862	ex-E Counties
	1873	0-4-2T class T7
	1894	Blank
	1904	0-6-0T class S56
86	1862	ex-E Counties
	1869	Blank
	1873	0-4-2T class T7
	1893	Blank
	1904	0-6-0T class S56

87	1862	ex-E Counties
	1867	2-2-2 class W
	1878	0-4-4T class E10
	1904	0-6-0-T class S56
88	1862	Blank
-90	1866	2-2-2 class W
	1878	0-4-4T class E10
	1904	0-6-0T class S56
91	1862	Blank
-93	1866	ex-London & Blackwall
	1878	0-4-4T class E10
	1905	2-4-2T class M15 (Holden)
94	1862	ex-E Counties
	1877	Blank
	1878	0-4-4T class E10
	1904	Blank
	1905	2-4-2T class M15 (Holden)
95	1862	Blank
	1866	ex-London & Blackwall
	1874	Blank
	1879	0-4-4T class E10
	1905	2-4-2T class M15 (Holden)
96	1862	Blank
	1866	ex-London & Blackwall
	1879	0-4-4T class E10
	1905	2-4-2T class M15 (Holden)
97	1862	Blank
	1866	ex-London & Blackwall
	1876	Blank
	1879	0-4-4T class E10
	1905	2-4-2T class M15 (Holden)
98	1862	Blank
	1866	ex-London & Blackwall
	1879	0-4-4T class E10
	1905	2-4-2T class M15 (Holden)
99	1862	ex-E Counties
	1866	ex-London & Blackwall
	1879	0-4-4T class E10
	1905	2-4-2T class M15 (Holden)
100	1862	Blank
	1866	ex-London & Blackwall
	1870	2-4-0 1 class (L7)
	1879	0-4-4T class E10
	1905	2-4-2T class M15 (Holden)
101	1862	ex-E Counties
	1866	ex-London & Blackwall
	1879	0-4-4T class E10
	1905	2-4-2T class M15 (Holden)
102	1862	Blank
	1866	ex-London & Blackwall
	1879	0-4-4T class E10
	1905	2-4-2T class M15 (Holden)
103	1862	ex-E Counties
	1875	Blank
	1878	2-4-0 ex-100
	1905	2-4-2T class M15 (Holden)

104	1862	ex-E Counties
	1870	2-4-0 1 class (L7)
	1905	2-4-2T class M15 (Holden)
105	1862	ex-E Counties
	1868	Blank
	1870	2-4-0 1 class (L7)
	1905	2-4-2T class M15 (Holden)
106	1862	ex-E Counties
	1870	2-4-0 1 class (L7)
	1904	Blank
	1905	2-4-2T class M15 (Holden)
107	1862	ex-E Counties
	1870	Blank
	1871	2-4-0 1 class (L7)
	1906	2-4-2T class M15 (Holden)
108	1862	ex-E Counties
	1876	Blank
	1878	2-4-0 ex-173
	1904	Blank
	1906	2-4-2T class M15 (Holden)
109	1862	ex-E Counties
	1868	2-4-0 116 class
	1885	Blank
	1906	2-4-2T class M15 (Holden)
110	1862	ex-E Counties
	1869	2-4-0 1 class (L7)
	1905	Blank
	1906	2-4-2T class M15 (Holden)
111	1862	ex-E Counties
	1869	2-4-0 6 class
	1883	Blank
	1907	2-4-2T class M15 (Holden)
112	1862	ex-E Counties
	1869	2-4-0 1 class (L7)
	1906	Blank
113	1862	ex-E Counties
	1869	2-4-0 1 class (L7)
	1903	Blank
114	1862	ex-E Counties
	1870	2-4-0 1 class (L7)
	1912	Blank
115	1862	ex-E Counties
	1870	2-4-0 1 class (L7)
	1902	Blank
116	1862	ex-E Counties
	1868	2-4-0 116 class
	1882	Blank
117	1862	ex-E Counties
	1876	Blank
	1878	2-4-0 ex-176
	c1909	Blank
118	1862	Blank
	1871	2-4-0 1 class (L7)
	1904	Blank
119	1862	Blank
	1871	2-4-0 1 class (L7)
	1884	0-6-0 class Y14 (Worsdell)

120	1862	2-4-0T class X
	1881	Blank
	1884	0-6-0 class Y14 (Worsdell)
121	1862	2-4-0T class X
	1883	Blank
	1884	0-6-0 class Y14 (Worsdell)
122	1862	2-4-0T class X
	1884	0-6-0 class Y14 (Worsdell)
123	1862	2-4-0T class X
	1883	Blank
	1884	0-6-0 class Y14 (Worsdell)
124	1862	2-4-0T class X
	1884	0-6-0 class Y14 (Worsdell)
125	1862	Blank
	1867	2-4-0 125 class
	1886	Blank
	1891	0-4-0T 'tram' class G15
	1921	0-6-0T 'tram' class C53
126	1862	Blank
	1867	2-4-0 125 class
	1887	Blank
	1892	0-4-0T 'tram' class G15
	1921	0-6-0T 'tram' class C53
127	1862	Blank
	1867	2-4-0 125 class
	1887	0-6-0 compound
	1892	0-4-0T 'tram' class G15
	1921	0-6-0T 'tram' class C53
128	1862	Blank
	1867	2-4-0 125 class
	1885	0-4-0T 'tram' class G15
	1914	0-6-0T 'tram' class C53
129	1862	Blank
	1867	2-4-0 125 class
	1885	0-4-0T 'tram' class G15
	1921	0-6-0T 'tram' class C53
130	1862	ex-E Counties
	1869	Blank
	1883	0-4-0T 'tram' class G15
	1910	0-6-0T 'tram' class C53
131	1862	ex-E Counties
	1883	0-4-0T 'tram' class G15
	1908	Blank
	1914	0-6-0T 'tram' class C53
132	1862	ex-E Counties
	1881	Blank
	1883	0-4-0T 'tram' class G15
133	1862	ex-E Counties
	1878	0-4-4T ex-170
	1897	0-4-0T 'tram' class G15
134	1862	ex-E Counties
	1871	Blank
	1872	0-4-4T 134 class
	1897	0-4-0T 'tram' class G15
135	1862	ex-E Counties
	1872	0-4-4T 134 class
	1903	0-6-0T 'tram' class C53

136	1862	ex-E Counties
	1869	Blank
	1872	0-4-4T 134 class
	1903	0-6-0T 'tram' class C53
137	1862	ex-E Counties
	1867	Blank
	1872	0-4-4T 134 class
	1908	0-6-0T 'tram' class C53
138	1862	ex-E Counties
	1872	0-4-4T 134 class
	1903	Blank
	1908	0-6-0T 'tram' class C53
139	1862	ex-E Counties
	1872	0-4-4T 134 class
	1908	0-6-0T 'tram' class C53
140	1862	Blank
-142	1864	2-4-2WT class V
	1880	0-4-4T/0-4-2T 140 class
	1903	2-4-2T class M15 (Holden)
143	1862	Blank or ex-E Counties
	1864	2-4-2WT class V
	1880	0-4-4T/0-4-2T 140 class
	1903	2-4-2T class M15 (Holden)
144	1862	Blank or ex-E Counties
	1865	2-4-2WT class V
	1880	0-4-4T/0-4-2T 140 class
	1903	2-4-2T class M15 (Holden)
145	1862	Blank
-149	1865	2-4-2WT class V
	1880	0-4-4T/0-4-2T 140 class
	1903	2-4-2T class M15 (Holden)
150	1862	Blank
	1865	2-4-2WT class V
	1889	0-6-0T class E22
151	1862	Blank
	1865	2-4-2WT class V
	1887	Blank
	1889	0-6-0T class E22
152	1862	ex-E Counties
	1865	2-4-2WT class V
	1887	Blank
	1889	0-6-0T class E22
153	1862	Blank
	1865	2-4-2WT class V
	1884	Blank
	1889	0-6-0T class E22
154	1862	ex-E Counties
	1863	Blank
	1865	2-4-2WT class V
	1887	Blank
	1889	0-6-0T class E22
155	1862	ex-E Counties
	1865	2-4-2WT class V
	1884	Blank
	1889	0-6-0T class E22

156	1862	ex-E Counties
-158	1865	2-4-2WT class V
	1887	Blank
	1889	0-6-0T class E22
159	1862	ex-E Counties
	1865	2-4-2WT class V
	1888	Blank
	1889	0-6-0T class E22
160	1862	Blank or ex-E Counties
	1865	Blank
	1871	2-4-0 1 class (L7)
	1901	0-6-0T class R24
161	1862	ex-E Counties
	1867	Blank
	1871	2-4-0 1 class (L7)
	1901	0-6-0T class R24
162	1862	ex-E Counties
	1872	0-4-4T 134 class
	1901	0-6-0T class R24
163	1862	ex-E Counties
	1867	Blank
	1872	0-4-4T 134 class
	1901	0-6-0T class R24
164	1862	ex-E Counties
	1872	0-4-4T 134 class
	1901	0-6-0T class R24
165	1862	Blank or ex-E Counties
	1865	Blank
	1872	0-4-4T 134 class
	1901	0-6-0T class R24
166	1862	ex-E Counties
-167	1868	Blank
	1873	0-4-4T 134 class
	1901	0-6-0T class R24
168	1862	Blank or ex-E Counties
	1865	Blank
	1873	0-4-4T 134 class
	1901	0-6-0T class R24
169	1862	Blank
	1873	0-4-4T 134 class
	1901	0-6-0T class R24
170	1862	ex-E Counties
	1873	0-4-4T 134 class
	1878	0-4-4T 61 class
	1908	2-4-2T class M15 (Holden)
171	1862	ex-E Counties
	1878	0-4-4T 61 class
	1908	2-4-2T class M15 (Holden)
172	1862	ex-E Counties
	1875	Blank
	1878	0-4-4T 61 class
	1908	2-4-2T class M15 (Holden)
173	1862	Blank or ex-E Counties
	1865	Blank
	1871	2-4-0 1 class (L7)
	1878	0-4-4T 61 class
	1908	2-4-2T class M15 (Holden)

174	1862	ex-E Counties
	1878	0-4-4T 61 class
	1908	2-4-2T class M15 (Holden)
175	1862	ex-E Counties
	1878	0-4-4T 61 class
	1908	2-4-2T class M15 (Holden)
176	1862	ex-E Counties
	1871	2-4-0 1 class (L7)
	1878	0-4-4T 61 class
	1908	2-4-2T class M15 (Holden)
177	1862	ex-E Counties
-178	1876	Blank
	1878	0-4-4T 61 class
	1908	2-4-2T class M15 (Holden)
179	1862	Blank or E Counties
	1865	Blank
	1878	0-4-4T 61 class
	1908	2-4-2T class M15 (Holden)
180	1862	ex-E Counties
	1872	Blank
	1878	0-4-4T 61 class
	1908	2-4-2T class M15 (Holden)
181	1862	ex-E Counties
-182	1878	0-4-4T 61 class
	1908	2-4-2T class M15 (Holden)
183	1862	ex-E Counties
	1870	Blank
	1878	0-4-4T 61 class
	1907	Blank
	1908	2-4-2T class M15 (Holden)
184	1862	ex-E Counties
	1876	Blank
	1878	0-4-4T 61 class
	1908	2-4-2T class M15 (Holden)
185	1862	ex-E Counties
	1873	0-4-4T 134 class
	1906	Blank
	1909	2-4-2T class M15 (Holden)
186	1862	ex-E Counties
	1872	0-4-4T 134 class
	1908	Blank
	1909	2-4-2T class M15 (Holden)
187	1862	ex-E Counties
	1872	0-4-4T 134 class
	1904	Blank
	1909	2-4-2T class M15 (Holden)
188	1862	Blank or ex-E Counties
	1865	Blank
	1872	0-4-4T 134 class
	1909	2-4-2T class M15 (Holdcn)
189	1862	ex-E Counties
	1869	Blank
	1872	0-4-4T 134 class
	1900	0-6-0T class R24
	1909	2-4-2T class M15 (Holden)

190	1862	ex-E Counties
-191	1871	Blank
	1873	0-4-4T 134 class
	1900	0-6-0T class R24
192	1862	ex-E Counties
-193	1870	Blank
	1873	0-4-4T 134 class
	1900	0-6-0T class R24
194	1862	ex-E Counties
-195	1869	Blank
	1873	0-4-4T 134 class
	1900	0-6-0T class R24
196	1862	ex-E Counties
	1872	Blank
	1873	0-4-4T 134 class
	1900	0-6-0T class R24
197	1862	ex-E Counties
	1871	Blank
	1873	0-4-4T 134 class
	1900	0-6-0T class R24
198	1862	ex-E Counties
	1870	Blank
	1873	0-4-4T 134 class
	1900	0-6-0T class R24
199	1862	ex-E Counties
	1871	Blank
	1873	0-4-4T 134 class
	1899	0-6-0T class R24
200	1862	ex-E Counties
	1872	0-4-0ST
	1895	Blank
	1897	0-4-4T ex-133
	1899	0-6-0T class R24
201	1862	Blank
	1867	0-6-0ST
	1889	Blank
	1897	0-4-4T ex-134
	1898	Blank
	1899	0-6-0T class R24
202	1862	Blank
	1867	0-6-0ST
	1887	Blank
	1899	0-6-0T class R24
203	1862	ex-E Counties
	1877	Blank
	1879	ex-W&B
	1889	Blank
	1899	0-6-0T class R24
204	1862	ex-E Counties
	1868	0-6-0T 204 class
	1895	Blank
	1899	0-6-0T class R24
205	1862	ex-E Counties
	1868	0-6-0T 204 class
	1895	Blank
	1899	0-6-0T class R24

206	1862	ex-E Counties
	1868	0-6-0T 204 class
	1895	Blank
	1899	0-6-0T class R24
207	1862	ex-E Counties
-208	1868	0-6-0T 204 class
	1890	Blank
	1899	0-6-0T class R24
209	1862	Blank
	1874	0-4-0ST 209 class (Adams)
210	1862	ex-E Counties
	1869	Blank
	1875	0-4-0ST 209 class (Adams)
	1915	Blank
	1921	0-4-0T class B74
211	1862	ex-E Counties
-219	1875	0-4-4T 61 class
	1907	2-4-2T class M15 (Holden)
220	1862	ex-E Counties
	1873	Blank
	1875	0-4-4T 61 class
	1907	2-4-2T class M15 (Holden)
221	1862	ex-E Counties
-224	1877	0-4-4T 61 class
	1907	2-4-2T class M15 (Holden)
225	1862	ex-E Counties
	1868	Blank
	1877	0-4-4T 61 class
	1907	2-4-2T class M15 (Holden)
226	1862	ex-E Counties
	1884	Blank
	1897	0-4-0ST 209 class (Holden)
	1907	Blank
	1914	0-4-0T class B74
227	1862	ex-E Counties
	1882	Blank
	1897	0-4-0ST 209 class (Holden)
	1907	Blank
	1913	0-4-0T class B74
228	1862	ex-E Counties
	1874	Blank
	1876	0-4-0ST 209 class (Adams)
	1914	0-4-0T class B74
229	1862	Blank or E Counties
	1865	Blank
	1876	0-4-0ST 209 class (Adams)
	1918	Blank
	1921	0-4-0T class B74
230	1862	Blank or ex-E Counties
	1865	Blank
	1878	0-4-0T 'tram'
	1884	4-4-0 compound class G16
	1903	0-4-0ST 209 class (Holden)
231	1862	ex-E Counties
	1879	Blank
	1880	0-4-4T class E10
	1903	0-4-0ST 209 class (Holden)

232	1862	ex-E Counties
	1868	Blank
	1880	0-4-4T class E10
	1907	2-4-2T class M15 (Holden)
233	1862	ex-E Counties
-235	1880	0-4-4T class E10
	1907	2-4-2T class M15 (Holden)
236	1862	ex-E Counties
	1880	0-4-4T class E10
	1904	Blank
	1906	2-4-2T class M15 (Holden)
237	1862	ex-E Counties
	1880	0-4-4T class E10
	1906	2-4-2T class M15 (Holden)
238	1862	ex-E Counties
	1874	Blank
	1880	0-4-4T class E10
	1905	Blank
	1906	2-4-2T class M15 (Holden)
239	1862	ex-E Counties
	1876	Blank
	1880	0-4-4T class E10
	1905	Blank
	1906	2-4-2T class M15 (Holden)
240	1862	ex-E Counties
-241	1876	Blank
	1880	0-4-4T class E10
	1906	2-4-2T class M15 (Holden)
242	1862	ex-E Counties
	1874	Blank
	1880	0-4-4T class E10
	1904	Blank
	1906	2-4-2T class M15 (Holden)
243	1862	ex-E Counties
	1876	Blank
	1880	0-4-4T class E10
	1906	2-4-2T class M15 (Holden)
244	1862	ex-E Counties
	1877	Blank
	1880	0-4-4T class E10
	1906	2-4-2T class M15 (Holden)
245	1862	ex-E Counties
	1876	Blank
	1879	4-2-2 245 class
	1892	Blank
	1893	0-6-0T class E22
246	1862	ex-E Counties
	1874	Blank
	1879	4-2-2 245 class
	1893	0-6-0T class E22
247	1862	ex-E Counties
	1876	Blank
	1879	4-2-2 245 class
	1893	0-6-0T class E22

248	1862	ex-E Counties
	1874	Blank
	1879	4-2-2 245 class
	1891	Blank
	1893	0-6-0T class E22
249	1862	ex-E Counties
-250	1879	4-2-2 245 class
	1891	Blank
	1893	0-6-0T class E22
251	1862	ex-E Counties
-252	1879	4-2-2 245 class
	1892	Blank
	1893	0-6-0T class E22
253	1862	ex-E Counties
	1879	4-2-2 245 class
	1891	Blank
	1893	0-6-0T class E22
254	1862	ex-E Counties
	1874	Blank
	1879	4-2-2 245 class
	1891	Blank
	1893	0-6-0T class E22
255	1862	ex-E Counties
	1877	4-4-0 265 class
	1896	Blank
	1899	0-6-0T class R24
256	1862	ex-E Counties
	1876	Blank
	1877	4-4-0 265 class
	1896	Blank
	1899	0-6-0T class R24
257	1862	ex-E Counties
	1877	4-4-0 265 class
	1896	Blank
	1899	0-6-0T class R24
258	1862	ex-E Counties
	1877	4-4-0 265 class
	1897	Blank
	1899	0-6-0T class R24
259	1862	ex-E Counties
-260	1877	4-4-0 265 class
	1895	Blank
	1899	0-6-0T class R24
261	1862	ex-E Counties
	1875	Blank
	1877	4-4-0 265 class
	1897	Blank
	1899	0-6-0T class R24
262	1862	ex-E Counties
	1877	4-4-0 265 class
	1897	Blank
	1899	0-6-0T class R24
263	1862	ex-E Counties
	1874	Blank
	1877	4-4-0 265 class
	1895	Blank
	1899	0-6-0T class R24

264	1862	ex-E Counties
	1877	4-4-0 265 class
	1896	Blank
	1899	0-6-0T class R24
265	1862	ex-E Counties
	1875	Blank
	1876	4-4-0 265 class
	1896	0-6-0T class R24
266	1862	ex-E Counties
-267	1876	4-4-0 265 class
	1896	0-6-0T class R24
268	1862	ex-E Counties
-269	1875	Blank
	1876	4-4-0 265 class
	1896	0-6-0T class R24
270	1862	ex-E Counties
	1876	4-4-0 265 class
	1895	Blank
	1896	0-6-0T class R24
271	1862	Blank
-272	1876	4-4-0 265 class
	1896	0-6-0T class R24
273	1862	Blank
	1876	4-4-0 265 class
	1895	Blank
	1896	0-6-0T class R24
274	1862	ex-E Counties
	1876	4-4-0 265 class
	1896	0-6-0T class R24
275	1862	ex-E Counties
-276	1876	Blank
	1880	2-2-2 ex-51/2
	1886	0-6-0T class T18
277	1862	ex-E Counties
	1879	Blank
	1880	2-2-2 ex-53
	1886	0-6-0T class T18
278	1862	ex-E Counties
	1876	Blank
	1880	2-2-2 ex-55
	1886	0-6-0T class T18
279	1862	ex-E Counties
	1875	Blank
	1880	2-2-2 ex-56
	1885	Blank
	1886	0-6-0T class T18
280	1862	ex-E Counties
-283	1880	2-2-2 ex-57-60
	1886	0-6-0T class T18
284	1862	2-2-2 class W
	1886	0-6-0T class T18
285	1862	2-2-2 class W
-288	1887	0-6-0T class T18
289	1862	Blank
-298	1865	2-2-2 class W
	1887	0-6-0T class T18

299	1862	Blank
-300	1866	2-2-2 class W
	1887	0-6-0T class T18
301	1862	ex-E Counties
	1874	4-4-0 class C8
	1878	2-2-2 ex-87
	1887	0-6-0T class T18
302	1862	ex-E Counties
	1874	4-4-0 class C8
	1878	2-2-2 ex-88
	1886	Blank
	1887	0-6-0T class T18
303	1862	ex-E Counties
	1874	Blank
	1878	2-2-2 ex-89
	1887	0-6-0T class T18
304	1862	ex-E Counties
	1874	Blank
	1878	2-2-2 ex-90
	1884	Blank
	1887	0-6-0T class T18
305	1862	ex-E Counties
	1876	Blank
	1878	4-4-0 ex-301
	1899	Blank
	1905	0-6-0T ex-189
306	1862	ex-E Counties
	1874	Blank
	1878	4-4-0 ex-302
	1898	Blank
307	1862	ex-E Counties
-309	1888	0-6-0T class T18
310	1862	ex-E Counties
	1887	Blank
	1888	0-6-0T class T18
311	1862	ex-E Counties
-312	1888	0-6-0T class T18
313	1862	ex-E Counties
	1886	Blank
	1888	0-6-0T class T18
314	1862	ex-E Counties
-317	1888	0-6-0T class T18
318	1862	ex-E Counties
	1885	Blank
	1888	0-6-0T class T18
319	1862	ex-E Counties
-321	1888	0-6-0T class T18
322	1862	ex-E Counties
-323	1884	Blank
	1888	0-6-0T class T18
324	1862	ex-E Counties
-325	1888	0-6-0T class T18
326	1862	ex-E Counties
	1884	Blank
	1888	0-6-0T class T18
327	1862	ex-E Counties
	1889	Blank
	1890	0-6-0T class R24

328	1862	ex-E Counties
	1891	Blank
	1890	0-6-0T class R24
329	1862	ex-E Counties
-332	1889	Blank
	1890	0-6-0T class R24
333	1862	ex-E Counties
	1886	Blank
	1890	0-6-0T class R24
334	1862	ex-E Counties
	1887	Blank
	1890	0-6-0T class R24
335	1862	ex-E Counties
-336	1889	Blank
	1890	0-6-0T class R24
337	1862	ex-E Counties
	1887	Blank
	1890	0-6-0T class R24
338	1862	ex-E Counties
	1890	0-6-0T class R24
339	1862	ex-E Counties
-345	1890	0-6-0T class R24
346	1862	ex-E Counties
	1886	Blank
	1890	0-6-0T class R24
347	1862	ex-E Counties
-348	1887	Blank
	1892	0-6-0T class R24
349	1862	ex-E Counties
	1891	Blank
	1892	0-6-0T class R24
350	1862	ex-E Counties
	1888	Blank
	1892	0-6-0T class R24
351	1862	ex-E Counties
-352	1891	Blank
	1892	0-6-0T class R24
353	1862	ex-E Counties
	1890	Blank
	1892	0-6-0T class R24
354	1862	ex-E Counties
	1884	Blank
	1892	0-6-0T class R24
355	1862	ex-E Counties
-356	1891	Blank
	1892	0-6-0T class R24
357	1863	2-4-0 class Y
	1891	Blank
	1892	0-6-0T class R24
358	1864	2-4-0 class Y
-362	1891	Blank
	1892	0-6-0T class R24
363	1864	2-4-0 class Y
	1889	Blank
	1892	0-6-0T class R24
364	1864	2-4-0 class Y
	1890	Blank
	1892	0-6-0T class R24

365	1864	2-4-0 class Y
-366	1891	Blank
	1892	0-6-0T class R24
367	1864	2-4-0 class Y
	1889	Blank
	1894	0-6-0T class R24
368	1864	2-4-0 class Y
	1884	Blank
	1894	0-6-0T class R24
369	1864	2-4-0 class Y
	1889	Blank
	1894	0-6-0T class R24
370	1864	2-4-0 class Y
	1891	Blank
	1894	0-6-0T class R24
371	1864	2-4-0 class Y
	1887	Blank
	1894	0-6-0T class R24
372	1864	2-4-0 class Y
-373	1891	Blank
	1894	0-6-0T class R24
374	1864	2-4-0 class Y
	1887	Blank
	1894	0-6-0T class R24
375	1864	2-4-0 class Y
-376	1891	Blank
	1894	0-6-0T class R24
377	1864	2-4-0 class Y
-378	1891	Blank
	1895	0-6-0T class R24
379	1865	2-4-0 class Y
-380	1891	Blank
	1895	0-6-0T class R24
381	1865	2-4-0 class Y
	1887	Blank
	1895	0-6-0T class R24
382	1865	2-4-0 class Y
	1891	Blank
	1895	0-6-0T class R24
383	1865	2-4-0 class Y
	1886	Blank
	1895	0-6-0T class R24
384	1865	2-4-0 class Y
-386	1891	Blank
	1895	0-6-0T class R24
387	1864	2-4-0 class Y
	1884	Blank
	1895	0-6-0T class R24
388	1864	2-4-0 class Y
	1885	Blank
	1895	0-6-0T class R24
389	1864	2-4-0 class Y
	1891	Blank
	1895	0-6-0T class R24
390	1864	2-4-0 class Y
	1884	Blank
	1895	0-6-0T class R24

391	1864	2-4-0 class Y
	1887	Blank
	1896	0-6-0T class R24
392	1864	2-4-0 class Y
	1890	Blank
	1896	0-6-0T class R24
393	1864	2-4-0 class Y
	1891	Blank
	1896	0-6-0T class R24
394	1864	2-4-0 class Y
	1885	Blank
	1896	0-6-0T class R24
395	1864	2-4-0 class Y
	1886	Blank
	1896	0-6-0T class R24
396	1864	2-4-0 class Y
	1891	Blank
	1896	0-6-0T class R24
397	1864	2-4-0 class Y
	1890	0-6-0T class R24
398	1864	2-4-0 class Y
	1885	Blank
	1890	0-6-0T class R24
399	1864	2-4-0 class Y
	1886	Blank
	1890	0-6-0T class R24
400	1864	2-4-0 class Y
	1888	Blank
	1890	0-6-0T class R24
401	1865	2-4-0 class Y
	1886	Blank
	1890	0-6-0T class R24
402	1865	2-4-0 class Y
	1887	Blank
	1890	0-6-0T class R24
403	1865	2-4-0 class Y
-404	1885	Blank
	1890	0-6-0T class R24
405	1865	2-4-0 class Y
-406	1890	0-6-0T class R24
407	1866	2-4-0 class Y
-409	1890	0-6-0T class R24
	1920	2-4-0 ex-1250-2
410	1866	2-4-0 class Y
	1886	Blank
	1891	0-6-0T class R24
	1920	2-4-0 ex-1253
411	1866	2-4-0 class Y
-416	1891	0-6-0T class R24
	1920	2-4-0 ex-1254-9
417	1867	0-6-0 417 class
-418	1890	Blank
	1891	2-4-0 class T26
419	1867	0-6-0 417 class
	1891	2-4-0 class T26
420	1867	0-6-0 417 class
	1890	Blank
	1891	2-4-0 class T26

421	1867	0-6-0 417 class
	1889	Blank
	1891	2-4-0 class T26
422	1867	0-6-0 417 class
-423	1891	2-4-0 class T26
424	1867	0-6-0 417 class
	1889	Blank
	1891	2-4-0 class T26
425	1867	0-6-0 417 class
	1890	Blank
	1891	2-4-0 class T26
426	1867	0-6-0 417 class
	1891	2-4-0 class T26
427	1867	0-6-0 417 class
	1889	Blank
	1891	2-4-0 class T26
428	1867	0-6-0 417 class
-431	1891	2-4-0 class T26
432	1868	0-6-0 417 class
	1891	2-4-0 class T26
433	1868	0-6-0 417 class
-434	1889	Blank
	1891	2-4-0 class T26
435	1868	0-6-0 417 class
-436	1890	Blank
	1891	2-4-0 class T26
437	1867	0-6-0 417 class
	1891	2-4-0 class T26
438	1867	0-6-0 417 class
	1889	Blank
	1891	2-4-0 class T26
439	1867	0-6-0 417 class
	1891	2-4-0 class T26
440	1868	0-6-0 417 class
-442	1891	2-4-0 class T26
443	1868	0-6-0 417 class
	1890	Blank
	1891	2-4-0 class T26
444	1868	0-6-0 417 class
-445	1889	Blank
	1891	2-4-0 class T26
446	1868	0-6-0 417 class
	1890	Blank
	1891	2-4-0 class T26
447	1868	0-6-0 417 class
-450	1892	2-4-0 class T26
451	1868	0-6-0 417 class
	1891	Blank
	1892	2-4-0 class T26
452	1868	0-6-0 417 class
	1889	Blank
	1892	2-4-0 class T26
453	1868	0-6-0 417 class
-454	1890	Blank
	1892	2-4-0 class T26
455	1869	0-6-0 417 class
	1892	2-4-0 class T26

456	1869	0-6-0 417 class	
	1890	Blank	
	1892	2-4-0 class T26	
457	1869	0-6-0 417 class	
	1891	Blank	
	1892	2-4-0 class T26	
458	1869	0-6-0 417 class	
	1890	Blank	
	1892	2-4-0 class T26	
459	1869	0-6-0 417 class	
-460	1892	2-4-0 class T26	
461	1869	0-6-0 417 class	
	1889	Blank	
	1892	2-4-0 class T26	
462	1869	0-6-0 417 class	
-463	1890	Blank	
	1892	2-4-0 class T26	
464	1869	0-6-0 417 class	
-465	1892	2-4-0 class T26	
466	1869	0-6-0 417 class	
	1891	Blank	
	1892	2-4-0 class T26	
467	1869	0-6-0 417 class	
-471	1892	2-4-0 class T26	
472	1869	0-6-0 417 class	
	1889	Blank	
	1892	2-4-0 class T26	
473	1869	0-6-0 417 class	
	1892	Blank	
	1893	2-4-0 class T26	
474	1869	0-6-0 417 class	
	1890	Blank	
	1893	2-4-0 class T26	
475	1869	0-6-0 417 class	
	1889	Blank	
	1893	2-4-0 class T26	
476	1869	0-6-0 417 class	
	1891	Blank	
	1893	2-4-0 class T26	
477	1871	0-6-0 477 class	
-486	1894	2-4-0 class T26	
487	1872	0-6-0 477 class	
-489	1894	2-4-0 class T26	
490	1872	0-6-0 477 class	
-496	1895	2-4-0 class T26	
497	1872	0-6-0 477 class	
-506	1896	2-4-0 class T26	
507	1872	0-6-0 477 class	
-511	1899	0-6-0 class Y14	(Holden)
512	1873	0-6-0 477 class	
	1899	0-6-0 class Y14	(Holden)
513	1873	0-6-0 477 class	
	1899	0-6-0 class Y14	(Holden)
	1921	Blank	
514	1873	0-6-0 477 class	
-518	1899	0-6-0 class Y14	(Holden)
519	1873	0-6-0 477 class	
	1898	Blank	
	1899	0-6-0 class Y14	(Holden)
520	1873	0-6-0 477 class	
-526	1899	0-6-0 class Y14	(Holden)
527	1878	2-6-0	
-528	1887	0-6-0 class Y14	(Holden)
529	1878	2-6-0	
	1886	Blank	
	1887	0-6-0 class Y14	(Holden)
530	1878	2-6-0	
-531	1887	0-6-0 class Y14	(Holden)
532	1879	2-6-0	
	1886	Blank	
	1888	0-6-0 class Y14	(Holden)
533	1879	2-6-0	
	1887	Blank	
	1888	0-6-0 class Y14	(Holden)
534	1879	2-6-0	
	1888	0-6-0 class Y14	(Holden)
535	1879	2-6-0	
	1887	Blank	
	1888	0-6-0 class Y14	(Holden)
536	1879	2-6-0	
-539	1888	0-6-0 class Y14	(Holden)
540	1879	2-6-0	
	1887	Blank	
	1888	0-6-0 class Y14	(Holden)
541	1879	2-6-0	
	1888	0-6-0 class Y14	(Holden)
542	1881	0-6-0T class M12	
	1897	Blank	
	1898	0-6-0 class N31	
	1911	Blank	
	1913	0-6-0 class Y14	(Holden)
543	1881	0-6-0T class M12	
-544	1897	Blank	
	1898	0-6-0 class N31	
	1913	0-6-0 class Y14	(Holden)
545	1881	0-6-0T class M12	
	1898	0-6-0 class N31	
	1913	0-6-0 class Y14	(Holden)
546	1881	0-6-0T class M12	
	1898	0-6-0 class N31	
	1910	Blank	
	1913	0-6-0 class Y14	(Holden)
547	1881	0-6-0T class M12	
	1896	Blank	
	1898	0-6-0 class N31	
	1912	Blank	
	1913	0-6-0 class Y14	(Holden)
548	1881	0-6-0T class M12	
	1898	0-6-0 class N31	
	1913	0-6-0 class Y14	(Holden)
549	1881	0-6-0T class M12	
	1898	0-6-0 class N31	
	1910	Blank	
	1913	0-6-0 class Y14	(Holden)

550	1881	0-6-0T class M12
	1898	0-6-0 class N31
	1911	Blank
	1913	0-6-0 class Y14 (Holden)
551	1881	0-6-0T class M12
	1898	0-6-0 class N31
	1912	Blank
	1913	0-6-0 class Y14 (Holden)
552	1882	0-6-0 552 class
	1905	Blank
	1906	0-6-0 class Y14 (Holden)
553	1882	0-6-0 552 class
-561	1906	0-6-0 class Y14 (Holden)
562	1882	2-4-0 class G14
	1898	0-6-0 class N31
	1912	0-6-0 class Y14 (Holden)
563	1882	2-4-0 class G14
	1898	0-6-0 class N31
	1911	Blank
564	1882	2-4-0 class G14
	1897	Blank
	1898	0-6-0 class N31
	1912	0-6-0 class Y14 (Holden)
565	1883	2-4-0 class G14
-566	1898	0-6-0 class N31
	1910	Blank
	1912	0-6-0 class Y14 (Holden)
567	1883	2-4-0 class G14
	1898	0-6-0 class N31
	1912	0-6-0 class Y14 (Holden)
568	1883	2-4-0 class G14
	1898	0-6-0 class N31
	1911	Blank
	1912	0-6-0 class Y14 (Holden)
569	1883	2-4-0 class G14
	1896	Blank
	1898	0-6-0 class N31
	1911	Blank
	1912	0-6-0 class Y14 (Holden)
570	1883	2-4-0 class G14
	1897	0-6-0 class N31
	1910	Blank
	1912	0-6-0 class Y14 (Holden)
571	1883	2-4-0 class G14
	1896	Blank
	1898	0-6-0 class N31
	1910	Blank
	1912	0-6-0 class Y14 (Holden)
572	1881	0-4-4T class E10
	1907	2-4-2T class M15 (Holden)
573	1881	0-4-4T class E10
	1906	Blank
	1907	2-4-2T class M15 (Holden)
574	1881	0-4-4T class E10
	1905	Blank
	1907	2-4-2T class M15 (Holden)

575	1882	0-4-4T class E10
	1906	Blank
	1907	2-4-2T class M15 (Holden)
576	1882	0-4-4T class E10
	1907	2-4-2T class M15 (Holden)
577	1882	0-4-4T class E10
	1906	Blank
	1907	2-4-2T class M15 (Holden)
578	1882	0-4-4T class E10
-584	1907	2-4-2T class M15 (Holden)
585	1883	0-4-4T class E10
-591	1907	2-4-2T class M15 (Holden)
592	1884	0-6-0 class Y14 (Worsdell)
-599		
600	1881	4-2-2 245 class
	1893	Blank
	1912	0-6-0 ex-41
601	1882	4-2-2 245 class
	1894	Blank
602	1882	4-2-2 245 class
	1894	Blank
	1897	0-6-0 class N31
	1910	Blank
603	1882	4-2-2 245 class
	1891	Blank
	1897	0-6-0 class N31
	1911	Blank
604	1882	4-2-2 245 class
	1891	Blank
	1897	0-6-0 class N31
605	1882	4-2-2 245 class
	1894	Blank
	1897	0-6-0 class N31
	1910	Blank
606	1882	4-2-2 245 class
	1894	Blank
	1897	0-6-0 class N31
	1911	Blank
607	1882	4-2-2 245 class
	1894	Blank
	1897	0-6-0 class N31
	1914	Blank
608	1882	4-2-2 245 class
	1893	Blank
	1897	0-6-0 class N31
	1910	Blank
609	1882	4-2-2 245 class
	1891	Blank
	1892	0-6-0 ex-800
610	1883	0-6-0 class Y14 (Worsdell)
-619		
620	1884	0-6-0 class Y14 (Worsdell)
-639		
640	1883	2-4-0 class G14
-643	1899	0-6-0 class Y14 (Holden)
644	1883	2-4-0 class G14
	1898	Blank
	1899	0-6-0 class Y14 (Holden)

645	1883	2-4-0 class G14
-649	1899	0-6-0 class Y14 (Holden)
650	1884	2-4-2T class M15 (Worsdell)
651	1884	2-4-2T class M15 (Worsdell)
	1915	Blank
652	1884	2-4-2T class M15 (Worsdell)
	1914	Blank
653	1884	2-4-2T class M15 (Worsdell)
-657		
658	1884	2-4-2T class M15 (Worsdell)
	1916	Blank
659	1885	2-4-2T class M15 (Worsdell)
-660		
661	1885	2-4-2T class M15 (Worsdell)
	1914	Blank
662	1885	2-4-2T class M15 (Worsdell)
-663		
664	1885	2-4-2T class M15 (Worsdell)
	1916	Blank
665	1885	2-4-2T class M15 (Worsdell)
-671		
672	1885	2-4-2T class M15 (Worsdell)
	1914	Blank
673	1885	2-4-2T class M15 (Worsdell)
	1915	Blank
674	1885	2-4-2T class M15 (Worsdell)
-679		
680	1885	0-6-0 class Y14 (Worsdell)
-693		
694	1886	0-6-0 class Y14 (Worsdell)
-695		
696	1885	0-6-0 class Y14 (Worsdell)
697	1886	0-6-0 class Y14 (Worsdell)
-699		
700	1885	4-4-0 compound class G16
	1892	2-4-0 class T19
701	1885	4-4-0 compound class G16
	1892	2-4-0 class T19
	1910	Blank
702	1885	4-4-0 compound class G16
	1892	2-4-0 class T19
	1920	Blank
703	1885	4-4-0 compound class G16
	1892	2-4-0 class T19
	1910	Blank
704	1885	4-4-0 compound class G16
-708	1892	2-4-0 class T19
709	1885	4-4-0 compound class G16
	1892	2-4-0 class T19
	1911	Blank
710	1886	2-4-0 class T19
711	1887	2-4-0 class T19
	1909	Blank
712	1887	2-4-0 class T19
-713		
714	1887	2-4-0 class T19
	1910	Blank
715	1887	2-4-0 class T19

716	1887	2-4-0 class T19
	1910	Blank
717	1887	2-4-0 class T19
-719		
720	1888	2-4-0 class T19
-722	1910	Blank
723	1888	2-4-0 class T19
	1909	Blank
724	1888	2-4-0 class T19
	1915	Blank
725	1888	2-4-0 class T19
	1920	Blank
726	1888	2-4-0 class T19
	1911	Blank
727	1888	2-4-0 class T19
	1916	Blank
728	1888	2-4-0 class T19
-735		
736	1888	2-4-0 class T19
	1911	Blank
737	1888	2-4-0 class T19
-739		
740	1888	2-2-2 class D27
	1889	2-4-0 class T19
	1912	Blank
741	1889	2-4-0 class T19
-742		
743	1889	2-4-0 class T19
	1914	Blank
744	1889	2-4-0 class T19
-745		
746	1889	2-4-0 class T19
	1909	Blank
747	1889	2-4-0 class T19
-748		
749	1889	2-4-0 class T19
	1909	Blank
750	1889	2-4-0 class T19
	1916	Blank
751	1889	2-4-0 class T19
752	1889	2-4-0 class T19
	1911	Blank
753	1889	2-4-0 class T19
	1910	Blank
754	1889	2-4-0 class T19
	1909	Blank
755	1889	2-4-0 class T19
	1911	Blank
756	1889	2-4-0 class T19
757	1889	2-4-0 class T19
	1911	Blank
758	1889	2-4-0 class T19
	1909	Blank
759	1889	2-4-0 class T19
	1912	Blank
760	1890	2-4-0 class T19
	1915	Blank

761	1890	2-4-0 class T19		811	1886	0-6-0 class Y14 (Holden)
	1909	Blank		-814		
762	1890	2-4-0 class T19		815	1887	0-6-0 class Y14 (Holden)
-763	1914	Blank		-829		
764	1890	2-4-0 class T19		830	1888	0-6-0 class Y14 (Holden)
	1912	Blank		-834		
765	1890	2-4-0 class T19		835	1889	0-6-0 class Y14 (Holden)
-767				-874		
768	1890	2-4-0 class T19		875	1890	0-6-0 class Y14 (Holden)
-769	1914	Blank		-894		
770	1891	2-2-2 class D27		895	1891	0-6-0 class Y14 (Holden)
	1904	2-4-0 ex-781		-930		
	1915	Blank		931	1892	0-6-0 class Y14 (Holden)
771	1891	2-2-2 class D27		-934		
	1904	2-4-0 ex-782		935	1891	0-6-0 ex-127
	1920	Blank			1914	Blank
772	1891	2-2-2 class D27		936	1892	0-6-0 class Y14 (Holden)
	1904	2-4-0/4-4-0 ex-783		-945		
773	1891	2-2-2 class D27		946	1897	0-6-0 class N31
	1904	2-4-0 ex-784			1916	Blank
	1910	Blank		947	1897	0-6-0 class N31
774	1891	2-2-2 class D27			1915	Blank
	1904	2-4-0 ex-785		948	1897	0-6-0 class N31
	1915	Blank		949	1897	0-6-0 class N31
775	1891	2-2-2 class D27			1913	Blank
	1904	2-4-0/4-4-0 ex-786		950	1897	0-6-0 class N31
776	1891	2-2-2 class D27			1910	Blank
	1904	2-4-0 ex-787		951	1897	0-6-0 class N31
	1921	Blank		952	1897	0-6-0 class N31
777	1891	2-2-2 class D27			1913	Blank
	1904	2-4-0/4-4-0 ex-788		953	1897	0-6-0 class N31
778	1891	2-2-2 class D27		-955	1910	Blank
	1904	2-4-0 ex-789		956	1897	0-6-0 class N31
	1921	Blank			1911	Blank
779	1891	2-2-2 class D27		957	1897	0-6-0 class N31
	1904	2-4-0/4-4-0 ex-790			1910	Blank
780	1892	2-2-2 ex-789		958	1897	0-6-0 class N31
	1906	2-4-2T class M15 (Holden)			1912	Blank
781	1892	2-4-0 class T19		959	1896	0-6-0 class N31
-788	1904	2-4-2T class M15 (Holden)		960	1896	0-6-0 class N31
789	1888	2-2-2 ex-740		-961	1912	Blank
	1892	2-4-0 class T19		962	1896	0-6-0 class N31
	1904	2-4-2T class M15 (Holden)			1911	Blank
790	1886	2-4-2T class M15 (Holden)		963	1896	0-6-0 class N31
	1892	2-4-0 class T19		-964		
	1904	2-4-2T class M15 (Holden)		965	1896	0-6-0 class N31
791	1886	2-4-2T class M15 (Holden)			1922	Blank
-799				966	1896	0-6-0 class N31
800	1886	0-6-0 class Y14 (Holden)			1910	Blank
	1892	2-4-2T ex-790		967	1896	0-6-0 class N31
801	1880	ex-Thetford & Watton		-968	1913	Blank
	1885	Blank		969	1894	0-6-0 class N31
	1886	0-6-0 class Y14 (Holden)			1910	Blank
802	1880	ex-Thetford & Watton		970	1894	0-6-0 class N31
-807	1886	0-6-0 class Y14 (Holden)		971	1894	0-6-0 class N31
808	1879	ex-Felixstowe			1909	Blank
-810	1886	0-6-0 class Y14 (Holden)		972	1894	0-6-0 class N31
					1910	Blank

973	1894	0-6-0 class N31
974	1894	0-6-0 class N31
	1911	Blank
975	1894	0-6-0 class N31
	1910	Blank
976	1894	0-6-0 class N31
-978		
979	1893	0-6-0 class N31
	1914	Blank
980	1893	0-6-0 class N31
-981		
982	1893	0-6-0 class N31
	1911	Blank
983	1893	0-6-0 class N31
-987		
988	1893	0-6-0 class N31
	1912	Blank
989	1894	0-6-0 class N31
-991	1911	Blank
992	1894	0-6-0 class N31
-993		
994	1894	0-6-0 class N31
	1917	Blank
995	1894	0-6-0 class N31
996	1894	0-6-0 class N31
	1913	Blank
997	1894	0-6-0 class N31
	1912	Blank
998	1894	0-6-0 class N31
999	1892	0-6-0 class N31
	1921	Blank
1000	1893	2-2-2 class D27
	1902	Blank
	1915	0-6-2T class L77
1001	1893	2-2-2 class D27
	1903	Blank
	1915	0-6-2T class L77
1002	1893	2-2-2 class D27
	1902	Blank
	1921	0-6-2T class L77
1003	1893	2-2-2 class D27
	1903	Blank
	1921	0-6-2T class L77
1004	1893	2-2-2 class D27
	1905	Blank
	1921	0-6-2T class L77
1005	1893	2-2-2 class D27
	1902	Blank
	1921	0-6-2T class L77
1006	1893	2-2-2 class D27
	1905	Blank
	1921	0-6-2T class L77
1007	1893	2-2-2 class D27
	1902	Blank
	1921	0-6-2T class L77
1008	1893	2-2-2 class D27
-1009	1904	Blank
	1921	0-6-2T class L77

1010	1893	2-4-0 class T19
	1916	Blank
	1921	0-6-2T class L77
1011	1893	2-4-0 class T19
	1915	Blank
	1921	0-6-2T class L77
1012	1893	2-4-0 class T19
-1013		
1014	1893	2-4-0 class T19
	1916	Blank
1015	1893	2-4-0 class T19
-1016		
1017	1893	2-4-0 class T19
	1916	Blank
1018	1893	2-4-0 class T19
1019	1893	2-4-0 class T19
	1911	Blank
1020	1895	2-4-0 class T19
-1021		
1022	1895	2-4-0 class T19
	1913	Blank
1023	1895	2-4-0 class T19
1024	1895	2-4-0 class T19
	1909	Blank
1025	1895	2-4-0 class T19
-1029		
1030	1897	2-4-0 class T19
-1033		
1034	1897	2-4-0 class T19
	1915	Blank
1035	1897	2-4-0 class T19
-1037		
1038	1897	2-4-0 class T19
	1910	Blank
1039	1897	2-4-0 class T19
1040	1902	2-4-2T class C32
-1049		
1050	Blank	
-1059		
1060	1895	2-4-2T class C32
-1069		
1070	1893	2-4-2T class C32
-1075		
1076	1894	2-4-2T class C32
-1089		
1090	1893	2-4-2T class C32
-1099		
1100	1898	0-4-4T class S44
-1103		
1104	1899	0-4-4T class S44
-1119		
1120	1900	0-4-4T class S44
-1133		
1134	1901	0-4-4T class S44
-1139		
1140	1916	0-6-0 class T77
-1148		

1149	1917	0-6-0 class T77
1150	1900	0-6-0 class F48
-1164		
1165	1901	0-6-0 class F48
-1188		
1189	1902	0-6-0 class F48 (G58)
1190	1902	0-6-0 class F48
-1204		
1205	1903	0-6-0 class F48
-1209		
1210	1905	0-6-0 class G58
-1219		
1220	1906	0-6-0 class G58
-1229		
1230	1910	0-6-0 class G58
-1237		
1238	1911	0-6-0 class G58
-1239		
1240	1912	0-6-0 class E72
-1248		
1249	1913	0-6-0 class E72
1250	1902	2-4-0 class T26
-1254	1920	0-6-0 class T77
1255	1902	2-4-0 class T26
-1259	1920	Blank
1260	1917	0-6-0 class T77
-1261		
1262	1918	0-6-0 class T77
-1267		
1268	1919	0-6-0 class T77
-1269		
1270	1920	0-6-0 class D81
-1274		
1275	1922	0-6-0 class D81
-1294		
1295	Blank	
-1299		
1300	1909	2-4-2T class Y65
-1309		
1310	1910	2-4-2T class Y65
-1311		
1312	Blank	
-1499		
1500	1911	4-6-0 class S69
1501	1912	4-6-0 class S69
-1504		
1505	1913	4-6-0 class S69
-1519		
1520	1914	4-6-0 class S69
-1533		
1534	1915	4-6-0 class S69
1539	1917	4-6-0 class S69
-1540		
1541	1920	4-6-0 class S69
-1547		
1548	1921	4-6-0 class S69
-1549		

1550	1920	4-6-0 class S69
-1553		
1554	1921	4-6-0 class S69
-1560		
1561	1920	4-6-0 class S69
-1570		
1571	Blank	
-1789		
1790	1911	4-4-0 class D56
-1799		
1800	1910	4-4-0 class D56
-1819		
1820	1909	4-4-0 class D56
-1829		
1830	1908	4-4-0 class D56
-1839		
1840	1906	4-4-0 class D56
-1847		
1848	1907	4-4-0 class D56
-1849		
1850	1903	4-4-0 class D56
-1853		
1854	1904	4-4-0 class D56
-1859		
1860	1903	4-4-0 class D56
-1869		
1870	1902	4-4-0 class S46
-1879		
1880	1901	4-4-0 class S46
-1889		
1890	1900	4-4-0 class S46

NORTH BRITISH RAILWAY

Introduction

The oldest part of the North British Railway was in the Monklands coalfields to the east of Glasgow around Coatbridge and Airdrie. Coal had been transported to Glasgow by the Monkland Canal from 1778, and to Edinburgh and the east by the Forth and Clyde Canal from 1790 and the Union Canal direct to Edinburgh from 1822. However, the eastbound journey was congested and slow, so in 1824 a group of coal owners, ironmasters and canal proprietors promoted the Monkland and Kirkintilloch Railway to connect with the Forth and Clyde canal at Kirkintilloch, and it was opened in October 1826 with the 4ft 6in gauge.

Although the Act authorised the use of locomotives, being the first Scottish Act to do so, it was not until May 1831 that two locomotives were purchased, the first to be built in Scotland. A tunnel at Bedlay with only 9ft headroom prevented the locomotives working through, so one locomotive worked each side and horse haulage continued through the tunnel until it was opened out in January 1832.

By 1845, six more railways had been built to the 4ft 6in gauge forming a continuous system; the Ballochney, which extended the Kipps branch of the M&K opened in 1828, the Glasgow, Garnkirk and Coatbridge (1831), the Pollok and Govan (1840), the Wishaw and Coltness (1833) and the Slamannan which extended the Ballochney Railway to a connection with the Union Canal (1841) and the Wilsontown, Morningside and Coltness, which was a continuation of the Wishaw and Coltness (1845). Of these, the GG&C, P&G and W&C were absorbed by the Caledonian Railway but the M&K, Slamannan and Ballochney railways were amalgamated as one company, Monkland Railways in 1848, having all been altered to standard gauge in 1847.

Meanwhile, a direct railway between Glasgow and Edinburgh had been mooted since 1824, but the Edinburgh and Glasgow Railway was not authorised until 1838 and opened in 1842. The E&G was engineered as a high-speed trunk railway in contrast to the Monkland railways with their many inclines, primarily intended for coal traffic (although passengers were carried) and laid out more like waggonways. On the E&G, high-speed passenger traffic was provided in addition to goods traffic, and both the Monkland railways and the E&G prospered in their different spheres to the extent that they acquired the Wilsontown, Morningside and Coltness in 1849, and started a secondary route from Edinburgh through Bathgate the same year.

The E&G had running powers over the Scottish Central Railway from Falkirk to Stirling, and worked the Stirling and Dunfermline Railway (opened 1849) from 1853, absorbing the Caledonian and Dumbartonshire Junction Railway in 1862.

The success of the E&G Railway encouraged other speculations for railways to connect with it. The Edinburgh, Leith and Granton Railway had already been authorised in 1836, but suffered from a shortage of capital and was only partially opened by August 1842, by which time the E&G Railway had already been operating to Haymarket for six months. The line was eventually completed in 1847 in the face of severe financial difficulties, but by then two new trunk lines had been authorised, the Edinburgh and Northern Railway and the North British Railway itself. The E&N, incorporated in 1845, purchased the virtually bankrupt EL&G in 1847 and changed its name to Edinburgh, Perth and Dundee Railway.

The route to the north faced the major obstacles of the Forth and Tay across which ferry services from Granton to Burntisland on the Forth, over which all services would have to pass, and from Tayport on the Tay to reach Dundee. Through services with a break of journey for the ferry were established to Perth on the Scottish Central Railway in July 1848, and Tayport was reached in 1850.

Further minor railways were opened in the Fifeshire region including the Fife and Kinross, Charleston (Charlestown) Railway and Harbour, West of Fife Mineral, Leslie and Leven and East of Fife. The North British as originally planned was concerned with the potential of traffic to the south-east of Edinburgh, initially as a purely local line along the coast to Dunbar. There was still no English railway north of Newcastle-upon-Tyne, and doubts were still being expressed about the viability of a second Anglo-Scottish line. However, by the time of incorporation on 4/7/1844, the prospectus had been revised and the projected line extended to Berwick-upon-Tweed, the Directors being convinced that a line would be built north from Newcastle. It was opened on 22/6/1846 with a branch line to the Royal Borough of Haddington from Longniddry. By this time the Newcastle and Berwick Railway had indeed been incorporated and reached the south bank of the Tweed at Tweedmouth on 1/7/1847 with a connecting ferry service.

Traffic was slow to develop initially but, after the opening on 29/8/1850 of the Royal Border Bridge at Berwick connecting the two railways, it began to grow and received a large boost with passengers travelling to the Great Exhibition in London in 1851. The East coast route to Scotland via the GN, NE and NB railways was duly established.

A branch from Reston to Duns (originally spelt Dunse) was opened on 15/8/1849, and the horse operated Edinburgh and Dalkeith Railway (the 'innocent' railway, incorporated 1826, opened 4/7/1831 - 10/1831) was acquired on 21/7/1845 and converted from 4ft 6in gauge to standard gauge on 7/7/1847. It had branches to Leith Harbour, Fishberrow, Musselburgh and Dalkeith. The North Berwick branch from Drem was opened to Williamstown on 13/8/1849 and to North Berwick on 17/6/1850.

In the meantime, the Edinburgh and Hawick Railway was authorised under NB auspices on 31/7/1845 and was opened on 1/11/1849. A branch from St Boswells to Kelso was opened on 17/6/1850 and extended to join the NE line from Tweedmouth through Coldstream on 1/6/1851.

The Jedburgh Railway from Roxburgh on the Kelso branch was opened on 17/1/1856, and was worked by the NB until absorbed on 3/7/1860; a branch line from Galashiels to Selkirk was opened on 5/4/1856.

The Peebles Railway, which formed a loop from the NB line between Eskbank and Galashiels, was leased by the NB in 1861. The Leadburn, Linton and Dolphinton Railway (incorporated 1862) was opened from Leadburn on the Peebles Railway on 4/7/1864 and absorbed by the NB on 31/7/1865. On 17/3/1867 it was joined by a branch of the Caledonian Railway from Carstairs.

On 21/7/1859, the Border Union Railway Act authorised the line from Hawick to Carlisle with branches from Riddings Junction to Langholm and Longtown to Gretna on the Caledonian Railway. The line was opened on 1/7/1862 and the NB began advertising the new route as the 'Waverley Route' by which it was known until its closure in 1969.

On the same date as the Border Union Railway, the Border Counties Railway (incorporated 1854) was opened from Riccarton Junction on the Border Union Railway to Hexham on the Newcastle to Carlisle line of the NE. The NB, who operated both Border railways, obtained running powers to Newcastle over this route and operated through services. A branch was opened from Reedsmouth to Morpeth on 1/5/1865 (Wansbeck Railway, incorporated 1859 and amalgamated with NB in 1862) connecting with the Blythe and Tyne Railway, crossing the NE main line by an overbridge. Connection with the NE was made 1871/2 and there was a branch from Scotsgap to Rothbury.

The Berwickshire Railway (incorporated 1862) extended the Duns branch to meet the Waverley line at Ravenswood between Melrose and Newtown St Boswells, which was the junction station for the branch. It was opened throughout on 2/10/1865, and also worked by the NB until amalgamated on 1/8/1876.

By leasing the Port Carlisle and Carlisle and Silloth Bay railways and docks in 1859, the NB enabled its goods traffic to reach the coast without having to pass through Carlisle station where the Caledonian Railway were in a strong position, diverting even NB locomotive spares over their own route to Edinburgh and Glasgow. The NB attempted to develop the port for passenger traffic also but without conspicuous success. The Port Carlisle and Silloth Bay companies were amalgamated in 1880.

£5 million had been spent on extending the railway from Hawick to Carlisle but revenue was disappointing. It had been built as a trunk route, but earned only branch line revenue and some NB Directors were in favour of selling it or even closing it. However, its significance, if not its profitability, increased when in 1876 the Midland Railway reached Carlisle and made agreement with the NB and the Glasgow and South Western railways for through expresses from St Pancras dividing at Carlisle, the Edinburgh portions going forward over the NB and the Glasgow portions over the G&SW in competition with the L&NW and the Caledonian Railways.

Despite this prestige service, however, it is doubtful if the Border Union section ever paid its way although it enabled Galashiels, Melrose and Hawick to have a through service to the south.

The mid-1860s were a period of severe financial strain on the company and stringent cut-backs were imposed on spending in all departments. Work in progress on the railway and in the works was held up, and suppliers were asked to delay delivery of orders in hand. This was the period when the company's fortunes, which had never been good, were at their lowest point. Train services were unreliable, and much of this was due to poor financial management. Prior to the amalgamation with the much more successful Edinburgh and Glasgow Railway in 1865, the NB was hardly a viable railway, only the Lothian coalfield and the Hawick to Edinburgh line providing any volume of traffic apart from the Anglo-Scottish traffic to Berwick which had still to develop. The amalgamation of the EP&D in 1862 had expanded the geographical area of the railway, but the necessity of ferries made it uncompetitive against the Caledonian Railway.

On the E&G section, the line between the two cities via Bathgate and Coatbridge was completed to Glasgow (College) in 1871. The E&G Campsie branch was extended by the Blane Valley Railway opening on 5/11/1866 for goods traffic and 1/7/1867 for passengers which, by means of the Strathendrick and Aberfoyle Railway, connected with the Forth and Clyde Junction Railway (leased by NB 1871) providing a through route from Glasgow (Queen Street) to Aberfoyle from its opening on 1/8/1882. Also connected with the Campsie branch was the Kelvin Valley Railway, authorised in 1873 and opened with NB operation to Kilsyth on 1/6/1878. The KV however was authorised as a line through the whole length of the valley to Maryhill on the Dumbarton line where a connection was made on 1/10/1879 but, except for a morning and evening train from Kilsyth to Maryhill and return from 29/10/1880 to 31/12/1880, the Maryhill to Torrance section saw only goods traffic. The KV was amalgamated on 1/8/1885 and from 2/7/1888 was extended by the Kilsyth and Bonnybridge Railway joining the Caledonian Railway Denny branch from Larbert. Both CR and NB trains operated between Kilsyth and Larbert, but it was not officially a joint line, merely a common one.

The City of Glasgow Union Railway was authorised on 29/7/1864 and when opened in December 1870 provided a link between the Glasgow and South Western Railway and the NB between the Glasgow and Paisley joint line and the Sighthill branch of the NB, avoiding the Caledonian Railway. The 6.25 miles from Pollok Junction to Springburn with a new bridge over the river cost £2 million, and north of the river there was a succession of tunnels and cuttings between deep retaining walls; it was steeply graded. The section from Dunlop Street to Springburn was not completed until 16/8/1875 for goods trains (its primary purpose - passenger trains operating to a temporary station at Dunlop Street) being extended to Bellgrove on the Coatbridge line on 1/6/1871 with through services to the Bathgate line from 1/9/1872. Passenger trains ran through to Barnhill from 1885 and right through to Springburn from 1887. South of the river services were extended to Govan and Paisley.

Links with the Caledonian were eventually made to the Barrhead and General Terminus line and also at Sighthill on the Buchanan Street line. A triangular junction connected the line with the new St Enoch station, opened in 1876 by the G&SW. Originally a joint line, it was partitioned in 1896, the NB taking over the section north of College West Junction and the G&SW the southern section, each company retaining running powers over the other section.

The Stobcross branch from Maryhill, authorised in 1870, was not opened until 20/10/1874 after encountering similar difficulties both engineering and legal as the CGU. The engineering works included a 30-chain diversion of the Forth and Clyde Canal, a viaduct over the Kelvin and many street bridges. There was also a branch from near Crow Road to Whiteinch on the Dumbarton Road from where the Whiteinch Tramway Company, operated by James and William Wood, conveyed the traffic over the road and across the fields to the river and the various yards and works. Horse haulage was used on this tramway until 1875 when a locomotive was obtained.

The Glasgow, Bothwell, Hamilton and Coatbridge Railway, incorporated in 1874 as an independent concern, was amalgamated with the NB in 1878 before it was fully open, and its four locomotives transferred to NB stock.

The Glasgow City and District Railway promoted by the NB enabled it to improve its crowded and inadequate station accommodation by building a line from near Bellgrove on the Coatbridge line across the city, with an underground station at Queen Street, to the Stobcross line near Partick. The new low-level station at Queen Street was only the fourth underground railway to be built. A new through station at High Street replaced the College station, and there was also a station at Charing Cross. The opening date was 15/3/1886 and on the same day a branch was opened to Hyndland. On 1/8/1886 a connecting spur from the Stobcross line to the Helensburgh line provided through running to the coast. A branch line was opened from High Street to Bridgeton Cross on 1/6/1892 and from 1/10/1896 the Dumbarton - Balloch Joint line provided a further link to the coast from Stobcross to Dalmuir via Yoker.

In Edinburgh the Waverley - Abbeyhill - Easter Road line gave access to Leith, and the Scotland Street tunnel of the Edinburgh, Leith and Granton Railway was closed in 1869. It has since been used for wagon storage, mushroom growing and storage for cars. Waverley station was extended between 1869-73 and again between 1892 and 1900. In 1873, the first sleeping cars to operate in the UK began running between Edinburgh and Kings Cross over the East Coast main line. Normally East Coast expresses did not stop at Berwick and NE locomotives worked through to Waverley. Only for a period of just over a year from 14th January 1897 to February 1898, when the NB unsuccessfully challenged these running powers in a legal action, were locomotives changed at Berwick.

Branches opened in the Edinburgh and Lothian areas were, Ormiston 1/5/1867 extended to Macmerry 1/5/1872; Penicuik (Penicuik Railway) 2/9/1872; Edinburgh Loanhead and Roslin Railway 23/7/1874 extended to Glencorse 2/7/1877; Edinburgh Suburban and Southside Junction Railway 1/12/1884; Eyemouth 13/4/1891; Giffard (a light railway from Ormiston) 14/10/1901; Corstorphine 1/2/1902.

The North British Hotel at Waverley Station in Edinburgh was opened on 15th October 1902.

The 'Lothian lines', which improved access to Leith docks from the Lothian coalfields, opened on 26/9/1915.

The route to the north is very largely the story of the Tay and Forth bridges, a story that has woven itself into the folklore of the nineteenth century with its dramatic ingredients of failure and success, tragedy and triumph.

The EP&D had introduced the world's first rail wagon ferry at Burntisland designed by its engineer Thomas Bouch. Named Leviathan, it began to operate on 1/3/1850.

Even so, the journey from Edinburgh to Dundee via the Granton-Burntisland and Tayport-Broughton Ferry ferries took at least 3 hours 20 minutes, although the straight line distance is only 46 miles.

Parliamentary bills for a bridge over the Tay were presented in 1864 and 1866, but failed because of doubts over the cost. However, under John Stirling of Kippendavie as NB Chairman, a further bill was passed in 1870 and Thomas Bouch, the younger brother of William Bouch, the Stockton and Darlington Railway locomotive engineer, was engaged to design it. He had left the EP&D in 1851 to run his own engineering consultancy business in Edinburgh. In this capacity he had engineered many of the Fifeshire lines and also lines south of Edinburgh and in the north of England, including several of the trans-Pennine lines of the Stockton and Darlington Railway, as well as the Sevenoaks to Maidstone line of the South Eastern railway. He had built viaducts at Barnard Castle, Deepdale, Belah and at Hownes Gill in Consett.

He had, however, a reputation for keeping costs to a minimum, which naturally found initial favour with the proprietors, but he lacked attention to detail and many of his structures had only marginal safety factors to withstand extraneous forces. Some of the railways he engineered subsequently complained that the work he was supposed to have supervised was plainly inadequate, and he would sometimes omit quite essential matters such as arranging with other railways for junctions to be made.

The two-mile-long, single-line bridge over the Tay which Bouch designed had eighty-five spans, of which thirteen were 'high girders' with the track running through them to give clearance for shipping. It was completed on 22/9/1877 and new rail connections to the bridge were opened on 1/1/1878. In June 1879, Queen Victoria crossed it and Bouch was knighted for his achievement on 26/6/1879.

Six months later on 28/12/1879 in a violent storm, whilst the last train of the day was crossing, the high girders in the centre were carried away and all seventy-five occupants of the train were drowned.

The Committee of Enquiry found against Bouch's design for the bridge and held him entirely to blame, although the NB could not escape some responsibility themselves. They had permitted trains to break the 25 mph speed limit and had been negligent in their own responsibility for supervising the contractors building the bridge. The effect on Bouch was devastating. It ruined his health, and he died ten months later in October 1880, aged 58.

Whilst the Bouch bridge was being built, the NB promoted the North British, Arbroath and Montrose Railway linking the Dundee and Arbroath Railway with their Montrose branch of the Scottish North Eastern Railway. Under the 1866 Act amalgamating the SNE with the Caledonian Railway, the NB had been granted running powers over the SNE system. This included the Dundee and Arbroath Railway, so by linking Arbroath and Montrose and carrying the line two miles north, the SNE main line to Aberdeen could be joined at Kinnaber Junction. This completed the East Coast main line and provided an alternative route to and from London, save only for the bridges over the Forth and Tay.

Incorporated in 1871, the line connected with the SNE Montrose to Bervie branch (opened 1/11/1865). It was opened from Arbroath to Lunan Bay on 8/11/1880 and throughout to Kinnaber Junction on 1/3/1881 but, because of the fall of the Tay bridge, was at first used only for local traffic.

This line had also been engineered by Thomas Bouch who designed the bridge over the South Esk at Montrose. This bridge was condemned in the light of the Tay Bridge disaster, being found to be out of perpendicular and curved instead of straight, as shown on the plans, and was demolished and rebuilt.

Bouch, however, did not live long enough to endure this final humiliation. Through trains began to operate over the line from 1/5/1883, with a considerable saving of time over the more circuitous CR route from Arbroath.

The Dundee and Arbroath Railway became a joint line from 1/2/1880 and the Montrose and Bervie Railway, which had been worked by the CR, was amalgamated with the NB on 18/7/1881.

The second Tay bridge was approved in 1881 and built by William Arrol, who also built the Forth Bridge and was knighted in 1890. Sixty yards to the west of the old structure with the piers exactly opposite the old ones, the new Tay bridge had double track and some of the girders from the first bridge were used in the second. It was opened on 11/7/1887. Thomas Bouch produced plans for two suspension bridges to cross the Forth, using the island of Inch Garvie in the middle of the Firth, in 1873, but work did not start as the Tay bridge was given priority. After the disaster, plans were cancelled, although approach lines were built to Dalmeny and Inverkeithing.

A new project was set up in 1881, the Forth Bridge Railway Committee as a joint venture, the NB contributing 35%, the Midland 30% and 35% shared between the NE and the GN.

The cantilever bridge designed by Sir John Fowler and his partner Sir Benjamin Baker, the Forth Bridge, is of steel rather than cast iron, imperfections in which had contributed to the failure of the first Tay bridge. The three double cantilevers with two central suspended spans total 5,349ft 6in long with two approach viaducts of 1,978ft on the south side and 968ft 3½in on the north, giving a total length of 8,295ft 9½in. All members under compression are of tubular form and circular shape wherever possible, and all members under tensile stress are open lattice girders. Weighing 50,000 tons, it is the largest railway bridge ever built although the Quebec Bridge over the St Lawrence (now a road bridge) has a single span of 1,800ft which is longer than the two 1,710ft spans of the Forth bridge. Fifty-seven men lost their lives during the construction of the Forth Bridge, and it was opened on 4/3/1890 by the Prince of Wales. Now well past its centenary, it was acclaimed throughout the World as a structural masterpiece.

Lines north of the bridge were doubled and uprated to main line standard, and a new main line constructed from Mawcarse to Hilton Junction (Bridge of Earn) through Glenfarg. New lines in Fife were also opened as follows: Tillicoultry to Rumbling Bridge (1869-71) joining the Fife and Kinross line at Hopefield (Devon Valley Railway); Thornton Junction - Buckhaven - Methil (1881-7) joining the Leven Railway; Cameron Bridge to Lochty 18/8/1898; Alloa - Kincardine - Culross - Dumfermline (1893-1906).

With the two bridges open, the way was clear for the famous 'railway races' between the East and West coast routes from London to Aberdeen, which culminated in 1895 and ended on safety grounds. In effect, of course, these 'races' ended at Kinnaber Junction because from there both trains had to use the same track.

The other big expansion of the NB was the West Highland Railway, promoted independently but backed by the NB, who worked the line to Fort William. The project was opposed by the Highland Railway who feared that the line would be extended through the Great Glen to Inverness.
The Act was passed in 1889. From Craigendoran on the Helensburgh line by the Gareloch and Loch Long to Tarbert, the line ran to Ardlui at the head of Loch Lomond. It then passed through Glen Falloch on the west side to cross the CR Callender and Oban line at Crianlarich. Climbing through Tyndrum to Bridge of Orchy, it then crossed the bleak Rannoch Moor for 33 miles at a summit of 1350 feet. Descending to the shore of Loch Treig to Tulloch, it then avoided Ben Nevis by passing through Glen Spean to Fort William. The formidable engineering works, including 350 viaducts and 50 overbridges, exceeded the £540,000 capital and further loans were needed. One Director, JH Renton, contributed a large amount to save the project, and his effigy was cut on a granite slab at Rannoch station.
The line to Fort William was opened on 7/8/1894. A branch to Banavie was authorised by the original Act, and this was opened on 31/5/1895.
As the railway opened in 1894, a second Act authorised an extension to Mallaig on the coast with further engineering features requiring 100 cuttings and no fewer than 11 tunnels.
The Mallaig extension was built with a government guarantee of 3% of part of the capital in addition to a similar guarantee from the NB Railway, and this caused a Parliamentary battle (the then Liberal Party being opposed to such government intervention) causing a delay in passing the Act.
Robert McAlpine was the contractor and several of the bridges were of concrete, including one with a span of 127 ft, then the largest span in this material. The biggest engineering feature was Glenfinnan viaduct, built on a 12 chain curve with 21 arches at a height of 100 ft. The extension was opened on 1st January 1901.
The Invergarry and Fort Augustus Railway was promoted largely by Lord Burton, a local landowner. Authorised in 1896, it ran from Spean Bridge on the West Highland line to Fort Augustus on the shores of Loch Ness. Its construction led to sparring between the Highland Railway and the NB, the former still fearing extension to Inverness. A bill for this extension failed in Parliament but, when the I&FA opened on 22/7/1903, it was worked by the HR not the NB, despite the HR having no direct connection. The extension of the line to a pier on the loch side, which required a swing bridge over the Caledonian canal locks in Fort Augustus, closed in 1907. The extension cost a quarter of the total cost of £350,000. In 1908 the HR withdrew their working arrangement, and the NB worked the line until 1911 when it closed for two years.
The NB took over the West Highland Railway on 31/12/1908, and purchased the I&FA for £25,000 on 1/8/1913, reopening it as a NB branch.

Locomotive Superintendents

Robert Thornton	1846-51	Resigned
William Smith	1851-54	Dismissed
Hon Edmund George Petre	1854	Dismissed
William Hurst	1855-66	Dismissed
Thomas Wheatley	1867-74	Resigned
Dugald Drummond	1875-83	Resigned
Matthew Holmes	1882-1903	Retired
William Paton Reid CBE	1904-19	Retired
Walter Chalmers	1920-23	Formation of LNER

The original NB locomotives had been ordered from Hawthorn's before Thornton's appointment and numbers 1-4 and 7 (delivered before the railway opened) were hired to the Edinburgh and Glasgow Railway in the meantime.
A total of seventy locomotives were obtained from Hawthorn's, and considerable difficulty was experienced from broken crank axles that began a chronic backlog of locomotive repairs which was to plague the NB for years.
A comprehensive works for locomotives and rolling stock was set up at St Margaret's, Meadowbank in Edinburgh.

Thornton grappled with the problems on the Hawthorn locomotives, but when his
solutions only made matters worse he was dismissed for incompetence in 1851.
The NB style of management was always somewhat autocratic, very much in the
traditional master and servant tradition. Even Reid in the twentieth century had to
suffer humiliations that many engineers would not have tolerated, and the NB never
granted its engineers the kind of autonomous authority they enjoyed on many other
railways.
Thornton's successor, William Smith, fared little better, and he too was dismissed
after a heated exchange with a committee of Directors when they complained that a
quarter of the Company's locomotives were not fit for traffic, awaiting repair in the
works. The Board called in William Hurst and Emmott of the Lancashire and Yorkshire
Railway to give them an independent report which was not favourable to Smith. In
addition it seems that Smith was just as unpleasant a man as the Board were employers
at this time.
The Hon Edmund George Petrie was then appointed, which proved a very mistaken decision
as he was a very young man and proved to be quite out of his depth on locomotive
matters and the ongoing critical situation.
St Margaret's works now being totally overwhelmed with repair work, Petrie was
instructed to scour the land for private firms able to take on some of the repairs.
To help alleviate the situation six locomotives were hired from the GN.
The Board, whose own competence can be called into question, demanded solutions
without providing suitable resources and the strain drove Petrie to drink. Within a
year of his appointment, he was dismissed for intoxication. Some solution to the
problem came when William Hurst, who had been one of the authors of the previous
report, applied for the job and was appointed. Hurst had been Locomotive
Superintendent of the Manchester and Bolton Railway at Salford, moving to the Miles
Platting works of the L&Y the following year. He had other connections with Scotland
being a director of the Scottish Wagon Company, a finance company.
Gradually, he succeeded in producing some order out of the chaos, rebuilding some of
the Hawthorn's, and also producing the first locomotives to be built for the company
at St Margaret's works.
In 1862, the EP&D locomotives came into NB ownership. The EP&D had workshops at
Burntisland established in 1847 under Robert Nicholson as Superintendent. Five
locomotives are recorded as being built there, but facilities were poor and these
probably used parts of older locomotives, as the railway had an agreement with the
Scottish Central Railway for locomotive work to be carried out in their workshops at
Perth.
The Cowlairs works of the Edinburgh and Glasgow Railway in Glasgow, one of the oldest
railway owned works, were much better equipped than St Margaret's, and after the
Edinburgh and Glasgow Railway amalgamated with the NB in 1865 this became the main NB
works in 1866, the last locomotives being built at St Margaret's in 1869, after which
it only dealt with repairs.
The first Locomotive Superintendent of the E&G was William Paton who designed the
express singles numbers 52 *Orion* and 58 *Sirius*, as well as four locomotives designed
for assisting trains on Cowlairs bank out of Queen St station.
The latter were not too successful, so trains continued to be assisted by a winding
engine attached to the train engine and slipped without stopping as the train over-
rode it. This system was only discontinued in November 1908.
Paton was unfortunate, in 1845, to be convicted of sending out a Bury locomotive in an
unfit state causing an accident when it failed for lack of steam, and was run into by
another train. In the absence of a proper signalling system, stalled locomotives were
a hazard, and the unfortunate Paton was found guilty of culpable homicide under
Scottish law and sentenced to twelve months imprisonment.
He was succeeded by William Steel Brown in 1861, and from 1863, by SW Johnson who
remained under Hurst for a year after the amalgamation until he left to become
Locomotive Superintendent of the Great Eastern Railway in 1860 (qv).
Shortly afterwards, Hurst was implicated in underhand dealings with his Scottish Wagon
Company, and was given six months notice on 16/8/1866, returning to the L&Y.
Thomas Wheatley apprenticed on the Leeds and Selby Railway, afterwards working for the
Midland and Manchester, Sheffield and Lincolnshire railways, becoming Southern

Divisional Superintendent of the L&NW in 1862 succeeding James Edward McConnell, and could therefore be regarded as well qualified when appointed to the NB.
He introduced the first internal cylinder 4-4-0s in the UK, one of which went down with the Tay bridge, but was recovered.
Of the amalgamated companies, the E&G locomotive stock was the best, reflecting its relative prosperity, but Wheatley was faced with having to replace many of the others with larger and more powerful machines. He reorganised the works, and because of the continuing financial restraints, many new locomotives utilised parts from older ones when they were withdrawn. Four- and five-foot, six-coupled, goods engines were built with 2-4-0s for secondary traffic.
Another financial scandal in 1874 resulted in Wheatley's resignation, and had he not done so it is likely that he too would have been dismissed. He became general engineer of the little Wigtownshire Railway, which can only have been regarded as a demotion after Wolverton and Cowlairs.
Dugald Drummond, aged 35, on his first appointment as Locomotive Superintendent had worked under William Stroudley at Cowlairs when Stroudley had been works manager, and had followed him to the Highland Railway in 1869. He was thus greatly influenced by Stroudley's designs, and adopted many features of these in the locomotives he designed for the NB. His *Abbotsford* 4-4-0s became a classic type on the NB as well as the Caledonian, Highland and London and South Western railways. He also brought from Brighton a practice of naming locomotives after places where they were in use.
Westinghouse brake systems were introduced with the inauguration of through services from London St Pancras for which services his 4-4-0s were intended. He introduced the 0-4-4T arrangement to the NB which was continued by his successors.
In general, he brought about a transformation in the locomotive affairs of the company. A number of Cowlairs men who transferred with him included his brother Peter, later to become Locomotive and Carriage and Wagon Superintendent of the Highland and Glasgow and South Western railways, and the results of his combined team were beneficial for the NB.
They also did much to establish Drummond's formidable reputation, which led to him being offered and accepting the Locomotive Superintendency of the Caledonian Railway. Like his predecessors at Cowlairs, it is probable that Drummond also enjoyed pecuniary advantages from his period of office, but unlike them his conduct was never called into question.
Matthew Holmes was the son of a foreman at the E&G's Haymarket Works. After apprenticing with Hawthorn & Co at Leith, he joined the E&G himself and was eventually appointed Chief Inspector and Assistant to Drummond. He was greatly respected by all the men under him, and during this period of twenty-one years, the longest period of office, the modernisation introduced by Drummond was steadily maintained, further 4-4-0s being added, together with six-coupled tender and tank engines.
Under Holmes, stability was finally achieved in the locomotive department.
After Holmes retired due to ill health, he was succeeded by WP Reid the son of Robert Reid the E&G Railway's Carriage and Wagon Superintendent. He apprenticed under Holmes at Cowlairs, and after periods at Balloch, Dunfermline, Dundee and St Margaret's works, he was appointed as assistant to Holmes.
In addition to continuing and developing the Drummond/Holmes designs, including the *Scott* 4-4-0s, he introduced the famous North British Atlantics in 1906. An 0-6-2T design in 1909, and 4-4-2Ts in 1911 and 1915, were also new to the NB, and superheating enabled much more powerful goods and passenger locomotives to be produced.
From 1st September 1913, Reid introduced a power classification system for locomotives denoted by a single letter similar to that used on the Midland Railway. Letters A to G were for goods and shunting engines, and H to R (except O and Q) for passenger engines. As this was purely a power classification, several different types of both tender and tank engines could have the same letter, so because the letters are not very useful in identifying a particular class, they have not been used in the text.

The full list was as follows:

	Type	Class	LNE class
A	0-6-2T	858	N14, N15
B	0-6-0	848	J35
	0-6-0	8	J37 (Superheated WP 165 lbs/sq in)
C	0-6-0	100	J32
	0-6-0	604	J36
D	0-6-0	566	J33
	0-6-0	34 & 497	J34
	0-6-0T	795	J83
E	0-6-0	396	J31
	0-6-0ST	229	J81
	0-6-0ST	251	J84 (As rebuilt from 0-6-0)
	0-6-0ST	130	J85
	0-6-0ST	226/8	J86
F	0-6-0T	836	J88
G	0-4-0ST	32	Y9
H	4-4-2	868	C11 (Saturated as built)
I	4-4-2	509	C10 (Superheated as built and as rebuilt from 868 class)
J	4-4-0	895	D29
	4-4-0	400	D30 (Superheated as built)
K	4-4-0	317	D26
	4-4-0	882	D32
	4-4-0	331	D33
	4-4-0	149	D34 (Superheated as built)
L	4-4-2T	438	C16
	4-4-0	695	D36 (Superheated rebuild)
M	4-4-2T	1	C15
	4-4-0	476	D27, D28 (Rebuilds)
	4-4-0	574	D31 (Rebuilds)
	4-4-0	633	D31 (Rebuilds)
	4-4-0	729	D31 (Rebuilds)
	0-4-4T	239	G9
N	4-4-0	592	D25
	4-4-0	693	D35
P	4-4-0T	494	D50
	2-4-0	418	E7
	0-4-4T	586	G7
	0-4-4T	157	G8 (Rebuilt from 0-4-2T)
R	4-4-0T	72	D51
	0-6-0T	165	J82
S	0-6-0	8	J37 (Superheated WP 175 lbs/sq in

0-4-0 no 1011 and 'petrol engine no 1' were unclassified.

Reid was awarded the CBE in 1920 (after his retirement at the end of 1919) for his contribution to the war effort.
Walter Chalmers was also apprenticed at Cowlairs, and became responsible for the inspection of new materials and purchase of rolling stock. He became Chief Draughtsman in 1906.
In his short tenure before the LNER took over in 1923, his principle achievement was the improved version of Reid's Atlantic.
Driving position was on the left.

LNER Renumbering
Under the temporary scheme introduced in 9/1923, NB numbers were suffixed by the letter B. From 2/1924 until the 1946, renumbering NB numbers had 9000 added.

BR Renumbering
In common with other LNE locomotives, BR added 60000 to the 1946 LNER numbers.

NORTH BRITISH RAILWAY

Constituent Companies

Monkland and Kirkintilloch Railway (4ft 6in gauge)

Incorporated 17/5/1824. Opened 10/1826.
This was the first railway authorised to use locomotives in its original Act of
Parliament, but locomotives were not introduced until 10/5/1831. It connected with
the Forth and Clyde canal at Kirkintilloch, offering a shorter journey for eastbound
coal than the Monkland canal.
Gauge altered to standard 26-7/7/1847.
Amalgamated with Ballochney and Slamannan Railways as **Monkland Railways** 14/8/1848.
Even before amalgamation, there was close co-operation between the above companies
having common interests and several of the Directors were on the Boards of the other
companies. Until late in 1838, the M&K used the Ballochney Railway works at
Greenside, Kipps. From late 1838, the M&K used their new works at Moss-side, Kipps.
This works survived as 'Kipps Wagon-shop' until the mid-1960s. At least five
locomotives were built by the M&K.

17 locomotives as below (records are sparse and in addition there may have been
others):

0-4-0 Built by Murdoch & Aitken, Glasgow.
DW 3ft 9in; Cyls (vertical) 10½ x 24.
These were the first locomotives to be built in Scotland, and were designed by George
Dodds, the Ballochney Railway engineer. They were of the Killingworth type, the two
vertical cylinders sunk into the boiler barrel over the axle centres with ball and
socket joints on the coupling rods. There was a single firetube halfway down the
barrel where a tube plate was fitted.

Name	Date	
Monkland	5/1831	Scrapped about 1846
Kirkintilloch	9/1831	
	6/1841	Sold to Wishaw & Coltness Railway, renamed *Jenny*
		(see Volume 4 page 18)

0-4-0 Built by M&K Railway at Greenside, Kipps.
DW 4ft 0in; Cyls (vertical) $10^3/8$ x 24.
Built by George Dodds, and believed to be similar to Killingworth type locomotives
above. Name and date of numbering not known.

No	Date	
3	c5/1834	Disposal not known. Replaced 1857.

0-4-0 Built by M&K Railway at Greenside, Kipps.
DW 4ft 0in; Cyls (vertical) 10½ x 24
George Dodds died in 1835, but engineering work was carried on by his son, William
Dodds, and this is believed to have been a further Killingworth type engine.

No	Name	Date	
4	*Victoria*	c1837/8	Disposal not known. Replaced 1843.

0-4-0 Built by M&K Railway at Moss-side, Kipps.
DW 4ft 0in; Cyls 13 x 20.
Inside cylinder engine of conventional design.

Name	Date	
Atlas	1840	Disposal not known.

0-4-0 Built by M&K Railway at Moss-side, Kipps.
DW 4ft 0in; Cyls 13 x 20.
Inside cylinder engine of conventional design.

Name	Date	
Atlas	1840	Disposal not known.

0-4-0 Built by M&K Railway at Moss-side, Kipps.
DW 4ft 6in; Cyls 14 x 20.

Name	Date	
Zephyr	1841/2	Disposal of these locomotives is not known but it is
Sirocco	1841/2	possible that parts of these and those above were used to
		build further locomotives, possibly two in number.

0-4-0 Built by Neilson & Co. Works nos below.
DW 4ft 6in; Cyls 14 x 20.
M&K numbering not known, disposal not known.

Works no	Approx date	
4	1843	Replaced 1857
5	1843	Replaced 1857
10	1844	
11	1844	
12	1844	
13	1844	
24	1847	
25	1847	
26	1847	
27	1847	

Ballochney Railway (4ft 6in gauge)
Incorporated 5/1826, opened 1828.
Extension of the Kipps branch of the Monkland & Kirkintilloch Railway using horse haulage and two inclines worked by stationary winding engines. M&K locomotives operated on the railway when introduced, but one locomotive is believed to have been built by the company. Gauge altered to standard 26-7/7/1847. Amalgamated with Monkland & Kirkintilloch and Slamannan Railways as **Monkland Railways** 14/8/1848.

1 locomotive as under:

Details not known but built by the Ballochney Railway at Greenside, Kipps.

Name	Date	
Ballochney	1836	Disposal not known.

Other locomotives may have been built but there are no records.

Slamannan Railway (4ft 6in gauge)

Incorporated 3/7/1835. Opened 5/8/1840 from Arbuckle branch of Ballochney Railway to Causwayend on Union Canal. Interchange with Edinburgh and Glasgow Railway as well as Union Canal from 26/1/1844. With the Monkland & Kirkintilloch, Wilsontown, Morningside and Coltness, Glasgow Garnkirk and Coatbridge, Wishaw and Coltness and the Pollock and Govan, these railways formed a continuous 4ft 6in gauge system in the Airdrie, Motherwell and Coatbridge district. The latter three companies however were taken over by the Caledonian Railway (see Volume 4). The Slamannan Railway was worked by the M&K from 1842 and the gauge altered to standard 26-7/7/1847. Amalgamated with M&K and Ballochney railways as **Monkland Railways** 14/8/1848.

3 locomotives as under:

2-2-2 Built by Jas M Rowan & Co, Glasgow.
DW 5ft 0in; Cyls 15 x 18

Name	Date	
Boanerges	1839	Sold to Wishaw & Coltness Railway 1842. See Volume 4 page 18.
Borealis	1839	Sold to Wishaw & Coltness Railway 1842, and renamed *Mercury*. See Volume 4 page 18.

0-4-0 Built by Murdoch, Aitken & Co, Glasgow.
Details not known.

Name	Date	
Glenellrigg	1841	Disposal not known.

Wilsontown, Morningside and Coltness Railway - 4ft 6in gauge.

Incorporated 1841. Opened Chapel Colliery (Coltness) to Longridge 6/1845.
Extension for 8¾ miles of Wishaw and Coltness Railway.
Company transferred to Edinburgh and Glasgow Railway 28/7/1849 who opened a Bathgate to Longridge connection on 1/5/1850, but locomotives acquired by Monkland Railways.
Presumed converted to standard gauge at the same date as W&C, 1/6/1849.

6 locomotives as under (Monkland Railways numbers not known):

0-4-2 Built by R&W Hawthorn & Co. Works nos below.
DW 5ft 0in; Cyls 14 x 21.

Name	Date*	Works no	
Fireking	1843*	396*	All three locomotives
Allanton	1844	448*	withdrawn
Torch	1846	453	before 1865

* Works numbers given in SLS Journal Vol 23 page 146 and Vol 24 page 203 (1946/7) are Suspect for the given dates by comparison with other orders in the same range of numbers, 1846/7 being more consistent. If the early date of 1843 for *Fireking* is correct the possibility that it was purchased from the contractor building the line arises.

Type uncertain built by Neilson & Co, Works nos 14,15 & 31.
DW not ascertained; Cyls 16 x 20. No record of names, if any.

Works nos	Date	
14	1846	All three locomotives
15	1846	withdrawn
31	1848	before 1865

Monkland Railways

Incorporated 14/8/1848 by amalgamation of the above three companies. Slamannan line
extended to Borrowstones (B'ness) 17/3/1851 crossing Edinburgh and Glasgow Railway.
Blackstone to Bathgate (E&G Railway) opened 1855 (goods), 1856 (passengers).
Amalgamated with Edinburgh and Glasgow Railway 31/7/1865. Combined company absorbed
by North British Railway 1/8/1865. Locomotive numbering was introduced on 11/5/1852
but nos uncertain.

30 locomotives as under (plus one ex-Stirling & Dunfermline, not confirmed):

0-6-0 Built by R&W Hawthorn & Co, Works no 698.
DW 5ft 0in; Cyls 16 x 22.
Possibly numbered between 23-6, built c1848. Disposal not known. Not taken into NB
Railway stock.

0-4-0 Built by Neilson & Co.
DW 4ft 6in; Cyls 14 x 20.

Possible no	Date	
between 23-6	1849	To North British Railway **275** 1865
	1867	Rebuilt
	1875	Sold to R&I Easton

0-6-0 Built by R&W Hawthorn & Co.
DW 5ft 0in; Cyls 16 x 24.
Double framed, similar to NB 137 (ex-Edinburgh, Perth & Dundee). Described as 'heavy
luggage engine'.
1852

no	Name	Date	
22	*Achilles*	1850	To NB **276** 1865
		1852	Name removed
		1874	To duplicate list 276A
		1880	Withdrawn

0-4-0 Built by R&W Hawthorn & Co.
DW 5ft 0in; Cyls 15 x 18.
Locomotives of the North British Railway 1846-82 (SLS) states that this locomotive may
have been built for the Glasgow, Dumfries and Carlisle Railway.
1852

no	Date	
not known	1851	To NB **270** 1865
	1867	Rebuilt
	1876	To duplicate list 270A
	1894	Withdrawn

0-6-0 Built by R&W Hawthorn & Co, Works nos 776 (uncertain 1851), 999/1000 (1856).
DW 4ft 6in; Cyls 16 x 24; Double framed. Rebuilt DW 5ft 0in; WB 7ft 3in + 6ft 9in.

		NB no		Duplicate		
1852 no	Date	1865	Rebuilt	no	date	Withdrawn
31*	1851	**277**	1866	277A	1879	1883
33	1856	**278**	1866	278A	1876	1884
34	1856	**279**	1866	279A	1879	1882

* Presumably renumbered as second no 31 recorded in 1855.

0-4-0 Built by R&W Hawthorn & Co, Works nos 868 (uncertain 1852), 908, 935/6 (1854/5).
DW 4ft 6in; WB 7ft 9in; Cyls 15 x 20; Double framed, no dome, stovepipe chimney.
Four-wheel tenders. No 30 had a tall brass safety valve on the boiler. No 27 was to
have been called *Hermes*, but naming ceased in 1852 when numbers were introduced.

		NB no		Duplicate		
No	Date	1865	Rebuilt	no	date	Withdrawn
27	1852	**271**	1867	271A	1879	
				874	1895	1896
30	1854	**272**	1867	272A	1880	
				875	1895	
				1075	1901	1902
31	1855	**273**	1867	273A	1880	1888
32	1855	**274**	1867	274A	1877	1887

0-6-0 Built by R&W Hawthorne & Co, Works no 790.
DW 5ft 0in; Cyls 16 x 24; Ex-Stirling and Dunfermline (see page 140). Not confirmed.

0-4-0ST Built by Sharp Stewart & Co, Works no 695.
DW 3ft 9in; Cyls 15 x 22.

No	Date	
28	1852	Rebuilt 0-4-2 at unknown date. To NB **281** 1865.
	1876	To duplicate list 281A and withdrawn same year

0-4-0ST Built by Neilson & Co.
DW 3ft 6in; Cyls 12 x 18.

	Date	
No not known	1855	To NB **282** 1865
	1866	Withdrawn

0-4-2 Built by Neilson & Co (N). Works nos below.
R&W Hawthorne & Co (H).
DW 5ft 0in; Cyls 16 x 22 o/s; Standard goods engine; Tall conical dome with square
base over firebox.

		Works	NB no	Rebuilt	Duplicate		
No	Date	no	1865	0-6-0	no	date	Withdrawn
35	11/1856	N353*	**295**		295A	1877	1882
36	1859	N461	**296**	1867/8	296A	1879	1889
37	1860	N536	**297**	1867/8	297A	1875	1882
38	1860	N556	**298**	1867/8			1875
39	1862	N740	**299**		299A	1880	1891
40	1862	N741	**300**		300A	1879	1890
3	1857	H	**304**	1867/8	304A	1876	1880
4	1857	H	**305**	1867/8	305A	1876	1882

* Not confirmed

0-4-2 Built by Neilson & Co.
DW 5ft 0in; Cyls 15 x 22; Modification of standard goods.

Nos not		NB no	Rebuilt	Duplicate		
known	Date	1865	0-6-0	no	date	Withdrawn
	1863	**301**	1867/8	301A	1879	1890
	1864	**302**		302A	1879	1886
	1864	**303**		303A	1879	1882

0-4-0ST Built by Neilson & Co. Works nos 812, 932.
DW 3ft 6in; WB 5ft 9in; Cyls 12 x 18 o/s.

Nos not		NB no	Duplicate		
known	Date	1865	no	date	Withdrawn
	1862	**313**	313A	1877	1886
	1864	**314**	314A	1877	1892

0-4-0ST Built by Neilson & Co.
DW 3ft 6in; WB 4ft 10in; Cyls 10 x 18 o/s.
Purchased second-hand from Shaw, Thompson & Moore. Believed built for James Gowan of
Dunkeld and named *Dunkeld*.

No not	Date	
known	built	
	1862	Date of purchase not ascertained. To NB **315** 1865.
	1877	To duplicate list 315A
	1884	Withdrawn

0-4-2ST Built by Neilson & Co. Works no 406.
DW 5ft 0in; WB 7ft 5½in + 6ft 5½in; Cyls 15½in x 22.

No	date	
5	1857	To NB **316** 1865
	1868	Rebuilt 0-6-0ST DW 4ft 2in; Cyls 16 x 22
	1884	To duplicate list 316A
	1894	Withdrawn

0-4-0 Built by R&W Hawthorn & Co.
DW 5ft 0in; WB 8ft 0in; Cyls 15 x 20.

Nos not		NB no		Duplicate		
known	Date	1865	Rebuilt	no	year	Withdrawn
	1864	**268**	1875 Cyls 16 x 20	268A	1882	
			DW 4ft 0in.	820	1895	
				1020	1901	1921
	1864	**269**		269A	1887	
				821	1895	
				1021	1901	1921

Caledonian and Dumbartonshire Junction Railway

Incorporated 26/6/1846.
Opened Bowling to Balloch 15/7/1850. Formed joint Board of Management with **Glasgow,
Dumbarton and Helensburgh Railway** (incorporated 15/8/1855, opened Cowlairs to Bowling
and Dalreoch Junction to Helensburgh 31/5/1858) with the trading title of
Dumbartonshire Railways. Joined Edinburgh and Glasgow Railways at Cowlairs, but owing
to failure to agree terms with the E&G trains, ran to the Caledonian station at
Buchanan St until 30/6/1858, thereafter to the E&G Queen St Station. In 1851, Patrick
Stirling held his first post as Locomotive Superintendent on this railway. Trains
divided at Dumbarton for Balloch and Helensburgh. Absorbed by Edinburgh and Glasgow
Railway 14/8/1862.

9 Locomotives as under:

2-2-2 Built by Stark and Fulton, Glasgow in 1849.
DW 5ft 0in; Cyls 12 x 16.
Purchased from contractor.

No	Date	
1	1849	Disposal
2	1849	not known

2-2-2WT Built by Neilson & Co. Works nos 38/9.
DW 5ft 0in; Cyls 14 x 20.
These locomotives had copper fireboxes and brass tubes, 500 gallon tenders with 50
cubic feet of coke capacity.

No	Date	Rebuilt 2-4-0T	E&G no	NB no	
3	1850	1851	9	**309**	1871 Withdrawn
4	1850	1851	10	**310**	1882 To duplicate list 310A 1874

2-2-0WT Built by Neilson & Co. Works no 42.
DW 5ft 0in; WB 10ft 8in + 5ft 0in; Cyls 10 x 15.
Became NBR Inspection engine/saloon. Frequently referred to as 'The Cab'.

No	Date	
5	1850	Originally named *Wee Scotland*
	1858	Rebuilt 2-2-2
	1862	To E&G no 88. Renumbered 13 in 1864.
	1865	To NB **312**
	1868	Rebuilt with inspection saloon
	1882	Rebuilt
	1884	To duplicate list 312A
	1895	Rebuilt and renumbered 879
	1901	Renumbered 1079
	1911	Sold

2-2-2WT Built by Neilson & Co. Works No 45
DW 5ft 6in; Cyls 14 x 20.

No	Date	
6	1850	To E&G 11 1862, NB **311** 1865. Withdrawn 1872.

2-4-0 Built by John Jones & Son, Liverpool in 1857.
DW 5ft 0in (or 4ft 6in); Cyls 17 x 20 o/s.
Records of DW size differ, and some records give 0-4-2 instead of 2-4-0. The
locomotive, which was not delivered until 1858, is thought to have been of the 'Crewe'
type.

No	Date	E&G no 1862	NB no 1865	Withdrawn
9	1858	82*	**308**	1874

* E&G number not certain

2-4-0 Built by John Jones & Sons, Liverpool.
DW 6ft 0in; Cyls 16 x 22 o/s 'Crewe' type.

No	Date	E&G no 1862	NB no 1865	Duplicate no	year	Withdrawn
7	1858	8	**306**	306A	1879	1882
8	1858	22	**307**			1872

Stirling and Dunfermline Railway

Incorporated 16/7/1846.
Opened Dunfermline (Edinburgh & Northern) to Oakley 13/12/1849, to Alloa 28/8/1850 and Stirling 1/7/1852. Stirling and Tillicoultry and Alloa Harbour branch 3/6/1851.
Worked Edinburgh & Glasgow Railway (who had running powers over the Scottish Central Railway from Falkirk to Stirling) from 8/1853 through a separate **Stirling and Dunfermline Committee**. Company vested in the Edinburgh and Glasgow Railway 1858 (locos to E&G stock 1854).

7 Locomotives as under (no record of numbering):

0-6-0 Built by R&W Hawthorn & Co. Works no 790.
DW 5ft 0in; Cyls 16 X 24; Double Frames.
      Date
(i)   1852   To E&G 1854 but no record of E&G no. May have been transferred
              to Monkland Railways in compensation for damages.
       1865   Rebuilt DW 4ft 9in; Cyls 16¼ x 24, which was regarded as a
              renewal and to NB no **280**
       1895   To duplicate list no 876. Withdrawn 1899 (replaced 1893).

0-4-2 Built by Simpson & Co, Aberdeen.
DW 5ft 0in; Cyls 15 x 21; Double frames.

		E&G no	NB no			Duplicate		
	Date	1854	1865	Rebuilt		no	year	Withdrawn
(ii)	1851	60	**247**	1866 Cyls 16 x 22		247A	1892	
				WB 7ft 1½in				
				+ 7ft 1½in		872	1895	
				1885		1072	1901	1907
(iii)	1851	61	**248**	1867 Cyls 16 x 22				
				WB 7ft 9in + 7ft 1in				
				1873		248A	1892	1895

0-4-2 Built by Neilson & Co. Works nos 72-4
DW 5ft 0in; Cyls 15 x 20; o/s frames.
Boilers and tubes were supplied from Cowlairs from spares.

		E&G no	NB no	
	Date	1854	1865	Withdrawn
(iv)	1854	68	**253**	1870
(v)	1854	66	**251**	1867
(vi)	1854	67	**252**	1871

2-2-2T Built by Neilson & Co. Works no 76, 1850.
DW 5ft 0in; Cyls 10 x 15; Adams patent light engine and coach purchased from stock to work the Tillicoultry branch. It was not very efficient and was replaced on this service.
(vii) 1851   To E&G no 69 in 1854
       1865   To NB no **254**. Withdrawn 1870.

Edinburgh and Glasgow Railway

Incorporated 4/7/1838.
Opened Glasgow (Queen St) to Edinburgh (Haymarket) 21/2/1842. Extended to Edinburgh
North Bridge (later Waverley) 1/8/1846; Falkirk to Shieldhill branch opened 28/8/1847;
Slamannan Junction branch 28/8/1847; Lenzie to Campsie branch 5/7/1848. Leased
Edinburgh and Bathgate Railway (incorporated 1847) in 1848; opened Ratho to Bathgate
12/11/1849; Bathgate to Longridge 1/5/1850; Bathgate to Coatbridge 11/8/1862.
Absorbed Caledonian and Dumbartonshire Junction and Glasgow, Dumbarton and Helensburgh
Railways 1862, and worked Glasgow and Milngavie Junction Railway (incorporated 1861,
opened Westerton-Milngavie 21/4/1863). Amalgamated with North British Railway
1/8/1865. Line extended from Coatbridge to Glasgow (College) 1/4/1871.
Locomotive Superintendent: William Paton. Locomotive names removed by NBR.

120 Locomotives as under, plus one not confirmed:

0-4-0 or 2-2-0 Built by E Bury & Co.
DW 5ft 0in (0-4-0), 5ft 6in (2-2-0); Cyls 13 x 18. Bar frames.
One of these six locomotives was a passenger 2-2-0 the others being for goods traffic,
0-4-0. Some accounts give a different order for the names.

No	Name	Date	Scrapped or withdrawn	
8	*Pallas*	1841	1862	
9	*Napier*	1841	1863	(replaced 1862)
10	*Smeaton*	1841	1864	(replaced 1862)
11	*Watt*	1841	1864	(replaced 1862)
12	*Savery*	1841	1866	(replaced 1865)
13	*Bell*	1841	1863	

2-2-0 Built by E Bury & Co.
DW 5ft 6in; Cyls 13 x 18; Bar frames.
Various accounts give different names. Alternatives shown below. Rebuilt with six
wheels by 1854 and later as 0-4-2T. DW 5ft 0in; Cyls 14 x 18.

No	Name	Date	Rebuilt	NB No 1865	Withdrawn
14	*Davy* or	1841	6 wheel by 1854		
	Baird		0-4-2T 1856	**263**	1873
15	*Rennie* or	1842	2-2-2-0 1845-49		
	Baird or		0-4-2T 1858	**264**	1871
	Brindley				
16	*Telford* or	1842	6 wheel by 1854		
	Murdoch		0-4-2T 1859	**265**	1871
17	*Galileo* or	1842	6 wheel by 1854		
	Newcomen		0-4-2T 1862	**266**	1872

2-2-2 Built by R&W Hawthorn & Co. Works nos 333-9.
DW 5ft 6in; Cyls 13 x 18; Outside frames.
No 1 possibly named *Archimedes*, no 2 named *Euclid*, others not known.

No	Date	
1	1841	Replaced 1861
2	1841	Rebuilt 14in cyls by 1867; DW 6ft 0in.
		To NB **220** 1865. Withdrawn 1870.
3	1841	Replaced 1861
4	1841	Replaced 1860
5	1841	Replaced 1860. Possibly sold to Edinburgh, Perth and Dundee
		Railway but not confirmed. Did not enter NB stock.
6	1841	Replaced 1862
7	1841	Replaced 1861

2-2-2 Built by R&W Hawthorn & Co. Works nos 546-51.
DW 6ft 0in; Cyls 16 x 18; Originally fitted with Hawthorn expansion valve gear but
this was not found satisfactory and was changed to link motion. Intended for express
passenger trains.

	Known	NB no	
No	names	1865	Withdrawn
34	*Niger*	**219**	1871
35			(replaced 1866)
36			(replaced 1866)
37	*Asia*	**221**	1871
38			by 1865
39	*America*	**222**	1873

2-2-2 Built by B Hick & Co.
DW 5ft 6in; WB 6ft 9¾in + 5ft 11³/₈in; Cyls 15 x 22 o/s; Blr 3ft 6in x 10ft 0in.
Firebox 4ft 0⁵/₁₆in x 3ft 9³/₈in x 3ft 11in high; Large dome behind chimney.

No	Date	
42	1846/7	Sold to Stockton and Darlington Railway no 93 *Uranus*, 3/1855.
		See Volume 5A page 73.
43	1846/7	Sold to Stockton and Darlington Railway no 94 *Neptune*, 3/1855.
		See Volume 5A page 73.

2-2-2 Built by Neilson & Co. Works nos 16-21.
DW 6ft 0in; Cyls 15 x 20; Neilson patent valves fitted. Rebuilt as goods engines and
cylinders renewed.

	Known		Rebuilt	NB no	
No	name	Date	0-4-2 DW 5ft 0in	1865	Withdrawn
44	*Mercury*	1847/8	1852/3	**243**	1868
45		1847/8	1852/3		by 1865
46	*Mars*	1847/8	1852/3	**244**	1868
47		1847/8	1852/3		by 1865
48	*Ceres*	1847/8	1852/3	**245**	1868
49	*Juno*	1847/8	1852/3	**246**	1868

2-2-2 Built by Sharp Brothers. Works nos below.
DW 5ft 6in; Cyls 15 x 20. Standard Sharp Single.

			Works		NB no	Duplicate		
No	Name	Date	no	Rebuilt	1865	no	year	Withdrawn
50	*Vesta*	1847	452	1864	**225**			1882
51	*Astraeu*	1847	464*		**226**			1870
52	*Diana*	1847	465*	1866 no dome	**227**	227A	1890	
						871	1895	by 1901
53	*Hebe*	1847	466*		**228**			1870
54	*Jupiter*	1848	479		**229**			1871
55	*Saturn*	1848	487		**230**			1871

* Not confirmed

2-2-2 Built by E&G Railway at Cowlairs.
DW 6ft 0in; LW 4ft 0in; TW 3ft 6in; Cyls 15 x 20.
Centre dome; o/s frames; Gooch valve gear. It was intended to build twenty but only
two were completed.

			NB no	
No	Name	Date	1865	Withdrawn
58	*Sirius*	1848	**223**	1868
59	*Orion*	1848	**224**	1871

2-2-2 Built by Beyer Peacock & Co. Works nos 21-6, 133/4.
DW 6ft 6in; LW & TW 3ft 6in; WB 7ft 3in + 7ft 3in; Cyls 16 x 20;
Blr 3ft $11^7/8$in x 10ft 1in; THS 1011 sq ft; WP 130-140 lbs/sq in;
Wt 22¾ tons. Charles Beyer design. Double frames with outside bearings on LW and TW,
no dome, weatherboard, open splashers, smokebox wing plates, safety valve on flush
firebox. Four wheel tender. Names applied 1880.

1880 No Name	Date	1862 no	Rebuilt	NB no 1865	Duplicate no	Duplicate year	Withdrawn
82 *Polmont*	1856	6	1875: stovepipe chimney & dome, cab sheets added 1897: Holmes blr and Westinghouse brake	213	803	1895	
					1003	1900	1909
83 *Lenzie*	1856	23	1880: Cyls 16 x 22 cab and dome	214	804	1895	
					1004	1900	1909
84 *Newcastle*	1856	42	1880: as 214	215	805	1895	
					1005	1901	1905
85 *Dullatur*	1856	43	1873: DW 6ft 0in, dome, stovepipe chimney 1885: 16 x 22 cyls, DW 6ft 6in, cab & dome	216	806	1895	
					1006	1901	1912
86 *Castlecary*	1856	56	1880: as 214	217	807	1895	
					1007	1909	1901
87 *Winchburgh*	1856	57	1880: as 214	218	808	1895	
					1008	1901	1907
1 *Haymarket*	1861		1880: as 214	211	801	1895	
					1001	1900	1910
2 *Corstorphine*	1861		1880: as 214	212	802	1895	
					1002	1900	1910

0-4-0 Built by E Bury & Co in 1846.
DW 5ft 0in; Cyls 16 x 20; Bar frames.
Built for Edinburgh, Leith and Granton Railway but not taken up.

No	Name	Date	Rebuilt	NB no 1865	Withdrawn
31	*Mersey*	1846	0-4-2 by 1854. Probably DW 4ft 6in Cyls 15 x 20 early 1860s	261	1873
32	*Medway*	1846	0-4-2 by 1854.	267	1867
33	*Edinburgh*	1846	Exploded at Stirling and scrapped. Possibly rebuilt 0-4-2 as nos 31/2.	5/1865	

2-4-0 Built by R&W Hawthorn & Co. Works no 340-2.
DW 5ft 0in; Cyls 13 x 18. Names not known.

No	Date	
18	1841	Sold to Edinburgh, Perth and Dundee Railway 1850 but withdrawn by 1865
19	1841	Withdrawn by 1865
20	1841	Withdrawn by 1865

2-4-0 Built by Sharp Brothers. Works nos 781/2.
DW 5ft 6in; Cyls 15 x 20.
Double framed with six wheel tender.

No	Date		NB no 1865	Duplicate no	Duplicate year	Withdrawn
64	1854	Cylinders altered to 16in diameter. Records give 1867 but works plate was dated 1871*	231	231A	1891	1894
65	1854	Cylinders altered to 16in in 1867*	232	232A	1891	1891

* Evidence of 1871 plate comes from a photograph of 231 in which the date is visible.
Date of 16in cylinders fitted on 232 is presumed from the records.

2-4-0 Built by Beyer Peacock & Co. Works nos 139-42.
           E&G Railway/NB Railway at Cowlairs.
DW 6ft 0in; LW 3ft 6in; WB 6ft 8in + 7ft 10in; Cyls 16 x 20.
Beyer Peacock locomotives (1859/61) had brass domes, outside bearings on LW, pull out
regulator, spectacle board with four wheel o/s framed tender, 1720 gallon capacity.
Cowlairs locos (1865/7) had no domes and were slightly larger although the boiler was
smaller. No 239 was turned out with a rounded cab similar to Fletcher's on the NE
Railway. This coupled version of the Beyer singles was equally successful, and they
were rebuilt by Drummond and Holmes with cabs and 16 x 22 cylinders, some with domes.
Names applied 1880.

			Rebuilt	NB no	Duplicate		
No	Name (1880)	Date	16 x 22 cyls	1865	no	year	Withdrawn
40	*Alexandria*	1859/60	1881	**237**	1026	1909	1910
41	*Bathgate*	1860	1881	**238**	1027	1909	1910
4	*Stirling*	1860	1882	**233**	1022	1909	1911
7	*Kincardine*	1861	1881	**234**	1023	1909	1914
12	*Dunbar*	1865	1886	**235**	1024	1909	1914
(35)	*Aberdeen*	1866	1886	**236***	1025	1909	1910
-	*Falkirk*						
	renamed						
	Stonehaven	1867	1901	**239***	1028	1909	1911

* Turned out 1866/7 as NB 236 & 239.

2-4-0 Built by E&G Railway/NB Railway at Cowlairs.
DW 6ft 0in; LW 4ft 2in; Cyls 16¼ x 22.
Designed by William Steel Brown during a short period as Locomotive Superintendent and
completed by his successor SW Johnson, these locomotives differed from the Beyer
design being without domes, having bell-topped chimneys and with all the springs on
the locomotive and tender being above the running plate. The driving wheel springs
had compensating levers, and the safety valves were over the firebox. Contrary to E&G
and NB practice, the reversing lever and gear was on the right-hand-side, and this
anomaly was never corrected. Rebuilt with larger cylinders as below by Holmes with
cab and dome.

			NB no	Duplicate		
No	Date	Rebuilt	1865	no	year	Withdrawn
101	1862	1882: 16½ x 24 cyls				
		1898: 17 x 24 cyls	**351**	1007	1909	1915
102	1862	1882: 16½ x 24 cyls				
		1897: 17 x 24 cyls	**352**	1008	1909	1915
103	1863	1888-9: 17 x 24 cyls	**353**	1009	1909	1912
104	1863	1882: 16½ x 24 cyls				
		1889: 17 x 24 cyls	**354**	1012	1909	1913
105	1864	1889: 17 x 24 cyls	**355**	1017	1909	1914
106	1864	1889: 17 x 24 cyls	**356**	1019	1909	1912
-	1866	1888: 17 x 24 cyls	**349***	1003	1909	1912
-	1867	1888: 17 x 24 cyls	**350***	1005	1909	1913

* Turned out 1866/7 as NB 349/50.

0-4-2 Built by R&W Hawthorn & Co.
DW 4ft 6in; TW 3ft 6in; Cyls 14 x 21; Double frames.
The first two of these locomotives, delivered in early 1844 had Hawthorn's patent
valve gear. The others were all rebuilt as 0-4-2 tanks by the E&G Railway. Names
removed by NB Railway.

			NB no	
No	Name	Date	1865	
23		1843		Possibly renumbered 83* in 1862, and definitely
				renumbered 109 in 1864. Not taken into NB stock.
25	*Ferguson*	1843	255	To duplicate stock 255A 1873. Withdrawn 1876.
26	*Henry Ball*	1843	256	Withdrawn 1872
27	*Pambour*	1844	257	Withdrawn 1870

28   *Tredgold*   1844   **258**   Withdrawn 1873

* Renumbering of no 23 has frequently been stated as 88, but 83 seems more logical as no 88 was already in use (ex-C&DJt well-tank). The above supposition would mean that numbers were exchanged between 23 and 83.

0-4-2 Built by R&W Hawthorn & Co.
DW 4ft 6in; LW 3ft 6in; Cyls 15 x 21; THS 259 sq ft.
Similar to above 0-4-2s, but with larger diameter cylinders. Rebuilt 0-4-2T by E&G Railway.

No	Name	Date	NB no 1865	Withdrawn
29	*Forth*	1846	**259**	1875
30	*Tyne*	1846	**260**	1873

0-4-2 Built by R&W Hawthorn & Co.
DW 5ft 0in; Cyls 14 x 21.
Details uncertain. May have been rebuilt as a tank engine with 5ft 1in DW and 15 x 24 cyls in 1862, and was certainly rebuilt again in 1868.

No	Date	
24	1850	To NB no **242**, 1865
	1876	To duplicate list 242A. Withdrawn 1880.

0-4-2 Built by Neilson & Co. Works nos 33/4
DW 5ft 1in; Cyls 16 x 20; Double frames.

No	Date	
56	1848	Withdrawn 1862
57	1848	Withdrawn 1862

0-4-2 Built by Neilson & Co.
DW 5ft 0in; Cyls 16 x 20.
Purchased from stock for working the Wilsontown branch at £1700 each.

No	Date		NB no 1865	Duplicate no	year	Withdrawn
62	1851	Both rebuilt 0-6-0.	**249**	249A	1887	1890
63	1851	16 x 22 cyls in 1867	**250**	250	1892	
				873	1895	by 1901

0-4-2 Built by Neilson & Co. Works nos 94-5 (or 85-90) 1855, 330-5 1856/7.
DW 5ft 0in; Cyls 16 x 22 o/s.

No	Date	Rebuilt	NB no 1865	Duplicate no	year	
70	1855		**283**	283A	1875	Sold 1876
71	1855		**284**	284A	1875	Sold 1876
72	1855		**285**			Scrapped 1875
73	1855		**286**			Scrapped 1870
74	1855		**287**			Sold 1876
75	1855	1870: 0-6-0 DW 4ft 0in Cyls 16½ x 22 o/s	**288**	288A	1879	Scrapped 1890
76	1855	1869: 0-6-0 as 288	**289**	289A	1879	Scrapped 1887
77	1856	1867: 0-6-0 as 288	**290**	290A	1879	Scrapped 1884
78	1856		**291**			Sold 1875. Scrapped 1876.
79	1856		**292**	292A	1876	Scrapped 1878
80	1856	7/1872: 0-6-0 16 x 26 cyls & listed as a renewal	**293**	293A	1894	
				881	1895	
				1081	1901	Scrapped 1907
81	1857	1870: 0-6-0 as 288	**294**	294A	1882	Disposal not known

0-4-2 Built by Beyer Peacock & Co. Works nos 143-50, 135-8.
                    E&G Railway at Cowlairs.
DW 5ft 1in; TW 3ft 6in or 3ft 8in; WB 7ft 3in + 7ft 0in (BP),
7ft 9in + 7ft 1in (Cowlairs); Cyls 16 x 22; Blr 4ft 0in diam;
THS 1019.6 sq ft (BP), 900.5 sq ft (Cowlairs); Wt 26 tons 11 cwt (BP),
28 tons 12 cwt (Cowlairs).
Beyer 0-4-2 version of 2-4-0 with same features, open splashers and outside bearings
on TW. The cylinders however were inclined at 1 in 12. Left-hand lever reverse,
brass dome on Beyer locomotives (1859-62) but Cowlairs locomotives (1864) did not have
domes and nos 331/2 were turned out with Stroudley style window cabs. After the
Wheatley period rebuilds had domes and GN type cabs. Names were applied in 1880.
1000 gallon tenders.

| | | | | NB no | Duplicate | | |
No	Name (1880)	Date	Rebuilt	1865	no	year	Withdrawn
89	*Jamestown*	1859	1871 short cab, 1895	**317**	1058	1903	1915
90	*Balloch*	1859	1875, 1895	**318**	1059	1903	1912
91		1859	1887	**319**	1060	1903	1913
92	*Balfron*	1859	1882	**320**	1061	1903	1911
93	*St Ronans*	1861	1882	**321**	1062	1903	1911
94	*Coldarvan*	1861	1882	**322**	1063	1903	1911
95	*Cardrona*	1861	1882	**323**	1064	1903	1912
96		1861	1887	**324**	1065	1903	1912
97	*Peebles*	1862	1882	**325**	1066	1903	1911
98	*Renton*	1862	1871 (weatherboard), 1895	**326**	1067	1903	1913
99		1862	1885	**327**	1068	1903	1911
100		1862	1892 0-6-0ST* o/s cyls	**328**	1069	1903	1913
83		1864	1889	**329**	1029	1906	1912
84		1864	1892	**330**	1031	1906	1913
85		1864	1882	**331**	1032	1909	1913
86		1864	1892	**332**	1033	1909	1914
87		1864	1891	**333**	1034	1909	1912
88		1864	1891	**334**	1035	1909	1912

* As an 0-6-0ST, no 328 was used on the Causeway End branch.

0-4-2 Built by E&C Railway at Cowlairs.
DW 5ft 0in; Cyls 15 x 22; Double frame.
Reputed to have been built from parts of old locomotives.
No   Date
(33) 1866   Turned out as NB **262**
      1888   Rebuilt 0-4-2T, Cyls 16 x 22
      1894   To duplicate list 262A
      1895   Renumbered 880
      1901   Renumbered 1080. Withdrawn 1907.

2-2-2WT Built by G England & Co in 1850.
DW 4ft 6in; LW & TW 3ft 0in; Cyls 9 x 12.
This locomotive was hired for trials for a time being intended for 'light express
services' and was purchased in 1856.
No   Name   Date
88   *England* 1856   Renamed *Little Scotland*
                1860-2 Possibly renumbered 5
                        Withdrawn by 1865

2-2-2WT Built by Neilson. Works no 43.
DW 5ft 0in; Cyls 10 x 14 o/s; WB 10ft 8in + 5ft 0in.
Also purchased in connection with light express services as C&DJt no 5 rebuilt.
No   Name   Date
18   *Atalanta* 1850   Scrapped 1864

0-6-0WT Built by E&G Railway at Cowlairs.
DW 4ft 3½in; Cyls 15½ x 25 o/s; Firebox 4ft 0in long, 4ft 6in deep;
THS 808 sq ft; Wt 26½ tons. Inclined cylinders, large centre dome, valve chest above
cylinders.
This locomotive and no 22 below were intended for hauling (rather than banking) trains
up Cowlairs incline, but they were not successful due to poor balancing, so the
winding engine was reverted to. 200-gallon tank below smokebox, screw brakes with
steam brake on rear wheels. Water jets to clean rails, two safety valves of spring
loaded type, one on dome and the other over the firebox. Sand boxes on either side of
smokebox.

No	Name	Date	
21	*Hercules*	1844	Scrapped c1862

0-6-0T Built by E&G Railway at Cowlairs.
DW 4ft 9in; Cyls 16½ x 25.
Larger cylindered version of no 21 but still not successful.

No	Name	Date	
22	*Samson*	1844	Scrapped by 1865

0-6-0 Built by R&W Hawthorn & Co. Works no 532.
DW 5ft 0in; Cyls 18 x 24.
Following the failure of nos 21 & 22, these two locomotives were intended for banking
trains on the Cowlairs incline. They had outside frames. Hawthorn design possibly
modified by Paton. The stationary engine was still preferred (attached to the train
engine) and these locomotives were transferred to mineral work, but the wheelbase was
too long for the sharp curves on these lines hence their sale. DW 4ft 3in on S&D.

No	Name	Date	
40	*Hawthorn*	1847-8	Sold to Stockton and Darlington Railway
41	*Miller*	1847-8	See Vol 5A page 73

0-4-0T Built by E&G Railway at Cowlairs
DW not certain; Cyls 15 x 22 (inclined); Blr 8ft 0in long approximately.
A further attempt to provide locomotive haulage on the Cowlairs incline. This
locomotive was coal burning on the MW Ivison system of combustion assisted by a jet of
steam. Large central dome. Jets of water to clean rails.

No	Date	
61	1850	Scrapped soon afterwards. (Replaced 1854.)

There is a possibility that there were plans to build a further Cowlairs banking
engine for which the number 60 was reserved, and this might have been a tender version
of the above four-coupled tank engine, but there is no evidence that this was ever
built.
Some researchers, including Jas F McEwan, have maintained that the 0-4-0ST built by
Andrew Barclay & Co (Works no 3) which was purchased by the NB Railway from colliery
owners in 1866 (see page 164) was originally an Edinburgh & Glasgow locomotive, built
in 1859, and numbered 88 in 1860 and 21 in 1862, but subsequently sold. It has been
stated that the order was passed to Andrew Barclay by Neilson's.

Edinburgh, Leith and Granton Railway

Incorporated 13/8/1836 as Edinburgh and Newhaven. Name changed and route amended 1/7/1839.
Opened: Canonmills (later Scotland St) and Trinity 8/1842 with horse haulage Trinity to Granton 19/2/1846, Bonnington Junction to Leith 5/1846, throughout to Canal St station (between North and Waverley bridges in tunnel from Scotland St) 17/5/1847. Locomotives used north of the tunnel, but probably not until completion of the line May 1847. Trains descended by gravity through the tunnel on a 1 in 27 grade and were hauled up by stationary engine.
Purchased by Edinburgh and Northern Railway 27/7/1847.

It is very doubtful if this company ever actually owned any locomotives. It was originally intended to obtain locomotives for the opening of the northern section, but capital was short and horses were used instead (forcing the company to sell the original coaches to the Wishaw and Coltness Railway and obtain lighter ones). By the time the line was completed in 1847, the company was in deep financial difficulty. As already noted three locomotives ordered from E Bury & Co built in 1846 had been diverted to the Edinburgh and Glasgow Railway. The three engines listed below are known to have worked on the Granton section, but their origins are obscure, and the possibility is that they were contractor locomotives; purchase would be by the Edinburgh, Perth and Dundee Railway, possibly not until the early 1850s.

0-4-2 Built by Hawthorn of Leith in 1845.
DW 4ft 6in; TW 3ft 0in; Cyls 13 x 20.
Cylinders also recorded as 14 x 20. Possibly rebuilt 2-2-2T in 1850
EP&D

no	Date	
31	1847	To NB no **141** 1862
	1868	Sold to James Russell & Son

0-4-0 Built by Hawthorn of Leith in 1847
DW 4ft 0in; WB 6ft 0in; Cyls 13 x 16
EP&D

no	Date	
30	1847	To NB no **140** 1862. Withdrawn 1870.
32	1847	To NB no **142** 1862
	1860	Rebuilt 0-4-2. DW 4ft 6in; WB 6ft 0in + 4ft 9in; Cyls 13 x 20 but listed in 1867 as 0-6-0.
	1875	Sold to Glentore Colliery.

Edinburgh and Northern Railway

Incorporated 31/7/1845. Purchased Edinburgh, Leith and Granton Railway 27/7/1847, and name changed to **Edinburgh, Perth and Dundee Railway**.
Opened Burntisland to Cupar and Lindores 20/9/1847; Lindores to Glenburnie (Newburgh) 9/12 1847; extended to junction with Scottish Central Railway at Hilton and through service to Perth commenced 25/7/1848. Cupar to Leuchars 17/5/1848 and Tayport 17/5/1850. Thornton Junction to Crossgates 4/9/1848 and Dunfermline 13/12/1849. Goods branches opened to Kirkaldy Harbour 10/1848, Pettycur Harbour 2/1849. Ferry services operated between Granton and Burntisland, and Tayport and Broughty Ferry. Worked St Andrews Railway (incorporated 1851, opened 1/7/1852), and Kinross-shire Railway (incorporated 1857, opened 20/6/1860). Cowdenbeath to Fife and Kinross Railway at Kinross opened 20/6/1860. Amalgamated with NB Railway 19/7/1862.

46 Locomotives as under. EP&D nos given below are those existing in 1862. Earlier nos if different from these are not known, nor are the nos carried by the one (or possibly two) locomotives purchased from the Edinburgh and Glasgow Railway mentioned above. NB numbers probably not allotted until about 1865.

2-2-0 Built by R&W Hawthorn & Co in 1847.
DW 4ft 0in; Cyls 13 x 16.
Origin uncertain. Probably obtained second-hand c1860 but not confirmed.

	NB no			
No	1862-5	Rebuilt		Withdrawn
41	**151**	1860 0-4-0 Cyls 14 x 16; DW 3ft 10in		1877
42	**152**			1870

2-2-2 Built by R&W Hawthorn & Co. Works nos 494-6, 617.
DW 6ft 0in; LW & TW 3ft 0in; Cyls 15 x 21.
Similar to NB Railway 33 class. Rear axle behind firebox, elliptical springs with
adjustable adhesion.

		NB no		Duplicate		
No	Date	1862-5	Rebuilt	no	year	Withdrawn
14	1848	**124**				1871
15	1848	**125**	1866 o/s cyls	125A	1882	1884
16	1848	**126**				1871
17	1848	**127**				1871

2-2-2 Built by EP&D Railway at Burntisland.
DW 6ft 0in; Cyls 15 x 20; WB 6ft 8in + 6ft 8in.
Crewe type. Recorded as new 1867.

No	Name	Date	
37	*Oakley*	1861	To NB Railway no **147** 1862-5 and name removed
			6/1868 New boiler and tubes. Withdrawn 1882.

0-4-0 Built by R&W Hawthorn & Co in 1847
DW 3ft 10in; Cyls 13 x 16. Possibly built as 0-4-2.
Probably obtained second-hand in 1850s but not confirmed.

	NB no	
No	1862-5	
36	**146**	Rebuilt 0-4-2ST when sold to Thomas Wheatley in 1870.
		See Vol 4 page 133. To Wigtownshire Railway no 2 1875.

0-4-0 Built by R&W Hawthorn & Co in 1847.
DW 4ft 0in; Cyls 13 x 16.
Probably obtained second-hand in 1850s but not confirmed.

	NB no	
No	1862-5	
39	**149**	Withdrawn 1871

0-4-0 Built by Hawthorn of Leith.
DW 4ft 6in; Cyls 14 x 18.
No 48 was built for the operation of the Kinross-shire Railway.

		NB no	Duplicate			
No	Date	1862-5	no	year		Withdrawn
43	c1860	**153**	153A	1876		1889
48	8/1861	**158**	158A	1877	Rebuilt 0-4-0ST; DW 3ft 6in;	
					Cyls 14 x 18 o/s, and restored	
	Renumbered				to Capital list 1883	
	1883	**404**	404A	1894		
			882	1895		1899

0-4-2 Built by R&W Hawthorn & Co. Works nos 497-504, 615/6.
DW 5ft 0in; Cyls 15 x 21. Variations in TWB from 12ft 8in to 13ft 5in. Intended for
passenger trains. Initial order.

| | | NB no | | Duplicate | | |
No	Date	1862-5	Rebuilt	no year	Withdrawn
1	8/1847	**111**		111A 1880		1885
2	8/1847	**112**				1870
3	8/1847	**113**	0-4-2ST Cyls 14½ x 21	113A 1873		1875*
			(date not recorded)			
4	8/1847	**114**				1870
5	8/1847	**115**				1867
6	8/1847	**116**	Cyls 15 x 22 by 1867			1870
7	8/1847	**117**	Cyls 15 x 22 by 1867			1870
8	9/1847	**118**				1870
19	1/1848	**129**				1871
20	1/1848	**130**	Cyls 15 x 22 by 1867			1870

* Sold to Thomas Wheatley for Wigtownshire Railway.

0-4-2 Built by R&W Hawthorn & Co. Works nos 673/4.
DW 5ft 0in; Cyls 15 x 21.
Although having the same DW & cyls, these two locomotives differed from each other in
some respects, particularly the WB.

| | | NB no | | |
No	Date	1862-5	Rebuilt	Withdrawn
25	1849	**135**	2-4-0 by 1867	1868
26	1849	**136**	2-4-0 by 1867	1873

0-6-0 Built by R&W Hawthorn & Co. Works nos 505-9, 611/2.
DW 4ft 6in; Cyls 15 x 24.
Initial order for goods engines. Similar to NB Railway 27 class.

| | | NB no | | |
No	Date	1862-5		Withdrawn
9	1847	**119**		1870
10	1847	**120**	Possibly rebuilt 2-4-0. LW 3ft 6in.	1867
11	1847	**121**		1870
12	1847	**122**		1867
13	1847	**123**	Rebuilt 1867. To duplicate list 123A 1877.	1880
22	1848	**132**		1870
23	1848	**133**		1872

0-6-0 Built by R&W Hawthorne & Co. Works nos 610, 613/4.
DW 4ft 6in; Cyls 16 x 24.
Large cylinder version of above. Probably an amendment to initial order.

| | | NB no | | |
No	Date	1862-5		Withdrawn
21	1847/8	**131**		1869
24	1847/8	**134**		1869
18	1847/8	**128**	Rebuilt 2-2-2 1861 and named *Alva* (removed by NB Railway). To duplicate list 128A, 1881.	1882

0-6-0 Built by R&W Hawthorn. Works no 680.
DW 5ft 0in; WB 7ft 3in + 6ft 7in; Cyls 16 x 24; o/s frames, no dome.
Described as 'Heavy luggage engine'.

No	Date	
27	1851	To NB Railway no **137** 1862-5
	by 1867	Rebuilt WB 7ft 2in + 6ft 6½. By 1868 Cyls 16¼ x 24.
	1885	To duplicate list 137A. Withdrawn 1892.

0-6-0 Built by R&W Hawthorn. Works nos 681/2.
DW 5ft 0in; WB 7ft 3in + 6ft 7in; Cyls 18 x 24; o/s frames, no dome.

No	Date	NB no 1862-5	Rebuilt	Duplicate no	year	Withdrawn
28	1851	**138**	By 1867 WB 7ft 2in + 6ft 6½in			
			Cyls 16 x 14			
			By 1868 Cyls 16¼ x 24	138A	1883	1890
29	1851	**139**	By 1868 Cyls 16¼ x 24	139A	1876	1880

0-6-0 Built by Hawthorn of Leith.
DW 5ft 0in; WB 7ft 3in + 6ft 7½in; Cyls 16 x 22.

No	Date	NB no 1862-5	Withdrawn
44	1856	**154**	1869
45	1856	**155**	1869

0-6-0 Built by Neilson & Co.
DW 5ft 0in; WB 6ft 10¼in + 7ft 1in; Cyls 16 x 24

No	Date	NB no 1862-5	
38	1861	**148**	Withdrawn 1884. May have replaced locomotive ex-Edinburgh & Glasgow Railway.
46	1861	**156**	To duplicate list 156A, 1886. Withdrawn 1889.

0-6-0 Built by EP&D Railway at Burntisland.
DW 5ft 0in; WB 7ft 0in + 7ft 3in; Cyls 16 x 24.

No	Date	NB no 1862-5	Withdrawn	
40	1861	**150**	1883	
35	1862	**145**	1889	May have replaced locomotive ex-Edinburgh & Glasgow Railway
50	1862	**160**	1885	

0-6-0 Built by EP&D Railway at Burntisland.
DW 5ft 0in; Cyls 16 x 24. WB similar to Neilson locomotives above.

No	Date	
49	1862	NB Railway **159**, 1862-5
	1886	To Duplicate list 159A
	1895	Renumbered 863. Latterly had a Holmes dome with two safety valves and 'stovepipe' chimney. Withdrawn 1896.

2-4-0T Built by R&W Hawthorn. Works nos 675/6.
DW 5ft 6in; Cyls 14 x 20.

No	Date	NB no 1862-5	Rebuilt	Duplicate no	year	Withdrawn
33	1850	**143**	1867: 0-4-2T Cyls 12 x 18			
			DW 4ft 9in as NB 20 class	143A	1881	1882
34	1850	**144**	By 1867, 2-2-2 Cyls 14 x 18			1874

No 47 was the property of the Leslie Railway - see below.

Fife and Kinross Railway

Incorporated 16/7/1855.
Opened Ladybank (EP&D Railway) to Strathmiglow 6/7/1857 and Kinross 1858. The company
was amalgamated with the EP&D Railway in a separate Act when the EP&D was amalgamated
with the NBR in 1862

2 Locomotives as under:

0-4-0 Built by Hawthorns of Leith.
DW 4ft 6in; Cyls 14 x 18 o/s; Inside frames.

Name	Date	
Loch Leven Castle	1857	To NB Railway no **161**, 1862
	1877	To duplicate list 161A
	1884	Rebuilt 0-4-0ST and restored to Capital list **312**
	1894	To duplicate list 312A
	1895	Renumbered 834
	1901	Renumbered 1034. Withdrawn 1906.
Falkland Castle	1857	To NB Railway no **162**, 1862
	1877	To duplicate list 162A. Withdrawn 1878.

Charleston Railway and Harbour

Privately constructed as a waggonway c1792. Converted to edge rails c1841, serving
coal pits in the Dunfermline and Charlestown area. Incorporated as Charleston (*sic*)
Railway and Harbour 8/8/1859. Transferred to West of Fife Mineral Railway 1/8/1861.

1 Locomotive as under:

0-4-2 Built by Hawthorn of Leith.
DW 4ft 6in; Cyls 14 x 18.

Date	
1857	To NB **163**, 1862
1866	Rebuilt 0-6-0 Cyls 13 x 18 o/s
1882	To duplicate list 163A. Withdrawn 1891.

West of Fife Mineral Railway

Incorporated 1856.
Opened Dunfermline to Killernie with Halbeath and Roscobie branches 5/1858.
Amalgamated with NB Railway 29/7/1862.

4 Locomotives as under:

0-4-0 Built by Hawthorn of Leith in 1852.
DW 4ft 0in; Cyls 12 x 18; WB 5ft 4in.
Presumably obtained second-hand but origin unknown. Became the smallest NB
locomotive.

To NB **164** in 1862. May have been rebuilt as a 0-4-0T.
Sold to J Watson 1868.

0-4-0ST Built by Neilson & Co in 1858.
DW 3ft 6in; Cyls 14 x 18.
Some records state that this locomotive was built for Elgin Colliery, and give DW as
5ft 0in; Cyls 14 x 20. In the 1867 NB list it was classed as a tender engine.

Date	
1858	To NB Railway **165**, 1862
1875	To duplicate list 165A. Withdrawn 1882.

```
0-4-0ST Built by Neilson & Co.
DW 3ft 6in; Cyls 13 x 18.
Date
1858    To NB Railway no 166, 1862
1875    To Duplicate list 166A
1881    Rebuilt and restored to Capital list 24
1885    To duplicate list 24A
1895    Renumbered 833
1901    Renumbered 1033. Withdrawn 1903.

0-4-0ST Built by Neilson & Co.  Works no 483.
DW 3ft 6in; Cyls 14 x 20.
Date
1858    To NB Railway no 167, 1862
1873    Rebuilt
1877    To duplicate list 167A.  Withdrawn 1887.
```

Leslie Railway

Incorporated 7/7/1857.
Opened Markinch (EP&D Railway) to Leslie 1/2/1861.
The line was worked by the EP&D/NB Railway, but the company owned its own locomotive.
The EP&D included this locomotive in its numbering scheme, although it was not its
property. The locomotive was transferred to NB stock in 1869, presumably by purchase
as the company was not amalgamated with the NB Railway until 1872.

1 Locomotive as under:

```
0-4-0 Built by Hawthorn of Leith between 1855 and 1861.
DW 4ft 6in; Cyls 14 x 18.  As EP&D 43 and 48.  EP&D no allotted c1861.
EP&D    NB no
no      1869
47      157     To duplicate list 157A, 1877.  Withdrawn 1878.
```

Leven and East of Fife Railway

Incorporated 7/1861 by amalgamation of Leven Railway (incorporated 1852) and East of
Fife Railway (incorporated 1855).
Opened Thornton Junction (EP&D Railway) to Leven 3/7/1854 (Leven Railway); Leven to
Kilconquar 8/7/1857; to Anstruther 1863 (East of Fife Railway). Amalgamated with NBR
1877 and line extended to St Andrews 1887.

5 Locomotives as under:

```
0-4-0 Built by Hawthorn of Leith.
DW 4ft 6in; Cyls 14 x 18 o/s; Dome over firebox.
Built for Leven Railway.  It is not certain whether the locomotive was delivered in
time for the opening of the railway in 1854.
Date
1854/5  Sent to Cowlairs to be rebuilt as 0-4-0ST in 1872.  DW 3ft 6in.
1877    To NB Railway no 481
1883    To duplicate list 481A
1895    Renumbered 836
1901    Renumbered 1036.  Withdrawn 1907.
```

0-4-0 Built by Hawthorn of Leith in 1857.
DW 4ft 6in; Cyls 14 x 18 o/s.
NB 484 was delivered new to the East of Fife Railway, but NB 485 (although built in
1857) was not acquired until 1863.
Date
1857   To NB Railway no **484**, 1877
1884   To duplicate list 484A
1885   Rebuilt 0-4-0ST
1895   Renumbered 839
1901   Renumbered 1039. Withdrawn 1911.
1863   To NB Railway no **485**, 1877. Scrapped 11/1877.

0-4-0 Built by Black Hawthorn, Gateshead.
DW 3ft 6in; Cyls 14 x 20 o/s.
Date
1870   To NB Railway no **482**, 1877
1883   To duplicate list 482A
1885   Rebuilt 0-4-0ST
1895   Renumbered 837
1901   Renumbered 1037. Date of withdrawal not known.

0-4-0 Built by Black Hawthorn, Gateshead.
DW 4ft 5in; Cyls 14 x 20 o/s.
May have been built as a tank engine.
Date
1874   To NB Railway no **483**, 1877
1883   To duplicate list 483A
1885   Rebuilt 0-4-0ST
1895   Renumbered 838
1901   Renumbered 1038. Withdrawn 1912.

Peebles Railway

Incorporated 8/7/1853.
Opened Eskbank to Peebles 4/7/1855, to Galashiels 18/6/1866 forming a loop from NBR
via Penicuik, Leadburn and Innerleithen.
Leased by NB Railway 8/1861. Amalgamated with NB 13/7/1876.

4 Locomotives as under:

2-4-0T Built by Neilson & Co. Works nos 317/8.
DW 5ft 0in; Cyls 15 x 20 0/s.
Passenger engines with outside frames.

Name	Date	NB no 1861	Rebuilt	Duplicate no	year	Withdrawn
St Ronans	1855	**86**	2-4-0 15½ x 20 cyls by 1867			1871
Tweed	1855	**87**	2-4-0 15½ x 20 cyls by 1867			
			1868 16 x 20 cyls	87A	1879	1882

0-4-2 Built by Hawthorn of Leith.
DW 4ft 6in; TW 3ft 0in; Cyls 16 x 24 o/s. Goods engines.

Name	Date	NB no 1861	Duplicate no	year	Withdrawn
Roslyn Castle	1856	**89**	89A	1877	1880
Neidpath Castle	1857	**88**	88A	1877	1878

Port Carlisle Dock and Railway
Carlisle and Silloth Bay Railway and Dock

Incorporated 4/8/1953 (PCD&R) and 1855 (C&SBR&D).
Opened 22/5/1854 (goods), 22/6/1854 (passengers) converting former Carlisle Canal to the Solway Firth. C&SB opened Drumburgh to Silloth 4/9/1856, dock opened 3/8/1859. Unofficially also known as Solway Railway.
The NB Railway entered into a working agreement with these two companies in 1859, although at this date the NB had only reached Hawick. All rolling stock was transferred to the NBR and in 1862, when the Border Union Railway was completed to Carlisle, the working arrangement was converted into a lease and amalgamation took place on 12/8/1880.

3 Locomotives as under:

2-4-0T Built by R&W Hawthorn & Co. Works no 924.
DW 5ft 0in; LW 3ft 6in; Cyls 15 x 20.
Built for PCD&R.

Name	Date	
Solway	1855	To NB Railway no **100**, 1859
	1876	To duplicate list 100A
	1877	Sold to CH Paterson, Glasgow.

2-4-0 Built by R&W Hawthorn & Co. Works no 965 (H).
                R Stephenson & Co. Works no 1099 (S).
DW 5ft 0in; LW 3ft 0in; Cyls 15 x 20.

Name	Date	
Silloth (H)	1856	To NB Railway no **101**, 1859
renamed	1868	Rebuilt
Barrock	1881	Withdrawn
Dixon (S)	1857	To NB Railway no **102**, 1859
	1872	Withdrawn

Forth and Clyde Junction Railway

Incorporated 1853.
Opened Stirling to Buchlyvie 18/3/1856, throughout to Balloch (C&DJt) 26/5/1856.
Worked by Scottish Central Railway until 7/2/1860. Leased to NB Railway 8/1871 and locomotives transferred to NB stock. Company absorbed by LNER in 1923.

4 Locomotives as under:

2-4-0 Built by Brassie, Jackson, Betts & Co.
DW 5ft 0in; LW 3ft 3in; Cyls 16 x 22 o/s.
Allan type with inclined cylinders. Slotted splashers over leading DW. Dome on firebox.

Date	NB no 1861	Duplicate no	year	Withdrawn	
1859	**401**	401A	1879	1880	
1859	**402**			1879	
1859	**403**	403A	1879	1882	
1859	**404**	404A	1882		Rebuilt by Wheatley in 1874 with four
		835	1895		wheel tender with oval slots above axle
		1035	1901	1903	boxes to provide access to springs

Glasgow, Bothwell, Hamilton and Coatbridge Railway

Incorporated 16/7/1874.
Opened Shettleston to Hamilton 1/11/87 (goods), 1/4/1878 (passengers); Hamilton Castle to Whifflet (NB) 1/11/1878 (goods), 1/5/1879 (passengers).
Trains ran over NB Railway from Shettleston to Glasgow (College).
Amalgamated with NB Railway 8/1878.

4 Locomotives as under:

0-6-0T Built by Dubs & Co. Works nos 980-3.
DW 4ft 7in; Cyls 18 x 24; WP130 lbs/sq in.
Purchase price £2050 each. Bell-mouth chimneys, Ramsbottom safety valve on firebox.
Enclosed cab with rounded edges. 3-ring boiler, lever reverse, front sanding.
Westinghouse brake was replaced by steam brake. Holmes increased WP to 140 lbs/sq in
and decreased heating surface

No	Date	NB no 1861	Duplicate no	year	Withdrawn
4	1877	**502**	1372	1920	1921
3	1877	**503**	1373	1920	1921
2	1877	**504**	1374	1920	1923
1	1877	**505**	1375	1920	1921

NORTH BRITISH RAILWAY

Thornton Locomotives 1846-52

2-2-2 Built by R&W Hawthorn & Co. Works nos 459-64.
DW 6ft 0in; LW & TW 3ft 6in; Cyls 16 x 18.
Express passenger engines. Open footplate without weatherboard. Central dome.

No	Date	Rebuilt	Duplicate no	year	Withdrawn
33	1847	1867	33A	1881	1882
34	1847	1865	34A	1879	1882
35	1847	1853 O/s bearings on LW & TW			
		1863	35A	1879	1880
36	1847	1868 Cyls 15 x 18. Hurst chimney.			1890
37	1847	1868 2-4-0 Double frames, cyls 16 x 21	37A	1890	1893
38	1847	1869 2-4-0 Cyls 16 x 24, curved running plate, stovepipe chimney, no dome, brass safety valve over firebox, 1702 gallon tender			
		5/1893 Cyls 17 x 24, Holmes cab and domed boiler	1126	1910	1912

2-2-2 Built by R&W Hawthorn & Co.
DW 7ft 0in; LW & TW 4ft 0in; WB 7ft 1in + 7ft 7in; Cyls 16 x 20; Blr (oval) 4ft 0in
high, 3ft 10in wide x 10ft 8in; WP 120 lbs/sq in; WT 27 tons.
This locomotive was to the same design as York Newcastle and Berwick no 180 *Plews*,
built by Hawthorn in 12/1848 (Vol 5A page 29). It worked on the same duties as the
Crampton no 55 below. Purchase price £2375. Open splashers.

No	Name	Date
57	*The Queen*	1849 Withdrawn by 1867

(2-2)-2-0 Built by EB Wilson & Co.
DW 7ft 0in; LW 4ft 6in and 3ft 9in; Cyls 16½ x 20 o/s.
One of six locomotives built by Wilson, to the Crampton patent, the other five being
purchased by the Eastern Counties Railway (see page 15). The price was £2800, and
they had Gooch valve gear and no dome. A four-wheel tender was provided.

No	Date	
55	1849	
	1855	Rebuilt by R Stephenson & Co probably as 2-2-2
	1864	Rebuilt 2-2-2, DW 6ft 0in and dome on original boiler
	1/1867	Rebuilt DW 6ft 1½in, LW 4ft 4½in, TW 3ft 7¼in; Cyls 16 x 20. No dome and o/s bearings on LW & TW. Stovepipe chimney. Steel framed tender in place of earlier wooden framed one.
	1894	To duplicate list 55A
	1895	Renumbered 809
	1897	Rebuilt with Drummond boiler and Holmes cab and chimney
	1901	Renumbered 1009. Withdrawn 1907.

0-4-2 Built by R&W Hawthorn & Co.
DW 5ft 0in; TW 3ft 6in; WB 6ft 9in + 4ft 9in; Cyls 14 x 21. Double frames.
First engines delivered. Intended for passenger traffic. All were scrapped between
1863 and 1873. Replacement dates below.

No	Date	Rebuilt	Replaced
1	1846		1870
2	1846		1871
3	1846		1870
4	1846		1870
5	1846		1870
6	1846		1871

No	Date	Rebuilt		
7	1846	1856		1868
8	1846			1873
9	1846			1872
10	1846	1855-6 by R Stephenson & Co.		1872
11	1846			1872
12	1846	1855-6 by R Stephenson & Co.		1871
13	1846			1873
14	1846			1871
15	1846	1857 as 2-2-2		1871
16	1846			1872

0-4-2 Built by R&W Hawthorn & Co.
DW 4ft 6in; TW 3ft 0in; Cyls 14 x 21.
Goods engine version of 1 class above.

No	Date	Rebuilt	Duplicate no	year	
17	1846				Renewed 1868
18	1846				Withdrawn 1872
19	1846	1867/8 0-6-0T	19A	1882	Withdrawn 1890
20	1846	Possibly rebuilt tank engine (or no 22)			Withdrawn 1856
					Scrapped 1857
21	1846	1867/8 0-6-0T	21A	1885	
			843	1895	Withdrawn 1899
22	1846				Sold 1857*
23	1846	1865	23A	1875	Withdrawn 1880
24	1846	1859 2-2-2 DW 5ft 6in.			
		1868 Cyls 14½ x 21			Withdrawn 1881
25	1846				Withdrawn 1871
26	1846				Withdrawn 1872

* Eventually purchased by North Eastern Railway and renewed as 0-6-0, their no 415 in
  2/1862 (Vol 5A page 97).

2-4-0 Built by R&W Hawthorn & Co. Works nos 568-75.
DW 4ft 9in; LW 3ft 0in; Cyls 16 x 21.
Passenger engines. DW possibly 4ft 10in later. Cyls 15 x 21 by 1867.

No	Date	Rebuilt	Duplicate no	year	
39	1847	DW 5ft 0in by 1867			Withdrawn 1872
40	1847				Renewed 1873
41	1847				Withdrawn 1871
42	1847	DW 5ft 0in by 1867			Withdrawn 1874
43	1847				Withdrawn 1871
44	1847				Withdrawn 1873
45	1847	DW 5ft 0in by 1867, 1870 0-6-0	45A	1891	
		Cyls 16 x 24	819	1895	Withdrawn 1895
46	1847	DW 5ft 0in by 1867, 1868 0-6-0			
		DW 4ft 6in; Cyls 15 x 24			Withdrawn 1878

2-4-0 Built by R&W Hawthorn & Co. Works nos 584-91. 1849-51.
DW 5ft 0in; LW 3ft 6in; Cyls 16 x 20.
Similar to 39 class above.

No	Date	Rebuilt	
56	1851		Withdrawn 1868
58	1851		Withdrawn 1868
59	1851		Withdrawn 1869
60	1851	1868 Cyls 16¼ x 21	Withdrawn 1882
61	1851		Withdrawn 1874
62	1851		Withdrawn 1873
63	1851		Renewed 1873

0-6-0 Built by R&W Hawthorn & Co. Works nos 474-79.
DW 4ft 3in; Cyls 15 x 24.
Built for Lothians coal traffic and became known as Dalkeith coal engines.

No	Date	Rebuilt	Duplicate no	year	
27	1846	1855; 1868: Cyls 16¼ x 24	27A	1882	Withdrawn 1887
28	1846	1867: DW 4ft 6in; Cyls 16 x 24	28A	1882	Withdrawn 1886
29	1846				Sold 1855*
30	1846	1868: Cyls 16¼ x 24	30A	1882	Withdrawn 1893
31	1846				Sold 1855
32	1846				Sold 1855**

* Sold 1855 to Marleyhill Co, Newcastle for their London depot.
  To North London Railway 1859. See Vol 2A page 56.
** Sold 1855 to Londonderry Railway. See Vol 5A page 85.

0-6-0 Built by R&W Hawthorn & Co. Works nos 576-83.
DW 4ft 3in; Cyls 18 x 24.
Heavy goods engines.

No	Date	Rebuilt	Duplicate no	year	Withdrawn
47	1848	Cyls later 16½in diam; 1874 DW 4ft 2in	47A	1875	
			847	1895	
			1047	1901	1902
48	1848	Cyls later 16½in diam			1871
49	1848				1855
50	1848	Cyls later 17in diam; 1869 DW 4ft 2in	50A	1890	
			830	1895	
			1030	1901	1910
51	1848	Cyls later 17in diam			1872
52	1848	Cyls later 17in diam	52A	1882	1884
53	1848	Cyls later 17in diam			1871
54	1848	Cyls later 17in diam			1871

0-6-0 Built by R&W Hawthorn & Co. Works nos 592-6, 599, 598, 597.
DW 4ft 9in; Cyls 18 x 24.
Similar in design to 47 class above. No dome. Cyls reduced to 17in diam by 1858.

No	Date	Rebuilt	Renumbered no	year	Duplicate no	year	Withdrawn
64	1850	1872: Cyls 16 x 24	9	1872	9A	1890	
					814	1895	
					1014	1901	1912
65	1850	1872: Cyls 16 x 24	10	1872	10A	1890	
					815	1895	
					1015	1901	1912
66	1850	1858 after explosion at			11A	1890	
		Burnmouth 7/1858.			816	1895	
		1872: Cyls 16 x 24	11	1872*	1016	1901	1912
67	1850				67A	1882	
					848	1895	1895
68	1851				68A	1891	
					849	1895	1905
69	1851						1874
70	1851		14	1871	14A	1890	
					817	1895	
					1017	1901	1903
71	1851-2				71A	1874	1876

* Replaced 1870.

Hurst Locomotives 1855-68

0-4-2 Built by W Fairbairn & Son.
DW 5ft 0in; TW 3ft 6in; Cyls 17 x 24.
When Hurst came to the NB Railway from the Lancashire and Yorkshire Railway, he was
instrumental in diverting these locomotives, which the L&Y had decided were surplus to
their requirements, to his new employers. Already delivered to the L&Y, they were
duly sent to St Margaret's. They were similar to the LNW (NE division) 71 class and
were to John Ramsbottom's design (Vol 2A pp 67/8). Nos 72/3, which had cast iron
wheels, cost £2920 each, and 74/5 with wrought iron wheels were £3000 each.

			Duplicate		
No	Date	Rebuilt	no	year	Withdrawn
72	1855	1867: Cyls 16 x 24; Hawthorn blr	72A	1880	c1882
73	1855	1867: Cyls 16 x 24; Hawthorn blr	73A	1880	1882
74	1855	1867: Cyls 16 x 24;			1882
75	1855	1867: Cyls 16 x 24; Hawthorn blr			1882

2-4-0 Built by Neilson & Co. Works nos below (N).
           Dubs & Co. Works nos below (D).
DW 6ft 0in; LW 4ft 0in; Cyls 16 x 20.
Replacements for Hawthorn singles. Nos 90-5 had a brass dome with a flared top and
Hurst copper-capped chimney. Open splashers on leading DW and rectangular splasher on
trailing DW. Spring balance safety valve over firebox. O/s bearings on LW. Nos 341-
6 had a taller dome cover with two slots in the leading DW splasher, and the sandboxes
were incorporated with the rear splashers. Nos 385-93 had no domes, and it has been
stated that these 12 locomotives were to the design of SW Johnson, Locomotive
Superintendent of the Edinburgh and Glasgow Railway 1864-6. All locomotives had only
tender hand brakes when built, Westinghouse brakes being fitted in 1891-2.

		Works		Duplicate		
No	Date	no	Rebuilt	no	year	Withdrawn
90	1861	N677	1874	90A	1888	1889
91	1861	N678	1874	91A	1888	
				859	1895	1897
92	1861	N679	1874	92A	1888	1889
93	1861	N680	1874	93A	1888	
				860	1895	1895
94	1861	N681	1874	94A	1888	1890
95	1861	N682	1874	95A	1888	
				861	1895	1896
341	1866	D72		341A	1889	1892
342	1866	D73		342A	1889	
				877	1895	Not recorded
343	1866	D74		343A	1889	
				878	1895	Not recorded
344	1866	D75		344A	1889	1889
345	1866	D76		345A	1889	1892
346	1866	D77		346A	1889	1889
382	1866	N1290	1888: Cyls 16 x 22			
			1891: Holmes cab/blr	1044	1909	1911
383	1866	N1291	1888 & 1891 as 382	1049	1910	1911
384	1866	N1292	1888 & 1891 as 382	1057	1910	1913
385	1866	N1293	1888 & 1891 as 382	1062	1910	1911
386	1866	N1297	1888 & 1891 as 382	1111	1910	1911
387	1866	N1298	1888 & 1891 as 382	1115	1910	1912
388	1866	N1299	1888 & 1891 as 382	1116	1910	1911
389	1868	N1350	1888 & 1891 as 382	1117	1910	1914
390	1868	N1351	1888 & 1891 as 382	1118	1910	1913
391	1868	N1352	1888 & 1891 as 382	1119	1910	1913

392	1868	N1353	1888 & 1891 as 382		1120	1910	1912
393	1868	N1354	1888 & 1891 as 382		1121	1910	1913

0-4-0 Built by NB Railway at St Margaret's.
DW 4ft 6in; WB 7ft 2in; Cyls 13 x 20 o/s.
For work on Lothian colliery branches.

		Duplicate		
No	date	no	year	Withdrawn
109	1865	109A	1880	1893
184	1866	184A	1882	1891

0-4-0 Built by NB Railway at St Margaret's.
DW 4ft 9in; WB 7ft 2in; Cyls 13 x 20 o/s.
Similar to 109/184 above.

No   Date
110 1865   To duplicate list 110A, 1880. Withdrawn 1891.

0-6-0 Built by NB Railway at St Margaret's.
DW 5ft 0in; Cyls 15 x 24.
Hurst copper topped chimney, replaced by Wheatley 'stovepipe'.

			Duplicate		
No	Date	Rebuilt	no	year	Withdrawn
76	1860	1873	76A	1884	
			850	1895	1897
77	1860	1870	77A	1884	
			851	1895	By 1906

0-6-0 Built by NB Railway at St Margaret's.
DW 5ft 0in; WB 7ft 3in + 7ft 5in; Cyls 15½ x 24.
Similar to 76/8 above.

No   Date
78 1861   Rebuilt 1876
      1884   To duplicate list 78A
      1895   Renumbered 852
      1901   Renumbered 1052. Withdrawn by 1908.

0-6-0 Built by NB Railway at St Margaret's.
DW 5ft 0in; WB 7ft 1in + 6ft 8in; Cyls 15½ x 24.
Shorter wheelbase version of 0-6-0s above.

No   Date
79 1861   Rebuilt 1874
      1884   To duplicate list 79A
      1895   Renumbered 853
      1901   Renumbered 1053. Withdrawn 1904.

0-6-0 Built by Hawthorn of Leith (H).
              R Stephenson & Co. Works nos below (S).
              Dubs & Co. Works nos below (D).
DW 5ft 0in; WB 7ft 1in + 6ft 8in;
Cyls 15 x 24 (sometimes recorded as 15½ x 24).
Together with 76-9 above these were referred to as 'Third class six wheel coupled'.
Weatherboard only. Stephenson engines had Stephenson link motion and lever reverse
with raised firebox and large brass centre dome.
The Dubs engines weatherboard had a bent top and the sandboxes were integral with the
leading splashers instead of being separate.

		Works			Duplicate		
No	Date	no	Rebuilt		no	year	Withdrawn
80	1861	H	1873 Cyls 17 x 24		80A	1884	
					854	1895	
					1054	1901	1902

81	1861	H	1872 Cyls 17 x 24	81A	1885	
				855	1895	
				1055	1901	1902
82	1862	H	(Cyls sometimes recorded 16 x 24)	82A	1884	
			1874 Cyls 17 x 24	856	1895	
				1056	1901	1902
83	1862	H	(Cyls sometimes recorded 16 x 24)	83A	1884	
			1874 Cyls 17 x 24	857	1895	
				1057	1901	1903
84	1862	H				1880
						(Scrapped 4/82)
85	1862	H	1874 Cyls 17 x 24	85A	1885	
				858	1895	By 1901
168	1863	S1461		168A	1886	1889
169	1863	S1462	Cyls later 16 x 22	169A	1886	
				864	1895	1898
170	1863	S1463		170A	1885	1886
171	1863	S1464				1880
172	1863	S1465		172A	1889	1893
173	1863	S1466	Cyls later 16 x 22	173A	1890	
				865	1895	1900
174	1863	S1519		174A	1883	1885
175	1863	S1520				1880
176	1864	S1563	Cyls later 16 x 22	176A	1890	
				866	1895	1901
177	1864	S1564	Cyls later 16 x 22	177A	1892	
				867	1895	1900
178	1864	S1565				1883
179	1864	S1566		179A	1891	1893
180	1864	S1567	Cyls 16 x 22	180A	1892	
				868	1895	1897
181	1864	S1568		181A	1892	
				869	1895	1896
182	1864	S1569	Cyls later 16 x 22	182A	1892	
				870	1895	1896
183	1864	S1570		183A	1891	1895
185	1865	D32	Cyls later 16 x 22	1037	1908	1913
186	1865	D33	Cyls later 16 x 22	1038	1908	1912
187	1865	D34	Cyls later 16 x 22	1040	1908	Not recorded
188	1865	D35	Cyls later 16 x 22	1041	1908	1911
189	1865	D36	1885 Cyls 16 x 22	1043	1908	1912
190	1865	D37	Cyls later 16 x 22	1044	1908	1909
191	1865	D38	Cyls later 16 x 22	1045	1908	1911
192	1865	D39	Cyls later 16 x 22	1047	1908	1912
193	1865	D40	1885 Cyls 16 x 22	1048	1908	1912
194	1865	D41	1874 Cyls 16 x 22	1050	1908	1913
195	1865	D42	Cyls later 16 x 22	1051	1908	Not recorded
196	1865	D43	Cyls later 16 x 22	1052	1908	1912
197	1865	D44	1888 Cyls 16 x 22	1053	1909	1912
198	1865	D45	Cyls later 16 x 22	1054	1909	1914
199	1865	D46	Cyls later 16 x 22	1055	1909	1912
200	1865	D47	1888 Cyls 16 x 22	1056	1909	1912
201	1865	D48	DW 4ft 0in; Cyls 16 x 22			
			'2nd class six wheel coupled'			1909
202	1865	D49	Cyls later 16 x 22	1074	1909	1909
203	1865	D50	Cyls later 16 x 22	1075	1909	1909
204	1865	D51	Cyls later 16 x 22	1076	1909	1909
205	1865	D52	Cyls later 16 x 22	1077	1909	1909
206	1865	D53	Cyls later 16 x 22	1078	1909	1911
207	1865	D54	Cyls later 16 x 22	1080	1909	1914
208	1865	D55	1885 Cyls 16 x 22	1081	1910	1912

364	1866	D108	Cyls later 16 x 24		1104	1909	1914
365	1866	D109	Cyls later 16 x 24		1105	1909	1912
366	1866	D110	Cyls later 16 x 24		1106	1909	1913
367	1866	D111	Cyls later 16 x 24		1107	1909	1912
368	1866	D112	Cyls later 16 x 24		1108	1909	1912
369	1866	D113	Cyls later 16 x 24		1109	1909	1914
370	1866	D114	Cyls later 16 x 24		1110	1909	Not recorded
371	1866	D115	Cyls later 16 x 24		1111	1909	1909
372	1867	D116	Cyls later 16 x 24		1112	1909	1912
373	1867	D117	Cyls later 16 x 24		1113	1909	1911
374	1867	D118	Cyls later 16 x 24		1042	1910	Not recorded
375	1867	D119	Cyls later 16 x 24		1063	1910	1911

2-2-2WT Built by NB Railway at St Margaret's.
DW 5ft 0in; LW & TW 3ft 6in; WB 6ft 0in + 6ft 0in; Cyls 12 x 18 (later 13 x 18).
Weatherboard only, dome on first boiler ring. This locomotive, and no 31 below, were built for the Selkirk and Sedburgh branches. They were the first to be built at St Margaret's.

No	Date	
32	1856	To duplicate list 32A, 1874
	1875	Sold to Thomas Wheatley for the Wigtownshire Railway (no 1). See Vol 4 page 133.

2-2-2WT Built by NB Railway at St Margaret's.
DW 5ft 0in; LW & TW 3ft 6in; WB 6ft 10in + 6ft 0in; Cyls 12 x 18 (later 13 x 18).
Similar to no 32 above except for wheelbase.

No	Date	
31	1856	To duplicate list 31A, 1874
	4/1877	Sold to Thomas Wheatley for the Wigtownshire Railway (no 5). See Vol 4 page 133.

0-4-2WT Built by NB Railway at St Margaret's and Burntisland.
DW 4ft 9in; TW 3ft 6in; WB 6ft 6in + 6ft 6in and (later engines) 7ft 0in + 7ft 0in; Cyls 12 x 18
Branch tank engine. No dome, raised firebox, slots in coupled wheel splashers.
Accounting records seem to indicate that the original no 20 built in 1857 (the third locomotive built at St Margaret's) was sold, and a second replacement built in 1860, but other records are vague on this point (*Locomotives of the North British Railway 1846-1882* SLS page 20). All were built at St Margaret's except no 108, which was built in the former EP&D works at Burntisland. In addition, EP&D no 33 was rebuilt to this class at Burntisland (see page 151). Some, if not all, had the cylinders increased in diameter to 13in.

No	Date	Rebuilt	Duplicate no	year	Scrapped or Withdrawn	
20	1857				1876	Hired to Girvan and Portpatrick Junction Railway contractors during construction. Rebuilt 0-4-2ST and named *Lochinvar*.
22	1857		22A	1877	1885	
29	1860		29A	1878	1882	
49	1860				1878	
96	1861	Cyls 13 x 18			1878	
97	1862	Cyls 13 x 18	97A	1878	2/1882	
98	1862	Cyls 13 x 18	98A	1881	4/1882	
99	1862	Cyls 13 x 18	99A	1882	1885	
103	1863	Cyls 13 x 18	103A	1881	1884	
104	1863	Cyls 13 x 18	104A	1881	1882	
105	1864	Cyls 13 x 18	105A	1881	1882	
106	1864				1878	

107   1864 Cyls 13 x 18   107A 1878   1886
108   1864   1878

0-4-0ST Built by Dick & Stevenson, Airdrie in 1865.
DW 3ft 0in; Cyls 12 x 18.
Purchased from G Simpson, colliery owner, Wilsontown, 1866.
No   Date
240 1866   Probably to duplicate list 240A, 1878. Withdrawn 1887.

0-4-0ST Built by Andrew Barclay & Co. Works no 3 in 1859.
DW 3ft 0in; Cyls 10 x 18.
Purchased from G Simpson 1866. See note on page 147.
No   Date
241 1866   Probably to duplicate list 241A, 1876. Withdrawn 1890 and sold
               to Macfarlane Strang, Lochburn Ironworks, Maryhill, Glasgow.

0-6-0ST Built by Dubs & Co. Works no 56.
DW 4ft 2in; Cyls 16 x 22.
Ordered by Edinburgh and Glasgow Railway for the Ballochney inclines on the Monkland
Railways in anticipation of the amalgamation. No cab or weatherboard. Hurst copper-
topped chimney, central dome with Salter safety valve. There were compensating beams
between the leading and centre wheel springs. Double sets of buffers were provided
for colliery wagons. Rebuilt with Holmes chimneys, domes and cabs with flared
bunkers.
No   Date
282 6/1866 Rebuilt Cyls 16 x 24, 1895/6
         1910   To duplicate list 1076. Withdrawn 1921.

0-6-0ST Built by Dubs & Co. Works no 120/1.
DW 4ft 1in; Cyls 16 x 22.
Ordered by NB Railway. As no 282 except for slightly smaller DW, and also
rebuilt by Holmes as 282.

		Rebuilt	Duplicate		
No	Date	Cyls 16 x 24	no	year	Withdrawn
209	11/1867	1895/6	1069	1910	1921
210	12/1867	1895/6	1073	1910	1920

Wheatley Locomotives 1867-74

0-4-0 Built by NB Railway at Cowlairs.
DW 5ft 3in; WB 7ft 6in; Cyls 15 x 24; THS 929 sq ft.
Built from parts of scrapped locomotives, only the boiler being new. No dome, raised
firebox with safety valve in flared brass casing. 'stovepipe' chimney, semi open
splashers. There were hand brakes on engine and tender and double buffers were
fitted. Four wheel tender. The former no 358 was the last 0-4-0 tender engine in use
on a main line railway. The new boilers fitted in 1899 and 1902 had domes.
LNE class Y10.

No	Date	Rebuilt	Duplicate no	year	LNE no 9/1923	Withdrawn
357	1868	1899; 4/1902 Cyls 16 x 22;	357A	1892		
		Blr 4ft 0¾in x 10ft 7½in;	810	1895		
		WP 140 lbs/sq in;	1010	1901		4/1921
		Wt 27 tons 18 cwt.				
		1911 DW 4ft 3in, steam brake				
		and cab.				
358	5/1868	7/1902 Cyls 16 x 22, blr as 357.	358A	1892		
		1911 DW 4ft 3in, steam brake and	811	1895		
		cab.	1011	1901	(1011B)	12/1925*

* Sold for scrap 1/1926. The 2/1924 no 10011 was never applied.

0-4-0 Built by Neilson & Co in 1866.
DW 5ft 0in; Cyls 16 x 22.
Purchased from John Watson, Balquatstone colliery, Glasgow. Brass domes over firebox,
weatherboard and dumb buffers.

No	Date	Rebuilt	Duplicate no	year	Withdrawn
394	1867	1887	394A	1894	
			812	1895	
			1012	1901	1906
395	1867	1885	395A	1894	
			813	1895	
			1013	1901	1911

2-4-0 Built by NB Railway at Cowlairs.
DW 6ft 6in; LW 4ft 0in; Cyls 17 x 24.
Cylinders might have originally been 16in diameter. No dome, flush boilers with
flared safety valve over firebox. Front 'paddle box' splasher and rear box splasher
with coupling rod splashers between them. Weatherboard with two circular spectacles.
Bell-topped chimney. Holmes rebuild in 1890 had curved splashers, smoke box wing-
plates, round cab and dome with safety valve attached. The sandboxes were under the
running plate and incorporated in the splashers. Westinghouse brake equipment was
fitted.

No	Date	Rebuilt	Duplicate no	year	Withdrawn
141	1869	1890	1158	1912	1915
164	1869	1890	1160	1912	1915

2-4-0 Built by NB Railway at Cowlairs.
DW 5ft 0in; Cyls 16 x 22.
Renewals of earlier Hawthorn 2-4-0s (see page 158). Round-top firebox flush with
boiler. Only a tender hand brake was provided. The springs were underslung.

No	Date	Duplicate no	year	Withdrawn
40	1873	40A	1890	
		827	1895	1900

```
63    1873    63A    1890
              829    1895
             1029    1901    1903
```

2-4-0 Built by NB Railway at Cowlairs.
DW 6ft 0in; LW 3ft 9in; WB 7ft 3in + 7ft 9in; Cyls 16 x 22; WP 140 lbs/sq in. Centre
dome enclosing the safety valves. Wheatley cab, sandboxes under running plate, solid
splashers. Rebuilt 1890/1 with Holmes boilers 4ft 5in x 10ft 1in; THS 1061 sq ft and
side window cabs. (428 earlier had a Drummond cab). Cyls 17 x 24; DW 6ft 1in; LW 4ft
2½in. All but two rebuilt 1915. WP 150 lbs/sq in with Reid blrs. Wt 37 tons 2 cwt.
Names were applied by Drummond but removed after he left c1883/4.
LNE class E7.

No	Date	Name	Rebuilt as above	Duplicate no	year	LNE nos no	date	Withdrawn
418	8/1873	Bonnybridge	3/1891			1239B	9/1923	
			3/1915	1239	1914	(9986)	1924	
						(10239)	1924	5/1925
419	1873	Gogar	1890	1240	1914			1914
424	7/1873	Dunfermline	1/1891			1245B	9/1923	
			2/1915	1245	1915	(9987)	1924	
						(10245)	1924	7/1925
425	7/1873		7/1890			1246B	9/1923	
			2/1915	1246	1915	(9988)	1924	
						10246	9/1924	9/1925
426	7/1873		9/1890			1247B	9/1923	
			2/1915	1247	1915	9989	6/1924	
						10247	9/1924	10/1927
427	1873	Linlithgow	1890	1248	1915			1918
428	8/1873	Ratho	1/1891			1249B	9/1923	
			1/1915	1249	1915	9990	6/1924	
						10249	9/1924	8/1926
429	8/1873		10/1890			1256B	9/1923	
			2/1915	1256	1915	(9991)	1924	
						(10256)	1924	12/1925

4-4-0 Built by NB Railway at Cowlairs.
DW 6ft 6in; LW 2ft 9in; WB 6ft 0in + 6ft 8^3/8in + 7ft 7in; Cyls 17 x 24;
THS 981 sq ft; Wt 38 tons.
These were the earliest inside cylinder, inside frame 4-4-0s, a type which was to
become so numerous. Flush boiler with safety valve over firebox and centre dome. No
224 was the locomotive of the train which went down with the Tay bridge on 28/12/1879,
but was recovered after three months immersion with only superficial damage. It was
rebuilt in 1885 as a compound on the Nisbet system (Nisbet was Holmes's cousin) with
four cylinders working in tandem 2HP 13 x 24 and 2LP 30 x 12. It was converted back
to simple expansion in 1887 with Holmes cab, boiler, chimney and wing plates. No 264
was similarly rebuilt by Holmes in 1893. A 1652 gallon tender was provided.

No	Date	Rebuilt	Duplicate no	year	Withdrawn
224	1871	1885 4-cyl compound.			
		1887 Simple expansion.			
		1897	1192	1913	1919
264	1871	1893	1198	1913	4/1917*

* On withdrawal no 1198 was used as a stationary boiler by Malt Barns, Ladybank for a
  short period.

4-4-0 Built by NB Railway at Cowlairs.
DW 6ft 6in; LW 3ft 4in; WB 6ft 0in + 6ft $8^3/_8$in + 7ft 9in; Cyls 17 x 24.
These were the locomotives intended for use on the through service over the Midland
Railway from St Pancras to Edinburgh which began in 1876, but only no 421 was tried on
this service being fitted with Westinghouse brake for the purpose (the first
locomotive so fitted). It was quickly found to be inadequate for this duty. Similar
to 224/264 above with centre dome. The front coupled splasher was of the 'paddle box'
type, the rear splasher following the curve of the wheel with a coupling rod splasher
in addition. Rebuilt with Holmes boilers and features.

			Duplicate		
No	Date	Rebuilt	no	year	Withdrawn
420	1873	1887	1241	1914	1915
421	1873	1887	1242	1914	1918
422	1873	1890	1243	1914	1918
423	1873	1890	1244	1914	1914

0-6-0 Built by NB Railway at Cowlairs.
DW 4ft 3in; Cyls 16 x 24; Blr 4ft 0¾in x 9ft 10in.
The first 18 locomotives below were constructed using parts from old locomotives and
consequently there were several variations. Many had no domes with brass safety
valves over the firebox. Front and rear sanding. Weatherboards with tender hand
brake only. Holmes rebuilt 12 of them with the original wheelbase, the weight then
being 37¼ tons. Nos 2, 41, 43,86,223 and 265 were rebuilt with a shorter wheelbase,
weight 31 tons 16 cwt.

			Duplicate		
No	Date	Rebuilt	no	year	Withdrawn
251	1867	Holmes blr 37¼ tons	1075	1910	1915
1	1870	1898 Holmes blr 37¼ tons	1150	1911	1916
3	1870	1896 Holmes blr 37¼ tons	1151	1912	1915
4	1870	1900 Holmes blr 37¼ tons	1152	1912	1920
5	1870	1896 Holmes blr 37¼ tons	1153	1912	1915
253	1870	Holmes blr 37¼ tons	1174	1912	1920
254	1870	Holmes blr 37¼ tons	1175	1912	1913
66	1870	Holmes blr 37¼ tons	1161	1912	1912
25	1871	1897 Holmes blr 37¼ tons	1185	1913	1915
223	1871	Holmes blr 31 tons 16 cwt	1191	1913	1915
2	1871	1888 Holmes blr 31 tons 16 cwt	1181	1913	1914
6	1871	1894 Holmes blr 37¼ tons	1182	1913	1916
15	1871	1897 Holmes blr 37¼ tons	1184	1913	1915
41	1871	1887 Holmes blr 31 tons 16 cwt	1186	1913	1914
43	1871	1900 Holmes blr 31 tons 16 cwt	1187	1913	1914
86	1871	1888 Holmes blr 31 tons 16 cwt	1176	1913	1914
252	1871	1900 Holmes blr 37¼ tons	1196	1913	1920
265	1871	1901 Holmes blr 31 tons 16 cwt	1199	1913	1915

The following were built with cabs with abbreviated roof and domes forward of centre.
All were rebuilt 0-6-0ST, and later fitted with Holmes boilers the same dimensions as
the original boiler THS 878.5 sq ft; WP 140 lbs/sq in; WB 6ft 9in + 7ft 9in; Wt 36
tons 11 cwt. On rebuilding to saddle tank, the cabs were replaced by front and rear
weatherboards with spectacles only, the lower part of the cab sheet remaining. When
reboilered, the dome remained in the original position to avoid altering the tanks
which had a capacity of 760 gallons. Steam brakes were fitted to all, except 440
which had already been withdrawn in 1915, about 1916. Three of these locomotives
survived to become LNER class J84.

		Rebuilt		Duplicate		LNE nos		
No	Date	0-6-0ST	New blr	no	date	no	date	Withdrawn
430	10/1873	1892	1/1898	1257	11/1915	1257B	9/1923	
						(10257)		1/1924
431	10/1873	1891	1/1895	1258	11/1915			5/1921

432	10/1873	1891	6/1900	1259	11/1915	1259B (10001) (10259)	9/1923	6/1924
433	1873	1894	5/1900	1260	5/1916			8/1921
434	1873	1890	7/1900	1261	6/1916			12/1919
435	1873	1893	11/1900	1262	6/1916			9/1921
436	1873	1891	12/1900	1263	6/1916			8/1922
437	1873	1890	1/1901	1264	6/1916			4/1921
438	1873	1894	5/1897	1265	12/1915			9/1921
439	1873	1893	4/1897	1266	1/1916			1/1919
440	1873	1891	12/1892	(1267)				4/1915
441	1873	1889	7/1900	1268	1/1916			11/1921
442	1873	1890	7/1900	1269	1/1916			8/1921
443	12/1873	1890	1/1901	1270	1/1916	1270B	9/1923	7/1923
444	1873	1889	6/1897	1271	3/1916			9/1921
445	1874	1889	1/1901	1272	2/1916			10/1920
446	1874	1895	6/1897	1273	2/1916			7/1919
447	1874	1890	1/1898	1274	3/1916			1/1919
448	1874	1890	11/1895	1275	4/1916			7/1921
449	1874	1889	6/1900	1276	4/1916			3/1919

0-6-0 Built by Neilson & Co, works nos below.
Dubs & Co, works nos below.
NB Railway at Cowlairs.
DW 5ft 0in; WB 7ft 3in + 7ft 9in; Cyls 17 x 24; Blr 4ft 2in x 10ft 4⁵/₈in;
WP 140 lbs/sq in.
These were the main line goods engines of the Wheatley period. Rebuilt by Holmes.
Blr 4ft 5in x 10ft 1in; THS 1059 sq ft; Wt 31 tons 13 cwt with round cabs, Holmes
chimneys and safety valves on the dome. In 1913, working pressure was increased to
150 lbs/sq in. Sand boxes under the running plate originally supplied the leading
wheels only, but after rebuilding additional boxes also supplied the rear wheels.
Holmes also fitted steam and Westinghouse braking, 49 having the former and 39 the
latter. 38 of the class were again rebuilt by Reid with the same dimensions but,
except for nos 7 and 340 rebuilt in 1909, with the safety valves over the firebox. 26
of the Westinghouse braked locomotives were also equipped with vacuum brake control at
this period. Those with Westinghouse brake are marked with * in the rebuild column
below, and dual fitted locomotives **. Four more had Westinghouse brakes and some
rebuild dates are not recorded. DW later 5ft 1¾in. LNE class J31.

The following were built by Neilson & Co. Works nos 1278-89. They originally had
tapered Johnson style chimneys with dome and spring-loaded safety valve over the
firebox. They had weatherboards, box-shaped side sheets and coupling rod splashers.
The chimneys were replaced by Wheatley 'stovepipe' type until rebuilt by Holmes. Nos
347/8 were delivered as 400/1, but renumbered before entering traffic. No 381 was no
3 in the Stockton and Darlington Centenary procession in July 1925 following its
withdrawal in April. For this occasion it was reconstructed with a weatherboard and
Wheatley chimney, lettered NBR but in green LNE livery. After scrapping the green
painted wheels were fitted to no 10227.

				Duplicate		LNE nos		
No	Date	Rebuilt as above		no	date	no	date	Withdrawn
396	12/1867	12/1893*	10/1916**	1122	8/1910	(9945) 10122	1924 12/1925	8/1927
397	1867			1123	1910			1921
398	1867			1124	1910			10/1911
399	1868	1888		1125	1910			1913
347	1868	1884		1136	1910			1915
348	2/1868	11/1886*	5/1913**	1137	12/1910	(9948) (10137)	1924 1924	2/1925

No	Date	Rebuilt as above		Duplicate no	date	LNE nos no	date	Withdrawn
376	5/1868	1888*	6/1913**	1070	3/1910	(9985)	1924	
						(10070)	1924	8/1924
377	1868			1071	1910			1916
378	1868			1072	1910			1913
379	1868			1077	1910			1915
380	5/1868	4/1893*	3/1914**	1082	4/1910	(9943)	1924	
						(10082)	1924	8/1925
381	5/1868	6/1892*	4/1916	1114	4/1910	(9944)	1924	
						(10114)	1924	4/1925
								See above

The following were built by Dubs & Co. Works nos 260-73. They had bell-topped chimneys with copper top (replaced by Wheatley pattern until rebuilt), Naylor safety valves on the firebox, weatherboard with narrow side panels and coupling rod splashers. Some had brass domes. Outside framed tenders with concealed springs. Latterly nos 1146/7 had tender weatherboards.

No	Date	Rebuilt as above		Duplicate no	date	LNE nos no	date	Withdrawn
7	1868	1884	1909	1004	1910			1922
57	1868	1886		1128	1910			1918
335	12/1868	10/1893*	4/1916**	1133	11/1910	(9947)	1924	
						(10133)	1924	2/1925
336	12/1868	3/1894*		1134	12/1910			10/1923
337	1868	1883		1135	1910			1913
338	1/1869	11/1893*	10/1916**	1141	10/1911	(9951)	1924	
						(10141)	1924	4/1925
339	2/1869	5/1892*	3/1916**	1142	10/1911	(9952)	1924	
						(10142)	1924	11/1925
340	2/1869	4/1892*	9/1909	1143	11/1911	(9953)	1924	
						(10143)	1924	1/1925
359	2/1869	7/1893*		1144	12/1911	(9954)	1924	
						(10144)	1924	2/1926
360	1869			1145	1911			1913
361	3/1869	7/1886*	5/1913*	1146	1911	(9955)	1924	
						10146	1/1926	10/1928
362	3/1869	10/1893*	7/1917**	1147	1/1912	(9956)	1924	
						(10147)	1924	2/1926
363	3/1869	6/1893*	3/1914**	1148	10/1912	(9957)	1924	
						(10148)	1924	12/1924
400	3/1869	7/1885*	6/1913**	1149	9/1912	(9958)	1924	
						(10149)	1924	11/1925

The following were built at Cowlairs. There were many variations, as in the interests of economy odd boilers, wheels and tenders from old locomotives were used for the six batches in 1869, 1870, 1871, 1872 1874 and 1875, the final batch being turned out after Drummond had taken over. Earlier batches had the safety valves over the firebox, later ones on the dome. Similarly the older locomotives had a weatherboard only with a box splasher. Later ones had a short cab and box splasher and the final version had the cab sides brought down to be combined with a small rear splasher. No 119 had a round cab fitted before rebuilding and all had 'stovepipe' chimneys until rebuilt. In later times, nos 1132/80/90, 1178 and 1224 had tender weatherboards and 1132 & 1178 were fitted with steam-heating equipment when rebuilt in 1916 and 1914 respectively. No 1164 was provided with cut down chimney and dome to clear a low bridge at Gartverrie siding in 1921. Three others were so altered, 1208 by 1923, and the LNE altered 10206 in 1/1925 and 10180 in 11/1925 for the same duty.

No	Date	Rebuilt as above		Duplicate no	date	LNE nos no	date	Withdrawn
115	1869			1131	1910			1921
243	6/1869	7/1892*	9/1916**	1138	9/1911	(9949)	1924	
						(10138)	1924	7/1924

120	8/1869	12/1894*	11/1916**	1132	11/1910	(9946)	1924	
						(10132)	1924	12/1925
244	1869			1139	1911			1920
245	12/1869	1884*	3/1916	1140	10/1911	(9950)	1924	
						(10140)	1924	9/1924
114	6/1870	7/1894*	7/1917**	1162	4/1912	(9959)	1924	
						10162	9/1925	1/1927
116	1870			1163	1912			1921
117	6/1870	4/1892	4/1914	1164	5/1912	(9960)	1924	
						(10164)	1924	8/1925
118	1870			1165	1912			1917
119	6/1870	10/1895*	7/1917**	1166	6/1912	(9961)	1924	
						10166	4/1926	3/1932
121	1870			1167	1912			1920
122	1870			1154	1912			1920
12	1/1871	3/1892*	2/1916**	1183	2/1913	(9964)	1924	
						(10183)	1924	12/1924
127	1871	3/1894	1914	1179	3/1913			1921
129	2/1871	4/1888*	4/1913**	1180	3/1913	(9963)	1924	
						10180	11/1925	8/1927
53	4/1871	6/1888*	4/1916**	1189	5/1913	(9966)	1924	
						(10189)	1924	10/1924
219	6/1871	4/1897*	10/1916**	1190	5/1913	(9967)	1924	
						(10190)	1924	11/1925
48	7/1871	5/1888*	7/1912**	1188	4/1913	(9965)	1924	
						10188	12/1925	9/1928
124	1871			1177	1913			1919
126	7/1871	3/1894*	3/1914**	1178	2/1913	(9962)	1924	
						(10178)	1924	8/1925
246	8/1871	4/1894*	7/1912	1195	5/1913	(9968)	1924	
						(10195)	1924	12/1924
257	1871			1197	1913			1914
267	8/1871	7/1889*	5/1913**	1200	1913			9/1923#
						#Sold for scrap 5/1924		
309	1871			1201	1913			1913
16	1872			1202	1913			1914
26	1872			1203	1913			1916
64	4/1872	6/1897*	8/1917	1206	1913	(9970)	1924	
						10206	1/1925	4/1937#
						#Steam brake from 1925		
102	1872			1207	1913			1920
133	5/1872	1/1894	2/1914	1208	1913	(9971)	1924	
						(10208)	1924	9/1924
266	1872			1213	1913			1915
307	10/1872	7/1896		1214	1913			9/1923
407	1872			1217	1913			1920
408	1872			1218	1913			1915
409	1872			1219	1914			1920
410	1872			1220	1914			1917
411	7/1872	7/1895*		1221	1914			2/1923
412	1872			1222	1914			1920
413	7/1872	1/1894*	10/1916	1223	1914	(9972)	1924	
						(10223)	1924	5/1924
414	8/1872	12/1894*	6/1917**	1224	1914	(9773)	1924	
						(10224)	1924	4/1925
415	1872			1225	1914			1919
416	1872			1226	1914			1920
417	10/1872	1885*	3/1914**	1227	1914	(9774)		
						10227	10/1925	12/1926#
						#Cut up 2/1927		

No	Date	Renum	Dup no	year	Withdrawn
47	1874		1280	1916	1921
54	1874		1281	1916	1917
61	1874		(1282)		1916
65	1874		1283	1916	1920
69	1874		1284	1916	1921
70	1874		1285	1916	1922
71	1874		(1253)		1915
276	1874		1286	1916	1918
450	1874		1277	1915	1920
451	1874		1278	1915	1919
452	1874		1279	1915	1915
23	1875		(1251)		1915
31	1875		(1252)		1915
142	1875		1288	1916	1919
275	1875		1292	1916	1920
283	1875		1293	1916	1920
285	1875		(1254)		1915
291	1875		1295	1916	1920
298	3/1875	1/1895	1296	1916	6/1923
453	1875		1287	1916	1917

0-6-0 Built by the NB Railway at St Margaret's.
DW 4ft 6in; Cyls 16¼ x 24.
Renewal of earlier no 17 of 1846 (0-4-2 17 class).

No	Date
17	1868
	1890 To duplicate list 17A
	1895 Renumbered 818
	1898 Rebuilt DW 4ft 7in; Cyls 16 x 22
	1901 Renumbered 1018. Withdrawn 1914.

0-6-0 Built by the NB Railway at St Margaret's.
DW 5ft 0in; WB 7ft 6in + 7ft 6in; Cyls 16¼ x 24.
Double frames, no dome, known as 'Longbacks'. Assembled from parts of scrapped locomotives so consequently many variations. No 154 was a renewal of EP&D 0-6-0 no 44 (NB 154) of 1856 and had total wheelbase 13ft 10½in. Weatherboards only, no 135 having the top bent over and on 155 the top was elongated. 'Stovepipe' chimneys. Rebuilt by Holmes. Cyls 16 x 24; Wt 49 tons 11 cwt; 1648 gallon tender.

No	Date	Rebuilt	Duplicate no	year	Withdrawn
56	1868	Period 1888-98	1127	1910	1913
58	1868		1129	1910	1913
59	1868	1888	1130	1910	1913
131	1869	Period 1888-98	1155	1912	1914
134	1869		1156	1912	1914
135	1869		1157	1912	1913
154	1869		1027	1910	1912
155	1869		1159	1912	1914

0-4-0ST Built by NB Railway at Cowlairs.
DW 3ft 0in; WB 4ft 6in; Cyls 11 x 18 o/s.
Built for use at Leith Docks. Hand brake only, front and rear sanding.

No	Date	Duplicate no	year	Withdrawn
18	1872	18A	1883	
		831	1895	
		1031	1901	1906
311	1872	311A	1883	
		832	1895	
		(1032)	1901	1901

0-6-0ST Built by NB Railway at Cowlairs.
DW 4ft 0in (nominal, see below); WB 7ft 0in + 7ft 0in; Cyls 16 x 24.
Shunting and short distance goods engines. The DW dimension originally given as a
nominal 4ft 0in was latterly 4ft 3in. No 130 is recorded as having 4ft 2in wheels
originally. The wheels, as on some of the Wheatley 0-6-0s had T section spokes and
were cast iron. No 130 was also recorded as having WB 7ft 0in + 7ft 0½in.
'Stovepipe' chimneys, flared domes with inset safety valve forward of centre DW,
coupling rod splashers. The bunker had a flared top and the tank capacity was 690
gallons. Rebuilt by Holmes blr 4ft 0¾in x 9ft 6in; THS 840.63 sq ft;
WP 140 lbs/sq in; Wt 34 tons 4 cwt; with new tanks, chimney, smokebox, rear
weatherboard and steam brake instead of only hand brake. LNE class J85.

No	Date	Rebuilt	Duplicate no	date	Withdrawn
130	6/1870	4/1895	1168	6/1912	9/1924 (LNE no 9999 not applied)
132	1870	7/1898	1169	7/1912	1919
152	1870	7/1898	1170	9/1912	1920
258	1872	1/1894	1212	11/1913	4/1921
8	1873	1/1899	1228	12/1914	2/1919
13	1873	7/1899	1229	1/1915	2/1920
44	1873	9/1898	1230	1/1915	11/1920
260	1873	11/1898	1236	4/1915	4/1921
263	1873	11/1898	1238	11/1915	8/1920

0-6-0ST Built by NB Railway at Cowlairs.
DW 4ft 3in; WB 7ft 3in + 7ft 9in; Cyls 16 x 24; Wt 36 tons 3 cwt.
This locomotive appears to have been a hybrid between the shunting locomotives above
and the passenger locomotives below, having the wheelbase of the latter but smaller
wheels. Rebuilt by Holmes, blr 4ft 0¾in x 10ft 2in; THS 900.5 sq ft.
WP 140 lbs/sq in; Wt 37 tons 2 cwt; Holmes chimney and fittings replacing the Wheatley
variety.

No	Date	Rebuilt	Duplicate no	date	Withdrawn
220	10/1870	1902	1171	1912	11/1922

0-6-0ST Built by NB Railway at Cowlairs.
DW 5ft 0in; WB 7ft 3in + 7ft 9in; Cyls 16 x 24; Wt 36¼ approx.
These were passenger engines, and appeared in pea green with black and white lining.
'Stovepipe' chimney; wrought iron wheels; dome between leading and centre DW; rear and
forward weatherboarding; 740 gallon tanks. As rebuilt by Holmes with Holmes chimney
and Blr 4ft 0¾in x 10ft 2in; THS 900.5 sq ft; WP 140 lbs/sq in. The weight was
approximately 37¼ tons. No 228 was fitted with Westinghouse brake in the Holmes
period. LNE class J86.

No	Date	Rebuilt	Duplicate no	date	Withdrawn
226	10/1870	12/1901	1172	11/1912	1919
228	10/1870	11/1901	1173	11/1912	10/1924*

* No 1173 withdrawn 3/1920 but reinstated.
  LNE nos 10173 and 10000 not applied.

0-6-0ST Built by NB Railway at Cowlairs.
DW 5ft 0in; WB 7ft 0in + 7ft 3in; Cyls 17 x 24; Blr 4ft 0¾in x 9ft 7in; Wt 36 tons 6
cwt. Similar to above passenger engines but with larger cylinders and shorter
wheelbase. Rebuilt by Holmes as above with boilers of the same dimensions. THS
859.36 sq ft; WP 140 lbs/sq in; Wt 35 tons 14 cwt; 740 gallon tank. No 405 was fitted
with a Drummond cab in 1910 for a short period. Westinghouse brake was fitted to
several by the 1890s in addition to the original hand brake. Some were later fitted
with steam brakes including some previously Westinghouse fitted. LNE class J81.

No	Date	Rebuilt	Duplicate no	date	Withdrawn
229	1871	7/1901	1193	5/1913	6/1921
230	1871	11/1901	1194	5/1913	9/1921

39	1872	6/1895	1204	11/1913	10/1922	
51	1872	1/1902	1205	11/1913	1/1920	
149	1872	7/1901	1209	9/1913	11/1921	
221	1872	12/1895	1210	9/1913	4/1921	
256	1872	1/1902	1211	9/1913	9/1921	
405	1872	3/1902	1215	12/1913	1/1922	
406	2/1872	1/1902	1216	12/1913	2/1924	LNE no 10216 not applied
62	1873	7/1901	1231	1/1915	12/1921	
113	1873	7/1901	1232	1/1915	10/1920	
136	1873	10/1901	1233	9/1915	10/1922	
222	1873	1/1902	1234	4/1915	4/1921	
255	1873	12/1901	1235	4/1915	4/1921	
261	1873	1/1902	1237	4/1915	4/1921	

0-6-0ST Built by NB Railway at Cowlairs.
DW 3ft 6in (except as below); WB 5ft 6in + 5ft 6in; Cyls 13 x 18. Shunters for Forth
and Tay ferry stations. Either nos 42 or 308 had 4ft 3in wheels in addition to no
146. Built with cabs. Hand brake only.

No	Date	Duplicate no	date	Withdrawn
32	1874	32A	1887	
		822	1895	
		1022	1901	1907
42	1874	42A	1887	
		823	1895	
		1023	1901	1906
144	1874	144A	1887	
		824	1895	
		1024	1901	1906
146	1874	146A	1887	
		825	1895	
		1025	1901	1907
308	1874	308A	1887	
		828	1895	
		1028	1901	1903
310	1874	310A	1887	
		826	1895	
		1026	1901	1907

0-6-0ST Built by NB Railway at Cowlairs.
DW 4ft 6in; Cyls 16 x 22. Probably renewals from parts of scrapped locomotives.
Double frames, 'stovepipe' chimneys, flared dome and weatherboard. Sand boxes above
the running plate.

No	Date	Duplicate no	date	Withdrawn
112	1870	112A	1883	
		844	1895	
		1044	1901	1908
140	1870	140A	1885	
		845	1895	1899
286	1870	286A	1883	
		846	1895	
		1046	1901	1910

Drummond Locomotives 1875-84

2-2-2 Built by Neilson & Co.
DW 7ft 0in; LW & TW 4ft 6in; WB 7ft 9in + 7ft 9in; Cyls 17 x 24; Blr 4ft 4in diam; THS
1225 sq ft; WP 140 lbs/sq in; Wt 37 tons 18 cwt.
Based on LBSC *Grosvenor* class. Dome on rear boiler ring. Ramsbottom safety valves,
Stroudley feed water heating later removed. Screw reverse, steam brakes replaced by
Westinghouse.

No	Date	Name	Withdrawn
474	1876	*Glasgow*	1910
475	1876	*Berwick*	1910

4-4-0 Built by Neilson & Co 1877/8. Works nos 2147-50, 2384-7.
NB Railway at Cowlairs 1879.
DW 6ft 6in; LW 3ft 6in; WB 6ft 6in + 6ft 7in + 9ft 0in; Cyls 18 x 26; Blr 4ft 6¼in x
10ft 3½in; THS 1099.3 sq ft; WP 150 lbs/sq in; Wt 44¼ tons.
These were the locomotives for the through expresses to Edinburgh from the Midland
Railway at St Pancras, and did much to establish Drummond's reputation. The Neilson
locomotives originally had steam brakes with Westinghouse brake control on the train
with no co-ordination between them. The Cowlairs locomotives were built with
Westinghouse brakes, and the Neilson Locomotives were so converted in the early 1890s.
All had a cutaway cab, central dome with Ramsbottom safety valve, coupling rod
splashers and smokebox wing plates. A triangular sand box was incorporated with the
DW splashers. Vertical screw reverse, six wheel tenders of 2500 gallons capacity had
outside bearings, slotted frames and underslung frames. THS had become 1080.96 sq ft
by about 1888 and WP reduced to 140 lbs/sq in.
Rebuilding was commenced by Holmes on 1902, and completed by Reid in 1904.
Cyls 18¼ x 26; Blr 4ft 8in x 10ft 3½in; THS 1350 sq ft; WP 175 lbs/sq in. After
rebuilding, nos 476/88/90 ran with Holmes 3500 gallon tenders, but by 1922 no 1321
(ex-476) had a Holmes 2500 gallon tender as also fitted to nos 10361/87 by the LNE in
1924. The 1902 rebuilds had side window cabs, Wt 47 tons 18 cwt, and became LNE class
D28. All the rebuilds had the sand boxes under the running plate.
Popularly known as *Abbotsford* class because Neilson's official photograph depicted no
479 with that name, nos 486/7 were originally sent to Aberdeen to work the northern
section from Burntisland but, after the fall of the Tay Bridge in December 1879, were
moved south to the Carlisle section and in consequence of Drummond's practice of using
names appropriate to their location they were renamed. All the names were removed by
Holmes by 1900.

No	Date	Name	Rebuilt	Duplicate no	date	LNE nos no	year	Withdrawn
476	5/1877	*Carlisle*	6/1902	1321	1/1919	(9992)	1924	
						(10321)	1924	11/1924
477	6/1877	*Edinburgh*	7/1904	1322	1/1919	(9993)	1924	
						(10322)	1924	12/1924
478	6/1877	*Melrose*	7/1902	1323	1/1919	(9319)	1924	
						(10323)	1924	9/1924
479	7/1877	*Abbotsford*	7/1902	1324	1/1919	(1324B)	1923	12/1923
486	1878	*Aberdeen*	6/1904	1360	12/1919			2/1922
	1880	renamed *Eskbank*						
487	10/1878	*Montrose*	7/1904	1361	12/1919	(9994)	1924	
	1880	renamed *Waverley*				10361	10/1924	7/1926
488	1878	*Galashiels*	7/1902	1362	12/1919			9/1921
489	1878	*Hawick*	7/1902	1363	12/1919			6/1922
490	1879	*St Boswells*	6/1902	1371	5/1920			11/1921
491	1/1879	*Dalhousie*	7/1904	1387	2/1920	(9995)	1924	
						10387	10/1924	9/1926
492*	2/1879	*Newcastleton*	7/1904	1388	6/1920	(9996)	1924	
						(10388)	1924	12/1924
493*	1879	*Netherby*	6/1904	1389	7/1920			6/1921

* No 492 was in an accident at Dunbar on 3/1/1898.
  No 493 took part in Stephenson Centenary 9/6/1881.

0-6-0 Built by NB Railway at Cowlairs. Works nos below.
Neilson & Co. Works nos below.
DW 5ft 0in; WB 7ft 6in + 7ft 9in; Cyls 18 x 26; Blr 4ft 6¼ x 10ft 3½in; THS 1099.3 sq
ft; WP 140 lbs/sq in; Wt 39 tons 15 cwt.
Heavy goods locomotive. Similar to Stroudley LBSC class C of 1871 but more powerful.
Lever reverse, Adams patent safety valve replaced by 'lock up' type after explosion of
no 465. Steam brakes were standard but nos 278, 461/73 were additionally fitted with
vacuum ejectors when rebuilt in 1901. No 454 might also have been so fitted for a
time. Nos 456/8 and possibly 459 had the steam brake substituted by Westinghouse. No
153 was fitted with Moreton's valve gear in 1890, with cylinders increased to 19 x 26,
but reverted to Stephenson link motion and 18in cylinders when rebuilt in 1901.
Tenders were of 2500 gallons capacity. Before rebuilding, working pressure was
increased to 150 lbs/sq in. THS was also altered to 1080.96 sq ft. Rebuilt by
Holmes, WB 7ft 6in + 8ft 0in; Blr 4ft 6¼in x 10ft 2¼in; THS 1235.13 sq ft; Wt 39½
tons, with Holmes round cabs instead of Drummond cutaway type. LNE class J32.
The following were built at Cowlairs:

No	Date	Rebuilt	Duplicate no	year	LNE nos no	year	Withdrawn
100	1876	1/1899	1297	1917	(9975)	1924	
					(10297)	1924	12/1924
153	1876	1890 as above					
		10/1901	1298	1917	(1298B)	1923	10/1923
242	1876	11/1901	1300	1919	(1300B)	1923	1/1924
270	1876	4/1899	1301	1919			4/1922
278	1876	7/1901	1302	1919			2/1922
281	1876	1/1899	1303	1919			4/1921
287	1876	10/1900	1304	1919	(9976)	1924	
					(10304)	1924	12/1924
292	1876	10/1900	1305	1918			4/1923
304	1876	10/1900	1307	1918			10/1921
139	1877	12/1902	1329	1918	(1329B)	1923	10/1923
305	1877	1/1903	1337	1918	(9981)	1924	
					(10337)	1924	4/1925
315	1877	10/1898	1339	1918	(9982)	1924	
					(10339)	1924	11/1924

The following were built by Neilson & Co. Works nos 2112-17, 2131-44.

No	Date	Rebuilt	Duplicate no	year	LNE nos no	year	Withdrawn
454	1876	11/1899	1308	1918			1/1922
455	1876	10/1901	1309	1918			4/1921
456	1876	12/1902	1310	1918	(1310B)	1923	10/1923
457	1876	10/1902	1311	1918	(9977)	1924	
					(10311)	1924	12/1924
458	1876	1/1903	1312	1918	(9978)	1924	
					(10312)	1924	12/1924
459	1876	11/1899	1313	1918			9/1921
460	1876	12/1902	1314	1918	(9979)	1924	
					(10314)	1924	6/1924
461	1876	7/1901	1315	1918	(9980)	1924	
					(10315)	1924	8/1924
462	1876	12/1899	1316	1918			5/1922
463	1876	10/1900	1317	1918			6/1922
464	1876	10/1900	1318	1918			2/1922
465	12/1876	1883*					
		10/1900	1319	1918	(1319B)	1923	2/1924
466	1877	1/1900	1340	1918			7/1922
467	1877	12/1902	1341	1918			4/1923
468	1877	9/1898	1342	1918			9/1922
469	1877	1/1903	1343	1918	(10343)	1924	5/1924

470	1877	10/1899	1344	1919	(1344B)	1923	9/1923
471	1877	12/1899	1345	1919	(9983)	1924	
					(10345)	1924	2/1925
472	1877	12/1898	1346	1919	(9984)	1924	
					(10346)	1924	11/1924
473	1877	7/1901	1347	1919			7/1922

* After explosion at Dunbar 1/9/1882.

0-6-0 Built by NB Railway at Cowlairs.
DW 5ft 0in; WB 7ft 6in + 7ft 9in; Cyls 17 x 24.
Standard goods. Lever reverse. Steam brake. Rebuilt by Holmes,
Blr 4ft 5in x 10ft 1in; THS 1061 sq ft; WP 150 lbs/sq in; Wt 37 tons 13 cwt but
Drummond cabs retained. Nos 290 & 35 were converted to Westinghouse brake prior to
rebuilding. On rebuilding some were altered to 17 x 26 cyls but others retained 17 x
24 cylinders as indicated below. The cylinders from no 1376 were transferred to 497
class no 513 in November 1922. LNE class J34.

No	Date	Rebuilt			Duplicate no	year	LNE nos no	year	Withdrawn
34	1879	10/1904	17 x 24		1376	1919			11/1922
35	1879	4/1905	17 x 24		1379	1919	(9346)	1924	
							(10377)	1924	10/1924
87	1879	6/1906	17 x 24		1364	1919	(9341)	1924	
							(10364)	1924	7/1925
271	1879	1/1905	17 x 26		1365	1919	(9342)	1924	
							(10365)	1924	6/1925
277	1879	8/1907	17 x 26		1366	1919	(9343)	1924	
							(10366)	1924	10/1924
279	1879	4/1906	17 x 24		1367	1919			3/1923
288	1879	12/1903	17 x 24		1368	1919	(1368B)	1923	1/1924
289	1879	11/1907	17 x 24		1369	1919	(9344)	1924	
							(10369)	1924	5/1925
290	1879	10/1904	17 x 24		1370	1919	9345	5/1924	
							10370	8/1924	1/1926
296	1879	1/1900	17 x 26		1378	1919			7/1921
401	1879	3/1899	17 x 26		1384	1919			2/1922
402	1879	11/1898	17 x 26		1385	1919			6/1922
403	1879	4/1904	17 x 24		1386	1919	(9704)	1924	
							(10386)		8/1924

0-6-0 Built by Dubs & Co. (Nos 497-501). Works nos 1217-21.
             NB Railway at Cowlairs.
DW 5ft 0in; WB 7ft 6in + 7ft 9in; Cyls 17 x 26.
Standard goods. Larger cylindered version of 17 x 24 locomotives above. Rebuilt by
Holmes as above. Only no 524 (rebuilt in 1/1892 after a head-on collision with no 501
on the Almond Viaduct at Todds Mill, Bo'ness, which caused it to fall sixty feet from
the viaduct) was given a Holmes round cab, the others retaining the Drummond cab.
After rebuilding, apart from those few locomotives above retaining 17 x 24 cylinders,
all in effect became one class. Locomotives believed converted from steam brake to
Westinghouse were 501, 84, 507/8/11/15/17/21/3-5/7/30/1/8/41/3/4, 163, 548/52/3/5-
7/65, 286, 481 from the 1890s. Of these, 501/7/44 additionally had vacuum ejectors,
and 540/58 were converted to Westinghouse brake by the LNE in July 1923.
LNE class J34.

No	Date	Rebuilt	Duplicate no	year	LNE nos no	year	Withdrawn
497	1879	3/1900	1393	1919	(9481)	1924	6/1924
498	1879	8/1904	1394	1919	(9482)	1924	
					(10394)	1924	11/1925
499	1879	7/1904	1395	1919	(9483)	1924	
					(10395)	1924	8/1924
500	1879	12/1905	1396	1919			1/1923

501	1879	1/1904	1397	1919	(9529)	1924	*
					(10397)	1924	8/1924
300	1879	3/1900	1379	1919			4/1921
301	1879	1/1904	1380	1919	(9703)	1924	
					(10380)	1924	10/1925
302	1879	2/1900	1381	1919			5/1923
303	1879	8/1904	1382	1919			9/1921
306	1879	7/1907	1383	1919			6/1923
46	1880	12/1907	1400	1920	(9530)	1924	
					(10400)	1924	8/1925
84	1880	12/1905	1403	1920			8/1922
171	1880	4/1907	1407	1920			7/1923
175	1880	1/1904	1408	1920			2/1922
272	7/1880	11/1905	1409	1920	9538	5/1924	
					10409	9/1924	3/1926
273	1880	6/1907	1410	1921	(9544)	1924	
					(10410)	1924	8/1925
506	1880	5/1906	1412	1920			6/1923
507	1880	1/1908	1413	1920	(9545)	1924	
					(10413)	1924	10/1925
508	1880	10/1907	1414	1920			6/1923
509	1880	7/1906	1415	1920	(9549)	1924	
					(10415)	1924	3/1926
510	1880	2/1899	1416	1920	(1416B)	1923	9/1923
511	1880	6/1907	1417	1920	(9559)	1924	
					(10417)	1924	2/1925
512	1880	1/1900	1418	1920	(9560)	1924	
					(10418)	1924	8/1924
513	1880	11/1905**	1419	1920	(9565)	1924	
					(10419)	1924	1/1926
514	1880	4/1904	1420	1920	(9693)	1924	
					(10420)	1924	6/1925
515	1880	11/1907	1421	1920	(9694)	1924	
					(10421)	1924	3/1925
516	1880	10/1907	1422	1920	(9696)	1924	
					(10422)	1924	11/1925
517	1880	3/1904	1423	1920			2/1923
128	1881	11/1907	1430	1920	(9697)	1924	
					(10430)	1924	10/1924
143	3/1881	3/1899	1431	1920	(1431B)	1923	9/1923
518	1881	11/1904	1432	1920	(9638)	1924	
					(10432)	1924	1/1925
519	1881	9/1907	1472	1923	(9699)	1924	
					(10472)	1924	9/1924
520	4/1881	12/1905	1473	1923			6/1923
521	1881	1/1906	1474	1923	(9700)	1924	
					(10474)	1924	8/1924
522	1881	1/1905	1475	1923	(9701)	1924	
					(10475)	1924	3/1925
523	1881	4/1907	1476	1923	(9702)	1924	
					(10476)	1924	12/1926
524	1881	1/1892	1477	1923	(9316)	1924	*
					(10477)	1924	12/1924
525	1881	1/1906	1478	1923	(1478B)	1923	9/1923
526	1881	1/1906	1479	1923	(1479B)	1923	3/1924
527	1881	4/1906	(1480)	1923			2/1923
528	1881	9/1907	1481	1923			7/1923
529	1881	6/1907					7/1923
530	11/1881	12/1905					5/1923
531	11/1881	9/1907			(9531)	1924	1/1925

532	1881	1/1908	(9532)	1924	10/1924
533	12/1881	10/1907	(9533)	1924	10/1925
534	1/1882	5/1906	9534	9/1924	10/1927
535	1/1882	7/1906	(9535)	1924	7/1925
536	1/1882	12/1898	9536	5/1924	11/1924
537	1/1882	5/1907	(9537)	1924	11/1925
538	1/1882	5/1907			5/1923
539	1/1882	10/1904	(9539)	1924	10/1924
540	3/1882	3/1904	(9540)	1924	11/1925
541	1882	9/1904	(9541)	1924	2/1925
542	4/1882	8/1907	(9542)	1924	4/1926
543	1882	5/1906	(9543)	1924	9/1925
544	4/1882	4/1904			4/1923
545	4/1882	12/1903			8/1923
27	7/1882	9/1904	27B	9/1923	
			(9027)	1924	1/1926
28	7/1882	3/1907	(9028)	1924	10/1924
30	7/1882	7/1907	(9030)	1924	3/1924
125	7/1882	1/1904			5/1923
163	7/1882	3/1905	9163	5/1924	4/1926
184	7/1882	2/1900	(9184)	1924	9/1924
548	10/1882	1/1899	(9548)	1924	4/1925
549	10/1882	4/1905			7/1923
550	10/1882	7/1907	9550	8/1924	1/1928
551	1882	8/1904	(9551)	1924	6/1925
552	11/1882	7/1907	(9552)	1924	11/1924
553	11/1882	3/1906	9553	5/1924	11/1925
554	2/1883	4/1907	(9554)	1924	7/1925
555	1883	7/1907	(9555)	1924	10/1925
556	3/1883	3/1904	(9556)	1924	12/1924
557	4/1883	6/1907	(9557)	1924	10/1924
558	4/1883	11/1907	(9558)	1924	10/1925
559	5/1883	6/1906			8/1923
560	5/1883	7/1907			7/1923
561	6/1883	11/1904	(9561)	1924	12/1924
562	6/1883	11/1904	(9562)	1924	4/1925
563	6/1883	11/1905	(9563)	1924	4/1925
564	6/1883	6/1906	(9564)	1924	1/1925
565	6/1883	12/1905			6/1923
18	7/1883	5/1907	(18B)	1923	12/1923
138	7/1883	6/1906	9138	6/1924	1/1928
286	7/1883	12/1907	(9286)	1924	10/1925
311	7/1883	6/1907	(9311)	1924	11/1924
481	7/1883	1/1905	(481B)	1923	9/1923
482	7/1883	1/1906	(482B)	1923	11/1923

* Nos 501 and 524 in Accident Todds Mill, Bo'ness 28/11/1890.

** No 513, 17 x 24 cyls ex-1376 fitted 11/1922.

0-4-2T Built by NB Railway at Cowlairs.
DW 5ft 9in; TW 4ft 6in; Cyls 17 x 24; THS 1075 sq ft; WP 140 lbs/sq in; Wt 45 tons.
Based on LBSC Stroudley *Sydenham* class for the Helensburgh line. The tanks had 980
gallons capacity and condensers originally provided were soon removed.
Rebuilt 0-4-4T - TW 3ft 6in; WB 7ft 6in + 8ft 0in + 6ft 6in; WP 150 lbs/sq in; Wt 47
tons 17 cwt approximately. Tank capacity increased to 1290 gallons and THS 1143 sq
ft. Westinghouse control equipment added to original steam brakes, later substituted
for Westinghouse brake on locomotive as on train. Lever reverse, sand boxes in
splashers.
Rebuilt by Reid with Holmes boilers standard with 494 class 4-4-0Ts. Blr 4ft 5in x
10ft 1in; THS 1051.4 sq ft and steam-heating apparatus provided. In late NBR period,

no 1320 became dual-brake fitted with Westinghouse and vacuum ejector. Names removed about 1883. LNE class G8.

No	Date	Name	Rebuilt 0-4-4T	4-4-0T Boiler	Duplicate no	year	LNE nos no	year	With- drawn
157	6/1877	*Dumbarton*	1881/2	7/1905	1320	1918	(9283)	1924	
	1879	renamed					(10320)	1924	9/1925
		Markinch							
167	6/1877	*Cardross*	1881/2	7/1905	1334	1918	(9323)	1924	
	1879	renamed					(10334)	1924	5/1925
		Dundee							
314	6/1877	*Craigendoran*	1881/2	7/1905	1338	1918	(9328)	1924	
	1879	renamed					(10338)	1924	5/1925
		Lochee							
480	6/1877	*Roseneath*	1881/2	7/1905	1325	1918	(9284)	1924	
	1879	renamed					(10325)	1924	10/1924
		Burntisland							
89	7/1877	*Gareloch*	1881/2	7/1905	1327	1918	(9321)	1924	
	1879	renamed					(10327)	1924	5/1925
		Ladybank							
88	7/1877	*Helensburgh*	1881/2	7/1905	1326	1918	(9285)	1924	
	1879	renamed					(10326)	1924	1/1925
		Kirkaldy							

4-4-0T Built by Neilson & Co. Works nos 2420-2.
DW 6ft 0in; LW 3ft 6in; WB 6ft 6in + 6ft 7in + 8ft 0in; Cyls 17 x 26;
Blr 4ft 5in x 10ft 1in; THS 1174 sq ft; WP 140 lbs/sq in; Wt 46 tons 16 cwt.
Built for fast trains on the Helensburgh line. Central dome, Ramsbottom safety valve,
screw reverse. Steam brakes with Westinghouse train brake control was substituted by
Westinghouse brake on locomotive and train. No 1390 had vacuum ejector added about
1922. THS later 1123 sq ft and WP increased to 150 lbs/sq in. Rebuilt with Holmes
boilers as on 0-4-4Ts above. THS 1051.4 sq ft; Wt 47 tons 4 cwt. Names removed about
1883. LNE class D50.

No	Date	Name	Rebuilt	Duplicate no	year	LNE nos no	year	Withdrawn
494	4/1879	*Craigendoran*	5/1905	1390	1919	9231	4/1924	
						10390	9/1924	3/1926
495	4/1879	*Roseneath*	6/1905	1391	1919	9232	5/1924	
						10391	8/1924	2/1926
496	5/1879	*Helensburgh*	7/1905	1392	1919	(9268)	1924	
						(10392)	1924	5/1924

4-4-0T Built by NB Railway at Cowlairs.
DW 5ft 0in; LW 2ft 6in; WB 5ft 0in + 5ft 10½in + 7ft 0in; Cyls 16 x 22; Blr 3ft 10in x
8ft 8½in; THS 647.46 sq ft; WP 140 lbs/sq in; Wt 35 tons 4 cwt.
Branch passenger engines with solid bogie wheels and 655 gallon tanks. Brakes were
originally steam on locomotive with Westinghouse train brake control, but this was
supplanted by Westinghouse brake throughout during the late Holmes period. No 19 had
vacuum ejectors added about 1908, and by 1916 nos 67, 105/11 were dual-fitted as also
was no 268 by about 1921. New boilers of the same type fitted to the rebuilt Drummond
0-6-0Ts below were provided by Reid. THS 666.06 sq ft. Names were removed about
1883/4 and it is possible that there were other renamings not recorded.
LNE class D51.

No	Date	Name	New Boiler	Duplicate no	year	LNE nos no	year	Withdrawn
72	1880	*Morpeth*	7/1910	1401	1920	(10025)	1924	
						(10401)	1924	10/1924
73	1880	*Rothbury*	7/1908	1402	1920	(10026)	1924	
						(10402)	1924	9/1925
109	9/1880	*Uddingston*	5/1910	1404	1920	(10027)	1924	
						(10404)	1924	9/1924

110	1880	*Kinross*	5/1909	1405	1920	(1405B)	1923	12/1923
111	1880	*Clackmannan*	6/1910	1406	1/1921	(10028)	1924	
						10406	9/1925	4/1933
299	8/1880	*Hamilton*	7/1910	1411	2/1921	(10029)	1924	
						10411	2/1926	10/1930
33	1881	*Bellgrove*	5/1910	1424	7/1921	(1424B)	1923	10/1923
98	5/1881	*Aberfoyle*	3/1910	1425	6/1921	(10030)	1924	
						10425	6/1925	10/1931
101	5/1881	*Anstruther*	1/1911	1426	6/1921	(10031)	1924	
						10426	2/1926	10/1929
103*	6/1881	*Montrose*	5/1909	1427	6/1921	(10032)	1924	
						10427	9/1925	3/1928
104	5/1881	*Roslin*	5/1910	1428	8/1921	(10033)	1924	
						10428	4/1925	8/1931
105	5/1881	*Penicuik*	7/1909	1429	9/1921	(10034)	1924	
						10429	3/1925	8/1931
19	1882	*Strathendrick*	1/1911	1454	7/1921	(1454B)	1923	12/1923
60	6/1882	*Airdrie*	6/1909	1455	7/1921	(10035)	1924	
						(10455)	1924	10/1924
74	5/1882	*Coatbridge*	7/1909	1456	7/1921	(10036)	1924	
		renamed				10456	2/1925	9/1931
		Whiteinch						
		renamed *Coatbridge*						
75	6/1882	*Sunnyside*	6/1910	1457	7/1921	(10037)	1924	
						(10457)	1924	9/1924
99	1882	*Roxburgh*	1/1911	1458	7/1921	(10038)	1924	
						10458	7/1925	5/1933
147	6/1882	*Slamannan*	6/1910	1459	7/1921	(10039)	1924	
						10459	6/1925	4/1929
225	1882	*Milngavie*	7/1909	1460	7/1921	(10040)	1924	
						(10460)	1924	3/1926
294	1882	*Clydebank*	6/1909	1461	7/1921	(10041)	1924	
						10461	3/1925	10/1932
52	1/1883	*Dirleton*	7/1910	1462	7/1921	(10042)	1924	
						10462	3/1925	8/1933
67	1/1883	*Clarkston*	5/1909	1463	7/1921	(1463B)	1923	12/1923
174	2/1883	*Lennoxtown*	7/1910	1464	7/1921	(10043)	1924	
						10464	8/1925	5/1929
268	1/1883	*Bothwell*	5/1910	1465	7/1921	(10044)	1924	
						10465	11/1925	7/1928
76	1884	(naming	12/1910	1466	7/1921	(10045)	1924	
		ceased)				(10466)	1924	11/1924
77	9/1884		1/1911	1467	7/1921	(10046)	1924	
						10467	6/1925	8/1929
78	1884		6/1909	1468	7/1921	(10047)	1924	
						(10468)	1924	9/1924
79	10/1884		6/1910	1469	7/1921	(10048)	1924	
						10469	9/1924	1/1927
316	1884		6/1908	1470	7/1921	(10049)	1924	
						(9394)	1924	
						(10470)	1924	6/1925
483	10/1884		12/1910	1471	7/1921	(10050)	1924	
						(9395)	1924	
						10471	9/1925	8/1927

* No 103 was exhibited in Newcastle at the Stephenson Centenary in 1881.

0-6-0T Built by NB Railway at Cowlairs.
DW 4ft 6in; WB 6ft 4in + 6ft 10in; Cyls 15 x 22; Blr 3ft 10in x 8ft 8½in; THS 738 sq ft; WP 140 lbs/sq in; Wt 33 tons 9 cwt.

Based on LBSC Stroudley *Terrier* class but bigger and more powerful. The original cylinders had four valve faces with double exhaust ports later replaced by conventional type. Ramsbottom safety valves, 600 gallon tanks, coal capacity 24 cwt increased to 1½ tons with coal rails. The first ten originally had crosshead driven feed pumps and condenser water heating, but the remainder had injectors which were also substituted on the earlier ones and the condensers removed. The cab and bunker were only 6ft 0¾in wide and the buffer beams projected above the footplate. Hand brakes were replaced by steam brakes from 1881 on some locomotives, but by the late Holmes period all had Westinghouse brakes and Westinghouse train brake control. Rebuilt by Reid with new boilers pitched 3in higher at 6ft 6in. THS 666 sq ft; WP 140 lbs/sq in; Wt 36 tons. The original boilers were latterly recorded as having THS 701 sq ft, and had the older type of non-lifting injectors, but the new boilers had the more modern combination injectors. The first eleven had the Wheatley type of number plate with raised numbers, the remainder the Drummond type. Names were removed about 1883. LNE class J82.

No	Date	Name*	New Boiler	Duplicate no	year	LNE nos no	year	Withdrawn
165	11/1875	Coatbridge	7/1909	1289	2/1917	(1289B)	1923	10/1923
		renamed						
		Bo'ness*						
166	11/1875	Bothwell	4/1908	1290	3/1917			11/1922
	1882	renamed Newport						
259	11/1875	Bellshill	12/1910	1291	5/1917	(10002)	1924	
		renamed Queensferry				(10291)	1924	1/1925
284	11/1875	Airdrie	4/1910	1294	4/1916	(10003)	1924	
		renamed Grahamston				(10294)	1924	12/1924
241	1/1876	Roslin	3/1910	1299	6/1917	(10004)	1924	
		renamed Penicuik				(10299)	1924	1/1925
	1881	renamed Bervie						
297	1/1876	Penicuik	6/1910	1306	8/1918	(10005)	1924	
		renamed Leith				(10306)	1924	2/1925
123	4/1877	Westfield	5/1908	1328	6/1918	(10006)	1924	
						(10328)	1924	11/1926
151	5/1877	Dalmuir	4/1910	1330	7/1918	10007	6/1924	
		renamed Guard Bridge				10330	8/1924	1/1926
158	5/1877	North Berwick	7/1909	1331	7/1918	(10008)	1924	
		renamed Meadowbank				(10331)	1924	7/1925
161	4/1877	Partick	4/1909	1332	7/1918	(10009)	1924	
		renamed Buckhaven				(10332)	1924	6/1925
162	5/1877	Milngavie	4/1910	1333	8/1918	(10010)	1924	
		renamed Loch Leven				(10333)	1924	2/1925
274	1877	Dalkeith	7/1909	1335	8/1918	(10012)	1924	
						(10335)	1924	6/1925
295	5/1877	Bellgrove	4/1909	1336	8/1918	(10013)	1924	
	1881	renamed Carnoustie				(10336)	1924	12/1925
20	11/1877	Haddington	7/1910	1348	2/1920	(10014)	1924	
						(10348)	1924	1/1925
22	3/1878	Langholm	5/1908	1349	2/1920	(10015)	1924	
						(10349)	1924	11/1924
29	3/1878	Granton	4/1910	1350	2/1920	(10016)	1924	
						(10350)	1924	2/1925
49	5/1878	Sunnyside	6/1910	1351	2/1920	(10017)	1924	
		renamed Gretna				(10351)	1924	8/1924
96	6/1878	Arbroath	4/1910	1352	2/1920	(10018)	1924	
						(10352)	1924	9/1926
97	7/1878	Bonnington	4/1909	1353	2/1920	(10019)	1924	7/1924
106	7/1878	Slamannan	5/1908	1354	2/1920	(10020)	1924	
	1880	renamed Tayport				(10354)	1924	10/1924

107	7/1878	*Uddingston*	7/1909	1355	3/1920	(9018)	1924	
	1880	renamed *Leuchars*				(10335)	1924	12/1924
108	6/1878	*Hamilton*	7/1910	1356	3/1920	(10026)	1924	
		renamed *St Andrews*				(10356)	1924	2/1925
240	1/1878	*Coatbridge*	7/1909	1357	3/1920	(10022)	1924	
	1880	renamed *Polton*				(10357)	1924	12/1924
313	1/1878	*Clydebank*	5/1909	1358	6/1920	10023	5/1924	
	1880	renamed *Musselburgh*				10358	9/1924	8/1926
485	1/1878	*Yoker*	6/1910	1359	12/1919	(10024)	1924	
	1882	renamed *Blairadam*				(10359)	1924	11/1924

* No complete record of names is available. The name *Bo'ness* may have been *Bo-ness* with a hyphen rather than an apostrophe.

0-4-0ST Built by Neilson & Co. Works nos 2935/6.
DW 3ft 8in; WB 7ft 0in; Cyls 14 x 20.
Neilson standard design. Wooden dumb buffers, hand brakes.
Rebuilt: Blr 3ft $9^5/8$in x 10ft $4^3/8$in; THS 788 sq ft; WP 130 lbs/sq in; Wt 14 tons 3 cwt. The footplate roof, which had previously been open at the sides, had side panels added in 1931 (no 10101 in October and 10102 in August) converting into a cab. Steam brakes were added by BR in 1948/9 as under. Holmes continued the class with similar locomotives built at Cowlairs, and rebuilt as above to form one class which became LNER Y9 (see page 194).

No	Date	New boiler	Steam brake	Duplicate no	date	LNE nos no	date	BR no	App- lied	With- drawn
546	1882	3/1915	2/1949	901	7/1899	(9941)	1924			
				1101	1901	10101	7/25			
						8092	11/46	68092	2/49	2/1953
547	1882	12/1913	5/1948	902	7/1899	9942	7/24			
				1102	1901	10102	9/24			
						8093	8/46	68093	5/48	5/1955

Holmes Locomotives 1883-1903

4-4-0 Built by NB Railway at Cowlairs.
DW 6ft 6in; LW 3ft 6in; WB 6ft 6in + 6ft 7in + 8ft 3in; Cyls 17 x 26; Blr 4ft 5in x
10ft 1in; THS 1059 sq ft; WP 140 lbs/sq in; Wt 43½ tons.
Built for Edinburgh-Glasgow expresses, the boiler was standard with Holmes 17in
cylinder 0-6-0s, and were fitted with the Cowlairs incline rope guide on the bogie.
All had Westinghouse brake. Vacuum ejectors were added before 1923. Sandboxes were
incorporated in the leading splasher. 2500 gallon tenders. Steam heating apparatus
added by 1908. Extensively rebuilt by Reid - WB 6ft 6in + 6ft 7in + 9ft 0in; Cyls 18¼
x 26; Blr 4ft 8^1/$_8$in x 10ft 3^3/$_8$in; THS 1266.1 sq ft; WP 175 lbs/sq in; Wt 46 tons 8
cwt; with side window cabs and vertical screw reverse instead of lever type. In 1918-
22, they became one class with rebuilds of 633 and 729 classes below.
LNE class D31 (D31/1, 11/1927-1935).

			LNE nos			
No	Date	Rebuilt	1923	1924	Applied	Withdrawn
574	6/1884	7/1911	574B	9574	11/1924	6/1934
575	6/1884	7/1911	575B	9575	4/1926	2/1937
576	7/1884	7/1911	576B	9576	10/1924	6/1933
577	7/1884	7/1911	577B	9577	1/1926	5/1934
578	7/1884	7/1911	578B	9578	3/1925	7/1933
579	7/1884	7/1911	579B	9579	6/1924	8/1933

4-4-0 Built by NB Railway at Cowlairs.
DW 7ft 0in; LW 3ft 6in; WB 6ft 6in + 6ft 7in + 9ft 3in; Cyls 18 x 26; Blr 4ft 6in
(maximum) x 10ft 3½in; THS (Nos 592-7) 1102 sq ft, (Nos 598-603) 1126 sq ft; WP 150
lbs/sq in; Wt 45¼ tons.
Built for Aberdeen expresses. The boilers were lap jointed, the front ring being 4ft
5in in diameter. Westinghouse brakes, vacuum ejectors being added to Westinghouse
train brake control by 1908. Steam-heating apparatus was added about 1901. Vertical
screw reverse. Cowlairs rope guide fitted until about 1901. Rebuilt with new
boilers, side window cab and Reid chimneys. These boilers were butt jointed 4ft 4in
diameter; THS 1106.18 sq ft; Wt 46 tons 4 cwt. Air sanding replaced previous gravity
feed. Smokebox wing plates were retained but removed 1921-6.
LNE class D25.

			LNE nos			
No	Date	Rebuilt	1923	1924	Applied	Withdrawn
592*	4/1886	6/1911	592B	9592	1/1925	9/1932
593	9/1886	3/1911	593B**	(9593)		10/1926
594	10/1886	7/1911	594B**	(9594)		11/1926
595	4/1887	4/1911	595B	9595	7/1924	3/1932
596	4/1887	5/1911	596B	9596	6/1925	7/1933
597	3/1887	5/1911	597B**	(9597)		10/1926
598	2/1888	4/1911	598B	9598	8/1925	10/1930
599	2/1888	6/1911	599B	9599	1/1926	2/1930
600	2/1888	5/1911	600B	9600	9/1925	9/1928
601	3/1888	4/1911	601B	9601	7/1924	4/1926
602	3/1888	4/1911	602B**	(9602)		4/1926
603	3/1888	6/1911	603B	9603	3/1925	3/1928

* No 592 exhibited at Edinburgh International Exhibition 1886.
** These locomotives carried 'B' suffix.

4-4-0 Built by NB Railway at Cowlairs.
DW 6ft 6in; LW 3ft 6in; WB 6ft 6in + 6ft 7in + 9ft 0in; Cyls 18 x 26; Blr 4ft 8^1/$_8$in x
10ft 3½in; THS (1890 locomotives) 1266 sq ft, (others) 1350 sq ft; Wt 46 tons.
Enlarged version of 574 class introduced to work traffic over the newly-opened Forth
Bridge. Nos 213-8, which were primarily intended for working through expresses from
the Midland Railway, were fitted with dual train brake systems - Westinghouse and
vacuum as well as Westinghouse brakes on the engine when built. The others had vacuum
fitted ejectors fitted later. 2500 gallon tenders. Steam-heating apparatus added by
1908. Rebuilt by Reid and Chalmers becoming one class with rebuilds of 574 and 729

classes (18¼ cyls and a rebuilds of 574 class above) with side window cabs and Reid chimneys and vertical screw reverse in place of lever action. Smokebox wing-plates removed in Chalmers period. Those rebuilt by Chalmers from 12/1921 had modifications in the springing and a straight shorter chimney instead of the outwardly tapered pattern. From 11/1927 the LNE classified these as D31/2 and the others as D31/1. Before this date and after 1935 the classification was simply D31.

No	Date	Rebuilt	LNE nos 1923	1924	app-lied	1946 no	app-lied	BR nos	app-lied	With-drawn
633	5/1890	9/1918	633B	9633	4/26					1/1939
634	5/1890	1/1919	634B	9634	6/25					11/1935
635	5/1890	10/1918	635B	9635	4/24	2059	8/46	62059	9/48	
								62281	8/49	12/1952
636	6/1890	1/1918	636B	9636	12/25					11/1937
637	6/1890	10/1918	637B	9637	3/25					4/1936
638	6/1890	9/1918	638B	9638	8/24					5/1937
639	8/1890	12/1918	639B	9639	2/26					10/1935
640	8/1890	12/1918	640B	9640	12/24					10/1936
641	8/1890	10/1918	641B	9641	1/26					5/1937
642*	9/1890	9/1922	642B	9642	12/24	2060	5/46	62060	10/48	
								62282	6/49	2/1950
36	9/1890	9/1918	36B	9036	12/24					6/1935
37	9/1890	12/1918	37B	9037	10/25					5/1935
262	11/1894	10/1920	262B	9262	1/25					8/1937
293	12/1894	10/1920	293B	9293	2/25					1/1938
312	1/1895	1/1921	312B	9312	12/24					12/1938
404	1/1895	11/1922	404B	9404	9/25	2062	6/46			3/1948
211	1/1895	9/1922	211B	9211	11/24					9/1937
212	1/1895	3/1921	212B	9212	5/24					4/1937
213	6/1895	10/1920	213B	9213	4/25					3/1939
214	6/1895	10/1920	214B	9214	9/26					5/1939
215	6/1895	10/1920	215B	9215	9/25	(2061)				9/1946
216	6/1895	11/1920	216B	9216	5/24					11/1937
217	7/1895	10/1920	217B	9217	10/24					10/1939
218	7/1895	2/1921	218B	9218	9/24					7/1937

* No 642 was in an accident at Dunbar on 3/1/1898.

4-4-0 Built by NB Railway at Cowlairs.
Blr 4ft 6¼ x 10ft 2¼in; THS 1235.13 sq ft; WP 150 lbs/sq in; Wt 43 tons 6 cwt. Designed for the West Highland line and known as 'West Highland bogies'. DW 5ft 7in; LW 3ft 6in; WB 6ft 6in + 6ft 7in + 8ft 2in; Cyls 18 x 24. These were Holmes least successful 4-4-0s. Lever reverse, gravity sanding, 2500 gallon tenders, Westinghouse brake, smokebox wing-plates. Nos 55, 341/3-6, 395, 700/2/3 had vacuum ejectors added by 1919. Only no 695 was rebuilt. WB 6ft 6in + 6ft 7in + 9ft 1in; Cyls 19 x 26; Blr 4ft 8¹/₈in x 10ft 3³/₈in; THS 1062.3 sq ft plus superheater 220 sq ft; WP 165 lbs/sq in; Wt 49 tons 11 cwt. This was the only Holmes locomotive to be superheated and air sanding was provided instead of gravity feed and the smokebox wing-plates removed. No 695, of course, got a side window cab on rebuilding, but the others retained the original Holmes round cab. The LNE classified the unrebuilt locomotives, of which only seven reached LNE ownership, D35 and no 695 D36. No 695 was converted back to saturated state with a D31 boiler, THS 1266.5 sq ft; WP 175 lbs/sq in; Wt 49 tons 14 cwt by the LNE in 5/1936.

No	Date	Rebuilt	Duplicate no	date	LNE nos no	date	Withdrawn
693	1894		1446	1920			9/1921
694	1894		1447	1920			9/1921
695	1/1894*	2/1919 19 x 26 S'heat					
		5/1936 Saturated			9695	3/1924	5/1943
696	1/1894*		1448	4/1921	(9998)	1924	
					(10448)	1924	10/1924
697	1/1894*		1449	3/1921			5/1923

698	1894	(1433)			1920
699	1894	1450	1920		11/1922
700	1894	1451	1920		4/1921
701	4/1894	1452	7/1921		5/1923
55	5/1894	1434	4/1921		3/1923
394	1894	1444	1920		6/1922
395	1894	1445	1920		5/1922
227	1896	(1435)			1920
231	1896	1436	1920		12/1922
232	1896	1437	1920		10/1921
341	1896	1438	1920		9/1921
342	1/1896	1439	4/1921	(9997) 1924	
				(10439) 1924	11/1924
343	1896	1440	1920		9/1921
344	1896	1441	1920		7/1921
345	4/1896	1442	4/1921		2/1923
346	1896	1443	1920		10/1921
702	1896	(1398)			1919
703	1896	(1399)			1919
704	3/1896	1453	10/1921	(1453B) 1923	1/1924

* Date to stock. Built 9/1893.

4-4-0 Built by NB Railway at Cowlairs.
DW 6ft 6in; LW 3ft 6in; WB 6ft 6in + 6ft 7in + 9ft 0in; Cyls 18¼ x 26; Blr 4ft 8^1/8in
x 10ft 3^3/8in; THS 1350 sq ft; WP 175 lbs/sq in; Wt 47¼ tons.
Similar to 633 class but built with 18¼ diameter cylinders, combination injectors and
steam heating apparatus. Westinghouse brake for engine and train, vacuum ejectors
being added before 1923. Larger 3500 gallon tenders. Rebuilt by Reid and Chalmers
becoming one class with rebuild of 574 and 633 classes (dimensions as 574 class
above). LNE class D31 Chalmers rebuild from 12/1921 had certain modifications and
from 11/1927 to 1935 these were classified D31/2 and the others D31/1.

No	Date	Rebuilt	LNE nos 1923	1924	app-lied	1946 no	app-lied	BR nos	app-lied	With-drawn
729	3/1898	12/1921	729B	9729	3/25	(2063)				3/1946
730	4/1898	12/1920	730B	9730	11/25					12/1937
731	4/1898	1/1922	731B	9731	10/24	2064	7/46	(62064)		8/1948
732	5/1898	4/1922	732B	9732	12/25	2065	9/46	62065	7/48	4/1949
733	5/1898	10/1922	733B	9733	5/24	2066	6/46	(62066)		5/1948
734	5/1898	5/1922	734B	9734	3/24	2067	9/46			10/1946
735	7/1898	4/1922	735B	9735	2/25					3/1939
736	7/1898	3/1922	736B	9736	12/24					7/1931
737	7/1898	12/1920	737B	9737	2/26					5/1939
738	7/1898	2/1922	738B	9738	6/24					6/1939
739	7/1898	9/1922	739B	9739	4/25	2068	8/46			7/1947
740	7/1898	6/1922	740B	9740	1/25	2069	9/46			11/1947
765	9/1899	2/1921	765B	9765	3/25	(2070)				11/1946
766	9/1899	6/1922	766B	9766	12/24					6/1937
767	9/1899	9/1922	767B	9767	3/25	2071	8/46			10/1946
768	11/1899	12/1921	768B	9768	6/24	2072	10/46	62072	7/48	
								62283	6/49	2/1951
769	11/1899	12/1921	769B	9769	7/24	2073	9/46			12/1947
770	11/1899	4/1922	770B	9770	10/24	2074	1/46			3/1946

4-4-0 Built by NB Railway at Cowlairs.
DW 6ft 6in; LW 3ft 6in; WB 6ft 6in + 7ft 7in + 9ft 6in; Cyls 19 x 26; Blr 4ft 8^1/8in x
11ft 4in; THS 1577 sq ft; WP 200 lbs/sq in; Wt 52 tons.
Holmes's largest 4-4-0. He was taken ill during the construction of these locomotives
and died before they entered traffic. They were built with side window cabs more
associated with Reid than Holmes although there is no reason to connect Reid with the
design. Indeed Reid did not add to the initial order for 12 locomotives and turned

his attention to his Atlantic design instead. WP was reduced to 190 lbs/sq in. Steam reversing gear and air sanding was provided, and steam heating apparatus was also fitted when built. Westinghouse brake. Vacuum ejectors additionally fitted to nos 323-8 when built and the others so fitted by 1916. Smokebox wing-plates removed from 1922 except on 317/9/21/8. Although generally reported to be very efficient their existence was only short. LNE class D26.

No	Date	Duplicate nos allotted	LNE nos 1923	1924	Applied	Withdrawn
317	5/1903	(1485)	317B	(9317)		8/1924
318	6/1903	(1486)	318B	9318	3/1924	7/1925
319	6/1903	(1483)				9/1922
320	6/1903	(1487)	320B	(9320)		1/1925
321	1903	(1484)				11/1922
322	7/1903	(1488)	322B	9322	8/1924	2/1925
323	9/1903	(1489)				2/1923
324	9/1903	(1490)	324B	9324	7/1924	12/1924
325	10/1903	(1491)	325B	9325	4/1924	7/1926
326	10/1903	(1492)	326B	9326	5/1924	8/1925
327	10/1903	(1493)	327B	9327	3/1924	11/1925
328	1903	(1482)				7/1922

0-6-0 Built by NB Railway at Cowlairs.
DW 5ft 0in; WB 7ft 6in + 8ft 0in; Cyls 17 x 26; Blr 4ft 5in x 10ft 1in; Wt 38 tons 8 cwt.
Standard goods with Holmes modifications including increase of 3in in wheelbase. The first 24 had Drummond type cutaway cabs, the remainder having Holmes round cabs. The first 12 had Drummond type 2500 gallon tenders with underslung springs, the remainder with the springs above the axles and of the same capacity. Safety valves on the dome. The earlier locomotives had steam brake but nos 582-5, 82, 148, 83 and all those built with Holmes cab had Westinghouse brake. Nos 566/9 had vacuum ejectors as well. New boilers THS 1059 sq ft; WP 150 lbs/sq in; Wt 37 tons 16 cwt were fitted with improved injectors and safety valves on the firebox although nos 80/112/50/56/484/568/9/71/80/1/3/5 continued to have them on the dome. LNE class J33.

No	Date	New boiler	LNE nos 1923	1924	Applied	Withdrawn
566	11/1883	12/1912	566B	(9566)		6/1925
567	11/1883	3/1912	567B	9567	7/1925	5/1929
568	12/1883	1/1912	568B	9568	1/1926	4/1928
569	1883	2/1908	569B	(9569)		6/1925
570	12/1883	2/1913	570B	9570	2/1925	1/1929
571	12/1883	12/1911	571B	9571	9/1924	10/1927
572	1/1884	8/1912	572B	9572	4/1926	5/1932
573	1884	4/1912	573B	(9573)		7/1925
112	2/1884	1/1912	112B	9112	5/1925	12/1930
150	2/1884	1/1912	150B	9150	11/1924	4/1929
178	1/1884	4/1912	178B	9178	10/1924	1/1927
484	2/1884	3/1908	484B	9484	4/1924	12/1966
580	11/1884	1/1912	580B	9580	11/1924	11/1926
581	11/1884	1/1912	581B	9581	11/1924	8/1927
582	11/1884	7/1912	582B	9582	3/1924	3/1927
583	12/1884	1/1912	583B	(9583)		7/1924
584	12/1884	4/1912	584B*	(9584)		6/1928
585	12/1884	1/1912	585B	9585	3/1924	6/1928
80	2/1885	12/1911	80B	9080	10/1924	4/1929
81	3/1885	3/1912	81B	9081	8/1925	9/1929
82	3/1885	4/1913	82B	9082	4/1924	8/1931
148	3/1885	12/1912	148B	9148	7/1924	6/1926
83	6/1885	3/1912	83B	9083	7/1925	12/1928
85	8/1885	3/1912	85B	(9085)		1/1929
140**	6/1885	3/1912	140B	(9140)		4/1926

24	7/1885	2/1913	24B	9024	12/1924	12/1930
21	8/1885	3/1912	21B	9021	1/1926	10/1931
137	11/1885	3/1912	137B	9137	6/1925	5/1928
160	11/1885	3/1912	160B	9160	9/1925	4/1928
170	1/1886	2/1913	170B	(9170)		10/1927
156	3/1887	1/1912	156B	9156	6/1924	8/1927
159	3/1887	1/1912	159B	9159	10/1925	9/1932
168	3/1887	12/1912	168B	9168	2/1926	4/1931
169	6/1887	9/1912	169B	9169	3/1924	12/1938
269	6/1887	9/1912	269B	9269	8/1925	6/1928
249	6/1887	12/1912	249B	9249	3/1926	12/1938

* No 584 was the only locomotive to carry the 'B' suffix.
** No 140 and all subsequently listed had Holmes cab.

0-6-0 Built by NB Railway at Cowlairs.
                Neilson & Co. Works nos below.
                Sharp Stewart & Co. Works nos below.
DW 5ft 0in; WB 7ft 6in + 8ft 0in; Cyls 18 x 26; Blr 4ft 6¼in x 10ft 2¼in; THS 1244.68 sq ft (later 1235.13 sq ft); WP 140 lbs/sq in (150 lbs/sq in from 1900); Wt 40 tons 4 cwt.
In 1888 Holmes commenced building standard goods engines with 18in diameter cylinders, and construction went on until the end of 1900, by which time it was the largest class numerically on the system. Those built before 1897 had steam brakes and those from 1897 onwards, Westinghouse brakes, but there were alterations noted below. Some had vacuum train brake equipment in addition. 2500 gallon tenders. Rebuilt with new boilers, side window cab and Reid chimneys. Blr 4ft 8^1/$_8$in x 10ft 2¼in pitched 1½in higher at 7ft 4½in; THS 1309 sq ft; WP 160 lbs/sq in; Wt 41 tons 19 cwt. From 1938 THS was 1235.5 sq ft. 'B' suffixes for interim number scheme 9/23-2/24 are not known to have been carried on any locomotives of this class. LNE class J36.
From 1928, Cowlairs subdivided the class, those rebuilt before 1921, which had laminated springs on the leading and driving axle and helical on the trailing axle, being J36/1, and those rebuilt by Chalmers 1921-3, with helical springs throughout, were J36/2, although this subdivision was never officially recognised, and it is probable that most were standardised on the Reid pattern.
The following were built at Cowlairs. Additional fittings listed below: S bk = steam brake reinstated; S/H = steam heating apparatus; TC = tender cab; Vac = Vacuum ejector; W bk = Westinghouse brake; XSB = Extended smokebox.

No	Date	New boiler	Fittings	LNE nos no	date	BR no	app-lied	Withdrawn
604	8/1888	2/1916		9604	9/25			
				5210	10/46	65210	4/49	10/1962*
605**	8/1888	8/1915		9605	12/25			6/1934
606	8/1888	7/1916		9606	9/24			6/1933
607	8/1888	8/1915	Vac & TC by NB	9607	10/26			8/1934
608**	8/1888	11/1914		9608	1/25			6/1937
609	8/1888	8/1915		9609	5/25			5/1934
613	7/1889	8/1915	Vac & S/H by NB	9613	7/25			2/1936
614	7/1889	10/1914		9614	12/25			12/1937
615**	7/1889	6/1914	TC by NB	9615	5/24			4/1935
616	9/1889	5/1916		9616	10/25			9/1937
617	9/1889	10/1913		9617	11/25			
				5211	7/46	65211	10/48	7/1962
618	9/1889	7/1916		9618	11/24			2/1936
619	10/1889	2/1916		9619	7/25			10/1935
620**	10/1899	10/1913		9620	6/25			6/1937
621**	10/1889	10/1913		9621	12/24			4/1937
622	11/1889	11/1914	W bk by NB	9622	10/25			
			S bk 11/45	5213	6/46	65213	10/52	4/1957*
145	11/1889	7/1916		9145	11/26			8/1935
172	11/1889	7/1916	W bk by NB	9172	11/24			
				5212	6/46			7/1947*

623	1/1890	12/1916						
				9623	3/24			
				5214	9/46	65214	3/48	11/1963
624	1/1890	3/1918						
				9624	4/25			8/1937
625	1/1890	6/1914	W bk by NB					
			S bk 7/45					
				9625	11/25			
				5215	7/46	65215	6/48	4/1950
626	1/1890	7/1914						
				9626	5/25			12/1935
627**	1/1890	6/1915						
				9627	10/25			4/1936
628**	1/1890	6/1915						
				9628	11/26			
				5216	11/46	65216	9/48	4/1962*
629	3/1890	3/1918						
				9629	3/25			8/1937
630	3/1890	11/1914						
				9630	10/25			3/1936
631**	3/1890	5/1915						
				9631	11/25			3/1939
632	4/1890	5/1914 TC by BR						
				9632	2/25			
				5218	12/46	65218	10/49	10/1962
173	4/1890	8/1918						
				9173	2/26			4/1936
176**	4/1890	7/1913 TC by BR						
				9176	8/25			
				5217	7/46	65217	11/48	10/1962*
643**	2/1891	11/1913 TC by 1938						
				9643	12/24			
				5219	9/46			7/1947
644	2/1891	3/1916						
				9644	7/25			
				5220	12/46			3/1948
645	2/1891	4/1921						
				9645	4/25			
				5221	7/46	65221	9/50	7/1959
646**	2/1891	11/1913						
				9646	4/24			
				5222	6/46	65222	4/48	11/1963
647**	2/1891	10/1913						
				9647	6/25			
				5223	10/46			9/1947
648**	2/1891	11/1915 TC by 1938						
				9648	7/24			
				5224	10/46	65224	12/48	5/1963
649	4/1891	3/1917						
				9649	3/26			
				5225	10/46	65225	7/48	10/1957
650**	4/1891	11/1915 TC 1946-8						
				9650	7/24			
				5226	12/46	(65226)		4/1951
651	5/1891	6/1919						
				9651	11/25			
				5227	10/46	65227	8/50	8/1961
652	5/1891	1/1917						
				9652	2/26			
				5228	10/46	65228	3/48	12/1962
653	5/1891	12/1916						
				9653	9/25			
				5229	10/46	65229	11/49	5/1960
654	5/1891	10/1921						
				9654	6/24			
				5230	11/46	65230	5/48	10/1962
655	7/1891	9/1917						
				9655	12/25			
				5231	11/46	65231	9/48	4/1952
656	7/1891	3/1918 TC by NB						
			XSB 1905***					
				5232	10/46	65232	6/49	10/1961
657**	7/1891	11/1913						
				9657	7/24			
				5233	6/46	65233	8/48	12/1960
658	7/1891	5/1916 Vac by NB						
				9658	3/25			
				5234	9/46	65234	3/48	4/1967
659**	8/1891	9/1915						
				9659	9/26			
				5235	7/46	65235	1/49	10/1961
660**	8/1891	10/1913						
				9660	11/25			
				5236	6/46	65236	3/48	4/1956
661**	11/1891	5/1915						
				9661	5/25			1/1939
662**	11/1891	10/1913						
				9662	7/25			4/1937
179	11/1891	1/1922						
				9179	4/25			12/1937
45	12/1891	3/1917						
				9045	4/26			
				5246	9/46	65246	5/48	1/1962
68	12/1891	7/1914 W bk by NB						
			Vac 4/25, S bk 5/45					
				9068	4/25			
				5247	7/46	65247	7/48	7/1959

183	12/1891	12/1915		9183	8/25		
				5248	10/46	65248	9/48	5/1956

* The following were withdrawn in 1939 but reinstated.

No	Withdrawn	Reinstated
9604	12/1939	1/1940
9622	5/1939	9/1939
9172	12/1939	1/1940
9628	7/1939	9/1939
9176	5/1939	10/1939

** The following were taken over by the Railway Operating Department of the War
Department to work supply trains in France in 1917. On their return in 1919,
they were given names associated with the war which were painted on the centre
splasher above the works plate following the curve of the splasher. For the most
part, these names were maintained during the LNER period despite temporary
obliterations when locomotives were repaired and repainted especially at non-NB
Works. (See *Locomotives of the LNER Part 5* page 218, RCTS.)

No	To ROD	Returned	Named
605	11/1917	7/1919	*St Quentin*
608	10/1917	4/1919	*Foch*
615	10/1917	6/1919	*Verdun*
620	10/1917	5/1919	*Rawlinson*
621	10/1917	6/1919	*Monro*
627	11/1917	4/1919	*Petain*
628	10/1917	4/1919	*Byng*
631	10/1917	6/1919	*Aisne*
176	10/1917	5/1919	*French*
643	10/1917	5/1919	*Arras*
646	10/1917	5/1919	*Somme*
647	10/1917	6/1919	*Albert*
648	10/1917	5/1919	*Mons*
650	10/1917	5/1919	*Haig*
657	10/1917	5/1919	*Plumer*
659	10/1917	4/1919	*Gough*
660	10/1917	6/1919	*Horne*
661	11/1917	4/1919	*Ole Bill*
662	11/1917	4/1919	*Birdwood*

*** No 656 was fitted with an early form of superheating in 1905 which went under the
trade name of *New Century* with an extended smokebox in which compressed air and
steam was superheated prior to admission to the cylinders. Although economy in
coal and water was reported it was soon reconverted back to normal.

The following were built by Neilson & Co. Works nos 4382-96. Fittings below:
S bk = steam brake reinstated; TC = Tender cab; T Wbd = Tender weatherboard;
Vac = vacuum ejector added; W bk = Westinghouse brake.

No	Date	New boiler	fittings	LNE nos no	date	BR no	app-lied	Withdrawn
663	10/1891	5/1916	TC by NB	9663	3/26			
				5237	9/46	65237	7/48	11/1962
664	10/1891	12/1916		9664	8/24			
				5238	9/46	65238	4/49	7/1951
665	10/1891	9/1916	Vac by NB	9665	4/25			4/1931
666*	10/1891	11/1914		9666	10/24			11/1935
667	10/1891	12/1916	T Wbd by BR	9667	9/24			
				5239	11/46	65239	10/48	1/1961
668	11/1891	6/1916		9668	3/24			
				5240	12/46	65240	9/48	5/1952
669	11/1891	12/1916		9669	9/24			
				5241	10/46	65241	5/48	10/1962
670	11/1891	1/1916		9670	9/24			
				5242	10/46	65242	3/48	8/1957

```
671   11/1891  12/1919           9671  12/24                 7/1937
672   12/1891   8/1913           9672   5/26                 1/1931
673*  12/1891  12/1915           9673   8/24
                                 5243  11/46  65243   6/48   7/1966
674   12/1891   9/1919           9674   4/24                 4/1943
675   12/1891   6/1914 W bk & Vac by NB 9675  2/25
                          S bk 2/46     5244  10/46  65244  10/49   8/1957
676*  12/1891   6/1915           9676   5/24                10/1926**
677   12/1891   3/1917           9677  12/24
                                 5245   9/46  65245   8/49   5/1951
```

```
*  To ROD 1917-19.  See above.
        No    To ROD    Returned    Named
        666   10/1917   6/1919      Marne
        673   11/1917   6/1919      Maude   Preserved at Bo'ness.
        676   10/1917   7/1919      Reims   (Not Rheims as sometimes recorded)
** No 9676 was damaged beyond repair in the Linlithgow accident on 21/12/1925
   also involving no 9756.
```

The following were built by Sharp Stewart & Co. Works nos 3768-82. Fittings below:
S bk = steam brake reinstated; S/H = Steam heating apparatus; TC = Tender cab; T Wbd =
Tender weatherboard; Vac = vacuum ejector added; W bk = Westinghouse brake.

```
              New                    LNE nos              app-
No    Date    boiler  fittings       no    date  BR no  lied  Withdrawn
678   2/1892   7/1916                9678   3/26
                                     5249   9/46  65249   3/48  10/1960
679   2/1892   3/1918 Vac & T Wbd    9679   7/24
                      by NB          5250  10/46  65250   4/48   2/1957
680   2/1892   2/1916 TC by 1938     9680   4/25
                      T Wbd by BR    5251   6/46  65251  11/49  11/1963
681   2/1892   3/1917                9681  12/24
                                     5252  10/46  65252   3/49   5/1960
682*  2/1892   5/1915                9682   5/25
                                     5253   9/46  65253   9/48   5/1963
683   2/1892   5/1915 W bk by NB     9683   9/24
                      S bk 2/46      5254   6/46  65254   9/48   4/1951
684   2/2892   1/1918 Vac by NB      9684  11/24
                                     5255  10/46  65255  11/49   9/1951
685   2/1892   8/1916                9685   4/24
                                     5256   8/46 (65256)         4/1948
686   2/1892   7/1919                9686   9/25
                                     5257  10/46  65257   6/49  10/1962
687   2/1892  12/1915 W bk & Vac by NB 9687  7/26
                      TC by 1938     5258   7/46  65258   6/48   3/1962
                      S bk 2/43
688   2/1892  12/1916 Vac & S/H by NB 9688   8/25
                      T Wbd by BR    5259   7/46  65259   9/49   7/1959
689   3/1892  12/1915                9689   8/25
                                     5260   9/46  65260   3/48  10/1962
690   3/1892   5/1916 TC by BR       9690   3/24
                                     5261   9/46  65261  12/49   6/1963
691   3/1892   8/1915 Vac & TC by NB 9691   2/25
                                    (5262) allotted            6/1945
692   3/1892   2/1917                9692   6/25
                                     5263   7/46                10/1946
```

```
* To ROD 1917-19 see above.
      No    To ROD    Returned    Named
      682   11/1917   5/1919      Joffre
```

The following were built at Cowlairs. Fittings below: S/H = Steam heating apparatus; TC = Tender cab; Vac = vacuum ejector added.

No	Date	New boiler	fittings	LNE nos no	date	BR no	app-lied	Withdrawn
247	7/1892	11/1919		9247	8/24			
				5264	10/46	65264	6/50	7/1952
248	7/1892	1/1920		9248	5/24			
				5265	9/46	65265	10/48	12/1963
357	7/1892	11/1919		9357	3/25			
				5266	3/46	65266	7/48	5/1962
358	7/1892	10/1919		9358	2/25			
				5267	3/46	65267	8/48	11/1966
611*	8/1892	7/1914		9611	9/24			
				5268	6/46	65268	6/48	11/1962
612*	8/1892	11/1914		9612	11/24			
				5269	6/46			7/1947
177	1/1893	5/1922		9177	3/24			
				5274	10/46	65274	5/48	12/1950
180	1/1893	3/1921		9180	12/24			
				5275	9/46	65275	1/51	12/1962
181	3/1893	7/1915		9181	4/24			
				5270	6/46	65270	2/51	2/1958
182	3/1893	8/1919		9182	6/24			
				5271	3/46	65271	4/50	8/1952
250	3/1893	5/1923		9250	1/26			
				5272	9/46			8/1947
280	3/1893	4/1921		9280	4/24			
				5273	12/46	65273	7/48	11/1963
705	6/1896	3/1922		9705	2/26			
				5276	9/46	65276	10/49	3/1961
706	6/1896	6/1922	Vac by NB	9706	9/24			
				5277	10/46	65277	9/48	6/1963
707	6/1896	6/1921		9707	3/25			
				5278	6/46	65278	12/48	1/1952
708	6/1896	3/1918	Vac & S/H by NB	9708	4/25			
			TC by 1938	5279	9/46	65279	6/48	3/1951
709	6/1896	3/1918	Vac by NB	9709	12/24			
				5280	11/46	65280	1/50	5/1962
710	6/1896	3/1918	Vac by NB	9710	7/25			
				5281	6/46	65281	9/48	7/1961
711	11/1896	5/1922	Vac by NB	9711	10/25			
				5282	6/46	65282	6/50	1/1966
712	11/1896	10/1919		9712	9/24			
				5283	10/46	65283	5/48	12/1952
713	11/1896	4/1921	TC by 1938	9713	5/25			
				5284	7/46			7/1947
714	11/1896	11/1922		9714**	1/26			
				5285	10/46	65285	8/49	11/1963
715	12/1896	5/1919		9715	11/25			
				5286	11/46	65286	11/48	2/1952
716	12/1896	5/1923		9716**	4/24			
				5287	10/46	85287	6/49	6/1963

* To ROD 1917-19 see above.

No	To ROD	Returned	Named
611	11/1917	6/1919	*Allenby*
612	10/1917	6/1919	*Ypres*

** Nos 9714/6 were fitted with short chimneys and domes and low cab in 2/1937 and 4/1937 for working Gartverrie Siding.

The following were built at Cowlairs with Westinghouse brakes instead of steam brakes.
Most were converted to steam brake by the LNER. Fittings below: S bk = Steam brake;
S/H = Steam heating apparatus; TC = Tender cab; T Wbd = Tender weatherboard;
Vac = Vacuum ejector.

No	Date	New boiler	fittings	LNE nos no	date	BR no	app-lied	Withdrawn
717	4/1897	2/1918	S bk 12/43	9717	12/25			
				5288	10/46	65288	2/49	6/1967
718	4/1897	3/1919	S bk 8/45	9718	3/26			
				5289	10/46			3/1948
719	4/1897	5/1921	S/H by NB	9719	5/25			
			S bk 3/47	5290	11/46	65290	12/48	8/1963
720	5/1897	2/1922	S/H by NB	9720	12/24			
			Vac 12/24	5291	6/46	65291	6/48	11/1950
			S bk 4/46					
721	5/1897	3/1921	S bk 9/42	9721	8/24			
				5292	9/46	65292	12/48	2/1951
722	6/1897	5/1923	S/H by NB	9722	3/26			
			Vac by 3/26	5293	9/46	65293	9/48	11/1962
			S bk & TC 10/48					
723	7/1897	6/1921	Vac & S/H by NB	9723	2/25			
			S bk 4/46	5294	10/46	65294	5/48	3/1950
724	7/1897	11/1919	S/H & T Wbd	9724	1/25			
			by NB	5295	12/46	65295	9/48	4/1961
725	7/1897	1/1922	S bk 6/47	9725	5/24			
				5296	10/46	65296	12/50	2/1962
726	7/1897	6/1922	Vac & S/H by NB	9726	3/24			
			S bk 12/47	5297	10/46	65297	12/50	1/1966
727	7/1897	8/1922	S/H by NB	9727	1/25			
			Vac 10/26	5298	9/46	65298	1/49	3/1951
			S bk 2/47					
728	7/1897	9/1922	Vac & S/H by NB	9728	3/25			
			S bk 6/45	5299	7/46			10/1947
741	10/1898	6/1921	S/H by NB	9741	5/25			5/1943
742	10/1898	4/1921	S bk 3/45	9742	11/24			
				5300	10/46	65300	12/48	7/1962
743	10/1898	7/1922	Vac & S/H by NB	9743	3/24			
				5301	9/46			2/1947
744	10/1898	11/1919		9744	4/26			
				5302	8/46			7/1947
745	10/1898	1/1920	S bk 11/46	9745	7/24			
			TC by BR	5303	7/46	65303	12/48	12/1962
746	10/1898	11/1921	TC by LNE	9746	7/24			
			S bk 12/44	5304	12/46	65304	9/48	10/1962
747	12/1898	12/1922	S/H by NB	9747	5/25			
			S bk 6/43	5305	11/46	65305	3/48	2/2962
748	1/1899	5/1921	T Wbd by LNE	9748	8/25			
			S bk 3/45	5306	10/46	65306	2/49	7/1962
749	1/1899	11/1921	Vac by NB	9749	2/25			
			T Wbd by LNE	5307	10/46	65307	11/48	12/1963
			S bk 2/45					
750	1/1899	5/1921		9750	9/26			
				5308	11/46	65308	11/48	6/1951
751	1/1899	7/1921	Vac by NB	9751	2/26			
			S bk 1/46	5309	11/46	65309	4/48	6/1964
752	1/1899	12/1919	S bk 7/49	9752	8/25			
				5310	7/46	65310	7/49	7/1962
753	3/1899	4/1921	Vac 2/26	9753	2/26			
			S bk 10/45	5311	11/46	65311*	3/50	11/1963
754	3/1899	12/1921	S/H by NB	9754	1/26			
			Vac & S bk 4/30	5312	11/46	65312	4/48	11/1962

```
755   3/1899   12/1921  S/H by NB          9755    12/24
                        Vac by 1928        5313     7/46   65313    6/48    7/1962
                        S bk 3/45
756   4/1899    2/1923  S/H by NB          9756**   5/25
                        S bk 6/43          5314     9/46   65314    1/49    8/1955
757   4/1899    3/1921  S/H by NB          9757     5/26
                        Vac 5/26           5315    11/46   65315   10/48    4/1962
                        S bk 12/45
758   4/1899    5/1919  Vac by NB          9758    11/24
                        S bk 1/43          5316     9/46   65316    4/48   12/1962
                        TC by BR
759   5/1899   10/1921  Vac & S/H by NB    9759     5/25
                        TC by 1938         5317     7/46   65317   12/48    7/1960
                        S bk 10/45
                        T Wbd by BR
760   5/1899    2/1921  S bk 2/48          9760     6/25
                                           5318     7/46   65318    5/50    5/1962
761   5/1899    5/1919  Vac by 6/35        9761     5/25
                        S bk 11/42         5319     7/46   65319   10/48   11/1966
                        T Wbd by LNE
762   5/1899   11/1921  Vac by NB          9762     7/26
                        S bk 10/46         5320     6/46   65320   10/48    4/1962
763   5/1899    6/1922  Vac & S/H by NB    9763     5/25
                        S bk 6/47          5321     9/46   65321    9/48   11/1962
764   6/1899    2/1922  S/H by NB          9764     6/26
                        Vac 6/26           5322     6/46   65322    2/50    7/1951
                        S bk 12/45
771   1/1900   10/1921  S/H & Vac by NB    9771    12/25
                        S bk 12/41         5323     3/46   65323    6/50   12/1963
                        T Wbd by LNE
772   1/1900    5/1923  S/H by NB          9772     7/25
                        Vac 5/23 S bk 2/46 5324     2/46   65324    7/48    2/1957
773   1/1900    9/1921  S bk 5/43          9773    10/24
                                           5325     2/46   65325   12/49   11/1963
774   1/1900   11/1922  S/H & Vac by NB    9774     4/25
                        S bk 12/43         5326     3/46                   10/1946
775   1/1900    3/1922  S bk 5/43          9775    10/25
                                           5327     3/46   65327    5/48   11/1965
776   1/1900    8/1922  S/H & Vac by NB    9776     8/26
                        S bk 12/45         5328     3/46                    3/1948
777   3/1900    2/1918  S bk 3/46          9777     1/25
                                           5329     3/46   65329    1/50   12/1963
778   3/1900    5/1923  S/H by NB          9778     5/26
                        Vac 5/23           5330     2/46   65330    8/48    6/1962
                        S bk 10/46
779   3/1900   11/1922  S/H & Vac by NB    9779    10/25
                        TC by 1938         5331     2/46   65331    4/52    8/1963
                        S bk by 5/54
780   3/1900    3/1921  S/H by NB          9780     1/25
                        Vac 12/25          5332     1/46                    8/1947
                        S bk 4/45
781   5/1900    8/1922  S/H & Vac by NB    9781     3/26
                        S bk 3/43          5333     2/46   65333   11/48    9/1959
782   5/1900    7/1921  S bk 5/45          9782     9/25
                                           5334     2/46   65334    4/49   10/1962
783   7/1900    9/1922  S/H & Vac by NB    9783     2/25
                        S bk 4/46          5335     1/46   65335    2/49   11/1963
                        T Wbd by BR
```

784	7/1900	5/1923	S/H by NB	9784	2/26			
			Vac 5/23, S bk 4/43	5336	2/46			10/1947
785	7/1900	3/1918	S/H by NB	9785	5/24			
			Vac 7/26	5337	3/46	(65337)		4/1948
			S bk 1/43					
786	7/1900	11/1919	S bk 4/47	9786	9/25			
				5338	3/46	65338	7/49	12/1963
787	7/1900	11/1921	S/H by NB	9787	6/25			
			Vac by 1928	5339	5/46	65339	10/51	3/1961
			S bk 12/42					
788	7/1900	10/1921	S/H & Vac by NB	9788	10/25			
			S bk 10/44	5340	7/46	65340	10/48	1/1952
			T Wbd by BR					
789	12/1900	5/1922	S bk 7/43	9789	4/25			
				5341	4/46	65341	7/48	7/1963
790	12/1900	1/1922	S bk 11/46	9790	4/25			
				5342	11/46	65342	6/48	2/1960
791	12/1900	2/1920	Vac by NB	9791	8/26			
			S bk 4/30	5343	12/46	65343	3/52	2/1960
792	12/1900	8/1918	Vac & S bk 4/48	9792	8/25			
				5344	9/46	65344	4/48	11/1962
793	12/1900	2/1923	Vac 2/23	9793	8/25			
			S bk 11/42	5345	9/46	65345	4/48	6/1967
			TC by BR					
794	12/1900	6/1919	S/H by NB	9794	6/24			
			Vac 6/24	5346	6/46	65346	9/48	6/1964
			S bk 2/43					

* No 65311 was unofficially named *Haig* in 6/1955.
** No 9756 was involved in the Linlithgow accident on 21/12/1925.

0-4-0ST Built by NB Railway at Cowlairs.
DW 3ft 8in; WB 7ft 0in; Cyls 14 x 20; Blr 3ft $9^5/_8$in x 10ft $4^3/_8$in.
Based on Neilson design of 546/7 (see page 182) with which they became one class.
Wooden dumb buffers, hand brakes. Some had four-wheel tenders adding to the meagre 18
cwt coal capacity. Rebuilt with new boilers THS 788 sq ft; WP 130 lbs/sq in; Wt 14
tons 3 cwt. Steam brake fitted to some from 1920. Overall roof over footplate had
cab sides added by LNE from 1929. LNE class Y9.
(C/S - cab sides; S bk = steam brake)

No	Date	New boiler	fittings	Duplicate no	date	LNE nos no	date	BR no	app- lied	With- drawn
32	1887	9/1916	C/S 11/29	892	11/97	(9933)	1924			
			S bk 8/35	1092	1901	10092	3/26			
						8094	11/46	68094	10/48	4/1955
42	1887	3/1915	C/S 10/31	894	11/97	(9935)	1924			
				1094	1901	10094	10/25			
						8095	11/46	68095	8/48	12/1962*
144	1887	10/1916	C/S 5/31	897	11/97	(9938)	1924			
				1097	1901	10097	11/24			
						8096	11/46	(68096)		5/1954
146	1887	12/1913	C/S 2/32	898	6/99	(9939)	1924			
			S bk 8/51	1098	1901	10098	11/25			
						8097	11/46	68097	5/48	10/1958
308	1887			899	7/99					
				1099	1901				Sold 11/1921	
310	1887	2/1915	C/S 12/32	900	7/99	(9940)	1924			
				1100	1901	10100	8/25			
						8098	9/46	68098	9/51	12/1954
341	1889	9/1916	C/S 8/31	883	1/96	9835	5/24			
			S bk 11/50	1083	1901	10083	9/24			
						8099	11/46	68099	11/50	11/1956

```
342  1889 12/1913 C/S 11/31   884  1/96 (9927) 1924
               S bk 6/48     1084  1901 10084  6/27
                                   8100  9/46  68100   6/48  5/1960
343  1889                     885  1/96
                             1085  1901                          7/1922
344  1889                     886  1/96
                             1086  1901                         11/1921
345  1889  2/1915 C/S 9/31    887  1/96 (9928) 1924
               S bk 4/36     1087  1901 10087  3/26              8/1938
346  1889 12/1913 S bk by     888  1/96 9929  4/24
               1928          1088  1901 10088 10/24
               C/S 6/31**          8101  9/46  68101  1/49 10/1962
  9 11/1890  3/1920 S bk 3/20       9009  4/24
               C/S 4/32            8104  5/46  68104  6/49 10/1962
 10 11/1890 12/1913 C/S 1/32        9010  4/25
                                   8105  5/46  68105  5/48  4/1955
 11 11/1890  8/1917 S bk 10/26      9011 10/26
               C/S 3/31            8106  5/46  68106 12/50  8/1957
 14 12/1890 12/1913 C/S 8/32        9014  7/26
                                   8107  5/46  68107 11/50 12/1953
 17 12/1890  5/1917 C/S 5/33        9017  9/25
                                   8108  5/46  68108 11/52 11/1959
 40 12/1890  3/1915 C/S 2/32    893 11/97 (9934) 1924
                             1093  1901 10093  2/25
                                   8103  8/46 (68103)         6/1954
 50  1/1891  4/1915 C/S 1/31    895 11/97 10095  1/26
                             1095  1901  8111  8/46  68111  3/48  3/1953
 63  1/1891  2/1920 S bk 2/20   896 11/97 (9937) 1924
               C/S 12/32     1096  1901 10096 11/25
                                   8112  8/46  68112 12/51  1/1955
227  1/1891  8/1916 C/S 8/30    889  5/96 (9930) 1924
               S bk 11/51    1089  1901 10089 11/24
                                   8102  9/46  68102 11/51 12/1958
231  6/1891  6/1917 C/S 2/31    890  5/96 (9931) 1924
                             1090  1901 10090  3/26
                                   8109  8/46 (68109)         4/1954
232  6/1891  9/1916 C/S 5/30    891  5/96 (9932) 1924
               S bk 2/48     1091  1901 10091  9/24
                                   8110  9/46  68110  9/54  8/1961
610  6/1891                     903  7/99
                             1103  1901
                                  (1103B) 1923                12/1923
 32 11/1897  4/1920 S bk 2/27       9032 10/24
               C/S 10/30           8113  7/46  68113 11/48  1/1958
 40 11/1897  7/1917 C/S & S bk      9040 11/25
               10/32               8114  7/46  68114 11/48  9/1960
 42 11/1897  9/1916 C/S 7/31        9042  2/25
               S bk 3/51           8115  7/46  68115  3/51  7/1957
 50 11/1897  3/1923 S bk 3/23       9050  9/26
               C/S 9/32            8116  7/46  68116  1/49  2/1958
 63 12/1897  5/1923 S bk 5/23       9063 10/25
               C/S 10/32           8117  7/46  68117  5/48  7/1962
144 12/1897  3/1923 S bk 3/23       9144  1/26
               C/S 1/33            8118  7/46  68118  7/48 10/1958
146  6/1899  4/1923 S bk 4/23       9146  9/25
               C/S 6/30            8119  7/46  68119  1/51 10/1961
308  7/1899  5/1920 S bk 5/20       9308  4/26
               C/S 9/32            8120  7/46  68120  7/49  8/1955
310  7/1899  1/1920 S bk 1/20       9310 11/24
               C/S 1/31            8121 11/46  68121 12/49  7/1955
```

547	8/1899	5/1920	S bk 5/20		9547	11/26		
			C/S 8/31		8123	7/46	68123	4/50	8/1960
546	8/1899	8/1917	C/S 12/31		9546	4/26		
					8122	7/46	68122	4/51	8/1955
610	9/1899	5/1917	C/S 8/34		9610	3/24		
			S bk 12/42		8124	7/46	68124	2/54	9/1959

* No 68095 preserved as NB 42 at Bo'ness.
** No 10088 also fitted with vacuum ejector in 1937.

0-4-0ST Builders unknown.
Dimensions not known.
Purchased 1889 from Gartness Coal and Iron Co.

No	Date	
610	1889	
	1891	To duplicate list 610A
	1895	Renumbered 840
	1901	Allotted no 1040 but scrapped

0-4-0ST Built by A Barclay & Co. in 1884. Works no 313.
DW 3ft 6in; Cyls 14 x 22.
Purchased 1889 from Methil Dock Co.

No	Date	
611	1889	
	1892	To duplicate list 611A
	1895	Renumbered 841
	1901	Allotted no 1041 but scrapped

0-4-0ST Built by Grant Ritchie & Co, Kilmarnock in 1887. Works no 174.
DW 3ft 6in; Cyls 14 x 22 o/s.
Purchased 1889 from Methil Dock Co. Named *Jubilee* when purchased.

No	Date	
612	1889	
	1892	To duplicate list 612A
	1895	Renumbered 842
	1901	Renumbered 1042. Scrapped by 1904.

0-4-0ST Built by A Barclay & Co. in 1891. Works no 700.
DW 2ft 11in; Cyls 13 x 20.
Purchased 1901 from a 'Mr Wood'.

No	Date	
835	1901	Withdrawn by 1923.

0-4-4T Built by NB Railway at Cowlairs.
DW 5ft 9in; TW 3ft 6in; WB 7ft 6in + 8ft 3in + 6ft 6in; Cyls 17 x 24; Blr 4ft 5in x
10ft 1in; THS 1026 sq ft (586-91), 1059 sq ft (90-5); Wt 49 tons 12 cwt.
Similar to Drummond 157 class as rebuilt. Rebuilt with new boilers with combination
injectors THS 1059 sq ft; Wt 51 tons 14 cwt. Originally all had Westinghouse brakes
only, but vacuum ejectors were added at the dates below.
A front footstep was added during the Reid period, as was the steam heating apparatus.
Tanks which held 1281 gallons were wider than the cabs. The first two rebuilds, nos
91 and 588, retained the safety valves on the dome as on the original boilers, but all
later rebuilds had them over the firebox. LNE class G7.

No	Date	New boiler	Vacuum ejector	LNE no*	Applied	Withdrawn
586	4/1886	12/1912	4/1925	9586	4/1925	11/1926
587	5/1886	12/1912	by 1920	9587	9/1925	8/1926
588	7/1886	1/1912	11/1925	9588	11/1925	4/1931
589	8/1886	4/1913	by 1920	9589	7/1925	7/1930
590	8/1886	4/1913	4/1913	9590	2/1926	6/1930
591	9/1886	4/1913	12/1924	9591	12/1924	2/1927

90	1/1889	4/1913	4/1913	9090	4/1924	9/1926
91	1/1889	12/1911	3/1925	9091	3/1925	5/1932
92	1/1889	11/1911	by 1920	9092	10/1924	9/1930
93	1/1889	4/1913	5/1924	9093	5/1924	1/1927
94	2/1889	12/1912	not fitted	9094	10/1924	2/1927
95	2/1889	12/1912	3/1926	9095	10/1924	4/1931

* 'B' suffixes 9/1923-2/1924 not applied.

0-6-0T Built by Neilson & Co. Works nos below.
Sharp Stewart & Co. Works nos below.
DW 4ft 6in; WB 7ft 6in + 8ft 0in; Cyls 17 x 26; Blr 4ft 5in x 10ft 1in; THS 1050 sq ft; WP 150 lbs/sq in; Wt 45 tons 5 cwt.
Intended for shunting and trip working all were built with steam brakes but twelve were soon altered to Westinghouse for carriage shunting, and by 1916 also had vacuum ejectors. Rebuilt with new boilers THS 1049.5 sq ft, the dome height being reduced from 12ft 3½in to 11ft 6^7/8in, and with Ross pop safety valves. LNE class J83.

The following were built by Neilson & Co. Works nos 5733-52. No 805 had Westinghouse brake fitted in place of steam late in the NB period, and had vacuum ejectors fitted also. It was altered back to steam brake in 9/1944.
BR 68449 was also fitted with vacuum ejectors in 10/1952.

No	Date	New boiler	LNE no*	App-lied	1946 no	App-lied	BR no	App-lied	Withdrawn
795	8/1900	6/1924	9795	6/24	8442	4/46	68442	7/50	1/1962
796	8/1900	6/1924	9796	6/24	8443	4/46	68443	12/50	2/1961
797	9/1900	10/1924	9797	10/24	8444	4/46	68444	5/51	1/1960
798	9/1900	10/1924	9798	10/24	8445	4/46	68445	12/49	10/1962
799	9/1900	6/1924	9799	6/24	8446	4/46	68446	11/48	3/1956
800	9/1900	5/1924	9800	5/24	8447	3/46	68447	8/48	2/1961
801	9/1900	11/1924	9801	11/24	8448	3/46	68448	4/50	10/1962
802	9/1900	5/1924	9802	5/24	8449	3/46	68449	8/48	9/1958
803	9/1900	2/1925	9803	2/25	8450	3/46	68450	8/50	12/1957
804	9/1900	4/1924	9804	4/24	8451	3/46	68451	9/49	2/1958
805	3/1901	2/1925	9805	2/25	8452	3/46	68452	3/50	6/1958
806	3/1901	12/1924	9806	12/24	8453	5/46	68453	1/50	10/1962
807	3/1901	11/1924	9807	11/24	8454	5/46	68454	9/50	2/1962
808	3/1901	9/1924	9808	9/24	8455	3/46	68455	4/48	5/1956
809	3/1901	2/1925	9809	2/25	8456	5/46	68456	4/48	1/1961
810	3/1901	9/1924	9810	9/24	8457	5/46	68457	9/48	3/1960
811	3/1901	5/1924	9811	5/24	8458	5/46	68458	5/50	1/1962
812	3/1901	5/1924	9812	5/24	8459	5/46	68459	8/50	5/1961
813	4/1901	12/1924	9813	12/24	8460	5/46	68460	7/50	11/1958
814	4/1901	2/1925	9814	2/25	8461	4/46	68461	5/48	6/1958

* 'B' suffixes 9/1923-2/1924 not applied so far as is known.

The following were built by Sharp Stewart & Co. Works nos 4723-42. Nos 825-34 had Westinghouse brake fitted in place of steam soon after building and, by 1916, also had vacuum ejectors. No 816 became dual-fitted with Westinghouse and vacuum late in the NB period. Altered back to steam brake and vacuum on dates below. All dual-fitted locomotives had steam heating apparatus. BR 68466 had vacuum ejectors fitted in 12/1952 and 68470 in 2/1953.

No	Date	New boiler	S brake reinstated	LNE no*	App-lied	1946 no	App-lied	BR no	App-lied	With-drawn
815	4/1901	12/1924		9815	12/24	8462	4/46			9/1947
816	4/1901	1/1925	7/45	9816	1/25	8463	6/46	68463	6/50	11/1958
817	4/1901	5/1924		9817	5/24	8464	4/46	68464	7/48	3/1958
818	4/1901	8/1924		9818	8/24	8465	5/46	68465	5/48	8/1957
819	4/1901	11/1924		9819	11/24	8466	4/46	68466	9/48	12/1958
820	4/1901	11/1924		9820	11/24	8467	6/46	68467	5/48	9/1959
821	4/1901	9/1924		9821	9/24	8468	5/46	68468	7/50	6/1959

```
822  4/1901  3/1925              9822  3/25  8469  5/46  68469 12/48 10/1956
823  4/1901  1/1925              9823  1/25  8470  5/46  68470 10/49 10/1962
824  4/1901 12/1924              9824 12/24  8471  5/46  68471 10/50  8/1961
825  4/1901 10/1924      8/44    9825 10/24  8472  6/46  68472  5/48  2/1962
826  4/1901 10/1924      6/45    9826 10/24  8473  3/46  68473  4/50  5/1956
827  4/1901 12/1924     12/44    9827 12/24  8474  1/46  68474  7/50  4/1958
828  5/1901 10/1924      4/47    9828 10/24  8475  1/46  68475  7/50  3/1958
829  5/1901  8/1924      2/44    9829  8/24  8476  1/46  68476  4/48  3/1956
830  5/1901  4/1924     12/44    9830  4/24  8477  5/46  68477  8/49 12/1962
831  5/1901  2/1925      3/45    9831  2/25  8478  5/46  68478 10/49 11/1958
832  5/1901  4/1924      9/44    9832  4/24  8479  3/46  68479  6/50 10/1962
833  5/1901  1/1925     12/44    9833  1/25  8480  5/46  68480  5/51  3/1959
834  5/1901 11/1924      1/44    9834 11/24  8481  4/46  68481  5/48  2/1962
```
* 'B' suffixes 9/1923-2/1924 not applied so far as is known.

Reid Locomotives 1904-23

4-4-0 Built by NB Railway at Cowlairs.
DW 6ft 0in; LW 3ft 6in; WB 6ft 6in + 7ft 7in + 9ft 6in; Cyls 19 x 26; Blr 5ft 1¼in
(max) x 11ft 4in (lap jointed front ring 5ft 0in, rear ring 5ft 1¼in diameter); THS
1760 sq ft; WP 175 lbs/sq in; Wt 53 tons.
Mixed traffic (intermediate). Most had Cowlairs rope guide until the cessation of
rope haulage in 11/1908. 3525 gallon tenders. Dual brake equipment, steam brake
substituted for Westinghouse 1935/6. Steam reverse altered to screw type at the same
time. Steam heating apparatus provided. WP increased to 180-190 lbs/sq in. Rebuilt
with butt jointed boiler 5ft 0in diameter with superheater THS 1153.14 sq ft + 192.2
sq ft superheater; WP 180 lbs/sq in; Wt 53 tons 14 cwt. One boiler built in 1933 was
4ft 10⅜in diameter, and had a heating surface of 1186.2 sq ft being fitted to no 9889
from 11/1933-11/1937, no 9883 from 2/1938-3/1944 and no 9882 from 4/1945-4/1948. From
1946, standard heating surface was 1255 sq ft plus 192.92 sq ft superheater. Smokebox
wing-plates were removed 1922-4. Raven cab signalling was installed in nos 9882/7/8
from 1929 to the mid 1930s. LNE class D32.

No	Date	Super-heated	Steam brake	LNE nos* no	date	Allotted BR no	Withdrawn
882	10/1906	8/1924	6/1936	9882	8/1924		
				2443	9/1946	(62443)	3/1948
883	11/1906	2/1924	7/1936	9883	12/1925		
				2444	9/1946	(62444)	9/1948
884	11/1906	12/1925	9/1936	9884	12/1925*		
				2445	9/1946	(62445)	12/1949
885	12/1906	11/1923	4/1936	9885	9/1924		
				2446	9/1946	(62446)	9/1948
886	12/1906	11/1924	4/1936	9886	11/1924		
				2447	12/1946		12/1947
887	12/1906	9/1924	12/1935	9887	9/1924		
				2448	4/1946	(62448)	9/1948
888	12/1906	9/1923	3/1935	9888	8/1925		
				2449	4/1946	(62449)	11/1948
889	12/1906	1/1924	9/1935	9889	9/1925		
				2450	3/1946	(62450)	2/1948
890	1/1907	8/1923	8/1935	9890	5/1925		
				2451	9/1946	62451**	3/1951
891	1/1907	2/1926	6/1935	9891	2/1926		
				2452	3/1946		11/1947
892	1/1907	11/1924	7/1935	9892	11/1924		
				2453	8/1946	(62453)	5/1948
893	1/1907	8/1923	2/1935	9893	1/1925		
				2454	9/1946	(62454)	9/1948

* No 884 carried 'B' suffix until 12/1925.
** BR 62451 applied 2/49.

4-4-0 Built by North British Locomotive Co. Works nos below.
NB Railway at Cowlairs.
DW 6ft 6in; LW 3ft 6in; WB 6ft 6in + 7ft 7in + 9ft 6in; Cyls 19 x 26; Blr 5ft 0in (max) x 11ft 4in (lap-jointed front ring 4ft 10¾in diameter, rear ring 5ft 0in; THS 1618.2 sq ft; WP 190 lbs/sq in; Wt 54 tons 16 cwt.
Scott class built to haul through expresses from the Midland Railway. Dual-brake facilities and steam heating apparatus were provided. Smokebox wing-plates were removed 1921-3. Rebuilt with superheated boilers THS 1153.14 sq ft + 192.92 sq ft superheater. From 1938 boiler and firebox heating surface was 1255.7 sq ft. Steam brakes substituted for Westinghouse 1933-6 and air sanding converted to gravity. Original steam reverse gear altered to screw type. 4325 gallon tenders.
LNE class D29.

The following were built by the North British Locomotive Co. Works nos 18856-61.

No	Date	Name	Super-heated	Steam brake	LNE nos* no	date	BR no	App-lied	With-drawn
895	7/1909	_Rob Roy_	4/25	12/33	9895	4/25			
					2400	6/46	(62400)		4/1948
896	7/1909	_Dandy Dinmont_	3/32	11/35	9896	4/25			
					2401	6/46	(62401)		11/1949
897**	8/1909	_Redgauntlet_	10/32	12/34	9897	1/26			
					2402	6/46	(62402)		6/1949
898	8/1909	_Sir Walter Scott_	11/25	9/36	9898	11/25			
					2403	6/46	(62403)		3/1948
899	8/1909	_Jeanie Deans_	6/31	4/35	9899	10/24			
					2404	6/46	(62404)		8/1949
900	9/1909	_The Fair Maid_	6/34	7/35	9900	2/25			
					2405	7/46	62405	3/49	2/1951

* 'B' suffixes 9/1923-2/1924 not applied so far as is known
** No 897 had Phoenix superheating installed temporarily in 1897

The following were built at Cowlairs:

No	Date	Name	Super-heated	Steam brake	LNE nos* no	date	BR no	App-lied	With-drawn
243	9/1911	_Meg Merrilies_	1/33	12/35	9243	5/25			
					2406	6/46	(62406)		10/1949
244	10/1911	_Madge Wildfire_	6/26	7/36	9244	5/24			
					2407	12/46			12/1947
245	10/1911	_Bailie Nicol Jarvie_	5/32	2/36	9245	4/24			
					2408	5/46			11/1947
338	10/1911	_Helen MacGregor_	8/35	8/35	9338	7/24**			
					2409	4/46	(62409)		10/1948
339	10/1911	_Ivanhoe_	6/31	4/35	9339	4/24**			
					2410	7/46	62410	5/49	1/1952
340	11/1911	_Lady of Avenel_	11/25	11/34	9340	11/25			
					2411	6/46	62411	7/48	11/1952
359***	12/1911	_Dirk Hatteraick_	10/32	3/35	9359	5/25			
					2412	6/46	62412	2/49	9/1952
360	12/1911	_Guy Mannering_	10/30	1/35	9360	1/25			
					2413	6/46	62413	3/49	8/1950
361	12/1911	_Vich Ian Vohr_	8/36	5/35	9361	6/24			
					(2414)				2/1946
362	12/1911	_Ravenswood_	7/33	3/36	9362	1/25			
					2415	12/46			7/1947

* 'B' suffixes 9/1923-2/1946 not carried as far as is known.
** No 9338 in accident at Haymarket (Edinburgh) 28/7/1924.
   No 9339 in accident at Cowlairs 30/1/1942.
*** No 359 had Weir feed water heating from 1914-19.

4-4-0 Built by NB Railway at Cowlairs.
DW 6ft 0in; LW 3ft 6in; WB 6ft 6in + 7ft 7in + 9ft 6in; Cyls 19 x 26; Blr 5ft 0in
(max) x 11ft 4in (lap jointed as *Scott* (895) class above); THS 1618.2 sq ft; WP 190
lbs/sq in; Wt 54 tons 1 cwt.
Mixed traffic version of *Scott* class similar to 882 class but with higher pitched
boiler and heavier. WP later reduced to 180 lbs/sq in, original steam reversing gear
altered to screw type. Rebuilt with superheated boilers THS as *Scott* class above.
Dual-braking systems until steam brakes substituted for Westinghouse 1935/6.
LNE class D33.

No	Date	Super-heated	Steam brake	LNE nos* no	date	BR no	App-lied	Withdrawn
331	10/1909	2/1935	2/1935	9331	12/25			
				2460	8/46	62460	6/49	8/1951
864	10/1909	12/1928	11/1935	9864	8/25			
				2455	10/46	62455	9/48	12/1949
865	10/1909	6/1933	11/1935	9865	5/25			
				2456	4/46			12/1947
866	11/1909	4/1936	4/1936	9866	12/25			
				2457	6/46	62457	4/48	6/1952
867	11/1909	11/1927	7/1935	9867	4/25			
				2458	2/46	(62458)		9/1949
894	11/1909	11/1925	4/1935	9894	11/25			
				2459	9/46	62459	5/48	9/1951
332	12/1909	3/1926	11/1935	9332	8/24			
				2461	9/46	62461	7/49	6/1951
333	12/1909	3/1934	6/1935	9333	8/24			
				2462	6/46	62462	12/49	11/1952
382	12/1909	4/1934	7/1935	9382	7/24			
				2463	4/46	(62463)		3/1948
383	1/1901	7/1933	5/1935	9383	9/24			
				2464	6/46	62464	2/49	9/1953
384	2/1910	7/1930	9/1935	9384	7/25			
				2465	12/46			9/1947
385	2/1910	11/1935	11/1935	9385	8/24			
				2466	2/46	62466	12/48	10/1951

* 'B' suffix 9/1923-2//1924 not applied so far as is known.

4-4-0 Built by NBR at Cowlairs.
DW 6ft 6in; LW 3ft 6in; WB 6ft 6in + 7ft 7in + 9ft 6in; Cyls 20 x 26; Blr 5ft 0in
(max) x 11ft 4in (lap jointed as *Scott* class above); THS (nos 400, 363) 1306.6 sq ft +
266.4 sq ft superheater, remainder 1285.5 + 355.2 sq ft superheater; WP 165 lbs/sq in;
Wt (nos 400, 363) 57 tons 6 cwt, others 57 tons 16 cwt.
Superheated *Scotts*. Nos 400 and 363 had Schmidt superheaters with 8in piston valves
and were classified D30/1 by the LNER. The remainder had Robinson superheaters with
24 elements and 10in piston valves. These became D30/2. Standard 22 element
superheaters of the Robinson pattern were fitted, and from 1924, THS was 1153.14 sq ft
+ 192.02 sq ft superheater and 1255.7 sq ft with the same superheater from 1938.
Smokebox wing-plates were removed in 1922. Steam reverse on nos 400 and 363 was
changed to screw type, and all the later ones had screw reverse when built. Dual-
brake equipment until Westinghouse changed to steam 1935-7. As on previous 4-4-0
classes, later boilers were butt-jointed and still later were of single plates.

No	Date	Name	Steam brake	LNE nos* no	date	BR no	App-lied	With-drawn
400	9/1912	*The Dougal Cratur*	5/36	9400	12/24			6/1945
363	10/1912	*Hal o'the Wynd*	9/36	9363	11/25			
				2417	9/46	62417	5/48	1/1951
409	4/1914	*The Pirate*	10/35	9409	1/26			
				2418	5/46	62418	8/48	8/1959
410	4/1914	*Meg Dods*	8/35	9410	5/24			
				2419	1/46	62419	3/49	9/1957

No	Built	Name								Withdrawn
411	4/1914	Dominie Sampson	5/35	9411	2/25					
						2420	5/46	62420	10/48	9/1957
412	4/1914	Laird o'Monkbarns	11/36	9412	3/25					
						2421	6/46	62421	5/48	6/1966
413	5/1914	Caleb Balderstone	3/35	9413	2/26					
						2422	6/46	62422	12/49	12/1958
414	6/1914	Dugald Dalgetty	11/35	9414	2/25					
						2423	6/46	62423	12/48	12/1957
415	6/1914	Claverhouse	2/35	9415**	7/24					
						2424	6/46	62424	5/48	8/1957
416	6/1914	Ellangowan	5/35	9416	10/24					
						2425	11/46	62425	2/49	7/1958
417	7/1914	Cuddie Headrigg	1/36	9417	5/25					
						2426	9/46	62426	2/49	6/1960
418	7/1914	Dumbiedykes	5/35	9418	8/24					
						2427	11/46	62427	11/48	4/1959
419	9/1914	The Talisman***	10/35	9419	12/24					
						2428	11/46	62428	9/49	12/1958
420	10/1914	The Abbot	9/36	9420	10/25					
						2429	11/46	62429	1/50	8/1957
421	10/1914	Jingling Geordie	6/35	9421	7/25					
						2430	8/46	62430	5/50	1/1957
422	10/1914	Kenilworth	3/36	9422	6/24					
						2431	10/46	62431	3/50	10/1958
423	10/1914	Quentin Durward	11/36	9423	2/25					
						2432	6/46	62432	3/48	12/1958
424	6/1915	Lady Rowena	6/35	9424	9/24					
						2433	9/46			11/1947
425	7/1915	Kettledrummle	9/35	9425	10/25					
						2434	10/46	62434	5/48	4/1958
426	7/1915	Norna	9/35	9426	9/25					
						2435	10/46	62435	4/50	12/1957
427	8/1915	Lord Glenvarloch	12/35	9427	6/25					
						2436	10/46	62436	7/48	6/1959
428	8/1915	Adam Woodcock	5/36	9428	3/24					
						2437	11/46	62437	10/50	6/1958
497	12/1920	Peter Poundtext	6/37	9497	10/24					
						2438	10/46	62438	2/49	10/1957
498	11/1920	Father Ambrose	11/36	9498	11/24					
						2439	1/46	62439	7/48	10/1959
499	11/1920	Wandering Willie	8/35	9499	3/25					
						2440	12/46	62440	6/49	7/1958
500	11/1920	Black Duncan	5/36	9500	5/24					
						2441	3/46	62441	3/49	8/1958
501	12/1920	Simon Glover	3/36	9501	1/26					
						2442	4/46	62442	11/48	6/1958

*   'B' suffix 9/1923-2/1924. No record of applications.
**   No 9415 in accident at Hyndland 16/11/1925.
*** Ran as *Talisman* without the definite article 12/1931-2/1938 and from 5/1940-3/1947.

4-4-0 Built by NBR at Cowlairs.
DW 6ft 0in; LW 3ft 6in; WB 6ft 6in + 7ft 7in + 9ft 6in; Cyls 20 x 26; Blr 5ft 0in x 11ft 4in; THS 1153.14 sq ft + 192.92 sq ft superheater. WP 165 lbs/sq in; Wt 57 tons 4 cwt.
Superheated intermediate named after Scottish Glens and thus popularly known as the *Glen* class. The boilers and superheaters were of the same size as those fitted to the previous 4-4-0s when superheated, but nos 307, 405-8 originally had Schmidt superheaters, the others having Robinson type which were adopted as standard. Working pressure was raised to 180 lbs/sq in on some locomotives. 4235 gallon tenders.

Smokebox wing plates were removed 1922-4. Dual braking, but Westinghouse brake altered to steam brake 1935-7, the air sanding being altered to gravity at the same time. Five had tender cabs provided for snow plough working, and in the LNE period eight had spark arrestors fitted for working the West Highland line (nos 2469/70/2-4/7/9/80). LNE class D34.

No	Date	Name	Steam brake	LNE nos* no	date	BR no	App- lied	With- drawn
149	9/1913	*Glen Finnan*	9/35	9149	2/25			
				2467	10/46	62467	4/48	8/1960
221	9/1913	*Glen Orchy*	10/35	9221	4/26			
				2468	11/46	62468	11/48	9/1958
256	9/1913	*Glen Douglas*	9/35	9256	8/25			
				2469	6/46	62469	12/49	12/1959**
258	9/1913	*Glen Roy*	6/35	9258	5/25			
				2470	9/46	62470	9/48	5/1959
266	10/1913	*Glen Falloch*	5/35	9266	12/24			
				2471	11/46	62471	4/49	3/1960
307	12/1913	*Glen Nevis*	3/36	9307	10/25			
				2472	4/46	62472	10/49	10/1959
405	12/1913	*Glen Spean*	3/36	9405	6/26			
				2473	11/46	(62473)		5/1949
406	12/1913	*Glen Croe*	11/35	9406	5/24			
				2474	7/46	62474	3/50	6/1961
407	12/1913	*Glen Bleasdale*	1/36	9407	5/24			
				2475	7/46	62475	5/50	6/1959
408	12/1913	*Glen Sloy*	12/36	9408	11/24			
				2476	6/46	(62476)		2/1950
100	5/1917	*Glen Dochart*	6/36	9100	5/24			
				2477	1/46	62477	5/50	10/1959
291	5/1917	*Glen Quoich*	9/35	9291	5/24			
				2478	7/46	62478	11/48	12/1959
298	5/1917	*Glen Sheil*	3/36	9298	9/24			
				2479	3/46	62479	3/48	6/1961
153	6/1917	*Glen Fruin*	11/35	9153	3/24			
				2480	6/46	62480	12/49	10/1959
241	7/1917	*Glen Ogle*	6/35	9241	5/25			
				2481	6/46	(62481)		9/1949
242	3/1919	*Glen Mamie*	3/35	9242	6/25			
				2482	5/46	62482	5/48	3/1960
270	3/1919	*Glen Garry*	5/35	9270***	6/24			
				2483	6/46	62483	12/48	4/1959
278	4/1919	*Glen Lyon*	11/36	9278***	10/25			
				2484	6/46	62484	11/49	11/1961
281	4/1919	*Glen Murran*	7/35	9281	12/25			
				2485	6/46	62485	5/48	3/1960
287	4/1919	*Glen Gyle*	9/35	9287***	5/25			
				(2486)				2/1946
504	4/1920	*Glen Aladale*	4/35	9504***	4/24			
				2488	3/46	62488	5/48	10/1960
503	5/1920	*Glen Arklet*	11/35	9503	6/24			
				2487	3/46	62487	12/48	9/1959
490	5/1920	*Glen Dessary*	6/36	9490	2/25			
				2489	9/46	62489	2/50	12/1959
502	5/1920	*Glen Fintaig*	11/35	9502	12/24			
				2490	3/46	62490	6/49	2/1959
505	5/1920	*Glen Cona*	5/35	9505	8/25			
				2491	4/46			12/1947
34	6/1920	*Glen Garvin*	6/35	9034	12/24			
				2492	7/46	62492	4/49	6/1959
35	6/1920	*Glen Gloy*	11/35	9035	5/25			
				2493	5/46	62493	9/50	9/1950

```
492   7/1920  Glen Gau           9/36   9492***  7/25
               renamed Glen Gour         2494    1/46   62494   9/48   4/1959
493   7/1920  Glen Luss          6/35   9493     8/24
                                         2495    6/46   62495  12/48   4/1961
494   8/1920  Glen Loy           7/36   9494     5/24
                                         2496    3/46   62496   6/48  11/1961
495   8/1920  Glen Mallie        8/36   9495     1/25
                                         2497    5/46   62497   4/48   2/1960
496   9/1920  Glen Moidart       1/37   9496     6/25
                                         2498   10/46   62498   5/48   3/1960
```

*   No record of 'B' suffixes applied to numbers 9/1923-2/1924.
**   No 256 preserved at Glasgow Transport Museum. It also had a spark arrestor fitted
     for a short period in 1919.
*** Tender cabs:
```
     9270  12/1938 later removed
     9278  11/1938 later removed
     9287  12/1938
     9504  12/1938
     9492  11/1938 later removed
```

4-4-2 Built by North British Locomotive Co. Works nos below.
             R Stephenson & Co. Works nos below.
DW 6ft 9in; LW 3ft 6in; TW 4ft 3in; WB 6ft 6in + 5ft 9½in + 7ft 3in + 8ft 3in; Cyls 20
x 28 o/s; Blr 5ft 6in x 15ft 0in; THS 2256.2 sq ft; WP 200 lbs/sq in; Wt 76 tons 14
cwt.
Similar to Great Central Atlantic class 8B, also built by the NB Loco Co late in 1905,
having the same wheelbase and possibly produced from the same drawings. Belpaire
firebox boilers. Large size of cylinders necessitated them being placed outside the
frames. The 1906 locomotives had narrow cabs, 7ft 8in wide, and steam reversing gear.
The RS&Co batch of 1911 had wider 8ft 6¹/8in cabs and lever reverse, although NB
locomotive drawings continued to show the narrow cab, resulting in some published
drawings and models built from them to be incorrect. 4240 gallon tenders. WP reduced
to 190 lbs/sq in and THS to 2223.96 from 1912. Dual brakes and steam heating
connections at rear but Westinghouse brake replaced by steam brake 1930-2.
Superheated from 1912 THS 1803.8 sq ft + Robinson superheater 385 sq ft with 'long
loop' and cylinders enlarged to 21in diameter. WP 180 lbs/sq in; Wt 74 tons 8 cwt.
Wide cabs and lever reverse fitted to 1906 locomotives. With the introduction of
power classification (see pages 131-2) the superheated locomotives were rated class H
and the saturated ones class I. From 1922 'short loop' superheaters of 263 sq ft were
fitted and from about 1924 22 element superheaters instead of 24 element reduced the
superheater heating surface to 241.1 sq ft. THS of boiler and firebox was now 1779.55
sq ft. The LNE classified those still saturated (all from the 1911 batch) as C10 and
the superheated ones as C11. Air sanding was replaced by gravity feed when
Westinghouse equipment removed. Plans for streamlining were not proceeded with.
The following were built by NB Loco Co. Works nos 17369-82 with narrow cabs and steam
reverse until superheated.

No	Date	Name*	Super-heated	Steam brake	LNE nos 1923	1924	Applied	Withdrawn
868	7/1906	Aberdonian	5/1915	9/31		9868	5/24	9/1933
869	7/1906	Dundonian	5/1920	5/30	869B	9869	5/24	10/1935
	4/1912	renamed Bonnie Dundee						
870	7/1906	Bon Accord	6/1919	5/32		9870	6/24	5/1937
871	7/1906	Thane of Fife	10/1921	6/32		9871	1/25	1/1935
872	7/1906	Auld Reekie	6/1921	11/31		9872	4/24	8/1935
873	7/1906	Saint Mungo	9/1915	6/30		9873	2/25	11/1934
874	8/1906	Dunedin	5/1921	7/31		9874	6/25	5/1933
875	8/1906	Midlothian	12/1920	2/31	875B	9875	3/25	11/1939**
876	8/1906	Waverley	2/1921	3/32	***	9876	7/24	5/1937
877	8/1906	Liddesdale	4/1921	4/30		9877	5/24	4/1936
878	8/1906	Hazeldean	9/1919	1/30		9878	3/24	11/1936

No	Date	Name							
879	8/1906	*Abbotsford*	9/1920	4/32	879B	9879	4/25	11/1936	
880	8/1906	*Tweeddale*	1/1917	2/32		9880	8/25	10/1936	
881	8/1906	*Borderer*	6/1917	6/31		9881	11/25	11/1936	

* RCTS *Locomotives of the LNER part 3A* gives an explanation of the meaning of the names.
** No 9875 was withdrawn 12/1937 and reinstated 6/1938. It was intended for preservation but due to the outbreak of war was withdrawn 11/1939 and scrapped.
*** No 876 ran as 'LNE 876' in 1923-4.

The following were built by R Stephenson & Co. Works nos 3428-33 with larger domes, modified frames, wide cabs and lever reverse.

No	Date	Name	Super-heated	Steam brake	LNE nos 1923	1924	App-lied	Withdrawn
901	7/1911	*St Johnstoun*	6/1925	5/30	901B	9901	6/25	12/1937
902	7/1911	*Highland Chief*	11/1923	6/31	902B	9902	5/25	10/1936
903	8/1911	*Cock o'the North*	9/1924	12/31		9903	9/24	5/1937
	5/1934	renamed *Aberdonian*						
904	8/1911	*Holyrood*	11/1924	4/31		9904	11/24	8/1936
905	8/1911	*Buccleuch*	5/1924	4/31		9905	5/24	9/1937
906	8/1911	*Teribus*	7/1924	5/31		9906	7/24	2/1937

0-6-0 Built by North British Locomotive Co. Works nos below.
                NB Railway at Cowlairs.
DW 5ft 0in; WB 7ft 9in + 9ft 0in; Cyls 18½ x 26; Blr 5ft 4¼in (max) x 10ft 5³/₈in; THS 1748 sq ft (except nos 329/30 see below); WP 180 lbs/sq in; Wt 50 tons 9 cwt. Heavy goods locomotives. Boiler pitched 9in higher than Holmes 0-6-0s at 8ft 0in. Lap-jointed boiler originally, front ring 5ft 3in diam, rear ring 5ft 4¼in. 3500 gallon tenders. Nos 329/30 had different boilers when built (first two built at Cowlairs 1906, details below) and all locomotives constructed before December 1908 had piston valves, but from this date slide valves were adopted. The LNE classified the piston valve engines J35/1 except nos 329/30 which were J35/2, and the remaining locomotives with slide valves were J35/3. Superheating was carried out by the LNE, THS 1243.33 sq ft + 176.39 sq ft superheater, Wt 51 tons 4 cwt and these became J35/4. From 1938 THS was 1232.9 sq ft + 176.39 sq ft superheater, Wt 50¾ tons and superheated locomotives with piston valves were classified J35/5 (Wt 51½ tons). All except the second Cowlairs batch (1910-13) had Westinghouse brakes and some were dual-fitted with vacuum train brake equipment. Steam brakes were substituted by the LNE. NB Loco Co engines had tapered chimneys with a shallow cap, the Cowlairs chimneys, later fitted to most of the class, had a deeper cap.

The following were built by North British Locomotive Co. Works nos 17322-31.

No	Date	Super-heated	Vacuum fitted	Steam brake	LNE nos* no	date	BR no	App-lied	Withdrawn
848	6/1906	9/1925	7/27	1/47	9848	9/25			
					4460	6/46	64460	3/48	9/1959
849	6/1906	1/1925	7/27	3/48	9849	1/25			
					4461	7/46	64461	3/48	10/1961
850	6/1906	2/1925	6/27	11/51	9850	2/25			
					4462	9/46	64462	10/48	11/1960
851	6/1906	11/1936		9/47	9851	5/24			
					4463	10/46	64463	4/49	9/1960
852	6/1906	2/1925	1/27	12/47	9852	2/25			
					4464	9/46	64464	4/49	5/1958
853	6/1906	3/1926			9853	5/24			
					4465	10/46			12/1947
854	6/1906	6/1925		10/46	9854	6/25			
					4466	2/46	64466	12/48	7/1959
855	6/1906	11/1932			9855	10/24			
					4467	6/46			11/1947

```
856   6/1906  6/1925  8/27   8/48  9856   6/25
                                   4468  10/46  64468  8/48   5/1960
857   6/1906  5/1925                9857   5/25
                                   4469   7/46               12/1946
```
* No record 'B' suffixes applied 9/1923-2/1924.

The following were built at Cowlairs. Nos 329/30 had boilers with a shorter firebox
(6ft 0in instead of 6ft 4in) and had THS 1794 sq ft being classified J35/2 by the LNE
(Wt 48 tons 14 cwt). They were converted to standard boilers as J35/1 in 3/1924 and
1/1926 respectively. From no 191 in 12/1908 slide valves were fitted instead of
piston valves (LNE J35/3). No 329 had a Phoenix superheater fitted experimentally for
a short period in 1911 and no 191 had Raven cab signalling fitted from 9/1928 until
2/1936.

No	Date	Super-heated	Vacuum fitted	Steam brake	LNE nos* no	date	BR no	App-lied	Withdrawn
329	7/1906	12/1931	6/27	3/48	9329	1/27			
					4470	10/46	64470	8/49	2/1962
330	7/1906	5/1935		5/48	9330	1/26			
					4471	9/46	64471	5/48	6/1961
185	7/1908	8/1937	11/26	4/50	9185	9/25			
					4472	1/46	64472	4/50	3/1962
186	7/1908	3/1925		11/47	9186	3/25			
					4473	5/46	64473	3/50	12/1959
187	7/1908	12/1936		6/51	9187	9/25			
					4474	5/46	64474	4/48	10/1961
188	7/1908	6/1926		9/48	9188	6/24			
					4475	6/46	64475	9/48	4/1959
189	8/1908	7/1925	7/27	11/47	9189	7/25			
					4476	10/46	64476	10/49	5/1961
190	8/1908	3/1926	2/46	2/46	9190	4/24			
					4477	7/46	64477	8/48	11/1961
191	12/1908	2/1936	2/34	2/36	9191	12/24			
					4478	1/46	64478	3/48	8/1962
192	12/1908	8/1938		10/47	9192	10/25			
					4479	9/46	64479	3/50	12/1961
193	12/1908	4/1936	7/27	4/50	9193	6/24			
					4480	5/46	64480	4/50	9/1962
194	12/1908	11/1933	5/27	11/45	9194	3/25			
					4481	1/46			2/1947
195	12/1908	1/1938	4/27	9/47	9195	4/24			
					4482	12/46	64482	7/50	6/1961
196	1/1909	8/1932	8/27	1/46	9196	5/25			
					4483	4/46	64483	1/50	6/1960

* No record 'B' suffixes applied 9/1923-2/1924.

The following were built by North British Locomotive Co.
Works nos 18880-9 and 18955-64 (1909) and 19085-94 (1910), 1910 batch originally
18¼ x 26 cyls.

No	Date	Super-heated	Vacuum fitted	Steam brake	LNE nos* no	date	BR no	App-lied	Withdrawn
197	8/1909	7/1935		8/47	9197	3/24			
					4484	4/46	64484	6/49	9/1959
198	8/1909	11/1933		3/48	9198	7/24			
					4485	5/46	64485	3/48	3/1959
199	9/1909	11/1931		8/47	9199	10/24			
					4486	4/46	64486	4/50	9/1958
200	9/1909	4/1923		7/47	9200	8/24			
					4487	11/46	64487	10/49	4/1960
201	9/1909	10/1935		3/47	9201	2/25			
					4488	1/47	64488	4/49	10/1961

No	Date				LNE no	date	BR no	Applied	Withdrawn
202	9/1909	10/1937	7/27	6/45	9202	8/25			
					4489	6/46	64489	5/48	6/1961
203	9/1909	5/1925	9/27	7/47	9203	5/25			
					4490	11/46	64490	4/49	12/1959
204	9/1909	7/1930	6/27	1/47	9204	9/24			
					4491	1/47	64491	6/48	12/1962
205	9/1909	7/1933	9/26	6/48	9205	1/25			
					4492	9/46	64492	6/48	2/1959
206	9/1909	8/1933		7/48	9206	12/25			
					4493	6/46	64493	7/48	11/1960
364	11/1909	8/1925	1/28	12/47	9364	8/25			
					4494	9/46	64494	6/48	6/1961
365	11/1909	5/1926		10/47	9365	5/24			
					4495	11/46	64495	11/50	6/1958
366	11/1909	4/1936	12/26	1/47	9366	12/24			
					4496	11/46	64496	9/48	10/1959
367	11/1909	4/1932	12/26	1/49	9367	1/25			
					4497	7/46	64497	1/49	4/1962
368	11/1909	12/1932		11/50	9368	2/25			
					4498	1/47	64498	4/48	9/1959
369	12/1909	3/1925	6/27	12/47	9369	3/25			
					4499	10/46	64499	9/48	10/1962
370	12/1909	10/1932		2/47	9370	9/24			
					4500	11/46	64500	9/49	6/1961
371	12/1909	12/1936	6/27	3/51	9371	7/24			
					4501	4/46	64501	4/48	8/1959
372	12/1909	8/1934		12/47	9372	3/24			
					4502	4/46	64502	11/48	9/1960
373	12/1909	5/1929			9373	3/24			
					4503	6/46			9/1947
207	3/1910	9/1932		4/51	9207	11/25			
					4512	5/46	64512	9/48	9/1960
208	3/1910	8/1932	12/26	11/49	9208	12/26			
					4513	10/46	64513	11/49	9/1959
374	3/1910	11/1933		5/48	9374	4/24			
					4504	5/46	64504	5/48	9/1960
375	3/1910	1/1940	10/26	1/50	9375	12/24			
					4505	6/46	64505	1/50	10/1961
376	3/1910	3/1936		4/48	9376	7/25			
					4506	9/46	64506	4/48	12/1959
377	3/1910	5/1928	10/27	12/50	9377	3/26			
					4507	10/46	64507	3/48	1/1962
378	3/1910	9/1934			9378	11/25			
					(4508)				10/1946
379	3/1910	9/1939	4/27	3/48	9379	6/24			
					4509	6/46	64509	12/49	10/1959
380	4/1910	9/1931	9/28	2/46	9380	7/24			
					4510	10/46	64510	9/48	11/1962
381	4/1910	7/1925	6/28	3/47	9381	7/25			
					4511	10/46	64511	9/48	10/1959

* No record 'B' suffixes 9/1923-2/1924.

The following were built at Cowlairs with steam brakes instead of Westinghouse.

		Super-	LNE nos*			App-	
No	Date	heated	no	date	BR no	lied	Withdrawn
38	9/1910	12/1941	9038	3/25			
			4514	10/46	64514	1/49	2/1962
56	9/1910	4/1935	9056	6/25			
			4515	3/46	64515	12/48	11/1961
57	10/1910	12/1933	9057	11/24			
			4516	3/46	64516	5/48	6/1959

58	10/1910	5/1938	9058	11/24			
			4517	4/46	64517	8/48	10/1958
59	10/1910	8/1932	9059	9/25			
			4518	7/46	64518	2/49	11/1961
115	10/1910	5/1934	9115	3/25			
			4519	10/46	64519	3/48	4/1962
120	11/1910	11/1933	9120	1/26			
			4520	10/46	64520	7/48	9/1959
335	12/1910	3/1936	9335	8/25			
			4521	11/46	64521	1/51	4/1959
336	12/1910	12/1938	9336	12/25			
			4522	7/46	64522	7/48	1/1959
337	12/1910	7/1942	9337	6/25			
			4523	10/46	64523	9/48	2/1961
347	12/1910	11/1934	9347	2/25			
			4524	11/46	64524	6/48	3/1961
348	1/1911	9/1930	9348	4/25			
			4525	10/46	64525	3/49	7/1962
220	11/1912	7/1927	9220	4/26			
			4528	10/46	64528	1/49	9/1958
226	11/1912	12/1937	9226	8/24			
			4526	5/46	64526	9/48	3/1958
228	12/1912	2/1933	9228	2/26			
			4527	3/46	64527	11/48	6/1962
253	12/1912	4/1936	9253	9/24			
			4529	10/46	64529	1/49	9/1960
254	12/1912	8/1925	9254	3/24			
			4530	9/46	64530	10/48	10/1959
86	2/1913	12/1934	9086	4/25			
			4531	10/46	64531	10/48	7/1961
124	2/1913	3/1934	9124	7/25			
			4532	4/46	64532	8/48	11/1961
126	3/1913	7/1927	9126	8/25			
			4533	5/46	64533	9/50	1/1962
127	3/1913	12/1929	9127	1/25			
			4534	11/46	64534	5/48	5/1961
129	3/1913	5/1927	9129	10/25			
			4535	1/46	64535	6/49	11/1961

* No record 'B' suffixes 9/1923-2/1924.

0-6-0 Built by NB Railway at Cowlairs.
                North British Locomotive Co. Works nos below.
DW 5ft 0in; WB 7ft 9in + 9ft 2in; Cyls 19½ x 26; Blr 5ft 4¼in (max) x 10ft 5³/₈in; THS
1407.62 sq ft + 324.6 sq ft superheater; WP 175 lbs/sq in (load class S see below) and
165 lbs/sq in (load class B); Wt 54 tons 14 cwt.
Superheated version of 848 class. Boiler originally lap-jointed as 848 class. The
first ten originally had Schmidt superheater, the others Robinson pattern which became
standard. Nos 296/300-3/6/13/401-3/70-3/85-9/91 had the higher pressure and were
designated load class S, the others being load class B. By 1923, nos 167/468/9/76-80
and 455 had become load class S and 403 had become class B. Intended for express
goods traffic rather than passenger they were provided with steam brakes rather than
Westinghouse (except for the final batch built in 1921), but vacuum ejectors were also
provided for working vacuum fitted goods stock. From 1931, however, 22 were fitted
with steam heating apparatus to enable them to work vacuum fitted passenger trains
between 1931 and 1937 and a further two in 1944. The final batch were built with
Westinghouse and vacuum ejectors. Tenders had 3500 gallons capacity. Subsequent
alterations to heating surface were as follows:
From 1918 THS 1407.62 sq ft + 208.25 sq ft superheater.
        1924 THS 1243.43 sq ft + 176.39 sq ft superheater.
        1938 THS 1232.9 sq ft + 176.39 sq ft superheater.

LNE class J37.
The following were built at Cowlairs.

No	Date	LNE nos* 1924	Applied	1946	Applied	BR no	Applied	Withdrawn
8	12/1914	9008	9/25	4536	5/46	64536	11/48	5/1959
13	12/1914	9013	1/25	4537	6/46	64537	6/48	6/1964
44	12/1914	9044	11/25	4538	7/46	64538	4/50	12/1959
62	1/1915	9062	3/24	4539	10/46	64539	8/48	9/1961
113	1/1915	9113	11/25	4540	10/46	64540	2/49	12/1962
136	4/1915	9136	9/24	4541	11/46	64541	7/49	7/1964
222	4/1915	9222	5/26	4542	10/46	64542	8/48	10/1961
255	4/1915	9255	11/25	4543	12/46	64543	5/48	12/1962
260	4/1915	9260	9/24	4544	10/46	64544	5/50	12/1962
261	5/1915	9261	4/24	4545	10/46	64545	8/48	6/1962
263	11/1915	9263	7/24	4546	11/46	64546	5/49	5/1964
429	11/1915	9429	10/25	4547	11/46	64547	8/49	12/1966
430	11/1915	9430	4/25	4548	10/46	64548	12/49	11/1963
431	11/1915	9431	9/25	4549	11/46	64549	8/50	7/1964
432	12/1915	9432	2/26	4550	6/46	64550	7/48	12/1963
433	5/1916	9433	2/25	4551	11/46	64551	2/49	9/1963
434	5/1916	9434	3/24	4552	9/46	64552	2/49	10/1964
435	6/1916	9435	12/24	4553	11/46	64553	1/49	3/1962
436	6/1916	9436	3/25	4554	10/46	64554	4/48	1/1964
437	6/1916	9437	6/25	4555	11/46	64555	3/49	10/1964
292	8/1918	9292	5/24	4567	10/46	64567	8/48	3/1960
297	8/1918	9297	8/24	4569	10/46	64569	8/48	12/1966
304	8/1918	9304	3/24	4570	5/46	64570	7/48	11/1966
454	8/1918	9454	4/24	4574	9/46	64574	1/50	12/1962
455	9/1918	9455	7/24	4575	10/46	64575	5/48	12/1963

* No record 'B' suffixes 9/1923-2/1924

The following were built by the North British Locomotive Co. Works nos 21925-58
(6/1918-1/1919), 22268-77 (11/1919-12/1919), 22490-9 (12/1919-1/1920), 22668-82
(12/1920-2/1921).

No	Date	LNE nos* 1924	Applied	1946	Applied	BR no	Applied	Withdrawn
88	6/1918	9088	3/24	4556	11/46	64556	2/50	12/1962
89	6/1918	9089	3/24	4557	11/46	64557	5/48	10/1963
123	6/1918	9123	2/25	4558	10/46	64558	4/48	9/1965
139	6/1918	9139	10/24	4559	2/46	64559	5/48	11/1963
151	7/1918	9151**	4/24	4560	10/46	64560	6/48	3/1961
157	7/1918	9157	4/24	4561	9/46	64561	8/50	5/1964
158	7/1918	9158	4/25	4562	9/46	64562	3/49	11/1963
161	7/1918	9161	4/25	4563	10/46	64563	11/50	10/1964
162	7/1918	9162	2/26	4564	11/46	64564	9/49	6/1964
167	7/1918	9167	5/24	4565	8/46	64565	11/49	10/1961
274	8/1918	9274	6/24	4566	9/46	64566	8/48	4/1962
295	8/1918	9295**	5/25	4568	11/46	64568	1/50	8/1963
305	8/1918	9305	4/24	4571	4/46	64571	4/49	10/1965
314	8/1918	9314	2/26	4572	10/46	64572	3/49	9/1964
315	8/1918	9315	11/24	4573	10/46	64573	12/49	10/1964
456	8/1918	9456	11/24	4576	9/46	64576	12/48	4/1967
457	9/1918	9457	4/25	4577	9/46	64577	12/49	8/1966
458	9/1918	9458	12/25	4578	10/46	64578	4/49	5/1962
459	9/1918	9459	3/24	4579	9/46	64579	9/49	12/1963
460	9/1918	9460	4/24	4580	10/46	64580	5/48	10/1965
461	10/1918	9461	11/24	4581	9/46	64581	12/50	12/1962
462	10/1918	9462	4/24	4582	10/46	64582	5/48	11/1963
463	10/1918	9463	2/26	4583	10/46	64583	3/50	12/1963
464	10/1918	9464	9/25	4584	10/46	64584	4/49	7/1959

465	11/1918	9465	9/25	4585	9/46	64585	12/48	1/1965***
466	11/1918	9466	9/24	4586	10/46	64586	1/50	6/1964
467	11/1918	9467**	10/25	4587	10/46	64587	2/49	6/1964
468	11/1918	9468	2/25	4588	10/46	64588	3/48	6/1966
469	11/1918	9469	7/25	4589	9/46	64589	7/48	5/1963
476	12/1918	9476	5/25	4590	10/46	64590	12/49	5/1962
477	1/1919	9477	6/25	4591	10/46	64591	7/49	10/1964
478	1/1919	9478	10/25	4592	10/46	64592	12/48	7/1965
479	1/1919	9479	4/24	4593	10/46	64593	8/48	11/1963
480	1/1919	9480	5/24	4594	9/46	64594	6/49	12/1962
470	11/1919	9470	5/24	4596	10/46	64596	6/50	4/1961
471	11/1919	9471	8/24	4597	10/46	64597	2/50	8/1966
472	11/1919	9472	3/25	4598	10/46	64598	10/49	9/1962
473	11/1919	9473	8/25	4599	10/46	64599	3/50	10/1965
313	11/1919	9313	9/25	4595	3/46	64595	4/48	3/1966
485	11/1919	9485	10/25	4600	10/46	64600	7/48	7/1963
486	11/1919	9486	6/24	4601	9/46	64601	9/50	12/1962***
487	11/1919	9487**	7/25	4602	7/46	64602	5/48	4/1967
488	11/1919	9488**	12/24	4603	7/46	64603	11/50	12/1963
489	12/1919	9489**	2/26	4604	9/46	64604	4/49	8/1962
296	12/1919	9296	6/26	4605	11/46	64605	3/49	6/1964
300	12/1919	9300	12/25	4606	10/46	64606	10/50	7/1966
301	12/1919	9301	7/25	4607	3/46	64607	12/48	8/1962
302	12/1919	9302	12/25	4608	2/46	64608	4/49	8/1966
303	1/1920	9303	12/24	4609	9/46	64609	4/48	12/1962
306	1/1920	9306	10/25	4610	4/46	64610	4/48	2/1966
401	1/1920	9401	3/25	4611	9/46	64611	6/49	4/1967
402	1/1920	9402	4/24	4612	10/46	64612	3/48	12/1962***
403	1/1920	9403	11/24	4613	11/46	64613	5/48	1/1964
491	1/1920	9491	6/26	4614	2/46	64614	8/48	12/1964
46	12/1920	9046	1/25	4615	12/46	64615	12/49	12/1962***
72	12/1920	9072**	4/24	4616	6/46	64616	11/49	12/1963
73	12/1920	9073**	6/24	4617	6/46	64617	6/49	12/1962***
84	12/1920	9084**	12/24	4618	6/46	64618	11/48	10/1966
109	12/1920	9109	6/24	4619	6/46	64619	4/49	12/1963
110	12/1920	9110	8/24	4620	6/46	64620	8/48	4/1967
111	1/1921	9111**	11/25	4621	6/46	64621	12/48	5/1965
171	1/1921	9171**	4/25	4622	5/46	64622	3/49	12/1962
175	1/1921	9175	1/25	4623	6/46	64623	10/50	11/1966
272	1/1921	9272	12/24	4624	5/46	64624	6/48	1/1966
273	1/1921	9273	3/25	4625	6/46	64625	4/48	9/1965
299	2/1921	9299	11/25	4626	10/46	64626	6/49	11/1963
506	2/1921	9506**	3/24	4627	3/46	64627	5/48	10/1963
507	2/1921	9507**	11/24	4628	3/46	64628	5/48	3/1962
508	2/1921	9508**	8/25	4629	3/46	64629	12/48	10/1963

* No record 'B' suffixes 9/1923-2/1924.
** Fitted with steam heating apparatus.

No 9151	1944		No 9073	1931-7
9295	1944		9084	1931-7
9467	1931-7		9111	1931-7
9487	1931-7		9171	1931-7
9488	1931-7		9506	1931-7
9489	1931-7		9507	1931-7
9072	1931-7		9508	1931-7

*** Withdrawals:
   1/1965 was the statistical date for withdrawal of 64585. Actual date was
   30/12/1964
   No 64601 returned to operating stock 'on loan' 2/1963-4/1963
   No 64612 returned to operating stock 'on loan' 1/1963-4/1963
   No 64615 returned to operating stock 'on loan' 1/1963-4/1963
   No 64617 returned to operating stock 'on loan' 1/1963-2/1963

The following were built at Cowlairs with Westinghouse brakes and vacuum ejectors.
Steam brakes substituted 1945-51 on locomotives marked **.
Steam heating to all 1931-7.

		LNE nos*						
No	Date	1924	Applied	1946	Applied	BR no	Applied	Withdrawn
517	6/1921	9517**	4/26	4630	5/46	64630	9/48	9/1962
98	6/1921	9098**	9/24	4631	2/46	64631	9/48	12/1962***
101	6/1921	9101**	3/25	4632	2/46	64632	5/50	12/1965
103	1921	9103	5/26	4633	10/46	64633	3/48	6/1964
33	7/1921	9033	2/26	4634	9/46	64634	4/49	1/1964
128	8/1921	9128	8/25	4636	10/46	64636	3/48	10/1964
104	8/1921	9104	6/25	4635	10/46	64635	4/50	12/1962***
105	9/1921	9105	10/25	4637	9/46	64637	11/50	8/1962
143	9/1921	9143	1/26	4638	9/46	64638	5/48	12/1962
518	1921	9518	10/24	4639	5/46	64639	10/49	12/1962

*   No record 'B' suffixes 9/1923-2/1924.
**   Steam brakes substituted for Westinghouse 1945-51.
*** No 64631 returned to operating stock 'on loan' 1-5/1963.
     No 64635 returned to operating stock 'on loan' 1-4/1963.

0-4-4T Built by North British Locomotive Co. Works nos 18868-79.
DW 5ft 9in; TW 3ft 6in; WB 7ft 6in + 8ft 3in + 6ft 6in; Cyls 18 x 26; Blr 4ft 8^{1}/8in x
10ft 2¾in; THS 1309 sq ft; WP 175 lbs/sq in; Wt 58 tons 6 cwt.
Similar to Holmes 0-4-4Ts, but larger for local passenger working. The boilers were
standard with the Reid 4-4-2Ts and 0-6-2Ts below, and with the Holmes 604 class 0-6-0s
after rebuilding by Reid. 1345 Gallon tanks. By 1923 THS was 1258 sq ft and from
1938 1235.5 sq ft. Westinghouse brakes and steam heating connections at both ends.
As on the Holmes 0-4-4Ts, rear sanding was delivered between the bogie wheels. Vacuum
ejectors were added later as under. LNE class G9.

		Vacuum	LNE nos*		
No	Date	ejector	1924	applied	Withdrawn
239	9/1909	8/1926	9239	6/1924	7/1936
334	9/1909	10/1926	9334	5/1924	2/1939
349	9/1909	c1920	9349	6/1925	7/1936
350	10/1909	c1920	9350	12/1924	1/1939
351	10/1909	11/1925	9351	11/1925	11/1939
352	10/1909	c1920	9352	5/1925	6/1937
353	10/1909	c1920	9353	2/1925	10/1937
354	10/1909	12/1923	9354	1/1926	9/1936
355	10/1909	c1920	9355	3/1925	9/1939
356	10/1909	2/1927	9356	4/1924	5/1939
474	11/1909	3/1926	9474	3/1926	1/1939
475	10/1909	11/1925	9475	10/1924	11/1940

* No record 'B' suffixes 9/1923-2/1924.

4-4-2T Built by Yorkshire Engine Co. Works nos 1066-95.
DW 5ft 9in; LW 3ft 6in; TW 3ft 9in; WB 6ft 6in + 6ft 7in + 8ft 3in + 7ft 6in ; Cyls 18
x 26; Blr 4ft 8^{1}/8in x 10ft ¼in; THS 1309 sq ft; WP 175 lbs/sq in; Wt 68 tons 16 cwt.
The change from front coupled tanks to leading bogie and radial trailing axle for
local passenger working had the benefit of a considerable increase in tank capacity to
1990 gallons. Later THS was 1222 sq ft approximately and in the late 1930s, 1235.5 sq
ft. Westinghouse brake and vacuum ejector were provided with steam heating
connections at both ends and air sanding. The Westinghouse equipment on these engines
was retained. Nicknamed 'Yorkies'. LNE class C15.

		LNE nos*						
No	Date	1924	Applied	1946	Applied	BR no	Applied	Withdrawn
1	12/1911	9001	7/1925	7452	5/1946	67452	8/1948	2/1956
3	1/1912	9003	10/1924	7454	5/1946	67454	2/1949	6/1954

		1924	Applied	1946	Applied	BR no	Applied	Withdrawn
4	3/1912	9004	11/1925	7455	5/1946	67455	4/1948	2/1955
5	4/1912	9005	4/1925	7456	5/1946	67456	6/1951	9/1954
122	5/1912	9122	8/1924	7457	7/1946	67457	5/1951	6/1955
131	6/1912	9131	10/1924	7458	7/1946	67458	9/1948	3/1956
134	7/1912	9134	5/1925	7459	7/1946	67459	9/1950	10/1955
135	8/1912	9135**	10/1924	7460	1/1946	67460	6/1948	4/1960
141	9/1912	9141	4/1925	7461	7/1946	(67461)		12/1954
155	10/1912	9155	6/1924	7462	7/1946	67462	6/1950	6/1954
164	11/1912	9164	11/1925	7463	10/1946	67463	7/1948	9/1955
2	12/1912	9002	3/1926	7453	5/1946	67453	2/1950	1/1954
6	1/1913	9006	2/1925	7464	5/1946	67464	12/1948	8/1953
12	2/1913	9012	9/1924	7465	5/1946	(67465)		11/1954
15	2/1913	9015	10/1925	7466	6/1946	67466	10/1949	4/1956
25	3/1913	9025	12/1925	7467	10/1946	67467	3/1949	3/1955
41	3/1913	9041	3/1925	7468	5/1946	67468	4/1950	10/1953
43	4/1913	9043	7/1924	7469	7/1946	67469	5/1950	9/1954
48	4/1913	9048	5/1924	7470	11/1946	(67470)		12/1954
53	5/1913	9053	12/1924	7471	7/1946	(67471)		12/1952
265	7/1913	9265	11/1924	7472	10/1946	67472	11/1948	4/1956
267	7/1913	9267	10/1925	7473	7/1946	67473	7/1950	12/1954
309	8/1913	9309	2/1925	7474	3/1946	67474**	9/1948	4/1960
16	8/1913	9016	4/1924	7475	5/1946	67475**	10/1948	4/1954
26	10/1913	9026	4/1925	7476	7/1946	67476	2/1949	9/1954
39	10/1913	9039	5/1924	7477	11/1946	67477	12/1949	9/1954
51	11/1913	9051	7/1924	7478	11/1946	67478	2/1949	2/1956
64	11/1913	9064	6/1924	7479	10/1946	67479	2/1949	1/1954
102	12/1913	9102	11/1924	7480	3/1946	67480	11/1950	2/1956
133	12/1913	9133	5/1925	7481	7/1946	67481	9/1948	2/1956

* No record 'B' suffixes 9/1923-2/1924.
** Fitted for vacuum operated push and pull working between Craigendoran and
   Arrochar: No 9135 10/1940, 67474 9/1954, 67475 10/1950.

4-4-2T Built by North British Locomotive Co.
Works nos 21203-17 (1915/16), 22683-8 (1921).
DW 5ft 9in; LW 3ft 6in; TW 3ft 9in; WB 6ft 6in + 6ft 8½in + 8ft 3in + 7ft 6in; Cyls 19
x 26; Blr 4ft 8^{1}/8in x 10ft 2¼in; THS 1025 sq ft + 220 sq ft superheater (1915), 1009
sq ft + 220 sq ft (1921); WP 165 lbs/sq in; Wt 72½ tons.
Superheated version of 1 class above, WB 1½in longer. NB Loco Co records gave WP as
175 lbs/sq in, but railway records show the lower pressure as above. Tank capacity
2080 gallons, piston valves instead of slide valves. Westinghouse brakes and vacuum
ejectors, air sanding which were retained. As on the saturated 1 class 4-4-2Ts,
smokebox wing-plates were also retained. There were several variations of tube-plate,
and changes in the superheater from the original long loops to short loop, and the
adoption for a period of 16 element heaters instead of 18 element. Principal
variations were as follows:
c1923 THS 933.23 sq ft + superheater (18 element short loop) 142.25 sq ft
 1924 THS 915.54 sq ft + superheater (16 element) 126.4 sq ft
 1938 THS 868.52 sq ft + superheater (18 element) 142.2 sq ft.
From 3/1943 to 2/1947, no 9349 ran with a saturated boiler (THS 1235.5 sq ft).
LNE class C16.

		LNE nos*						
No	Date	1924	Applied	1946	Applied	BR no	Applied	Withdrawn
438	12/1915	9438	6/1925	7482	9/1946	67482	5/1949	10/1959
439	12/1915	9439	4/1925	7483	1/1946	67483	4/1949	4/1956
440	12/1915	9440	5/1924	7484	7/1946	67484	10/1949	4/1960
441	12/1915	9441	7/1925	7485	7/1946	67485	9/1948	4/1961
442	12/1915	9442	3/1925	7486	7/1946	67486	11/1948	4/1960
443	1/1916	9443	1/1926	7487	7/1946	67487	5/1948	10/1959
444	2/1916	9444	1/1925	7488	11/1946	67488	6/1952	10/1959

445	2/1916	9445	12/1925	7489	5/1946	67489	2/1949	2/1961
446	2/1916	9446	4/1925	7490	7/1946	67490	3/1948	4/1960
447	3/1916	9447	6/1926	7491	10/1946	67491	6/1949	3/1960
448	4/1916	9448	3/1924	7492	10/1946	67492	6/1948	3/1960
449	4/1916	9449	1/1925	7493	7/1946	67493	5/1949	4/1956
450	4/1916	9450	1/1925	7494	4/1946	67494	12/1951	2/1961
451	4/1916	9451	3/1925	7495	3/1946	67495	11/1949	5/1956
452	5/1916	9452	10/1924	7496	7/1946	67496	1/1949	3/1960
511	2/1921	9511	6/1924	7497	4/1946	67497	4/1950	10/1959
512	2/1921	9512	10/1925	7498	3/1946	67498	9/1948	8/1955
513	2/1921	9513	3/1924	7499	3/1946	67499	9/1948	11/1955
514	3/1921	9514	6/1924	7500	3/1946	67500	1/1953	10/1959
515	3/1921	9515	9/1925	7501	3/1946	67501	1/1949	4/1960
516	3/1921	9516	6/1925	7502	3/1946	67502	11/1948	4/1960

* No record 'B' suffixes 9/1923-2/1924.

0-6-0T Built by NB Railway at Cowlairs.
DW 3ft 9in; WB 5ft 3in + 5ft 9in; Cyls 15 x 22 o/s; Blr 3ft 10in x 8ft 8½in; THS 651.2
sq ft; WP 130 lbs/sq in; Wt 36¼ tons (1904/5, 1909), 38 tons 14 cwt (1912, 1919).
Dock shunting tank also used in restricted yards with sharp curves. The 1912 and 1919
locomotives had safety valves on the firebox instead of the dome, and combination
injectors were introduced on the 1909 batch. All had right-hand instead of left-hand
drive and no smokebox wing-plates. The 1904/5 batch were reboilered with combination
injectors and Ross 'pop' valves on the firebox in 1925. The increased weight of the
latter locomotives was accounted for by the fact that they had solid plate frames
instead of slotted frames. All had steam brakes and dumb buffers. Two of the class
were fitted with vacuum equipment for shunting vacuum fitted freight stock by BR, nos
68332 in 11/1952 and 68335 in 11/1953.
LNE class J88.

| | | LNE nos* | | | | | | |
No	Date	1924	Applied	1946	Applied	BR no	Applied	Withdrawn
836	12/1904	9836	12/1924	8320	7/1946	68320	3/1950	6/1960
837	12/1904	9837	6/1924	8321	7/1946	68321	9/1949	6/1958
838	12/1904	9838	3/1925	8322	7/1946	68322	4/1948	12/1958
839	12/1904	9839	7/1924	8323	7/1946	68323	1/1950	10/1956
840	1/1905	9840	7/1924	8324	3/1946	68324	6/1948	7/1958
841	1/1905	9841	4/1925	8325	1/1946	68325	12/1950	3/1961
842	9/1905	9842	3/1925	8326	3/1946	68326	3/1951	10/1959
843	9/1905	9843	6/1925	8327	7/1946	68327	7/1951	7/1958
844	9/1905	9844	4/1925	8328	7/1946	68328	1/1952	3/1958
845	10/1905	9845	12/1924	8329	7/1946	68329	5/1949	2/1959
846	10/1905	9846	4/1925	8330	7/1946	68330	5/1949	8/1958
847	10/1905	9847	3/1925	8331	7/1946	68331	1/1949	3/1959
233	3/1909	9233	3/1927	8332	4/1946	68332	11/1949	8/1960
234	3/1909	9234	4/1925	8333	1/1946	68333	5/1948	3/1958
235	3/1909	9235	11/1924	8334	3/1946	68334	4/1949	6/1959
236	3/1909	9236	8/1926	8335	3/1946	68335	6/1950	10/1962
237	4/1909	9237	3/1926	8336	5/1946	68336	3/1949	5/1962
238	4/1909	9238	2/1925	8337	6/1946	68337	10/1951	11/1955
66	4/1912	9066	10/1925	8338	6/1946	68338	7/1949	9/1961
114	4/1912	9114	5/1925	8339	1/1946	68339	10/1951	10/1958
116	5/1912	9116	4/1924	8340	3/1946	68340	7/1949	2/1958
117	5/1912	9117	2/1925	8341	5/1946	68341	3/1951	11/1954**
118	5/1912	9118	6/1925	8342	5/1946	68342	6/1950	2/1962
119	6/1912	9119	3/1924	8343	6/1946	68343	10/1949	10/1960
121	6/1912	9121	5/1925	8344	6/1946	68344	2/1950	1/1961
130	7/1912	9130	9/1925	8345	1/1946	68345	7/1951	12/1962
132	7/1912	9132	8/1925	8346	1/1946	68346	9/1948	10/1962
152	7/1912	9152	2/1925	8347	3/1946	68347	8/1952	8/1958
277	9/1919	9277	3/1925	8348	6/1946	68348	11/1949	8/1958
290	9/1919	9290	12/1924	8349	5/1946	68349	10/1950	8/1960

288	10/1919	9288	6/1925	8353	6/1946	68353	7/1948	2/1962
289	10/1919	9289	7/1925	8354	1/1946	68354	3/1951	9/1960
87	11/1919	9087	3/1925	8350	7/1946	68350	7/1948	7/1962
271	11/1919	9271	11/1925	8351	5/1946	68351	2/1951	1/1957
279	11/1919	9279	1/1925	8352	6/1946	68352	6/1948	6/1960

* No record 'B' suffixes 9/1923-2/1924.
** No 68341 scrapped after running away on 1 in 25 Kirkaldy Harbour branch with
nineteen wagons and falling into the harbour.

A small tank engine described as 'contractors type' was purchased from Finlayson of
Airdrie second-hand in 1/1915, and was numbered 1250 in the Duplicate list. It was
not taken into LNER stock.

0-6-2T Built by North British Locomotive Co. Works nos below.
                R Stephenson & Co. Works nos below.
                LNE Railway at Cowlairs.
DW 4ft 6in; TW 3ft 9in; WB 7ft 6in + 8ft 0in + 7ft 0in; Cyls 18 x 26; Blr 4ft 8^1/8in x
10ft 2¼in; THS 1309 sq ft; WP 175 lbs/sq in; Weights as below.
Intended as goods engines supplementing the Holmes 0-6-0s with larger boiler standard
with Reid 0-4-4Ts (239 class above), the saturated Reid 4-4-2Ts (1 class) and the
rebuilt 18-inch Holmes 0-6-0s (604 class). The class divided into three groups
recognised by the LNE as N14, N15/1 and N15/2 as below. NB Loco Co drawings and also
those of Stephenson's showed an additional 10 sq ft of heating surface in the firebox
making THS 1319 sq ft. By 1923 THS was 1258 sq ft and by 1938 1235.5 sq ft. Steam-
heating apparatus was fitted in late NB and early LNE period.

The following were built by North British Locomotive Co. Works nos 18862-7 and had
shorter cabs with longer bunkers with coal capacity of 4 tons 8 cwt - 4½ tons and tank
capacity of 1631 gallons. When built, only Westinghouse brakes were fitted, but
vacuum ejectors were added late in the NB period to nos 858-62 and to LNE 9863 in
2/1925. Safety valves were originally on the domes. Wt 62 tons 10 cwt.
LNE class N14.

		LNE nos*						
No	Date	1924	Applied	1946	Applied	BR no	Applied	Withdrawn
858	9/1909	9858	4/1926	9120	10/1946	69120	4/1949	3/1954**
859	9/1909	9859	3/1924	9121	7/1946			9/1947***
860	9/1909	9860	8/1926	9122	8/1946			11/1947
861	9/1909	9861	4/1925	9123	10/1946			12/1947
862	9/1909	9862	1/1926	9124	6/1946	69124	12/1948	11/1950
863	9/1909	9863	2/1925	9125	10/1946	69125	12/1948	3/1954

* No record 'B' suffixes 9/1923-2/1924.
** No 858 fitted with Scarab oil burning system 1921 (a few months only).
*** No 859 fitted with Holden oil burning system 1921 (a few months only).

The following were built by the North British Locomotive Co. Works nos 19159-64 with
longer cabs and shorter bunkers, coal capacity 3½-4 tons and tank capacity 1586
gallons with Westinghouse brakes only. Vacuum ejectors added at dates below. Three
converted to steam brake and vacuum by BR. Safety valves on firebox. Wt 62 tons 1
cwt. LNE class N15/2

		Vacuum	Steam	LNE nos*			App-		App-	With-
No	Date	ejector	brake	1924	Applied	1946	lied	BR no	lied	drawn
7	6/1910	3/25		9007	3/24	9126	5/46	69126	6/48	2/1962
154	6/1910	11/25**	10/53	9154	11/25	9127	11/46	69127	1/51	6/1959
209	6/1910	10/24		9209	10/24	9128	10/46	69128	10/50	10/1962
210	6/1910	7/24		9210	7/24	9129	1/46	69129	8/49	12/1958
251	6/1910	by 1923	7/48	9251	6/25	9130	5/46	69130	7/48	12/1957
282	7/1910	by 1923	11/53	9282	2/26	9131	8/46	69131	10/50	2/1962

* No record 'B' suffixes 9/1923-2/1924.
** Assumed date.

The following were built by the North British Locomotive Co. Works nos 19165-76 (1910), 19828-47 (1912), 20164-72 (1913), 21218-29 (1916/17), with the longer cabs as 1910 batch above, but with steam instead of Westinghouse brakes. Vacuum ejectors added at dates below. Wt 60 tons 18 cwt. LNE class N15/1.

No	Date	Vacuum ejector	LNE nos* 1924	Applied	1946	App-lied	BR no	App-lied	Withdrawn
386	6/1910		9386	1/26	9132	1/46	69132	7/49	11/1960
387	6/1910		9387	7/24	9133	8/46	69133	12/49	8/1960
388	7/1910	8/48	9388	10/24	9134	8/46	69134	8/48	3/1961
389	7/1910		9389	10/24	9135	1/46	69135	8/48	10/1962
390	7/1910		9390	10/25	9136	12/46	69136	1/49	5/1961
391	7/1910		9391	8/25	9137	5/46	69137	6/48	5/1962
392	7/1910	1/48	9392	12/24	9138	6/46	69138	1/51	10/1962
393	7/1910		9393	12/25	9139	2/46	69139	10/48	4/1958
396	8/1910		9396	3/25	9140	6/46	69140	3/49	6/1958
397	8/1910		9397	3/25	9141	8/46	69141	11/48	9/1960
398	8/1910		9398	5/24	9142	9/46	69142	7/48	1/1958
399	8/1910		9399	4/24	9143	2/46	69143	11/49	9/1960
907	7/1912	8/48	9907	1/26	9144	9/46	69144	8/48	2/1960
908	7/1912		9908	9/25	9145	4/46	69145	6/48	3/1960
909	7/1912		9909	10/24	9146	9/46	69146	4/49	7/1959
910	8/1912		9910	1/26	9147	11/46	69147	1/49	6/1958
911	8/1912		9911	12/24	9148	6/46	69148	12/50	6/1958
912	8/1912		9912	6/25	9149	10/46	69149	4/48	3/1960
913	8/1912		9913	7/25	9150	6/46	69150	8/48	10/1962
914	8/1912		9914	8/24	9151	11/46	69151	5/50	2/1959
915	8/1912		9915	11/24	9152	6/46	69152	12/48	12/1958
916	8/1912		9916	4/25	9153	8/46	69153	9/48	9/1958
917	8/1912		9917	7/24	9154	11/46	69154	6/48	11/1959
918	8/1912		9918	5/25	9155	8/46	69155	9/48	9/1962
919	8/1912		9919	9/25	9156	6/46	69156	7/48	2/1962
920	8/1912		9920	11/24	9157	11/46	69157	7/49	4/1958
921	8/1912		9921	5/24	9158	10/46	69158	8/48	5/1958
922	8/1912		9922	11/24	9159	3/46	69159	7/48	10/1961
923	8/1912	11/52	9923	4/24	9160	6/46	69160	3/50	8/1958
924	8/1912		9924	2/24	9161	11/46	69161	2/51	8/1960
925	8/1912		9925	10/25	9162	11/46	69162	4/50	3/1959
926	8/1912	5/54	9926	1/26	9163	6/46	69163	9/48	2/1962
219	5/1913		9219	12/24	9185	2/46	69185	4/48	7/1959
223	5/1913	11/53	9223	9/24	9164	11/46	69164	6/48	4/1959
224	5/1913		9224	10/25	9165	4/46	69165	11/49	5/1960
229	5/1913		9229	9/25	9166	11/46	69166	7/49	12/1959
230	5/1913	7/48	9230	12/25	9167	9/46	69167	7/48	12/1957
246	5/1913		9246	5/25	9168	5/46	69168	4/49	2/1960
252	5/1913		9252	4/25	9169	5/46	69169	5/48	2/1959
257	5/1913		9257	5/24	9170	5/46	69170	2/50	1/1960
264	5/1913		9264	5/24	9171	5/46	69171	7/50	6/1960
47	8/1916		9047	10/25	9172	7/46	69172	3/51	11/1958
54	8/1916		9054	10/24	9173	6/46	69173	4/50	1/1961
61	9/1916		9061	8/24	9174	11/46	69174	9/48	11/1958
65	9/1916		9065	9/25	9175	7/46	69175	4/48	10/1958
69	10/1916		9069	3/25	9176	8/46	69176	12/49	8/1959
70	12/1916		9070	8/25	9177	11/46	69177	8/49	8/1960
276	1/1917	8/50	9276	11/25	9179	6/46	69179	6/48	9/1960
453	1/1917	3/53	9453	10/25	9180	9/46	69180	8/50	3/1961
142	2/1917	3/48	9142	6/26	9181	7/46	69181	4/51	2/1962
165	3/1917	**	9165	4/25	9182	4/46	69182	12/50	9/1959
166	3/1917	4/36	9166	4/24	9183	11/46	69183	3/49	11/1961

259   3/1917   9259   7/24   9184   6/46   69184   10/48   11/1960
*   No record 'B' suffixes 9/1923-2/1924.
** No 9165 was equipped with Westinghouse brake plus vacuum ejectors in 3/1929 and was
   reclassified as N15/2. Changed back to steam vacuum 7/1955.

The following were built by North British Locomotive Co. Works nos 22278-87 as above
(LNE N15/1), but were provided with vacuum ejectors when built in addition to steam
brakes. These ejectors were removed in 1922-3, but no 9029 was changed to
Westinghouse plus vacuum in 3/1929 becoming N15/2 with no 9165 above, and was changed
back to steam brake plus vacuum in 11/1953. Nos 9049 and 9097 had vacuum equipment
reinstated as below.

No	Date	Vacuum reinstated	LNE nos* 1924	Applied	1946	Applied	BR no	Applied	Withdrawn
20	2/1920		9020	12/25	9186	5/46	69186	3/48	7/1959
22	2/1920		9022	5/24	9187	6/46	69187	5/48	12/1959
29	2/1920	**	9029	9/25	9188	6/46	69188	12/49	10/1962
49	2/1920	1/48	9049	8/25	9189	11/46	69189	11/50	4/1958
96	2/1920		9096	1/25	9190	8/46	69190	6/48	8/1960
97	2/1920	4/36	9097	5/25	9191	2/46	69191	5/51	10/1962
106	2/1920		9106	9/24	9192	11/46	69192	7/49	3/1959
107	3/1920		9107	8/24	9193	7/46	69193	12/49	8/1958
108	3/1920		9108	1/25	9194	2/46	69194	3/50	10/1960
240	3/1920		9240	10/25	9195	12/46	69195	12/49	3/1958

*   No record 'B' suffixes 9/1923-2/1924.
** To N15/2 see above.

The following were ordered in 1922 from R Stephenson & Co, but were not delivered
until 1923, with steam brakes only. Works nos 3851-60. Only no 69203 had vacuum
ejector added by BR in 12/1953. They were delivered with NB numbers and there is no
record of 'B' suffixes being added 9/1923-2/1924. LNE class N15/1.

No	Date	LNE nos* 1924	Applied	1946	Applied	BR no	Applied	Withdrawn
519	1/1923	9519	10/1925	9196	4/1946	69196	4/1949	10/1962
520	1/1923	9520	8/1925	9197	5/1946	69197	9/1948	12/1959
521	2/1923	9521	3/1925	9198	5/1946	69198	5/1948	6/1960
522	2/1923	9522	2/1925	9199	4/1946	69199	4/1948	5/1961
523	3/1923	9523	12/1925	9200	12/1946	69200	12/1948	6/1958
524	3/1923	9524	10/1925	9201	1/1947	69201	5/1948	1/1958
525	3/1923	9525	3/1925	9202	7/1946	69202	2/1949	5/1960
526	3/1923	9526	2/1926	9203	12/1946	69203	11/1948	6/1958
527	3/1923	9527	8/1925	9204	1/1947	69204	11/1948	7/1962
528	3/1923	9528	10/1925	9205	11/1946	69205	12/1949	2/1960

* No record 'B' suffixes 9/1923-2/1924.

The LNER constructed a further 20 N15/1s at Cowlairs from 10/1923 to 4/1924, nos 19B,
23B, 31B, 52B, 55B, 60B, 67B, 71B, 74B-79B, 99B, 125B, 9147, 9174, 9225 and 9227. All
these had steam brakes and there were no further alterations. They became 9206-12,
9178 and 9213-24 in 1946.

Chalmers Locomotives 1921-2

4-4-2 Built by North British Locomotive Co. Works nos 22689/90.
DW 6ft 9in; LW 3ft 6in; TW 4ft 3in; WB 6ft 6in + 5ft 9½in + 7ft 3in + 8ft 3in; Cyls 21
x 28 o/s; Blr 5ft 6in x 15ft 0in; THS 1803.8 sq ft + 263 sq ft superheater; WP 180
lbs/sq in; Wt 74 tons 18 cwt.
Superheated Atlantics as Reid Atlantics after superheating. THS later 1779.5 sq ft +
241/1 sq ft superheater. Westinghouse brake and vacuum train brake control. Lever
reverse, 4240 gallon tenders. Proposals to streamline these and the Reid Atlantics
drawn up in 2/1936 were not carried out. Brakes altered to steam plus vacuum by LNE
as below. LNE class C11.

No	Date	Name	Steam brake	LNE no 1924*	Applied	Withdrawn
509	6/1921	*Duke of Rothesay*	12/1930	9509	6/1925	2/1937
510	6/1921	*The Lord Provost*	9/1931	9510	2/1925	9/1936

* 'B' suffix 1923/4 not applied.

Simplex petrol engine built by Motor Rail and Tram Co, works no 2037 3/1921.
DW 3ft 1in; WB 5ft 7in; Wt 8 tons approximately.
Purchased 1922 and replaced a horse for shunting at Kelso. LNE class Z6.

Date
   1922 'Petrol engine no 1'
 8/1927 Cab added at Cowlairs
 8/1928 Transferred to Ware. Caught fire on 12/5/1929 but repaired.
 7/1930 Numbered 8431
   1942 Allocated no 7592 but never carried
12/1943 Reclassified Y11
 6/1946 Renumbered 8189
12/1948 BR no 68189 applied
 5/1949 Renumbered 15099. Withdrawn 11/1956.

NORTH BRITISH RAILWAY

NUMBER INDEX

45	1847	2-4-0/	
		0-6-0	39 class
	1891	0-6-0	604 class
46	1847	2-4-0/	
		0-6-0	39 class
	1879	Blank	
	1880	0-6-0	497 class
	1920	0-6-0	8 class
47	1848	0-6-0	47 class
	1874	0-6-0	396 class
	1916	0-6-2T	858 class
48	1848	0-6-0	47 class
	1871	0-6-0	396 class
	1913	4-4-2T	1 class
49	1848	0-6-0	47 class
	1856	Blank	
	1860	0-4-2WT	20 class
	1878	0-6-0T	165 class
	1920	0-6-2T	858 class
50	1848	0-6-0	47 class
	1891	0-4-0ST	32 class
	1897	0-4-0ST	32 class
51	1848	0-6-0	47 class
	1872	0-6-0ST	229 class
	1913	4-4-2T	1 class
52	1848	0-6-0	47 class
	1883	4-4-0T	72 class
	1922	Blank	
53	1848	0-6-0	47 class
	1871	0-6-0	396 class
	1913	4-4-2T	1 class
54	1848	0-6-0	47 class
	1872	Blank	
	1874	0-6-0	396 class
	1916	0-6-2T	858 class
55	1849	(2-2)-2-0	
	1894	4-4-0	693 class
56	1851	2-4-0	56 class
	1868	0-6-0	56 class
	1910	0-6-0	848 class
57	1849	2-2-2	
	1868	0-6-0	396 class
	1910	0-6-0	848 class
58	1851	2-4-0	56 class
	1868	0-6-0	56 class
	1910	0-6-0	848 class
59	1851	2-4-0	56 class
	1869	0-6-0	56 class
	1910	0-6-0	848 class
60	1851	2-4-0	56 class
	1882	4-4-0T	72 class
61	1851	2-4-0	56 class
	1874	0-6-0	396 class
	1916	0-6-2T	858 class
62	1851	2-4-0	56 class
	1873	0-6-0ST	229 class
	1915	0-6-0	8 class
63	1851	2-4-0	56 class
	1873	2-4-0	40 class (renewal)
	1891	0-4-0ST	32 class
	1897	0-4-0ST	32 class
64	1850	0-6-0	64 class
	1872	0-6-0	396 class
	1913	4-4-2T	1 class

65	1850	0-6-0	64 class
	1873	Blank	
	1874	0-6-0	396 class
	1916	0-6-2T	858 class
66	1850	0-6-0	64 class
	1870	0-6-0	251 class
	1912	0-6-0T	836 class
67	1850	0-6-0	64 class
	1883	4-4-0T	72 class
	1922	Blank	
68	1851	0-6-0	64 class
	1891	0-6-0	604 class
69	1851	0-6-0	64 class
	1874	0-6-0	396 class
	1916	0-6-2T	858 class
70	1851	0-6-0	64 class
	1872	Blank	
	1874	0-6-0	396 class
	1916	0-6-2T	858 class
71	1851-2	0-6-0	64 class
	1874	0-6-0	396 class
	1916	Blank	
72	1855	0-4-2	72 class
-73	1880	4-4-0T	72 class
	1920	0-6-0	8 class
74	1855	0-4-2	72 class
-75	1882	4-4-0	72 class
	1922	Blank	
76	1860	0-6-0	
-77	1884	4-4-0T	72 class
	1922	Blank	
78	1861	0-6-0	
-79	1884	4-4-0T	72 class
	1922	Blank	
80	1861	0-6-0	80 class
-81	1885	0-6-0	566 class
82	1862	0-6-0	80 class
-83	1885	0-6-0	566 class
84	1862	0-6-0	80 class
	1880	0-6-0	497 class
	1920	0-6-0	8 class
85	1862	0-6-0	80 class
	1885	0-6-0	566 class
86	1861	ex-Peebles	
	1871	0-6-0	251 class
	1913	0-6-0	848 class
87	1861	ex-Peebles	
	1879	0-6-0	34 class
	1919	0-6-0T	836 class
88	1861	ex-Peebles	
-89	1877	0-4-2T	157 class
	1918	0-6-0	8 class
90	1861	2-4-0	90 class
-95	1889	0-4-4T	586 class
96	1861	0-4-2WT	20 class
	1878	0-6-0T	165 class
	1920	0-6-2T	858 class
97	1862	0-4-2WT	20 class
	1878	0-6-0T	165 class
	1920	0-6-2T	858 class
98	1862	0-4-2WT	20 class
	1881	4-4-0T	72 class
	1921	0-6-0	8 class

232	1865	ex-E&G	
	1891	0-4-0ST	32 class
	1896	4-4-0	693 class
	1922	Blank	
233	1865	ex-E&G	
-235	1909	0-6-0T	836 class
236	1866	2-4-0	(E&G)
	1909	0-6-0T	836 class
237	1865	ex-E&G	
-238	1909	0-6-0T	836 class
239	1867	2-4-0	(E&G)
	1909	0-4-4T	239 class
240	1865	Blank	
	1866	0-4-0ST	
	1878	0-6-0T	165 class
	1920	0-6-2T	858 class
241	1866	0-4-0ST	
	1876	0-6-0T	165 class
	1917	4-4-0	149 class
242	1865	ex-E&G	
	1876	0-6-0	100 class
	1917	4-4-0	149 class
243	1865	ex-E&G	
-245	1869	0-6-0	396 class
	1911	4-4-0	895 class
246	1865	ex-E&G	
	1869	Blank	
	1871	0-6-0	396 class
	1913	0-6-2T	858 class
247	1865	ex-E&G	(S&D)
-248	1892	0-6-0	604 class
249	1865	ex-E&G	
	1887	0-6-0	566 class
250	1865	ex-E&G	
	1893	0-6-0	604 class
251	1865	ex-E&G	(S&D)
	1867	0-6-0	251 class
	1910	0-6-2T	858 class
252	1865	ex-E&G	(S&D)
	1871	0-6-0	251 class
	1913	0-6-2T	858 class
253	1865	ex-E&G	(S&D)
-254	1870	0-6-0	251 class
	1912	0-6-0	848 class
255	1865	ex-E&G	
	1873	0-6-0ST	229 class
	1915	0-6-0	8 class
256	1865	ex-E&G	
	1872	0-6-0ST	229 class
	1913	4-4-0	149 class
257	1865	ex-E&G	
	1871	0-6-0	396 class
	1913	0-6-2T	858 class
258	1865	ex-E&G	
	1872	0-6-0ST	130 class
	1913	4-4-0	149 class
259	1865	ex-E&G	
	1875	0-6-0ST	165 class
	1917	0-6-2T	858 class
260	1865	ex-E&G	
	1873	0-6-0ST	130 class
	1915	0-6-0	8 class

261	1865	ex-E&G	
	1873	0-6-0ST	229 class
	1915	0-6-0	8 class
262	1865	ex-E&G	
	1894	4-4-0	633 class
263	1865	ex-E&G	
	1873	0-6-0ST	130 class
	1915	0-6-0	8 class
264	1865	ex-E&G	
	1871	4-4-0	
	1913	0-6-2T	858 class
265	1865	ex-E&G	
	1871	0-6-0	251 class
	1913	4-4-2T	1 class
266	1865	ex-E&G	
	1872	0-6-0	396 class
	1913	4-4-0	149 class
267	1865	ex-E&G	
	1871	0-6-0	396 class
	1913	4-4-2T	1 class
268	1865	ex-Monkland	
	1883	4-4-0T	72 class
	1922	Blank	
269	1865	ex-Monkland	
	1887	0-6-0	566 class
270	1865	ex-Monkland	
	1876	0-6-0	100 class
	1919	4-4-0	149 class
271	1865	ex-Monkland	
	1879	0-6-0	34 class
	1919	0-6-0T	836 class
272	1865	ex-Monkland	
-273	1880	0-6-0	497 class
	1921	0-6-0	8 class
274	1865	ex-Monkland	
	1877	0-6-0T	165 class
	1918	0-6-0	8 class
275	1865	ex-Monkland	
	1875	0-6-0	396 class
	1917	Blank	
276	1865	ex-Monkland	
	1874	0-6-0	396 class
	1917	0-6-2T	858 class
277	1865	ex-Monkland	
	1879	0-6-0	34 class
	1919	0-6-0T	836 class
278	1865	ex-Monkland	
	1876	0-6-0	100 class
	1919	4-4-0	149 class
279	1865	ex-Monkland	
	1879	0-6-0	34 class
	1919	0-6-0T	836 class
280	1865	ex-E&G	(S&D)
	1893	0-6-0	604 class
281	1865	ex-Monkland	
	1876	0-6-0	100 class
	1919	4-4-0	149 class
282	1865	ex-Monkland	
	1866	0-6-0ST	
	1910	0-6-2T	858 class
283	1865	ex-E&G	
	1875	0-6-0	396 class
	1917	Blank	

284	1865	ex-E&G	
	1875	0-6-0T	165 class
	1917	Blank	
285	1865	ex-E&G	
	1875	0-6-0	396 class
	1916	Blank	
286	1865	ex-E&G	
	1870	0-6-0ST	112 class
	1883	0-6-0	497 class
287	1865	ex-E&G	
	1876	0-6-0	100 class
	1919	4-4-0	149 class
288	1865	ex-E&G	
-290	1879	0-6-0	34 class
	1919	0-6-0T	836 class
291	1865	ex-E&G	
	1875	0-6-0	396 class
	1917	4-4-0	149 class
292	1865	ex-E&G	
	1876	0-6-0	100 class
	1918	0-6-0	8 class
293	1865	ex-E&G	
	1894	4-4-0	633 class
294	1865	ex-E&G	
	1882	4-4-0T	72 class
	1922	Blank	
295	1865	ex-Monkland	
	1877	0-6-0T	165 class
	1918	0-6-0	8 class
296	1865	ex-Monkland	
	1879	0-6-0	34 class
	1919	0-6-0	8 class
297	1865	ex-Monkland	
	1876	0-6-0T	165 class
	1918	0-6-0	8 class
298	1865	ex-Monkland	
	1875	0-6-0	396 class
	1917	4-4-0	149 class
299	1865	ex-Monkland	
	1880	4-4-0T	72 class
	1921	0-6-0	8 class
300	1865	ex-Monkland	
-302	1879	0-6-0	497 class
	1919	0-6-0	8 class
303	1865	ex-Monkland	
	1879	0-6-0	497 class
	1920	0-6-0	8 class
304	1865	ex-Monkland	
	1876	0-6-0	100 class
	1918	0-6-0	8 class
305	1865	ex-Monkland	
	1877	0-6-0	100 class
	1918	0-6-0	8 class
306	1865	ex-E&G	(C&DJ)
	1879	0-6-0	497 class
	1920	0-6-0	8 class
307	1865	ex-E&G	(C&DJ)
	1872	0-6-0	396 class
	1913	4-4-0	149 class
308	1865	ex-E&G	(C&DJ)
	1874	0-6-0ST	32 class
	1887	0-4-0ST	32 class
	1899	0-4-0ST	32 class
309	1865	ex-E&G	(C&DJ)
	1871	0-6-0	396 class
	1913	4-4-2T	1 class
310	1865	ex-E&G	(C&DJ)
	1874	0-6-0ST	32 class
	1887	0-4-0ST	32 class
	1899	0-4-0ST	32 class
311	1865	ex-E&G	(C&DJ)
	1872	0-4-0ST	18 class
	1883	0-6-0	497 class
312	1865	ex-E&G	(C&DJ)
	1884	ex-161A	
	1895	4-4-0	633 class
313	1865	ex-Monkland	
	1878	0-6-0T	165 class
	1919	0-6-0	8 class
314	1865	ex-Monkland	
	1877	0-4-2T	157 class
	1918	0-6-0	8 class
315	1865	ex-Monkland	
	1877	0-6-0	100 class
	1918	0-6-0	8 class
316	1865	ex-Monkland	
	1884	4-4-0T	72 class
	1922	Blank	
317	1865	ex-E&G	
-328	1903	4-4-0T	317 class
329	1865	ex-E&G	
-330	1906	0-6-0	848 class
331	1865	ex-E&G	
-333	1909	4-4-0	331 class
334	1865	ex-E&G	
	1909	0-4-4T	239 class
335	1865	Blank	
-337	1868	0-6-0	396 class
	1910	0-6-0	848 class
338	1865	Blank	
-340	1869	0-6-0	396 class
	1911	4-4-0	895 class
341	1865	Blank	
-346	1866	2-4-0	90 class
	1889	0-4-0ST	32 class
	1896	4-4-0	693 class
347	1865	Blank	
	1868	0-6-0	396 class
	1910	0-6-0	848 class
348	1865	Blank	
	1868	0-6-0	396 class
	1911	0-6-0	848 class
349	1865	ex-E&G	
-356	1909	0-4-4T	239 class
357	1866	Blank	
-358	1868	0-4-0	
	1892	0-6-0	604 class
359	1866	Blank	
-362	1869	0-6-0	396 class
	1911	4-4-0	895 class
363	1866	Blank	
	1869	0-6-0	396 class
	1912	4-4-0	400 class
364	1866	0-6-0	80 class
-371	1909	0-6-0	848 class

372	1867	0-6-0	80 class		476	1877	4-4-0	476 class
-373	1909	0-6-0	848 class			1918	0-6-0	8 class
374	1867	0-6-0	80 class		477	1877	4-4-0	476 class
-375	1910	0-6-0	848 class		-479	1919	0-6-0	8 class
376	1868	0-6-0	396 class		480	1877	0-4-0T	157 class
-381	1910	0-6-0	848 class			1919	0-6-0	8 class
382	1866	2-4-0	90 class		481	1877	ex-L&EF	
	1909	4-4-0	331 class		-482	1883	0-6-0	497 class
383	1866	2-4-0	90 class		483	1877	ex-L&EF	
-385	1910	4-4-0	331 class			1884	4-4-0T	72 class
386	1866	2-4-0	90 class		484	1877	ex-L&EF	
-388	1910	0-6-2T	858 class			1884	0-6-0	566 class
389	1868	2-4-0	90 class		485	1877	ex-L&EF	
-393	1910	0-6-2T	858 class			1878	0-6-0T	165 class
394	1867	0-4-0				1919	0-6-0	8 class
-395	1894	4-4-0	693 class		486	1878	4-4-0	476 class
396	1867	0-6-0	396 class		-489	1919	0-6-0	8 class
-398	1910	0-6-2T	858 class		490	1879	4-4-0	476 class
399	1868	0-6-0	396 class			1920	4-4-0	149 class
	1910	0-6-2T	858 class		491	1879	4-4-0	476 class
400	1869	0-6-0	396 class			1920	0-6-0	8 class
	1912	4-4-0	400 class		492	1879	4-4-0	476 class
401	1871	ex-F&CJ			-493	1920	4-4-0	149 class
-403	1879	0-6-0	34 class		494	1879	4-4-0T	494 class
	1920	0-6-0	8 class		-496	1920	4-4-0	149 class
404	1871	ex-F&CJ			497	1879	0-6-0	497 class
	1883	ex-158A			-501	1920	4-4-0	400 class
	1895	4-4-0	633 class		502	1879	ex-GBH&C	
405	1872	0-6-0ST	229 class		-505	1920	4-4-0	149 class
-406	1913	4-4-0	149 class		506	1880	0-6-0	497 class
407	1872	0-6-0	396 class		-508	1921	0-6-0	8 class
-408	1913	4-4-0	149 class		509	1880	0-6-0	497 class
409	1872	0-6-0	396 class		-510	1921	4-4-2	509 class
-417	1914	4-4-0	400 class		511	1880	0-6-0	497 class
418	1873	2-4-0	418 class		-516	1921	4-4-2T	438 class
-419	1914	4-4-0	400 class		517	1880	0-6-0	497 class
420	1873	4-4-0	420 class			1921	0-6-0	8 class
-423	1914	4-4-0	400 class		518	1881	0-6-0	497 class
424	1873	2-4-0	418 class			1921	0-6-0	8 class
-428	1915	4-4-0	400 class		519	1881	0-6-0	497 class
429	1873	2-4-0	418 class		-533			
	1915	0-6-0	8 class		534	1882	0-6-0	497 class
430	1873	0-6-0	251 class		-545			
-432	1915	0-6-0	8 class		546	1882	0-4-0ST	546 class
433	1873	0-6-0	251 class		-547	1899	0-4-0ST	32 class
-437	1916	0-6-0	8 class		548	1882	0-6-0	497 class
438	1873	0-6-0	251 class		-553			
-442	1915	4-4-2T	438 class		554	1883	0-6-0	497 class
443	1873	0-6-0	251 class		-565			
-444	1916	4-4-2T	438 class		566	1883	0-6-0	566 class
445	1874	0-6-0	251 class		-571			
-449	1916	4-4-2T	438 class		572	1884	0-6-0	566 class
450	1874	0-6-0	396 class		-573			
-452	1916	4-4-2T	438 class		574	1884	4-4-0	574 class
453	1875	0-6-0	396 class		-579			
	1917	0-6-2T	858 class		580	1884	0-6-0	566 class
454	1876	0-6-0	100 class		-585			
-465	1918	0-6-0	8 class		586	1886	0-4-4T	586 class
466	1877	0-6-0	100 class		-591			
-469	1918	0-6-0	8 class		592	1886	4-4-0	592 class
470	1877	0-6-0	100 class		-594			
-473	1919	0-6-0	8 class		595	1887	4-4-0	592 class
474	1876	2-2-2			-597			
-475	1909	0-4-4T	239 class					

598	1888	4-4-0	592 class
-603			
604	1888	0-6-0	604 class
-609			
610	1889	0-4-0ST	
	1891	0-4-0ST	32 class
	1899	0-4-0ST	32 class
611	1889	0-4-0ST	
-612	1892	0-6-0	604 class
613	1889	0-6-0	604 class
-622			
623	1890	0-6-0	604 class
-632			
633	1890	4-4-0	633 class
-642			
643	1891	0-6-0	604 class
-677			
678	1892	0-6-0	604 class
-692			
693	1894	4-4-0	693 class
-694	1921	Blank	
695	1894	4-4-0	693 class
696	1894	4-4-0	693 class
-697	1922	Blank	
698	1894	4-4-0	693 class
-700	1921	Blank	
701	1894	4-4-0	693 class
	1922	Blank	
702	1896	4-4-0	693 class
-703	1920	Blank	
704	1896	4-4-0	693 class
	1922	Blank	
705	1896	0-6-0	604 class
-716			
717	1897	0-6-0	604 class
-728			
729	1898	4-4-0	729 class
-740			
741	1898	0-6-0	604 class
-747			
748	1899	0-6-0	604 class
-764			
765	1899	4-4-0	729 class
-770			
771	1900	0-6-0	604 class
-794			
795	1900	0-6-0T	795 class
-800			

In 1895, nos 801-882 were used for duplicate list locomotives formerly on the 'A' list. From 1/1896 to 7/1899, nos 883-903 were used for further locomotives transferred to the duplicate list. In 1900/01, all duplicate list locomotives were renumbered 1001-1103.

801	1900	0-6-0T	795 class
-804			
805	1901	0-6-0T	795 class
-834			
835	1901	0-4-0ST	
836	1904	0-6-0T	836 class
-839			

840	1905	0-6-0T	836 class
-847			
848	1906	0-6-0	848 class
-857			
858	1909	0-6-2T	858 class
-863			
864	1909	4-4-0	331 class
-867			
868	1906	4-4-2	868 class
-881			
882	1906	4-4-0	882 class
-893			
894	1909	4-4-0	331 class
895	1909	4-4-0	895 class
-900			
901	1911	4-4-2	868 class
-906			
907	1912	0-6-2T	858 class
-926			

From 1900/01, nos 1001 up were duplicate list numbers including those renumbered from 801-903, the highest number reached being 1481 in 1922.

GREAT NORTH OF SCOTLAND RAILWAY

Introduction

The Great North of Scotland was promoted as a railway from Inverness to Aberdeen with powers to amalgamate with the Aberdeen Railway. Its aims reflected in its rather grand title, but on the direct route from Aberdeen to Inverness it got no further than Keith. Powers granted in 1847 to amalgamate with the Aberdeen Railway did not come to fruition, and the Aberdeen Railway amalgamated instead with the Scottish Midland Junction to the south as the Scottish North Eastern. By taking over the working of the Morayshire Railway, the Great North reached Elgin over that company's line from Craigellachie.
The difficulty of raising capital forced the company to modify its plans, and the initial Act of 1846 was for a line from Kittybrewster, near Aberdeen, to Huntly.
The company had made a successful bid to buy the ailing Aberdeenshire Canal (incorporated 1796, opened 6/1805) for £36,000 in 1845 but, surprisingly, powers for the transfer of the canal were omitted from the Act, which caused legal difficulties.
The canal ran from Aberdeen harbour to Port Elphinstone, near Inverurie, and it was decided to construct the Inverurie to Huntly section of the railway first using the canal to transport supplies. Even so it was the summer of 1852 before the Directors could authorise the contractors, Mitchell and Dean, to begin work. The first sod was cut on 25th November 1852 at Oyne near Inverurie.
Despite a harsh winter in 1853, which brought work to a standstill, the Huntly section was completed swiftly, whilst lawyers still struggled to reach individual settlements with each canal shareholder and mortgagees. In an effort to break the legal log jam, possibly with the tacit approval of the Directors, Mitchell and Dean resorted to the desperate measure of breaching the canal, draining the pound above Kintore into the river Don, stranding several boats and causing bad feelings locally.
The breach was temporarily repaired and the boats refloated, but it did have the effect of speeding the legal transfer of the canal. Work could then start on the section to Kittybrewster using the bed of the canal for a little under half the distance.
The line from Kittybrewster to Huntley was opened on 12th September 1854 for goods and on 20th September 1854 for passengers after an opening ceremony on 19th September.
Meanwhile, Inverness parties led by the Earls of Grant and Seafield, impatient for a link with Aberdeen, promoted the Inverness and Nairn and the Inverness and Aberdeen Junction Railways which were incorporated in 1854 and 1856 to complete the line from Aberdeen to Keith. These companies became part of the Highland Railway.
The GNS line from Huntly to Keith was authorised in 1855 and opened on 11th October 1856, and the I&AJ line to Keith was opened 18th August 1858 linking Inverness to Aberdeen, where the Great North line had been extended from Kittybrewster to Aberdeen Waterloo using the line of the remaining section of canal. This extension was opened 24th September 1855 for goods and 1st April 1856 for passengers. A branch from Inverurie to Old Meldrum was opened on 1st July 1856. (Inverury and Old Meldrum Junction Railway, worked by the GNS).
Connections and probably some through coaches were made and exchanged between the GNS and the I&A at Keith, but it was not until 1908 that there was any through working of locomotives.
A through route to the south was now available over the Scottish North Eastern and the Scottish Central, but a change of stations was necessary as the Aberdeen Railway had established its terminus at Guild Street from 2nd August 1854, which was also being used by trains of the Deeside Railway.
The Great North worked the Aberdeen and Turriff Railway and its extension, the Banff Macduff and Turriff Extension Railway, opened to Turriff on 5th September 1857 and Macduff on 4th June 1860. Also worked was the Alford Valley Railway from Kintore to Alford, opened on 21st March 1859. Another worked company was the Formantine and Buchan Railway, opened from Dyce to Mintlaw on 18th July 1861, and extended to Peterhead on 3rd July 1862 and Maud Junction to Fraserburgh on 24th

April 1865. A further extension to Peterhead harbour was opened on 9th August 1865. The need for a shorter route to the south from Inverness could not be denied and its opening by the Inverness and Aberdeen Junction Railway in 1863, becoming the Highland Railway in 1865, diverted through traffic away from the GNS, including the mails, and brought the two companies into competition.

Despite financial difficulties the Great North extended the Keith and Dufftown Railway (opened 19th February 1862 for goods, 21st February 1862 for passengers) with which it had a working agreement as the Strathspey Railway to Nethy Bridge on 1st July 1863, and to join the Highland at Boat of Garten on 1st August 1866. This line connected with the Morayshire Railway at Craigellachie, the working of which was taken over by the Great North in 1863. Another working agreement in 1863 was the Banffshire Railway to Banff and Portsoy.

Until 1866, the only portion of the system that the company owned outright was the main line from Aberdeen to Keith. All the rest, which exceeded it in mileage, was under working arrangements with nominally independent companies. However, on 1st August 1866 all of the above companies, except the Morayshire and Banffshire, which had their own locomotives (qv), were merged with the GNS.

In 1866, the Scottish North Eastern became part of the Caledonian and there was some discussion of an amalgamation with the GNS also. This did not come about, but agreement was reached for a new through joint station in Aberdeen, the GNS opening a line from Kittybrewster through the Denburn Valley on 4th November 1867, the cost having been shared by the two companies.

Shortly before this, the Deeside Railway, which had at one time looked to be absorbed by the SNE, was leased by the Great North on 1st September 1866 (qv).

A new and more convenient station was opened at Macduff on 1st July 1872, and a new coast line from Portsoy was opened to Tochineal on 1st April 1884, and to Garmouth on 5th April 1886 (goods) 1st May 1886 (passengers), from where it connected with a line from Elgin already opened on 12th August 1884, making a second Great North route to Elgin in addition to the original route via the Highland Railway from Keith.

In 1887, a suburban service was introduced between Dyce and Aberdeen which eventually reached a schedule of twenty trains a day, and in 1894 a similar service was provided on the Deeside line between Aberdeen and Culter. Additional stations were opened and these trains became known as 'Subbies'.

On 2nd August 1897, the Cruden Bay branch from Ellon on the Buchan line to Boddam was opened.

Throughout the 19th century, relations with the Highland Railway were punctuated by frequent disputes over through services and connections, the Highland reluctant to accept Elgin as an official exchange point in addition to Keith, and the Great North supporting schemes which would give it access to Inverness.

In 1897, the GNS applied to Parliament for running powers into Inverness, and although this was not granted it did establish Elgin as an official exchange point and through services were increased to eight, four via Keith and four via Elgin.

Relations between the two companies improved to the point where in 1905 there was a proposal to amalgamate from 1907. Although this was approved by both boards the Highland Board did not feel that it had sufficient support from shareholders and the scheme was dropped.

In 1908, however, it was agreed that certain trains could be worked through to and from Inverness and Aberdeen by locomotives of either company. Due to wartime pressures on the Highland Railway, the Great North worked all trains to Inverness from late 1914 until at least 1916, and ran some 500,000 miles over Highland metals during the war as a whole. The St Combs branch from Fraserburgh was opened on 1st July 1903 under the Light Railways Act, and worked 'one engine in steam' without signals.

At Cruden Bay, an hotel was opened in 1899 one mile from the railway and connected to it by an electric tramway to 3ft 6½in gauge. Two single-deck tramcars and three goods trailers were provided.

The Station Hotel at Aberdeen was purchased by the company in 1910, and between May 1913 and July 1914 the joint station was completely rebuilt, but the outbreak of war delayed the completion of the work until 1920.

The Great North were also pioneers of motorbus services. Starting in 1904 with a service between Braemar and Ballater, services were introduced to Aberchirder, Cluny, Echt, Midmar, Newburgh, Bellabeg, Tomintoul, Corgaff, Rosehearty, New Aberdour and Methlick. These services were continued and further developed by the LNER.

Locomotive Superintendents

Daniel Kinear Clark	1853-5	Resigned
James Folds Ruthven	1855-7	Resigned
William Cowan	1857-83	Retired
James Manson	1883-90	Resigned
James Johnson	1890-94	Resigned
William Pickersgill	1894-1914	Resigned
Thomas E Heywood	1914-23	Formation of LNER

Clark was appointed in October 1853 before the railway was opened and the company's first locomotive works at Kittybrewster were still being constructed. He had served an apprenticeship at Thomas Edington & Son in Glasgow and had been employed by the North British Railway. He was a exceptionally gifted engineer, and set up an engineering consultancy at the early age of thirty.
For the opening of the railway he designed and ordered from William Fairburn & Sons of Manchester twelve 2-4-0s, seven intended for passenger working and five for goods. Only two of these arrived in time for the opening to Huntly with three arriving soon after. As the first two were soon out of action, one due to a collision at Kittybrewster and the other with a mechanical defect, the other three had to handle all traffic until the end of the year. The goods engines were not delivered until the summer and autumn of 1855. A locomotive with driver was hired from the Lancashire & Yorkshire Railway from 8/55 until 11/55.
At this time, Clark was also working on his book, *Railway Machinery*, which was the first and most comprehensive text book on the subject, published in 1855, and he obviously hoped to combine his writing and consultancy work with his GNS duties. However, he had agreed to a condition in his contract that he should reside in Aberdeen and be responsible for supervision of the Kittybrewster works. The Board were not prepared to accept his assertion that this could be left to an assistant, and as he was not willing to move he resigned. He later published other technical works, *Railway Locomotives* (1856, 1860), *Manual Rules for Mechanical Engineers* (1877, 1884) and *Tramways and their Construction and Working* (1878, 1881).
He was succeeded by his works foreman John Folds Ruthven who, presumably, was the man he intended to supervise the works anyhow. Ruthven ordered four more 2-4-0s, which were basically as the first seven passenger engines but with a smoke consuming device invented by Clark, and two 0-4-0WTs from Beyer Peacock which gave excellent service banking and shunting for some sixty years before being sold, one of them still being in service as late a 1943. He resigned in 1867 to enter private practice in association with Clark.
Born in Edinburgh, William Cowan had worked in the locomotive department of the Arbroath and Forfar Railway in 1839, and subsequently the Edinburgh and Glasgow Railway and the Great Northern Railway.
Further 2-4-0s, similar to the previous goods engines, were ordered from Stephenson's and also had Clark's smoke consuming equipment These were the last 2-4-0s constructed for the GNS, the 4-4-0s then being adopted as standard. Out of some 163 locomotives built by or for the company, no less than 112 were 4-4-0s and there were never any 0-6-0s.
Cowan continued to provide outside cylinders however, as on the 2-4-0s, and his 4-4-0s were amongst the earliest in the UK.
After Cowan's retirement, Manson introduced inside cylindered 4-4-0s. He had been manager of the Kilmarnock works of the Glasgow and South Western Railway after a period serving as a marine engineer with the Bibby Line, and had also been apprentice at Kilmarnock under Patrick Stirling.
Polished brass domes were supplanted by round-topped, cast-iron, ones in the centre of the boiler on his locomotives, and Salter safety valves replaced Ramsbottom ones on the firebox. Clark's smoke consuming apparatus was retained in a modified form.

Westinghouse brake was introduced on class N when built in the place of steam brake
and earlier locomotives so fitted.
The two locomotives of class N were the only ones built at Kittybrewster, probably
from parts supplied by outside firms. The works could only hold four locomotives
under cover, and much repair work had to be done in the open.
The Manson 4-4-0 design became the standard form. Nine six-coupled tank engines for
shunting were also used on the Aberdeen suburban services. He also invented an
automatic tablet exchange apparatus.
James Johnson trained under his father, Samuel Johnson, at Derby and returned there
after his resignation from the Great North.
With class S, which came out in 1893, use of the Clark smoke consuming device was
discontinued. The 0-4-4Ts class R, built for the Aberdeen suburban services, had been
designed by Manson, but Johnson introduced modifications making the boiler, valve gear
and fireboxes standard with the 4-4-0s.
Johnson also incorporated certain Midland features in his designs, such as chimneys
and safety valves placed on domes, which were altered by Pickersgill to firebox
mountings.
William Pickersgill had spent all of his previous working life on the Great Eastern
Railway, where he had been a pupil at Stratford in 1876 and a Whitworth Exhibitioner.
His class T 4-4-0s were similar to the Johnson class S, but with closed domes and
safety valves on the firebox. However, his class V of 1899, although basically to the
same design, had side window cabs. Eight of this class were built at the new works
opened at Inverurie in 1902. Kittybrewster subsequently took on the work of
maintaining the motorbuses.
He also introduced two rail motors which were tried out on the Aberdeen suburban
services and on the Lossiemouth and St Combs branches but were not very successful.
Pickersgill left in 1914 to become Locomotive Superintendent of the Caledonian, and
Thomas Heywood, who had been assistant Locomotive Superintendent on the Taff Vale
Railway, was appointed.
Four 0-4-2T shunting engines were delivered in 1915, and it was not until 1920 that
further 4-4-0s of his design were turned out, two built at Inverurie, to class F.
These differed little from class V in appearance, but were fitted with Robinson
superheaters. Others from earlier classes were superheated subsequently. The LNER
regarded classes V and F as one class, D40.
A new livery was introduced in 1917 in place of the previous green with various shades
at different periods with locomotives now painted black lined with yellow and red.
This was applied to class F with the company crest on the leading splashers below the
curved brass nameplates.
Driving position was on the left.

LNER Renumbering

Under the temporary scheme introduced in 9/1923, the GNS was allotted the suffix
letter S but not many locomotives carried this. From 2/1924 until the 1946
renumbering GNS numbers had 6800 added.

BR Renumbering

In common with the other LNE locomotives, BR added 60000 to the 1946 LNER numbers.

GREAT NORTH OF SCOTLAND RAILWAY

Absorbed Companies

Morayshire Railway

Incorporated 10th July 1846. Opened 10th August 1852 Lossiemouth to Elgin; 23rd August 1858 Orton (Inverness and Aberdeen Junction Railway) to Rothes with running powers over I&AJR between Elgin and Orton. Inadequacy of locomotives (see below) and slack working practices caused the I&AJR to withdraw running powers, causing Orton to Rothes branch to be worked independently. 23rd December 1858; Rothes to Dandaleith. Direct line Elgin to Rothes opened 30th December 1961 (goods), 1st January 1862 (passengers). Working taken over by the GNS 1st July 1863, and extension from Dandaleith to connect with the GNS at Craigellachie opened on same date. Orton to Rothes section closed 1866. Company amalgamated with the GNS 1881.

4 Locomotives as under:

2-2-0T Built by Neilson & Co. Works nos 51/2.
DW 5ft 6in or 5ft 0in; LW 3ft 0in; Cyls 10 x 16 (vertical); WP 120 lbs/sq in; Wt 14 tons; Vertical boiler. Designed by J Samuel of the Eastern Counties Railway. These locomotives were very inadequate for the traffic and were partly the cause of the withdrawal of I&AJR running powers.

No	Name	Date	
1	*Elgin*	1852	In collision head on with no 2, 23rd April 1857, killing the engineer Mr Taylor
		1863	Still in use in 1863, but transferred to the GNS at nil valuation and probably soon withdrawn
2	*Lossiemouth*	1852	In collision with no 1, 23rd April 1857, as above
		1859	Withdrawn. Out of use and taken over by the GNS at nil valuation and not put into stock.

Pending delivery of nos 3 & 4 Neilson's arranged for a locomotive to be hired from the Caledonian and Dumbarton Railway.

2-4-0ST Built by Neilson & Co. Works nos 487 & 663.
No 3 - DW 4ft 10in; Cyls 12 x 18 o/s; THS 615 sq ft; Wt 25 tons.
No 4 - DW 4ft 9½in; Cyls 14 x 18 o/s; THS 674 sq ft; Wt 22 tons.
No domes. Copper capped chimneys. Side and saddle tanks. Sheet iron cabs added later. Names removed by the GNS.

No	Name	Date	1863 GNS no	Rebuilt	Sold or Scrapped
3	*Glen Grant*	6/1859	**41**	1874	1/1885
4	*Lesmurdie*	2/1861	**42**	1874	7/1883

Deeside Railway

Incorporated 6th July 1846. Opened 8th September 1853, Ferryhill to Banchory; 2nd December 1859, Banchory to Aboyne. Operated by Aberdeen Railway from Ferryhill until 1854. Running powers to Aberdeen Guild St from 8/1854. Leased by the GNS 1st September 1866, and extension to Ballater opened 17th October 1866. Amalgamated with the GNS 31st August 1875. Livery was dark blue with black lining.

8 locomotives as under. (It would seem likely that the intention was to number these 39, 49-54 in the GNS stock, but this was amended to 39, 49-53 when Deeside No 3 was found to be unserviceable.)

0-4-2T Built by Hawthorn's of Leith. (No 2 works no 157*).
Similar to Banffshire locomotives. DW 4ft 6in; Cyls 13 x 18 o/s.

No	Date		
1	2/1854	Sold 5/1865	
2	12/1854	To GNS, **39** 1867. Scrapped 7/1883.	

* The works no of 157 is suspect at this date. Nos 83/4 are recorded for Caledonian 184/5 in 1852 and the next recorded works number is 152 for a South African order as late as 1859.

0-4-2 Built by Dodds & Co, Rotherham.
DW 4ft 6in; Cyls 14¼ x 22.
Dodds patent valve gear.

No	Date	
3	1854	Taken over by GNS at nil valuation and broken up due to inefficient operation circa 3/1871

0-4-2 Built by Hawthorn's of Leith in 1856 (No 5 works no 195).
DW 4ft 6³/8in; Cyls 15¼ x 24 o/s. As Banffshire Railway *Keith* 28 tons.
Four wheel tender.

		1867	
No	Date	GNS no	Scrapped
4	3/1857	**49**	1876
5	7/1859	**50**	5/1876

0-4-2 Built by Hawthorn's of Leith. (No 6 works no 232).
Dimensions similar to 4 and 5.
Six wheel tender, 2000 gallons water, 2 tons coal.

		1867	
No	Date	GNS no	
6	6/1860	**51**	Withdrawn 11/1878
8	9/1866	**53**	Withdrawn 11/1878

0-4-2 Purchased from GNS ex-Banff, Portsoy & Strathisla no 4 (see below) possibly replacing no 1. Date of purchase 3/1864 numbered 7.

Banffshire Railway

Incorporated 27th July 1857 as the **Banff, Portsoy and Strathisla Railway**. Opened 2nd
August 1859, Grange to Banff and branch Tillynaught to Portsoy. Name changed to
Banffshire Railway 1st February 1863, and worked by the GNS from that date.
Amalgamated with the GNS 31st August 1867.

4 locomotives as under:

0-4-2T Built by Hawthorn's of Leith. Works nos 172/3.
DW 5ft 0in or 5ft 2in; TW 3ft 0in; Cyls 12½ or 13 x 16 or 18; Wt 20 tons.
Front weatherboard. Raised firebox, dome on top with Salter safety valve.

			1863			
No	Name	Date	GNS no	Rebuilt	Scrapped	
1	*Banff*	1859	**37**	1874	6/1885	Both sold to contractor
2	*Portsoy*	1859	**38**	1874	6/1885	on Elgin coast line.

Nos 3 & 4 have been quoted in reverse order with one of them (no 3 according to JF
McEwan, *Locomotives of the Caledonian Railway*, Locomotive Magazine Volume 48 page 73
(1942) and no 4 according to HA Vallance, *The Great North of Scotland Railway*) having
been purchased second-hand from the Scottish Central Railway ex-their no 23 (Vol 4
page 24). The Great North of Scotland Railway Association in their abstract no 17
(October 1989) state that both were built by Hawthorn's of Leith, and were supplied
new, quoting Banffshire Board minutes. Only one of Hawthorn's works numbers is known,
and as the Hawthorn works list has not survived, it is not possible to verify this
from that source.
The Scottish Central 0-4-2 no 23 was in an accident in 1860 and was removed from
stock. The possibility must be considered, therefore, that it was reconstructed after
the accident, perhaps by Hawthorn's of Leith, which could account for the Banffshire
Board being informed that it was new, but this can only be speculation.
The GNSRA also quote identical measurements for both locomotives, but also state that
no 3 was like Deeside no 5, and no 4 was like Deeside no 3, which had differing
dimensions.

0-4-2 Built by Hawthorn's of Leith. Works no 196 (1858).
DW 4ft 6in; Cyls 15 x 21; Wt 28 tons. Purchased from stock.
Domed firebox. Salter safety valves. Hawthorn standard design.

No	Name	Date	
3	*Keith*	11/1859	
		1863	To GNS **39** and name removed
		3/1864	Sold to Deeside Railway as above
		1867	To GNS **52**
		7/1877	Withdrawn

0-4-2 See above.

No	Name	Date	
4	*Strathisla*	7/1861	
		1863	To GNS no **40** and name removed
		1878	Renumbered **63**
		10/1879	Withdrawn

GREAT NORTH OF SCOTLAND RAILWAY

Clark Locomotives 1854-57

2-4-0 Built by Fairbairn & Sons.
DW 5ft 6in; LW 3ft 6in; Cyls 15 x 20 o/s; THS 749 sq ft (1-7), 966 sq ft (15-18);
Wt 23¼ tons; WP 130 lbs/sq in.
Outside bearings on LW, raised firebox, tall bell-mouth chimney, dome on firebox. No
cab when built, but weatherboards added to 1854 batch, and when built on 1857 batch
together with sandboxes. Dome was brass with Salter safety valve, and chimneys were
originally copper capped. Sanding front and rear. Livery was a medium shade of green
without lining, red buffer beams with number plate on footplate side sheet. Four-
wheel tender. Nos 15-18 were originally 16 x 22 cyls, with eccentric crank pins, and
had smoke prevention apparatus. The GNSRA quotes earlier withdrawal dates which would
obviate transfer to A list.

| | | Duplicate | | |
No	Date	no	date	Withdrawn
1	7/1854	1A	12/1878	1879 or 6/1878 Stirling type cab 1860s
2	7/1854	2A	1/1879	1880 or 6/1878
3	8/1854	3A	1/1879	1882 or 10/1879
4	9/1854	4A	5/1888	1897/8
5	9/1854	5A	2/1887	1892 To Engineering Department c1883
6	10/1854	6A	12/1887	1890 or 1886 Stirling type cab mid 1880s.
7	12/1854	7A	5/1888	Rebuilt about 1883 with cab as above.
				Scrapped about 1898-1900.
15	4/1857	15A	5/1884	1883/4 Rebuilt 15½in cyls later reverting
				to 15in. Rounded cab as above 1860s.
16	4/1857	16A	5/1884	1883/4 Rebuilt as 15
17	5/1857	17A	4/1888	1892 Stirling type cab mid 1880s
18	5/1857	18A	5/1888	1891 Stirling type cab mid 1880s

2-4-0 (goods) Built by Fairbairn & Sons.
DW 5ft 0in; LW 3ft 6in; Cyls 15 x 20 o/s; THS 808 sq ft.
Originally ordered as 0-6-0. Apart from smaller DW, otherwise as 1 class. Sandboxes
and weatherboards added as 1 class and Stirling type cabs in mid 1880s.

| | | Duplicate | | |
No	Date	no	date	Withdrawn
8	6/1855			1883/4 Stirling type cab 1860s
9	6/1855			1887/8
10	8/1855	10A	4/1888	1888
11	9/1855			1883
12	10/1855	12A	5/1890	1897 To Engineering Dept in place of no 5

Ruthven Locomotives 1855-6

0-4-0WT Built by Beyer Peacock & Co. Works nos 19 & 20.
DW 4ft 6in; Cyls 15 x 24 o/s; Blr 4ft 2in x 11ft 0in; THS 890 sq ft later 798 sq ft;
WP 130 lbs/sq in; Wt 24 tons later 25 tons.
Large dome on centre of boiler. 350 gallons water. 1 Ton of coal. Cab added later.
Rebuilt 1876 without change of appearance. Rebuilt by Pickersgill with flush boiler
instead of raised firebox, dome on centre of boiler with safety valve and cab
replaced. Believed to have had spectacle plate added before cab fitted. Clark smoke
prevention apparatus. £1850 each.

| | | Duplicate | | Rebuilt | |
No	Date	no	date	flush blr	
13	12/1855	13A	6/1890	6/1887	Sold 12/1916 to James Barclay*
14	1/1856	14A	6/1890	5/1887	Sold 12/1916 to James Barclay*.
					Resold 1919 to Tareni Colliery, Pontarve,
					Glamorgan. Still in service 1943.

* Both hired 1915 to War Department at Lenabo airship station.

Cowan Locomotives 1859-79

2-4-0 Built by R Stephenson & Co. Works nos 1281-9.
DW 5ft 1in (19-24), 5ft 6in (25-7); Cyls 16 x 22 o/s; THS 965.6 sq ft later 1036 sq
ft; WP 120 lbs/sq in, later 140 lbs. Weatherboards, drop gate and sanding gear.
Clark smoke consuming apparatus. Raised firebox, open splashers and cabs. Later
class B. Four wheel tender. 950 gallons water, 2 tons coal.

No	Date	Duplicate no	date	Rebuilt		Withdrawn
19	12/1859	19A	2/1896	1/1882		6/1905
20	12/1859	20A	2/1896	3/1881	Westinghouse brake and six wheel tender	12/1900
21	1/1860	21A	2/1896	5/1883	Westinghouse brake as 20	4/1907
22	2/1860	22A	2/1896	8/1882	Westinghouse brake as 20	4/1907
23	4/1860	23A	3/1896	12/1882	Steam brake	6/1904
24	5/1860	24A	3/1896	2/1880	Steam brake	1/1902
25	5/1861	25A	10/1899	8/1882		4/1907
26	5/1861	26A	10/1899	3/1881		4/1907
27	5/1861			11/1882	Westinghouse brake retaining four wheel tender	4/1909

4-4-0 Built by R Stephenson & Co. Works nos 1290-2, 1431-6.
DW 5ft 1in; Cyls 16 x 22 o/s; Blr 3ft 9¾in x 11ft 4½in; THS 965.6 sq ft later 1036 sq
ft; WP 120 lbs/sq in later 140 lbs/sq in; Wt in wo 32tons 10cwt (engine), 15tons 10cwt
(tender).
The last three of the order for 19 class were altered to 4-4-0, and six more were
added to the order. These small mixed-traffic locomotives had outside frame bogies,
open splashers, raised fireboxes with bell-shaped dome on top, small weatherboard and
four wheel tenders. Domes were brass with Salter safety valve attached. In the early
1880s Cowan rebuilt them with more modern inside frame bogies and cabs with the
footplate side plate extended forward and larger sand boxes on the leading side of the
DW splashers. The cabs were not all the same and others (eg 32) had shorter cabs.
All the cabs had large cut outs. No 32 also had a six-wheel tender at this time. Nos
28 and 34 were eventually fitted with steam brake, the others having Westinghouse.
The tall bell-mouth chimneys were retained after rebuilding. (34.5 tons).
Later **class H**.

No	Date	Duplicate no	date	Rebuilt	Withdrawn
28	1/1862	28A	3/1913	3/1883	10/1913
29	1/1862			12/1880	8/1905
30	2/1862	30A	1915	3/1883	12/1917
31	5/1863*			8/1880	8/1905
32	5/1863	32A	8/1915	7/1881	12/1917
33	8/1863	33A	9/1913	7/1881	10/1913
34	9/1863	34A	3/1915	12/1881	10/1920**
35	1/1864	35A	9/1914	4/1882	10/1920**
36	1/1864			4/1882	11/1910

* No 31 exploded at Nethy Bridge 13/9/1878
** Intended for replacement 1916

4-4-0 Built by Neilson & Co. Works nos 1182-7.
DW 5ft 6½in; LW 3ft 0in; WB 6ft 0in + 6ft 6in + 8ft 0in; Cyls 16 x 24 o/s; Blr 4ft
1⅞in x 10ft 11in; THS 1049 sq ft later 1046 sq ft; WP 140 lbs/sq in; Wt 36 tons.
Generally similar to above for mixed traffic duties on the Fraserburgh line, but with
larger DW and boiler. Inside frame bogie with splashers. Brass dome on raised
firebox and Salter safety valves. Drop gate. 1050 gallon four wheel tender holding 2
tons of coal. Rebuilt with cabs and larger flush boilers 4ft 4in x 10ft 6in; THS 1046
sq ft with centre dome and Salter safety valve but without drop grate. Tall copper-
capped chimney retained. As rebuilt weight was 37.25 tons. Four later had six-wheel
tenders, nos 43/4/6 with 2100 gallons capacity and no 48 with 1800 gallons and 4 tons
coal. All were eventually fitted with Westinghouse brake, and no 48 was dual-fitted
in 1906. These locomotives were given a more elaborate livery, grass green with black
and red lining. Later **class K**. The LNE classified them D47/2, but only three came
into LNE stock, and none carried LNE numbers.

| | | Duplicate | | | | Allotted |
No	Date	no	date	Rebuilt	Withdrawn	LNE no
43	3/1866	43A	4/1915	5/1890	8/1921	
44	3/1866	44A	4/1915	11/1890	6/1925	6844A
45	3/1866	45A	7/1921	2/1891	7/1925	6845A*
46	3/1866			2/1890	7/1921	
47	4/1866	47A	9/1920	8/1890	8/1921	
48	4/1866	48A	10/1920	11/1889	6/1925	6848

* No 45A in stock until 11/1925 to appear at Darlington Centenary then to Works pilot
  Inverurie pending possible preservation but broken up shortly after.

4-4-0 Built by Neilson & Co. Works nos 2069-74.
DW 5ft 6½in; LW 3ft 0in; WB as class K; Cyls 17 x 24 o/s; Blr 4ft 4¼in diameter; THS
1107.4 sq ft; WP 140 lbs/sq in; Wt 39 tons 13 cwt.
Larger version of class K above, but built with cabs and smoke consuming apparatus.
Six-wheel tenders with o/s springs. Rebuilt by Pickersgill with Johnson type chimney
in place of original, closed central domes and larger boilers 4ft 6in x 10ft 0in. THS
1118.5 sq ft; WP 150 lbs/sq in; Wt as rebuilt 41 tons 3 cwt. Ramsbottom safety
valves. No 54 later provided with a side-window cab (as fitted by Pickersgill), and
by 1923 was dual-fitted with vacuum brake control together with Westinghouse brake
fitted to all. Plainer chimneys substituted. Later **class L**. LNE class D47/1 but LNE
numbers not carried.

| | | Duplicate | | | | Allotted |
No	Date	no	date	Rebuilt	Withdrawn	LNE no
49	3/1876	49A	10/1920	8/1898	10/1924	6849A
50	3/1876*	50A	10/1920	7/1899	10/1924	6850A
54	4/1876	54A	11/1920	9/1897	10/1924	6854A
55	3/1876			3/1900	8/1924	6855
56	4/1876			12/1901	9/1924	6856
57	4/1876					
	Renumbered					
52	9/1876*	52A	10/1920	6/1897	1/1926	6852A

* No 50 in accident near Newmachar 1920
  No 52 in accident at Knock 7/1896

4-4-0 Built by Neilson & Co. Works nos 2351-9.
DW 5ft 7in; LW 3ft 0½in; WB 6ft 0in + 6ft 6½in + 8ft 0in; Cyls 17½ x 26 o/s; Blr 4ft
4¼in diameter; THS 1107.4 sq ft; WP 140 lbs/sq in; Wt 41 tons.
Similar to class L with dome on raised firebox, Salter safety valves and copper-capped
chimney. Dome was brass and the cab side sheet was curved to form a splasher over
rear coupled wheels. Leading splasher was slotted. 1959 gallon six-wheel tender
holding 3 tons of coal. Built with steam brake, nos 51/3 had Westinghouse brake
equipment by 1885, the others by 1898. Rebuilt with larger flush boiler 4ft 6in x
10ft 0in; THS 1118.5 sq ft; WP 150 lbs/sq in with painted central dome and Ramsbottom
safety valves on firebox. Johnson type chimney in place of original and slotted
splashers filled in. When rebuilt weight was 42 tons 4 cwt.
Later **class M**. LNE class D45. T/E = Tablet exchange apparatus.

No	Date	Rebuilt			LNE no	applied	Withdrawn
57	8/1878	1/1900	T/E	4/1915	(6857)		6/1925
58	8/1878	11/1903	T/E	9/1914	6858	12/1924	5/1927
59	8/1878	9/1898	T/E	3/1917	6859	12/1924	7/1926
60	9/1878	4/1897	T/E	8/1919	(6860)		9/1925
61	9/1878	5/1900	T/E	6/1919	6861	12/1924	4/1926
62	10/1878*	5/1904	T/E	4/1916	(6862)		6/1926
40	10/1878	10/1896	T/E	11/1914	6840	3/1925	6/1932
51	11/1878	1/1899			6851	4/1925	1/1927
53	11/1878	10/1903	T/E	10/1921	6853	11/1924	3/1927

* No 62 in accident at Knock 7/1896. Rebuilt with square cab, two side windows and
raised roof instead of cut-out.

4-4-0 Built by Neilson & Co. Works nos 2360-1.
DW 6ft 1in; LW 3ft 0½in; WB 6ft 0in + 6ft 6in + 8ft 0in; Cyls 17½ x 26 o/s; Blr 4ft
4¼in diameter; THS 1107.4 sq ft; WP 140 lbs/sq in; Wt 41.25 tons.
Class C. As class M with larger DW. Rebuilt as class M with larger flush boilers, as
detailed for class M with the same modifications to chimneys, safety valves and
splashers. Brass beading was retained. LNE class D39.

No	Date	Rebuilt	LNE no	applied	Withdrawn
1	12/1878	2/1897	(6801)		8/1925
2	1/1879	10/1904	6802	10/1924	6/1926
3	1/1879	2/1898	6803	10/1924	2/1927

Manson Locomotives 1884-90

4-4-0 Built by Kitson & Co. Works nos 2668-73.
DW 6ft 0in; LW 3ft 0in; WB 5ft 6in + 7ft 2in + 8ft 0in; Cyls 17½ x 26 o/s; Blr 4ft 4in diameter; THS 1036 sq ft; WP 140 lbs/sq in; Wt 37 tons 2 cwt.
Class A. Manson introduced the first inside cylinder 4-4-0s to the GNS. Tall square cab with roof not quite covering the footplate with cut-out and rear and leading splashers. The six-wheel tender was 2000 gallons with 3 tons of coal. Centre covered painted dome, Ramsbottom safety valves. Tablet exchange apparatus fitted by the GNS. At first they had screw reverse, but lever reverse was substituted. Wing-plates on the smokebox were later removed. Rebuilt with larger boilers 4ft 6in x 10ft 2in; THS 1144 sq ft; WP 150 lbs/sq in; Wt 41 tons 13 cwt. Both original and rebuilt boilers were flush-top type. The original Manson built-up chimneys were replaced by the GNS standard cast type when rebuilt, and the dome cover was amended. No 64 ran with a four-wheel tender and later 66/7. No 67 was fitted with a tender cab. Four-wheel tenders were 1050 gallons with 2 tons coal. These were as fitted to classes K and L. All had Westinghouse brake as built.
LNE class D44.

No	Date	Rebuilt	LNE No	applied	Withdrawn
63	8/1884	10/1905	(6863)		7/1924
64	8/1884	10/1905	(6864)		11/1925
65	8/1884	1/1912	6865	12/1925	8/1926
66	9/1884	4/1912	(6866)		11/1925
67	9/1884	6/1906	6867	12/1926	10/1932
68	10/1884	7/1906	(6868)		1/1925

4-4-0 Built by Kitson & Co. Works nos 2838-40.
DW 5ft 6in; LW 3ft 0in; Cyls 17½ x 26 o/s; Other dimensions as class A; Wt 36.5 tons.
Class G. As class A but with smaller DW. Rebuilt as class A with larger boilers and modified as class A. Wt 41¼ tons. Steam-heating fitted at dates below.
LNE class D48.

No	Date	Rebuilt	Steam heating	LNE no	applied	Withdrawn
69	5/1885	12/1905	3/1920	6869	9/1925	11/1934
70	5/1885	9/1906	11/1918	6870	12/1924	6/1928
71	5/1885	12/1911	12/1921	6871	9/1924	1/1928

4-4-0 Built by the GNS at Kittybrewster.
DW 5ft 7in; LW 3ft 1in; WB 5ft 6in + 7ft 4½in + 8ft 4in; Cyls 17½ x 26 o/s; Blr 4ft 6in x 10ft 6in; THS 1187.7 sq ft; WP 140 lbs/sq in; Wt 40 tons.
Class N. First and only locomotives built at Kittybrewster from parts supplied by Kitson or Neilson, similar to previous Manson 4-4-0s. The names were later removed, and they were reboilered THS 1159 sq ft; WP 165 lbs/sq in increasing weight to 42.25 tons. As with previous classes, the Manson chimneys were replaced by cast ones. Wing-plates were retained on number 6 but not on number 5. Both had Westinghouse brake as built, with Ramsbottom safety valves, but the LNE substituted Ross pop valves. LNE class D46.

No	Name	Date	Reboilered	LNE no	applied	Withdrawn
5	*Kinmundy*	2/1887	4/1915	6805*	2/1925	4/1936
6	*Thomas Adam*	12/1887	8/1917	6806	5/1925	2/1932

* Before 2/1925 no 5 carried LNE livery without 'S' suffix as 'LNE 5'

4-4-0 Built by Kitson & Co. Works nos 3059-67.
DW 6ft 0½in; LW 3ft 9½in; WB 5ft 6in + 7ft 5in + 8ft 9in; Cyls 18 x 26; Blr 4ft 6in x
10ft 6in; THS 1193.7 sq ft; WP 140 lbs/sq in; Wt 41 tons 9 cwt.
Class O. Similar to previous classes. Westinghouse brake. Five were superheated,
THS 860 sq ft + 140 sq ft superheater; WP 160 lbs/sq in; Wt 44 tons 8 cwt, no 74 with
Schmidt superheater the others with Robinson type. The saturated ones were reboilered
with boilers of the same size. Three were dual-fitted with vacuum brake control by
1923, the others except 6807/9 so fitted by the LNE. Bogies were swing link and the
slide valves were placed on top of the cylinders actuated by rocking shafts. The
saturated ones had THS 1165 sq ft; WP 165 lbs/sq ft; chimneys replaced by cast type.
LNE class D42.

No	Date	Reboilered	Superheated	Dual fitted	LNE no	applied	Withdrawn
10	4/1888	5/1916		8/1916	6810	12/1924	11/1939
17	4/1888		1/1920	1911	6817	4/1924	
					(2076)		2/1946
18	5/1888		7/1920	1936	6818	9/1924	12/1939
4	5/1888	8/1915		3/1926	6804	2/1925	4/1935
7	5/1888	2/1917			6807*	6/1924	4/1945
9	5/1888	12/1916			6809	2/1925	11/1939
72	6/1888		12/1920	1936	6872	9/1925	12/1938
73	6/1888		1/1920	4/1926	6873**	4/1926	4/1937
74	6/1888		4/1916***	4/1916	6874	2/1925	5/1939

*   No 6807 allotted number 2075 in 1943 renumbering scheme
**   No 6873 ran without 'S' suffix before 4/1926 as 'LNE 73'
*** Schmidt superheater 177 sq ft replaced by Robinson type by LNE.

4-4-0 Built by R Stephenson & Co. Works nos 2695-7.
DW 6ft 0½in; LW 3ft 9½in; Cyls 18 x 26; Blr 4ft 6in x 10ft 6in; THS 1193.7 sq ft; WP
150 lbs/sq in. Other dimensions as class O.
Class P. As class O but eight-wheel 3000 gallon tender holding 3 tons of coal. About
1922-3, six-wheel tenders were substituted. Two rebuilt with Robinson superheating
(details as class O) increasing weight to 46 tons 7 cwt. Nos 6812/4 reverted to
saturated steam after 1923 (THS 1165 sq ft) although 6814 was later superheated again.
LNE class D43.

No	Date	Superheated	LNE no	applied	Withdrawn
12	5/1890	5/1917 until 6/1932	6812	3/1924	1/1938
13	6/1890	*	6813	11/1924	6/1937
14	6/1890	10/1917 until 1/1928 & from 2/1931.	6814	6/1925	11/1936

* Saturated boiler 11/1916

4-4-0 Built by R Stephenson & Co. Works nos 2698-700.
DW 6ft 6½in; LW 3ft 9½in; Cyls 18 x 26; THS 1193.7 sq ft; WP 150 lbs/sq in; Wt 42.5
tons. Other details as class O.
Class Q. Eight-wheel tenders as class P. Two were superheated as classes O and P, no
75 with Robinson and no 77 with Schmidt superheaters. No 76 was reboilered with
saturated steam, THS as classes O and P. Rebuilt weights were 47 tons saturated, 47
tons 1 cwt superheated. Six-wheel tenders substituted about 1922-3. LNE class D38.

No	Date	Reboilered	Superheated	LNE no	applied	Withdrawn
75	8/1890		7/1917	6875	8/1925*	1/1938
76	8/1890	5/1914		6876	4/1925	2/1931
77	9/1890		10/1913	6877	5/1925	9/1937

* No 6875 was dual fitted 11/1926

0-6-0T Built by Kitson & Co. Works nos 2651-5.
DW 4ft 6in; WB 6ft 10in + 6ft 10in; Cyls 16 x 24; Blr 4ft 0in x 10ft 6in; THS 762 sq ft; WP 140 lbs/sq in; Wt 37 tons 7 cwt.
Class D. Hand brake only, but nos 15/16/39/42 were fitted with Westinghouse brake by 1890 and nos 8 & 11 shortly afterwards. The original chimneys were replaced by Johnson type. When built, steam sanding was provided, but this was converted to gravity feed. No 8 was fitted with safety guards ('cowcatchers') for working the St Combs service, increasing the weight by 4.5 tons. Reboilered THS 846 sq ft; WP 150 lbs/sq in (as fitted to E class when built) increasing weight to 42 tons. As new, these were the first UK locomotives to be fitted with side doors to the footplate. Ramsbottom safety valves were latterly replaced by Ross pop type. LNE class J90.

No	Date	Reboilered	LNE no	applied	Withdrawn
8	5/1884	5/1908	6808	6/1925	4/1932
11	5/1884	12/1910	6811	*	6/1934
15	5/1884	10/1911	6815	12/1925	4/1935
16	5/1884	1/1908	6816	10/1924	5/1935
39	6/1884	11/1907	6839**	7/1925	5/1934
42	6/1884	6/1911	6842	8/1924	3/1936

* Date of application not recorded
** No 39 ran without suffix 'S' before 7/1925 as 'LNE 39'

0-6-0T Built by Kitson & Co. Works nos 2835-7.
DW 4ft 6in; WB 6ft 10in + 6ft 10in; Cyls 16 x 24; Blr 4ft 0in x 10ft 6in; THS 756 sq ft later 846 sq ft; WP 140 lbs/sq in later 150 lbs/sq in; Wt 43 tons 5 cwt.
Class E. All built with Westinghouse brake. Boilers exchangeable with D class after the latter had been reboilered. Original chimneys replaced by Johnson type. No 38 fitted with safety guards for St Combs service. Steam heating apparatus fitted at dates below. LNE class J91.

No	Date	Reboilered	Steam heating	LNE no	applied	Withdrawn
37	6/1885	3/1911	5/1921	6837	3/1925	6/1931
38	6/1885	11/1911	5/1920	6838	8/1924	7/1933
41	6/1885	8/1908	4/1919	6841	10/1925	6/1934

Johnson Locomotives 1893

4-4-0 Built by Neilson & Co. Works nos 4640-6.
DW 6ft 1in; LW 3ft 9½in; WB 5ft 6in + 7ft 6½in + 8ft 9in; Cyls 18 x 26; Blr 4ft 6in x
10ft 6in; THS 1207 sq ft; WP 165 lbs/sq in; Wt 43 tons 18 cwt.
Class S. Centre open top domes, six wheel 3000 gallon tender holding 5 tons of coal.
Westinghouse brake. Nos 79 and 81 were dual-fitted with vacuum brake control, and all
were so fitted by LNE. The open-top domes were retained but original 'lock up' safety
valves were replaced by Ramsbottom safety valves before 1923. Reboilered with 213
tubes instead of 220 giving THS of 1172.5 sq ft (1044 sq ft from 1924, LNE diagram
88); Wt 44 tons 18 cwt. Two had single-plate boilers instead of the original three-
ring telescopic fitted in 1946/7, THS 1182.4 sq ft (LNE diagram 88B). Steam heating
applied at dates below. LNE class D41.

No	Date	Reboilered	Steam heating	Dual fitted	LNE no	app-lied	BR no	app-lied	With-drawn
78	12/1893	8/1918	7/1913	3/1927	6878	6/24			
					2225	11/46	62225	12/48	2/1953
79	12/1893	2/1919	6/1916	by 1910	6879	11/25			
					(2226)				7/1946
80	12/1893	11/1915	3/1915	by LNE	6880	11/24			
		8/1946 (88B)			2227	10/46	62227	11/48	3/1951
81	12/1893	2/1919	9/1913	by 1910	6881	12/24			
					2228	10/46	62228	9/48	2/1952
82	12/1893	3/1921	1/1916	7/1926	6882	7/26			
		3/1947 (88b)			2229	9/46	62229	5/48	12/1951
83	12/1893	6/1919	10/1914	7/1927	6883	3/25			
					2230	8/46	62230	4/49	3/1952

0-4-4T Built by Neilson & Co. Works nos 4631-9.
DW 5ft 1in; TW 3ft 0½in; WB 7ft 6in + 9ft 0in + 5ft 6in; Cyls 17½in x 26; Blr 4ft 6in
x 10ft 6in; THS 1207 sq ft; WP 165 lbs/sq in; Wt 53 tons 15 cwt.
Class R. Built for the Aberdeen local service, these had 1200 gallon tanks and
carried 2 tons of coal in bunkers to which coal rails were later added, Ramsbottom
safety valves. Westinghouse brake. Reboilered THS 1172.5 sq ft at dates below. Wt
53 tons 17 cwt. Steam heating apparatus was fitted to all in 1915 except 84/6 fitted
in 1916, and 87 not fitted until 1922. LNE class G10.

No	Date	Reboilered	LNE no	applied	Withdrawn
84	11/1893	7/1916	6884	11/1926	11/1937
85	11/1893	4/1921	6885	11/1925	10/1937
86	11/1893	8/1916	6886	9/1925	11/1937
87	11/1893	2/1922	6887	3/1926	
			7505	4/1946	8/1947
88	11/1893	11/1918	6888	6/1925	8/1937
89	12/1893	8/1921	6889	3/1925	1/1940
90	12/1893	4/1921	6890	7/1925	8/1937
91	12/1893	11/1918	6891	11/1924	10/1937
92	12/1893	7/1922	6892	6/1925	5/1939

Pickersgill Locomotives 1895-1915

4-4-0 Built by Neilson & Co. Works nos 4877-90, 5212-23.
DW 6ft 1in; LW 3ft 9½in; Cyls 18 x 26. Details as class S.
Class T. As class S, but with closed domes (some with flat tops) and Ramsbottom
safety valves as built. Reboilered as class S including fitting of single-plate
boilers (88B) by LNE to eleven of the class. Westinghouse brake, but three dual-
fitted by 1910 and the others by LNE. The LNE classed these as one class with class S
as D41.

No	Date	Reboilered	Steam heating	Dual fitted	LNE no	app-lied	BR no	app-lied	With-drawn
93	12/1895	12/1920	12/1912	by LNE	6893	1/25			
					2237	10/46			12/1946
94	12/1895	by LNE	9/1915	11/1906	6894	4/24			
					2238	9/46	62238	3/48	8/1948
95	12/1895	by LNE	1/1915	by LNE	6895	2/25			
					2239	11/46			12/1947
96	12/1895	by LNE	10/1915	11/1926	6896	6/24			
					2240	9/46	62240	4/48	10/1949
97	12/1895	8/1917	6/1912	1936	6897	10/25			
					2241	11/46	62241	4/49	2/1953
98	12/1895	12/1920*	7/1915	1936	6898	4/24			
		7/1933 (88B)			2242	10/46	62242	10/48	2/1953
		(until 5/42)							
99	12/1895	by LNE	9/1913	4/1927	6899	9/24			
					2243	9/46	62243	8/48	1/1951
100	2/1896	3/1921	7/1912	by LNE	6900	10/25			
					2244	10/46			7/1947
19	2/1896	12/1920	10/1913	1937	6819	4/24			
					2231	9/46	62231	4/48	11/1952
20	2/1896	1920	7/1912	by 1910	6820	6/24			
		6/1947 (88B)			2232	9/46	62232	9/48	10/1951
21	2/1896	by LNE*	6/1914	1937	6821	10/25			
		1/1936 (88B)			(2233)				9/1946
22	2/1896	by LNE	11/1913	10/1926	6822	6/24			
					2234	10/46	62234	4/48	11/1949
23	3/1896	by LNE	1/1917	by LNE	6823**				
		6/1945 (88B)			2235	10/46	(62235)		5/1950
24	3/1896	by LNE	2/1917	by LNE	6824	9/24			
					2236	10/46			12/1947
101	9/1897	by LNE	6/1912	9/1926	6901	4/24			
					2245	9/46			12/1947
102	9/1897	by LNE*	3/1915	1936	6902	10/24			
		8/1946 (88B)			2246	9/46	62246	10/48	8/1951
103	9/1897	1923	12/1912	11/1927	6903**				
					2247	9/46	62247	5/48	10/1950
104	9/1897	by LNE	11/1913	1937	6904	1/26			
		4/1947 (88B)			2248	9/46	62248	8/49	10/1952
105	9/1897	by LNE*	10/1915	by LNE	6905	6/26			
		4/1933 (88B)			2249	11/46	62249	5/48	10/1950
		(until 10/1936 and from 1/1942 until 3/1946)							
106	9/1897	by LNE	12/1915	by LNE	6906	6/25			
					2250	8/46			12/1947
107	2/1898	by LNE	5/1913	11/1906	6907	9/24			
					2251	9/46	62251	3/49	6/1951
108	2/1898	2/1921	5/1912	1936	6908	9/26			
					2252	8/46	62252	11/48	11/1951

```
109  2/1898  by LNE*     4/1913    4/1927   6909    **
             12/1934 (88B)                   2253    9/46               1/1947
             (until 7/1945)
110  2/1898  1923       11/1912  by LNE     6910    **
             11/1943 (88B)                   2254    9/46               1/1947
111  2/1898  by LNE      5/1913    3/1927   6911    **
                                             2255   10/46  62255  5/48  5/1952
112  2/1898  12/1916     2/1915      1937   6912    **
             7/1947 (88B)                    2256   10/46  62256  9/49  12/1952
```

* Fitted with extended smokebox as follows in period 1928-31:
    No 6898 later removed
    No 6821 retained
    No 6902 subsequently removed and later replaced
    No 6905 later removed
    No 6909 later removed
** Date of application not recorded. Fitted with Macallan variable blast pipe
from 1898-1916.

4-4-0 Built by Neilson Reid & Co.   Works nos 5602-6
               GNS at Inverurie.
DW 6ft 1in; LW 3ft 9½in; Cyls 18 x 26; Details as class S.
Class V. As classes S and T, but provided with side-window cab in place of previous
cut-out type, increasing weight to 46 tons 7 cwt. Built with steam heating equipment
except 27/9/31/6, which were fitted later. Westinghouse brake, but three dual-fitted
by the GNS and the others by the LNE. Reboilered as class S including fitting of
single-plate boilers by LNE (88B). LNE class D40.

The following were built by Neilson Reid & Co.

No	Date	Reboilered	Dual fitted	LNE app-lied no	app-lied	BR no	app-lied	Withdrawn
113	10/1899	2/1918*	6/1908	6913	5/24			
		9/1951 (88B)		2262	10/46	62262	2/49	10/1955
114	10/1899	12/1916*	1935	6914	11/24			
		1/1933 (88B)		(2263)				3/1946
115	10/1899	3/1917*	6/1908	6915	**			
		4/1936 (88B)		2264	8/46	62264	4/48	3/1957
		(until 10/1943						
		& from 12/1953)						
116	10/1899	by LNE	1935	6825	4/24			
	Renumbered			2260	10/46	62260	12/48	8/1953
25	1/1900							
117	10/1899	by LNE	6/1908	6826	5/24			
	Renumbered							
26	1/1900	2/1943 (88B)		2261	9/46	62261	6/48	2/1953
		(until 11/1944)						

The following were built by the GNS at Inverurie.

No	Date	Reboilered	Steam heating	Dual fitted	LNE app-lied no	app-lied	BR no	app-lied	With-drawn
27	4/1909	by LNE	11/1911	1935	6827	9/25			
		11/1953 (88B)			2265	10/46	62265	3/49	12/1956
29***	7/1909	by LNE	12/1911	1935	6829	2/26			
		8/1946 (88B)			2267	9/46	62267	10/48	8/1956
		(until 3/46							
		& from 12/53).							
31	6/1910	5/1928*	4/1916	1935	6831	11/25			
		11/1940 (88B)			2268	5/46	62268	12/48	7/1956

36	8/1910	8/1928*	7/1913	1935	6836	12/25			
		3/1935 (88B)			2272	9/46	62272	12/48	3/1955
		(until 11/1941							
		& from 4/1951)							
28	3/1913	6/1930*	as built	1935	6828	2/26			
		3/1936 (88B)			2266	9/46			1/1947
33	10/1913	by 1930	as built	1935	6833	8/25			
		5/1951 (88B)			2269	8/46	62269	2/49	9/1955
35	9/1914	12/1930*	as built	10/1927	6835	10/24			
		12/1935 (88B)			2271	5/46	62271	4/48	11/1956
		(until 11/1941							
		& from 4/1951							
		until 3/1955)							
34	3/1915	c1930	as built	11/1926	6834	7/24			
					2270	8/46	62270	12/48	9/1953

* Fitted with extended smokebox as follows:
   No 6913 after 1931
   No 6914 3/1929
   No 6915 after 1931
   No 6831 5/1928 later removed
   No 6836 8/1928 later removed
   No 6828 6/1930
   No 6835 12/1930 later removed
** Date of application not recorded
*** No 29 entered traffic as 116 but was immediately renumbered

0-2-2T Rail Motor. Built by Andrew Barclay & Sons. Works nos 1056/7.
DW 3ft 7in; Cyls 10 x 16 o/s; Vertical boiler 9ft 6in x 6ft 0in; THS 500 sq ft; WP 150 lbs/sq in; Wt 27 tons 7 cwt (engine approx); Total wt 47 tons.
Walschaerts valve gear. Seating 45 passengers. **Class W.**

No	Date	Withdrawn	
29	7/1905	8/1909	Believed both separated from coach portion and converted to 0-4-0Ts about 1907
31	8/1905	8/1909	Boilers used for stationary work 3/1912

Heywood Locomotives 1915-20

4-4-0 Built by North British Locomotive Co. Works nos 22561-6.
                    GNS at Inverurie.
DW 6ft 1in; LW 3ft 9½in; Blr as class S; THS 860 sq ft + 140 sq ft superheater, other
details as class S; Wt 48 tons 13 cwt.
Class F. Side-window cab as class V. Superheated boiler. All built with steam
heating equipment and dual-fitted Westinghouse brakes and vacuum brake control. Later
boilers were THS 796 sq ft + 140 sq ft superheater. The LNE classed these with the
saturated class V as D40 without subdivision.

The following were built by North British Locomotive Co:

No	Name	Date	LNE no	App-lied	BR no	App-lied	Withdrawn
47	Sir David Stewart	9/1920*	6847	7/25			
			2275	11/46	62275	7/48	12/1955
48	Andrew Bain	10/1920*	6848	8/25			
			2276	8/46	62276	10/48	8/1955
49	Gordon Highlander	10/1920**	6849	12/24			
			2277	8/46	62277	11/48	6/1958
50	Hatton Castle	10/1920	6850	7/24			
			2278	8/46	62278	1/49	7/1955
52	Glen Grant	10/1920	6852	6/24			
			2279	9/46	62279	12/48	5/1955
54	Southesk	10/1920	6854	6/24			
			2280	8/46			1/1947

The following were built at Inverurie:

No	Name	Date	LNE no	App-lied	BR no	App-lied	Withdrawn
45	George Davidson	6/1921	6845	5/26			
			2273	9/46	62273	7/48	1/1955
46	Benachie	9/1921	6846	7/25			
			2274	10/46	62274	5/49	9/1955

* No 6847 ran with a saturated boiler from 7/25 until 1/28
  No 6848 ran with a saturated boiler from 11/46 until 3/47
** No 62277 was restored by BR at Inverurie in 11/59, and is preserved as GNS 49
  Gordon Highlander at Glasgow Transport Museum. In 1921 it was fitted with Scarab
  oil fuel system. Nicknamed '*The Sodger*'.

0-4-2T Built by Manning Wardle & Co. Works nos 1858/9.
DW 4ft 0in; TW 2ft 9in; WB 6ft 3in + 6ft 6in; Cyls 14 x 20 o/s; Blr 3ft 9in x 10ft
6in; THS 600 sq.ft; WP 165 lbs/sq.in (later 150 lbs/sq.in);
Wt 30 tons 9 cwt. (later 30 tons 18 cwt.)
Class Y. Aberdeen docks shunters. Purchased from stock (built 1/1915).
Steam brake. 450 Gallon tanks, 1 ton coal.
LNE class Z5.

No	Date	LNE no	applied	1946 no	applied	BR no	applied	Withdrawn
116	1/1915							
	renumbered							
30	8/1915	6830	7/1925	8192	9/1946	68192	11/1948	4/1960
117	1/1915							
	renumbered							
32	8/1915	6832	10/1925	8193	9/1946	68193	4/1949	4/1956

0-4-2T Built by Manning Wardle & Co. Works nos 1884/5.
DW 3ft 6in; TW 2ft 6in; WB 5ft 3in + 5ft 10in; Cyls 13 x 20 o/s; Blr 3ft 5in x 8ft
10in; THS 498 sq ft; WP 165 lbs/sq in (later 150 lbs/sq in); Wt 25 tons 17 cwt.
Class Y. Aberdeen docks shunters.   Steam brake.   450 Gallon tanks, 1 ton coal.
Classed by LNE with class Y above as Z5.

No	Date	LNE no	applied	1946 no	applied	BR no	applied	Withdrawn
116	8/1915							
	renumbered							
43	4/1916	6843	8/1924	8190	9/1946	68190	6/1948	4/1960
117	8/1915							
	renumbered							
44	4/1916	6844	9/1924	8191	10/1946	68191	8/1948	3/1959

GREAT NORTH OF SCOTLAND RAILWAY

NUMBER INDEX

No	Year				No	Year			
1	1854	2-4-0			39	1863	ex-Banffshire		
	1878	4-4-0	class C			1867	ex-Deeside		
2	1854	2-4-0				1884	0-6-0T class D		
-3	1879	4-4-0	class C		40	1863	ex-Banffshire		
4	1854	2-4-0				1878	4-4-0	class M	
	1888	4-4-0	class O		41	1863	ex-Banffshire		
5	1854	2-4-0				1885	0-6-0T class E		
-6	1887	4-4-0	class N		42	1863	ex-Morayshire		
7	1854	2-4-0				1884	0-6-0T class D		
	1888	4-4-0	class O		43	1866	4-4-0	class K	
8	1855	2-4-0	goods		-44	1915	0-4-2T class X		
	1884	0-6-0T class D			45	1866	4-4-0	class K	
9	1855	2-4-0	goods		-46	1921	4-4-0	class F	
11	1855	2-4-0	goods		47	1866	4-4-0	class K	
-10	1888	4-4-0	class O		-48	1920	4-4-0	class F	
	1884	0-6-0T class D			49	1867	ex-Deeside-50		
12	1855	2-4-0	goods			1876	4-4-0	class L	
	1890	4-4-0	class P			1920	4-4-0	class F	
13	1855	0-4-0WT			51	1867	ex-Deeside		
-14	1890	4-4-0	class P			1878	4-4-0	class M	
15	1857	2-4-0			52	1867	ex-Deeside		
-16	1884	0-6-0T class D				1876	4-4-0	ex-57	
17	1857	2-4-0				1920	4-4-0	class F	
-18	1888	4-4-0	class O		53	1867	ex-Deeside		
19	1859	2-4-0	class B			1878	4-4-0	class M	
-20	1896	4-4-0	class T		54	1876	4-4-0	class L	
21	1860	2-4-0	class B	1920			4-4-0	class F	
-24	1896	4-4-0	class T		55	1876	4-4-0	class L	
25	1861	2-4-0	class B		-56				
-26	1900	4-4-0	ex-116/7		57	1876	4-4-0	class L	
27	1861	2-4-0	class B			1878	4-4-0	class M	
	1909	4-4-0	class V		58	1878	4-4-0	class M	
28	1862	4-4-0	class H		-62				
	1913	4-4-0	class V		63	1878	0-4-2	ex-40	
29	1862	4-4-0	class H			1880	Blank		
	1905	Rail motor				1884	4-4-0	class A	
	1909	4-4-0	class V		64	1884	4-4-0	class A	
30	1862	4-4-0	class H		-68				
	1915	0-4-2T ex-116			69	1884	4-4-0	class G	
31	1863	4-4-0	class H		-71				
	1905	Rail motor			72	1888	4-4-0	class O	
	1910	4-4-0	class V		-74				
32	1863	4-4-0	class H		75	1890	4-4-0	class Q	
	1915	0-4-2T ex-117			-77				
33	1863	4-4-0	class H		78	1893	4-4-0	class S	
	1913	4-4-0	class V		-83				
34	1863	4-4-0	class H		84	1893	0-4-4T class R		
	1915	4-4-0	class V		-92				
35	1864	4-4-0	class H		93	1895	4-4-0	class T	
	1915	4-4-0	class V		-99				
36	1864	4-4-0	class H		100	1896	4-4-0	class T	
	1910	4-4-0	class V		101	1897	4-4-0	class T	
37	1863	ex-Banffshire			-106				
-38	1885	0-6-0T class E							

107	1898	4-4-0	class T
-112			
113	1899	4-4-0	class V
-115			
116	1899	4-4-0 class V	
	1900	Blank	
	1909	4-4-0 class V	
	1909	Blank	
	1915	0-4-2T class Y	
	1915	Blank	
	1915	0-4-2T class X	
	1916	Blank	
117	1899	4-4-0	class V
	1900	Blank	
	1915	0-4-2T class Y	
	1915	Blank	
	1915	0-4-2 class X	
	1916	Blank	

COLNE VALLEY AND HALSTEAD RAILWAY

Incorporated 30/6/1856. Opened Chappell (GE) to Halstead 16/4/1860, to Hedingham 1/7/1861, to Yeldham 26/5/1862, to Haverhill South 10/5/1863. Connection to Haverhill North (GE). Line worked under contract by Sir Daniel Gooch from 1/1/1865 until 1/1/1867, and by CB Sperling until 15/6/1867. GE locomotives also hired. In Receivership 1874-85. To LNE 1923.

14 Locomotives as under (not numbered until 1902).

2-2-2WT Built by Sharp Roberts & Co 12/1844. Works no 275.
DW 5ft 6in; Cyls 15 x 18.
Purchased from LBSC Railway (no 45, built for Brighton, Croydon & Dover Joint no 88, later LBSC 50 rebuilt from 2-2-2 2/1851). On the CV&H, brake blocks on LW and DW were on right side only.
Date
7/1860   Date of withdrawal not known

2-4-0 Built by R Stephenson & Co 9/1842. Works no 358.
DW 4ft 6in; Cyls 14 x 18. O/s frames.
Purchased from Eastern Counties Railway (page 16) having been built for the North Midland Railway (no 70, Vol 3A page 21). When built, cylinders were 14 x 20 and it had Dodds motion. On CV&H was LW 3ft 0in with dome on firebox.
Date
1861   Date of withdrawal not known

2-4-0WT Built by Manning Wardle & Co. Works nos 34, 59, 661.
DW 5ft 0in; LW 3ft 9in; TWB 14ft 0in; THS 720 sq ft; 490 gallon tanks. These three locomotives were owned by Charles Brewster of Little Maplestead, and were on hire to CV&H. Livery originally dark green, later brown.

Date	Name	
1861	*Brewster*	Scrapped 1887
1862	*Colne*	Scrapped 1887
1863	*Halstead*	Sold to a colliery at Wigan. Said to be still at work in 1911.

2-4-0T Built by George England & Co.
DW 3ft 8in; Cyls (see below).
These two locomotives were on hire from William Munro, the contractor who built the line. An article in *Locomotive Magazine* Volume 17 (1911) stated that they were built in 1860 but James W Lowe, *British Steam Locomotive Builders*, Goose & Son 1975, gives the building date as 1863. There is also a discrepancy on the cylinder sizes, *Locomotive Magazine* stating 11 x 17 and Lowe 11 x 16. A pamphlet published by the Colne Valley Railway Preservation Society in 1977 records cylinders as 11 x 13. The side tanks extended from the rear of the coupled wheels to the centre of the leading wheels. Narrow bunker, safety valves on smokebox, tall bell-capped chimney. Individual wheel splashers.

Name
Cam   Both returned to William Munro
Colne   after about twelve months

0-4-2T Built by Neilson & Co. Works no 2204.
DW 5ft 3in; TW 3ft 7in; TWB 14ft 6in; THS 752.6 sq ft.
Similar to GE class T7 tanks. Dome on front section of boiler with Salter safety valves. The original cab roof was narrower than the footplate, the supports inset from the tank sides with rounded corners. Rebuilt in 1888 by Hawthorn Leslie with a supplementary tank over each leading DW, but separated from the original tanks to allow room for the fitting of a Westinghouse brake pump. At this time the locomotive was a dark red. The supplementary tanks were removed at Haverhill in 1911 and Ramsbottom safety valves fitted. The cab was also rebuilt in 1888 with flush sides and full width roof in conventional style. The original chimney was replaced with a stovepipe type in 1888, a shorter one of the built-up type replacing it in 1911.

1902
no   Date
1   1877   Rebuilt as above. Withdrawn by LNE 1923.

0-6-0T Built by Sharp Stewart & Co. 1873. Works no 2358 (or 2359).
DW 3ft 6in; Cyls 16¼ x 20 o/s.
Purchased from makers having been returned by Cornwall Minerals Railway, for whom it
was built (no 10). On the CV&H it was green with rear weatherboard.
Date   Name
1879   *Haverhill*
1889   Sold to South Hetton Coal Co (No 2) and full cab fitted
1948   Scrapped

0-6-0ST Built by Beyer Peacock & Co. 1860. Works no 190.
DW 5ft 0in; Cyls 16 x 24; THS 929 sq ft; WP 120 lbs/sq in; Wt approx 32.5 tons.
Purchased from Crompton & Shawcross, Strangeways Hall colliery in 1883, having been
rebuilt for North London Railway (no 42, Vol 2A page 56) as 0-4-2ST, and sold to above
1873. Rebuilt 0-6-0ST as above on 1877 by Fletcher Jennings & Co (works no 154), and
stovepipe chimney substituted for original copper-topped one.
Date
1883   Purchased as above but not named
1894   Sold to South Hetton Coal Co, later Sutton Pit no 3. Scrapped 1902.

2-4-2T Built by Hawthorn Leslie & Co. Works nos 2079/80/83.
DW 5ft 1in; LW & TW 3ft 1in; WB 6ft 9in + 7ft 0in + 6ft 8in; THS 919 sq ft;
Wt 43 tons. Rebuilt by GER at Stratford with two-ring boiler
instead of three-ring but still with dome on front ring behind chimney. THS 1038.49
sq ft; WP 140 lbs/sq in; 1200 gallon tanks; 2.5 tons coal capacity; Wt 44 tons 12 cwt.
No 4 had rounded edge to tank top. LNE class F9.
1902

no	Name	Date	Rebuilt	LNE no	Applied	Withdrawn
2	*Halstead*	6/1887	1896	8312	6/1924	1/1930
3	*Colne*	7/1887	1897	8313	10/1924	12/1927
4	*Hedingham*	1/1894	1902			9/1923

0-6-2T Built by Hudswell Clarke & Co. Works no 836.
DW 4ft 6in; TW 3ft 8in; WB 7ft 0in + 7ft 0in + 6ft 0in; Blr 4ft 3in x 9ft 8³/8in: THS
974.4 sq ft; WP 150 lbs/sq in; Wt 50tons 3 Cwt.
1300 gallon tanks; 2.5 tons coal capacity. Westinghouse brake. Black with vermilion
lining. Used principally on goods trains. WP increased to 160 lbs/sq in by 1916 but
later reduced again to 150 lbs/sq in.

No	Date	LNE no	Applied	Withdrawn
5	8/1908	8314	3/1924	1/1928

EAST AND WEST YORKSHIRE UNION RAILWAY

Incorporated 2/8/1883. Opened 20/5/1891 Rothwell to Lofthouse (GN) with branches to Beeston colliery and Thorp. Worked South Leeds Junction Railway (incorporated 1893, opened 4/1895 from Rothwell to Stourton (MR) with branch to Aire and canal at Thwaite lock). Light Railway Order 1897 authorised branch from Robin Hood to Royds Green (lower). No passenger services except for short period from 4/1/1904 until 30 /9/1904 when a service was operated from Leeds (Wellington) to Stourton and Robin Hood for which MR 0-4-4Ts nos 6 and 1265 (later 1226 and 1239) were hired. Some traffic worked by colliery engines and GN. To LNE 7/1923.

10 Locomotives as under:

0-6-0ST Built by Manning Wardle & Co 1861. Works no 21.
DW 3ft 1in (or 3ft 2in); Cyls 11 x 17.
Purchased from a contractor.
Date
1894   Believed named *Henrietta* when purchased, but not numbered on E&WYU.
        Referred to as 'green engine 21' by maker's number.
        Sold to Meakin & Dean, Birkenhead and later to Hundred of Manhood &
        Selsey Tramway no 4 *Sidlesham*.

0-6-0ST Built by Manning Wardle & Co. Works nos 1307/8, 1489.
DW 4ft 0in; WB 6ft 6in + 8ft 0in; Blr 4ft 0in x 10ft 0in; THS 963 sq ft; Wt 39 tons 12 cwt; 850 gallon tanks.
No 1 originally had Marshall valve gear. LNE class J84.

No	Date	Altered and rebuilt		LNE no	Applied	Withdrawn
1	6/1895	4/1904	Vacuum ejector for passenger working.	3112	7/1924	6/1930
2	7/1895	4/1915	New frames 6in longer. Wt 42 tons.	3113	11/1924	12/1928
3*	9/1900					7/1923

* Replaced first no 3 below

0-6-0ST Built by Manning Wardle & Co. Works no 1325.
DW 3ft 6in; Cyls 15 x 20 (or 15 x 22); THS 743 sq ft; Wt 29 tons 3 cwt; 700 gallon tanks.

No	Date	
3	1895	Sold 1899 to Wath Main Colliery no 7

0-6-2T Built by Manning Wardle & Co. Works nos 1398, 1433/4.
DW 3ft 9in; TW 3ft 0in; WB 5ft 0in + 4ft 6in + 8ft 0in; Blr 3ft 10⁷/₈in x 12ft 6in; THS 963 sq ft; WP 140 lbs/sq in (later 150 lbs/sq in); Wt 44 tons; 900 gallon tanks; 2 tons coal capacity.
THS was 1039 sq ft by 1923. Steam brake. No 4 rebuilt 0-6-0ST by Manning Wardle. WB 6ft 3in + 8ft 3in; Blr 3ft 10in x 14ft 5in; THS 888 sq ft; 1000 gallon tanks; 2 tons coal capacity; Wt 40 tons.
WP 140 lbs/sq in on all three by 1923. No 3114 had saddle tank from 3113 fitted at Doncaster in 7/1929, as 3113 was not broken up until 5/1929 reducing capacity to 850 gallons, and smokebox door from 3113 also fitted.
LNE class 0-6-2ST N19, 0-6-0ST J85.

No	Date	Rebuilt as above	LNE no	Applied	Withdrawn
4	9/1898	8/1919, 7/1929	3114	10/1925	2/1933
5	5/1899		3115	3/1925	3/1928
6	6/1899				7/1923 (cracked frame)

0-6-0ST Built by Hudswell Clarke & Co 1889. Works no 362.
DW 4ft 0in; Cyls 14 x 22 o/s.
Purchased from Messrs Charlesworth (Collieries) 1902.

No	Date	
7	1902	Resold to Messrs Charlesworth 1904

0-4-0ST Built by Black Hawthorn & Co 1878. Works no 424.
DW not recorded; Cyls 12 x 19.
Purchased second-hand about 1902.

No	Date	
8	c1902	Scrapped or sold c1906.

MID-SUFFOLK LIGHT RAILWAY

Authorised by Light Railway Order 1900. Opened 20/9/1904 Haughley (adjacent to
Haughley GE) to Cratfield with a branch from Kenton to Debenham for goods traffic.
Passenger services operated from Haughley to Laxfield from 29/9/1905. In Receivership
from 5/1907, Cratfield extension and Debenham branch abandoned. Taken over by LNE
1/7/1924.

3 Locomotives as under:

0-6-0T Built by Hudswell Clarke & Co. Works nos 711, 807.
DW 3ft 4in; WB 6ft 0in + 6ft 0in; Cyls 14 x 20; Blr 3ft 8in x 8ft 10in; THS 547.28 sq
ft; WP 140 lbs/sq in; Wt 30 tons; 650 gallon tanks; 1 ton 6 cwt coal capacity.
Steam brake and Westinghouse brake pump. DW later 3ft 4½in. No 1 rebuilt 7/1917 with
new firebox THS 487.16 sq ft and in 1919 with 13½ x 20 cyls. Wt 29 tons 3 cwt and
tank capacity reduced to 570 gallons. No 3 rebuilt with new cylinders of the same
size in 3/1916 and new firebox 9/1921. WP later 150 lbs/sq in. Also ran as 2-4-0T
with leading DW disconnected. Names were soon removed. All rebuilds carried out at
Stratford GE. LNE class J64.

No	Name	Date	Rebuilt	LNE no	Applied	Withdrawn
1	*Haughley*	11/1904	7/1917, 11/1919	8316	9/1925	1/1928
3	*Laxfield*	4/1909	3/1916, 9/1921			8/1924

2-4-0T Built by Hudswell Clarke & Co. Works no 723.
DW 3ft 4in; WB 5ft 9in + 5ft 0in; Cyls 13 x 20; Blr 3ft 8in x 8ft 4in; THS 514 sq ft;
WP 140 lbs/sq in; Wt 27 tons 15 cwt. Rebuilt 0-6-0T in 1905. Wt 28 tons. Steam brake
and Westinghouse pump. Sand boxes above running plate. THS 463.36 sq ft by 1923.
LNE class J64

No	Name	Date	Rebuilt 0-6-0T	LNE no	Applied	Withdrawn
2	*Kenton* (later removed)	3/1905	1905	8317	3/1925	12/1929

MIDLAND AND GREAT NORTHERN JOINT RAILWAY

Introduction

West of King Lynn, two companies were worked by the Great Northern. The Norwich and Spalding, a scheme originally supported by the East Anglian Railway, was incorporated on 4/8/1853. Despite its title, the only sections constructed were from Spalding to Holbeach opened 9/8/1858 (goods) and 15/11/1858 (passengers), extended to Sutton Bridge 1/7/1862. The link with Lynn was completed by the Lynn and Sutton Bridge, incorporated 6/8/1861 and opened 1/11/1864, except for Sutton Bridge itself over the river Nene.
These two companies combined with the Spalding and Bourn (sic) incorporated 29/7/1862, but not then completed, to amalgamate as the Midland and Eastern from 23/7/1862 with joint working between the Midland Railway and the GN. The Spalding and Bourn was opened on 1/8/1866, and after the purchase of the company controlling Sutton Bridge, a new combined road and rail swing bridge was opened on 18/7/1867 connecting the L&SB with the N&S lines.
The Midland also worked the Peterborough, Wisbech and Sutton, incorporated 28/7/1863, and opened 1/6/1866 (goods) 1/8/1866 (passengers), which had running powers over the M&E to Sutton Bridge.
The system through to Lynn was now complete from Peterborough (GN and Midland). East of Lynn, the Lynn and Fakenham and the Yarmouth and North Norfolk (both qv) operated their own traffic. The two companies were amalgamated from 1/7/1883 as the Eastern and Midlands, and connected by a line from North Walsham to Melton Constable opened on 5/4/1883. From 1/7/1883, the M&E and the PW&S west of Lynn were also amalgamated into the E&M.
Joint working of the lines west of Lynn by the MR and the GN continued with the combined locomotive stock of the L&F and the Y&NN working east of Lynn, although the E&M did operate a daily Cromer to Peterborough express after 1887 in the summer only. The line from Melton Constable to Cromer (Beach) was opened on 16/6/1887.
Due to its piecemeal construction, the main line suffered from reversals necessary at Kings Lynn and Spalding even for goods trains. In addition, the Cromer line junction at Melton Constable was on the west side of the station only, attaining an easterly direction after rounding a long sharp curve. This permitted through working between Norwich and Cromer but east-west trains had to reverse.
The most inconvenient was Kings Lynn which was, of course, a Great Eastern station, and in and out amounted to a detour of some three miles. An avoiding line some 4.5 miles long was opened on 1/1/1886 from Bawsey to South Lynn, where a new station was built. Main line trains stopped here, and a connecting train provided a service to the GE station which became an E&M branch line using the former western link line. The former eastern link from Gaywood junction to Bawsey was lifted. An avoiding line for freight trains was eventually completed at Spalding in 1893.
The Midland and Great Northern Joint was incorporated on 9/6/1893 when the two companies jointly took over the Eastern and Midland, effective from 1/7/1893, and established a joint committee. The E&M locomotive works were at Melton Constable, and these were taken over by the joint committee retaining the engineer in charge of the works and the locomotives, William Marriott, MInstCE.
To enable the M&GN to work the whole system, additional locomotives were ordered. The arrangements were similar to that on the Somerset and Dorset, the Midland controlling the locomotive stock from Derby, the permanent way and engineering department being the responsibility of the Great Northern.
An additional connection with the Midland was opened in 1893 (goods) and 1894 (passengers) by extending the line from Bourne to a junction at Little Bytham.
A joint line with the GE, the Norfolk and Suffolk Joint Railway (incorporated 1898) was opened from North Walsham to Mundesley-on-Sea on 1/7/1898, extended to Cromer 3/8/1906 and Yarmouth (Beach) to Lowestoft 13/7/1903.
The MR and GN were replaced by the LMS and LNE in 1923, but the original title was retained although no new locomotives were provided despite the last addition to stock being in 1910. The LNE took over the line on 1/10/1936.

CONSTITUENT COMPANIES

Yarmouth and North Norfolk Railway

Originally authorised under the Regulation of Railways Act 1868 as the Great Yarmouth
and Stalham Light Railway 26/7/1876 incorporated 27/5/1878 as Y&NN. Opened Yarmouth
to Ormsby 7/8/1877, to Hemsby 16/5/1878, to Martham 15/7/1878, to Catfield 17/1/1880,
to Stalham 3/7/1880, to North Walsham 13/6/1881. Amalgamated with Yarmouth Union
Railway (incorporated 26/8/1880, opened 15/5/1882 connecting Y&NN to the Great Eastern
at Yarmouth. To Eastern and Midlands 1/7/1883 with Lynn and Fakenham, and connected
to the latter by a line from North Walsham to Melton Constable opened 5/4/1883.

7 Locomotives as under (names only).

0-6-0ST Built by Fox Walker & Co. Works nos 338/9.
DW 3ft 7in; WB 4ft 10in + 4ft 10in; Cyls 13 x 20 o/s; Blr 4ft 4^7/8in x 8ft 0in; THS
458.5 sq ft; WP 140 lbs/sq in; Wt 24.5 tons; 550 gallon tanks.

		E&M no	M&GN no	
Name	Date	1883	1894	
Ormsby	5/1877	15	**15**	Sold 1900
Stalham	7/1877	16	**16**	To Duplicate list 16A 5/1905
				To LNE 016A 1936
				Withdrawn 1937

0-6-0ST Built by Black Hawthorn & Co. Works nos 416, 517.
DW 3ft 4½in (later 3ft 6in); WB 5ft 3½in + 5ft 6in; Cyls 14 x 20 o/s; THS 556.5 sq ft;
WP 140 lbs/sq in (later reduced to 120 lbs); Wt 26 tons; 665 gallon tanks, 3 tons of
coal. Safety valves on centre dome and on firebox.

		E&M no	M&GN no	Duplicate		
Name	Date	1883	1894	no	date	
*Ida**	1877	7	**7**	7A	1894	Sold through TW Ward 1894 to
						Ibstock Brick & Tile Co. No 2
						Scrapped 7/1928
*Aylsham**	1881	17	**17**	17A	1894	Replaced 1901, scrapped 1902

* Names removed by E&M.

The following three locomotives were originally intended for South America.

4-4-0T Built by Hudswell Clarke & Co. Works no 208.
DW 4ft 6in; LW 2ft 4in; WB 4ft 10in + 5ft 10½in + 6ft 9in; Cyls 14 x 20 o/s; Blr 3ft
7in x 9ft 6½in; THS 565.8 sq ft; WP 140 lbs/sq in (later reduced to 130 lbs); Wt 34
tons; 750 gallon tanks increased to 835 gallons. 17 Cwt coal; DW & LW increased by
1½in with thicker tyres. Green livery. Safety valves on dome and on firebox.
Rebuilt Blr 3ft 10in x 8ft 10in; THS 821.7 sq ft; Firebox 4ft 3in long x 3ft 10in
wide.

Name	Date		
North Walsham	9/1878		
		1883	To Eastern & Midland 32
		1886	Renumbered 41
		1894	Rebuilt to M&GN **41** class B
		1904	Withdrawn. To stationary work Melton

4-4-0T Built by Hudswell Clarke & Co. Works nos 210 & 232.
DW 4ft 6in; LW 2ft 4in; WB 4ft 10in + 5ft 10½in + 6ft 9in; Cyls 15 x 20 o/s; Blr 3ft
9in x 9ft 0½in; THS 623 sq ft; WP 140 lbs/sq in (later reduced to 130 lbs); Wt 33 tons
10 cwt (*Martham*), 34 tons (*Great Yarmouth*); 750 gallon tanks (*Martham*), 800 gallon
tanks (*Great Yarmouth*), increased to 835 gallons. 17 Cwt coal (*M*), 25 Cwt coal (*GY*);
DW & LW increased by 1½in with thicker tyres. Green livery. Safety valves on dome
and on firebox. Rebuilt Blr 3ft 10in x 8ft 10in; THS 821.7 sq ft; Firebox 4ft 3in
long x 3ft 10in wide.

Name	Date	
Martham	5/1879	
	1883	To Eastern & Midlands 31
	1886	Renumbered 40
	1894	Rebuilt. To M&GN **40** class B.
	1917	Sold to War Department*, scrapped 1934
Great Yarmouth	10/1881	
	1883	To Eastern & Midlands 19
	1894	To M&GN **19** class B
	1903	Rebuilt
	1917	Sold to War Department*, scrapping date unknown

* Transferred to Midland Railway 1906 for branch line working in part exchange for
  Midland 0-4-4Ts nos 141-3 until about 1910. Received Deeley smokeboxes and
  chimneys. Converted for push/pull working with ex-Pullman car. See also ex-Lynn &
  Fakenham 4-4-0s M&GN nos 8 & 10.

Lynn and Fakenham Railway

Incorporated 13/7/1876. Opened Gaywood Junction (GE Kings Lynn) to Massingham
16/8/1879, to Fakenham (West) 16/8/1880, to Guestwick 19/1/1882, to Lenwade 1/7/1882,
throughout to Norwich (City) 2/12/1882. To E&M 1/7/1883.

10 Locomotives as under:

4-4-0T Built by Hudswell Clarke & Co. Works no 209.
DW 4ft 7in; LW 2ft 5in; WB as Y&NN *North Walsham*; Cyls 14 x 20 o/s. Other dimensions
similar to *North Walsham*. Originally intended for a South American order. Rebuilt
details as Y&NN 4-4-0Ts and cyls increased to 15 x 20.

Name	Date	
Hillington	11/1878	
	1883	To Eastern & Midlands 8 (name removed)
	1894	Rebuilt. To M&GN **8** class B.
	1917	Sold to War Department*
	c1920s	Sold to Ormiston Colliery, Scrapped 1935

* Transferred to Midland Railway 1906 for branch line working. A photograph in
  Railway Magazine Vol 18 page 375 (1906) shows it coupled to an ex-Pullman car
  Converted for motor working on the Hemel Hempstead branch. The Midland exchanged it
  and nos 10/19/40 for MR 0-4-4Ts 141-3. Returned to M&GN 1912 having been painted
  crimson lake and fitted with Deeley smokebox and chimney.

4-4-0T Built by Hudswell Clarke & Co. Works nos 211, 224 & 231.
DW 4ft 7in; LW 2ft 5in; WB as Y&NN *North Walsham*; Cyls 15 x 20 o/s. Other dimensions
similar to *North Walsham*. Originally intended for a South American order. Rebuilt
details as Y&NN 4-4-0Ts. *Norwich* and *Kings Lynn* had 800 gallon tanks, 25 cwt coal
bunker 3in higher. Wt 34 tons.

Name	Date	
Fakenham	6/1879	
	1883	To Eastern & Midlands 9 (name removed)
	1894	To M&GN **9** class B
	1899	Rebuilt
	1909	To Duplicate list 9A*

```
                1932   Withdrawn (cut up 1933)
Norwich         6/1879
                1883   To Eastern & Midlands 10 (name removed)
                1894   To M&GN 10 class B
                1896   Rebuilt Cyls 16 x 20
                1917   Sold to War Department, to Woolmer Instructional
                       Military Railway at Longmoor*
                1923   Rebuilt by Yorkshire Engine Co
                1930   Withdrawn & used for re-railing practice at Woolmer
                1953   Scrapped
Kings Lynn      1881
                1883   To Eastern & Midlands 20 (name removed)
                1894   To M&GN 20 class B
                1903   Rebuilt
                1909   To Duplicate list 20A
                1931   Withdrawn (cut up 1933)
```

* Transferred to Midland Railway 1906 for working branch lines in exchange for Midland 0-4-4Ts 141-3 together with 8/19/40 and converted for push/pull working with ex-Pullman car. Returned to M&GN 1912 having been painted crimson lake and fitted with Deeley smokebox and chimney.

0-6-0ST Built by Black Hawthorn & Co. Works no 503.
DW 3ft 4½in; Cyls 14 x 20 o/s. All dimensions as Y&NN *Ida*.

```
Name        Date
Holt        1879
renamed     1883   To Eastern & Midlands 6 and name removed
Chairman    1894   To M&GN 6 and to duplicate list 6A
            1894   Sold through TW Ward to Ibstock Brick & Tile Co becoming no 1
                   Ibstock. Scrapped 1940.
```

0-6-0T Built 1874 by Sharp Stewart & Co. Works nos 2370-2.
DW 3ft 6in; WB 5ft 0in + 6ft 0in; Cyls 16 x 20 o/s; Blr 4ft $0^3/8$in x 8ft 2in; THS 823.5 sq ft; WP 140 lbs/sq in; Raised firebox casing 3ft 11in x 4ft 0in; Firebox 3ft 3in x 3ft $4^1/8$in x 4ft 5½in; Wt 30 tons 16 cwt. 780 gallon tanks. 15 cwt coal. Purchased from Sharp Stewart having been returned to them by the Cornwall Minerals Railway (their nos 15-17). As these locomotives had been originally designed to work in pairs, there was no rear bunker, only a back plate. The L&F rebuilt them, removing the backplate and attaching four wheel tenders. After this rebuilding, weight was recorded as 29½ tons. DW later 3ft 7½in. Chocolate brown livery. Sandboxes on either side of smokebox. No 3 was rebuilt as 2-4-0 in 1891. DW 4ft 7in; Cyls 16 x 20 o/s; LW 3ft 6in; 876 gallon tender (4 wheel).

	L&F		ex-CM	E&M No	Rebuilt	M&GN	Duplicate	
Name**	no	Date	no	1883	2-4-0	no	date	Withdrawn*
Blakeney	3	12/1880	15	3	1891	3A	1894	1899
Reepham	2	12/1880	16	2		2A	1894	1894***
Melton Constable	1	12/1880	17	1		1A	1894	1898

* Officially Nos 1A, 2A & 3A were rebuilt as shunting engines, but this would appear to have been for accountancy purposes as wheels only appear to have been reused on some of the 'rebuilds'. They should therefore be classified as 'replacements'.
** Names removed by E&M.
*** The 'replacement' for no 2A was not constructed until 1903/4 (Sources differ on the date).

0-4-0ST Built by Hudswell Clarke & Co. Works nos 183 (10/1878), 192 (12/1880).
DW 2ft 6in; WB 5ft 0in; Cyls 8 x 15; Blr 2ft 3in x 7ft 1½in; THS 172 sq ft; WP 140 lbs/sq in (later reduced to 120 lbs); Wt 11 tons 10 cwt; 260 gallon tanks; 7½ cwt coal. Purchased from Wilkinson & Jarvis, contractors in 1881. *Vici* had minor variations.

		E&M no	M&GN no	Duplicate		
Name	Date	1883	1894	no	date	
Alpha	1881	4	4	4A	1894	Sold to Colman & Co, Norwich in 1920
Vici	1881	5	5	5A	1894	Withdrawn c1932-4

Eastern and Midlands Railway

Incorporated 18/8/1882 with effect from 1/7/1883 by amalgamation of the Yarmouth & North Norfolk, Yarmouth Union and Lynn and Fakenham and absorption of Midland and Eastern and Peterborough, Wisbech and Sutton (both worked jointly by MR and GN). Cromer (Beach) line opened 16/6/1887.

4-4-0 Built by Beyer Peacock & Co. Works nos 2105-8*, 2338-41, 2794/5/8, 2939-42.
* Ordered by Lynn & Fakenham.
DW 6ft 0in; LW 3ft 0in; WB 6ft 6in + 6ft 9in + 8ft 2in; Cyls 17 x 24 o/s; Blr 4ft 2in x 10ft 3½in; THS 1083 sq ft and 1009.8 sq ft; WP 140 lbs/sq in; Wt 38 tons 7¼ cwt. 2000 gallon tenders carrying 2 tons of coal. Tall brass-capped chimneys, separate coupling rod splashers, rear sanding on tender. Perhaps influenced by GE practice, these locomotives were supplied with Westinghouse brake, but this was replaced by the M&GN with vacuum ejector and steam brake in common with MR and GN practice, except for the final 1888 batch which always had dual brake systems.
The second batch (1883) had taller domes. GN chimneys replaced the originals. At the first rebuilding the boilers were replaced with Midland class C boilers 4ft 2in x 10ft 6in; THS 1246 sq ft; WP 160 lbs/sq in; Wt 41 tons 3 cwt with 3000 gallon tenders carrying 3 tons of coal. At the second rebuild, the cabs were enlarged with circular spectacles instead of rectangular and both front and rear sanding on the locomotive, and additional sandbox being placed behind the leading splasher to supply the rear sanders. The height of the leading splasher was increased slightly to be equal in height to the rear sandbox to meet it an inch or two above the splasher. Nos 21-31 had extended smokeboxes from 1907 and 32-5 had them on the second rebuild. From 1919, boilers 4ft 3in x 10ft 6in were fitted THS 1072.38 sq ft. The M&GN classified them as class A, but after the first rebuild they were known as 'A rebuild'. Presumably because of their intention to withdraw this class, the LNE did not allot a class number and they continued to be known a 'A rebuild'. Those not already withdrawn were given LNE duplicate numbers.

No	Date	M&GN no 1894	First rebuild	Second rebuild	LNE nos no	applied	Withdrawn
21	3/1882	21	1896	1914			1936
22	3/1882	22	1898	1915			1936
23	3/1882	23	1895	11/1919	(023)		2/1937
24	3/1882	24	1898	1914			1936*
25	11/1883	25	1906	6/1920	025	6/1937	5/1941
26	11/1883	26	1904	5/1923	(026)		11/1936
27	11/1883	27	1905	3/1927	027	11/1936	2/1937
28	11/1883	28	1905	2/1925	(028)		2/1938
29	11/1886	29		1906			1933
30	11/1886	30		1906			1933
31	11/1886	31		1907			1933
32	1888	32		1907**			1936
33	1888	33		1908**			1933
34	1888	34		1908**			1933
35	1888	35		1909**			1936

* The boiler of no 25 was fitted to the frames of no 24 in 1936 and the resulting engine numbered 25.
** Nos 32-5 were rebuilt with extended cab roof and 33-5 also had tender weatherboard.

0-6-0T Built by Sharp Stewart & Co. Works nos 2360/1, 2368/9, 2373 (1874).
DW 3ft 6in; Cyls 16¼ x 20 o/s. Dimensions as L&F nos 1-3.
Purchased from Sharp Stewart by L&F on behalf of, but prior to, the formation of the
amalgamating companies (E&MR), having been returned to them by the Cornwall Minerals
Railway (their nos 11-14 & 18). As with the Cornwall Mineral's saddle tanks purchased
by the L&F for their own use, the backplates were removed and 1150 gallon tenders
attached. They were given the same numbers as on the CM. Nos 13, 14 & 18 were
rebuilt as 2-4-0 as L&F no 3 with Westinghouse brake.

		Rebuilt	M&GN	Duplicate		
No	Date	2-4-0	no 1894	no	date	Withdrawn
11	3/1881		**11**	11A	9/1894	1899*
12	3/1881		**12**	12A	11/1894	1902*
13	3/1881	1891	**13**	13A	11/1894	1898
14	3/1881	1892	**14**	14A	11/1894	1897*
18	3/1881	1890	**18**	18A	11/1894	1895

* Nos 11/12 & 13 were officially rebuilt to M&GN class MR 0-6-0T on these dates but in
actual fact were scrapped with wheels only being reused.

2-4-0 Built by Rothwell & Company, Union Foundry, Bolton in 1857. Builders nos
160/165.
DW 5ft 2in; LW 3ft 9in; WB 6ft 0in + 8ft 3in; Cyls 17 x 20 o/s; WP 120 lbs/sq in; Wt
22½ tons.
Purchased from L&NW as their numbers 1858 and 1976. Previously L&NW 379/1118/1101 and
384/1802/1112. Originally Lancaster & Carlisle no 3 *Sedgewick* and no 8 *Luck of
Edenhall* (see Vol 2A page 36 - no 1858 wrongly shown as 1855). When built, DW was 5ft
0in; Cyls 15 x 20. Crewe type with Allan valve gear. 1800 gallon tender holding 3
tons coal.

No   Date
29   11/1883
       1885   Renumbered **42**
       1891   Rebuilt with Stephenson valve gear and E&M chimney.
              Front and rear sanding.
       1893   Replaced. Possibly to Duplicate list.
       c1895 Broken up
30   11/1883
       1885   Renumbered **43**
       1893   Replaced. To Duplicate list 43A.
       c1895 Broken up

MIDLAND AND GREAT NORTHERN JOINT RAILWAY

Incorporated 9/6/1893 effective from 1/7/1893 taking over the Eastern and Midlands
Railway.

80 Locomotives as under:

4-4-0 Built by Sharp Stewart & Co. Works nos 3988-4013, 4190-6.
              Beyer Peacock & Co.   Works nos 4066-72.
DW 6ft 6in; LW 3ft 3in; WB 6ft 0in + 7ft 0½in + 8ft 6in; Cyls 18½ x 26; Blr 4ft 3in x
10ft 6in; THS 1242 sq ft; WP 160 lbs/sq in; Wt 42 tons 12 cwt (later 42 tons 18 cwt);
2950 gallon tender, 3 tons coal.

Class C
Similar to Midland Railway 2808 class with MR class B boiler, which was 3-ring 4ft 1in
to 4ft 3in diameter. The original boilers, where not replaced, were re-tubed having
THS 1099 sq ft and, by 1937, 1078 sq ft. Vacuum train brake control and locomotive
steam brake were adopted as standard. Smokeboxes were extended from 1907 with a
shorter chimney, and the cab roof was extended rearwards. Only forward sanding was
provided, and rear sanding was only added later in the M&GN period. Steam heating
equipment was replaced latterly, being completed by the LNE. DW was later 6ft 6½in;
LW 3ft 3½in.
Three were reboilered with MR H boilers. These boilers were 4ft 8in to 4ft 9½in in
diameter; WP 175 lbs/sq in; Firebox 7ft 0in long as against 5ft 11in on the B class
boiler. No 39 had the Hx type; THS 1428 sq ft, nos 55 & 5 (ex-55) the H1 type with
1347 sq ft. Later the MR G6 Belpaire boiler was introduced which was 4ft 1in to 4ft
2in in diameter with extended smokebox THS 1078 sq ft; Wt 44 tons 7 cwt and the MR G7
Belpaire boiler 4ft 8in to 4ft 9¹/8in diameter also with extended smokebox THS 1394 sq
ft later 1384 sq ft. The G6 boiler had the 5ft 11in firebox and the G7 7ft 0in
firebox (Wt 49 tons 18 cwt). The three above which had the H type boiler all later
had the G7 boiler. Both G6 and G7 boilers had a working pressure of 175 lbs/sq in.
The LNE classified the unrebuilt locomotives as D52, those with G6 boilers D53, and G7
boilers D54. Those with G6 and G7 boilers had Ramsbottom safety valves replaced by
Ross pop type. All were given LNE duplicate numbers.

The following were built by Sharp Stewart & Co:

| | | 1896 | | LNE | | |
No	Date	no	Rebuilt	no	Applied	Withdrawn
36	5/1894		5/1929 G6 Belpaire blr	(036)		1/1937
37	5/1894			(037)		2/1937
38	5/1894			038	12/1937	9/1943
39	5/1894		1908 Hx blr			
			1/1924 G7 Belpaire blr	(039)		2/1937
42	5/1894			042	11/1936	6/1940
43	5/1894			043	9/1937	6/1943
44	6/1894		5/1930 G6 Belpaire blr	044	7/1937	8/1941
45	6/1894		1909 G7 Belpaire blr			
			1934 Tapered stove-pipe			
			chimney	(045)		11/1936
46	6/1894		1915 G7 Belpaire blr	046	3/1937	3/1943
47	6/1894			047	7/1937	6/1942*
48	7/1894			(048)		11/1937
49	7/1894		2/1931 G6 Belpaire blr	049	10/1937	9/1941
50	7/1894		11/1929 G6 Belpaire blr	050	9/1937	
				(2052)***		1/1945
51	8/1894	1	1915 G7 Belpaire blr			
			1932 B boiler	01	10/1936	11/1937
52	8/1894	2	1913 G7 Belpaire blr			
			1931 G6 Belpaire blr	02	1/1937	5/1943

```
53    8/1894    3    1910 G7 Belpaire blr
                     1932 B boiler         (03)              6/1937
54    8/1894    4    1914 G7 Belpaire blr
                     1933 B boiler         (04)              2/1938**
55    8/1894    5    1908 H1 boiler
                     7/1925 G7 Belpaire blr
                     1935 B boiler         05    11/1936    7/1937
56    8/1894    6    8/1930 G6 Belpaire blr 06   10/1937    3/1944
57    8/1894    7    1912 G7 Belpaire blr
                     1933 B boiler         07    10/1936    6/1937
11    9/1894                               011    9/1937    8/1942
12    11/1894                              012   11/1937    8/1942
13    11/1894                              013    5/1937    9/1941
14    11/1894                              (014)            2/1937
17    11/1894                              (017)           10/1937
18    11/1894                              (018)            2/1937
51    8/1896         1915 G7 Belpaire blr  051    9/1937    5/1943
52    8/1896         1913 G7 Belpaire blr  052   10/1936    2/1943
53    8/1896         1910 G7 Belpaire blr  053    7/1937    1/1940
54    9/1896         1914 G7 Belpaire blr  054    1/1937   10/1939**
55    9/1896         1908 H1 boiler
                     7/1925 G7 Belpaire blr
                     1934 Tapered stove pipe
                     chimney.              055    4/1937   11/1943
56    9/1896         1912 G7 Belpaire blr
                     1934 Tapered stove-pipe
                     Chimney               056    2/1937   11/1943
57    9/1896         1912 G7 Belpaire blr  (057)            2/1937
```

*   No 047 was destroyed by enemy action at Norwich City station
** After withdrawal of no 22 in 1936 its 3000 gallon tender was attached to
     no 54 and later to no 4
*** Allotted 1946 number

The following were built by Beyer Peacock & Co:

```
                            LNE
No    Date     Rebuilt      no     Applied   Withdrawn
74    10/1899               (074)            5/1937
75    10/1899               (075)            2/1937
76    10/1899*              076    11/1936   7/1943
77    11/1899  12/1930 G6 Belpaire blr. 077  10/1937
                            (2054)**         1/1945
78    11/1899               078    11/1936   2/1938
79    11/1899               079    11/1936   2/1937
80    11/1899               (080)            2/1937
```

* Accident Hillington 7/3/1909
** Allotted 1946 number

0-6-0 Built by Neilson & Co. Works nos 5032-9 (£2345 each).
          Kitson & Co. Works nos 3873-80 (£2830 each).
DW 5ft 2½in; WB 8ft 0in + 8ft 6in; Cyls 18 x 26; Blr 4ft 2in x 10ft 6in; THS 1240 sq
ft; WP 150 lbs/sq in; Firebox 5ft 11in long x 4ft 0½in wide; Wt 38 tons 16 cwt (later
40 tons 13 cwt); 3250 gallon tender; 5 tons coal.
Class D As 2284 batch of MR 1873 class. B class boiler. Steam brake plus vacuum
train brake control. Wheels later 5ft 3in. Heating surface varied, 1252 sq ft being
also recorded as the original and WP increased to 160 lbs/sq in. Later with 196 tubes
THS was recorded as 1099 sq ft (1909), 1088 sq ft (1910), 1079.5 sq ft (1916) and with
194 tubes, 1069 sq ft (post 1923), 1089 sq ft (1936), 1078 sq ft (1937). Nos
59/60/1/4/5/70/3 were fitted with carriage heating equipment, and the LNE so fitted
062/9/71. Nos 62 and 69 were reboilered with MR H boilers 4ft 8in diameter; THS 1428
sq ft; WP 175 lbs/sq in. By 1915 THS of these boilers was 1315.5 sq ft. Both were

again reboilered with MR G7 Belpaire boilers as were nos 68 and 71. These had
extended smokeboxes; THS 1384 sq ft; WP 175 lbs/sq in; Wt 46 tons 11 cwt. The LNE
classified unrebuilt locomotives J40 and the G7 boilered ones J41. LNE duplicate
numbers. Midland chimneys were replaced, and 2950 gallon tenders attached to some.
No 58, and also others of the unrebuilt locomotives, had cab roof extended as did the
G7 boilered ones. Those fitted with H class boilers had cab side panels enlarged.

The following were built by Neilson & Co:

No	Date	Rebuilt	LNE no	Applied	Withdrawn
58	8/1896		058*	10/1936	9/1938
59	8/1896		059	8/1937	
			(4100)**		6/1944
60	8/1896		060	11/1937	5/1941
61	8/1896		061	1/1939	12/1942
62	8/1896	1906 H boiler			
		12/1923 G7 Belpaire boiler	062	5/1937	10/1939
63	9/1896		(063)		2/1937
64	9/1896		064	by 5/1937	
			(4101)**		3/1944
65	9/1896		065	9/1937	
			(4102)**		3/1944

* Retained M&GN livery
** Allotted 1946 number

The following were built by Kitson & Co:

No	Date	Rebuilt	LNE no	Applied	Withdrawn
66	3/1899		(066)		10/1937*
67	3/1899		(067)		1/1937*
68	4/1899	8/1921 G7 Belpaire boiler	(068)		11/1936*
69	4/1899	1909 H boiler			
		1/1928 G7 Belpaire boiler	069	3/1937	7/1942
70	4/1899		070	1/1938	
			(4103)**		3/1944
71	4/1899	6/1921 G7 Belpaire boiler	071	5/1937	7/1943
72	4/1899		(072)		10/1937*
73	4/1899		073	9/1937	5/1941

* Not taken into LNE stock
** Allotted 1946 number

0-6-0 Built by Dubs & Co. Works nos 3933-44.
DW 5ft 1½in; WB 7ft 3in + 8ft 3in; Cyls 17½ x 26; Blr 4ft 5in x 10ft 1in; THS 1126 sq
ft; WP 175 lbs/sq in; Firebox 5ft 6in long x 4ft 0½in wide; Wt 42 tons 2½ cwt; 3170
gallon tenders, 4-5 tons coal.
Class DA As GN class J5, these twelve locomotives having actually been ordered as GN
nos 1161-72. Wheels later 5ft 2in. Extended smokeboxes and spark arrestors fitted
from 1907. WP 170 lbs/sq in by 1923.
From 1920 they were rebuilt with 4ft 8in diameter boilers as GN class J4 becoming LNE
class J3. THS 1235 sq ft; Wt 42 tons 12 cwt. Eight reverted to 4ft 5in boilers as
LNE class J4 with 2800 gallon tenders.

		Rebuilt		LNE		1946		
No	Date	J3	J4	no	Applied	no	Applied	Withdrawn
81	10/1900	6/1927		081	4/1938	4156	6/1946	9/1947
82	10/1900	8/1921	3/1937	082	3/1937	4157	8/1946	8/1947
83	10/1900	1/1921		083	1936	4158	6/1946	7/1951*
84	10/1900	12/1924	1/1937	084	1/1937	4159	8/1946	8/1947
85	10/1900	4/1926	2/1937	085	2/1937	4160	5/1946	12/1951**

```
86  10/1900  10/1927            086  1/1937   4161  6/1946   9/1947***
87  10/1900  5/1925   6/1937    087  6/1937   4162  12/1946  12/1950*
88  10/1900  11/1920            088  1936     4163  6/1946   1/1949*
89  10/1900  2/1926   4/1937    089  4/1937   4164  8/1946   8/1947
90  11/1900  12/1926  2/1937    090  2/1937   (4165)         7/1946
91  10/1900  1/1927   5/1937    091  5/1937   (4166)         1/1946
92  11/1900  10/1921  2/1937    092  2/1937   4167  6/1946   7/1948*
*      BR number not applied
**     BR number 64160 applied 11/1948
***    No 4161 withdrawn 7/1939, reinstated 10/1939
```

0-6-0T Built by M&GN at Melton Constable.
DW 3ft 6½in; WB 6ft 3in + 7ft 6in; Cyls 16 x 20 o/s; Blr 3ft 11in x 9ft 7in; THS 737
sq ft (later 729.8 sq ft); WP 140-150 lbs/sq in; Firebox 4ft 3in long x 3ft 10in wide;
Wt 37 tons 13¾ cwt; 800 gallon tanks; 1½ tons coal.
Shunting Class. Some parts including wheels from ex-Cornwall Minerals tanks were used
in construction, and they were officially regarded as rebuilds, which is presumably
why seven of them originally had duplicate numbers, but this was only for accounting
purposes as they were really new locomotives. Steam brake plus vacuum control was
fitted, and they had laminated springs on the leading axle, twin-coil springs on the
centre (driving) axle and inverted laminated springs mounted transversely on the rear
axle.
LNE class J93.

		Renumbered	LNE		1946		
No	Date	no	date	no	Applied	no	Applied	Withdrawn
14A	10/1897	98	1907	098	8/1937	8482	8/1946	1/1947
1A	8/1898	93	1907	093	12/1937			6/1944
11A	4/1899	96	1907	096	3/1937	8484	8/1946	5/1948*
3A	12/1899	95	1907	095	5/1937	8485	8/1946	12/1947
15	1/1901			015	11/1937			12/1945
17A	3/1902	99	1907	099	3/1937			7/1945
12A	12/1902	97	1907	097	2/1938			3/1943
2A	1/1904	94	1907	094	12/1937	8488	8/1946	1/1948*
16	5/1905			016	5/1938	8489	12/1946	8/1949*

* BR numbers not applied. No 096 had a stovepipe chimney fitted in 1941. Vacuum
pipes were removed latterly. No 094 had vacuum pipes removed by 1946. No 8489 had
a stovepipe chimney fitted by 1949. No 8485 had a stovepipe chimney shorter than
the above fitted by 1947. Vacuum pipes were removed by 1946.

4-4-2T Built by M&GN at Melton Constable.
DW 6ft 0in; LW 3ft 0in; TW 3ft 6½in; WB 6ft 6in + 7ft 0in + 8ft 6in + 7ft 6in; Cyls
17¾ x 24 o/s; THS 1232 sq ft; WP 160 lbs/sq in; Firebox 5ft 11in long x 4ft 0½in wide;
Wt 68 tons 9 cwt; 1650 gallon tanks; 2 tons coal.
Class A. Designed by GB Clarke, chief draughtsman, using some 4-4-0 parts and
referred to as 'rebuilds', but given capital list numbers. Nos 20 and 9 had extended
smokeboxes. Accordingly weight of no 41 was recorded in 9/1920 as 65½ tons. In order
to improve forward view the tanks were given sloping top, reducing capacity to 1600
gallons. THS was later 1099 sq ft (196 instead of 240 tubes) and later still 1078 sq
ft (194 tubes).
LNE class C17 from 7/1942.

		LNE		
No	Date	no	Applied	Withdrawn
41	12/1904	041	9/1937	1/1944 (No 7503 allotted 1943)
20	2/1909	020	11/1937	4/1942
9	3/1910	09	5/1937	7/1944 (No 7504 allotted 1943)

EASTERN AND MIDLANDS RAILWAY and MIDLAND AND GREAT NORTHERN JOINT RAILWAY

NUMBER INDEX

1	1883 ex-L&F			66	1899 0-6-0 Class D	
-6	1894 Blank			-73		
	1896 4-4-0 ex-51-6			74	1899 4-4-0 Class C	
7	1883 Ex-Y&NN/L&F-80			-80		
	1894 Blank			81	1900 0-6-0 Class D	
	1896 4-4-0 ex-57			-92		
8	1883 Ex-L&F Class B			93	1907 0-6-0T Shunting ex-1A-3A	
	c1916 Blank			-95		
9	1883 Ex-L&F Class B			96	1907 0-6-0T Shunting ex-11A-12A	
	1910 4-4-2T			-97		
10	1883 Ex-L&F Class B			98	1907 0-6-0T Shunting ex-14A	
	c1916 Blank			99	1907 0-6-0T Shunting ex-17A	

 1   1883 ex-L&F
-6   1894 Blank
     1896 4-4-0 ex-51-6
 7   1883 Ex-Y&NN/L&F-80
     1894 Blank
     1896 4-4-0 ex-57
 8   1883 Ex-L&F Class B
     c1916 Blank
 9   1883 Ex-L&F Class B
     1910 4-4-2T
10   1883 Ex-L&F Class B
     c1916 Blank
11   1883 0-6-0T Ex-Cornwall Minerals
-14 1894 4-4-0 Class C
15   1883 ex-Y&NN
     1901 0-6-0T Shunting
16   1883 Ex-Y&NN
     1905 0-6-0T Shunting
17   1883 Ex-Y&NN
     1894 4-4-0 Class C
18   1883 0-6-0T Ex-Cornwall Minerals
     1894 4-4-0 Class C
19   1883 Ex-Y&NN Class B
     c1916 Blank
20   1883 Ex-L&F Class B
     1909 4-4-2T
21   1882 4-4-0 Class A
-24
25   1883 4-4-0 Class A
-28
29   1883 2-4-0 Ex-L&NW
-30 1886 4-4-0 Class A
     1934 Blank
31   1883 Ex-Y&NN Class B
     1886 4-4-0 Class A
     1934 Blank
32   1883 Ex-Y&NN Class B
     1887 Blank
     1888 4-4-0 Class A
33   1888 4-4-0 Class A
-34 1934 Blank
35   1888 4-4-0 Class A
36   1894 4-4-0 Class C
-39
40   1886 4-4-0T Ex-31
     c1916 Blank
41   1886 4-4-0T Ex-32
     1904 4-4-2T
42   1885 2-4-0 Ex-29/30
-43 1894 4-4-0 Class C
44   1894 4-4-0 Class C
-50
51   1896 4-4-0 Class C
-57
58   1896 0-6-0 Class D
-65

66   1899 0-6-0 Class D
-73
74   1899 4-4-0 Class C
-80
81   1900 0-6-0 Class D
-92
93   1907 0-6-0T Shunting ex-1A-3A
-95
96   1907 0-6-0T Shunting ex-11A-12A
-97
98   1907 0-6-0T Shunting ex-14A
99   1907 0-6-0T Shunting ex-17A

BIBLIOGRAPHY

Abbreviations

BRJ	*British Railway Journal*
BRM	*British Railway Modelling*
Bylines	*Railway Bylines*
Eng	*The Engineer*
Engg	*Engineering*
Eng Mech	*English Mechanic*
GEJ	*Great Eastern Journal* Great Eastern Railway Society
GNSRA	*Great North Review*: Great North of Scotland Railway Association
HMRS	*Journal of the Historical Model Railway Society*
L&R	*Locomotives and Railways*
LI	*Locomotives Illustrated*
Loco Mag	*Locomotive Magazine* (Vol 1 [1896] was *Moore's Monthly Magazine*, from Vol 22 [1916] *Locomotive, Railway Carriage and Wagon Review*)
Mech Eng	*Mechanical Engineer*
MGNRC	*Bulletin of the Midland & Great Northern Circle*
Mod Back	*Modellers Backtrack*
Mod Eng	*Model Engineer*
Mod Rlys	*Model Railways* (formerly *Model Railway News*)
Modern R	*Modern Railways* (formerly *Trains Illustrated*)
MRC	*Model Railway Constructor*
MRJ	*Model Railway Journal*
MRN	*Model Railway News* (later *Model Railways*)
NBRSG	*Journal of the North British Railway Study Group*
New Soc	*Newcomen Society Transactions*
Railways	*Railways* (from Vol 14 [1953] *Railway World*)
Rly Eng	*Railway Engineer*
Rly Mag	*Railway Magazine*
Rly Mod	*Railway Modeller*
Rly Wld	*Railway World* (formerly *Railways*)
RO	*Railway Observer* Journal of the Railway Correspondence and Travel Society
RTM	*Railway and Travel Monthly*
SLS	*Journal of the Stephenson Locomotive Society*
Stm Days	*Steam Days*
TI	*Trains Illustrated* (from Vol 14 [1961] *Modern Railways*)

Various organisations exist for the study of the companies covered in this volume and all have helped to bring this bibliography up to date. If you would like to find out more about their activities, and possibly become involved yourself, their websites can be found as follows:

Colne Valley Railway	http://www.colnevalleyrailway.co.uk/
Great Eastern Railway Society	http://www.gersociety.org.uk/
Great North of Scotland Railway Association	http://www.gnsra.org.uk/
Midland & Great Northern Circle	http://www.mgncircle.org.uk/
Mid-Suffolk Light Railway Museum	http://www.mslr.org.uk/
North British Railway Study Group	http://www.nbrstudygroup.co.uk/

GREAT EASTERN RAILWAY

Constituent Companies

Eastern Counties Railway
Loco Mag Vol 6 pp 180, 196 (1901); Vol 7 pp 79, 111 (1902); Vol 8 pp 75,160, 196,
          228, 296, 368, 440 (1903); Vol 9 pp 112,170, 224, 368 (1903);Vol 10 p 189
          (1904); Vol 11 p 59 (1905); Vol 12 pp 21, 75, 165 (1906); Vol 13 pp 3, 13,
          43 (1907); Vol 14 pp 3, 61 (1908); Vol 43 pp 79, 126, 140, 195, 228, 265,
          296, 367, 396 (1937); Vol 44 pp 53, 127, 186, 261, 358 (1938); Vol 45 pp
          56, 111 (1939); Vol 54 pp 169, 176 (1948)
GEJ   Vol 2 Issue 15
Sinclair 2-4-0 Class Y
Loco Mag Vol 14 p 61 (1908)
SLS   Vol 29 p 299 (1953)
2-2-2 Nos 61-7
GEJ   Vol 6 Issue 59
Early Ballast Engines
GEJ   Vol 9 Issue 84
Enfield **Steam carriage**
Vertical Boiler Locomotives and Railmotors Built in Great Britain, RAS Rowland,
    Oakwood Press 1989
GEJ   Vol 3 Issue 26
RO   Vol 42 pp 434-6 (1972)
Crampton
Mod Eng   Vol 109 pp 550-1 (1953)

Northern and Eastern Railway
Loco Mag Vol 7 p 42 (1902)

Norfolk Railway (Yarmouth & Norwich)
The First Railway in Norfolk G Dow, LNER 1944, 1947
Loco Mag Vol 10 pp 2, 21, 57, 101, 138 (1904)

Newmarket Railway
Loco Mag Vol 10 p 138 (1904)
GEJ   Vol 1 Issue 10

East Anglian Railway
The Lynn and Dereham Railway, Stanley C Jenkins, Oakwood Press 1993
The Lynn and Hunstanton Railway and the West Norfolk Branch, Stanley C Jenkins,
    Oakwood Press 1987
Loco Mag Vol 11 p 21 (1905)
Rly Mag   Vol 25 pp 331, 401 (1909) HH Meik
GEJ   Vol 2 Issue 16

Eastern Union Railway
East Anglia's First Railway, Hugh Moffat, Terence Dutton 1987
The Eastern Union Railway, HF Hilton, LNER 1946
Loco Mag Vol 11 pp 98, 149, 189 (1905)
          Vol 13 p 204 (1907)
Rly Mag   Vol 25 p 513 (1909)
          Vol 26 p 43 (1910) HH Meik

London and Blackwall Railway
Stepney's Own Railway, JE Connor, Connor and Butler 1987
Loco Mag Vol 10 p 171 (1904)
          Vol 15 p 89 (1909)
GEJ   Vol 2 Issue 19

Waveney Valley Railway
Loco Mag   Vol 15 p 45 (1909)
GEJ   Vol 2 Issue 14

Wivenhoe and Brightlingsea Railway
The Fighting Branch: Wivenhoe and Brightlingsea Railway, Paul Brown, Scribe 1975
Wivenhoe and Brightlingsea Railway, Paul Brown, Ian Henry Publications 1985, 1995
Loco Mag   Vol 17 p 75 (1911)
GEJ   Vol 1 Issue 10

Thetford and Watton Railway
Loco Mag   Vol 17 p 76 (1911)
GEJ   Vol 1 Issue 10

Felixstowe Railway
The Felixstowe Railway, HI Quayle & GT Bradbury, Oakwood Press 1978
Loco Mag   Vol 17 p 75 (1911)
Rly Mag   Vol 48 p 73 (1921) JF Gairns
GEJ   Vol 1 Issue 10

General Surveys
Aspects of East Anglian Steam: Vol 1: Liverpool Street, JD Mann, South Anglia
    Publications 1989
Aspects of East Anglian Steam: Vol 2: On Eastern Branch Lines and the M&GN, Part 1,
    JD Mann, South Anglia Publications 1991
Aspects of East Anglian Steam: Vol 3: The GER 1950-1962, JD Mann, South Anglia
    Publications 1992
Aspects of East Anglian Steam: Vol 5:On Eastern Branch Lines and the M&GN, Part 2,
    JD Mann, South Anglia Publications 1992
Aspects of East Anglian Steam: Vol 6:Norwich to Liverpool Street and Southend Routes,
    JD Mann, South Anglia Publications 1993
The Colour of Steam Vol 9 - The Great Eastern Line, RC Riley, Atlantic 1990
Great Eastern Album, RC Riley, Ian Allan 1968
GER Locomotives 1858-1924, Lyn D Brooks, GER Society Information sheet L100/1-12
Great Eastern Articles in the Railway Press, GER Society 1981
Great Eastern Locomotives 1900-22, C Langley Aldrich, The Author 1942,
    Fowler & Son 1944
Great Eastern Locomotives 1923 with additions to 1943, C Langley Aldrich,
    The Author 1944
Great Eastern Locomotives Past and Present 1862-1948, C Langley Aldrich,
    The Author 1949
The Great Eastern Railway, Cecil J Allen, Ian Allan 1955, 1956, 1959, 1961, 1967, 1975
The Great Eastern Railway, Gavin Smith, The History Press 2007
Great Eastern Railway: A Selection of 7mm Locomotive Drawings Reproduced from
    Locomotive Magazine, M Sharman (compiled), Oakwood Press 1987
Great Eastern Railways: A Pictorial Collection, JD Mann, South Anglia 1975
The Great Eastern Since 1900, C Philips, Ian Allan 1985
The Life and Times of the Great Eastern Railway, Paar & Gray, The Book Castle 1991
Locomotives of the GER, Locomotive Magazine Extracts 1901-13, AW Wright, GER Society
    Information sheets L104-8
Locomotives of the GER, Locomotive Magazine Extracts 1937-8, AW Wright, GER Society
    Information sheet L110
The Locomotives of the Great Eastern Railway 1862-1954, C Langley Aldrich,
    The Author 1955
The Locomotives of the Great Eastern Railway 1862-1962, C Langley Aldrich,
    The Author 1969
Stratford Works Locomotive List, Lyn D Brooks, GER Society Information sheet L115
GEJ   Vol 2 Issue 14, Locomotive Policy - Sinclair and Worsdell
GEJ   Vol 2 Issue 18, Locomotive Policy - James Holden
GEJ   Vol 7 Issue 69, GER Locomotives and the Continent
GEJ   Vol 8 Issue 75, GERS 20th Anniversary Review - GE Locomotive History

Rly Mag   Vol 49 p 1 (1921), Stratford Works, JF Gairns
HMRS   Vol 4 p 29, Stratford Works (photos)
Railways   Vol 6 p 67 (1945), Adams Locomotives
Rly Wld   Vol 45 p 346 (1984), Massey Bromley
Railways   Vol 4 p 162 (1943), Holden Locomotives
LI   No 116 *GE Jazz Engines, N7s and Their Predecessors* (1997)
Loco Mag   Vol 16 pp 68-70, 91, 185, 215-6 (1910); Vol 17 pp 30-2, 124-5 (1911)
            Vol 19 p 58 (1913); *Locomotives of the GER*, ACW Lowe [See also *passim*]
L&R   Vol 2 pp 51, 131 (1901); Vol 3 pp 37, 54, 88, 113 (1903) *Early Locomotives*
SLS   Vol 27 pp 125-9, 355 (1951), *Some old Engines*
Rly Mag   Vol 43 pp 9, 86, 151, 241, 295, 364 (1918), *Locomotive and Train*
            Working in the Latter Part of the 19th Century, EL Ahrons
            Also republished by Heffer, edited by LL Asher, Vol 1 1951
Loco Mag   *Famous Locomotive Engineers*, C Hamilton Ellis
            Vol 44 pp 383-6 (1938), Part 8 - Robert Sinclair
            Vol 45 pp 51-5 1939), Part 9 - William Adams
            Vol 45 pp 115-18 (1939), Part 10 - Thomas W Worsdell
            Vol 45 pp 313-18 (1939), Part 13 - Samuel W Johnston
            Vol 48 pp 110-15 (1942), Part 20 - James Holden

See also works having information *inter alia* at end.

Locomotive Types

2-2-2 Sinclair
Loco Mag   Vol 14 p 191 (1908)
            Vol 15 p 223 (1909)
Eng   Vol 24 (1867)
D27 Holden
Loco Mag   Vol 18 p 119 (1912)
Eng   Vol 71 (1891)
Mod Eng   Vol 93 pp 422-4 (1945)
GEJ   Vol 4 Issue 47
4-2-2 Bromley
Loco Mag   Vol 17 p 51 (1911)
Eng Mech   Vol 37 pp 268, 314 (1886)
L&R   Vol 1 p 228 (1900)
MRN   Vol 39 p 180 (1963)
P43 Holden
Loco Mag   Vol 18 p 120 (1912)
Rly Eng   Vol 19 (1898)
MRN   Vol 25 p 144 (1949)
    No 17 fitted for oil fuel:
    Rly Eng   Vol 20 (1899 working drawing), Vol 22 (1901)
2-4-0 Sinclair
Loco Mag   Vol 14 pp 4. 61 (1908)
Railways   Vol 4 pp 104, 140, correspondence p 173 (1943)
Johnson
Loco Mag   Vol 15 pp 107, 130, 223 (1909)
MRN   1 Class Vol 27 p 94 (1951)
Mod Eng   1 Class Vol 114 pp 700-1 (1956)
G14 Worsdell
Loco Mag   Vol 18 p 10 (1912)
Eng Mech   Vol 37 p 199 (1886)
Eng   Vol 55 (1883, working drawing)
Engg   Vol 36 (1883, working drawing)
Rly Eng   Vol 5 (1884)
GEJ   Vol 2 Issue 18
T19 Holden
Loco Mag   Vol 18 pp 119, 150 (1939)

SLS   Vol 15 pp 17, 64, 71, 135 (1939)
           Vol 20 p 183 (1944)
Eng   Vol 79 (1895)
Engg   Vol 45 (1888, working drawing)
Rly Eng   Vol 12 (1891, working drawing)
GEJ   Vol 1 Issues 7 & 9
HMRS   Vol 2 p 104
BRJ   GE Edition pp 13-22 (1989), Lyn D Brooks
LI   No 92 *GWR & LNER Group 2-4-0s*, JWP Rowledge (1993)
Rly Mod   Vol 15 p 320 (1964); Vol 16 p 80 (1965)
   No 761 fitted for oil fuel:
   Eng   Vol 78 (1894)
   Engg   Vol 58 (1894, working drawing), Vol 63 (1897)
   Rly Eng   Vol 12 (1891)

T26 Holden
Locomotives of the LNER Part 4, RCTS 1968
Loco Mag   Vol 18 p 169 (1912)
SLS   Vol 16 p 199 (1940)
Engg   Vol 53 (1892, working drawing)
Rly Wld   Vol 16 p 130 (1955); Vol 22 p 106 (1961)
Mod Rlys   Vol 13 p 94 (1984)
GEJ   Vol 6 Issues 58 & 59
RO   Vol 25 pp 73-5, 106-7, 142-4 (1955); Vol 26 pp 255-6
           Vol 27 pp 174-5 (1956), P Proud
           Vol 3 pp 31-2 (1931), JE Kite; Vol 11 p 21 (1939)
LI   No 92 *GWR & LNER Group 2-4-0s*, JWP Rowledge (1993)

4-4-0 Adams
MRN   Vol 38 p 384 (1962)

C8 Johnson
Loco Mag   Vol 16 pp 113, 239 (1910)

G16 Compound, Worsdell
Loco Mag   Vol 18 p 199 (1912)
Eng   Vol 59 (1885, part working drawing); Vol 83 (1897)

T19 Holden rebuilt from 2-4-0
Locomotives of the LNER Part 3C, RCTS 1981
Rly Mod   Vol 37 p 501 (1986)
HMRS   Vol 2 p 74
MRC   Vol 1 p 150 (1934); Vol 4 p 46 (1937); Vol 15 p 7 (1948)
GEJ   Vol 1 Issues 7 & 9
RO   Vol 10 p 352 (1938)

S46, D56 *Claud Hamilton*
Locomotives of the LNER Part 3C, RCTS (1981)
Loco Mag   Vol 18 p 183 (912)
SLS   Vol 15 pp 17, 64, 71, 135 (1939); Vol 16 pp 10,14,48,56,101,153,
           171, 198, 235 (1940); Vol 17 pp 32, 70, 110, 156, 195, 211,
           correspondence p 180 (1941); Vol 18 pp 66, 129, 145,
           correspondence pp 96, 202 (1942), KACR Nunn
L&R   Vol 1 p 45 (1900)
Rly Eng   Vol 22 (1901, working drawing)
GEJ   Vol 4 Issue 46
LI   No 42 *GER 'Claud Hamilton' 4-4-0s*, John Booth (1985)
RO   Vol 10 p 352 (1938)
Railways   Vol 8 p 125 (1947)
Rly Wld   Vol 21 p 69 (1960); Vol 24 p 338 (1963); Vol 31 p 18 (1970)
TI   Vol 1 issue 7 p 4, correspondence p 23; Vol 6 p 116 (1953);
           Vol 8 p 332 (1955); Vol 14 p 113, correspondence p 255 (1961)
Rly Mag   Vol 73 pp 139, 152 (1933); Vol 74 pp 127, 397 (1934);
           Vol 75 p 306 (1934); Vol 76 p 219 (1935)
Mod Eng   Vol 123 pp 264, 326, 394, 456 (1960)
MRN   Vol 34 p 58 (1958)

Rly Mod   Vol 40 p 374 (1989)
   Fitted for oil fuel:
   Rly Eng   Vol 42 (1921)
Superheated *Claud Hamilton*
Rly Mag   Vol 52 p 492 (1923) Rebuilt from D56
SLS   Vol 8 p 23 (1932)
0-6-0
Johnson
Loco Mag   Vol 15 p 167 (1909) 417 class
           Vol 16 p 23 (1910) 477 class
Engg   Vol 13 (1872) 477 class
Bromley
Loco Mag   Vol 17 p 173 (1911)
Eng Mech   Vol 37 p 411 (1886)
Y14 Worsdell/Holden
Locomotives of the LNER Part 5 RCTS 1966, 1984
Rebirth of an Engine: The Story of Our J15, M&GN Joint Railway Society
Loco Mag   Vol 18 pp 34, 212 (1912)
Eng Mech   Vol 37 p 411 (1886)
SLS   Vol 8 p 230 (1932); Vol 28 p 305 (1952)
           On war service: Vol 29 p 119 (1953)
Eng   Vol 89 (1900)
Engg   Vol 37 (1884, working drawing)
GEJ   Vol 1 Issues 2 & 3; Vol 3 Issues 36 & 37
Rly Eng   Vol 11 (1890)
RO   Vol 11 p 113 (1939)
           Vol 16 pp 36-7, 60-1 (1946) P Proud
Rly Mag   Vol 100 p 239 (1954)
Compound 0-6-0 Holden
Loco Mag   Vol 18 p 233 (1912)
N31 Holden
Locomotives of the LNER Part 5, RCTS 1966,1984
Loco Mag   Vol 18 p 213 (1912)
RO   Vol 11 p 113 (1939)
F48, G58 Holden
Locomotives of the LNER Part 5, RCTS 1966,1984
Loco Mag   Vol 18 p 233 (1912)
L&R   Vol 1 p 140 (1900)
RO   Vol 11 p 113 (1939)
           Vol 27 pp 228-30, 262-4 (1957) P Proud
T77, D81 Hill
Locomotives of the LNER Part 5, RCTS 1966,1984
Eng   Vol 122 (1916)
Rly Eng   Vol 37 (1916)
RO   Vol 11 p 100, 113 (1900)
           Rebuilt by Gresley: Rly Mag Vol 77 p 437 (1935)
2-6-0
Loco Mag   Vol 17 p 15 (1911)
Engg   Vol 29 (1889, working drawing)
GEJ   Vol 4 Issue 42
MRN   Vol 38 p 101 (1962)
4-6-0
Locomotives of the LNER Part 2B, RCTS 1975
Loco Mag   Vol 19 p 16 (1913)
SLS   Vol 8 p 230 (1932)
Eng   Vol 113 (1912, part working drawing)
Engg   Vol 93 (1912)
Rly Eng   Vol 33 (1912, part working drawing); Vol 34 (1913)
GEJ   Vol 7 issues 67 & 68
RO   Vol 10 p 226 (1938)

TI   Vol 8 p 69 (1947); Vol 12 p 361, correspondence pp 516, 570 (1951);
            Vol 13 p 62 (1952)
Railways   Vol 6 p 188 (1945)
Rly Wld   Vol 24 p 213 (1963); Vol 30 p 296, correspondence p 464 (1969)
MRC   Vol 1 p 130 (1934)
LI   No 77 *GER 4-4-0s* JWP Rowledge (1991)
Rly Mod   **Gresley rebuild B12/3** Vol 23 p 352 (1972)
Rly Mag   Vol 103 p 680 (1957)

0-4-0ST
Locomotives of the LNER Part 9B, RCTS 1977
Loco Mag   **No 200 *The Chairman*** Vol 16 p 161 (1910)
GEJ   Vol 2 Issue 14
Loco Mag   Vol 19 p 109 (1913)
SLS   Vol 19 p 224 (1943)
RO   Vol 12 pp 82-4 (1940)
GEJ   Vol 8 Issue 80
Rly Wld   Vol 45 p 599 (1984)
Mod Rlys   Vol 2 pp 671, 854, 909 (1972)

0-4-0T
Locomotives of the LNER Part 9B, RCTS 1977
MRC   Vol 2 pp 156, 172 (1935)
SLS   Vol 8 p 230 (1932)

0-4-0T Tram
Locomotives of the LNER Part 9B, RCTS 1977
Vertical Boiler Locomotives and Railmotors built in Great Britain, RAS Abbott,
    Oakwood Press 1989 p 87
Loco Mag   Vol 16 p 262 (1910); Vol 18 p 53 (1912); Vol 19 p 109 (1913)
Mod Rlys   Vol 13 p 82 (1984)
Rly Mod   Vol 12 p 163 (1961)
HMRS   Vol 4 p 35
RO   Vol 12 p 82 (1940)

0-4-2T
Loco Mag   **Class T7 Johnson** Vol 16 p 3 (1910)
Mod Rlys   Vol 11 p 759 (1982)
Loco Mag   **Class K9 Adams** Vol 16 p 261 (1910)

2-4-0WT Sinclair
Loco Mag   Vol 15 p 44 (1909)

2-4-2WT Sinclair
Loco Mag   Vol 15 p 64 (1909)
MRN   Vol 21 p 177 (1945)
GEJ   Vol 7 Issue 63

2-4-2T
M15 Worsdell/Holden
Locomotives of the LNER Part 7, RCTS 1964, 1983
Loco Mag   Vol 18 p 73 (1912); Vol 19 p 39 (1913)
SLS   Vol 19 p 141 (1943); Vol 38 p 41 (1962)
Eng   Vol 59 (1885, working drawing); Vol 110 (1910)
Rly Eng   Vol 6 (1885)
Rly Mod   Vol 3 p 127 (1952)
Mod Rlys   Vol 5 pp 130, 239 (1976)
RO   Vol 11 p 24 (1939)

C32 Holden
Locomotives of the LNER Part 7, RCTS 1964, 1983
Loco Mag   Vol 19 p 39 (1913)
Rly Eng   Vol 15 (1894, working drawing)
SLS   Vol 29 p 222, correspondence p 371 (1953)
RO   Vol 11 p 24 (1939)
            Vol 21 pp 22-3 (1951) P Proud

G69, Y65 SD Holden
Locomotives of the LNER Part 7, RCTS 1964, 1983

Loco Mag   Vol 19 pp 39-40 (1913)
Rly Eng   Vol 30 (1909)
Railways   Vol 10 p 62 (1949)
Mod Rlys   Vol 5 p 130 (1976)
GEJ   Vol 1 Issue 6
RO   Vol 11 p 24 (1939)
0-4-4Ts & 2-4-2Ts
SLS   Vol 32 p 32 (correspondence, 1956)
TI   Vol 11 p 647 (1950)
0-4-4T
Great Eastern Railway 0-4-4Ts, Great Eastern Railway Society 1979
Loco Mag   Vol 42 pp 45-8 (1936)
Johnson
Loco Mag   Vol 16 p 67 (1910); Vol 17 p 30 (1911)
Adams
Loco Mag   Vol 16 p 185 (1910)
Bromley
Eng Mech   Vol 37 p 411 (1886)
Loco Mag   Vol 17 pp 30, 124 (1911)
L&R   Vol 1 p 158 (1900)
SLS   Vol 20 p 117 (1944)
S44 Holden
Locomotives of the LNER Part 7, RCTS 1964, 1983
Loco Mag   Vol 19 p 58 (1913)
GEJ   Vol 1 Issue 3
RO   Vol 11 p 38 (1939)
0-6-0T & 0-6-0ST
Great Eastern Railway 0-6-0Ts, P Proud, RCTS c1955
Previously published in Railway Observer as below
RO   Vol 24 pp 8-11, 34-5, 65-6, 101-4, 135-7, 276 (1954)
            Vol 11 pp 243, 283 (1939)
LI   No 142 *Great Eastern Railway 0-6-0s, LNER classes J14-J20* (2002)
Johnson
Loco Mag   Vol 15 pp 108, 203 (1909)
Eng   Vol 27 (1869, working drawing)
Engg   Vol 6 (1868)
Crane tanks rebuilt from above
Locomotives of the LNER Part 9B (1977)
RO   Vol 4 p 103 (1932); Vol 12 p 107 (1940)
Bromley
Loco Mag   Vol 17 p 173 (1911)
MRJ   Vol 1 pp 9, 41, 80 (1985) M12 in 4mm
T18, R24, S56, E22 Holden
Locomotives of the LNER Part 8A, RCTS 1970, 1983
Loco Mag   Vol 19 p 58 (T18), p 77 (R24), p 78 (S56), p 109 (E22) (1913)
Rly Eng   Vol 14 (1893) T18
Railways   Vol 6 pp 121, 153, 167, 185 (1945) T18
RO   Vol 11 p 281 (1939)
Rly Mod   Vol 39 p 130 (1988) S56
Mod Rlys   Vol 1 p 390 (1970) S56
SLS   Vol 33 p 215 (1957) S56
Mod Eng   Vol 103 p 484 (1950)
Hill
Locomotives of the LNER Part 8A, RCTS 1970, 1983
Loco Mag   Vol 19 p 78 (1913)
SLS   Vol 8 p 230 (1932)
RO   Vol 11 p 281 (1939)
0-6-0T 'Tram'
Locomotives of the LNER Part 8A, RCTS 1970, 1983
Loco Mag   Vol 19 p 109 (1913)

Mod Rlys   Vol 13 p 82 (1984)
RO   Vol 11 p 281 (1939)
0-6-2T
Locomotives of the LNER Part 9A, RCTS 1977
Eng   Vol 119 (1915); Vol 133 (1922)
SLS   Vol 8 p 231 (1932)
RO   Vol 11 pp 346-7 (1939)
Railways   Vol 1 pp 78, 93 (1940)
Rly Wld   Vol 18 p 67 (1957)
GEJ   Vol 6 Issue 60
0-10-0WT
Eng   Vol 95 p 135 (1903, working drawing)
Engg   Vol 75 p 111 (1903, working drawing)
Mech Eng   Vol 11 p 450 (1903)
Rly Eng   Vol 24 p 74 (1903, working drawing)
Loco Mag   Vol 8 p 259, Tests p 177, (1903); Vol 12 p 207 (1906)
Rly Mag   Vol 12 p 423 (1903); Vol 19 p 499 (1906)
L&R   Vol 4 p 4 (1903)
SLS   Vol 28 pp 321-2, 328 (1952)
New Soc   Vol 27 p 169; Vol 28 p 263 (WO Skeat, Paper from Vol 27 also
           published separately by Stephenson Locomotive Society
Rly Wld   Vol 18 p 105, correspondence pp 189, 228 (1957); Vol 25 p 293 (1964)

Standard Locomotive Details
Rly Eng   Vol 19 (1898, working drawing)
MRC   Vol 15 p 48 (1948) 4-4-0 smokebox

Tenders
GEJ   Vol 1 Issues 2, 7, 8, 10

Holden's patent system for oil burning locomotives
Rly Mag   Vol 117 p 352 (1971) WO Skeat
Rly Wld   Vol 21 p 238 (1960)

Operation
Great Eastern Railway Engine Sheds Part 1, C Hawkins & G Reeve, Wild Swan 1986
Great Eastern Railway Engine Sheds Part 2, C Hawkins & G Reeve, Wild Swan 1987
I Tried to Run a Railway, GF Fiennes, Ian Allan 1967
The Last Word in Steam Operated Suburban Train Services, Railway Gazette 1920
Steam in the Blood, RHN Hardy, Ian Allan 1971
The Stour Valley Railway - A History, BDJ Walsh, Connor & Butler 1987
Stour Valley Railway Through Time (2 volumes), Andy T Wallis, Amberley 2011

NORTH BRITISH RAILWAY

Constituent Companies

Monkland and Kirkintilloch Railway
The Monkland and Kirkintilloch Railway, D Martin, Strathkelvin District Libraries
and Museums (Auld Kirk Museum Publications No 2) 1976
The Monkland and Kirkintilloch Railway and Associated Railways, D Martin,
Strathkelvin District Libraries and Museums 1995
Loco Mag   Vol 37 p 356 (1931); Vol 47 p 78 (1941)
           Vol 51 pp 83, 99 (1945) *The First Locomotive built at Glasgow*, HF Hilton
Slamannan Railway
The Monkland and Kirkintilloch Railway and Associated Railways, D Martin,
Strathkelvin District Libraries and Museums 1995
Loco Mag   Vol 47 p 79 (1941)
SLS   Vol 33 p 207 (1957)
Monkland Railway
The Monkland and Kirkintilloch Railway and Associated Railways, D Martin,
Strathkelvin District Libraries and Museums 1995
Loco Mag   Vol 48 p 158 (1942)
Caledonian and Dunbartonshire Junction Railway
SLS   Vol 11 pp 151-2 (1935)
Stirling and Dunfermline Railway
Loco Mag   Vol 48 p 158 (1942)
SLS   Vol 12 p 159 (1936)
Edinburgh and Glasgow Railway
SLS   Vol 12 pp 156-63 (1036); Vol 13 pp 38, 287 (1937)
           The Edinburgh and Glasgow Railway and its Locomotives, John McInnes
Loco Mag   Vol 48 pp 3, 48, 94, 125, 156 (1942) *Cowlairs Commentary*, Stirling Everard
SLS   **Bury Locos**   Vol 19 pp 133, 183 (1943)
           Mixed Traffic 2-4-0, 0-4-2 Vol 22 pp 141-2, correspondence 214 (1946)
           Vol 23 pp 146-8 (1947) *Notes in Detail*
           Vol 24 pp 203, 289, (1948) correspondence
           Vol 33 p 207 1957) *Railway Notes of 1857*
NBRSG   Issues 41, 44 *The Beyer Peacock Locomotives of the Edinburgh and Glasgow
           Railway*, Dr Euan Cameron
SLS   Vol 22 p 144 (1946) **Paton Singles**
           Vol 16 pp 130, 184 (1940) **2-2-2 Nos 9,10, 11 & 58**, L Ward
Loco Mag   Vol 33 p 252 (1927)
Rly Mag   Vol 2 p 292 (1898); Vol 25 p 512 (1909)
Leven and East of Fife Railway
Loco Mag   Vol 49 p 125 (1943)
Solway Railway
Loco Mag   Vol 20 p 130 (1914)
Forth and Clyde Junction Railway
Loco Mag   Vol 49 p 62 (1943)
Glasgow, Bothwell, Hamilton and Coatbridge Railway
Loco Mag   Vol 49 p 125 (1943)
West Highland Railway
The Story of the West Highland, G Dow, LNER 1946
Mountain Moor and Loch, Sir Joseph Causton & Son 1894. Republished as *Victorian
Travel on the West Highland Line*, House of Lochar 2002
The West Highland Railway, John Thomas, David & Charles/Macdonald 1965, 1966, David
& Charles 1976, 1984
The West Highland Railway, John Thomas (Updated PJG Ransome), House of Lochar 1998
Early Locomotives
NBRSG   Issue 34 pp 25-31 (1988); No 35 pp 30-2 (1988)
           The First North British Locomotives, PAT Collar

General Surveys

Burntisland: Fife's Railway Port, Peter Marshall, Oakwood Press 2001
The Development of the NBR Passenger Locomotive in the Victorian Era, Dr Euan Cameron,
     privately published in aid of the Gosforth-Uganda Appeal 1995
The Drummond Brothers, a Scottish Duo, JE Chacksfield, Oakwood Press 2005
The First Railway across the Border, G Dow, LNER 1946
Locomotives of the North British Railway 1846-82, Stephenson Locomotive Society 1970
NBR Locomotives, a Design Survey, GWM Sewell, privately published 2002
North British Album, AA Maclean, Ian Allan 1975
The North British Railway, C Hamilton Ellis, Ian Allan 1955, 1959
The North British Railway in Northumberland, GWM Sewell, Merlin 1992
The North British Railway: Volume 1 (1844-1879), John Thomas, David & Charles 1969
The North British Railway: Volume 2 (1879-1922), John Thomas, David & Charles 1975
The Springburn Story, John Thomas, David & Charles/Macdonald 1964

Loco Mag	Vol 48 p 190 (1942); Vol 49 pp 20,60,92,124,156 (1943);
	Vol 50 pp 29, 51, 155, 191 (1944); Vol 51 pp 24, 59, 90, 152, 171 (1945)
	Cowlairs Commentary, Stirling Everard
Rly Mag	Vol 46 pp 222, 325, 370 (1920); Vol 47 pp 31, 89, 175 (1920) *Locomotive and*
	Train Working in the Latter Part of the 19th Century, EL Ahrons.
	Also republished by Heffer 1954 edited by LL Asher, Vol 3
RTM	Vol 14 (1916) *Dugald Drummond's Locomotives for the Scotch Railways No 1:*
	North British, CES Littlejohn
Rly Mag	Vol 32 p 489-94 (1913), *Express Passenger Locomotives of the North British*
	Railway, Alex K Bowman
	Vol 76 pp 275, 437 (1935); Vol 77 p 277 (1935); Vol 78 p 139 (1936)
	Vol 79 p 138 (1936), *Notes on Scottish Locomotives and Railway Working*
	1895-1910: V: North British, SR Yates
	Vol 114 p 168 (1968), *A Succession of Superintendents*, Campbell Highet
Loco Mag	Vol 44 pp 192, 231 (1938), *Famous Locomotive Engineers, Part 5: Dugald*
	Drummond
Rly Wld	Vol 18 p 77 (1957); Vol 20 p 382 (1959); Vol 35 p 132 (1974)
	Vol 38 pp 48, 194, correspondence p 344 (1977)
SLS	Vol 21 pp 115-16 (1945), *Miscellany*; Vol 22 pp 143, 147 (1946) Notes
	Vol 12 pp 165, 223 (1936), *The Drummond Locomotives of the North British*
	Railway, JF McEwan
	Vol 33 p 207 (1957), *Railway Notes of 1857*
LI	No 170 *An LNER Miscellany* (2008)
NBRSG	Issue 63 pp 7-13, *First Locomotives on the NBR (R&W Hawthorn 0-4-2)*,
	GW Hewit
	Issue 63 pp 14-5, *NBR Locomotives Nos 17-26 (0-4-2)*, Bruce Murray
	Issue 91 pp 16-9, issue 92 pp 28-31, issue 93 pp 22-6, *Notes on Scottish*
	Locomotive & Railway Working 1895-1910, NBR, SR Yates (previously
	published in *Railway Magazine* 1935-1936)
	Issue 82 pp 26-7, *Locomotives by Hawthorn's of Leith*, JB Rowley
	Issue 96 pp 4-46, issue 100 pp 26-46, *NBR Locomotive Liveries 1946-1922*,
	Allan Rodgers
	Issue 114 pp 3-13, *Holmes Period Locomotive Liveries*, Ray Kitching

See also works having information *inter alia* at end.

Locomotive Types

Singles

L&R	Vol 2 p 97 (1901) Old Singles
Loco Mag	Vol 48 pp 190-1 (1942) 2-2-2, 4-2-0;
	Vol 49 pp 21-2, 29 (1943) 2-2-2 No 36, 2-2-2WT;
	Vol 49 p 93 Drummond
Eng	Vol 23 (1877, working drawing) Drummond 474/5
MRN	Vol 32 p 78 (1956) No 475 *Berwick*
SLS	Vol 16 pp 130, 184 (1940) 2-2-2WTs 309-312 (ex-E&G and C&D Joint), L Ward
	Vol 27 p 116 (1951), 'The Cab' (ex-C&D Joint)

0-4-0
Locomotives of the LNER Part 6C, RCTS 1984
MRN   Vol 21 p 100 (1945)
Rly Wld   Vol 25 p 75 (1964)
Rly Mod   Vol 17 p 310 (1966)
SLS   Vol 21 p 150 (1945) Nos 357/8 Rebuilt
Loco Mag   Vol 48 p 190 (1942) Nos 394/5
RO   Vol 12 pp 82-5 (1940)

2-4-0
Locomotives of the LNER Part 4, RCTS 1968, 1984
SLS   Vol 22 p 141 (1946) Hurst; Vol 35 p 238 (1959) Brief notes
Loco Mag   Vol 49 pp 60-1 (1943) Wheatley
RO   Vol 11 pp 21, 24 (1939)
NBRSG   Issue 83 pp 22-4, *NBR No 38 (Wheatley 2-4-0)*, GWM Sewell
           Issue 86 pp 21-2, *Further Reflections on Wheatley's No 38 (2-4-0)*,
              GWM Sewell
           Issue 86 pp 22-6, *Some Notes to a Drawing of NBR No 38 (2-4-0)*, Dr Euan
              Cameron
           Issue 105 pp 3-10, *Hurst's 90/341/382 class 2-4-0 Express Passenger
              Locomotives*, Dr Euan Cameron

4-4-0
Locomotives of the LNER Part 4, RCTS 1968, 1984
TI   Vol 7 pp 207, 233, correspondence pp 305, 395, 482 (1954)
Railways   Vol 3 p 16 (1942); Vol 8 p 146 (1947)
Wheatley (4-4-0)
Loco Mag   Vol 49 pp 60-1 (1943)
Rly Mag   Vol 51 p 296 (1922) No 224
L&R   Vol 4 p 23 (1903) Nos 224, 264
Eng   Vol 62 (1886, working drawing) No 224 rebuilt as a compound
NBRSG   Issue 41 p 12, issue 45 p 17 *Nos 224 & 264: A History in Drawings*, Dr Euan
              Cameron; issue 54 pp 2-15, 420 class, Dr Euan Cameron
           Issue 107 pp 10-18, *The Tay Bridge Engine, Wheatley's 4-4-0 No 224*, Dr Euan
              Cameron
RO   Vol 32 pp 246-48, 333-5 (1962), 420 class, W Hennigan
Drummond (4-4-0)
Eng   Vol 45 (1898, working drawing), 476 class and tender
Loco Mag   Vol 49 pp 93-4 (1943)
SLS   Vol 12 p 168 (1936)
NBRSG   Issue 30 p 11; issue 31 p 31, AW Miller
           Issue 50 p 32, *The Abbotsfords and Their Stepchildren*, Dr Euan Cameron
           Issue 106 pp 12-20, *Drummond's Abbotsford 476 class 4-4-0s*, Dr Euan Cameron
RO   Vol 10 pp 292, 363 (1938)
Holmes (4-4-0)
L&R   Vol 4 p 34 (1903), 592 class
Eng   Vol 47 (1879, working drawing); Vol 83 (1897), 592 class and tender
           Vol 79 (1895); Vol 83 (1897), 633 class
Eng Mech   Vol 44 p 91 (1893), 574 class
Rly Eng   Vol 13 (1892, working drawing); Vol 14 (1893), 693 class and tender
MRN   Vol 21 p 170 (1945), 633 class
Rly Mod   Vol 17 p 54 (1966), 633 class
SLS   Vol 29 pp 229/9 (1953), Drummond and Holmes, power class M
           Vol 20 p 80 (1944), 693 class
Engg   Vol 58 (1894, working drawing), 693 class and tender
RO   Vol 10 pp 292, 363 (1938); Vol 6 pp 67-8 (1934), Brief notes
NBRGS   Issue 104 pp 9-13, *Holmes 574 class 4-4-0s*, Dr Euan Cameron
           Issue 113 pp 3-11, *Holmes 592 Class 4-4-0s*, Dr Euan Cameron
           Issue 114 pp 24-9, *Holmes 317 Class 4-4-0s*, Dr Euan Cameron
Reid (4-4-0)
LI   No 96 *Reid North British 4-4-0s* Patrick Russell
Engg   Vol 113 (1922), Superheated *Scotts*
SLS   Vol 22 p 145 (1946); Vol 24 p 228 (1948), Saturated *Scotts*

	Vol 29 p 290 (1953), Superheated *Scotts*;
	Vol 43 pp 237/8 (1967), Proposed names not used
MRC	Vol 8 pp 146, 161 (1941), Superheated *Scotts*
Loco Mag	Vol 51 p 24 (1945), Superheated *Scotts*
Rly Mod	Vol 19 p 372 (1968), *Glen*
Mod Eng	Vol 124 pp 527, 587, 648 (1961)
	Vol 127 p 408 (1962), *Glen*, Robin Orchard
RO	Vol 10 pp 292, 363 (1938)
NBRSG	Issue 81 pp 18-23, *The Second Intermediates (NBR class K Reid 4-4-0s)*, Bill Lynn
	Issue 101 pp 20-7, *The Scott Characters (Names of Reid's 4-4-0s)*, AF Nisbet

0-6-0

Locomotives of the LNER Part 5, RCTS 1966, 1984

LI	No 137 *The North British Railway 0-6-0s*

Hurst (0-6-0)

NBRSG	Issue 89 pp 18-22, 32, *The Hurst 0-6-0 Locomotives of the NBR*, Paul Smith
	Issue 112 pp 5-18, *Hurst's 0-6-0 Goods Engines*, Dr Euan Cameron

Wheatley (0-6-0)

Loco Mag	Vol 49 pp 20, 60, 93, 124 (1943); Vol 50 p 156 (1944)

Drummond (0-6-0)

Eng	Vol 43 (1877)
L&R	Vol 2 p 92 (1901)
RO	Vol 11 p 180 (1939)
NBRSG	Issue 103 pp 11-15, *Drummond's 18-in Goods 0-6-0s*, Dr Euan Cameron
	Issue 108 pp 15-23, *Drummond and Holmes 17-in Goods 0-6-0s*, Dr Euan Cameron

Holmes (0-6-0)

Loco Mag	Vol 50 p 151 (1944)
MRN	Vol 14 p 149 (1938), 604 class
RO	Vol 11 pp 100, 180 (1938)
NBRSG	Issue 99 pp 27-31, *NBR C class (LNER J36) Names*, Paul Smith
	Issue 108 pp 15-23, *Drummond and Holmes 17-inch Goods 0-6-0*, Dr Euan Cameron

Reid (0-6-0)

Rly Eng	Vol 27 (9106), 848 class and tender
Loco Mag	Vol 50 p 192 (1944), 848 class
	Vol 51 pp 24-5 (1945), 8 class, superheated (load class S)
Rly Mod	Vol 19 p 88 (1968), 848 class, p 152 (1968), 8 class
MRN	Vol 38 p 308 (1962), 8 class
Mod Rlys	Vol 2 p 372 (1972), 8 class
RO	Vol 11 pp 100, 180 (1938)

4-4-2

Locomotives of the LNER Part 3A, RCTS 1979

The North British Atlantics, John Thomas, David & Charles 1972

Rly Mag	Vol 76 pp 37, 298 (1935), *North British Atlantics*, JW Rattray
SLS	Vol 14 pp 169, 211, 224, 309 (1938), *North British Atlantics*, John T Rutherford MA
LI	No 62 *Reid NBR Atlantics and 4-4-2Ts*, Philip Atkins (1988)
TI	Vol 5 p 339, correspondence p 423 (1952)
Modern R	Vol 24 p 475 (1968)
Engg	Vol 84 (1907, working drawing), 868 class and tender
Rly Eng	Vol 27 (1906), 868 class
Loco Mag	Vol 50 pp 156, 191 (1944); Vol 51 p 125 (1945), 868 class
Rly Mod	Vol 27 pp 84-5 (1976), superheated 868 class
Eng	Vol 133 (1922), 509 class
Loco Mag	Vol 51 p 25 (1945) 509 class
RO	Vol 10 pp 262-3 (1938)

0-4-2T & 0-4-2WT

Locomotives of the LNER Part 7, RCTS 1964, 1983

Loco Mag	Vol 52 p 40 (1946), Hurst well tank
Rly Mag	Vol 76 p 353 (1935), *Drummond Tank Engines*, C Hamilton Ellis
SLS	Vol 27 p 172 (1951), Drummond 157 class

Loco Mag   Vol 49 p 94 (1943), Drummond 157 class
RO   Vol 11 p 38 (1939)
0-4-0ST
Locomotives of the LNER Part 9B, RCTS 1977
SLS   Vol 32 p 111 (1956), Hurst
Loco Mag   Vol 49 p 125 (1943); Vol 50 p 30 (1944), Drummond
SLS   Vol 28 pp 34, 55 (1952), Holmes
Loco Mag   Vol 50 pp 29-30, 52 (1944), Holmes
RO   Vol 28 p 291-2 (1958), Holmes; Vol 12 p 82 (1940)
MRN   Vol 43 p 508 (1967), Holmes
4-4-0T
Locomotives of the LNER Part 7, RCTS 1964, 1983
LI   No 151 *The North British Railway Six and Eight Wheeled Tank Locomotives*
Eng   Vol 47 (1879, working drawing)
Rly Mag   Vol 76 p 353 (1935), *Drummond Tank Engines*, C Hamilton Ellis
RO   Vol 6 pp 67-8 (1934), C Hamilton Ellis; Vol 10 p 423 (1938)
Loco Mag   Vol 49 p 125 (1943); Vol 50 p 29 (1944)
NBRSG   Issue 24 p 27; issue 24 p 51
            Issue 87 pp 16-8, *The Surviving Class D51 4-4-0Ts of the LNER (NBR Class R)*,
               JT Rutherford (previously published in SLS Journal 12/1930)
            Issue 110 pp 6-10, *Drummond's Small 4-4-0T 72 class*, Dr Euan Cameron
MRN   Vol 38 p 20 (1966)
MRC   Vol 44 p 114 (1977)
0-4-4T
Locomotives of the LNER Part 7, RCTS 1964, 1983
LI   No 151 *The North British Railway Six and Eight Wheeled Tank Locomotives*
Loco Mag   Vol 50 p 31 (1944), Holmes; Vol 50 p 192 (1944), Reid
RO   Vol 10 p 38 (1939); Vol 13 p 60 (1941)
MRN   Vol 32 p 7 (1956), Reid
0-6-0T & 0-6-0ST
Locomotives of the LNER Part 8B, 1971, 1983
LI   No 151 *The North British Railway Six and Eight Wheeled Tank Locomotives*
Loco Mag   Vol 48 p 157 (1942), Hurst saddle tank
Engg   Vol 28 (1878, working drawing), Drummond
Loco Mag   Vol 49 p 92 (1943), Drummond
Rly Mag   Vol 76 p 353 (1935), Drummond
SLS   Vol 21 p 187 (1945), Drummond
MRN   Vol 41 pp 60, 151 (1965), Holmes
SLS   Vol 50 p 12 (1952), Reid
Loco Mag   Vol 50 p 52 (1944), Reid
RO   Vol 11 p 243, 289 (1939)
NBRSG   Issue 109 pp 10-15, *Drummond's Passenger 0-6-0Ts 165 class*, Dr Euan Cameron
0-6-2T
Locomotives of the LNER Part 9A, RCTS 1977
LI   No 151 *The North British Railway Six and Eight Wheeled Tank Locomotives*
Loco Mag   Vol 50 p 192 (1944)
Rly Mod   Vol 18 p 276 (1967)
MRN   Vol 40 pp 220, 282, 393 (1964)
RO   Vol 11 pp 344, 374-5 (1939)
NBRSG   Issue 111 pp 19-29, *Reid's 0-6-2Ts*, Dr Euan Cameron
4-4-2T
Locomotives of the LNER Part 7, RCTS 1964, 1983
LI   No 62 *Reid NBR Atlantics and 4-4-2Ts*, Philip Atkins (1988)
SLS   Vol 20 pp 158, 206 (1944)
Engg   Vol 93 (1912, working drawing), 1 class saturated
Loco Mag   Vol 50 p 192 (1944)
RO   Vol 26 pp 7-9, 38-41 (1956), 1 class saturated, W Hennigan
            Vol 29 pp 33-5, 76-8 (1959), 438 class superheated, W Hennigan
            Vol 10 pp 259, 262
TI   Vol 6 pp 296, 394, correspondence p 474 (1953)

Standard Locomotive Details
Rly Eng   Vol 19 (1898, working drawings)

Petrol Shunter
SLS   Vol 33 p 48 (1957)
RO   Vol 12 p 107 (1940)

Saddle Tank Tender
MRN   Vol 5 p 217 (1929)

Wing plates
TI   Vol 7 p 75 (1954)

Duplicate List
NBRSG   Newsletter No 2 (1980) CJB Sanderson

GREAT NORTH OF SCOTLAND RAILWAY

Aberdeenshire's Lost Railways, Gordon Stansfield, Stenlake 2000

Banff, Moray & Nairn's Lost Railways, Gordon Stansfield, Stenlake 2000

Carriage Compendium, Great North of Scotland Railway Association 2010

Carriages of the Great North of Scotland Railway, by Keith Fenwick, Black Dwarf
Lightmoor 2009

Cruden Bay Hotel and its Tramway, Keith Jones, Great North of Scotland Railway
Association 2004

Directors, Dilemmas and Debt, Peter Fletcher, Great North of Scotland Railway
Association 2010

GNSR Locomotives, Abstract No 7, Great North of Scotland Railway Association, 1966
[Superseded by Abstract No 17]

GNSR Locomotives, Abstract No 17, Great North of Scotland Railway Association,
H Gordon and RP Jackson 1989

GNSR Wagons at the Grouping, Great North of Scotland Railway Association 2006

Great North Memories, 3 volumes, Great North of Scotland Railway Association

Great North of Scotland Railway, HA Vallance, David & Charles 1965, 1989

Great North of Scotland Railway Album, AE Glen, IA Glen & AG Dunbar, Ian Allan 1980

Great North of Scotland Railway Locomotives, Hugh Gordon, Irwell Press 2008

History of the Great North of Scotland Railway, Sir Malcolm Barclay-Harvey, Locomotive
Publishing Company 1940, 1949, Reprinted Ian Allan 1998

Little and Good: The Great North of Scotland Railway, WJ Scott, SLS 1972

Locomotives in North East Scotland, Abstract No 18, Great North of Scotland Railway
Association 1989

Locomotives of the Great North of Scotland Railway, MCV Allchin, Railway Hobbies
Ltd 1950

*Locomotives of the Great North of Scotland Railway as at 31st December 1922 with
Alterations to date* [List], AG Dunbar, The Author 1931

Moray Coast Railways, Rosemary Burgess and Robert Kinghorn, AUP 1990

Rails to Alford, Dick Jackson, Great North of Scotland Railway Association 2006

Railways of Aberdeen, Keith Jones, Great North of Scotland Railway Association 2000

Railways of Buchan, Keith Fenwick, Great North of Scotland Railway Association 2008

Railways of Keith, Keith Fenwick, Great North of Scotland Railway Association 2006

Railways of the Banff and Moray Coast, GR Maxtone, Keith & Dufftown Railway
Association 2005

Royal Deeside Line, AD Farr, David & Charles 1968

Royal Deeside's Railway - Aberdeen to Ballater, Dick Jackson, Great North of Scotland
Railway Association 1999

The Speyside Line, Dick Jackson, Great North of Scotland Railway Association 2006

Speyside Railways, Rosemary Burgess and Robert Kinghorn, AUP 1988

Stories of Royal Deeside's Railway, A Derek Farr, Kestrel Books 1971

LI   No 109 *Great North of Scotland Railway Locomotives* (1996)

Rly Mag   Vol 50 pp 55, 105, 161 (1922), *Locomotive and Train Working in the
          Latter Part of the Nineteenth Century*, EL Ahrons
          Also republished by Heffer, edited by LL Asher 1954, Vol 3

SLS   Vol 30 pp 303-320 (1954), All locomotives, brief details

Rly Mag   Vol 74 pp 44, 232, 427 (1934), *Notes on Scottish Locomotives and
          Railway Working 1895-1910: GNofS*

L&R   Vol 3 p 1 (1902), Passenger engines

GNSRA   Vol 3, Issue 11 (1966), *Locomotive Classification - Corrections to
          Errors in GNOSRA Abstract No 7*; Vol 16 Issue 63 (1979), *The Cruden
          Bay Hotel and its Tramway*; Vol 26 Issue 100 (1989), *Post Grouping
          Changes to Letters and Numbers on GNSR Locomotives*, WB Yeadon

RO   Vol 9 pp 365-7 (1937), *GNOSR Locomotives*, LM Hobday

See also works having information *inter alia* at end.

Locomotive Types

2-4-0
GNSRA   Vol 26 Issue 102 (1989), 19 class No 25
SLS   Vol 15 p 175 (1939), L Ward
4-4-0
Locomotives of the LNER Part 4, RCTS (1968)
RO   Vol 10 pp 252, 353 (1938)
SLS   Vol 15 p 175 (1939), L Ward, 28 class (H)
           Vol 24 pp 190-1 (1948), 43 class (K)
GNSRA   Vol 27 Issue 107, 109 (1990, 1991), 43 class (K), as built and rebuilt
           GNSR Class C, Abstract No 11, GNSRA, EWH Greig 1969
           GNSR Class A, Abstract No 19, GNSRA 1989
           Vol 5 Issue 17 (1968), *The Kittybrewster Twins*, Class N, Nos 5 & 6
SLS   Vol 26 p 175 (1950), Class O
Eng   Vol 79 (1895), Class O
Engg   Vol 49 (1895, working drawing), Class O
GNSRA   Vol 29 Issues 114/5 (1992), Class O
Eng   Vol 71 (1891), Class Q and tender
GNSRA   *GNSR Class T*, Abstract No 14, GNSRA 1979
Rly Eng   Vol 15 (1894), Vol 16 (1895), Class S
SLS   Vol 29 p 230 (1953), Classes S & T
Loco Mag   Vol 2 pp 19,29 (1897), Classes S & T
MRN   Vol 39 pp 140, 246 (1963), Classes S & T
Rly Mod   Vol 7 p 18 (1956), Classes S & T
GNSRA   Vol 6 Issue 20 (1969)
           Vol 9 Issues 33/4 (1972), Class F
           Vol 31 Issue 123 (1994), No 46 *Benachie*
SLS   Vol 34 p 274 (1958), Class F
Rly Wld   Vol 25 p 86 (1964), Class F
MRN   Vol 34 p 9 (1958), Class F
GNSRA   Vol 26 Issue 103 (1989), Class V
GNSRA   Vol 48 Issue 191 (2011), Class V
GNSRA   Vol 45 Issue 178 (2008), Class K
MRN   Vol 37 p 250 (1961), Class V
See also works having information *inter alia* at end
2-4-0T
GNSRA   Vol 24 Issue 93 (1987), The Morayshire 2-4-0 Tank Engines Nos 3 & 4
           (GNOS Nos 41 & 42)

0-4-0WT
SLS   Vol 15 p 175 (1939), L Ward
GNSRA   Vol 7 Issue 25 (1970)
           Vol 32 Issue 124 (1995)
           Vol 35 Issue 138 (1998)
           Vol 43 Issue 170 (2006)
           Vol 45 Issue 177 (2008)
0-4-4T
Locomotives of the LNER Part 7, RCTS 1964, 1983
Rly Wld   Vol 32 p 291 (1971); correspondence Vol 33 p 39 (1972)
Rly Mod   Vol 7 p 79 (1956)
GNSRA   Vol 5 Issue 18 (1968)
RO   Vol 11 p 38 (1939)
0-4-2T
Locomotives of the LNER Part 9B. RCTS 1977
MRC   Vol 35 p 215 (1968)
GNSRA   Vol 6 Issue 20 (1969)
RO   Vol 12 p 85 (1940)
0-6-0T
Locomotives of the LNER Part 8B, RCTS 1971, 1983
Rly Mod   Vol 6 p 240 (1955)

RO   Vol 11 pp 243, 289 (1939)
Rail Motor
Vertical Boiler Locomotives and Railmotors built in Great Britain, RAS Abbott,
   Oakwood Press 1989 p 16
Eng   Vol 100 (1905)
            Vol 102 (1906)
Engg   Vol 80 (1905, part working drawing)
            Vol 81 (1906, part working drawing)
GNSRA   Vol 30 pp 457-8 (1993), Gordon Hughes
            Vol 40 Issue 157 (2003)
            Vol 45 Issue 179 (2008)
Geared Locomotive
GNSRA   Vol 2 Issue No 6
            Vol 30 Issue No 116 pp 387-8 (1993) *The Great North's Geared
               Locomotive*, RP Jackson
Notes on Vacuum Fitted Locomotives
SLS   Vol 34 p 151 (1958)
Standard Locomotive Details
Rly Eng   Vol 119 (1898, working drawings)
HMRS   Vol 3 pp 45, 69, 97
            Vol 4 p 81
Operation
The 'Subbies': The Story of Aberdeen's Suburban Trains 1887-1987, Keith G Jones,
   GNSRA 1987

COLNE VALLEY AND HALSTEAD RAILWAY

Aspects of East Anglian Steam: Vol 4: The Stour and Colne Valley Line, JD Mann, South
    Anglia Publications 1992
*From Construction to Destruction: An Authentic History of the Colne Valley and
    Halstead Railway*, Edward P Willingham, Halstead & District Local History Society
    1989
Colne Valley Album, Michael Young, Apex Publications 1983
The Colne Valley and Halstead Railway, RA Whitehead & FD Simpson, Oakwood Press 1988
Colne Valley and Halstead Railway Through Time, Andy T Wallis, Amberley 2011
The Colne Valley Railway 1856-1923, C Portway, Colne Valley Railway Preservation
    Society incorporating *Locomotives of the CVR 1861-1923*, J Holbrook
The Colne Valley Railway: A Pictorial Survey, Colne Valley Railway Preservation
    Society 1977
Locomotives of the LNER Parts 7 & 9A, RCTS 1964, 1977, 1983
The Story of the Colne Valley, RA Whitehead & FD Simpson, Francis Ridgeway 1951
Loco Mag   Vol 17 pp 181, 196-7, 200, 222 (1911)
Rly Mag   Vol 9 p 417 (1901)
            Vol 53 p 85 (1923), JF Gairns
GEJ   Vol 8 Issue 76
SLS   Vol 29 p 32 (1953), 2-2-2WT ex-LBSC
RO   Vol 11 p 24, (1939) 2-4-2T
            Vol 11 p 344, 374-5, (1939) 0-6-2T
Loco Mag   Vol 14 p 154 (1908), 0-6-2T
BRJ   No 39 (1991), *Against the Trend in the Colne Valley*, Iain Rice

EAST AND WEST YORKSHIRE UNION RAILWAY

East and West Yorkshire Union Railways, DL Franks, Turntable Enterprises 1973
Locomotives of the LNER Part 7 & 8B, 1964, 1971, 1983
Loco Mag   Vol 39 pp 129-30 (1933)
Rly Mag   Vol 7 pp 113-8 (1900)
RO   Vol 11 pp 287, 289 (1939), 0-6-0ST
            Vol 11 p 344 (1939), 0-6-2T

MID-SUFFOLK LIGHT RAILWAY

Aspects of East Anglian Steam: Vol 2: On Eastern Branch Lines and the M&GN, Part 1,
    JD Mann, South Anglia Publications 1991
East Anglia Branch Lines & Byways, pp 139-150, J Brodribb, OPC 2000
East Anglian Magazine, October 1957, pp 716-8, *Building the Mid-Suffolk Light Railway*
Locomotives of the LNER Part 8A, RCTS 1970, 1983
The Mid-Suffolk Light Railway, NA Comfort, Oakwood Press 1963, 1986, 1997
The Mid-Suffolk Light Railway, P Paye, Wild Swan Publications 1986, 2003
BRM   Vol 13 No 1 (2005), *Liveries of Mid-Suffolk Light Railway* N Digby
GEJ   Vol 13 Issue 7, *The Mid-Suffolk Light Railway, Part 1* R Green
            Vol 13 Issue 8, *The Mid-Suffolk Light Railway, Part 2* R Green
Loco Mag   Vol 10 p 172 (1904)
            Vol 13 p 84-6 (1907)
            Vol 14 p 172 (1908)
Rly Mag   Vol 55 p 347-52 (1924)
            Vol 98 pp 607, 638 (1952)
RO   Vol 11 p 283 (1939)
TI   Vol 5 pp 373-7 (1952)
Railways   Vol 13 pp 232-4 (1952), *The Mid-Suffolk Light Railway Part 1*
            Vol 13 pp 283-4 (1952), *The Mid-Suffolk Light Railway Part 2*
Stm Days   No 67 pp 168-173 (1995), *East Anglian Sugar Beet Traffic in Days of Steam*
Bylines   Vol 5 Issue 4 (2000) pp 146-154, *The Mid-Suffolk Light Railway*
            Vol 13 Issue 5 (2008) pp 232-235, *The Mid-Suffolk Light Railway*

MIDLAND AND GREAT NORTHERN JOINT RAILWAY

Constituent Companies

Yarmouth and North Norfolk Railway
SLS   Vol 18 pp 196, 207 (1942)
          Vol 22 pp 201, 239 (1946)
          Vol 23, correspondence p 43 (1947)
RO   Vol 12 pp 296-7 (1940), EB Madeley
MRC   Vol 38 pp 52, 210 (1971)

Lynn and Fakenham Railway / Eastern and Midlands Railway
SLS   Vol 17 p 168 (1941)
          Vol 18 pp 44, 196, 207 (1942)
          Vol 23, correspondence p 43 (1947)
RO   Vol 13 pp 237-8, 261, 278 (1941), EB Madeley
MRC   Vol 38 p 84 (1971)

0-6-0T ex-Cornwall Minerals Railway
Locomotives of the Great Western Railway Part 3 [p 72], RCTS 1956
The Cornwall Minerals Railway and its Locomotives, Alan M Wells, M&GN Circle 1990.
Also same author, M&GN Circle Broadsheet No 7, 1984 including drawings, photographs
   and full details

4-4-0
Peacock A Class Locomotives of the Lynn and Fakenham Railway, Alan M Wells, M&GN
   Circle 1990
Also same author M&GN Circle Broadsheet No 11 1990 including drawings
Locomotives of the LNER Part 4, RCTS 1968, 1984
Mod Back   Vol 1 pp 272-80
RO   Vol 10 pp 263, 422 (1938)

General Surveys
Aspects of East Anglian Steam: Vol 2: On Eastern Branch Lines and the M&GN, Part 1,
   JD Mann, South Anglia Publications 1991
Aspects of East Anglian Steam: Vol 5:On Eastern Branch Lines and the M&GN, Part 2,
   JD Mann, South Anglia Publications 1992
Forty Years of a Norfolk Railway, W Marriott (Ed EW Beckett) M&GNJRS 1999
A Guide to the Midland & Great Northern Joint Railway, N Digby, Ian Allan 1993
An Illustrated History of M&GN Locomotives, RH Clark, Oxford Publishing Co 1990
*Liveries of the Midland & Great Northern Railways Joint Committee and its
   Constituents*, N Digby, M&GN Circle
Locomotives of the M&GN, Alan M Wells, HMRS & M&GN Circle 1980
The Midland and Great Northern Joint Railway, AJF Wrottesley, David & Charles 1970
The Midland and Great Northern Joint Railway, J Rhodes, Ian Allan 1979
The Midland and Great Northern Joint Railway (Railway World Special), MJ Clarke,
   Ian Allan 1990
The Midland and Great Northern Joint Railway and its Locomotives, RJ Essery,
   Black Dwarf Lightmoor 2009
*Midland & Great Northern Locomotives a Century Ago: Bedside Backtrack - Aspects of
   Railway History*, Edited David Jenkinson, Atlantic Transport Publications 1993
A Short History of the Midland and Great Northern Railway, RH Clark, Goose and Son
   1967
Rly Mag   Vol 23 pp 89, 217 (1909), *Midland and Great Northern Joint Railway,*
             HL Hopwood
          Vol 53 pp 126, 205 (1923), *Locomotive and Train Working in the Latter
             Part of the Nineteenth Century,* EL Ahrons. Also republished by Heffer
             edited by LL Asher 1954, Vol 3
          Vol 75 pp 135, 308 (1934), *Midland and Great Northern Railway Locomotive
             and Train Working*

	Vol 79 p 273 (1936), *Locomotives of the Midland and Great Northern Railway 1900-35*, FH Gillford
Loco Mag	Vol 27 pp 36, 62, 106, 108, 123, 144, 186, 221, 243, 276, 333 (1921), *M&GN Joint and its Locomotives*, PC Dewhurst
	Vol 44 p 16 (1938), Locomotive Notes
Railways	Vol 11 p 131 (1950); Vol 12 pp 145-7, 194-5, 233-4, 248 (1951), *Locomotives of the M&GNJR*, Alan M Wells. Also same author parts 1-7 in *Locomotive Pictorial* Vol 3 (parts 8-10, Railways Vol 12)
RO	Vol 3 pp 11-15 (1931), Brief Notes, A Crawshaw
LI	No 85 *M&GN Locomotives*, JWP Rowledge 1992
SLS	Vol 35 p 189, correspondence (1959)
MGNRC	Various issues of their *Bulletin*

See also works having information *inter alia* at end, and numerous references in the journal of the Midland and Great Northern Circle.

Locomotive Types

4-4-0
Locomotives of the LNER Part 4, RCTS 1968, 1984

Loco Mag	Vol 14 p 183 (1908)
	Vol 38 p 384 (1932), Rebuilt
MRC	Vol 10 pp 71, 75, 94 (1943)
	Vol 20 p 248 (1953), Class C
RO	Vol 10 p 422 (1938)
	Vol 14 pp 315-6 (1942/3)
	Vol 15 p 173 (1944/5), D Middleton, Class C

0-6-0
Locomotives of the LNER Parts 5 & 6A, RCTS 1966, 1982, 1984

Railways	Vol 11 p 44 (1950)
SLS	Vol 31 p 85 (1955), Class DA
MRN	Vol 39 p 60/61 (1963), Class D
RO	Vol 11 pp 100, 180 (1939)

4-4-2T
Locomotives of the LNER Part 7, RCTS 1964, 1983

Loco Mag	Vol 11 p 151 (1905)
MRC	Vol 27 p 36 (1960)
RO	Vol 10 p 263 (1938)

0-6-0T
Locomotives of the LNER Part 8B, RCTS 1971, 1983

MRC	Vol 38 p 122 (1971)
RO	Vol 12 p 110 (1940)
	Vol 20 pp 28-9 (1950), *The 'MR' 0-6-0Ts of the M&GNJR*, D Middleton

Locomotive Details

MRN	Vol 38 p 122 (1971), Tender lettering details
Rly Mag	Vol 74 p 61 (1934), M&GN Locomotives fitted with stovepipe chimneys

Locomotive Observations
Scenes from the Midland and Great Northern Railway, RH Clark, Moorland Publishing Co 1978

The following have information *inter alia*:

55 Years of East Anglian Steam, Dr Ian C Allen, OPC 1982
The Atlantic Era: The British Atlantic Locomotive, Martin Evans, Percival Marshall
    1961
BR Past & Present, No 12: East Anglia, Saunders & Adderson, SLP 1992
Britain's Light Railways, M Smith, Ian Allan 1994
British Atlantic Locomotives, Cecil J Allen, Ian Allan 1968
The British Steam Locomotive 1825-1925, EL Ahrons, Locomotive Publishing Co 1927,
    reprinted Ian Allan 1961
British Steam Locomotive Builders, James W Lowe, Goose & Sons 1975
Doctor on the Line, Dr Ian C Allen, Irwell Press 1992
East Anglia Branch Lines & Byways, J Brodribb, OPC 2000
East Anglia Railways Remembered, Leslie Oppitz, Countryside Books 1989
East Anglian Album, Dr Ian C Allen, OPC 1976
East Anglian Branch Line Album, Dr Ian C Allen, OPC 1977
East Anglian Steam (Five volumes), JD Mann, South Anglia
East Anglian Steam Gallery (Five volumes), JD Mann, South Anglia
Light Railway Era, J Scott-Morgan, Atlantic 1997
Light Railway Handbook, RW Kidner, Oakwood Press 1962
Locomotives at the Grouping Volume 2: London & North Eastern Railway, HC Casserley &
    SW Johnston, Ian Allan 1966
Lost Lines: Eastern, N Welbourne, Ian Allan 1995
Minor Railways of England and Their Locomotives, T Woodcock, Goose & Son 1970
The Scottish 4-4-0: Its Place in Railway History, Tom Middlemass, Atlantic Transport
    Publishers 1994
Scottish Locomotive History, Campbell Highet, George Allen & Unwin 1970
Standard Gauge Light Railways, RW Kidner, Oakwood Press 1954
Steam Around Ipswich, HN James, Trent Valley 1991
Steam in the Eastern Counties, J Brodribb, Ian Allan 1995
Suffolk In The Age Of Steam, R Jones, Countryside Books 2009
Suffolk's Railways in Old Postcards, D Cross, SB Publications 1993
Suffolk Steam Railways, D Kindred, Old Pond 2009
Yeadon's Register of LNER Locomotives, Willie B Yeadon, Numerous volumes covering
        every class of locomotive inherited or built by the LNER, published from 1990 to
        date by various publishers: Irwell Press (Vols 1 to 7), Challenger Publications
        (Vols 8 to 15) and Book Law Publications (Vols 16 to 50)
RO Vol 10 pp 151-4, 188-92, 224-8, 259-63, 291-6, 352-6, 363-7, 422-4, (1938)
    Vol 11 pp 21-7, 38-41, 100-3, 111-16, 166-73, 180-3, 243-7, 281-5, 287-91, 327-31,
        344-7, 373-6, (1939)
    Vol 12 pp 23-7, 31-4, 54-8, 82-5, 106-10, 139-43, 170-2 (1940)
    Vol 17 pp 126-8 (1947), *Locomotives of the LNER* (see also *passim*)
Republished as:
Locomotives of the LNER 1923-1937, KR Prentiss & P Proud, RCTS 1941

Kestrel Railway Books

The Cheshire Lines Railway between Glazebrook and Godley: A route of strategic importance by Bob Pixton

This line bypassed the city of Manchester, to the south, connecting the Manchester Sheffield & Lincolnshire Railway (later the Great Central Railway) with the Cheshire Lines route between Manchester and Liverpool. On its way, it connected with almost every other line in the district to create a vital artery for goods traffic. Much of the coal finding its way to south Lancashire and the docks at Liverpool passed along this line, and goods from the docks also used it to reach the conurbations east of the Pennines. Sections of the route were amongst the most intensively worked freight lines in the country.

The reader is taken along an imaginary journey, stopping at all the stations and other important features along the line. The main focus is the route between the two towns, but the traffic and the connections generating it are explored as they arise along the journey. From the author of the popular "Liverpool & Manchester" trilogy.

Softback: 136 pages, ISBN: 978-1-905505-21-0, Price £15.95

The Hidden Railways of Portsmouth and Gosport by Dave Marden

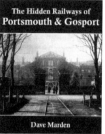

The lines around Portsmouth Harbour were operated mainly by the Admiralty and the Military. These secretive systems were often obscured by high walls, and glimpses would have been through closely-guarded gates, with the occasional sight of a train joining the main line. This book brings together data, illustrations and potted histories to give an insight into the operation of these concealed railways. The Portsmouth naval dockyard was home to over fifty locomotives over the years, and other associated facilities included the Naval Armament Depots at Gosport, the Gunnery School at HMS Excellent on Whale Island and the Army's presence at Hilsea Ordnance Depot – all of which are included.

Several large-scale construction projects also feature, as do railways and locomotives that do not quite fit into the Military or Contractors categories, such as the Stokes Bay Pier and the Lee-on-the-Solent railways. While these were not concealed from the public eye, they are of interest, and are appropriate to the theme of the book. Included for completeness are the dockyard branch lines, the industrial railway at Hilsea Gasworks, and Pounds Yard at Tipner. Although not exactly "hidden", they were beyond public access and fit well into this volume. Softback: 160 pages, ISBN: 978-1-905505-22-7, Price £17.95

Civil Engineers Wagons by David Larkin

David Larkin is well known for his study of British Railways goods wagons. In this new series, he presents the wagons of the civil engineering fleet. The books cover ballast wagons, on-track plant, and the other specialised wagons that comprised the fleet during the British Railways and British Rail eras. Profusely illustrated, these books include lot and diagram details, wagon number ranges, builders, and livery details of the vehicles.

Volume 1: British Railways 1948–1967
ISBN: 978-1-905505-23-4 *(available autumn 2011)*
Volume 2: Early British Rail 1968–1977
ISBN: 978-1-905505-24-1 *(available 2012)*
Volume 3: Later British Rail 1978–1994
ISBN: 978-1-905505-25-8 *(available 2013)*

All softback: 96 pages, Price £14.00

HUSH-HUSH: The Story of LNER 10000 by William Brown

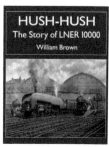

From his first encounter as a child with a model that seemed more like a spaceship than a locomotive, author William Brown has been fascinated by 10000. Meticulous research, involving hundreds of documents, has allowed him to piece together for the first time the true story of this intriguing part of LNER history, and the far-reaching effects it had on steam locomotive development.

The author took advantage of working at the National Railway Museum to seek out as much primary source material as he could find, culminating in the discovery of "the file" – a wide-ranging and motley collection of original North Road Works documentation relating to the locomotive. The sheer volume of information (including original memos from Gresley to Bulleid, Thompson, and the like) took years to sort and collate; the result is a book that, for the first time, chronicles the full story of Gresley's "Hush-Hush" project. Hardback: 128 pages, ISBN: 978-1-905505-15-9, Price £19.95

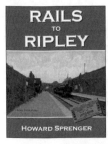

Rails to Ripley by **Howard Sprenger**
With the scenically beautiful Midland main line through the Peak District on one side, and the more workmanlike Erewash Valley line on the other, Ripley was surrounded by coal mines, potteries and agricultural land. Hard by Ripley, the Butterley Company sat like a spider in a web of industrial railway lines and canals.

Three lines eventually served the town, the earliest striking north-east from the Derwent valley and growing out of the railway town of Derby. From the Erewash Valley came another line that was destined to be the poorest and shortest lived. The third line, running east to west and linking the two great Midland Railway trunk routes from London to the north, bypassed Ripley, but provided the final link in the network of lines that this fascinating area spawned.
Softback:144 pages, ISBN: 978-1-905505-16-6, Price £17.95

The Salisbury and Dorset Junction Railway by **Nigel Bray**
The Salisbury & Dorset Junction Railway was built to consolidate the LSWR's domination of Hampshire and south Dorset, and to keep the GWR away from Bournemouth. It also gave Salisbury businessmen a more direct route to Poole and Weymouth. Almost half of the 18½-mile route was in Dorset, with less than five miles apiece in Wiltshire and Hampshire. Passing through three counties, it traversed contrasting landscapes and served a wide if thinly populated agricultural area.

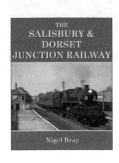

The water meadows between Downton and Fordingbridge produced cattle, milk and watercress. South-west of Fordingbridge, the clay soil had given rise to brick and tile manufacture centuries before the coming of the railway, enabling these industries to expand and distribute their wares over a much wider area. Year-round passenger traffic on the line was erratic, but it provided a useful diversionary and holiday route.
Softback:128 pages, ISBN: 978-1-905505-19-7, Price £17.95
Also available from us by this author: *Andover to Redbridge*

Northumberland & Durham Railway Pictorial, 1948-1967 by **Brian J. Dickson**
This pictorial review shows the changing railway scene in the adjoining counties of Northumberland and Durham from Nationalisation until the end of main-line steam in 1967. It contains well-captioned photographs of British Railways, National Coal Board and other private railways, laid out in date order to show the progression from almost exclusive steam working to total diesel working during this brief period of only 19 years.

Traffic was generated by the major industries of the region – steel, coal and shipbuilding. In addition, there were rural branch lines serving farms and communities in an era when mass car ownership was still a thing of the future. Both types of traffic, freight and passenger, found their way to the major routes connecting the towns and cities of the two counties with the East Coast Main Line to Edinburgh, Leeds and London.
Softback: 96 pages, ISBN: 978-1-905505-20-3, Price £14.95

Wagons of the British Railways and British Rail Eras by **David Larkin**
Profusely illustrated, these books include lot and diagram details, wagon number ranges, builders, and livery details of vehicles as diverse as Lowfit wagons, open wagons, containers and container wagons, mineral wagons, ventilated vans, railtanks, cattle wagons and brake vans. All softback: 96 pages
Wagons of the Early British Railways Era – A Pictorial Study of the 1948 to 1954 Period
ISBN: 978-0-9544859-8-6, Price: £13.00
Wagons of the Middle British Railways Era – A Pictorial Study of the 1955 to 1961 Period
ISBN: 978-1-905505-06-7, Price: £14.00
Wagons of the Final Years of British Railways – A Pictorial Study of the 1962 to 1968 Period
ISBN: 978-1-905505-08-1, Price: £14.00
Wagons of the Early British Rail Era – A Pictorial Study of the 1969 to 1982 Period
ISBN: 978-1-905505-10-4, Price: £14.00
Wagons of the Final British Rail Era – A Pictorial Study of the 1983 to 1995 Period
ISBN: 978-1-905505-17-3, Price: £14.00

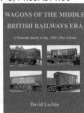

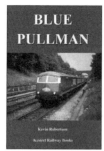

Blue Pullman by **Kevin Robertson**
The history of the Metropolitan-Cammell Blue Pullman units can be compared to a ride on a roller-coaster – indeed, that very comparison was made about the ride of these trains at the time, and their entry into service, and success on the line, followed a similar pattern.

Often referred to (incorrectly) as the forerunners of the HSTs, the Blue Pullmans had the similar advantage of a fixed formation and the quick turnaround times made possible as a result. However, where they did point towards the future was in the standard of service provided, and while this was only available to a privileged few, in later years, the speed and passenger facilities demonstrated by the sets would become the norm.

First published in 2005, and unavailable for some, the title has been reprinted due to popular demand.
Hardback: 168 pages, ISBN: 978-0-9544859-6-2, Price £19.95

Great Western Steam in Shakespeare Country by **Bob Pixton**
The GWR lines serving this rural part of Warwickshire took a long time to arrive. Opening in 1852, was a line from Birmingham to Oxford and the capital, and hard on its heels was a line to serve the market town of Stratford-upon-Avon. Opening to passengers in 1908 was a third line creating the triangle dealt with in this book – the Birmingham & North Warwickshire Railway, linking Stratford-upon-Avon with Birmingham through the Forest of Arden.

This book takes the reader on a journey along each of the lines. Firstly, along the original main line from Snow Hill to Leamington, and then over the branches to Stratford-upon-Avon. Completing the triangle is a return journey up the North Warwickshire line to Birmingham Moor Street. Softback: 136 pages, ISBN: 978-1-905505-13-5, Price: £15.95

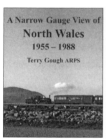

A Narrow Gauge View of North Wales 1955 – 1988 by **Terry Gough ARPS**
Most of the narrow gauge railways in North Wales were built primarily to transport slate within the quarries and to ports for transhipment to other parts of the UK and overseas. A few were built for the carriage of general merchandise and passengers, and two were built solely for tourists – a function which all the surviving lines now perform.

In 1954, Terry Gough decided it was time to see these railways for himself. Since that visit he has returned many times, and witnessed amazing transformations in the fortunes of several of the lines. As an enthusiastic and accomplished railway photographer, he has recorded these changes, and captured many wonderful scenes - some timeless, others merely transitory. All his photographs are supplemented with details about the various railways.
Hardback: 136 pages, ISBN: 978-1-905505-14-2, Price: £19.95

The Bideford, Westward Ho! & Appledore Railway by **Rod Garner**
The story of the Bideford, Westward Ho! & Appledore railway is not the traditional tale of the construction of a new railway. It has many of the usual ingredients – difficulties in raising capital and buying land, protracted negotiations regarding Parliamentary approval, and contractor troubles. However, a small group of local entrepreneurs had the drive and determination to create not just a railway, but a railway to serve a new town and a harbour that they also planned to build.

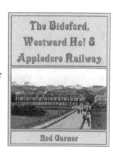

It is a story that has been told before, but as a local author, Rod Garner has been able to discover previously unpublished photographs and new information that adds to (and in some cases clarifies) that which has been published before.
Hardback: 120 pages, ISBN: 978-1-905505-09-8, Price: £17.95
Also available from us by this author: *The Torrington and Marland Light Railway*

The Alnwick Branch by **Bartle Rippon**
Although close to the east coast main line, the historic town of Alnwick was served by a branch line for nearly 120 years. Along with its famous castle and gardens, Alnwick boasted a majestic trainshed, all the more remarkable for being on a mere branch line.
Softback: 80 pages, ISBN: 978-1-905505-11-1, Price: £12.95

The Amble Branch by **Bartle Rippon**
Although much has been written about Northumberland's railways, one line – the branch line to Amble – has escaped detailed attention. Amble Junction marked the beginning of the 5-mile branch line to the seaside town of Amble, where coal was exported from Warkworth Harbour. Although a mineral line in essence, it flirted with a passenger service for some 50 years before returning to its original purpose
Softback: 72 pages, ISBN: 978-1-905505-05-0, Price: £10.95

Back list

- **Southampton's Quayside Steam** by **Dave Marden** Softback:160 pages, ISBN: 978-1-905505-02-9, Price: £16.95

- **A Further look at Southampton's Quayside Railways** by **Dave Marden** Softback:168 pages, ISBN: 978-1-905505-12-8, Price: £17.95

- **Liverpool & Manchester Volume 3: Lancashire & Yorkshire Lines** Softback: 144 pages, ISBN: 978-1-905505-07-4, Price £15.95

- **A Pictorial Guide to Southern Wagons and Vans** by **Terry Gough** Hardback with jacket: 160 pages, ISBN: 978-1-905505-04-3, Price: £25.00

- **LSWR Carriages Volume 3: Non-Passenger Carriage Stock** by **Gordon Weddell** Hardback with jacket: 168 pages, ISBN: 978-0-9544859-5-5, Price: £25.00

- **LSWR Carriages Volume 4: Goods, Departmental Stock and Miscellany** by **Gordon Weddell** Hardback with jacket: 176 pages, ISBN: 978-1-905505-01-2, Price: £25.00

- **The Torrington and Marland Light Railway** by **Rod Garner** Softback: 104 pages, ISBN: 978-0-9544859-7-9, Price: £14.00

- **Andover to Redbridge** by **Nigel Bray** Softback: 144 pages, ISBN: 978-0-9544859-4-8, Price: £17.95

- **Bulleid and the Turf Burner** by **Ernie Shepherd** Softback: 108 pages, ISBN: 978-0-9542035-8-0, Price: £17.95

- **The Story of the Southern USA Tanks** by **Howard Sprenger, Kevin Robertson, Clare Sprenger** Softback: 72 pages, ISBN: 978-0-9544859-3-1, Price: £13.95

- **The LSWR at Nine Elms – The Works and its Products 1839-1909** by **Barry Curl** Hardback with jacket: 368 pages, ISBN: 978-0-9542035-7-3, Price: £35.00

- **A Lifetime in Traction** by **Arthur Tayler** Softback: 96 pages, ISBN: 978-0-9544859-2-4, Price: £14.95

- **The Basingstoke and Alton Railway** by **Martin Dean, Kevin Robertson, Roger Simmonds** Hardback with jacket: 128 pages, ISBN: 978-0-9545617-0-3, Price: £18.95

- **Behind the Steam** by **Bill Morgan and Bette Meyrick** Hardback with jacket: 224 pages, ISBN: 978-0-9544859-0-0, Price: £14.95

- **Neyland – A Great Western Outpost** by **Richard Parker** Hardback with jacket: 152 pages, ISBN: 978-0-9542035-3-5, Price: £19.95

- **Great Western Halts Volume 2** by **Kevin Robertson** Hardback with jacket: 128 pages, ISBN: 978-0-9542035-2-8, Price: £18.95

- **Sutton Scotney: Life at a Country Station** by **Kevin Robertson** Softback: 60 pages, ISBN: 978-1-905505-00-5, Price: £7.95

- **Burghclere Signalman** by **Kevin Robertson** Softback: 40 pages, ISBN: 978-0-9542035-0-4, Price: £7.95

- **Winchester (Great Western)** by **Kevin Robertson** Softback: 48 pages, ISBN: 978-0-9542035-1-1, Price: £7.95

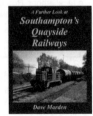

Our books are available from all good booksellers, or directly from:

Kestrel Railway Books, PO Box 269, Southampton, SO30 4XR
Telephone: 01489 798141
info@kestrelrailwaybooks.co.uk

We do not charge for postage to addresses in the UK.
For the latest news about our books, visit our web site at www.kestrelrailwaybooks.co.uk.
You can also follow us on Twitter and Facebook.